The Renaissance New Testament

Randolph O. Yeager

VOLUME EIGHTEEN

Rev. 4:1–22:21

PELICAN PUBLISHING COMPANY

GRETNA 1985

101178

Library of Congress Cataloging in Publication Data

Yeager, Randolph O.
    The Renaissance New Testament.

    Volumes 1-4 originally published in 1976-1978 by
Renaissance Press, Bowling Green, Ky.
    1. Bible. N.T.—Concordances, Greek. 2. Greek
language, Biblical. I. Title.
BS2302.Y4   1981   225.4'8'0321   79-28652
ISBN: 0-88289-159-6   (v. 18)

Manufactured in the United States of America

Published by Pelican Publishing Company, Inc.
1101 Monroe Street, Gretna, Louisiana 70053

To

my mother whose prayers for me were answered four years after her death, and to my dad who lived to hear me preach the gospel before he joined her in glory.

The Ideal and the Real

The Greek New Testament presents the divine ideal for the elect against a background of the real world in which he must live after he is born from above and before he is glorified.

From God's point of view there is no before and after — no sequence of events, for He is eternal and therefore not subject to time and space categories. Whom He did foreknow in what mortals call the eternal past He also predestined, called, justified and glorified. As far as God was concerned it was all done when He decreed that any of it should be done. But the Christian can look back to the days before he was saved. He can also review the days since he was saved and look forward to the days that remain until he is glorified. After that there is no problem, for when glorification comes he will have no further problems, either with the flesh or with the environment in which he must live.

Church historians may ponder the question as to whether the twentieth century Christian finds it more difficult to live the victorious life than members of the Body of Christ who lived in earlier days. The physical environment is more deleterious to health and happiness than it was before the rise of the factory system, the consequent urbanization with its slums, crowded conditions, rats, cockroaches, filth and disease, the chemical air pollution which seems inevitably to accompany advances in chemistry and the growing international tensions which threaten nuclear destruction.

The theological world has also changed, with the coming of more sophisticated media technology, which now permits widespread circulation of the printed page and universal coverage of radio and television. The first amendment of the United States constitution protects the right of preachers, teachers, philosophers and politicians, be they pundits, demagogues or snake oil salesmen to peddle their wares if they can pay for the time, and especially with the snake oil salesmen there seems to be no problem with the finances, as it is still true that the hand is quicker than the television camera eye and, as P.T.Barnum observed,"there is a fool born every minute." There are thousands who will send money which they ought to spend on their families or contribute to their local church to the television preacher who mistakes gastronomical reaction to too much pizza for a vision from the Lord. Anyone who sees Jesus, nine hundred feet tall standing atop an unfinished hospital building must be a messenger from the Lord who deserves all the money he can get.

We have had heresy in and out of the Church since the day that Eve ate the persimmon. The Gnostics have peddled their poison since the days of Zoroaster, with a generous assist from Origen in the third century and the holy rollers in the twentieth. We have always had the radical empiricism of Heraclitus, Locke,

Hume and Berkeley with an added existential twist in recent years. Kant has taught us that first century witnesses of Jesus and His words and works might reason their way to salvation, but that those of us who must depend upon the testimony of the New Testament by faith, cannot. We can toy with a splendid idea about Jesus but we cannot be certain that He ever lived, since we did not see Him.

Materialism tells us that there is nothing but atoms and the void, that thought is nothing more than a electro-chemical response in the synapse and that love is nothing more than a glandular motivation to propagate a race that might better be allowed to die and return to the dust.

Organic evolution assures us that progress is inevitable because change for the better has been resident in matter from the beginning. But this upward development is the reward given only to the winners of the struggle for survival which features the law of claw and fang. The human family was foreordained by sex to breed itself into poverty and starvation, since the economic rule of history is scarcity. There is not enough to go around so the big men kill the little people in order to eat, and the big corporations starve out the little business men, only to be absorbed by bigger corporations. In a world like that there is no place for a carpenter who said, "Blessed are the merciful for they shall obtain mercy."

Christians teach that certitude is available for those who keep faith, reason and experience in proper balance. Fanatics insist upon building their systems and governing their lives by playing up experience at the expense of reason, and rationalists glorify reason and despise experience. Neither has the faith without which it is impossible to please God.

The scenario for the elect child of God was written in eternity past when a sovereign God for reasons sufficient unto Himself decreed that He should be saved to live eternally in glory. The fact that He foreknew it did not depend upon the fact that He predestined it, nor did He predestine it because He had already foreknown it. There can be no progress with God and thus we can never arrange decisions or events on a cause and result scale as though God was forced to do one thing because He had previously done another thing. All that He thinks, knows, decides and executes are for Him in the glorious eternal present. God cannot be surprized nor taught nor corrected nor changed. Thus He has fixed the destination of His elect. But for us, the objects of His divine grace, love and power, there is the movement of time and space and therefore of history.

Jude tells us in his first verse that God has already set us apart and that He has preserved us until such time as He calls us to salvation. If Satan, the thief who comes only to kill and to steal and to destroy, goes to and fro in the earth and walks up and down in it, like a roaring lion, seeking whom he may devour, could kill us before God called us to salvation, the eternal purpose of God would be frustrated and God would be forced to admit that not all that He has planned can be done. That is why preservation for those who have been sanctified is promised until such time as they are called.

A man in a rescue mission meeting in New York City arose to witness for Christ, after the preacher had preached on Jude's first verse. He said that before he was saved he was an engineer on a locomotive pulling a long coal train through a tunnel in the Pennsylvania mountains. Half way through the long tunnel his train collided with another. Two days later the rescue crew succeeded in pulling the train out backward to find him and the dead fireman under the locomotive. Six weeks later he returned to work, not as an enginner but as an attendant in the roundhouse where the locomotives were housed, lubricated and refueled for the next trip. Someone pulled a lever and released tons of coal upon him. He was crushed but not killed. A third accident, the details of which escape my memory happened to him but again his life was preserved, just as Jude had promised. Then he was called by the Holy Spirit into the Body of Christ.

The Holy Spirit Who is omnipresent resides in and presides over human history on this planet in order to prevent hapless mortals from killing themselves and wiping out the race before He has called out from among the Gentiles a people for His name. Normally He permits events to occur in keeping with his natural laws of physics, chemistry, mathematics, the life sciences, *et al*, but He reserves the right to direct the course of history when otherwise foolish men are determined to play God. Who moved Napoleon to make the mistake of invading Russia in the winter? The laws of meteorology did the rest, as the merciless winter on the Russian steppes drove the remnant of the French army back. Who motivated Adolf Hitler to make the same mistake one hundred, thirty years later? What would have been the consequences, as they relate to Christian evangelism, if Napoleon had succeeded in his conquest and if Hitler had won World War II? The black plague wiped out half of Western Europe, but the other half survived. The Holy Spirit, Who is the Executive of the Godhead, will not allow circumstances and events to frustrate His eternal purpose.

It is easy for demographers to show that more than seventy per cent of the human race died in infancy and thus are assured of a home in heaven. I have discussed this in the present volume at pages 48 to 50. Thus the Holy Spirit has arranged to take them to heaven while they are safe, in order that others who survived to the age of discretion might be saved. If the infant death rate had been much less, the entire human race would have starved to death long before the time when God sent forth His Son, born of a woman, born under the law in order that He might redeem those who are under the law.

Paul argued for the theological interpretation of history on Mars Hill and the Athenian doctors who listened could not deny that it was so.

Now that he is sanctified and chosen in Him before the foundation of the world, that he should be holy and without blame before him, in love having been predestinated unto the adoption of children through Jesus Christ according to the purpose of His will, he is taken in infancy or protected from physical death until he reaches the time and place marked X where and when the Holy Spirit convinces him of sin, of righteousness and of judgment. What was his condition before the Holy Spirit tapped him on the shoulder and said, "Come. God wants you."? He was dead in trespasses and sins. He walked according to the course of this world. His thoughts and deeds were dictated by the prince of the power of the air, the unholy spirit who works like leaven works in dough, in the children of disobedience. He was the victim of the god of this world who had blinded his mind lest the light of the glory of the gospel of Christ should shine upon him. He was driven to godless deeds by the passions of his flesh which profits not at all.

Subject to demon possession, from which he will be eternally free after the Holy Spirit has made his body the divine temple, he indulges his despondant moods, entertains his confused thoughts, descends to the pig sty with his morals and visits his insane rages upon his victims. His id and ego divide the time between them as they dominate him. The voice of super ego is seldom heard and when heard it is ignored. Eros and thanatos, like Plato's black and white horses struggle within him. Ambivalence drives him to near insanity. He hates the light and revels in the darkness which he fancies covers his sins. Because he walks in the darkness he stumbles, falls and lies vomiting in the gutter. Or he preens himself at the country club, struts his pompous way about among his contemporaries, runs for congress and demonstrates that whoredom is practised in the intellectual as well as in the physical sphere.

But if he is one of God's elect, this period of sin and darkness is temporary. There will come the time when what he calls fate, but what has been arranged by the Holy Spirit, will present him with the gospel. He may have heard it often before, but this time he will *hear* it. Walter Taylor, the director of the Pacific Garden Mission on South State Street in Chicago, once consoled me as I was crestfallen because no one had responded to my gospel invitation at the close of the sermon. He placed his arm about my shoulders and said, "Don't be sad. These bums hear the gospel and hear the gospel and hear the gospel, and then one night they *hear* the gospel." He was correct. A week later when I preached again they who had heard the gospel *heard* the gospel. The difference was the convincing ministry of the Holy Spirit.

The sequence of events is set forth in Romans 10:13-15. Whosoever calls upon the name of the Lord shall be saved. But how can they call upon Him in whom they have not believed? And how can they believe in Him of whom they have not heard? And how shall they hear without a preacher? And how shall he preach if he is not sent? That is why Isaiah sang, "How beautiful upon the mountains are the feet of him that bringeth good tidings, that publishes peace." Obedient feet are beautiful feet, even when, in compliance with the Great Commission of our Lord, they walk the mountain paths to tell the story of Jesus and His love and grace. Those who are sent go; when they go they preach; when they preach sinners hear; when sinners hear they believe; when they believe they call upon the name of the Lord; when they call they are saved. Thus God has not only decreed the result but also the sequence of causes and results that bring the final result, as those who were ordained to eternal life believe.

When the Holy Spirit convinces the subject of His quest He talks about the proper things. He says nothing about moral reformation. The alcoholic is not scolded, nor advised to seek professional help. The libertine is not admonished to be pure. The murderer is not warned of the consequences of his violence. The mendacity of the liar is not exposed. Evangelists who spend their pulpit time lambasting the audience for their sins, should note that the Holy Spirit speaks to the unsaved only about his sin. He is a sinner because he has not believed upon Christ, Who is worthy of his trust because He is righteous as is evidenced by the fact that He has gone back to the Father and that is why we see Him no more. He is not out of sight because He is dead. He is gone because He arose from the dead and was invited back to the Father's right hand where He sits in repose until His enemies are made His footstool. Finally the Holy Spirit convinces the object of His quest that the prince of this world has been judged. Through death Messiah has destroyed him that had the power of death, that is the devil and has delivered them who through all of their lifetime were subject to bondage.

The Holy Spirit is sovereignly persuasive. He is God and as such He is omnipotent. He has never lost an argument. Theologians call this effectual call and irresistible grace. He is implementing the choice of Him Who said, "Ye have not chosen me but I have chosen you."

The sinner must repent and believe, but in his condition of spiritual death he cannot repent and believe, without the gift of repentance and the salvation which comes through faith. James, the pastor of the Jerusalem church came to understand that repentance is a gift of God, and said, "Then hath God granted repentance to the Gentiles." Paul also understood this and wrote that the fact that we are saved by grace through faith is the gift of God, not of works. The passage in Ephesians 2:8,9 does not say that faith is the gift of God, but that the fact that we are saved by grace through faith is God's gift.

When the sinner, chosen in Christ before the foundation of the world, and redeemed from the curse of the law at Calvary is effectually called by the Holy Spirit, he repents, believes and calls upon the name of the Lord. The promise is secure. He is saved. The Holy Spirit has breathed upon him because it was His sovereign decision to do so and the sinner heard his voice, although he had no idea of either the source or the destination of the Holy Spirit. Now he is baptized by the Holy Spirit into the Body of Christ. He is born from above, as a result of which he is now a "born one of God" because he has believed upon the name of the incarnate Christ. There is now in him a new creation, the result of the new birth. Paul called it the inner man. The baptism of the Holy Spirit, which is not to be confused with the filling of the Holy Spirit, is the occasion when the Holy Spirit comes in to dwell eternally and to make the body of the believer His temple. The heavenly resident in the temple can be grieved, unfortunately, but, fortunately He cannot be grieved away.

He not only convinces, brings the gifts of repentance and faith, induces the prayer for forgiveness, baptizes and indwells the body of the believer, but He also seals the believer as God's eternal property and thus announces to Satan and his demons that the body of the Christian is off limits to the hellish machinations of the nether world. Since the Spirit of Him who raised up Christ from the dead dwells in us He that raised up Christ from the dead will also quicken our mortal bodies at the rapture/resurrection. When the Lord descends from heaven with a shout and with the voice of the archangel and the last trump of God, the Holy Spirit will resurrect from the dust those who have died and catch up from mortal existence those who are alive and remain. We will meet the Lord in the air and begin our eternal association with Him, with Whom we have been associated in the intimacy of the trinity since the day He saved us.

All of this is the ideal plan of the sovereign God. It is ideal because of the perfect execution of it. From the moment in eternity when He chose us to the split second when we are raptured into His presence, no power of earth or hell has been able to frustrate the divine purpose. Everything will have gone according to the plan of Him Who is greater than he that is in the world.

So much for God's ideal plan and the ideal implementation of it. What about the real situation in which the Christian believer, the object of divine grace, finds himself in an unfriendly world society from the moment he is saved until the day of his physical death or rapture?

He is still in the world because he must be if he is to witness to the world the good news of the gospel of Christ. If God raptured into the divine presence every Christian the moment he was called and baptized into the Body of Christ, there would be no one left on earth to carry out the Great Commission. Though he enjoys the comfort and consolation of other Christians who, like him, are strangers in an unfriendly world, he is also confronted daily with the unsaved who are dead in trespasses and sins, driven by the demands of the flesh, brainwashed by the father of lies and thus convinced that the claims of Christianity cannot be sustained and incurably prejudiced against the Word of God. The Christian is also embarrassed by the countefeit representations of the holy rollers, who are getting rich on national television by performing "many wonderful works" in the name of the Lord. Once the paragon of virtue has spoken in what he calls tongues, healed the sick, raised the dead, cast out miscellaneous demons, stood on his crazy head, separated his followers from their money, sold his books, out of the depths of his abysmal ignorance of constitutional law criticized the Supreme Court and promoted the incipient Fascism of the political extreme right, by identifying it with orthodox Christianity, the unsaved world, whom the true Christian is trying to win to Christ, identifies him and his message with the ignorant fanaticism which he sees on television *ad infinitum ad nauseam.* The sinner may be dead in trespasses and sins and thus unable to come to Christ until he is enabled to do so by the Holy Spirit, but he is not stupid and he is able to tell the difference between a true gospel preacher and a snake oil salesman.

The Christian is also still motivated, tempted, often bored and sometimes annoyed by his own flesh. He is not a new creature, but he is the same old creature as before, but with the addition of a new creation as a result of regeneration. His flesh, which was not touched by the Holy Spirit when he was saved (although it will be glorified when the Lord returns), still demands fulfillment in terms of all of the sins, both physical and mental, which Paul suggests in Galatians 5:17. The Holy Spirit Who now dwells within him fights against the flesh and is fought against by the flesh. He produces His heavenly fruits which Paul lists in Gal.5:22,23. He is a battle ground on which is fought the fierce conflict between what comes natural for the flesh and what Abraham Lincoln called the "angels of our better nature." What he hates he nevertheless does and what he wants to do for Christ and His kingdom he somehow fails to do. In desperation he cries out, "O wretched man that I am. Who shall deliver me from this body of death" and then adds, "I thank God through Jesus Christ my Lord." This problem is greater for the babe in Christ than for the Christian who has grown in grace and in the knowledge of our Lord and Saviour Jesus Christ.

The Christian is always aware of the struggle that goes on between eros and thanatos within him, and he also sees in society the struggle between the social results of the flesh and those of the Spirit. Thus widespread inequity of wealth means poverty and physical degradation for the masses and the absurdity and

x

arrogant and heartless vulgarity of what Thorstein Veblen called "conspicuous consumption." While millions starve and other millions suffer pain for lack of medical care, the television commercials display the toys, gadgets, gewgaws, baubles and knicknacks, none of which have real social utility, at prices which would feed a poor family for a year. Even true Christians are guilty of salving their troubled conscience at Christmas time by buying a fifty dollar basket of food for the family on the wrong side of the tracks.

Something which the demagogues call private enterprise and *laissez faire*, supported by a classical theory of economics which was valid for the period before the rise of the factory system, which separated the worker from his tools, but which has long since lost its appeal for those who recognize that in the survival of the fittest, which the evolutionists talk about, the weak cannot survive without help from the strong, right wing fundamentalists, who somehow separate their theological gospel from its social implications, use their television influence to support the political party which seems to say that if a man cannot make his way in a capitalist society, let him make his way out of it.

When on Memorial Day Sunday we were asked to sing about America the Beautiful where "her alabaster cities gleam undimmed by human tears" I remarked to a Sunday School teacher who is abundantly aware of the superior quality of her Christian experience, that it seemed ironical for us to sing of alabaster and gleaming cities which are undimmed by human tears, when we have the slums of the nation's capital, the Bronx, Watts and Hough Avenue, she remarked that apparently the people who live in the ghettos, eat out of garbage cans and sleep in the warm air ducts on the streets of Washington, D.C. in the winter time, want it that way!

At a time when modernists emphasize the social gospel at the expense, and even denial of the theological gospel and the fundamentalists thump the tub for the theological gospel and vote for Social Darwinism, it is difficult for the babe in Christ to understand why he should study his Bible and try to grow in grace.

The institutional church makes imperious demands upon the time and energy of pastors, whose pulpit offerings suffer for the lack of time to study their Bibles. Not all preachers who offer their soporific outlines on Sunday morning reject the Bible as the Word of God. Some are so sure that the Bible is God's inerrant message to mankind that they have not read it and have not the ability to make clear what it teaches to the laity. A proof text, taken out of context can provide material for twenty minutes of tweedle dum and tweedle dee, while the congregation frets lest they be late for the tee shot off the first tee.

On the night of His arrest, shortly before He was betrayed and arrested in the Garden of Gethsemane, our Lord gave to Peter a special commission. He was told to strengthen his brethren. The Acts of the Apostles reveals Peter as a tower of strength to the early church, but his greatest contribution, pursuant to his commission is his contribution to the literature of the Greek New Testament. In his first epistle he tells the babe in Christ what to lay aside and in his second epistle he tells him what to add and the order in which to add it. Then he promises that if we follow his formula for Christian growth in grace, we will discover that "they make you neither barren nor unfruitful in the knowledge of our Lord and Saviour Jesus Christ" and adds the warning that "he that lacks these things is blind or myopic and has forgotten that he is saved.

Peter does not demand that the babe in Christ lay aside tobacco, beer, illicit sex or any of the other popular taboos. He does suggest that we lay aside the psychological sins, which are listed — malice, guile, envy, hypocrisy and evil speaking. He warns that these sins, if indulged sap our strength to the low point where we do not want the sincere milk of the Word of God, without which we cannot expect to grow in grace. Here Peter reveals one of the miracles of divine inspiration for he applies Plato's principle of the black horse/white horse team which the charioteer tries unsuccessfully to manage, and he anticipates Freud's psychic analysis in terms of eros (white horse) and thanatos (black). It is unlikely that Peter had ever heard of Plato and he could not have anticipated Freud. But Peter was taught by the Holy Spirit that malice and guile, hatred and evil speaking with the hypocrisy which these vicious negative attitudes produce, was enough to make the Christian so tired, after a day of hating others, that he had not the strength to read his Bible. In Freudian terms negative attitudes burn up the libido which Freud defined as "emotional or psychic energy derived from primitive biological urges and usually goal oriented." Sex was only a part of the eros; the rest of it is the urge to live and to grow. Peter is saying that after the babe in Christ lays aside the thanatos drive with its negative attitudes, he has available the entire libido which gives to him an intense desire for the sincere milk of the Word of God. Show to Peter and to me the Christian who cannot get enough of the sincere milk of the Word of God and we will show to you a mature child of God, who has found in the abundance of eternal life so much joy and so much to challenge him that he does not even think of the sins of the flesh which filled his life before he was saved.

Once we have laid aside the libido burning negatives, drink the milk of the Word of God and quickly outgrow the baby formula for the strong meat of Christian theology we add the things which Peter lists in 2 Peter 1:5-7. They must be added in the order in which he lists them, for each is instrumental to the addition of the next. It is by means of faith that we add the intellectual virtue of humility which is prerequisite to knowledge. Then, each in its turn, is necessary for the addition of the next. Suppose we continue to grow until we have added them all in abundance. Note the result: they (faith, virtue, knowledge, temperance, patience, godliness, brotherly kindness and charity) make you that you should not be barren nor unfruitful in the knowledge of the Lord. We do not learn how to win souls by reading a book or taking a course in a Bible Institute or Seminary. Peter's additions, if added in abundance, make us what the divine ideal, which called us in the first place, had in mind.

Thus Peter obeyed his commission, given to him by his Lord, just before he denied that he even knew Jesus. It is for those who wish to follow Peter's formula that *The Renaissance New Testament* has been written and which is now offered to the Christian reading public. It has been designed, organized and written with the Christian in view who would like to develop a strong appetite, first for the sincere milk and then for the strong meat of the Word. Field tested now, in part, for seven years, it has been proved to be as interesting and helpful to the laity, who have had no previous experience with Greek as to the clergy, some of whom have had Greek and some have not. For this I am profoundly and humbly grateful.

ΑΠΟΚΑΛΥΨΙΣ ΙΩΑΝΝΟΥ

The Heavenly Worship

(Revelation 4:1-11)

Revelation 4:1 - "After this I looked, and behold, a door was opened in heaven: and the first voice which I heard was as it were a trumpet talking with me, which said, Come up hither, and I will shew thee things which must be hereafter."

Μετὰ ταῦτα εἶδον, καὶ ἰδοὺ θύρα ἠνεῳγμένη ἐν τῷ οὐρανῷ, καὶ ἡ φωνὴ ἡ πρώτη ἣν ἤκουσα ὡς σάλπιγγος λαλούσης μετ' ἐμοῦ λέγων, Ἀνάβα ὧδε, καὶ δείξω σοι ἃ δεῖ γενέσθαι μετὰ ταῦτα.

"After this I looked, and lo, in heaven an open door! And the first voice, which I had heard speaking to me like a trumpet, said, 'Come up hither, and I will show you what must take place after this." ... RSV

Μετὰ (preposition with the accusative, time extent) 50.

ταῦτα (acc.pl.neut.of οὗτος, anaphoric in a time expression) 93.

εἶδον (1st.per.sing.aor.ind.of ὁράω, constative) 144.

καὶ (continuative conjunction) 14.

ἰδοὺ (exclamation) 95.

θύρα (nom.sing.fem.of θύρα, nominative absolute) 571.

ἠνεῳγμένη (perf.pass.part.nom.sing.fem.of ἀνοίγω, adjective, predicate position, restrictive, in agreement with θύρα) 188.

ἐν (preposition with the locative of place) 80.

τῷ (loc.sing.masc.of the article in agreement with οὐρανῷ) 9.

οὐρανῷ (loc.sing.masc.of οὐρανός, place) 254.

καὶ (continuative conjunction) 14.

ἡ (nom.sing.fem.of the article in agreement with φωνή) 9.

φωνὴ (nom.sing.fem.of φωνή, suspended subject) 222.

ἡ (nom.sing.fem.of the article in agreement with πρώτη) 9.

πρώτη (nom.sing.fem.of πρῶτος, in agreement with φωνή) 487.

ἥν (acc.sing.fem.of ὅς, direct object of ἤκουσα) 65.

ἤκουσα (1st.per.sing.aor.act.ind.of ἀκούω, constative) 148.

ὡς (comparative particle) 128.

σάλπιγγος (abl.sing.fem.of σάλπιγξ, comparison) 1507.

λαλούσης (pres.act.part.abl.sing.fem.of λαλέω, adjectival, predicate position, restrictive, in agreement with σάλπιγγος) 815.

μετ' (preposition with the genitive, accompaniment) 50.

ἐμοῦ (gen.sing.masc.of ἐμός, accompaniment) 1267.

λέγων (pres.act.part.nom.sing.masc.of λέγω, recitative) 66.

Ἀνάβα (2d.per.sing.2d.aor.act.impv.of ἀναβαίνω, command, ingressive) 323.

ὧδε (local adverb) 766.

καὶ (continuative conjunction) 14.

δείξω (1st.per.sing.fut.act.ind.of δείκνυμι, predictive) 359.

σοι (dat.sing.masc.of σύ, indirect object of δείξω) 104.

ἅ (acc.pl.neut.of ὅς, relative pronoun, direct object of δείξω) 65.

δεῖ (3d.per.sing.pres.impersonal ind. of δεῖ) 1207.

γενέσθαι (aor.inf.of γίνομαι, complementary) 113.

μετὰ (preposition with the accusative of time extent) 50.

ταῦτα (acc.pl.neut.of οὗτος, time extent) 93.

Translation - *"After these things I saw — and Look! An opened door in the heaven and the voice — the first one which I heard, like a trumpet, speaking with me, saying, 'Come up here and I will show you things which must happen later.'"*

Comment: ταῦτα is anaphoric. It refers to the introduction of Jesus to John (Rev.1:10-20) and the dictation by Jesus to John of the seven letters (Rev.2:1-3:22).

It is legitimate for the exegete who approaches the inspired record to construct a hypothetical model as a means of testing his hypothesis. If, on the basis of his research, internal evidence appears that tends to confirm the validity of his model, and if there is no internal evidence to dispute it, he may consider that his prior assumption is correct.

It is not legitimate for the student to approach the inspired text with a view to *proving* (not testing) that which he has already determined is true. If the model which is consistent with his predetermined conviction is not supported by the text, he must either abandon it or resort to torturing the text with his own ideas in terms of diction, grammar, syntax, context and *zeitgeist*. If one is determined to be subjective, he will find a way. Such an approach is foolish, since the Word of God teaches only what it teaches and it does not teach what eisegetes try to make it teach. Far better for the student to admit that his previous position was wrong than to incure the shame and guilt of tampering with the Word of God. If, despite his objectivity, he cannot determine what the text means by what it says, he should freely admit that he does not know. Only Gnostics know everything that God knows.

The pretribulation rapture model demands that the rapture of the believers will occur at the beginning of Daniel's 70th week. All exegesis must therefore be made to fit that assumption. If it is true no valid exegesis of other material will refute it. If it is false no valid exegesis of other material will support. Otherwise we have the Holy Spirit being inconsistent with Himself. And no evangelical will admit that.

If we divide the Revelation, on the basis of Revelation 1:19, as the Scofield Bible editors have, into three major divisions: Part I. *"The things which thou hast seen"* (Rev.1:1-20); Part II. *"The things which are": the seven churches*; and Part III. *"Things which shall be hereafter"* (Rev.4:1-22:21), and if we say that Chapters 2 and 3, *"The things which are"* present a picture of the church in the world from Pentecost to pretribulation rapture, then we must argue that the Body of Christ is not found upon the earth beyond Revelation 4:1, even though the Revelation points to saints on earth during the tribualtion frequently. We must also suppose a rapture at the beginning of Chapter 4. The theory says that the Philadelphians and as many of the Laodiceans that were saved (Rev.3:20-21) are caught up to meet the Lord for a seven year sojourn in the air, after which they and He will return to earth at Armageddon. If chapters 2 and 3 picture the church in the world during the church age, to which I agree, but exclude the church from the earthly scene during the tribulation, to which I dissent, the picture at the beginning of chapter 4 is of events at the beginning of the tribulation. To which I also agree. The issue is where the Body of Christ is during the tribuation? On earth or in the air above the earth? If we say that the Church will be gone from earth at the close of chapter 3, then it is convenient for us to interpret Μετὰ ταῦτα ("after these things") in a dispensational sense and conclude that the scene in heaven described in chapters 4 and 5 will occur after the church is raptured. But that is a deduction that must flow from the assumption that the rapture precedes the tribulation. Since that is the point at issue, such a position is a classic example of begging the question. We may not assume that the point in litigation is true and then use it as a part of the case which we are seeking to construct.

What other view of Μετὰ ταῦτα can we take? And let us remember that whatever view we take it must fit the context. After the Prolgoue (Rev.1:1-3) John offers the Introduction in which he describes his encounter with the Lord on Patmos. He says that our Lord dictated to him seven letters which he was ordered to commit to writing and send to the messengers of the seven churches, which were then in Asia Minor. He then says in Revelation 4:1 Μετὰ ταῦτα - "after these things" *viz*., events of Revelation 1:9-20) and the dictation of the letters of Revelation 2:1-3:22, "I heard the voice . . . " which had spoken to him before in Revelation 1:10. And what did the Lord say to him this time? That he was to come up to heaven in order to see the rest of what our Lord wished to show to him. How convenient, if one wishes to prove one's point, to say that

John's rapture is a type of the rapture of the church! But where does the Bible say that John is a type of anything or anybody? Why not say that Paul is a type of the raptured church because he had the same experience that John had (2 Cor.12:1-4). Both Paul and John were caught up to heaven for purposes of Christian education — Paul in the field of soteriology and John in the field of eschatology. And since each of these fields is essential to an understanding of the other, both Paul and John became mature theologians and were able to fulfill their Apostolic functions of writing the remainder of the New Testament literature. The Body of Christ had no further light on the subjects involved until the early part of the 19th century when a "charismatic" girl in Scotland had the vision upon the basis of which pretribulation rapture has been built. If God is still calling, anointing and inspiring apostles, prophets and purveryors of words of wisdom, without which we cannot understand the New Testament message, despite the fact that Paul says in 1 Cor.13:8 that those apostolic gifts of communication were phased out, then perhaps we should all stop studying the Word of God until the Holy Spirit gets it finished. But He has already told us in Revelation 2:2 that those who call themselves apostles and are not, are liars. If the Lord had not called end time "apostles" liars it would not be proper for us to call them liars. John's rapture in Rev.4:1,2 means the rapture of the church before the tribulation only because it must in order to build a logical model which leads with good logic and bad exegesis from a false assumption to a false conclusion. Let us indeed be logical, but let us also be exegetes, not eisegetes, for if eisegesis is legitimate then any one with an I.Q. to match his waist line can make the Bible teach anything you wish. All the children of God should go out and hang themselves since Judas did and Jesus said that we are to go and do likewise and that we must do it quickly (Mt.27:5; Lk.10:37b; John 13:27b).

If sound Biblical exegesis does not teach what we believe we must either admit error and change our views to conform to Scripture or we must eschew exegesis and resort to eisegesis. The latter policy may not involve loss of face, prestige, position or salary though it is certain to involve embarrassment and loss of reward at the judgment seat of Christ (2 Tim.2:15,16). Workmen who seek to avoid ridicule from bigots at the Bible conferences where they are featured speakers are headed for embarrassment at the judgment seat of Christ. Scripture teaches only what is there by the choice of the Author, the Holy Spirit. It does not necessarily teach what we hope is there. Thus the entire matter comes down to sound exegesis. What does the passage say? What do the words mean? What is the grammar and syntax? What the context? Under what circumstances and by whom and to whom was it written? We must remember that what it says must be consistent with what the Scriptures say every where else (2 Petere 1:20).

After what things did John see the open door in heaven and hear the trumpet voice? After the church age? After the rapture? Or after Christ had finished the dictation of the seven letters? Where did the dictation and writing take place? He was on earth — on the island of Patmos. When? In the latter part of the first century. *Cf.* comment on Rev.1:10. When John wrote Chapters 2 and 3 was he in the tribulation period? Has what he wrote had significance for Christians in the first century? Indeed it has. And for all Christians since? Without doubt for "all scripture is profitable . . . " (2 Tim.3:16,17). And will it have special significance for those Christians on earth during the tribualtion? More for them than for anyone else, because the *zeitgeist* will be right. They will be living in the times when the current events all about them will coordinate with that which our Lord will be telling them in the letters to the churches. Just as students of Psalm 22 who lived before the crucifixion received blessing from its study though they lived before the prophecy was fulfilled, so we now receive blessing from Revelation 2 and 3, but these passages will come into the sharpest focus in the days to come.

Thus when John says Μετὰ ταῦτα εἶδον - "after these things I saw . . . "he was relating his experiences in the order of their occurence. After Christ finished dictating, John saw . . . κ.τ.λ. This passage divides time into dispensations only for dispensationalists, who have taken their cue from the charismatic vision in Scotland 150 years ago.   Irving, J.N.Darby, W.E.Blackstone, R.A.Torrey and the Bible Institutes have perpetuated it.

The author abandoned pretribulation rapture in 1937. My present view, subject to change on grounds of good exegesis, is that the rapture of the Body of Christ will occur at the end of the tribulation at the same time when Jesus Christ returns to earth to take His place on David's throne. If I ever see the error of my position I will hasten to repudiate it, because I would rather face by brethren in embarrassment than to face my Lord as an "ashamed stonecutter" (2 Tim.2:15).

John saw the opened door in heaven. He saw Jesus, in vision, on the earth. The voice which he heard was the same one that he had heard in Rev.1:10, a few minutes before. This time the voice invited John up to heaven and promises to show him things scheduled on the divine time clock at some future time - *i.e.* future to John in the first century and future yet to us on 4 March 1984.

There is no way to determine whether the second μετὰ ταῦτα belongs to γενέσθαι of verse 1 or to ἐγενόμην of verse 2. No damange is done because it can with perfect consistency belong to both. What must be (ἃ δεῖ γενέσθαι) is chronologically after the dictation of the letters. John again found himself "in spirit" (ἐγενόμην ἐν πνεύματι) after Christ promised him to reveal the future. I have translated the second μετὰ ταῦτα as an adjunct of γενέσθαι, as did Weymouth (. . . "which are to heppen in the future"), while Goodspeed translates to join with ἐγενόμην (" . . . which must take place. Immediately after this I found myself in a trance . . . "). Both ideas are right. John is about to have the same experience that the two witnesses will have in the tribulation (Rev.11:12). It is also Paul's experience in 2 Cor.12:1-4; and Enoch's (Heb.11:5). Thus John was caught up in the first century, not the church in the 20th century or some later time. Of course it was necessary for him to be taken to heaven because what he is about to see is the throne room of the Almighty God in heaven, not on Patmos.

Verse 2 - "And immediately I was in the spirit: and behold a throne was set in heaven, and one sat on the throne."

εὐθέως ἐγενόμην ἐν πνεύματι, καὶ ἰδοὺ θρόνος ἔκειτο ἐν τῷ οὐρανῷ, καὶ ἐπὶ τὸν θρόνον καθήμενος,

"At once I was in the Spirit, and lo, a throne stood in heaven, with one seated on the throne!" . . . RSV

εὐθέως (temporal adverb) 392.

ἐγενόμην (1st.per.sing.aor.mid.ind.of γίνομαι, ingressive) 113.

ἐν (preposition with the instrumental, association) 80.

πνεύματι (instru.sing.neut.of πνεῦμα, association) 83.

καὶ (continuative conjunction) 14.

ἰδοὺ (exclamation) 95.

θρόνος (nom.sing.masc.of θρόνος, subject of ἔκειτο) 519.

ἔκειτο (3d.per.sing.imp.ind.of κεῖμαι, progressive description) 295.

ἐν (preposition with the locative of place) 80.

τῷ (loc.sing.masc.of οὐρανός, place) 9. .

οὐρανῷ (loc.sing.masc.of οὐρανός, place) 254.

καὶ (adjunctive conjunction joining substantives) 14.

ἐπὶ (preposition with the accusative, place description) 47.

τὸν (acc.sing.masc.of the article in agreement with θρόνον) 9.

θρόνον (acc.sing.masc.of θρόνος, rest) 519.

καθήμενος (pres.mid.part.nom.sing.masc.of κάθημαι, substantival, subject of ἦν understood) 377.

Translation - "Immediately I found myself in the Spirit and Look! A throne permanently established in heaven and upon the throne one sitting, . . . "

Comment: Is εὐθέως faster than ἐν ἀτόμῳ, ἐν ῥιπῇ ὀφθαλμοῦ (1 Cor.15:52)? John was immediately caught up to heaven. *Cf.* Paul's description of what happened to him in 2 Cor.12:1-4. And Enoch's (Heb.11:5). It was by the Holy Spirit or, as Goodspeed has it, as a result of a trance. In any case the Holy Spirit is about to transmit information to John which he will pass on to us.

The throne of God has always stood there as the imperfect tense in ἔκειτο indicates. *Cf.* John 20:12 where we have ἔκειτο in progressive duration - "where He had been lying" as opposed to progressive description - "where it has always stood" in Rev.4:2. Even during the time that Jesus was lying in the tomb in a repose that would not continue His throne was established in heaven in a position which will never be abandoned.

The One who is sitting on the throne in heaven is Christ (verses 8,9,10,11; 5:9-10). His description, which severely tests the power of human language to convey, is found in

Verse 3 - "And he that sat was to look upon like a jasper and a sardine stone: and there was a rainbow round about the throne, in sight like unto an emerald."

καὶ ὁ καθήμενος ὅμοιος ὁράσει λίθῳ ἰάσπιδι καὶ σαρδίῳ, καὶ ἶρις κυκλόθεν τοῦ θρόνου ὅμοιος ὁράσει σμαραγδίνῳ.

"And he who sat there appeared like a jasper and carnelian, and round the throne was a rainbow that looked like an emerald." . . . RSV

καὶ (continuative conjunction) 14.

ὁ (nom.sing.masc.of the article in agreement with καθήμενος) 9.

καθήμενος (pres.mid.part.nom.sing.masc.of κάθημαι, subject of ἦν understood) 377.

ὅμοιος (nom.sing.masc.of ὅμοιος, predicate adjective) 923.

ὁράσει (loc.sing.fem.of ὅρασις, sphere) 2982.

λίθῳ (instru.sing.masc.of λίθος, comparison) 290.

#5339 ἰάσπιδι (instru.sing.fem.of ἴασπις, comparison).

King James Version

jasper - Rev.4:3; 21:11,18,19.

Revised Standard Version

jasper - Rev.4:3; 21:11,18,19.

Meaning: A Phoenician word (Moulton & Milligan, 297). "A precious stone of divers colors (for some are purple, others blue, others green and others of the color of brass; Plin. h.n.37,37 (8); Rev.4:3; 21:11,18,19. (But many think (unquestionably) the diamond to be meant here; others the precious opal." (Thayer, 296).

καὶ (adjunctive conjunction joining nouns) 14.

#5340 σαρδίῳ (instru.sing.masc.of σάρδιον, comparison).

King James Version

sardine - Rev.4:3.
sardius - Rev.21:20.

Revised Standard Version

carnelian - Rev.4:3; 21:20.

Meaning: sard, sardius, a precious stone. "There are two kinds, concerning which Theophr. *de lapid.* 16, 5, para.30 ed. Schneid, says, τοῦ γὰρ σαρδίου τὸ μὲν διαφανὲς ἐροὑρότερον δὲ καλεῖται θῆλυ, τὸ δὲ διαφανὲς μέν μελάντερον δὲ καὶ ἄρσεν, the former of which is called carnelian (because flesh colored)." (Thayer, 569). LXX has σάρδιον in Ex.28:17; 36:17 (39:10) and Ezek.28:13, αἱματόεντα σάρδια, Orph. *de lapid.* 16,5). The latter *sard.* Rev.4:3; 21:20. Hence, the adjective σάρδιος, α ον. Sardine. *sc.* λίθον. See Exod.35:8.

καὶ (adjunctive conjunction joining nouns) 14.

#5341 ἶρις (nom.sing.fem.of ἶρις, subject of verb understood).

King James Version

rainbow - Rev.4:3; 10:1.

Revised Standard Version

rainbow - Rev.4:3; 10:1.

Meaning: rainbow - Rev.4:3; 10:1.

#5342 κυκλόθεν (adverbial).

King James Version

about - Rev.4:8.
round about - Rev.4:3,4.

Revised Standard Version

round - Rev.4:3,4.
all round - Rev.4:8.

Meaning: An adverb and adjective. From all sides; round about; surrounding. *Cf.* κυκλόω (#2509); κύκλος (#2183). Rev.4:3,4,8. Followed by a genitive in Rev.4:3,4 (adjectival) Adverbial in Rev.4:8.

τοῦ (gen.sing.masc.of the article in agreement with θρόνου) 9.
θρόνου (gen.sing.masc.of θρόνος, place description) 519.
ὅμοιος (nom.sing.masc.of ὅμοιος, predicate adjective) 923.
ὁράσει (loc.sing.fem.of ὅρασις, sphere) 2982.

#5343 σμαραγδίνῳ (instru.sing.masc.of σμαράγδινος, comparison).

King James Version

emerald - Rev.4:3.

Revised Standard Version

emerald - Rev.4:3.

Meaning: Cf. σμάραγδος (#5431). Made of emerald; of emerald; like an emerald - Rev.4:3.

Translation - "And the One seated there was in appearance like a jasper and a sardine stone; and a rainbow about the throne looked like an emerald."

Comment: The verb must be supplied. ὁράσει - a locative of sphere, followed by an instrumental of comparison. Note the adjective κυκλόθεν followed by the genitive, here and in verse 4, though in verse 8 it is used adverbially. The scene is too beautiful for words even if we were sure what colors are meant. The green rainbow around the throne challenges our imagination. John must have gasped. The description of the heavenly scene continues in verse 4.

(Note: On this day, 8 January 1975, the long hand manuscript of *The Renaissance New Testament* had advanced to this point. It had been a dark, blustering, cold and rainy day. All day long thunder had rolled and lightning had flashed across the dark sky — unusual weather for January in Kentucky. This afternoon I encountered ἶρις (#5341) for the first time in the New Testament and researched and wrote the analysis which appears here. At 4:15 p.m. the rain stopped and the sun shone brilliantly in the western sky. As Mrs. Yeager returned from the University she saw a gigantic double rainbow arching across the eastern sky. She came rushing into the house to tell me and we stood outside, gazing with rapture at the two distinct bands of red, golden and emerald which reached from horizon to horizon. The inner band was brillaint; the other band more pastel. That I should see my first double rainbow in 62 years on the day, indeed within the hour in which I first studied ἶρις in the Greek New Testament is not an omen, for we have only one sign (Mt.12:38-40) in the age of grace and we need no other. But God in His grace provided us with an illustration of what John saw above the throne of God. This rainbow had red and yellow in it. The one John saw was green. καὶ κυκλόθεν τοῦ θρόνου ὅμοιος ὁράσει σμαραγδίνῳ. How beautiful heaven must be.

Verse 4 - "And round about the throne were four and twenty seats: and upon the seats I saw four and twenty elders sitting, clothed in white raiment; and they had on their heads crowns of gold."

καὶ κυκλόθεν τοῦ θρόνου θρόνους εἴκοσι τέσσαρες, καὶ ἐπὶ τοὺς θρόνους εἴκοσι τέσσαρες πρεσβυτέρους καθημένους περιβεβλημένους ἐν ἱματίοις λευκοῖς, καὶ ἐπὶ τὰς κεφαλὰς αὐτῶν στεφάνους χρυσοῦς.

"Round the throne were twenty-four thrones, and seated on the thrones were twenty-four elders, clad in white garments, with golden crowns upon their heads." . . . RSV

καὶ (continuative conjunction) 14.

κυκλόθεν (adverbial) 5342.

τοῦ (gen.sing.masc.of the article in agreement with θρόνου) 9.

θρόνου (gen.sing.masc.of θρόνος, place description) 519.

θρόνους (acc.pl.masc.of θρόνος, direct object of εἶδον, verse 1) 519.

εἴκοσι (numeral) 2283.

τέσσαρες (numeral) 1508.

καὶ (adjunctive conjunction joining nouns) 14.

ἐπὶ (preposition with the accusative, rest) 47.

τοὺς (acc.pl.masc.of the article in agreement with θρόνους) 9.

θρόνους (acc.pl.masc.of θρόνος, rest) 519.

εἴκοσι (numeral) 2283.

τέσσαρες (numeral) 1508.

πρεσβυτέρους (acc.pl.masc.of πρεσβύτερος, direct object of εἶδον) 1141.

καθημένους (pres.mid.part.acc.pl.masc.of κάθημαι, adjectival, predicate position, restrictive, in agreement with πρεσβυτέρους) 377.

περιβεβλημένους (perf.pass.part.acc.pl.masc.of περιβάλλω, adjectival, predicate position, restrictive, in agreement with πρεσβυτέρους) 631.

ἐν (preposition with the locative of place) 80.

ἱματίοις (loc.pl.neut.of ἱμάτιον, place) 534.

λευκοῖς (loc.pl.neut.of λευκός, in agreement with ἱματίοις) 522.

καὶ (adjunctive conjunction joining nouns) 14.

ἐπὶ (preposition with the accusative, rest) 47.

τὰς (acc.pl.fem.of the article in agreement with κεφαλὰς) 9.

κεφαλὰς (acc.pl.fem.of κεφαλή, rest) 521.

αὐτῶν (gen.pl.masc.of αὐτός, possession) 16.

στεφάνους (acc.pl.masc.of στέφανος, direct object of εἶδον) 1640.

χρυσοῦς (acc.pl.masc.of χρύσεος, in agreement with στεφάνους) 4828.

Translation - "And in a circule around the throne I saw twenty-four thrones and upon the thrones twenty-four elders sitting, clothed in white garments and I saw upon their heads golden crowns."

Comment: John saw the 24 thrones encircling the throne of God and the 24 elders seated upon them, dressed in white and wearing golden crowns. It is totally idle to speculate about who these elders are and why there are 24 of them. The fact that the Levitical priesthood was divided into 24 groups, for purposes of division of labor in interesting, though not necessarily enlightening (2 Chron.24). *Cf.* Isa.24:23 where the LXX has πρεσβύτεροι for "ancients." Of course we may expect the pretribulation rapture teachers to claim that the elders represent the raptured church, whom they raptured in verse 1, despite the fact that there is nothing in Scripture to say that these elders are typical of anything or anyone. They are not the martyred saints of Rev.6:11, since those saints have not been killed yet. The same argument excludes those of Rev.7:9,11. Nor are they the group of Rev.19:14 who number many more than 24. These elders are not saints as their song of Rev.5:9-10 reveals. *Cf.* comment *en loc.* They belong to the heavenly order of things, and that is all that anyone who does not wish to be presumptuous can say about them. To say that the elders are the raptured church makes it incumbent upon such commentators to show that the church has indeed been raptured at this time point. Another example of *petitio principii*, which begs the question. The argument says, "The elders are the church which has been raptured because when the church was raptured they appeared in heaven as elders." !

The tribulation has not yet begun as John stands, looking at the heavenly scene. It begins when the Lamb takes off the first seal (Rev.6:1-2).

Verse 5 - "And out of the throne proceeded lightnights and thunderings and voices: and there were seven lamps of fire burning before the trhone, which are the seven spirits of God."

καὶ ἐκ τοῦ θρόνου ἐκπορεύονται ἀστραπαὶ καὶ φωναὶ καὶ βρονταί. καὶ ἑπτὰ λαμπάδες πυρὸς καιόμεναι ἐνώπιον τοῦ θρόνου, ἃ εἰσιν τὰ ἑπτὰ πνεύματα τοῦ θεοῦ,

"From the throne issue flashes of lightning, and voices and peals of thunder, and before the throne burn seven torches of fire, which are the seven spirits of God;" . . . RSV

καὶ (continuative conjunction) 14.

ἐκ (preposition with the ablative, source) 19.

τοῦ (abl.sing.masc.of the article in agreement with θρόνου) 9.

θρόνου (abl.sing.masc.of θρόνος, source) 519.

ἐκπορεύονται (3d.per.pl.pres.mid.ind.of ἐκπορεύομαι, progressive description) 270.

ἀστραπαὶ (nom.pl.fem.of ἀστραπή, subject of ἐκπονεύονται) 1502.

καὶ (adjunctive conjunction joining nouns) 14.

φωναὶ (nom.pl.fem.of φωνή, subject of ἐκπορεύονται) 222.

καὶ (adjunctive conjunction joining nouns) 14.

βρονταί (nom.pl.fem.of βροντή, subject of ἐκπορεύονται) 2117.

καὶ (continuative conjunction) 14.

ἑπτὰ (numeral) 1024.

λαμπάδες (nom.pl.fem.of λαμπάς, subject of εἰσίν understood, present periphrastic) 1529.

πυρὸς (gen.sing.neut.of πῦρ, description) 298.

καιόμεναι (pres.mid.part.nom.pl.fem.of καίω, present periphrastic) 453.

ἐνώπιον (preposition with the genitive of place description) 1798.

τοῦ (gen.sing.masc.of the article in agreement with θρόνου) 9.

θρόνου (gen.sing.masc.of θρόνος, place description) 519.

ἃ (nom.pl.neut.of ὅς, relative pronoun, subject of εἰσιν) 65.

εἰσιν (3d.per.pl.pres.ind.of εἰμί, aoristic) 86.

τὰ (nom.pl.neut.of the article in agreement with πνεύματα) 9.

ἑπτὰ (numeral) 1024.

πνεύματα (nom.pl.neut.of πνεῦμα, predicate nominative) 83.

τοῦ (gen.sing.masc.of the article in agreement with θεοῦ) 9.

θεοῦ (gen.sing.masc.of θεός, description) 124.

Translation - "And lightnings and voices and peals of thunder are coming out of the throne, and there are seven burning lamps before the throne which are the seven spirits of God."

Comment: There is no need to translate these present tenses as historical. John is describing what he is seeing. The throne of God is beautiful beyond description and majestic in power. Lightnings, voices and thunder speak of authority and power. The lamps before the throne burning brightly are identified, so we need not speculate. They represent the Holy Spirit, once again, as in Rev.1:4 and Rev.5:6, in the seven-fold plentitude of His sovereign power. Note that the virgins who awaited the coming of the Bridegroom had lamps such as these (Mt.25:1,3,4,7,8). The Holy Spirit who is always in the presence of God, Father and Son, burns in the lamps of all believers who yield to him (1 Cor.6:19; Eph.4:30; Gal.5:22,23 *al*). Two more elements in the thrilling description of the heavenly scene are added in

Verse 6 - "And before the throne was a sea of glass like unto crystal: and in the midst of the throne and round about the throne, were four beasts full of eyes before and behind."

καὶ ἐνώπιον τοῦ θρόνου ὡς θάλασσα ὑαλίνη ὁμοία κρυστάλλῳ. Καὶ ἐν μέσῳ τοῦ θρόνου καὶ κύκλῳ τοῦ θρόνου τέσαρρα ζῷα γέμοντα ὀφθαλμῶν ἔμπροσθεν καὶ ὄπισθεν.

"... and before the throne there is as it were a sea of glass, like crystal. And round the throne, on each side of the throne, are four living creatures, full of eyes in front and behind:" ... RSV

καὶ (continuative conjunction) 14.
ἐνώπιον (preposition with the genitive of place description) 1798.
τοῦ (gen.sing.masc.of the article in agreement with θρόνου) 9.
θρόνου (gen.sing.masc.of θρόνος, place description) 519.
ὡς (comparative particle) 128.
θάλασσα (nom.sing.fem.of θάλασσα, subject of ἔστι understood) 374.

#5344 ὑαλίνη (nom.sing.fem.of ὑάλινος, in agreement with θάλασσα).

King James Version

of glass - Rev.4:6; 15:2,2.

Revised Standard Version

of glass - Rev.4:6; 15:2,2.

Meaning: Cf. ὕαλος (#5428). A fragment of Corinna and occasionally in Greek writings from Aristophanes down - like glass; glassy. Smooth and transparent - Rev.4:6; 15:22 (Thayer, 633).

ὁμοία (nom.sing.fem.of ὅμοιος, in agreement with θάλασσα) 923.

#5345 κρυστάλλῳ (instr.sing.masc.of κρύσταλλος, comparison).

King James Version

crystal - Rev.4:6; 22:1.

Revised Standard Version

crystal - Rev.4:6; 22:1.

Meaning: Cf. κρύος - "ice." Anything congealed and transparent. The glassy sea was transparent - Rev.4:6; the water was clear - Rev.22:1.

καὶ (continuative conjunction) 14.
ἐν (preposition with the locative of place) 80.
μέσῳ (loc.sing.masc.of μέσος, place) 873.
τοῦ (gen.sing.masc.of the article in agreement with θρόνου) 9.
θρόνου (gen.sing.masc.of θρόνος, description) 519.
καὶ (adjunctive conjunction joining adverbial phrases) 14.
κύκλῳ (loc.sing.masc.of κύκλος, place) 2183.

τοῦ (gen.sing.masc.of the article in agreement with ϑρόνου) 9.

ϑρόνου (gen.sing.masc.of ϑρόνος, place description) 519.

τέσσαρα (nom.pl.fem.of τέσσαρεσ, in agreement with ζῷα) 1508.

ζῷα (nom.pl.neut.of ζῷον, subject of εἰσιν understood) 5086.

γέμοντα (pres.act.part.nom.pl.neut.of γέμω, adjectival, predicate position, in agreement with ζῷᾳ) 1457.

ὀφϑαλμῶν (gen.pl.masc.of ὀφϑαλμός, description) 501.

ἔμπροσϑεν (adverbial) 459.

καὶ (adjunctive conjunction joining adverbs) 14.

ὄπισϑεν (adverbial) 822.

Translation - *"And in front of the throne what looks like a glassy sea, like crystal. And in the midst of the throne-room and surrounding the throne are four living creatures full of eyes, before and behind."*

Comment: Note how John uses words like ἐνώπιον, μέσῳ, κύκλῳ, ἔμπροσϑεν and ὄπισϑεν either as adjectives with the gentive or adverbially. Since ἐν μέσῳ τοῦ ϑρόνου conflicts with κύκλῳ τοῦ ϑρόνου, we have translated with "throne room."

There is no hint in the text as to who or what these living creatures are. They remind us of Ezekial 1. Nothing more can be said with certainty. They belong to the heavenly order of things.

"We will understand it better bye and bye."

Verse 7 - "And the first beast was like a lion, and the second beast was like a calf, and the third beast had the face of a man, and the fourth beast was like a flying eagle."

καὶ τὸ ζῷον τὸ πρῶτον ὅμοιον λέοντι, καὶ τὸ δεύτερον ζῷον ὅμοιον μόσχω, καὶ τὸ τρίτον ζῷον ἔχων τὸ πρόσωπον ὡς ἀνϑρώπου, καὶ τὸ τέταρτον ζῷον ὅμοιον ἀετῷ πετομένῳ.

"the first living creature like a lion, the second living creature like an ox, the third living creature with the face of a man, and the fourth living creature like a flying eagle." . . . *RSV*

καὶ (continuative conjunction) 14.

τὸ (nom.sing.neut.of the article in agreement with ζῷον) 9.

ζῷον (nom.sing.neut.of ζῷον, subject of ἔστιν understood) 5086.

τὸ (nom.sing.neut.of the article in agreement with πρῶτον) 9.

πρῶτον (nom.sing.neut.of πρῶτος, in agreement with ζῷον) 487.

ὅμοιον (nom.sing.neut.of ὅμοιος, predicate adjective, in agreement with ζῷον) 923.

λέοντι (instru.sing.masc.of λέων, comparison) 4872.

καὶ (continuative conjunction) 14.

τὸ (nom.sing.neut.of the article in agreement with ζῷον) 9.

δεύτερον (nom.sing.neut.of δεύτερος, in agreement with ζῷον) 1371.

ζῶον (nom.sing.neut.of ζῶον, subject of ἔστιν understood) 5086.

ὅμοιον (nom.sing.neut.of ὅμοιος, predicate adjective) 923.

μόσχῳ (instru.sing.masc.of μόσχος, comparison) 2554.

καὶ (continuative conjunction) 14.

τὸ (nom.sing.neut.of the article in agreement with ζῶον) 9.

τρίτον (nom.sing.neut.of τρίτος, in agreement with ζῶον) 1209.

ζῶον (nom.sing.neut.of ζῶον, subject of ἔστιν understood in a present periphratic) 5086.

ἔχων (pres.act.part.nom.sing.masc.of ἔχω, present periphratic) 82.

τὸ (acc.sing.neut.of the article in agreement with πρόσωπον) 9.

πρόσωπον (acc.sing.neut.of πρόσωπον, direct object of ἔχων) 588.

ὡς (comparative particle) 128.

ἀνθρώπου (gen.sing.masc.of ἄνθρωπος, description) 341.

καὶ (continuative conjunction) 14.

τὸ (nom.sing.neut.of the article in agreement with ζῶον) 9.

τέταρτον (nom.sing.neut.of τέταρτος, in agreement with ζῶον) 1129.

ζῶον (nom.sing.neut.of ζῶον, subject of ἔστιν understood) 5086.

ὅμοιον (nom.sing.neut.of ὅμοιος, predicate ajdective) 923.

ἀετῷ (instru.sing.masc.of ἀετός, comparison) 1503.

#5346 πετομένῳ (pres.mid.part.instru.sing.masc.of πετάομαι, adjectival, predicate position, restrictive, in agreement with ἀετῷ).

    King James Version

    fly - Rev.4:7; 8:13; 14:6; 19:17.

    Revised Standard Version

    flying - Rev.4:7; 14:6; 19:17.
    flew - Rev.8:13.

Meaning: To fly. Of the comparison with a flying eagle - Rev.4:7; of angels - Rev.8:13; 14:6; of scavengers - Rev.19:17.

Translation - "And the first beast is like a lion, and the second beast is like an ox, and the third beast has a face like a man, and the fourth beast is like a flying eagle."

Comment: *Cf.* Ezek.1:5-10; 10:14. There is little more to say. When we get to heaven we will understand what the various appearances of these beasts indicate. That the lion, ox, man and eagle represent Christ Incarnate as King, Servant, Son of Man and Son of God has been suggested. Perhaps so but let us avoid eisegesis. We are not Gnostics who pretend to know it all.

Verse 8 - "And the four beasts had each of them six wings about him: and they were full of eyes within; and they rest not day and night, saying, Holy, Holy, Holy, Lord God Almighty, which was and is, and is to come."

καὶ τὰ τέσσαρα ζῷα, ἕν καθ' ἐναύτων ἔχων ἀνὰ πτέρυγας ἕξ,κὒκλόθεν καὶ
ἔσωθεν γέμουσιν ὀφθαλμῶν. καὶ ἀνάπαυσιν οὐκ ἔχουσιν ἡμέρας καὶ νυκτὸς
λέγοντες,Ἅγιος ἅγιος ἅγιος κύριος ὁ θεὸς ὁ παντοκράτωρ, ὁ ἦν καὶ ὁ ὤν καί ὁ
ἐρχόμενος.

*"And the four living creatures, each of them with six wings, are full of eyes all
round and within, and day and night they never cease to sing, 'Holy, holy, holy,
is the Lord God Almighty, who was and is and is to come.' " . . . RSV*

καὶ (continuative conjunction) 14.
τὰ (nom.pl.neut.of the article in agreement with ζῷα) 9.
τέσσαρα (nom.pl.neut.of τέσσαρες, in agreement with ζῷα) 1508.
ζῷα (nom.pl.neut.of ζῶον, subject of γέμουσιν) 5086.
ἕν (acc.sing.neut.of εἷς, distributive) 469.
καθ' (preposition with the accusative, distributive) 98.
ἕν (acc.sing.neut.of εἷς, distributive) 469.
αὐτῶν (gen.pl.neut.of αὐτός, partitive) 16.
ἔχων (pres.act.part.nom.sing.neut.of ἔχω, adjectival, in agreement with ἕν) 82.
ἀνὰ (preposition with the accusative, distributive) 1059.
πτέρυγας (acc.pl.fem.of πτέρυξ, direct object of ἔχων) 1480.
ἕξ (numeral) 1220.
κυκλόθεν (adverbial) 5342.
καὶ (adjunctive conjunction joining adverbs) 14.
ἔωθεν (adverbial) 672.
γέμουσιν (3d.per.pl.pres.act.ind.of γέμω, aoristic) 1457.
ὀφθαλμῶν (gen.pl.masc.of ὀφθαλμός, description) 501.
καὶ (continuative conjunction) 14.
ἀνάπαυσιν (3d.per.pl.pres.act.ind.of ἀναπαύω, aoristic) 955.
οὐκ (negative conjunction with the indicative) 130.
ἔχουσιν (3d.per.pl.pres.act.ind.of ἔχω, customary) 82.
ἡμέρας (gen.sing.fem.of ἡμέρα, time description) 135.
καὶ (adjunctive conjunction joining nouns) 14.
νυκτὸς (gen.sing.fem.of νύξ, time description) 209.
λέγοντες (pres.act.part.nom.pl.masc.of λέγω, recitative) 66.
Ἅγιος, nom.sing.masc.of ἅγιος, predicate adjective) 84.
ἅγιος (nom.sing.masc.of ἅγιος, predicate adjective) 84.
ἅγιος (nom.sing.masc.of ἅγιος, predicate adjective) 84.
κύριος (nom.sing.masc.of κύριος, subject of ἔστιν understood) 97.
ὁ (nom.sing.masc.of the article in agreement with θεὸς) 9.
θεὸς (nom.sing.masc.of θεός, apposition) 124.
ὁ (nom.sing.masc.of the article in agreement with παντοκράτωρ) 9.
παντοκράτωρ (nom.sing.masc.of παντοκράτωρ, apposition) 4325.
ὁ (nom.sing.masc.of the article, subject of ἦν) 9.
ἦν (3d.per.sing.imp.ind.of εἰμί, progressive duration) 86.
καὶ (adjunctive conjunction , joining substantives) 14.

ὁ (nom.sing.masc.of the article in agreement with ὤν) 9.

ὤν (pres.part.nom.sing.masc.of εἰμί, apposition) 86.

καὶ (adjunctive conjunction joining participles) 14.

ὁ (nom.sing.masc.of the article in agreement with ἐρχόμενος) 9.

ἐρχόμενος (pres.part.nom.sing.masc.of ἔρχομαι, substantival, apposition) 146.

Translation - "*And the four beasts, each having six wings above, are full of eyes round about and under the wings and they do not pause, day by day and night by night, as they say, 'Holy, Holy, Holy, Lord, the God, the Almighty One. The One who has always been, and who now is and who is the Coming one.*"

Comment: The distributive use of the numeral as in ἓν καθ' ἓν (Rev.4:8), Robertson, quoting Winer (Robertson, *Grammar*, 675) calls a "barbaric idiom, but it became common in later Greek." *Cf.* Mk.14:19; Rom.12:5; Rev.21:21. The participle here, as often is translated κατὰ σύνεσιν ("according to sense"). Most exegetes construe κυκλόθεν καὶ ἔσωθεν γέμουσιν ὀφθαλμῶν as belonging to πτέρυγας, not to ζῷα. It is the six wings, not the living creatures, that are full of eyes round about and within.

Once again we can only cite Isaiah 6:2; Ezek.1:18; 10:12 and leave the details of interpretation to the typologists, who are looking for evidence to support that which they have already determined to believe. These heavenly creatures are a part of the heavenly scene, who engage constantly, by day and night in praise to God.

Verse 9 - "*And when those beasts give glory and honour and thanks to him that sat on the throne, who liveth forever and ever. . .*"

καὶ ὅταν δώσουσιν τὰ ζῷα δόξαν καὶ τιμὴν καὶ εὐχαριστίαν τῷ καθημένῳ ἐπὶ τοῦ θρόνου τῷ ζῶντι εἰς τοὺς αἰῶνας τῶν αἰώνων,

"*And whenever the living creatures give glory and honor and thanks to him who is seated on the throne, who lives for ever and ever, . . .*" . . . *RSV*

καὶ (continuative conjunction) 14.

ὅταν (temporal adverb with the indicative in a definite temporal clause) 436.

δώσουσιν (3d.per.pl.fut.act.ind.of δίδωμι, definite temporal clause) 362.

τὰ (nom.pl.neut.of the article in agreement with ζῷα) 9.

ζῷα (nom.pl.neut.of ζῶον, subject of δώσουσιν) 5086.

δόξαν (acc.sing.fem.of δόξα, direct object of δώσουσιν) 361.

καὶ (adjunctive conjunction joining nouns) 14.

τιμὴν (acc.sing.fem.of τιμή, direct object of δώσουσιν) 1619.

καὶ (adjunctive conjunction joining nouns) 14.

εὐχαριστίαν (acc.sing.fem.of εὐχαριστία, direct object of δώσουσιν) 3616.

τῷ (dat.sing.masc.of the article in agreement with καθημένῳ) 9.

καθημένῳ (pres.mid.part.dat.sing.masc.of κάθημαι, substantival, indirect object of δώσουσιν) 377.

ἐπὶ (preposition with the genitive, place description) 47.

τοῦ (gen.sing.masc.of the article in agreement with θρόνου) 9.

θρόνου (gen.sing.masc.of θρόνος, place description) 519.

τῷ (dat.sing.masc.of the article in agreement with ζῶντι) 9.

ζῶντι (pres.act.part.dat.sing.masc.of ζάω, substantival, apposition) 340.

εἰς (preposition with the accusative of time extent) 140.

τοὺς (acc.pl.masc.of the article in agreement with αἰῶνας) 9.

αἰῶνας (acc.pl.masc.of αἰών, time extent) 1002.

τῶν (gen.pl.masc.of the article in agreement with αἰώνων) 9.

αἰώνων (gen.pl.masc.of αἰών, partitive) 1002.

Translation - "And whenever the beasts give glory and praise and thanks to Him who is sitting on the throne, to the One who is living into the ages of the ages. . ."

Comment: The element of contingency in ὅταν, which is normally found with the subjunctive is here joined with the future, which is somewhat less contingent. Verse 8 says that the living creatures sang their song of praise without ceasing. The idiom is unusual but it has precedent. If and when (or whenever) the four living creatures sing their song of praise to Christ, which may be a different song from that of verse 8, which is continuous, their song motivates the twenty-four elders also to worship (verse 10). *Cf.* ἐπί with the genitive in Mt.19:28; Rev.4:9,10) and with the accusative in Rev.3:20; 4:2. The Nestle text, following Westcott/Hort has τῷ θρόνῳ (locative) in the margin. Thus we have two (or three) cases with ἐπί and the same idea - rest and place description. Christ is utterly worthy (τιμήν). He has accomplished redemption (Psalm 110:1; Heb.1:3; 12:2 and others under #'s 377 and 420). He sits upon the throne, utterly triumphant (Mt.28:18; Eph.1:17-23). He has two essential achievements to His eternal credit - creation and redemption. Thus the twenty-four elders sing two songs: the creation song in Rev.4:11 and the redemption song in Rev.5:9,10.

The sentence which begins with the temporal clause in verse 9 continues in

Verse 10 - "The four and twenty elders fall down before him that sat on the throne, and worship him that liveth forever and ever, and cast their crowns before the throne, saying, . . ."

πεσοῦνται οἱ εἴκοσι τέσσαρες πρεσβύτεροι ἐνώπιον τοῦ καθημένου ἐπὶ τοῦ θρόνου καὶ προσκυνήσουσιν τῷ ζῶντι εἰς τοὺς αἰῶνας τῶν αἰώνων καὶ βαλοῦσιν τοὺς στεφάνους αὐτῶν ἐνώπιον τοῦ θρόνου λέγοντες

"the twenty-four elders fall down before him who is seated on the throne and worship him who lives for ever and ever; they cast their crowns before the throne, singing, . . . " . . . RSV

πεσοῦνται (3d.per.pl.fut.act.ind.of πίπτω, gnomic) 187.

οἱ (nom.pl.masc.of the article in agreement with πρεσβύτεροι) 9.

εἴκοσι (numeral) 2283.

τέσσαρες (numeral) 1508.

πρεσβύτεροι (nom.pl.masc.of πρεσβύτερος, subject of πεσοῦνται, προσκυνήσουσιν and βαλοῦσιν) 1141.

ἐνώπιον (preposition with the genitive of place description) 1798.

τοῦ (gen.sing.masc.of the article in agreement with καθημένου) 9.

καθημένου (pres.mid.part.gen.sing.masc.of κάθημαι, substantival, place description) 377.

ἐπὶ (preposition with the genitive of place description) 47.

τοῦ (gen.sing.masc.of the article in agreement with θρόνου) 9.

θρόνου (gen.sing.masc.of θρόνος, place description) 519.

καὶ (adjunctive conjunction joining verbs) 14.

προσκυνήσουσιν (3d.per.pl.fut.act.ind.of προσκυνέω, gnomic) 147.

τῷ (dat.sing.masc.of the article in agreement with ζῶντι) 9.

ζῶντι (pres.act.part.dat.sing.masc.of ζάω, substantival, indirect object) 340.

εἰς (preposition with the accusative of time extent) 140.

τοὺς (acc.pl.masc.of the article in agreement with αἰῶνας) 9.

αἰῶνας (acc.pl.masc.of αἰών, time extent) 1002.

τῶν (gen.pl.masc.of the article in agreement with αἰώνων) 9.

αἰώνων (gen.pl.masc.of αἰών, partitive) 1002.

καὶ (adjunctive conjunction joining verbs) 14.

βαλοῦσιν (3d.per.pl.fut.act.ind.of βάλλω, gnomic) 299.

τοὺς (acc.pl.masc.of the article in agreement with στεφάνους) 9.

στεφάνους (acc.pl.masc.of στέφανος, direct object of βαλοῦσιν) 1640.

αὐτῶν (gen.pl.masc.of αὐτός, possession) 16.

ἐνώπιον (preposition with the genitive of place description) 1798.

τοῦ (gen.sing.masc.of the article in agreement with θρόνου) 9.

θρόνου (gen.sing.masc.of θρόνος, place description) 519.

λέγοντες (prpes.act.part.nom.pl.masc.of λέγω, recitatitve) 66.

Translation - "... the four and twenty elders fall before the One who sits upon the throne and they worship Him who lives eternally and they cast their crowns before the throne, saying ..."

Comment: The verse is the multiple conclusion of the definite temporal clause which began in verse 9 with ὅταν δώσουσιν. *Cf.* comment. The four and twenty elders, whose cue is the praise given to Christ by the four living creatures, fall down, worship and cast their crowns before the throne of Christ. Thus it is clear, contrary to Gnostic teaching that rated Jesus Christ as only *primus inter pares* with other angels and heavenly creatures, He is the object of worship of all of them. Christ is not an angel, nor an elder nor a living creature. They worship Him (Phil.2:9-11; Eph.1:17-23). Indeed they say in verse 11 that He is the Creator.

Verse 11 - "Thou art worthy, O Lord, to receive glory and honour and power: for thou hast created all things and for thy pleasure they are and were created."

Ἄξιος εἶ, ὁ κύριος καὶ ὁ θεὸς ἡμῶν, λαβεῖν τὴν δόξαν καὶ τὴν τιμὴν καὶ τὴν δύναμιν, ὅτι σὺ ἔκτισας τὰ πάντα, καὶ διὰ τὸ θέλημά σου ἦσαν καὶ ἐκτίσθησαν.

"Worthy art thou, our Lord and God, to receive glory and honor and power, for thou didst create all things, and by thy will they existed and were created...."

... *RSV*

Ἄξιος (nom.sing.masc.of ἄξιος, predicate adjective) 285.

εἶ (2d.per.sing.pres.ind.of εἰμί, aoristic) 86.

ὁ (voc.sing.masc.of the article in agreement with κύριος, for κύριε) 9.

κύριος (voc.sing.masc.of κύριος, for κύριε, address) 97.

καὶ (adjunctive conjunction joining nouns) 14.

ὁ (voc.sing.masc.of the article in agreement with θεὸς, for θεέ) 9.

θεὸς (voc.sing.masc.of θεός, for θεέ, address) 124.

ἡμῶν (gen.pl.masc.of ἐγώ, relationship) 123.

λαβεῖν (2d.aor.act.inf.of λαμβάνω, complementary) 533.

τὴν (acc.sing.fem.of the article in agreement with δόξαν) 9.

δόξαν (acc.sing.fem.of δόξα, direct object of λαβεῖν) 361.

καὶ (adjunctive conjunction joining nouns) 14.

τὴν (acc.sing.fem.of the article in agreement with τιμὴν) 9.

τιμὴν (acc.sing.fem.of τιμή, direct object of λαβεῖν) 1619.

καὶ (adjunctive conjunction joining nouns) 14.

τὴν (acc.sing.fem.of the article in agreement with δύναμιν) 9.

δύναμιν (acc.sing.fem.of δύναμις, direct object of λαβεῖν) 687.

ὅτι (conjunction introducing a subordinate causal clause) 211.

σὺ (nom.sing.masc.of σύ, subject of ἔκτισας) 104.

ἔκτισας (2d.per.sing.aor.act.ind.of κτίζω, constative) 1284.

τὰ (acc.pl.neut.of the article in agreement with πάντα) 9.

πάντα (acc.pl.neut.of πᾶς, direct object of ἔκτισας) 67.

καὶ (continuative conjunction) 14.

διὰ (preposition with the accusative, cause) 118.

τὸ (acc.sing.neut.of the article in agreement with θέλημα) 9.

θέλημα (acc.sing.neut.of θέλημα, cause) 577.

σοῦ (gen.sing.masc.of σύ, possession) 104.

ἦσαν (3d.per.pl.imp.ind.of εἰμί, progressive duration) 86.

καὶ (adjunctive conjunction joining verbs) 14.

ἐκτίσθησαν (3d.per.pl.aor.pass.ind.of κτίζω, effective) 1284.

Translation - *"Worthy art thou, O Lord, even our God, to receive the glory and the honor and the power, because you created everything, and because of your will they have been and were created."*

Comment: The ὁ κύριος καὶ ὁ θεὸς is vocative just as we have it in John 20:28. Christ is here glorified because He is the Creator of all (τὰ πάντα). He created the universe because He chose to do so. He did not need to do so. The emanation theory of creation that Christ needed the universe and man for His fulfillment is not taught in Scripture. In Christ all fullness (πλήρωμα) dwells (Col.1:19; 2:9). Thus creation for Him was an act of grace and love, not an act of necessity. As the Creator of man and the universe He is also the creator of history. In Chapter 5 He appears in the role of the prime mover of historic events. The scene as it now stands has Christ supreme upon heaven's throne, receiving the adoration of all of heaven's creatures, as they ascribe to Him glory because He is the Creator (John 1:3; Col.1:16; Heb.1:2; 10-12).

We shall now see Him in the role as Redeemer and Judge.

The Scroll and the Lamb

(Revelation 5:1-14)

Revelation 5:1 - "And I saw in the right hand of him that sat on the throne a book, written within and on the backside, sealed with seven seals."

Καὶ εἶδον ἐπὶ τὴν δεξιὰν τοῦ καθημένου ἐπὶ τοῦ θρόνου βιβλίον γεγραμμένον ἔσωθεν καὶ ὄπισθεν κατεσφραγισμένον σφραγῖσιν ἑπτά.

"And I saw in the right hand of him who was seated on the throne a scroll written within and on the back, sealed with seven seals; " . . . *RSV*

Καὶ (continuative conjunction) 14.

εἶδον (1st.per.sing.aor.act.ind.of ὁράω, constative) 144.

ἐπὶ (preposition with the accusative of place description) 47.

τὴν (acc.sing.fem.of the article in agreement with δεξιὰν) 9.

δεξιὰν (acc.sing.fem.of δεξιός, place description) 502.

τοῦ (gen.sing.masc.of the article in agreement with καθημένου) 9.

καθημένου (pres.act.part.gen.sing.masc.of κάθημαι, substantival, possession) 377.

ἐπὶ (preposition with the genitive of place description) 47.

τοῦ (gen.sing.masc.of the article in agreement with θρόνου) 9.

θρόνου (gen.sing.masc.of θρόνος, place description) 519.

βιβλίον (acc.sing.neut.of βιβλίον, direct object of εἶδον) 1292.

γεγραμμένον (perf.pass.part.acc.sing.neut.of γράφω, adjectival, predicate position, restrictive, in agreement with βιβλίον) 156.

ἔσωθεν (adverbial) 672.

καὶ (adjunctive conjunction joining adverbs) 14.

ὄπισθεν (adverbial) 822.

#5347 κατεσφραγισμένον (perf.pass.part.acc.sing.neut.of κατασφραγίζω, adjectival, predicate position, restrictive, in agreement with βιβλίον).

    King James Version

seal - Rev.5:1.

    Revised Standard Version

seal - Rev.5:1.

Meaning: A combination of κατά (#98) and σφραγίζω (#1686). To seal; to close with seals. κατά indicates "under." Taken with ὄπισθεν - "sealed under, within and around." Of the Book of Judgment in Rev.5:1.

σφραγῖσιν (instru.pl.fem.of σφραγίς, means) 3886.
ἑπτά (numeral) 1024.

Translation - "And I saw in the right hand of the One sitting upon the throne a book, having been written within and upon the back, sealed with seven seals."

Comment: Note ἐπί with the accusative and also with the genitive - with the accusative of extent - firmly in His grasp; with the genitive of place description - upon the throne.

The Revelation without Daniel is indeed a book of total mystery and must always remain so. Commentators who do not see a connection between these two books say with justification that those of us who do see a connection must show where the two connect. We accept the challenge.

Here in the hand of God upon the throne is a sealed book. We shall see John bitterly disappointed when he fears that the book will remained sealed. Why should John be so anxious to have it opened? And what happens upon the earth when it is opened? The opening will occur in chapter six, and we shall see God's prophetic clock moving across the next seven years to culminate in the second coming of Christ. Once the countdown begins again there will be no more programmed holds. When the Lord takes the first seal from the book it will be "T minus 2520 days and counting."

The Book of Daniel was revealed to him in Babylon, when Israel was in captivity. It contains a great deal of information about the course of political history. Daniel was given the ability to understand visions and dreams (Daniel 1:17). Chapter two records Nebuchadnezzar's dream. The details were revealed to Daniel (Daniel 2:19). Note Daniel's statement after God had revealed to him the dream and its meaning (Daniel 2:20-22). This is political history to be enacted in the future. The dream is described in Daniel 2:31-36. The interpretation follows in verses 37-45.

We must understand that inspired Scripture has both local and prophetic significance. It means something to the people to whom it was originally given, but it also has meaning for future generations. This may be termed double imagery. Nebuchadnezzar of Babylon is identified as the head of gold (Daniel 2:38). Three more world kingdoms were to follow (verses 39,40). Babylon was succeeded by Media-Persia, who was succeeded by Greece under Alexander the Great and Greece in turn gave way to Imperial Rome.

There have been only four world governments in all of history — Babylon, Media-Persia, Greece and Rome. Since Rome's decline after A.D.476, no single power has ever been able to bring the world under its hegemony. Napoleaon came close; so did Hitler. But we had after Rome, first Feudalism and then the rise of nation states. Nationalism will continue to be the pattern until Daniel's 70th week. In the period of modern history, which may be said to have begun in the fifteenth century, various nation states have been predominant, but never unchallenged. Thus international wars have characterized modern history as first one and then other national powers have sought the total power over the globe once enjoyed by Babylon, Media-Persia, Greece and Rome. Thus the Holy Roman Empire of the Hapsburgs, in Vienna, the Hohenzollerns of Brandenburg-Prussia, the Bourbons of France, the Tudors and Stewarts of England, and in the 20th century the United States and Russia have influenced but never dominated the course of history.

Note Daniel 2:44,45. The stone cut out without hands (verse 35) became a great kingdom and filled the earth. This kingdom is of God's making. It shall never be destroyed. This stone is Christ (1 Peter 2:7,8), who shall sit on David's throne forever (2 Sam.7:10-17; Luke 1:30-33).

Daniel four has Nebuchadnezzar's dream of the tree and Daniel's interpretation. It predicted the fall of Babylon. The prophecy was fulfilled in chapter 5 with *Mene Mene Tekel Upharsin*, the Chaldean inscription on the wall at Belshazzar's feast, as Darius, the Mede became the shoulders of silver (Daniel 2:32), when Belshazzar was slain (Daniel 5:30,31).

Daniel's ministry continued in the courts both of Darius the Mede and of Cyrus the Persian (Daniel 6:28).

Daniel 7 carries us back, in a flashback, to the first year of Belshazzar of Babylon (Daniel 7:1). Another dream depicts, not parts of an image — head of gold, shoulders and arms of silver, belly of brass and legs of iron, as in Daniel 2, but, in different imagery, four beasts — a lion, a bear, a leopard and a fierce non-descript (Daniel 7:1-8). Note that just as the gold, silver, brass and iron image of Daniel 2 was replaced by a permanent Stone (Daniel 2:44,45), so the lion, bear, leopard and non-descript beasts are replaced by the Ancient of Days (Daniel 7:9-14). The second coming of Christ is depicted in Daniel 7:13,14 and His eternal kingdom on David's throne is established. Note the similarity between Daniel 7:9 and Revelation 1:14,15 and between Daniel 7:10 and Revelation 19:11*ff. Cf.* also Daniel 9:14 and Revelation 11:15-19. Note that His kingdom is permanent (Daniel 7:14; 2:44; 2 Sam.7:12-13; Lk.1:33; Rev.11:15). Note further how Daniel relates his interpretation of Belshazzar's dream to both ancient history (Daniel 7:17) and also to end-time events described in Revelation. *Cf.* Daniel 7:18-21 with Revelation 13:1-8. See the second coming of Christ in Daniel 7:22. End-time events are clearly described as Daniel interprets what had *local* application for him and for Israel and her captors at that time. This is double imagery.

Chapter 8 has Daniel's vision (Daniel 8:1-2). The ram and the he-goat depict Media and Persia (Daniel 8:20). The rough goat is Greece (Daniel 8:21). This prophecy also, as did those in Daniel 2 and 7, brings us to the second coming of Christ (Daniel 8:25). Clearly Daniel has portrayed historic events in his immediate future, from 586 B.C. to Messiah, as he pictures Babylon, Media-Persia, Greece and Rome, but he just as clearly pictures end-time events, identical to those in Revelation and leading to the second coming of Christ.

But Rome "fell" in A.D.476, in the sense that her police power over the world ended and 1500 years have since elapsed. Yet Christ has not come. Clearly this is a gap in the prophecy. This gap is explained in Daniel 9.

Following his prayer for wisdom (Daniel 9:1-19), Gabriel came to him (Daniel 9:20-23) and gave him the information which he sought as it related to Israel's future. This is what Daniel was praying about. We are dealing with a total of 490 years (70 times 7 years - Daniel 9:24). This program, which will run 490 years off of God's prophetic clock, will involve Israel and Jerusalem, the end of the Babylonian captivity, the Ezra and Nehemiah reforms, the presentation of Messiah to Israel as her King, the cross of Christ, the establishment of Christ's kingdom on David's throne, the end of all prohetic events and the anointing of Messiah. See all of this in Daniel 9:24. All of these events except the Messianic reign of Christ at His second coming, have already taken place. Of the 2400 years of history since the beginning of the 490 years, God's clock has run off 483 years. The time schedule is found in Daniel 9:25-26. The clock started with 490 years to run with the command given to Nehemiah, the king's cup bearer, to go back and rebuild Jerusalem. The first 49 years (7 weeks of years) were occupied in the return to Jerusalem and the rehabilitation of the city by Nehemiah, followed by the revival under Ezra. Four hundred, thirty four more years (62 times 7) brings us to the triumphal entry of Jesus (Matthew 21) when He offered Himself as Messiah to Israel (Zechariah 9). The last half of Daniel 9:25 was described in Nehemiah and Ezra. After the 434 years (from Nehemiah to Messiah), the first 49 years having first run from the original commission to rebuild Jerusalem, Christ was cut off, "not for himself" (verse 26). The crucifixion of Messiah stopped the clock with seven years (one week) still to be run off. The night came to replace God's day (John 9:4). When Christ died, God's prophetic clock stopped and He has had no concern with the events of human history since, except as He has directed the members of His Body, associated institutionally in various assemblies, to call out from among the Gentiles the elect (Acts 15:14; 13:48; Eph.3:4-6). When ungodly men said, "We will not have this man to reign over us" God took them at their word. World governments, since Calvary, have been administered only with the guidance of unregenerate human reason. Thus their tragic failure. The Holy Spirit, Who has been active and immanent in nature, in human personality and in history, without surrendering His transcendance, has controlled history since Calvary only to expedite the successful implementation of the world-wide missionary enterprise which has as its goal the effectual calling of the elect into the Body of Christ.

Only in this sense is it God's responsibility to run the world that nailed His Son to a cross. He has not failed. He has continued to carry out the function which Paul described as the mystery which had been given to him. This mystery will be complete at the end of the 70th week of Daniel (Rev.10:7).

Gabriel did not leave Daniel in the dark about the event that will mark the resumption of the count-down. The clock will start again, with no more programmed holds, when some dictator confirms to Israel the Abrahamic covenant, which is the basis for the Jewish claim to the land which God promised to Abraham. (Daniel 9:27). When that happens exactly seven years will remain until the prescribed 490 years have run their course, since the first 483 years brought Israel from Babylon, back to Jerusalem and on to Calvary.

This seven year span exactly fits the time span of the churches, seals and trumpets in the Revelation. Exactly half of it is defined in terms of days (Revelation 12:6), years (Revelation 12:14) and months (Revelation 13:5).

The 17th chapter of Revelation connects the four ancient kings of Daniel's day (Babylon, Media-Persia, Greece and Rome) with the three kings of the first three seals of Revelation 6. There are to be a total of seven, while the 8th is one of the preceding seven, namely the 5th. (Revelation 17:10 *cf.* comment, *en loc.*).

Daniel 10 and 11 gives more prophetic detail. Daniel was anxious to know more since God's history involves Israel. But further information was refused (Daniel 12:4), despite the fact that he begged for it (Daniel 12:8-9). Note that the book in which the entire story of the 490 years is written, is sealed. For how long? "To the time of the end" (Daniel 12:4,9).

So as we close the pages of the Book of Daniel we have a sealed book. But it is not to remain sealed forever. Only "until the time of the end" *i.e.* the last seven years of Daniel 9:27. This sealed book into which Daniel wanted so much to look further, dropped out of sight on earth, until now in Revelation 5:1, it reappears in the right hand of the Ancient of Days sitting upon His throne in heaven. We shall see that John was as bitterly disappointed as was Daniel when he feared that the book would not be opened, so that he could know the end of the story.

This is my argument that Daniel and Revelation must be studied together and that the Revelation covers the time period "of the end." Daniel 2:44,45; 7:9-14,22; 8:25 are the same event as Revelation 19:11, which occurs when the 6th and 7th seal, the 7th trumpet and the 7th vial judgments occur. The Ancient of Days, the Author of History (Acts 17:26-28) sits upon His heavenly throne with the book that was sealed against any further human research, until a future era, called "the time of the end". When the first seal comes off, the "time of the end" begins. When the last seal is removed, the 490 years of earmarked history will have been consummated.

It should be apparent from the foregoing that if the analysis which I have presented is incorrect then I do not know anything about the Revelation and the reader may as well stop reading.

The book in the hand of Him who sits upon the throne is the center of attention. It has been sealed for centuries, despite Daniel's desire to unseal it and investigate the rest of its contents. Will it be opened now? If it is opened, who is worthy to open it?

Verse 2 - "And I saw a strong angel, proclaiming with a loud voice, Who is worthy to open the book and to loose the seals thereof?"

καὶ εἶδον ἄγγελον ἰσχυρὸν κηρύσσοντα ἐν φωνῇ μεγάλῃ, Τίς ἄξιος ἀνοῖξαι τὸ βιβλίον καὶ λῦσαι τὰς σφραγῖδας αὐτοῦ;

"and I saw a strong angel proclaiming with a loud voice, 'Who is worthy to open the scroll and break its seals?' " . . . RSV

καὶ (continuative conjunction) 14.

εἶδον (1st.per.sing.aor.act.ind.of ὁράω, constative) 144.

ἄγγελον (acc.sing.masc.of ἄγγελος, direct object of εἶδον) 96.

ἰσχυρὸν (acc.sing.masc.of ἰσχυρός, in agreement with ἄγγελον) 303.

κηρύσσοντα (pres.act.part.acc.sing.masc.of κηρύσσω, adjectival, predicate position, restrictive, in agreement with ἄγγελον) 249.

ἐν (preposition with the instrumental, means) 80.

φωνῇ (instru.sing.fem.of φωνή, means) 222.

μεγάλῃ (instru.sing.fem.of μέγας, in agreement with φωνῇ) 184.

Τίς (nom.sing.masc.of τίς, interrogative pronoun, subject of ἐστιν understood in direct question) 281.

ἄξιος (nom.sing.masc.of ἄξιος, predicate adjective) 285.

ἀνοῖξαι (aor.act.inf.of ἀνοίγω, complementary) 188.

τὸ (acc.sing.neut.of the article in agreement with βιβλίον) 9.

βιβλίον (acc.sing.neut.of βιβλίον, direct object of ἀνοῖξαι) 1292.

καὶ (adjunctive conjunction joining infinitives) 14.

λῦσαι (aor.act.inf.of λύω, complementary) 471.

τὰς (acc.pl.fem.of the article in agreement with σφραγῖδος) 9.

σφραγῖδος (acc.pl.fem.of σφράγις, direct object of λῦσαι) 3886.

αὐτοῦ (gen.sing.neut.of αὐτός, possession) 16.

Translation - "And I saw a strong angel crying out with a loud voice, 'Who has the right to open the book and to unfasten its seals?' "

Comment: Heaven's court, the universal model of righteousness ("Let God be true but every man a liar") is confronted with an ethical problem. God holds in His hand the book, which, when unsealed, will loose the dogs of heaven's holy warfare upon a Christ rejecting world. Man's day (1 Cor.4:3) will end and God will reassume direct control over human history. His only concern since Calvary has been to work in and through His church, which is His Body, to call the elect. While this missionary enterprise has gone forward unregenerate man has stumbled along in his pitiable ignorance to achieve the "progress" that finds him at the end in a *cul de sac*. But now, as the seventh angel prepares to sound his trumpet (Revelation 10:7) the Body of Christ will become complete and our Lord will return to dictate earthly events again.

The problem is that the second coming of Christ involves judgment upon the unsaved. And in the seven years immediately prior to His coming, while the last remaining members of His Body are called and saved, there will be judgments upon the unsaved on the earth. The angel with the loud voice is asking who in heaven has the moral right to precipitate this program of judgment? At first it will seem that no one in heaven, earth or hell has such a right.

Verse 3 - "And no man in heaven, nor in earth, neither under the earth, was able to open the book, neither to look thereon."

καὶ οὐδεὶς ἐδύνατο ἐν τῷ οὐρανῷ οὐδὲ ἐπὶ τῆς γῆς οὐδὲ ὑποκάτω τῆς γῆς ἀνοῖξαι τὸ βιβλίον οὔτε βλέπειν αὐτό.

"And no one in heaven or on earth or under the earth was able to open the scroll or to look into it, . . . " . . . RSV

καὶ (continuative conjunction) 14.

οὐδεὶς (nom.sing.masc.of οὐδείς, subject of ἐδύνατο) 446.

ἐδύνατο (3d.per.sing.imp.mid.ind.of δύναμαι, progressive description) 289.

ἐν (preposition with the locative, place) 80.

τῷ (loc.sing.masc.of the article in agreement with οὐρανῷ) 9.

οὐρανῷ (loc.sing.masc.of οὐρανός, place) 254.

οὐδὲ (compound disjunctive particle) 452.

ἐπὶ (preposition with the genitive of place description) 47.

τῆς (gen.sing.fem.of the article in agreement with γῆς) 9.

γῆς (gen.sing.fem.of γῆ, place description) 157.

οὐδὲ (compound disjunctive particle) 452.

ὑποκάτω (improper preposition with the ablative of separation) 1429.

τῆς (abl.sing.fem.of the article in agreement with γῆς) 9.

γῆς (abl.sing.fem.of γῆ, separation) 157.

ἀνοῖξαι (aor.act.inf.of ἀνοίγω, complementary) 188.

τὸ (acc.sing.neut.of the article in agreement with βιβλίον) 9.

βιβλίον (acc.sing.neut.of βιβλίον, direct object of ἀνοῖξαι) 1292.

οὔτε (negative copulative conjunction) 598.

βλέπειν (pres.act.inf.of βλέπω, complementary) 499.

αὐτό (acc.sing.neut.of αὐτός, direct object of βλέπειν) 16.

Translation - "And not one man in the heaven, nor upon the earth, nor beneath the earth was able to open the book or to look into it."

Comment: The man who was so eagerly sought by the angel was not found, despite a universal search. The book could not be opened, nor could its contents be read, although all could see it from the outside. To open it involved the breaking of the seals, which would bring judgment upon the earth.

We shall see in verses 5 and 6 who was ethically worthy to open the seals, and upon what grounds His legal right exists. In verse 4, we find John, as eager to have the book opened as Daniel was disappointed to have it sealed (Daniel 12:4,8,9) and, we may add, for the same reason.

Verse 4 - "And I wept much, because no man was found worthy to open and to read the book, neither to look thereon."

κal ἔκλαιον πολὺ ὅτι οὐδεὶς ἄξιος εὑρέθη ἀνοῖξαι τὸ βιβλίον οὔτε βλέπειν αὐτό.

"and I wept much that no one was found worthy to open the scroll or to look into it." . . . RSV

καὶ (inferential conjunction) 14.

ἔκλαιον (1s.tper.sing.imp.act.ind.of κλαίω, inceptive) 225.

πολὺ (acc.sing.neut.of πολύς, adverbial) 228.

ὅτι (conjunction introducing a subordinate causal clause) 211.

οὐδεὶς (nom.sing.masc.of οὐδείς, subject of εὑρέθη) 446.

ἄξιος (nom.sing.masc.of ἄξιος, predicate adjective) 285.

εὑρέθη (3d.per.sing.aor.pass.ind.of εὑρίσκω, constative) 79.

ἀνοῖξαι (aor.act.inf.of ἀνοίγω, complementary) 188.

τὸ (acc.sing.neut.of the article in agreement with βιβλίον) 9.

βιβλίον (acc.sing.neut.of βιβλίον, direct object of ἀνοῖξαι) 1292.

οὔτε (negative copulative conjunction) 598.

βλέπειν (pres.act.inf.of βλέπω, complementary) 499.

αὐτό (acc.sing.neut.of αὐτός, direct object of βλέπειν) 16.

Translation - "So I began to sob bitterly because no one was found worthy to open the book nor to look into it."

Comment: πολύ must refer to the intensity of John's weeping, since its duration is indicated by the inceptive imperfect, which means that he began and continued to weep. καὶ is inferential. John was crying because of the unsuccessful search of verse 3, on the basis of which he concluded that the book would not be opened. No man was found worthy. In what respect? To open, once for all (aorist in ἀνοῖξαι) and to keep it open (present infinitive in βλέπειν) until everything in it has taken place on earth. Why should this distress John no much? For the same reason that Daniel was disappointed because the book was to be closed. The book, once unsealed, opened, and its plan executed will fulfill the prophecy of Daniel 9:24-27. All that God intends to do in human history is set forth in Daniel 9:24. Some of it in John's day (at the close of the first century A.D.) had been done. The first 483 years of it was history. The remaining seven years was prophecy (history in the future) for Daniel and for John and indeed for the rest of the family of God. Daniel was held hostage - a subject of a Gentile power in a foreign land. He longed for the fulfillment of the Messianic expectation (Psalm 137:1-9). He thirsted for God's judgment upon Israel's captors. Hence he was eager to know when God was going to accomplish the total program. Hence his disappointment that this information was to remain sealed until "the time of the end" which, after 2400 years (plus/minus) after Daniel's death, and 1900 years after John's death, is still future to living Christians on this day (13 March 1984). I pinpoint the time (3:30 p.m. EST) because the beginning of the "time of the end" is immanent (it could happen at any moment) and it has been since Calvary. There is nothing in Scripture to tell us how long the gap between the end of the 69th week of Daniel's prophecy and the beginning of the 70th week will be.

John too, like Daniel was persecuted — a subject of pagan Rome, the "legs of iron" (Daniel 2:33,40) and the non-descript beast (Daniel 7:7), just as Daniel was subject to pagan Media-Persia, the "shoulders of silver" (Daniel 2:32,39a) and the bear (Daniel 7:5). In other words, Daniel and John were separated in time by the first 483 years of the program. Daniel lived to see it begin. John was alive when it ended with the offering of Jesus as Israel's Messiah and His crucifixion. Both Daniel and John were eager for the last seven years to begin and run their course, since, at the end of them, Messiah will be anointed (Luke 1:30-33; 2 Samuel 7:12-17; Revelation 11:15). Daniel in Babylon and John on Patmos (Rev.1:9), the former an orthodox Jew anticipating Messiah's first coming, and the latter a Hebrew Christian anticipating Messiah's second coming, needed His divine rescue and vindication. Indeed so do all Christians who suffer for righteousness sake (Mt.5:10-12; 2 Tim.3:12; 1 Pet.4:12-14). Late 20th century Christians who are knowledgeable are watching eagerly, not the skies for the rapture is not the next event, but the newspapers and telecasts for the word that Daniel 9:27a has had its fulfillment. This is the same event as the removal of the first seal (Revelation 6:1,2; Daniel 9:27a).

John's disappointment was premature as we read in

Verse 5 - "And one of the elders saith unto me, Weep not: behold, the Lion of the Tribe of Judah, the Root of David, hath prevailed to open the book, and to loose the seven seals thereof."

καὶ εἷς ἐκ τῶν πρεσβυτέρων λέγει μοι, Μὴ κλαῖε, ἰδοὺ ἐνίκησεν ὁ λέων ὁ ἐκ τῆς φυλῆς Ἰούδα, ἡ ῥίζα Δαυίδ, ἀνοῖξαι τὸ βιβλίον καὶ τὰς ἑπτὰ σφραγῖδος αὐτοῦ.

"Then one of the elders said to me, 'Weep not; lo, the Lion of the tribe of Judah, the Root of David, has conquered, so that he can open the scroll and its seven seals.' " . . . *RSV*

καὶ (adversative conjunction) 14.

εἷς (nom.sing.masc.of εἷς, subject of λέγει) 469.

ἐκ (preposition with the ablative, partitive) 19.

τῶν (abl.pl.masc.of the article in agreement with πρεσβυτέρων) 9.

πρεσβυτέρων (abl.pl.masc.of πρεσβύτερος, partitive) 1141.

λέγει (3d.per.sing.pres.act.ind.of λέγω, historical) 66.

μοι (dat.sing.masc.of ἐγώ, indirect object of λέγει) 123.

Μὴ (negative conjunction with the imperative in a prohibition) 87.

κλαῖε (2d.per.sing.pres.act.impv.of κλαίω, prohibition) 225.

ἰδοὺ (exclamation) 95.

ἐνίκησεν (3d.per.sing.aor.act.ind.of νικάω, effective) 2454.

ὁ (nom.sing.masc.of the article in agreement with λέων) 9.

λέων (nom.sing.masc.of λέων, subject of ἐνίκησεν) 1872.

ὁ (nom.sing.masc.of the article in agreement with λέων) 9.

ἐκ (preposition with the ablative of source) 19.

τῆς (abl.sing.fem.of the article in agreement with φυλῆς) 9.

φυλῆς (abl.sing.fem.of φυλή, source) 1313.

Ἰούδα (gen.sing.masc.of Ἰούδα, description) 13.

ἡ (nom.sing.fem.of the article in agreement with ῥίζα) 9.

ῥίζα (nom.sing.fem.of ῥίζα, apposition) 293.

Δαυίδ (abl.sing.masc.of Δαυίδ, source) 6.

ἀνοῖξαι (aor.act.inf.of ἀνοίγω, consecutive) 188.

τὸ (acc.sing.neut.of the article in agreement with βιβλίον) 9.

βιβλίον (acc.sing.neut.of βιβλίον, direct object of ἀνοῖξαι) 1292.

καὶ (adjunctive conjunction joining nouns) 14.

τὰς (acc.pl.fem.of the article in agreement with σφραγῖδος) 9.

ἑπτὰ (numeral) 1024.

σφραγῖδος (acc.pl.fem.of σφραγίς, direct object of ἀνοῖξαι) 3886.

αὐτοῦ (gen.sing.neut.of αὐτός, description) 16.

Translation - "But one of the elders said to me, 'Stop crying. Look! The Lion from the tribe of Judah, the Root out of David, has been victorious and He will open the book and its seals."

Comment: καὶ is adversative. John is crying, but the elder orders him to stop it. (μὴ κλαῖε, the present imperative - "do not go on crying."). Only here in the New Testament does λέων refer to Christ, but *cf.* Gen.49:9-10, where Jacob vested the eternal throne rights over Israel in Judah and his line. *Cf.* comment on #13. The King must come from the tribe of Judah (Heb.7:14). Hence, Christ is here presented as Israel's King Messiah. He is not only descended from Judah, but also from the Davidic family (2 Sam.7:12-17; Isa.11:10; Rev.22:16). The "rod out of the stem of Jesse" refers to Jesse, David's father. *Cf.*#6. ἡ ῥίζα Δαυίδ (Rev.5:5) has τὴν κλεῖν Δαυίδ (Rev.3:7). The student should run all of the references to David (#6) and study Jesus in His Messianic functions as David's son and the heir to the promises of the Davidic covenant. He is the only man who has a legal right to sit on David's throne. *Cf.* comment on Mt.1:1. He has prevailed. He has succeeded (been victorious in His effort) in gaining the moral right to open the book. If it cannot be opened with probity then it must remain forever sealed and judgment will never be meted out against sin, for in God's moral universe, judgment must be righteous or there must be none (Rom.3:26). Only the Judge can judge (John 5:22; Mt.7:1,2) and the only Judge is Jesus Christ.

Why should Jesus judge and not some other? How did He qualify to be Judge? What is unique about Him? He has indeed conquered. Note the effective (culminative) aorist in ἐνίκησεν, with its emphasis upon the result of the completion of the action, not upon its inchoate action (ingressive).

The infinitive ἀνοῖξαι is both purpose and result, since purpose is conceived result. Jesus had not yet opened the book at the time of the elder's statement. The result awaits His action but His overcoming (ἐνίκησεν) was for the purpose of gaining the result. Jesus had completed all of the requirements for qualifying as the Judge to open the book. He has not yet opened it but He is about to do so. "The line of distinction" *i.e.* between purpose and result "is often very faint, if not, wholly gone" (Robertson, *Grammar*, 1089). Burton calls purpose "intended result." (*Moods and Tenses*, 148). We must exercise care not to indulge in overrefinement. Yet the Κοινή can be very precise and we should take full advantage of our privileges. Otherwise, we may as well stumble around with the English!

The elder told John to look for a lion - the King of Israel. John looked, but he saw a Lamb!

Verse 6 - "And I beheld, and, lo, in the midst of the throne and of the four beasts, and in the midst of the elders, stood a Lamb as it had been slain, having seven horns and seven eyes which are the seven spirits of God sent forth into all the earth."

Καὶ εἶδον ἐν μέσῳ τοῦ θρόνου καὶ τῶν τεσσάρων ζώων καὶ ἐν μέσῳ τῶν πρεσβυτέρων ἀρνίον ἑστηκὸς ὡς ἐσφαγμένον, ἔχων κέρατα ἑπτὰ καὶ ὀφθαλμοὺς ἑπτά, οἳ εἰσιν τὰ (ἑπτὰ) πνεύματα τοῦ θεοῦ ἀπεσταλμένοι εἰς πᾶσαν τὴν γῆν.

"And between the throne and the four living creatures and among the elders, I saw a Lamb standing, as though it had been slain, with seven horns and with seven eyes, which are the seven spirits of God sent out into all the earth;..."...

RSV

καὶ (continuative conjunction) 14.

εἶδον (1st.per.sing.aor.act.ind.of ὁράω, constative) 133.

ἐν (preposition with the locative, place) 80.

μέσῳ (loc.sing.masc.of μέσος, place) 873.

τοῦ (gen.sing.masc.of the article in agreement with θρόνου) 9.

θρόνου (gen.sing.masc.of θρόνος, description) 519.

καὶ (adjunctive conjunction joining substantives) 14.

τῶν (gen.pl.neut.of the article in agreement with ζῴων) 9.

τεσσάρων (gen.pl.neut.of τέσσαρες, in agreement with ζῴων) 1508.

ζῴων (gen.pl.neut.of ζῷον, description) 5086.

καὶ (adjunctive conjunction joining prepositional phrases) 14.

ἐν (preposition with the locative, place) 80.

μέσῳ (loc.sing.masc.of μέσος, place) 873.

τῶν (gen.pl.masc.of the article in agreement with πρεσβυτέρων) 9.

πρεσβυτέρων (gen.pl.masc.of πρεσβύτερος, description) 1141.

ἀρνίον (acc.sing.neut.of ἀρνίον, direct object of εἶδον) 2923.

ἑστηκὸς (perf.act.part.acc.sing.neut.of ἵστημι, adjectival, predicate position, restrictive, in agreement with ἀρνίον) 180.

ὡς (comparative particle) 128.

ἐσφαγμένον (perf.pass.part.acc.sing.neut.of σφάττω, consummative) 5292.

ἔχων (pres.act.part.nom.sing.masc.of ἔχω, adjectival, predicate position, restrictive, joined to ἀρνίον, for ἔχον) 82.

κέρατα (acc.pl.neut.of κέρας, direct object of ἔχων) 1851.

ἑπτὰ (numeral) 1024.

καὶ (adjunctive conjunction joining nouns) 14.

ὀφθαλμοὺς (acc.pl.masc.of ὀφθαλμός, direct object of ἔχων) 501.

ἑπτά (numeral) 1024.

οἱ (nom.pl.masc.of ὅς, relative pronoun, subject of εἰσιν) 65.

εἰσιν (3d.per.pl.pres.ind.of εἰμί, aoristic) 86.

τὰ (nom.pl.neut.of the article in agreement with πνεύματα) 9.

ἑπτὰ (numeral) 1024.

πνεύματα (nom.pl.neut.of πνεῦμα, predicate nominative) 83.

τοῦ (gen.sing.masc.of the article in agreement with θεοῦ) 9.

θεοῦ (gen.sing.masc.of θεός, description) 124.

ἀπεσταλμένοι (perf.pass.part.nom.pl.masc.of ἀποστέλλω, adjectival, predicate position, restrictive, in agreement with πνεύματα) 215.

εἰς (preposition with the accusative of extent) 140.

πᾶσαν (acc.sing.fem.of πᾶς, in agreement with γῆν) 67.

τὴν (acc.sing.fem.of the article in agreement with γῆν) 9.

γῆν (acc.sing.fem.of γῆ, extent) 157.

Translation - "But I saw within the throne area and amid the four living creatures and among the elders a Lamb standing, as one who had been slain, having seven horns and seven eyes which are the seven spirits of God which have been sent out into all the earth."

Comment: We can construe καί here as adversative. The elder told John to look for a Lion, but (καί) John saw a Lamb. *Cf.* the picture in Rev.4:6 for an idea of ἐν μέσῳ τοῦ θρόνου . . . τῶν πρεσβυτέρων.

Our Lord Jesus is indeed the Lion (verse 5) but in order to be the Judge He must first of all be a slain Lamb. Both the adjectival participles ἑστηκός and ἔχων fail to accord with ἀρνίον, with which they are joined in gender and case. Solecisms are common in the Revelation.

Note the characteristics necessary to qualify if one wishes to be worthy (ἄξιος) to rip the seals from the book. Such must be a King (verse 5). He must be a slain Lamb (verse 6). He must have all power given unto him (Mt.28:18). This He has with κέρατα ἑπτά. *Cf.*#1851. It seems clear that κέρας refers to power and authority while seven is the number of completion. Thus we have the King of the Jews, who died for redemptive purposes and rose again, who was invited to sit at the Father's right hand until His enemies are subdued (Psalm 110:1), and who, from His throne in the heavens, as Head over all things to His church which is His body (Eph.1:17-23) has sent the Holy Spirit to the ends of the earth to conduct the world-wide missionary enterprise, which, before it is complete, will have called out from among the Gentiles a people for His name(Acts 15:14-18). The seven spirits (*cf.* Rev.1:4; 3:1; 4:5; 5:6) represent the Holy Spirit in the sevenfold plentitude of His sovereign power as He goes into all the world (Mt.28:18-20) carrying the story of redemption and convincing the elect (John 16:7 -11).

Salvation must be purchased before a Judge can judge. Christ purchased it. It must also be offered or judgment cannot be made. The offer will have been made and accepted by those for whom He died before the final act of the judgment week occurs.

Note how prominently Christ's death is featured in this heavenly scene (Rev.5:6,9,12). Note how His death rescues the elect from damnation in Rev.13:8. *Cf.* comment. The Holy Spirit, in His world-wide quest for souls is referred to as God's perfect eyesight. With this in mind read Heb.4:13. Thus the Judge has full knowledge of every case that comes before Him, which is a prerequisite for every honest Judge. He also understands all of His saints (1 Peter 3:12). So, whether the Judge judges saints (1 Peter 3:12; Rev.11:18) or sinners (Heb.4:13; Rev.9:20; 20:10) He is perfectly informed.

Only in Christ, the Judge (John 5:22) does mercy and truth meet together and righteousness and peace kiss each other (Psalm 85:10). Truth sprang out of the earth (Isa.53:1) when He became incarnate and righteousness looked down from heaven when He was baptized (Mt.3:15). Thus the dilemma is resolved in Christ. He is now the all powerful Lion only because He became the totally submissive Lamb, who then arose with total authority (Mt.28:18) to send the Holy Spirit world-wide with the message of salvation. Thus there is no ethical reason why Jesus Christ cannot be the Judge. There is every reason why He should. As He steps forward to take the book, the opening of which begins Daniel's last seven year period, with an increasing crescendo of divine judgment, until, at the end, He comes in power, the heavenly hosts indicate that they understand that His judgments are "true and righteous all together." (Psalm 19:9,10,11).

Verse 7 - "And he came and took the book out of the right hand of him that sat upon the throne."

καὶ ἦλθεν καὶ εἴληφεν ἐκ τῆς δεξιᾶς τοῦ καθημένου ἐπὶ τοῦ θρόνου.

"and he went and took the scroll from the right hand of him who was seated on the throne." . . . *RSV*

καὶ (continuative conjunction) 14.

ἦλθεν (3d.per.sing.aor.mid.ind.of ἔρχομαι, constative) 146.

καὶ (adjunctive conjunction joining verbs) 14.

εἴληφεν (3d.per.sing.perf.act.ind.of λαμβάνω, aoristic present perfect) 533.

ἐκ (preposition with the ablative of separation) 19.

τῆς (abl.sing.fem.of the article in agreement with δεξιᾶς) 9.

δεξιᾶς (abl.sing.fem.of δεξιός, separation) 502.

τοῦ (gen.sing.masc.of the article in agreement with καθημένου) 9.

καθημένου (pres.mid.part.gen.sing.masc.of κάθημαι, substantival, possession) 377.

ἐπὶ (preposition with the genitive of place description) 47.

τοῦ (gen.sing.masc.of the article in agreement with θρόνου) 9.

θρόνου (gen.sing.masc.of θρόνος, place description) 519.

Translation - "And He came and took the book out of the right hand of Him who was sitting upon the throne."

Comment: We must supply τὸ βιβλίον from verse 8. There is controversy among the grammarians as to εἴληφεν. Is it a dramatic historical present perfect or equal to ἔλαβεν and thus preterit? If the former it indicates "an action completed in the past (but) conceived in terms of the present time for the sake of vividness." (Robertson, *Grammar*, 896). "Of the Historical Perfect in the sense of a Perfect which expresses a past completed action, the result of which the speaker conceives himself to be witnessing (as in the case of the Historical Present) there is no certain New Testament instance." (Burton, *New Testament Moods and Tenses*, 38). Simcox joins Burton against Robertson when he says that "no one but a doctrinaire special pleader is likely to deny that in Rev.5:7; 8:5, εἴληφεν, and in 7:14, εἴρηκα, are mere preterits in sense." (Simcox, *The Language of the New Testament*, 104, as cited in Robertson, *Ibid., 899*). Robertson calls εἴληφεν in Rev.5:7 "a striking instance" of the Dramatic Historical Present Perfect, "where John sees Jesus with the book in his hand." (*Ibid.,*897) He adds that "It is dull to make εἴληφεν here equal to ἔλαβεν." (*Ibid.*). John had been caught up to heaven and carried forward in time to the beginning of the last seven years before the second coming of Christ. Thus the action of Jesus in stepping forward and taking the book is not a past event in relation to the first century A.D. From the point of view of John, who was viewing a future event as though it were current, we can agree with Robertson and translate, "He has taken the book out of the hand of Him who sits upon the throne, and He now has it in His hand." This is the force of the historical present perfect. This is not "special pleading" in view of the assumption that the Revelation must be viewed in the futuristic sense.

John has been watching breathlessly. Overwhelmed by the majesty of the scene in the throne room of heaven, as reported in chapter 4, he is now delighted to learn that one has been found who is able to open the book. The action continues and John tells us as though in the present tense. "The Lion/Lamb has come forward and taken the book! He has it in His hand!" He who has won the right to initiate heaven's program which is designed to bring man's day to a halt and bring the unsaved to the bar of judgment, is here and the action is about to begin.

Our Lord's move to unseal the book is accompanied by a new song, begun by the four living creatures and the twenty-four elders and then joined by the angels and finally by every creature in heaven, earth, sea and under the earth. The theme is not "Glory to the Creator" as in chapter 4, but "Glory to the Redeemer."

Verse 8 - "And when he had taken the book the four beasts and four and twenty elders fell down before the Lamb, having every one of them harps and golden vials, full of odours, which are the prayers of the saints."

καὶ ὅτε ἔλαβεν τὸ βιβλίον, τὰ τέσσαρα ζῷα καὶ οἱ εἴκοσι τέσσαρες πρεσβύτεροι ἔπεσαν ἐνώπιον τοῦ ἀρνίου, ἔχοντες ἕκαστος κιθάραν καὶ φιάλας χρυσᾶς γεμούσας θυμιαμάτων, αἵ εἰσιν αἱ προσευχαὶ τῶν ἁγίων.

"And when he had taken the scroll, the four living creatures and the twenty-four elders fell down before the Lamb, each holding a harp, and with golden bowls full of incense, which are the prayers of the saints; . . ." . . . RSV

καὶ (continuative conjunction) 14.

ὅτε (conjunction introducing the indicative in a definite temporal clause) 703.

ἔλαβεν (3d.per.sing.aor.act.ind.of λαμβάνω, constative) 533.

τὸ (acc.sing.neut.of the article in agreement with βιβλίον) 9.

βιβλίον (acc.sing.neut.of βιβλίον, direct object of ἔλαβεν) 1292.

τὰ (nom.pl.neut.of the article in agreement with ζῷα) 9.

τέσσαρα (nom.pl.neut.of τέσσαρες, in agreement with ζῷα) 1508.

ζῷα (nom.pl.neut.of ζῶον, subject of ἔπεσαν and ᾄδουσιν) 5086.

καὶ (adjunctive conjunction joining nouns) 14.

οἱ (nom.pl.masc.of the article in agreement with πρεσβύτεροι) 9.

εἴκοσι (numeral) 2283.

τέσσαρες (numeral) 1508.

πρεσβύτεροι (nom.pl.masc.of πρεσβύτερος, subject of ἔπεσαν and ᾄδουσιν) 1141.

ἔπεσαν (3d.per.pl.aor.act.ind.of πίπτω, constative) 187.

ἐνώπιον (preposition with the genitive of place description) 1798.

τοῦ (gen.sing.neut.of the article in agreement with ἀρνίου) 9.
ἀρνίου (gen.sing.neut.of ἀρνίον, place description) 2923.
ἔχοντες (pres.act.part.nom.pl.masc.of ἔχω, adverbial, circumstantial) 82.
ἕκαστος (nom.sing.masc.of ἕκαστος, subject of ἔστιν understood) 1217.
κιθάραν (acc.sing.fem.of κιθάρα, direct object of ἔχοντες) 4232.
καὶ (adjunctive conjunction joining nouns) 14.

#5348 φιάλας (acc.pl.fem.of φιάλη, direct object of ἔχοντες).

King James Version

vial - Rev.5:8; 15:7; 16:1,2,3,4,8,10,12,17; 17:1; 21:9.

Revised Standard Version

bowls - Rev.5:8; 15:7; 16:;1,2,3,4,8,10,12,17; 17:1; 21:9.

Meaning: A broad, shallow bowl; a deep saucer. With reference to the heavenly receptacle containing the prayers of the saints - Rev.5:8. Those containing judgments to be poured out upon the world - Rev.15:7; 16:1,2,3,4,8,10,12,17; 17:1; 21:9.

χρυσᾶς (acc.pl.fem.of χρύσεος, in agreement with φιάλας) 4828.
γεμούσας (pres.act.part.acc.pl.fem.of γέμω, adjectival, predicate position, restrictive, in agreement with φιάλας) 1457.
θυμιαμάτων (gen.pl.neut.of θυμίαμα, description) 1793.
αἵ (nom.pl.fem.of ὅς, relative pronoun, subject of εἰσιν) 65.
εἰσιν (3d.per.pl.pres.ind.of εἰμί, aoristic) 86.
αἱ (nom.pl.fem.of the article in agreement with προσευχαὶ) 9.
προσευχαὶ (nom.pl.fem.of προσευχή, predicate nominative) 1238.
τῶν (gen.pl.masc.of the article in agreement with ἁγίων) 9.
ἁγίων (gen.pl.masc.of ἅγιος, possession) 84.

Translation - "And when He took the book, the four living creatures and the twenty-four elders fell before the Lamb, each having a harp and golden bowls full of incense, which are the prayers of the saints."

Comment: ὅτε introduces the definite temporal clause. Heaven's citizens — the living creatures and the elders know what is about to transpire. The text gives no hint as to why they each have a harp, but the golden bowls are explained. They contain the incense which is said to be the prayers which the Christians have sent up. There will be, at the time of the first seal event (Rev.6:1,2) seven years before the sixth and seventh seals terminate the tribulation period. During this time souls will still be saved. Christ has invited the Laodiceans to open the door and allow Him to come in (Rev.3:20,21). Not all of the elect will be saved until the days of the last judgment, when the seventh angel will begin to sound his trumpet (Rev.10:7). Thus, though man's day is soon to be terminated and "the day of the Lord" is soon to begin, with divine judgments falling upon godless men, God is not forgetting that some of the prayers of the saints are not yet answered. The same throne room of the Ancient of Days from which come thunders, lightnings, voices and divine judgments also contains on file in golden bowls the prayers which saints have prayed. No prayer that originates in the heart of the resurrected High Priest (Psalm 2:7,8; 110:1,4) and is formulated by the Holy Spirit (Jude 20) and which is uttered by a member of the Body of Christ on earth will go unanswered. Though judgments are soon to fall, the day of grace still has seven years to run.

We must take care to distinguish between what we call "prayer" and what God regards as prayer. Not all that is offered upon earth in liturgical worship and expressed in the rubrics of the lectionary, nor in the vapid and vacuous formulations of the Pharisees in the temple can be classified as prayer. Much public prayer, unfortunately, is pious pretense, designed not to impress God but the public. The Scriptures have established guide lines by which we can distinguish genuine from counterfeit prayer. The "if clauses" in John 14:13,14 and John 15:7 are not to be taken lightly. The assurance that what we pray becomes incense in the golden bowls in heaven is ours only when we are sure that God is listening. And He is not listening if we are praying for something that is contrary to His will (1 John 5:14,15). We may be sure that the prayer that is motivated by the Holy Spirit, Who indwells the believer, is consistent with the will of our Melchisedek High Priest. Thus it will be heard, and, if heard, answered. How important for us to pray, "Lord, teach us to pray. . . " (Luke 11:1). We learn to pray by praying. The motivation to pray is great when we remember that every real prayer is on file in heaven until it is answered.

The heavenly chorus bursts into singing with another theme added to the Creation hymn of Revelation 4:11. Everyone included in the song of verses 9 and 10 is also included in the perfume of the golden bowls which have been in the custodial care of the twenty-four elders.

Verse 9 - "And they sung a new song saying, Thou art worthy to take the book, and to open the seals thereof: for thou hast redeemed us to God by thy blood out of every kindred, and tongue, and people and nation; . . . "

καὶ ᾄδουσιν ᾠδὴν καινὴν λέγοντες, Ἄξιος εἶ λαβεῖν τὸ βιβλίον καὶ ἀνοῖξαι τὰς σφραγῖδος αὐτοῦ, ὅτι ἐσφάγης καὶ ἠγόρασας τῷ θεῷ ἐν τῷ αἵματί σου ἐκ πάσης φυλῆς καὶ γλώσσης καὶ λαοῦ καὶ ἔθνους,

"and they sang a new song, saying, 'Worthy art thou to take the scroll and to open its seals, for thou wast slain and by thy blood didst ransom men for God from every tribe and tongue and people and nation, . . . " . . . RSV

καὶ (continuative conjunction) 14.

ᾄδουσιν (3d.per.pl.pres.act.ind.of ᾄδω, aoristic) 4519.

ᾠδὴν (acc.sing.fem.of ᾠδή, direct object of ᾄδουσιν) 4518.

καινὴν (acc.sing.fem.of καινός, in agreement with ᾠδὴν) 512.

λέγοντες (pres.act.part.nom.pl.masc.of λέγω, recitatitve) 66.

Ἄξιος (nom.sing.masc.of ἄξιος, predicate nominative) 285.

εἶ (2d.per.sing.pres.ind.of εἰμί, static) 86.

λαβεῖν (2d.aor.act.ind.of λαμβάνω, complementary) 533.

τό (acc.sing.neut.of the article in agreement with βιβλίον) 9.

βιβλίον (acc.sing.neut.of βιβλίον, direct object of λαβεῖν) 1292.

καί (adjunctive conjunction joining infinitives) 14.

ἀνοῖξαι (aor.act.inf.of ἀνοίγω, complementary) 188.

τάς (acc.pl.fem.of the article in agreement with σφραγῖδος) 9.

σφραγῖδος (acc.pl.fem.of σφραγίς, direct object of ἀνοῖξαι) 3886.

αὐτοῦ (gen.sing.masc.of αὐτός, possession) 16.

ὅτι (conjunction introducing a subordinate causal clause) 211.

ἐσφάγης (2d.per.sing.2d.aor.pass.ind.of σφάττω, constative) 5292.

καί (adjunctive conjunction joining verbs) 14.

ἠγόρασας (2d.per.sing.aor.act.ind.of ἀγοράζω, culminative) 1085.

τῷ (dat.sing.masc.of the article in agreement with θεῷ) 9.

θεῷ (dat.sing.masc.of θεός, personal advantage) 124.

ἐν (preposition with the instrumental, means) 80.

τῷ (instru.sing.neut.of the article in agreement with αἵματί) 9.

αἵματί (instru.sing.neut.of αἷμα, means) 1203.

σου (gen.sing.masc.of σύ, possession) 104.

ἐκ (preposition with the ablative of source) 19.

πάσης (abl.sing.fem.of πᾶς, in agreement with φυλῆς, γλώσσης, λαοῦ and ἔθνους) 67.

φυλῆς (abl.sing.fem.of φυλή, source) 1313.

καί (adjunctive conjunction joining nouns) 14.

γλώσσης (abl.sing.fem.of γλῶσσα, source) 1846.

καί (adjunctive conjunction joining nouns) 14.

λαοῦ (abl.sing.masc.of λαός, source) 110.

καί (adjunctive conjunction joining nouns) 14.

ἔθνους (abl.sing.masc.of ἔθνος, source) 376.

Translation - "And they are singing a new song, saying, 'You are qualified to take the book and to open its seals, because you were slain and you have redeemed unto God by your blood from every tribe and dialect and people and nation."

Comment: The complementary infinitives λαβεῖν and ἀνοῖξαι repeat the thought of verse 6. The song is one of redemption — the song of the Lamb slain. Thus the Creator of Rev.4:11 is also the Redeemer of Revelation 5:6,9. *Cf.* Rev.14:3,3; 15:3,3.

The KJV, following the Textus Receptus, has ἡμᾶς after τῷ θεῷ, but αὐτούς after ἐποίησας in verse 10, and goes on with βασιλεύουσιν ἐπὶ τῆς γῆς. This reading supports the view that the four beasts and twenty-four elders are human saints, saved by Christ's blood and thus it supports the pretribulation rapture view that saints raptured in Rev.4:1 appear in heaven in Chapters 4 and 5. "Although the evidence for τῷ θεῷ is slight (A eth) this reading best accounts for the origin of the others. Wishing to provide ἠγόρασας with a more exactly determined object than is found in the words ἐκ πάσης φυλῆς κ.τ.λ. some scribes introduced ἡμᾶς either before τῳ θεῷ (94 2344 *al*) or after τῷ θεῷ (Sinaiticus 046 1006 1611 2013 *al*), while others replaced τῷ θεῷ with ἡμᾶς (1 2065* Cyprian *al*).

Those who made the emendations, however, overlooked the unsuitability of ἡμᾶς with αὐτούς in the following verse (where, indeed, the Textus Receptus reads ἡμᾶς but with quite inadequate authority)." (Metzger, *A Textual Commentary on the Greek New Testament*, 738). ἡμᾶς, which makes even the four beasts as well as the twenty-four elders objects of Christ's blood redemption (!) is inconsistent with βασιλεύσουσιν in verse 10 which is well supported. It makes no sense to say "You redeemed *us* and *they* shall reign upon the earth." *Cf.* Megzger's comment on verse 10.

Verse 10 - "And hast made us unto our God kings and priests: and we shall reign on the earth."

καὶ ἐποίησας αὐτοὺς τῷ θεῷ ἡμῶν βασιλείαν καὶ ἱερεῖς, καὶ βασιλεύσουσιν ἐπὶ τῆς γῆς.

. . . and hast made them a kingdom and priests to our God, and they shall reign on earth." . . . RSV

καὶ (continuative conjunction) 14.

ἐποίησας (2d.per.sing.aor.act.ind.of ποιέω, effective) 127.

αὐτοὺς (acc.pl.masc.of αὐτός, direct object of ἐποίησας) 16.

τῷ (dat.sing.masc.of the article in agreement with θεῷ) 9.

θεῷ (dat.sing.masc.of θεός, personal interest) 124.

ἡμῶν (gen.pl.masc.of ἐγώ, relationship) 123.

βασιλείαν (acc.sing.fem.of βασιλεία, double accusative) 253.

καὶ (adjunctive conjunction joining nouns) 14.

ἱερεῖς (acc.pl.masc.of ἱερεύς, double accusative) 714.

καὶ (continuative conjunction) 14.

βασιλεύσουσιν (3d.per.pl.fut.act.ind.of βασιλεύω, predictive) 236.

ἐπὶ (preposition with the genitive of place description) 47.

τῆς (gen.sing.fem.of the article in agreement with γῆς) 9.

γῆς (gen.sing.fem.of γῆ, place description) 157.

Translation - "And you have made them for our God a kingdom and priests, and they shall reign upon the earth."

Comment: Metzger adds, "Of the three variant readings it is obvious that βασιλεύσουσιν (2432 *al*) is a secondary development, arising from the introduction of ἡμᾶς in the preceding verse. (See the comments on verse 9). It is more difficult to choose between βασιλεύσουσιν supported by Sinaiticus P 1 94 1854 2053 2344 it_gig vg syr_ph cop_sa bo arm *al* and βασιλεύουσιν, supported by A 046 1006 1611 it_61 syr_h *al*. A majority of the Committee, noting that in 20.6 Codex Alexandrinus mistakenly reads βασιλεύουσιν for the future tense, preferred βασιλεύσουσιν here, as must suited to the meaning of the context." (*Ibid.*, 738).

The singers are not saints but they are singing a hymn of praise to Christ because of what He has done, and will do for the saints. As Redeemer, He has redeemed them (verse 9) and as King He has established for them a place in His kingdom and they shall reign upon the earth. *Cf.* Rev.20:4; 22:5; Rom.5:17.

Christ's redemption has been individually but not ethnically, linguistically, politically or nationally selective. The family of God, saved by His blood, comes from every part of earth. His Spirit has carried the message throughout the planet (Rev.5:6). Now His judgments are going to be felt all over the earth.

Verse 11 - "And I beheld, and I heard the voice of many angels round about the throne, and the beasts and the elders: and the number of them was ten thousand times ten thousand, and thousands of thousands."

Καὶ εἶδον, καὶ ἤκουσα φωνὴν ἀγγέλων πολλῶν κύκλῳ τοῦ θρόνου καὶ τῶν ζῴων καὶ τῶν πρεσβυτέρων, καὶ ἦν ὁ ἀριθμὸς αὐτῶν μυριάδες μυριάδων καὶ χιλιάδες χιλιάδων,

"Then I looked, and I heard around the throne and the living creatures and the elders the voice of many angels, numbering myriads of myriads and thousands of thousands, . . . " . . . RSV

Καὶ (continuative conjunction) 14.
εἶδον (1st.per.sing.aor.act.ind.of ὁράω, constative) 144.
καὶ (adjunctive conjunction joining verbs) 14.
ἤκουσα (1st.per.sing.aor.act.ind.of ἀκούω, ingressive) 148.
φωνὴν (acc.sing.fem.of φωνή, direct object of ἤκουσα) 222.
ἀγγέλων (gen.pl.masc.of ἄγγελος, description) 96.
πολλῶν (gen.pl.masc.of πολύς, in agreement with ἀγγέλων) 228.
κύκλῳ (loc.sing.masc.of κύκλος, place) 2183.
τοῦ (gen.sing.masc.of the article in agreement with θρόνου) 9.
θρόνου (gen.sing.masc.of θρόνος, place description) 519.
καὶ (adjunctive conjunction joining nouns) 14.
τῶν (gen.pl.neut.of the article in agreement with ζῴων) 9.
ζῴων (gen.pl.neut.of ζῶον, description) 5086.
καὶ (adjunctive conjunction joining nouns) 14.
τῶν (gen.pl.masc.of the article in agreement with πρεσβυτέρων) 9.
πρεσβυτέρων (gen.pl.masc.of πρεσβύτερος, description) 1141.
καὶ (continuative conjunction) 14.
ἦν (3d.per.sing.imp.ind.of εἰμί, progressive description) 86.
ὁ (nom.sing.masc.of the article in agreement with ἀριθμὸς) 9.
ἀριθμὸς (nom.sing.masc.of ἀριθμός, subject of ἦν) 2278.
αὐτῶν (gen.pl.masc.of αὐτός, description) 16.
μυριάδες (nom.pl.fem.of μυριάς, predicate nominative) 2473.
μυριάδων (gen.pl.fem.of μυριάς, partitive) 2473.
καὶ (adjunctive conjunction joining nouns) 14.
χιλιάδες (nom.pl.fem.of χιλιάς, predicate nominative) 2536.
χιλιάδων (nom.pl.fem.of χιλιάς, partitive) 2536.

Translation - "And I watched. And I began to hear the voices of many angels encircling the throne and of the living creatures and of the elders. And the number was untold myriads and thousands of thousands."

Comment: John watched and began to listen, as angels about the throne along with the four living creatures and the twenty-four elders numbering into myriads impossible to count were praising Christ. They are joined by all of God's creatures in verse 13 after which the four living creatures say, "Amen" and the elders worship (verse 14).

Verse 12 - "Saying with a loud voice, Worthy is the Lamb that was slain to receive power, and riches and wisdom, and strength, and honour, and glory, and blessing."

λέγοντες φωνῇ μεγάλῃ, Ἄξιός ἐστιν τὸ ἀρνίον τὸ ἐσφαγμένον λαβεῖν τὴν δύναμιν καὶ πλοῦτον καὶ σοφίαν καὶ ἰσχὺν καὶ τιμὴν καί δόξαν καὶ εὐλογίαν.

"saying with a loud voice, 'Worthy is the Lamb who was slain, to receive power and wealth and wisdom and might and honor and glory and blessing!'"..
                                                                    . RSV

λέγοντες (pres.act.part.nom.pl.masc.of λέγω, recitative) 66.

φωνῇ (instru.sing.fem.of φωνή, means) 222.

μεγάλῃ (instru.sing.fem.of μέγας, in agreement with φωνῇ) 184.

Ἄξιός (nom.sing.masc.of ἄξιος, predicate adjective) 285.

ἐστιν (3d.per.sing.pres.ind.of εἰμί, static) 86.

τὸ (nom.sing.neut.of the article in agreement with ἀρνίον) 9.

ἀρνίον (nom.sing.neut.of ἀρνίον, subject of ἐστιν) 2923.

τὸ (nom.sing.neut.of the article in agreement with ἐσφαγμένον) 9.

ἐσφαγμένον (perf.pass.part.nom.sing.neut.of σφάττω, adjectival, emphatic attributive position, ascriptive, in agreement with ἀρνίον) 5292.

λαβεῖν (2d.aor.act.inf.of λαμβάνω, complementary) 533.

τὴν (acc.sing.fem.of the article in agreement with the list of substantives following) 9.

δύναμιν (acc.sing.fem.of δύναμις, direct object of λαβεῖν) 687.

καὶ (adjunctive conjunction joining nouns) 14.

πλοῦτον (acc.sing.masc.of πλοῦτος, direct object of λαβεῖν) 1050.

καὶ (adjunctive conjunction joining nouns) 14.

σοφίαν (acc.sing.fem.of σοφία, direct object of λαβεῖν) 934.

καὶ (adjunctive conjunction joining nouns) 14.

ἰσχὺν (acc.sing.fem.of ἰσχύς, direct object of λαβεῖν) 2419.

καὶ (adjunctive conjunction joining nouns) 14.

τιμὴν (acc.sing.fem.of τιμή, direct object of λαβεῖν) 1619.

καὶ (adjunctive conjunction joining nouns) 14.

δόξαν (acc.sing.fem.of δόξα, direct object of λαβεῖν) 361.

καὶ (adjunctive conjunction joining nouns) 14.

εὐλογίαν (acc.sing.fem.of εὐλογία, direct object of λαβεῖν) 4060.

Translation - "Shouting in full cry, 'Worthy is the Lamb Who was slain to receive power and riches and wisdom and strength and honor and glory and blessing."

Comment: The repetition of adjunctive καὶ adds dignity and majesty to the production. Note how Georg Friedrich Handel exploits this idea in his phraseological structure in the final chorus of *The Messiah*. This rhetorical principle is known as polysyndeton. *Cf.*Phil.4:9; Rom.9:4; Rev.7:12; 1 Cor.15:4. Note that the article serves for all of the substantives, whereas in Rev.4:11; 5:13; 7:12 the article joins each quality.

Thus angels are added to the four living creatures and twenty-four elders in praise to the slaughtered Lamb. Note the perfect participial adjective in the emphatic attributive position, τὸ ἐσφαγμένον. Jesus, once slaughtered as God's Lamb (John 1:29) is always thereafter the Slaughtered Lamb, though eternally risen from the dead (Rom.6:9). The consequences of His death are durative.

The student should research #'s 687, 1050, 934, 2419, 1619, 361 and 4060 for an appreciation of the full extent of the heavenly praise given to the Lord Jesus Christ. It pleased the Father that in Him all fulness dwell (Col.1:19).

In verse 13 all of His creatures join the chorus.

Verse 13 - "And every creature which is in heaven, and on the earth, and under the earth and such as are in the sea, and all that are in them, heard I saying, Blessing, and honour, and glory, and power, be unto him that sitteth upon the throne, and unto the Lamb for ever and ever."

καὶ πᾶν κτίσμα ὃ ἐν τῷ οὐρανῷ καὶ ἐπὶ τῆς γῆς καὶ ὑποκάτω τῆς γῆς καὶ ἐπὶ τῆς θαλάσσης, καὶ τὰ ἐν αὐτοῖς πάντα, ἤκουσα λέγοντας, Τῷ καθημένῳ ἐπὶ τοῦ θρόνου καὶ τῷ ἀρνίῳ ἡ εὐλογία καὶ ἡ τιμὴ καὶ ἡ δόξα καὶ τὸ κράτος εἰς τοὺς αἰῶνας τῶν αἰώνων.

"And I heard every creature in heaven and on earth and under the earth and in the sea, and all therein, saying, 'To him who sits upon the throne and to the Lamb be blessing and honor and glory and might for ever and ever!'"... RSV

καὶ (continuative conjunction) 14.

πᾶν (acc.sing.neut.of πᾶς, in agreement with κτίσμα) 67.

κτίσμα (acc.sing.neut.of κτίσμα, direct object of ἤκουσα) 4748.

ὃ (acc.sing.neut.of ὅς, relative pronoun, in agreement with κτίσμα) 65.

ἐν (preposition with the locative of place) 80.

τῷ (loc.sing.masc.of the article in agreement with οὐρανῷ) 9.

οὐρανῷ (loc.sing.masc.of οὐρανός, place) 254.

καὶ (adjunctive conjunction joining prepositional phrases) 14.

ἐπὶ (preposition with the genitive of place description) 47.

τῆς (gen.sing.fem.of the article in agreement with γῆς) 9.

γῆς (gen.sing.fem.of γῆ, place description) 157.

καὶ (adjunctive conjunction joining prepositional phrases) 14.

ὑποκάτω (improper preposition with the genitive of place description) 1429.

τῆς (gen.sing.fem.of the article in agreement with γῆς) 9.

γῆς (gen.sing.fem.of γῆ, place description) 157.

καὶ (adjunctive conjunction joining prepositional phrases) 14.

ἐπὶ (preposition with the genitive of place description) 47.

τῆς (gen.sing.fem.of the article in agreement with θαλάσσης) 9.

θαλάσσης (gen.sing.fem.of θάλασσα, place description) 374.

καὶ (adjunctive conjunction joining substantives) 14.

τὰ (acc.pl.neut.of the article in agreement with πάντα) 9.

ἐν (preposition with the locative of place) 80.

αὐτοῖς (loc.pl.neut.of αὐτός, place, anaphoric) 16.

πάντα (acc.pl.neut.of πᾶς, direct object of ἤκουσα) 67.

ἤκουσα (1st.per.sing.aor.act.ind.of ἀκούω, constative) 148.

λέγοντας (pres.act.part.acc.pl.fem.of λέγω, recitatitve) 66.

Τῷ (dat.sing.masc.of the article in agreement with καθημένῳ) 9.

καθημένῳ (pres.mid.part.dat.sing.masc.of κάθημαι, substantival, personal advantage) 377.

ἐπὶ (preposition with the genitive of place description) 47.

τοῦ (gen.sing.masc.of the article in agreement with θρόνου) 9.

θρόνου (gen.sing.masc.of θρόνος, place description) 519.

καὶ (adjunctive conjunction joining substantives) 14.

τῷ (dat.sing.neut.of the article in agreement with ἀρνίῳ) 9.

ἀρνίῳ (dat.sing.neut.of ἀρνίον, personal advantage) 2923.

ἡ (nom.sing.fem.of the article in agreement with εὐλογία) 9.

εὐλογία (nom.sing.fem.of εὐλογία subject of ἔστω, understood - so with the substantives which follow) 4060.

καὶ (adjunctive conjunction joining nouns) 14.

ἡ (nom.sing.fem.of the article in agreement with τιμή) 9.

τιμή (nom.sing.fem.of τιμή) 1619.

καὶ (adjunctive conjunction joining nouns) 14.

ἡ (nom.sing.fem.of the article in agreement with δόξα) 9.

δόξα (nom.sing.fem.of δόξα) 361.

καὶ (adjunctive conjunction joining nouns) 14.

τὸ (nom.sing.neut.of the article in agreement with κράτος) 9.

κράτος (nom.sing.neut.of κράτος) 1828.

εἰς (preposition with the accusative of time extent) 140.

τοὺς (acc.pl.masc.of the article in agreement with αἰῶνας) 9.

αἰῶνας (acc.pl.masc.of αἰών, time extent) 1002.

τῶν (gen.pl.masc.of the article in agreement with αἰώνων) 9.

αἰώνων (gen.pl.masc.of αἰών, partitive genitive) 1002.

Translation - "And every creature which is in the heaven and upon the earth and under the earth and upon the sea and everything in them I heard saying, 'Blessing and honor and glory and sovereignty be to Him Who is sitting upon the throne and to the Lamb into the ages of the ages.' "

Comment: Note the distinction between Him Who sits upon the throne and the Lamb. Two of the Persons of the Triune Godhead are named. The fact that the Holy Spirit is not also named as worthy of praise does not mean that He is not also a Person in the Godhead. The praise comes from all animate creation who can speak.

In this vision John is carried forward in time. The time point is at the beginning of the tribulation. The first seal is removed as the next event (Rev.6:1). Yet John has all creatures praising God, the Ancient of Days and Jesus Christ, the slain Lamb. This comports with Philippians 2:9-11, but not with 2 Thessalonians 2:4; Revelation 13:5,6,7 or Revelation 16:9,10,11. The entire creation indeed will praise the exalted King-Priest, the Lord Jesus, but not before or during the tribulation. Thus John in Chapters 4 and 5 has the eternal point of view which is totally untrammelled by chronology. *Cf.* Romans 8:29-30 where the entire soteriological process is viewed in the aorist tense. Another example is found in Revelation 7:14 upon which *cf.* comment.

Verse 14 - "And the four beasts said, Amen. And the four and twenty elders fell down and worshipped him that liveth forever and ever."

καὶ τὰ τέσσαρα ζῷα ἔλεγον, ᾽Αμήν. καὶ οἱ πρεσβύτεροι ἔπεσαν καὶ προσεκύνησαν.

"And the four living creatures said, 'Amen!' and the elders ell down and worshipped." . . . RSV

καὶ (continuative conjunction) 14.

τὰ (nom.pl.neut.of the article in agreement with ζῷα) 9.

τέσσαρα (nom.pl.neut.of τέσσαρες, in agreement with ζῷα) 1508.

ζῷα (nom.pl.neut.of ζῶον, subject of ἔλεγον) 5086.

ἔλεγον (3d.per.pl.imp.act.ind.of λέγω, progressive description) 466.

καὶ (continuative conjunction) 14.

οἱ (nom.pl.masc.of the article in agreement with πρεσβύτεροι) 9.

πρεσβύτεροι (nom.pl.masc.of πρεσβύτερος, subject of ἔπεσαν and προσεκύνεσαν) 1141.

ἔπεσαν (3d.per.pl.aor.act.ind.of πίπτω, constative) 187.

καὶ (adjunctive conjunction joining verbs) 14.

προσεκύνεσαν (3d.per.pl.aor.act.ind.of προσκυνέω, ingressive) 147.

Translation - "And the four living creatures were saying, 'Amen.' And the elders fell down and began to worship."

Comment: God, the Holy Spirit has been active in human history since Calvary and Pentecost only in His function of calling out the elect, for whom Christ died, and incorporating them into the Body of Christ. He has been active in the Church, which is the Body of Christ, as He baptizes the believer at the time of regeneration (1 Cor.12:13) into the Body, indwells his body (1 Cor.6:19), infills upon request (Eph.5:18), endows with His gifts (1 Cor.12:1-11) and guides the believer in the use of His gifts (1 Cor.12-14). He seals the believer (Eph.1:13,14), thus assuring the redemption of the body at the rapture/resurrection (Rom.8:11). Though He is grieved when we drag Him into association with sin (Eph.4:30) He cannot be grieved away. He also produces His fruits in the psyche of the believer if He is given a chance (Gal.5:22,23). He guides the believer in his walk if given the opportunity and thus will prevent the fulfillment of the drives of the flesh (Gal.5:16). Thus the Holy Spirit is very active in human history but the sweep and scope of His work is for the primary purpose of completing through the regeneration, sanctification and glorification of the Body of Christ the redemptive process which God the Father ordained before the foundation of the world and which God, the incarnate Son, accomplished at the cross and at the empty tomb. The Holy Spirit's ministry is not to the world as such but to the elect in the world. He accomplishes this work by His convicting ministry as described in John 16:7-11. His work in directing the course of history is secondary to the primary task. Thus we can say that the Holy Spirit, though transcendant, is also immanent in nature, in the human spirit and in history in order to prevent the human race from destroying itself by the eccentric stresses in society which result from human depravity and lawlessness, which otherwise would bring the human story to a catastrophic end before all for whom Christ died could be saved or even be born.

Historians note the social, economic, political and philosophical evolution of man, as he stumbles about on the planet in his blindness, and we suggest various interpretations of history which are thought most plausibly and demonstrably to be the explanation. Objectivity, which is the *sine qua non* of good history suffers as writers who do not understand this, are enslaved by their "unplumbed prejudice or subconscious bias" (Sherman Kent, *Writing History*, 10). Schools of thought have become known as "the *official* historians of the third French Revoluation, the *national* historians of nineteenth century Germany, the *whig* historians of Victorian England, the *patriotic* historians of the United States." (*Ibid.*) The italcized adjectives indicate bias and the point of view. Such schools of thought have not passed the acid test set for historians by Leopold von Ranke, who demanded that we tell the story *wie es eigentlick gewesen* - "exactly how it happened." To achieve this we must "divorce the study of the past as much as humanly possible from the passions of the present." (G.P.Gooch, *History and Historians of the Nineteenth Century*, 96,97). The extent to which historians have been able to do this is the extent to which we have been able to understand how the Holy Spirit has been at work in history. But only theologians know why He has chosen to allow things to develop as He has. He has only one great design — He must call out from among the human race the individual members of the elect Body of Christ, who were purchased in the covenant of redemption, an agreement between the Father and the Son, the terms of which were ratified by the Father when He raised His Son from the dead (Psalm 2:7), seated Him at His own right hand (Psalm 110:1), declared Him to be the superior Melchisedek Priest (Psalm 110:4) and invited Him to pray for the salvation of His inheritance which would come from the uttermost parts of the earth. (Psalm 2:8).

The various interpretations of history shed some light upon the manner in which the Holy Spirit has presided in and over the course of history in His grand design to save mankind on this planet from himself until the last elect soul for whom Christ died has been born physically and then born again into the Church which is His Body. Thus geography, both in terms of climate and land forms, is seen as the explanation for how history has developed. It is thought by some that the greatest progress is made in the temperate zones where the annual temperature range is as much as one hundred degrees and where the diurnal range is thirty or forty degrees, and where annual rainfall is neither excessive in the rain forests of the sultry tropics or scant in the desert areas where temperatures may range on the same day from one hundred degrees at noon to twenty below at midnight.

Geographers have also pointed to the sinuosities of the Atlantic coast line of North America as an explanation for the development of localism within each of thirteen colonies in the seventeenth century, which became provincialism in the eighteenth century and produced the states' rights philosophy of Federalism, written into the Constitution in 1787 and precipitated the Civil War, "four-score and seven years later." If the Atlantic coast line had been like the Pacific coast line, which has only about three good harbors, there would have been fewer and larger colonies who would possibly have found more in common. For the first hundred years after Plymouth and Jamestown the colonies had more contact by sea with England than they had with each other. Thus a New England school teacher who migrated to South Carolina spoke of the strange mores and folkways of the southern people and southerners looked with some contempt upon Yankees.

Climate in the south which permitted a year-round growing season encouraged first the tobacco and then the cotton culture, which made human slavery profitable at first, whereas cold weather in New England made slavery unprofitable. One cannot afford to feed, clothe and house a slave and his rapidly growing family for twelve months in order to secure his services in a corn field for three months. Thus, say the cynical southern historians, it was not Christian ethics and an appreciation for civil rights, but economics that dictated that Yankees had no slavery. Furthermore northern rivers rush to the sea in New England from the highlands of northern mountain ranges which are not far from the coast and provide the water power for industry in the period before the steam engine was invented. Thus New England became industrial/agricultural, and developed the factory system in large cites, with their social problems, while the South, unable to move factory water wheels with the sluggish southern rivers, could only exploit the soil. The eastern mountain ranges, from the Green, White, Adirondack, Catskill and Allegheny ranges of New York and New England to the Blue Ridge of Virginia and the southern Appalachians are found further from the coast as they go toward the south and west. Thus the Potomac, the Rappahannock, the James, the Suwannee and the Apalachicola descend to the sea in much too leisurely a fashion to provide water power.

Frederick Jackson Turner advanced his famous "Thesis" which for him explained American development by the fact that as population migrated westward the frontier, defined by Turner as an area in which the population density is less than two per square mile, moved westward until in 1890 when the census report revealed that it had disappeared. Critics of the Turner Thesis take some delight in pointing out that since Turner implied, if he did not state that the westward moving frontier was the *only* source of American dynamics, it follows that the American economy has been in decline since the frontier disappeared nearly one hundred years ago.

Karl Marx, an atheistic materialist, and thus a thoroughgoing environmental determinist, viewed man as nothing more than a beast devoid of any ability to examine, analyze and manipulate his environment and thus unable to arrest the toboggan slide to destruction which the Classical economics of *laissez faire* capitalism had foisted upon the world following the invention of the steam engine and the industrial revolution. Thus we have his economic interpretation of history (*Das Kapital*).

One can teach both a boy and a monkey to ride a bicycle, but when the chain falls from the sprocket wheel, the boy has intelligence enough to examine his environment, discover the trouble, repair and replace the chain and ride on. The monkey does not have this intelligence and thus is victimized by an environment that he cannot understand and therefore cannot repair. Marx viewed man, not as the boy but as the monkey. Thus he was certain that the built-in economic injustice of the capitalist economy of David Ricardo, Thomas Malthus and John Stuart Mill could neither be detected nor eliminated and he therefore concluded that the capitalism of his day, in the mid-nineteenth century carried within it the seeds of its own destruction. Thus the modern industrial society of the classical economists of Western Europe, England and America was destined to fall before the proletarian revolution, with its law of bloody claw and fang, which Charles Darwin was soon to introduce as nature's only road to progress! The strong must survive and can do so only as the weak die. And that is good and proper because the strong are the only ones who have the inherent qualities which must be passed on to future generations. Thus the Social Darwinists were quick to take their cue, first from Marx and then from Darwin and preach against any attempt by Christians to introduce the social gospel of Christ. Herbert Spencer was inordinately proud of his remark that "To rescue a fool from the results of his folly is ultimately to fill the world with fools" and William Graham Sumner, Spencer's "little sir echo" at Yale University triumphantly told his classes that "if a man cannot make his way in this world let him make his way out of it." Thus the modifications of the old classical *laissez faire* capitalism which were suggested by Stanley Jevons, Gossen and Alfred Marshall, after Jeremy Bentham had parlayed the new marginal analysis of Jevons and Gossen into his legal positivism with its welfare state suggestion, had few disciples until the Roosevelt revolution of 1933 abandoned the Neo-Classicism of Marshall in favor of the new economics of John Maynard Keynes. Thus economists who are Christians and who thus reject Marx's atheistic and deterministic materialism, are prepared to agree with him that economics goes far to explain the development of history. If the classical capitalistic boy had not had the intelligence to look at his industrial bicycle, and discover the principle of diminishing marginal utility, as Gossen and Jevons did, and if Bentham had not discovered that the greatest utility is found in the "greatest good to the greatest number" and if Keynes had not discovered that a judicious redistribution of the wealth hurts the rich less than it helps the poor and that it results in sufficient consumer demand to sustain new investment and thus fuel the development of intelligent capitalism, Marx's dismal prophecies would have been fulfilled. It is significant that Lenin, Trotsky and Stalin, Marx's Bolshevik disciples had to make happen what Marx taught would happen automatically, not in England and America where the injustice of Classical Economics had done its exploitative worst, but in Russia where capitalism, in its incipient stage of development had not grown big enough to hurt enough people and reveal the unity of opposites, the escalation of conflict, both in quantity and quality, the negation of negation, the law of increasing misery and the revolution. Thus atheists, with their materialistic view that man is only an animal, are demonstrated by the relentless events of history, over which the Holy Spirit is presiding, to be fools or madmen. Marx's four laws of revolution were in development in the United States and England at the turn of the century, as the growing influence of the International Workers of the World attests. But the Keynesian reforms of the Roosevelt New Deal Revolution took the communist argument from the mouths of the workers who were no longer exploited and filled them with the nourishing food of better economic days. There are few Communist agitators within the ranks of either blue or white collar workers in America today, although there is widespread concern that right-wing Republicans will return America to the old Classical system which became defunct one hundred years ago.

To the geographic and economic interpretations of history can be added the racial interpretation of Hegel, who was convinced that his spiritual dialectic in the Rhine River valley of West Germany would merge thesis with antithesis to produce the synthesis of total enlightenment. Thus the Ayrans would become the "master race" not to burn, rape and slaughter as Adolf Hitler interpreted Hegel, but to lead the rest of the unenlightened world to the heavenly heights of German superiority!

Oswald Spengler, a German, unimpressed by Hegel's optimism that dialogue would ultimately elevate blue-eyed blonds to the status of Plato's Philosopher-King, and deeply depressed by the defeat of the Central Powers in World War I, conceived of society in terms of a biological unit, destined, after a period of youth and maturity to disintegrate into senility and final disintegration. Spengler's "Decline of the West" traced civilization across time from the Orient, ever westward, as the torch was passed first to the Middle East, then to Rome, later to Western Europe, and finally to the New World where its final days of agony would bring it to an end. Thus Spengler is regarded by those who can understand him as pessimistic as Hegel was optimistic. This morphological interpretation of history views human culture as it would an overripe potato. The only way it can get is worse.

Thomas Carlyle with his "Sartor Resartus" is generally regarded as the chief exponent of the "Great Man Theory" of history. For Carlyle the only significant history is biography. Critics debate whether great men make history or are made by the history which was in force when they appeared upon the scene. Would Abraham Lincoln have come to be regarded as one of our greatest presidents if he had come to power when there were no sectional differences in the United States? Would anyone have heard of Napoleon Bonaparte if there had been no French Revolution? Theologians point to Jesus of Nazareth as perhaps the only man great enough to influence history.

Arnold Toynbee in his *"A Study of History"* has argued that though each of the other interpretations of history has some value, all fail because each gives too much attention to one view and too little to the others. For Toynbee history reflects the progress of civilizations or societies rather than of nations. The work compares twenty-six civilizations in history each of which fell because it spent too much time responding to physical, environmental and economic challenges and too little time attending to moral, philosophical and religious affairs. This eclectic treatment pays attention to geography, climate, land forms, environmental problems, economics, racial and social problems and is criticized only because Toynbee insists that moral and religious values cannot be ignored by any culture with impunity.

The theological interpretation of history recognizes fully that as the Holy Spirit moves in the affairs of men, He does not ignore any of the elements that historians have seen as primary causation. He is God, sent forth by Jesus Christ to convict the world of sin, righteousness and judgment and to call effectually those who are to be saved. Thus He has presided over the course of nature, of men and of history and has seen the results of the curse which fell upon the world because of sin. If nature in its abnormal course had not been competitive and conflictive, if the law of claw and fang had not elminated the weak in favor of the strong, both the animal and human populations of the earth would have grown to the point where the scarce resources of the planet could not have sustained life and all life on this planet would have long since ceased. It is because much more than half of the human family born since the fall of Adam and Eve in Eden did not survive in the struggle beyond infancy that population pressure has not eliminated the race long ago.

Thus the Holy Spirit has chosen to carry out His mission in two ways. Those who die in infancy are members of the Body of Christ. Though they are sinners by nature they are not transgressors by choice. Thus, though they are not *saved* they are *safe*.

This idea seems always to be met with surprize when it is presented, as though some new thing were being set forth. Let the reader reflect upon the problem of population pressure, with its escalating demands for scarce food resources, with consequent poverty, malnutrition and lowered resistance to disease, as even for living space on the land.

Not until 1830 did the population of the earth reach one billion. This was 4000 years and 160 generations after the flood. In 1930 the population reached two billion. In 1960 there were three billion and in 1975 four billion. Current estimates in 1984 approach five billion and the projection is for eight billion by the year 2000. Thus, since 1830 we have seen a 100% increase in the first 100 years, a 50% increase in the next thirty and a 33 1/3% in the next fifteen years, while since 1975 another 25% increase has been experienced. This sudden acceleration in the rate of increase since 1830 has resulted from the discovery of the germ theory of disease, the increase in sanitation and the rising standard of living which resulted from the industrial revolution — what Alvin Toffler has called The Second Wave. If growth rates equal to those since 1830 had been experienced in the centuries before there would not be standing room upon the land surface of the earth and the human race would long since have starved to death.

Demographers know that in the long run population grows exponentially (in quantum leaps) when the net reproduction rate (NRR) exceeds unity. The NRR, by definition is the ratio of adult females to females of the immediately preceding generation. Thus if 100 mothers have 101 daughters who survive infancy and live to become mothers of the next generation, the NRR is 1.01. This means that if this ratio is maintained in the long run the population will increase 1% in every generation.

Many questions which must be answered if we are to approach this problem scientifically have been answered by demographic research only in the past two hundred years. Before 1750 data were either unavailable or available only in such form as to make objective conclusions most difficult if not impossible. But in the past 200 years we can conclude with a high degree of certitude that the following is true:

*The average first pregnancy occurred sometime between age 20 and age 25.

*Menopause occurred between ages 45 and 50. Thus the fertility period averages about 25 years.

*The first birth occurred within a year of marriage and later births were spaced at two and one half to five years. Thus the average number of children born to one union was between 5 and 6.

*The sex ratio between male and female has been 1:1.

*Demographers have exploded the Medieval myth of "one baby every year."

*Since a generation by definition is the average age of first pregnancy, there are, on balance four generations per century. There have thus been 160 generations since the flood.

*Demographers generally have considered a NRR of 1.01, which results in a cumulative increase of 1% in total population every generation as a high growth rate. This estimate however ignores long periods when the NRR was less than unity, due to famine, wars, pestilences and social conditions. For example the Black Death of the late 14th century wiped out perhaps half of the population of Western Europe. Wars that were especially bloody reduced the male population to the point that, in a monogamous culture, many eligible young women remained unmarried.

A NRR of unity of course results in zero population growth.

If we assume that each mother in her lifetime has three children who survive, then the NRR is 1.5 which yields a 50% increase in population every 25 years. If this were the case population pressure would long since have wiped out the race. If we assume that the NRR is 1.05 (100 mothers bear and rear to motherhood 105 daughters) the cululative increase in every generation would be 5%. And yet that is five times greater than the rate of growth that demographic historians agree is a high rate. Thus we must deduce that whatever the birth rate may be, the NRR must be much less due to the high infant mortality rate. If women, on balance had ten children (this number is too high according to records of the past 200 years), seven of whom died in infancy and three of whom did not, the number of surviving daughters would be 1.5 to yield a per generation increase of 50%. If 78% of babies born do not survive and 22% grow up, then the NRR would be 1.1

which again would yield a 10% cumulative increase in every quarter century. Exceptions to the average of course are always available. That is why the average figure must be used. Adam Smith says in *The Wealth of Nations* that some Scottish mothers had twenty children, eighteen of whom died in infancy. Thus two Scottish babies survived per family - and only one daughter. That Scotland's population did in fact grow in the past two hundred years proves that Smith's observation was an exception to the rule.

We have seen that the average number of children born per family was 5 or 6. If we assume the higher number and if two thirds of her children died and one third survived, and if one of the survivors was a girl, then the NRR would be unity which means zero population growth. Now, since there has been some population growth since the flood, which occurred approximately 2000 B.C. the scenario which I have presented above is too restrictive. The real situation has been somewhat better than that. Let us assume that the real NRR is 1.01. This would yield a cumulative growth rate of 1% every twenty-five years, a figure which demographers consider too high. Thus it must be somewhat less than 1.01 and perhaps somewhat more than 1.001. By computing each of these — 1.01_{160} and 1.001_{160} — we have the total population estimates of the earth in 1975. These figures can be compared to the population estimates for the earth in 1830, 1930, 1960 and 1975.

In order to give the reader who may be unacquainted with the use of logarithms an idea of what can be deduced when certain facts are given we offer the following:

There have been 160 generations of 25 years each since the flood. Let us begin with a population of 2. The population of the earth 4000 years (160 generations) later is 5 billion.

Let x equal NRR. Thus we have

$$160 \log x \text{ equals } \log 5 \text{ billion,}$$
$$160 \log x \text{ equals } 9.6990$$
dividing both sides of the equation by 160, we get
$$\log x \text{ equals } 0.0606, \text{ and}$$
x equals approximately 1.15. (Accurate to 3 significant figures)

Thus the NRR has been actually higher than that considered too high by demographers who have chosen to ignore other factors which we have mentioned *supra*, (page 48).

In order to gain an appreciation of the power of the quantum leaps involved when we assume a NRR which is too high we offer the following:

Assume 160 generations with a beginning population of 2 and terminal population of 5 billion. Then if NRR equals 2 (each mother produces two adult daughters), we have

$$\log \text{ population equals } 160 \log \text{ NRR}$$
$$\log \text{ population equals } 160 \ (0.3010) \text{ and}$$
$$\log \text{ population equals } 48.16 \text{ and}$$
population in 1975 equals 1.44 times 10_{48} which must be written as 144 followed by 46 zeros!

Just for the fun of it, let us ask how long after the flood the population of the earth would have grown to the point where upon the land area of the earth there would be standing room only, if NRR equals 2.

The land area of the earth is 57,280,000 square miles, which can be written as 5.73 times 10_7 square miles. Then

5.73 times 10_7 times 2.79 times 10_7 equals approximately 15.99 times 10_{14} square feet.

If we allocate 9 square feet to each person (a space three feet square) then

1.78 times 10_{14} people and

log population equals x log NRR, where x equals generations.

x equals log pop over log NRR

equals log 1.78 times 14 over log 2. Then

x equals 14.2504 over 0.3010 and

x equals 47.3 generations. Then

47.3 times 25 equals 1182.5 years.

Thus if the flood occurred 2000 B.C. and the NRR was 2 by the year 818 B.C. (sometime during the life of Elijah the prophet) the entire land area of the earth would have been filled with people - 9 square feet per person. Of course, long before this time the entire human and animal population of the earth would have starved to death. No man can grow enough food on the 9 square feet allotted to him to feed himself.*

The present NRR (in 1984)for the entire world is something more than 2.2, according to the best estimates of the United Nations World Food Organization. Thus, according to the formula the present world population of something more than 5 billion will double in the next twenty-five. This assumes that there will be enough food available to prevent widespread famine. The best authorites agree that we cannot feed the present population. The future therefore is dark for all except those who understand that God in His perfect wisdom is permitting these dreadful conditions in nature and in history in order to bring His redemptive purpose to fruition. We shall learn in Revelation 6:5-8 that the third and fourth seal judgments will bring famine and a struggle for survival that will devastate a fourth part of the globe.

Not since His resurrection from the dead and ascension to the Father's right hand in glory has our Lord been concerned about the affairs of earth during "man's day" (1 Cor.4:3) except to pray the Father for the completion of His Church, which is His Body. Now that the end of the age is in sight, our Lord moves to loose upon the earth the last round of divine judgment which will immediately precede His own personal return. The time for God once again actively to intervene in human history is at hand. We have seen that only in calling out the elect can the Holy Spirit be said to have been concerned with human history since Calvary. It has been night (John 9:4), since the Light of the

---

*I am indebted to Professor James McManamey for guidance in the proper use of logarithms.

World (John 8:12) was murdered. No unregenerate man has been able to work to produce net utility. God has chosen to allow the unsaved to direct events in keeping with his own wisdom. But God will act again. There remains seven more years in the divine program revealed to Daniel (Daniel 9:24-27). The clock is about to run again after a long hiatus that has extended from Calvary to the White Horse Rider of Revelation 6:1.

The army SNAFU (Situation Normal All Fouled Up) is man's admission that what he touches he confuses and corrupts. He simply is not intelligent enough to run the world. Even Plato saw this and begged for a Philospher-King. That King is Jesus Christ. But before He intervenes as He will do when He removes the first seal from Daniel's closed book, we must see that the entire creation is destined to admit that He is right and everyone else on earth is wrong. What the Judge of all the earth does (John 5:22) is right (Gen.18:25). The answer to Abraham's question, of course, is positive. But He will not act until all of heaven's angels, elders and living creatures sing His praises and worship Him, and after He has acted even His enemies, whom He has judged will join in and admit that He is Lord (Phil.2:10,11; Rev.5:13).

The material in chapters 4 and 5 is descriptive of the scene is heaven. It is chronologically parenthetical. The countdown clock has been on hold since our Lord's triumphal entry into Jerusalem two millenia ago. Revelation 1 introduces the Book and relates how John met Jesus. Revelation 2 and 3 is concerned with the dictation of the letters to the seven churches in Asia Minor in the first century. We have seen how this material will have special meaning to the Body of Christ on earth during the last seven years. With Revelation 6:1 the clock resumes the countdown of T minus 2520 days and counting. There are no more holds programmed into the program. The Christian who "has ears to hear what the Spirit is saying to the churches" (Rev.3:22) and who is alive on earth when the first seal is opened will be able to predict the day of the second coming of Christ. *Cf.* 1 Thess.5:4. That day will come as a thief only upon those whose ears (capacity to understand) are unable to hear. Exegetical deafness is chiefly caused by bigotry, conceit, prejudice and the lack of personal humility required to say that one has been mistaken.

The Seals

(Revelation 6:1-17)

Revelation 6:1 - "And I saw when the Lamb opened one of the seals, and I heard as it were the noise of thunder, one of the four beasts saying, Come and see."

Καὶ εἶδον ὅτε ἤνοιξεν τὸ ἀρνίον μίαν ἐκ τῶν ἑπτὰ σφραγίδων, καὶ ἤκουσα ἑνὸς ἐκ τῶν τεσσάρων ζώων λέγοντος ὡς φωνῇ βροντῆς, Ἔρχου.

"Now I saw when the Lamb opened one of the seven seals, and I heard one of the four living creatures say, as with a voice of thunder, 'Come.'" . . . *RSV*

Καὶ (continuative conjunction) 14.

εἶδον (1st.per.sing.aor.act.ind.of ὁράω, constative) 144.

ὅτε (conjunction introducing the indicative in a definite temporal clause) 703.

ἤνοιξεν (3d.per.sing.aor.act.ind.of ἀνοίγω, constative) 188.

τὸ (nom.sing.neut.of the article in agreement with ἀρνίον) 9.

ἀρνίον (nom.sing.neut.of ἀρνίον, subject of ἤνοιξεν) 2923.

μίαν (acc.sing.fem.of εἷς, direct object of ἤνοιξεν) 469.

ἐκ (preposition with the partitive genitive) 19.

τῶν (gen.pl.fem.of the article in agreement with σφραγίδων) 9.

ἑπτὰ (numeral) 1024.

σφραγίδων (gen.pl.fem.of σφραγίς, partitive) 3886.

καὶ (adjunctive conjunction joining verbs) 14.

ἤκουσα (1st.per.sing.aor.act.ind.of ἀκούω, constative) 148.

ἑνὸς (gen.sing.masc.of εἷς, objective genitive) 469.

ἐκ (preposition with the partitive genitive) 19.

τῶν (gen.pl.neut.of the article in agreement with ζῴων) 9.

τεσσάρων (gen.pl.neut.of τέσσαρες, in agreement with ζῴων) 1508.

ζῴων (gen.pl.neut.of ζῶον, partitive) 5086.

λέγοντος (pres.act.part.gen.sing.fem.of λέγω, adverbial, circumstantial) 66.

ὡς (comparative particle) 128.

φωνῇ (instru.sing.fem.of φωνή, means) 222.

βροντῆς (gen.sing.fem.of βροντή, description) 2117.

Ἔρχου (2d.per.sing.pres.mid.impv.of ἔρχομαι, command) 146.

Translation - "*And I was watching when the Lamb opened one of the seven seals, and I heard one of the four living creatures saying with a voice like thunder, 'Come'.*"

Comment: It is "passing strange" to quote the Bard (*Othello* I, 1604) that some suppose that the order of narration of events, the description of scenes and the presentation of explanatory material, presented in a book should also necessarily be the chronological order in which the events occur. To say that what happens on page ten must precede events which are described on page eleven, or that the material of the first chapters of a book must be antecedent in time to that which follows in later subsequent chapters is to make proper understanding of what is written impossible. The chronological order of events must be determined by the proper exegesis of the text, not by the order of pagination or the numerical and spatial arrangement of paragraphs, sections and chapters.

Let us suppose that a history of the American Civil War is written on a topical rather than a chronological basis. The period covered is four years beginning on April 12, 1861 and ending on April 19 ,1865. Topical history is written by presenting each topic that is germane to the story — each topic presented in its proper chronology of events *within the topic*, but with no attempt to connect the events within the topic with the time sequence of events described in other topical treatments. We can say that a soldier wrote a letter to his mother on the evening before he was killed in the Battle of Gettysburg, without saying whether Gettysburg was before or after Petersburg or Malvern Hill.

The monographic history of the Civil War should include topics such as the following: The cultural differences between the Southern colonies and those of the North, due to climate, geography, ethnic differences, etc. resulted in a Constitution in 1789 that was Federalistic in some areas and Nationalistic in others. Thus states' rights, provincialism, parochialism and localism prevailed, for example in the matter of human slavery, property taxation, franchise qualifications, etc., and the power of the National Government was recognized, for example, in the power of the Congress to contol interstate commerce. This must be understood if we are to understand why the eleven southern states thought that they had the constitutional right to secede from the union, and why Abraham Lincoln was convinced with equal certitude that they could not.

The ethical and legal questions relating to human slavery provide material for another monograph.

The industrial, demographic, social and religious differences between north and south provide another topic.

The fact that railroads ran east and west instead of north and south, with only a few exceptions, provided a great advantage to the North and an almost insuperable disadvantage to the Confederacy.

"Ohio, New York and Pennsylvania had in 1860 a combined population about equal to that of the whole South. . . . These three states had about nine million in 1860, approximately the equivalent of the South as distinguished from the border slave states," Maryland, Delaware, Kentucky and Missouri, which were slave holding states which did not join the eleven states of the Confederacy. (J.G.Randall, *The Civil War and Reconstruction,* 75). Of the nine million population of the South nearly half were slaves. The financial and industrial resources of the North far exceeded those of the South. The fact that the North already had functioning governments, at local, state and national levels, whereas the Confederacy was forced to establish these administrative offices anew gave the North a great advantage. These matters comprise material for another topical chapter.

The military, naval and international diplomatic stories provide other topics, as do the struggle between Lincoln and the Radical Abolitionists in the North, the opposition of northern Democrats, particularly in southern Indiana and Ohio, biographical material of officers, both North and South, the work of Clara Barton and the beginnings of the American Red Cross.

Finally no history of the Civil War would be complete without the story of the everyday life of the soldier in the field — his fears, his hopes, his feats of bravery and moments of panic, the love letters which he wrote to wives, parents, sweethearts and children, the songs he sang, the prayers he prayed and the pranks which he pulled. This part of the story has been admirably told by Professor Wiley of Emory University in his Billy Yank and Johnny Red stories.

Each chapter of the book, with its special attention to a single topic covers the same four year period, beginning in 1861 and ending with Appomattox. How distressed the author therefore would be if his reader assumed that chapter one covered the period from 1861 to 1865 and that chapter two, since it comes after chapter one in the book also comes after the events of chapter one and covers the period from 1865 to 1869. This reasoning dictates that each successive chapter covers the next four year period - 1869-1873, 1873-1877, etc. By the time the reader reaches the last chapter with its description of events, which also occurred in 1861-1865 he would conclude that the Civil War lasted into the 20th century.

This, of course is ridiculous. And yet it is the error of those who insist that the letters to the seven churches apply to events before the tribulation since chapters two and three come before chapter 4 and those following. The old rule that the seven trumpet judgments come out of the seventh seal and that the seven vials comes out of the seventh trumpet is another example of the same fallacy.

It is the assumption of this study as we have said before that churches, seals and trumpets are contemporareous and coterminous and that they extend, each with its own story to tell, from the beginning to the end of the seven year period. If this hypothesis is correct the evidence to support it must be found within the text itself and if such evidence is found we will find a correlation between events that will be overwhelming.

The student should look at the chart which depicts our hypothesis in *The Renaissance New Testament,* 17, 600. In order to study simultaneous scenarios the chart must be read vertically. Thus the material written to the first church (Ephesus) will have special meaning for Christians who are living in the days of the first seal and the first trumpet.

To follow the story across the seven years from beginning to end, we find the religious picture in chatpers two and three, the political picture with related events in Revelation 6:1-17; 8:1. The developing story of divine judgments upon the environment and the peoples of the earth is found in the story of the trumpets, while the last half of the period is covered also by the seven vials. All other material, *viz.*Rev.1:20; 4:1-5:14; 7:1-8:2-6; 10:1-11:14; 12:1-15:8; 17:1-22:5 is designed to describe and explain the events that occur in connection with and during the time that the clock is running. The clock is not running in these explanatory sections.

Some of the correlative evidence that links the prophecy of Daniel with the Revelation has already been presented. *Cf.* comment on Rev.5:1. Further correlative evidence is found in Rev.17:7-14, comment upon which the student should now read. Pursuant to that commentary it seems clear that the personality who emerges with the breaking of the first seal (Rev.6:1), who is called "The Rider on the White Horse" is the first king (dictator, ruler) of the "time of the end" series. He will be the fifth world ruler to exercise control over the entire world. The first four in the period between Babylon and Messiah's first coming were, in order, Babylon, Media-Persia, Greece and Rome. The fifth will be the Rider on the White Horse of Rev.6:2. Thus he is the fifth before his death and the eighth after his resurrection (Rev.17:10). We are dealing only with seven kings, but one of them, the fifth, rules the world briefly before his death and again as the eighth, for forty-two months after his restoration. Thus at mid-week, he will be the eighth, but one of the preceding seven. the author is embarrassed to state that for the first seven years as a Bible student, he misread Revelation 17:11 as "the beast that was, and is not, even he is the eighth, and is of the *seventh . . . "* instead of "is of the *seven.*" Thus I was trying to make the seventh king, the black horse rider of Rev.6:5,6, the source of the pale horse rider of Rev.6:7,8, the more detailed description of whom is found in Rev.13:1-8. Thus we have the results of careless reading and prejudicial manipulation of the Scripture.

Although this writer has made his share of snide remarks about chart prophecy preachers who would rather twist Scripture to conform to their chart than redesign the chart, perhaps the following will show what John appears to mean in Revelation 17:9-11.

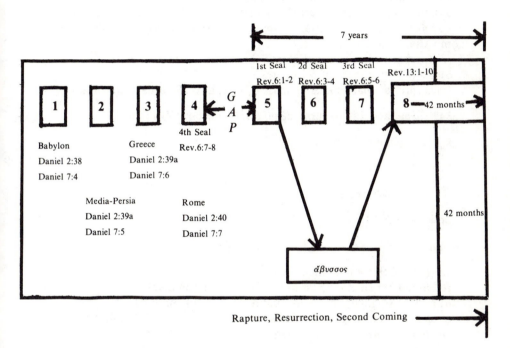

Verse 2 - "And I saw, and behold a white horse: and he that sat on him had a bow: and a crown was given unto him, and he went forth conquering and to conquer."

καὶ εἶδον, καὶ ἰδοὺ ἵππος λευκός, καὶ ὁ καθήμενος ἐπ' αὐτὸν τόξον, καὶ ἐδόθη αὐτῷ στέφανος, καὶ ἐξῆλθεν νικῶν καὶ ἵνα νικήσῃ.

"And I saw, and behold, a white horse, and its rider had a bow; and a crown was given to him, and he went out conquering and to conquer." . . . *RSV*

καὶ (continuative conjunction) 14.
εἶδον (1st.per.sing.aor.act.ind.of ὁράω, constative) 144.
καὶ (continuative conjunction) 14.
ἰδοὺ (exclamation) 95.
ἵππος (nom.sing.masc.of ἵππος, nominative absolute) 5121.
λευκός (nom.sing.masc.of λευκός, in agreement with ἵππος) 522.
καὶ (adjunctive conjunction joining substantives) 14.
ὁ (nom.sing.masc.of the article in agreement with καθήμενος) 9.
καθήμενος (pres.mid.part.nom.sing.masc.of κάθημαι, substantival, nominative absolute) 377.
ἐπ' (preposition with the accusative, rest) 47.
αὐτὸν (acc.sing.masc.of αὐτός, rest) 16.
ἔχων (pres.act.part.nom.sing.masc.of ἔχω, adverbial, circumstantial) 82.

#5349 τόξον (acc.sing.neut.of τόξον, direct object of ἔχων).

King James Version

bow - Rev.6:2.

Revised Standard Version

bow - Rev.6:2.

Meaning: A bow, designed for archery - Rev.6:2.

καὶ (continuative conjunction) 14.
ἐδόθη (3d.per.sing.aor.pass.ind.of δίδωμι, culminative) 362.
αὐτῷ (dat.sing.masc.of αὐτός, indirect object of ἐδόθη) 16.
στέφανος (nom.sing.masc.of στέφανος, subject of ἐδόθη) 1640.
καὶ (continuative conjunction) 14.
ἐξῆλθεν (3d.per.sing.aor.mid.ind.of ἐξέρχομαι, ingressive) 161.
νικῶν (pres.act.part.nom.sing.masc.of νικάω, adverbial, modal) 2454.
καὶ (adjunctive conjunction joining an adverb to a purpose clause) 14.
ἵνα (conjunction with the subjunctive, purpose) 114.
νικήσῃ (3d.per.sing.aor.act.subj.of νικάω, purpose) 2454.

Translation - "And as I was watching, Look! A white horse and the one who is sitting upon him! He has been given a bow and he has started out conquering and with the intent to conquer."

Comment: Note that after the interjection ἰδού, John employs the nominative absolute ἵππος λευκός καὶ ὁ καθήμενος . . . ἔχων, instead of the accusative case, as object of εἶδον. The excitement of the moment prompts ἰδού and the nominative absolute as often.

Satan's counterfeit will be riding a white horse, just as our Lord will do at His second coming seven years later (Rev.19:11,14). The Prince of Peace will bring millenial peace. Satan's counterfeit will bring false peace. This is clear from the fact that his successor (verse 4) will take peace from the earth and wage war.

It would seem logical to say that the White Horse Rider of Rev.6:2 will make his appearance at some time when war is either immanent or after hostilities have already begun. He cannot make false peace except in a time of threatened or actual military hostility. Note that he will carry a bow (a capability of waging war) but equipped with no arrow (no present intention of waging war). In other words he will negotiate peace between the warring parties using as his argument his threat to intercede with force himself. This is the current basis for world diplomacy of all major nations in the 20th century. The major powers, with great capability, even in terms of over-kill, nevertheless insist that the purpose is peace. The motto of Strategic Air Command in the United States is "Peace is our Profession." We do not suggest that SAC is the Beast of Rev.6:1,2, but the Beast when he comes, will enforce peace on earth for a short time. He will dominate the world scene for the first part (perhaps a year plus/minus) of the first half of the week of years.

World public opinion now is certain to look with favor that amounts to near worship upon anyone who succeeds in negotiating peace between the major powers, each of which is capable of starting the nuclear war that would terminate society on this planet. In 1914, and even in 1939, the world was so accustomed to war that peace, either between the Central Powers and the Allies after the Sarajevo crisis or between Hitler and the Allies, though viewed with relief, would not have brought the adulation that is certain to be given to him who can prevent nuclear war which no one can win. The difference is that future wars will be fought, both with conventional weapons and nuclear missiles. War before the development of nuclear fission and fusion was objectionable to all decent people. It is now unthinkable to all but mad men.

The White Horse Rider will receive a serious, perhaps a mortal wound and will be replaced by the Red Horse Rider, but he will be healed (restored, resurrected) in the middle of the week (Rev.13:5), after which he will be allowed to continue for forty-two months, which is the last half of the tribualtion period. The White Horse Rider of Rev.6:1,2 is the man that Daniel wrote about in Daniel 9:27a and the Pale Horse Rider of Rev.6:7,8 is the man of Daniel 9:27b. The rule of this Satan inspired monster, during the last forty-two months is described in Revelation 13, 17,18 and his fate is described in Revelation 19,20.

Those commentators who reject the "gap" in the 490 year period of Daniel 9:24-27 must show the second coming of Messiah only seven years after the crucifixion of Jesus, or they must put an entirely different interpretation on the entire book of Daniel. Post-millenialists, who reject a literal second coming of Christ, try to show that the sociological impact of institutional Christianity is what is meant by the last part of Daniel 9:24. This is the "theology of hope" so recently in vogue among those who mistake literal language for allegorical — a sort of "confident despair." To the tough minded social and behavioral scientist, particularly the economic historian who understands energy and raw material shortages, environmental pollution problems and the population explosion which has already populated the earth with more people than we can feed and is expected to add at least two billion more by the year 2000, this "confident despair- theology of hope" philosophy with its repudiation of Christ's supernatural intervention is incredibly and contemptibly naive - the intellectual vaporings of a retarded child.

Our hypothesis, with its contemporaneity and coterminality of churches, seals and trumpets (with vials beginning at the mid-week point), suggests that the events of the first seal (Rev.6:1-2) will occur at the same time as those of the first trumpet (Rev.8:7), and that the message of Christ to the Ephesus church (Rev.2:1-7) will be especially meaningful to the Body of Christ on the earth at the beginning of the tribulation week. Thus as the White Horse Rider confirms a peace agreement with Israel, in which he confirms the terms of the Abrahamic covenant for a period of seven years (Dan.9:27), and gains world-wide recognition as the long sought peacemaker in a war weary world, God will rain down hail, fire and blood upon the earth which will destroy one third of the trees and all of the cover crops (Rev.8:7). The unregenerate, deceived by the blandishments of the Beast who has brought peace instead of nuclear war, will suffer the judgments of the first trumpet but will regard them as an act of God, for which the Beast cannot be held responsible.

Further, this judgment plus the events which follow at the blast of the second trumpet (Rev.8:8,9) which is contemporary with the second seal (Rev.6:3,4) will contribute to the famine conditions of the third seal (Rev.6:5,6) and the third trumpet (Rev.8:10,11). The more we study the Revelation in keeping with this hypothesis the more the correlative evidence piles up in its favor and the more untenable all other interpretations become.

The student should arrange all of the details of the seals, trumpets and vials (the first vial occurs at mid-week) in parallel columns and study them with the assumption that they are contemporaneous and coterminus. If the sixth and seventh seal, the seventh trumpet and the seventh vial do not take place at the same time and if the details do not describe the same event, then we must believe that three identical sets of events will follow in chronological tandem with discernible periods of time intervening. For example the fifth trumpet judgment will torment men on earth for five months (Rev.9:5), while another time period, described as "an hour, and a day, and a month and a year" (Rev.9:15) is seen under the sixth trumpet judgment. The suggestion that from the seventh seal come the trumpets and from the seventh trumpet come the vials, forces us, if we accept it, to say that the events of Rev.6:12-17 occur one year, six months, a day and an hour before the seventh trumpet, which describes events and records speeches in heaven (Rev.11:15-18) some time before the events of Rev.16:17-21. The parallel columns which we have suggested can be seen on page 60. Accept our hypothesis and note the correlative harmony of Scripture. Deny it and note the problems that arise.

Will Christians on the earth when the week begins recognize the White Horse Rider? For what should we look? The answer is: for the confirmation of the Abrahamic covenant in keeping with Daniel 9:27. This is a matter of international diplomacy and it is not likely to escape the notice of the media, in view of the tinder box nature of the tensions which exist in the Middle East as the sons of Ishmael and the sons of Isaac glare at each other. Will the media discover and report the event if it is secretly negotiated? These are questions which cannot be answered with certainty before the fact, but the judgments of the first trumpet cannot be hidden from public knowledge! Christians in that day will be discerning special significance in Christ's message to the Ephesus church (Rev.2:1-7). The student should read this passage and imagine that he is upon the earth during the first seal/first trumpet days.

If we know when the Daniel 9:27 agreement is made we shall on that day become date setters for the second coming. (1 Thess.5:4). Our Lord said 1900 years ago that "No man knows (present tense in A.D.29) the day and hour" (Mt.24:36). He did not say that no man would ever know. *Cf.* comment on Mt.24:36-41 (*The Renaissance New Testament*, 3, 323-335). It seems clear that there will be no special effort to persecute Christians more than they have always been persecuted until the mid-point in the week (Rev.13:5). But no Christian will be hurt by the judgments of God which will be falling. They are reserved for the unsaved. Psalm 91:1-16 clearly teaches this glorious fact. *Cf.* especially Psalm 91:5-11. When, since it was written has Psalm 91 been fulfilled? And yet it must be fulfilled, just as Psalm 22 was fulfilled when Christ was crucified. Just as God distinguished between His covenant people Israel and the Egyptians during the period of the ten plagues, so will He again. He has not appointed His elect unto wrath (1 Thess.5:9). There are those who apparently believe that God is unable to do for the elect during the tribulation what He did for Israel during the Egyptian plagues, and that He must therefore rapture them to safety in the clouds before the tribulation judgments fall. He protected the Jews from flies (Exodus 8:23), murrain (Exodus 9:4-7), hail (Exodus 9:26), darkness (Exodus 10:23) and death (Exodus 12:13) *before* He took them out of Egypt.

Verse 3 - "And when he had opened the second seal, I heard the second beast say, Come and see."

Καὶ ὅτε ἤνοιξεν τὴν σφραγῖδα τὴν δευτέραν, ἤκουσα τοῦ δευτέρου ζώου λέγοντος, Ἔρχου.

"When he opened the second seal, I heard the second living creature say, 'Come!'" . . . *RSV*

Καὶ (continuative conjunction) 14.
ὅτε (conjunction introducing the indicative in a definite temporal clause) 703.
ἤνοιξεν (3d.per.sing.aor.act.ind.of ἀνοίγω, constative) 188.
τὴν (acc.sing.fem.of the article in agreement with σφραγῖδα) 9.
σφραγῖδα (acc.sing.fem.of σφραγίς, direct object of ἤνοιξεν) 3886.
τὴν (acc.sing.fem.of the article in agreement with δευτέραν) 9.
δευτέραν (acc.sing.fem.of δεύτερος, in agreement with σφραγῖδα) 1371.
ἤκουσα (1st.per.sing.aor.act.ind.of ἀκούω, constative) 148.
τοῦ (gen.sing.neut.of the article in agreement with ζώου) 9.
δευτέρου (gen.sing.neut.of δεύτερος, in agreement with ζώου) 1371.
ζώου (gen.sing.neut.of ζῶον, objective genitive after ἤκουσα) 5086.

6th and 7th Churches	6th and 7th Seals	7th Trumpet	7th vial
Philadelphia	earthquake	earthquake	earthquake - cities of nations fall
The open door to evangelize	sun dark		
Victory over false Jews	moon turns to blood	temple of God opened in heaven	Voice out of heaven, "It is done."
Promise of Rapture soon to come	stars fall		mountains and islands
	heaven rolled back as a scroll	destroy them that destroy the earth	Babylon destroyed
	mountains and islands moved	divine wrath has come	
	great men flee in terror	world kingdoms become Christ's	Jerusalem divided into three parts
	great day of His wrath is come	"He shall reign forever"	
		Christ begins to reign	
Laodicea		angry nations	
		judgement seat of Christ	
"neither cold nor hot"			lightnings
wretched, pitiable, poor, blind, naked		lightnings	voices
Christ knocks on the door and invites		voices	thunders
them to salvation.		thunderings	

λέγοντος (pres.act.part.gen.sing.neut.of λέγω, recitative) 66.
Ἔρχου (2d.per.sing.pres.mid.impv.of ἔρχομαι, command) 146.

Translation - *"And when he opened the second seal I heard the second living creature saying, 'Come.' "*

Comment: There must be some significance in the difference in the appearances of the living creatures (Rev.4:7) and therefore in the personalities which they introduce (Rev.6:1,3,5,7) but it escapes this writer. We must warn against fanciful interpretations. Unless the text itself spells out what the symbolism means, the only sensible policy dictates silence.

The KJV "Come and see" (Rev.6:1,3,5,7) is not well supported. Metzger says, "After ἔρχου, which is well supported by A C P I 1006 1611 1854 2053 vg copsa,bo *al*, several witnesses add (as though the verb "Come" were addressed to the Seer - it is possible to translate as Zahn prefers, 'Go')καὶ ἴδε (Sinaiticus 046 about 120 minuscules itgig syrph,h eth *al*) or καὶ βλέπε (296 2049 and Textus Receptus). The singular readings ὅτι ἔρχομαι (arm) and *et veni* (it61) are due to freedom in translation." The United Bible Societies' Commmittee prefers the text we have followed, which eliminates "and see" with a C degree of certitude. Without καὶ ἴδε, it is possible to interpret ἔρχου as an order directed to the riders, not an invitation to John. With reference to verse 3, Metzger adds "As in verse 1, after ἔρχου which is here well supported by A C P 046 1006 1611 1854 2053 vg syrph,h copsa,bo *al*, several witnesses (including Sinaiticus 1828 2073 2344 itgig,61 copbo ms *al*) add καὶ ἴδε, while a few others (296 2049 followed by the Textus Receptus) add καὶ βλέπε" (Metzger, *A Textual Commentary on the Greek New Testament*, 739,740). The same Committee decision applies to verses 5 and 7.

With reference to καὶ εἶδον in verses 2,5,8 the Committee concluded that "The words καὶ εἶδον are absent from 046 about 100 minuscules (most of which add καὶ ἴδε in verse 1. See previous comment) *al*. The Committee preferred to include the words (a) because of the preponderant testimony including Sinaiticus (A C ἴδον) P I 1006 1611 2053 2344 itgig vg syrh copbo arm *al*, and (b) because the omission can be either accidental (ΚΑΙΕΙΔΟΝΚΑΙΙΔΟΥ), or deliberate on the part of the copyists of the manuscripts which read καὶ ἴδε at the close of ver.1 (who therefore would naturally have regarded καὶ εἶδον as superfluous). The singular readings εἶδον (copsa) and καὶ ἤκουσα καὶ εἶδον (syrph) are due to freedom in translation" (*Ibid.*, 739). The same comments apply also to verses 5 and 8.

The second seal is contemporaneous with the second trumpet (Rev.8:8) and contemporary Christians will find Rev.2:8-11 particularly apropos. It is possible, and, at this point to me seems likely that the war of the second seal is the war of Ezekiel 38 and 39.

Verse 4 - "And there went out another horse that was red: and power was given to him that sat thereon to take peace from the earth, and that they should kill one another: and there was given unto him a great sword."

καὶ ἐξῆλθεν ἄλλος ἵππος πυρρός, καὶ τῷ καθημένῳ ἐπ' αὐτὸν ἐδόθη αὐτῷ λαβεῖν τὴν εἰρήνην ἐκ τῆς γῆς καὶ ἵνα ἀλλήλους σφάξουσιν, καὶ ἐδόθη αὐτῷ μάχαιρα μεγάλη.

"And out came another horse, bright red; its rider was permitted to take peace from the earth, so that men should slay one another; and he was given a great sword." . . . RSV

καὶ (continuative conjunction) 14.
ἐξῆλθεν (3d.per.sing.aor.mid.ind.of ἐξέρχομαι, constative) 161.
ἄλλος (nom.sing.masc.of ἄλλος, in agreement with ἵππος) 198.
ἵππος (nom.sing.masc.of ἵππος, subject of ἐξῆλθεν) 5121.

#5350 πυρρός (nom.sing.masc.of πυρρός, in agreement with ἵππος).

King James Version

red - Rev.12:3.
that is red - Rev.6:4.

Revised Standard Version

bright red - Rev.6:4.
red - Rev.12:3.

Meaning: Cf. πύρρος (#3502). Having the color of fire. Bright red - Rev.6:4, of the War Horse Rider; of Satan in Rev.12:3.

καὶ (continuative conjunction) 14.
τῷ (dat.sing.masc.of the article in agreement with καθημένῳ) 9.
καθημένῳ (pres.mid.part.dat.sing.masc.of κάθημαι, substantival, indirect object of ἐδόθη) 377.
ἐπ' (preposition with the accusative, rest) 47.
αὐτὸν (acc.sing.masc.of αὐτός, rest) 16.
ἐδόθη (3d.per.sing.aor.pass.ind.of δίδωμι, constative) 362.
αὐτῷ (dat.sing.masc.of αὐτός , indirect object of ἐδόθη, pleonastic) 16.
λαβεῖν (2d.aor.act.inf.of λαμβάνω, in apposition with ἐξουσίαν understood) 533.
τὴν (acc.sing.fem.of the article in agreement with εἰρήνην) 9.
εἰρήνην (acc.sing.fem.of εἰρήνη, direct object of λαβεῖν) 865.
ἐκ (preposition with the ablative of separation) 19.
τῆς (abl.sing.fem.of the article in agreement with γῆς) 9.
γῆς (abl.sing.fem.of γῆ, separation) 157.
καὶ (adjunctive conjunction joining an infinitive and a sub-final clause) 14.
ἵνα (conjunction with the subjunctive, sub-final) 114.
ἀλλήλους (acc.pl.masc.of ἀλλήλων, direct object of σφάξουσιν) 1487.
σφάξουσιν (3d.per.pl.for σφάξωσιν, aor.act.subj.of σφάττω, sub-final).5292.
καὶ (continuative conjunction) 14.
ἐδόθη (3d.per.sing.aor.pass.ind.of δίδωμι, constative) 362.
αὐτῷ (dat.sing.masc.of αὐτός, indirect object of ἐδόθη) 16.
μάχαιρα (nom.sing.fem.of μάχαιρα subject of ἐδόθη) 896.

μεγάλη (nom.sing.fem.of μέγας, in agreement with μάχαιρα) 184.

Translation - "And another fiery red horse came out, and to the one seated upon him was given power to take peace from the earth and the result was that they kill each other, and a great sword was given to him."

Comment: αὐτῷ in the second clause is pleonastic, though Robertson defends John against the charge of anacoluthon by calling it resumptive. It is clearly not needed as John has already written τῷ καθημένῳ. To the one who was seated on the red horse was given power to take the false and temporary peace, brought by the White Horse Rider (Rev.6:1,2) from the earth. By supplying ἐξουσίαν, we can construe the infinitive λαβεῖν as apposition. The ἵνα clause is sub-final. Violence on earth is a part of man's day (1 Cor.4:3; James 5:1-2). That we should have a future indicative σφάξουσιν after ἵνα, instead of an aorist subjunctive, may be due to a false reading, as we suggested above, though the idiom can be found elsewhere. Robertson suggests John 7:3; Acts 21:24; Lk.14:10; 1 Cor.9:18; Lk.20:10; 1 Cor.9:15; 1 Pet.3:1; Rev.8:3; 22:14 al. (Robertson, *Grammar*, 984).

The text does not divide between the first three seals the time span of 3 1/2 years which covers the first half of the tribulation. We know that the Pale Horse Rider of Rev.6:7,8 will continue for 42 months (the last half of the week of years). This is clear from Rev.13:5. The time point of the Red Horse Rider is that of Rev.17:10 a,b. When the Red Horse Rider appears, five of the kings will have fallen (Babylon, Media-Persia, Greece, Rome, in ancient history, and the fifth, the White Horse Rider of Rev.6:1,2) and "one is" *viz.*, the Red Horse Rider, who is the sixth of the seven. The seventh, the Black Horse Rider is found in Rev.17:10c, and it is added in Rev.17:10d that when he comes he will continue only for a short time. Events of the first two seals (Rev.6:1-4) are temporally coordinate with the events of the first two trumpets (Rev.8:6-8). Thus the scorched earth, with the destruction of one third of the trees and all of the cover crops (Rev.8:7) and the bloody oceans which will destroy one third of marine life, and the destruction of one third of the merchant marine (Rev.8:8) will cooperate with the war of Rev.6:3,4 to bring the famine of Rev.6:5,6. Food prices, both for vegetables, grain, fruit and sea food will rise, not only because of short supply but also because of the   reduction in trasport in international crowd as a result of the destruction of the ships. Thus we have the correlative evidence for our hypothetical scheme of interpretation. Let the student note all of this on the chart which follows on page 64. It is a more complete chart than the one in *The Renaissance New Testament*, 17, 600.

Verse 5 - "And when he had opened the third seal, I heard the third beast say, Come and See. And I beheld, and lo a black horse; and he that sat on him had a pair of balances in his hand."

Καὶ ὅτε ἤνοιξεν τὴν σφραγῖδα τὴν τρίτην, ἤκουσα τοῦ τρίτου ζῴου λέγοντος, Ἔρχου. καὶ εἶδον, καὶ ἰδοὺ ἵππος μέλας, καὶ ὁ καθήμενος ἐπ' αὐτὸν ἔχων ζυγὸν ἐν τῇ χειρὶ αὐτοῦ.

6th and 7th Churches	6th and 7th Seals	7th Trumpet	7th vial
Philadelphia	earthquake	earthquake	earthquake - cities of nations fall
The open door to evangelize	sun dark	temple of God opened in heaven	Voice out of heaven, "It is done."
Victory over false Jews	moon turns to blood	destroy them that destroy the earth	mountains and islands
Promise of Rapture soon to come	stars fall	divine wrath has come	Babylon destroyed
	heaven rolled back as a scroll	world kingdoms become Christ's	Jerusalem divided into three parts
	mountains and islands moved	"He shall reign forever"	
	great men flee in terror	Christ begins to reign	
Laodicea	great day of His wrath is come	angry nations	
		judgement seat of Christ	
"neither cold nor hot"		lightnings	lightnings
wretched, pitiable, poor, blind, naked		voices	voices
Christ knocks on the door and invites		thunderings	thunders
them to salvation.		great hail	hail

"When he opened the third seal, I heard the third living creature say, 'Come!' And I saw, and behold, a black horse, and its rider had a balance in his hand;" . . . RSV

Καὶ (continuative conjunction) 14.

ὅτε (conjunction introducing the indicative in a definite temporal clause) 703.

ἤνοιξεν (3d.per.sing.aor.act.ind.of ἀνοίγω, definite temporal clause, constative) 188.

τὴν (acc.sing.fem.of the article in agreement with σφραγῖδα) 9.

σφραγῖδα (acc.sing.fem.of σφραγίς, direct object of ἤνοιξεν) 3886.

τὴν (acc.sing.fem.of the article in agreement with τρίτην) 9.

τρίτην (acc.sing.fem.of τρίτος, in agreement with σφραγῖδα) 1209.

ἤκουσα (1st.per.sing.aor.act.ind.of ἀκούω, constative) 148.

τοῦ (gen.sing.neut.of the article in agreement with ζῴου) 9.

τρίτου (gen.sing.neut.of τρίτος, in agreement with σφραγῖδα) 1209.

ζῴου (gen.sing.neut.of ζῷον, objective genitive after a verb of hearing) 5086.

λέγοντος (pres.act.part.gen.sing.neut.of λέγω, recitative) 66.

Ἔρχου (2d.per.sing.pres.mid.impv.of ἔρχομαι, command) 146.

καὶ (adjunctive conjunction joining verbs) 14.

εἶδον (1st.per.sing.aor.act.ind.of ὁράω, constative) 144.

καὶ (continuative conjunction) 14.

ἰδοὺ (exclamation) 95.

ἵππος (nom.sing.masc.of ἵππος, nominative absolute) 5121.

μέλας (nom.sing.masc.of μέλας, in agreement with ἵππος) 523.

καὶ (adjunctive conjunction joining substantives) 14.

ὁ (nom.sing.masc.of the article in agreement with καθήμενος) 9.

καθήμενος (pres.part.nom.sing.masc.of κάθημαι, substantival, nominative absolute) 377.

ἐπ' (preposition with the accusative, rest) 47.

αὐτὸν (acc.sing.masc.of αὐτός, rest) 16.

ἔχων (pres.act.part.nom.sing.masc.of ἔχω, adverbial, circumstantial) 82.

ζυγὸν (acc.sing.masc.of ζυγός, direct object of ἔχων) 956.

ἐν (preposition with the locative, place) 80.

τῇ (loc.sing.fem.of the article in agreement with χειρὶ) 9.

χειρὶ (loc.sing.fem.of χείρ, place) 308.

αὐτοῦ (gen.sing.masc.of αὐτ ός, possession) 16.

Translation - *"And when he opened the third seal, I heard the third living creature saying, 'Come.' And I watched, and Look! A black horse and the one who was sitting on him, with a pair of balances in his hand!"*

Comment: ἔρχου can apply either to John who is thus invited to watch or to the black horse rider. Note, as in verses 1 and 3 that καὶ ἴδε is not supported by the best MSS authority. The scales in his hand must be interpreted in the light of verse 6. This rider is the seventh king of Rev.17:10, who will be on the scene only for a short time. He is the last king in the first half of the week since the next one appears at mid-week as announced in Mt.24:14; Dan.9:27b; 2 Thess.2:3,4,8-10;

Rev.13:1-10. He, the Black Horse Rider, is contemporary with the third trumpet judgment (Rev.8:10-11), the conditions under which, added to those of the first two, plus the devastation of the war of the second seal, contributes to the famine of the 3rd seal which is in view here. The church at this time will be reading the Pergamos letter (Rev.2:12-17) with its observations, rebuke and encouragement. Only those Christians who will be upon the earth at that time and experiencing the trials described can appreciate how these events and messages coordinate. God's word in that day will surely be our "shield and buckler" (Psalm 91:4).

Verse 6 - "And I heard a voice in the midst of the four beasts say, A measure of wheat for a penny, and three measures of barley for a penny; and see thou hurt not the oil and the wine."

καὶ ἤκουσα ὡς φωνὴν ἐν μέσω τῶν τερράρων ζώων λέγουσαν, Χοῖνιξ σίτου δηναρίου, καὶ τρεῖς χοίνικες κριθῶν δηναρίου καὶ τὸ ἔλαιον καὶ τὸν οἶνον μὴ αδδικήσης.

"and I heard what seemed to be a voice in the midst of the four living creatures saying, 'A quart of wheat for a denarius, and three quarts of barley for a denarius, but do not harm oil and wine!' " . . . RSV

καὶ (continuative conjunction) 14.

ἤκουσα (1st.per.sing.aor.act.ind.of ἀκούω, constative) 148.

ὡς (comparative particle) 128.

φωνὴν (acc.sing.fem.of φωνή, direct object of ἤκουσα) 222.

ἐν (preposition with the locative, place) 80.

μέσω (loc.sing.masc.of μέσος, place) 873.

τῶν (gen.pl.neut.of the article in agreement with ζώων) 9.

τεσσάρων (gen.pl.neut.of τέσσαρες, in agreement with ζώων) 1508.

ζώων (gen.pl.neut.of ζῷον, description) 5086.

λέγουσαν (pres.act.part.acc.sing.fem.of λέγω, recitatitve) 66.

#5351 Χοῖνιξ (nom.sing.fem.of χοίνιξ, nominative absolute).

King James Version

measure - Rev.6:6,6.

Revised Standard Version

quart - Rev.6:6,6.

Meaning: Thayer says, "a dry measure, containing four cotylae or two sextarii (*i.e.* less than our quart). As much as would support a man of moderate appetite for a day." Diog.Laert, 8,18 has ἡ χοῖνιξ ἡμερήσις τροφή - "one daily ration" - Fr.for one day. Moulton & Milligan say that ἡ χοῖνιξ equals 1.92 pints. Liddel & Scott agree. The fact that the price is inflated is shown by the fact that the price, (δηνάριον, #1278) was a normal day's wage. *Cf.* Mt.20:2,9,10,13. Thus a man worked all day long for less than one quart of wheat or less than three quarts of barley - Rev.6:6,6.

σίτου (gen.sing.masc.of σῖτος, partitive) 311.
δηναρίου (abl.sing.neut.of δηνάριον, comparison) 1278.
καὶ (adjunctive conjunction joining nouns) 14.
τρεῖς (nom.pl.fem.of τρεῖς, in agreement with χοίνικες) 1010.
χοίνικες (nom.pl.fem.of χοῖνιξ, nominative absolute) 5351.

#5352 κριθῶν (gen.pl.fem.of κριθή, partitive).

King James Version

barley - Rev.6:6.

Revised Standard Version

barley - Rev.6:6.

Meaning: Found only in the plural. Barley - Rev.6:6.

δηναρίου (abl.sing.neut.of δηνάριον, comparison) 1278.
καὶ (continuative conjunction) 14.
τὸ (acc.sing.neut.of the article in agreement with ἔλαιον) 9.
ἔλαιον (acc.sing.neut.of ἔλαιον, direct object of ἀδικήσῃς) 1530.
καὶ (adjunctive conjunction joining nouns) 14.
τὸν (acc.sing.masc.of the article in agreement with οἶνον) 9.
οἶνον (acc.sing.masc.of οἶνος, direct object of ἀδικήσῃς) 808.
μὴ (negative conjunction with the subjunctive, in a prohibition) 87.
ἀδικήσῃς (2d.per.sing.aor.act.subj.of ἀδικέω, prohibition) 1327.

Translation - "And I heard what sounds like a voice in the midst of the four living creatures saying, 'A quart of wheat for a day's wage and three quarts of barley for a day's wage, but the oil and the wine you must not damage."

Comment: Since τὸ δηνάριον was regarded as a normal day's wage (Mt.20:2,9,10,13) and a quart of wheat (one loaf) or three quarts of barley (three barley cakes) is enough food for one man-day, we have a picture of the inflation in the food market associated with famine. In the coming days men will be able to buy minimal subsistence for a day's wage. This is runaway inflation. It will be caused by the judgments of the first two trumpets and the war of the second seal. Note that the wheat, oil and wine (#'s 311, 1530, 808) will be traded actively in Babylon, Antichrist's capital city (Rev.18:13). Does this mean that μὴ ἀδικήσῃς refers to a cornering of the market of oil and wine? In any case we have a clear picture of famine conditions. Christians on earth during this time will be struggling with the problems discussed in Rev.2:1-29, as well as with the economic problems of the inflation. It is worth noting that the real value of money (purchasing power - command of goods and services) will be almost nil for all, saved and unsaved, who have it, but that after Antichrist appears in the middle of the week (4th seal), Christians will have no further need for money anyway (Rev.13:16,17). As the fourth seal is opened we find outselvs at mid-week.

Verse 7 - "And when he had opened the fourth seal, I heard the voice of the fourth beast say, Come and see."

Καὶ ὅτε ἤνοιξεν τὴν σφραγῖδα τὴν τετάρτην, ἤκουσα φωνὴν τοῦ τετάρτου ζῴου λέγοντος, Ἔρχου.

"When he opened the fourth seal, I heard the voice of the fourth living creature say, 'Come!' " . . . RSV

καὶ (continuative conjunction) 14.

ὅτε (conjunction introducing the indicative in a definite temporal clause) 703.

ἤνοιξεν (3d.per.sing.aor.act.ind.of ἀνοίγω, constative) 188.

τὴν (acc.sing.fem.of the article in agreement with σφραγῖδα) 9.

σφραγῖδα (acc.sing.fem.of σφραγίς, direct object of ἤνοιξεν) 3886.

τὴν (acc.sing.fem.of the article in agreement with τετάρτην) 9.

τετάρτην (acc.sing.fem.of τέταρτος, in agreement with σφραγῖδα) 1129.

ἤκουσα (1st.per.sing.aor.act.ind.of ἀκούω, constative) 148.

φωνὴν (acc.sing.fem.of φωνή, direct object of ἤκουσα) 222.

τοῦ (gen.sing.neut.of the article in agreement with ζῴου) 9.

τετάρτου (gen.sing.neut.of τέταρτος, in agreement with ζῴου) 1129.

ζῴου (gen.sing.neut.of ζῶον, possession) 5086.

λέγοντος (pres.act.part.gen.sing.neut.of λέγω, recitatitve) 66.

Ἔρχου (2d.per.sing.pres.mid.impv.of ἔρχομαι, command) 146.

Translation - "And when he opened the fourth seal, I heard the voice of the fourth living creature saying, 'Come.' "

Comment: The mid-week point has been reached (Dan.9:27b; Mt.24:15; 2 Thess.2:3,4; Rev.13:1-18; 12:6,7,8,9; 17:8-18; Rev.8:12-13; 9:1-11). At this point the countdown for the second coming of Christ will be T minus 3 1/2 years (Rev.12:14), 1260 days (Rev.12:6) or 42 months (Rev.13:5). By this time, of course, enlightened Christians on the earth will have had 3 1/2 years of ample opportunity to check world events against the Revelation and we will thus know exactly where we are on God's clock. Thus that day will not come upon us as a thief (2 Thess.5:4). It will be a time of revival as backslidden saints return to their first love (Rev.2:19). This is the time when the first major persecution of Christians will occur (Rev.13:7). Soon the Sardis epistle (Rev.3:1-6) will apply.

Verse 8 - "And I looked, and behold a pale horse; and his name that sat on him was Death and Hell followed with him. And power was given unto them over the fourth part of the earth to kill with sword, and with hunger, and with death, and with the beasts of the earth."

καὶ εἶδον, καὶ ἰδοὺ ἵππος χλωρός, καὶ ὁ καθήμενος ἐπάνω (αὐτοῦ) ὄνομα αὐτῷ (ὁ) Θάνατος, καὶ ὁ ᾅδης ἠκολούθει μετ᾽ αὐτοῦ. καὶ ἐδόθη αὐτοῖς ἐξουσία ἐπὶ τὸ τέταρτον τῆς γῆς, ἀποκτεῖναι ἐν ρομφαίᾳ καὶ ἐν λιμῷ καὶ ἐν θανάτῳ καὶ ὑπὸ τῶν θηρίων τῆς γῆς.

"And I saw, and behold a pale horse, and its rider's name was Death, and Hades followed him; and they were given power over a fourth of the earth, to kill with sword and with famine and with pestilence and by wild beasts of the earth." . . . *RSV*

καὶ (continuative conjunction) 14.

εἶδον (1st.per.sing.aor.act.ind.of ὁράω, constative) 144.

καὶ (continuative conjunction) 14.

ἰδοὺ (exclamation) 95.

ἵππος (nom.sing.masc.of ἵππος, nominative absolute) 5121.

χλωρός (nom.sing.masc.of χλωρός, in agreement with ἵππος) 2267.

καὶ (adjunctive conjunction joining substantives) 14.

ὁ (nom.sing.masc.of the article in agreement with καθήμενος) 9.

καθήμενος (pres.mid.part.nom.sing.masc.of κάθημαι, substantival, nominative absolute) 377.

ἐπάνω (improper preposition with the genitive of place description) 181.

αὐτοῦ (gen.sing.masc.of αὐτός, place description) 16.

ὄνομα (nom.sing.neut.of ὄνομα, nominative absolute) 108.

αὐτῷ (dat.sing.masc.of αὐτός, possession) 16.

ὁ (nom.sing.masc.of the article in agreement with Θάνατος) 9.

Θάνατος (nom.sing.masc.of θάνατος, predicate nominative) 381.

καὶ (continuative conjunction) 14.

ὁ (nom.sing.masc.of the article in agreement with ᾅδης) 9.

ᾅδης (nom.sing.masc.of ᾅδης, subject of ἠκολούθει) 947.

ἠκολούθει (3d.per.sing.imp.act.ind.of ἀκολουθέω, progressive description) 394.

μετ' (preposition with the genitive, accompaniment) 50.

αὐτοῦ (gen.sing.masc.of αὐτός, accompaniment) 16.

καὶ (continuative conjunction) 14.

ἐξουσία (nom.sing.fem.of ἐξουσία, subject of ἐδόθη) 707.

ἐπὶ (preposition with the accusative, extent) 47.

τὸ (acc.sing.neut.of the article in agreement with τέταρτον) 9.

τέταρτον (acc.sing.neut.of τέταρτος, extent) 1129.

τῆς (gen.sing.fem.of the article in agreement with γῆς) 9.

γῆς (gen.sing.fem.of γῆ, partitive) 157.

ἀποκτεῖναι (aor.act.inf.of ἀποκτείνω, in apposition with ἐξουσία) 889.

ἐν (preposition with the instrumental, means) 80.

ῥομφαίᾳ (instru.sing.fem.of ῥομφαία, means) 1904.

καὶ (adjunctive conjunction joining prepositional phrases) 14.

ἐν (preposition with the instrumental, means) 80.

λιμῷ (instru.sing.masc.of λιμός, means) 1485.

καὶ (adjunctive conjunction joining prepositional phrases) 14.

ἐν (preposition with the instrumental, means) 80.

θανάτῳ (instru.sing.masc.of θάνατος, means) 381.

καὶ (adjunctive conjunction joining prepositional phrases) 14.

ὑπὸ (preposition with the ablative, agent) 117.

τῶν (abl.pl.neut.of the article in agreement with ϑηρίων) 9.
ϑηρίων (abl.pl.neut.of ϑήριον, agent) 1951.
τῆς (gen.sing.fem.of the article in agreement with γῆς) 9.
γῆς (gen.sing.fem.of γῆ, description) 157.

Translation - "And I watched. And Look! A horse with a ghastly green color, and the one who sat upon him, named Death and Hades was following him. And power was given to them over one fourth of the earth, to kill with a sword and with famine and with pestilence and by the wild beasts of the earth."

Comment: The interjection ἰδοὺ is used with the nominative absolutes as before. The fourth seal presents, not one but two main characters, Death and Hades, who will have power to destroy 25% of the earth's population with war, famine, pestilence and the attacks of wild animals, no doubt in those areas of the earth where a decimated human population will put the animals back into ascendancy. Animals, now in danger of becoming extinct in the struggle for survival with man, with his superior intelligence and technology, will regain control. The earth in 1984 is already overpopulated with five billion people and a net reproduction rate in excess of two. Thus, in the absence of the events described in Rev.6:8 it is likely that the population of the earth will reach eight billion. Our verse says that one fourth of the people will be killed during the last half of the tribulation period. The war, early in the tribulation under the second seal will be resumed by the Antichrist and his satanic colleague. The famine and pestilence of the third and fourth seals will continue to do their ghastly work. Note the contribution to all of this of the first three trumpet judgments - scorched earth, trees and field crops destroyed, sea pollution, death of marine life, destruction of ships, polluted drinking water (Rev.8:7-11). Wild beasts, fighting for survival in the competition with man for minimal subsistence in a world-wide economy of reduced production will be out of control.

Let us not forget that the Holy Spirit is immanently supervisory, both in nature and in human history, as well as transcendant over them, and that the Body of Christ is not yet complete, nor will it be until the "days of the voice of the seventh angel when he shall begin to sound" (Rev.10:7). Many of those who will die during this period will be infants, while the Holy Spirit will direct the Christians to walk through the open doors for evangelism and reach the last elect soul for whom Christ died in order to witness to them the good news of the gospel of Christ. These doors will remain open, despite the efforts of Satan to close them. The Philadelphians, under the direction of the Holy Spirit will take full advantage of them (Rev.3:8). Some of their converts may be the Laodiceans, to whom the gospel invitation will still be extended (Rev.3:20). Others may be the Gentiles who will have professed falsely to be Jews, in order to gain recognition from the Antichrist, who will demand worship in the Jewish temple in Jerusalem (Rev.3:9; 2 Thess.2:4).

The student should study all of the other passages that describe in more detail the two Satanic characters of the fourth seal, both in their persons and works. They are the last of the personages revealed by the seal judgments. They appear in greater detail in Rev.13:1-10 and 13:11-18. Their connection with the first three seals and the Book of Daniel is explained in Rev.17:7-13. They will be destroyed by the Lamb (Rev.17:14) for He has the keys of "Hell and death". (*Cf.* Rev.1:18 for comment). That is to say that these two unsavory characters are completely under Christ's control. He will give them their little hour upon the earth, use them, judge them and send them to hell (Rev.19:20). Daniel (Dan.9:27), Jesus (Mt.24:15) and Paul (2 Thess.2:3-12) all allude to Antichrist. See also Dan.7:19-28 and compare with Rev.13:5-7. Compare Dan.7:25 with Rev.12:14. *Cf.* also Dan.8:23-25; 9:27; 11:36-45. Satan has always wanted to be God (Ezek.28:11-19; Isa.14:12-15; Gen.3:5; Mt.4:8-11; 2 Cor.4:4; Eph.2:1-2). For 3 1/2 years Satan's counterfeit Christ will be worshipped by all unregenerate people, except those elect souls (Acts 13:48) who are scheduled to be saved during the last half of the week, which we shall now term "The Great Tribulation - τῆς θλίψεως τῆς μεγάλης (Rev.7:14).

The Beast's promise to Israel, made 3 1/2 years before, when as the "fifth" he confirmed the Abrahamic covenant, will now be broken as he now, in the middle of the week, returns to power as the "eighth" who is one of the preceding seven (Rev.17:10,11). Israel will flee into the wilderness to escape him (Mt.24:15-22; Rev.12:6). The Beast will kill many of the saints (Rev.13:7). The evil and adulterous generation of that day, unwilling to accept the sign of Jonah (Mt.12:38-40) but "incurably religious" will have their signs (Rev.13:13-15). A Christ rejecting world will stand amazed in the Beast's presence. Jesus said, "I am come in my Father's name, and ye receive me not: if another shall come in his own name, him ye will receive" (John 5:43). Note the adulation that approaches worship of otherwise sophisticated people which is offered to Jeanne Dixon, Edgar Cayce, ouija boards, fakirs, gurus, swindlers, television snake oil salesmen and astrologers. It is interesting to see the Arminians who reject Ephesians 1:11, consult their horoscope in the daily newspaper. All except the elect (Mt.24:24) will be deceived by Antichrist and his colleague, the False Prophet. But the saints will be delivered from "the snare of the fowler" (Psalm 91:3,4) because God's truth will be our shield and buckler. Many shall do wickedly and none of the wicked shall understand, but the wise shall understand (Dan.12:10; 1 Thess.5:3-4).

We have seen that the Pale Horse Rider (Rev.6:7-8; 13:7) will kill some of the saints. It is to be expected then that some note should be taken of these martyred saints. Thus in the fifth seal passage we have souls of martyred saints under the altar in heaven. With the fourth and fifth seals God's countdown clock moves into the last half of the week. The count is now T minus 1260 days and counting. There are no more holds programmed into the divine scenario.

Verse 9 - "And when he had opened the fifth seal, I saw under the altar the souls of them that were slain for the word of God, and for the testimony which they held."

Καὶ ὅτε ἤνοιξεν τὴν πέμπτην σφραγῖδα, εἶδον ὑποκάτω τοῦ θυσιαστηρίου τὰς ψυχὰς τῶν ἐσφαγμένων διὰ τὸν λόγον τοῦ θεοῦ καὶ διὰ τὴν μαρτυρίαν ἣν εἶχον.

*"When he opened the fifth seal, I saw under the altar the souls of those who
had been slain for the word of God and for the witness they had borne;"... RSV*

Καὶ (continuative conjunction) 14.

ὅτε (conjunction introducing the indicative in a definite temporal clause) 703.

ἤνοιξεν (3d.per.sing.aor.act.ind.of ἀνοίγω, constative) 188.

τὴν (acc.sing.fem.of the article in agreement with σφραγῖδα) 9.

#5353 πέμπτην (acc.sing.fem.of πέμπτος, in agreement with σφραγῖδα).

King James Version

fifth - Rev.6:9; 9:1; 16:10; 21:20.

Revised Standard Version

fifth - Rev.6:9; 9:1; 16:10; 21:20.

Meaning: fifth - with reference to the seal (Rev.6:9), trumpet (Rev.9:1); vial
(Rev.16:10); gate of heaven (Rev.21:20).

σφραγῖδα (acc.sing.fem.of σφραγίς, direct object of ἤνοιξεν) 3886.

εἶδον (1st.per.sing.aor.act.ind.of ὁράω, constative) 144.

ὑποκάτω (improper preposition with the genitive of place description) 1429.

τοῦ (gen.sing.neut.of the article in agreement with θυσιαστηρίου) 9.

θυσιαστηρίου (gen.sing.neut.of θυσιαστήριον, place description) 484.

τὰς (acc.pl.fem.of the article in agreement with φυχὰς) 9.

φυχὰς (acc.pl.fem.of φυχή, direct object of εἶδον) 233.

τῶν (gen.pl.masc.of the article in agreement with ἐσφαγμένων) 9.

ἐσφαγμένων (perf.pass.part.gen.pl.masc.of σφάττω, substantival,
possession) 5292.

διὰ (preposition with the accusative, cause) 118.

τὸν (acc.sing.masc.of the article in agreement with λόγον) 9.

λόγον (acc.sing.masc.of λόγος, cause) 510.

τοῦ (gen.sing.masc.of the article in agreement with θεοῦ) 9.

θεοῦ (gen.sing.masc.of θεός, description) 124.

καὶ (adjunctive conjunction joining prepositional phrases) 14.

διὰ (preposition with the accusative, cause) 118.

τὴν (acc.sing.fem.of the article in agreement with μαρτυρίαν) 9.

μαρτυρίαν (acc.sing.fem.of μαρτυρία, cause) 1695.

ἣν (acc.sing.fem.of ὅς, relative pronoun, direct object of εἶχον) 65.

εἶχον (3d.per.pl.imp.act.ind.of ἔχω, progressive description) 82.

*Translation - "And when he opened the fifth seal I saw under the altar the souls
of those who had been slain because of the word of God and because of the
witness which they had been giving."*

Comment: The correlative evidence for our hypothesis that churches, seals,
trumpets and, in the last half of the week, vials are contemporaneous and

coterminous is abundant. In Rev.2:22 the Lord warned certain Christians just before the Beast arose (4th seal) that if they could no longer be used in His service, He would subject them to great tribulation and (verse 23) that some of them would be killed, whereas He told the survivors in the Sardis church (5th church contemporary with the 5th seal) that they had survived the first persecution because they still had work to do for God (Rev.3:2). Rev.13:7 tells us that the Beast when he came for his last 42 months (Rev.13:5) would kill some of the saints. Thus in the 5th seal we found his victims at the foot of God's altar in heaven. That these souls (not bodies, because their bodies are still on earth awaiting resurrection at the end of the week) are not martyrs of former days, but martyrs only recently killed, is clear from the present tense participle κατοικούντων in verse 10. Their murderers are still on earth when they ask God for vindication. So these martyrs are not the victims of Nero, Domitian or Adolf Hitler. They are the victims of the Beast and his gang of cutthroats still on earth. Note the perfect participle ἐσφαγμένων - "having been slain in past time and hence still slain." Note also that εἶχον is in the imperfect tense indicating that their testimony was consistent. They cry out to God for vengeance in

Verse 10 - "And they cried with a loud voice, saying, How long, O Lord, holy and true, dost thou not judge and avenge our blood on them that dwell on the earth?"

καὶ ἔκραξαν φωνῇ μεγάλῃ λέγοντες, Ἕως πότε, ὁ δεσπότης ὁ ἅγιος καὶ ἀληθινός, οὐ κρίνεις καὶ ἐκδικεῖς τὸ αἷμα ἡμῶν ἐκ τῶν κατοικούντων ἐπὶ τῆς γῆς;

"they cried out with a loud voice, 'O Sovereign Lord, holy and true, how long before thou wilt judge and avenge our blood on those who dwell upon the earth?'" . . . RSV

καὶ (continuative conjunction) 14.

ἔκραξαν (3d.per.pl.aor.act.ind.of κράζω, ingressive) 765.

φωνῇ (instru.sing.fem.of φωνή, means) 222.

μεγάλῃ (instru.sing.fem.of μέγας, in agreement with φωνῇ) 184.

λέγοντες (pres.act.part.nom.pl.masc.of λέγω, recitative) 66.

Ἕως (preposition in a temporal construction) 71.

πότε (temporal adverb) 1233.

ὁ (voc.sing.masc.of the article in agreement with δεσπότης) 9.

δεσπότης (voc.sing.masc.of δεσπότης, address) 1900.

ὁ (voc.sing.masc.of the article in agreement with ἅγιος) 9.

ἅγιος (voc.sing.masc.of ἅγιος, in agreement with δεσπότης) 84.

καὶ (adjunctive conjunction joining adjectives) 14.

ἀληθινός (voc.sing.masc.of ἀληθινός, in agreement with δεσπότης) 1696.

οὐ (negative conjunction with the indicative in indirect question) 130.

κρίνεις (2d.per.sing.pres.act.ind.of κρίνω, indirect question) 531.

καὶ (adjunctive conjunction joining verbs) 14.

ἐκδικεῖς (2d.per.sing.pres.act.ind.of ἐκδικέω, indirect question) 2623.

τὸ (acc.sing.neut.of the article in agreement with αἷμα) 9.

αἷμα (acc.sing.neut.of αἷμα, direct object of ἐκδικεῖς) 1203.
ἡμῶν (gen.pl.masc.of ἐγώ, possession) 123.
ἐκ (preposition with the ablative, source) 19.
τῶν (abl.pl.masc.of the article in agreement with κατοικούντων) 9.
κατοικούντων (pres.act.part.abl.pl.masc.of κατοικέω, substantival, source) 242.
ἐπὶ (preposition with the genitive of place description) 47.
τῆς (gen.sing.fem.of the article in agreement with γῆς) 9.
γῆς (gen.sing.fem.of γῆ, place description) 157.

Translation - "And they began to cry out with a loud voice saying, 'How long, O Lord, the holy and true one, will it be before you make a judgment and avenge our blood at the expense of those who are living on the earth?' "

Comment: *Cf.*#1233 for πότε with ἕως - "how long?" or "Until what time?" It is a natural question. The innate sense of justice that the martyrs had demanded that at some time God would vindicate them, since their deaths were the result of their faithful witness of His word (verse 9). God answers the question in

Verse 11 - "And white robes were given unto every one of them; and it was said unto them, that they should rest yet for a little season, until their fellowservants also and their brethren, that should be killed as they were, should be fulfilled."

καὶ ἐδόθη ἑκάστῳ στολὴ λευκή, καὶ ἐρρέθη αὐτοῖς ἵνα ἀναπαύσονται ἔτι χρόνον μικρόν, ἕως πληρωθῶσιν καὶ οἱ σύνδουλοι αὐτῶν καὶ οἱ ἀδελφοὶ αὐτῶν οἱ μέλλοντες ἀποκτέννεσθαι ὡς καὶ αὐτοί.

"Then they were each given a white robe and told to rest a little longer, until the number of their fellow servants and their brethren should be complete, who were to be killed as they themselves had been." . . . RSV

καὶ (continuative conjunction) 14.
ἐδόθη (3d.per.sing.aor.pass.ind.of δίδωμι, constative) 362.
αὐτοῖς (dat.pl.masc.of αὐτός, indirect object of ἐδόθη) 16.
ἑκάστῳ (dat.sing.masc.of ἕκαστος, indirect object of ἐδόθη) 1217.
στολὴ (nom.sing.fem.of στολή, subject of ἐδόθη) 2552.
λευκή (nom.sing.fem.of λευκός, in agreement with στολή) 522.
καὶ (continuative conjunction) 14.
ἐρρέθη (3d.per.sing.1st.aor.pass.ind.of ῥέω, constative) 116.
αὐτοῖς (dat.pl.masc.of αὐτός, indirect object of ἐρρέθη) 16.
ἵνα (conjunction with the future indicative in a sub-final object complementary clause) 114.
ἀναπαύσονται (3d.per.pl.fut.mid.ind.of ἀναπαύω, in a sub-final object clause) 955.
ἔτι (temporal adverb) 448.
χρόνον (acc.sing.masc.of χρόνος, time extent) 168.
μικρόν (acc.sing.masc.of μικρός, in agreement with χρόνον) 901.
ἕως (temporal adverb) 71.

πληρωθῶσιν (3d.per.pl.aor.pass.subj.of πληρόω, in an indefinite temporal clause) 115.

καὶ (correlative conjunction) 14.

οἱ (nom.pl.masc.of the article in agreement with σύνδουλοι) 9.

σύνδουλοι (nom.pl.masc.of σύνδουλος, subject of πληρωθῶσιν) 1276.

αὐτῶν (gen.pl.masc.of αὐτός, relationship) 16.

καὶ (adjunctive conjunction joining nouns) 14.

οἱ (nom.pl.masc.of the article in agreement with ἀδελφοὶ) 9.

ἀδελφοὶ (nom.pl.masc.of ἀδελφός, subject of πληρωθῶσιν) 15.

αὐτῶν (gen.pl.masc.of αὐτός, relationship) 16.

οἱ (nom.pl.masc.of the article in agreement with μέλλοντες) 9.

μέλλοντες (pres.act.part.nom.pl.masc.of μέλλω, adjectival, emphatic attributive position, in agreement with ἀδελφοὶ) 206.

ἀποκτέννεσθαι (pres.pass.inf.of ἀποκτείνω, complementary) 889.

καὶ (emphatic conjunction) 14.

αὐτοί (nom.pl.masc.of αὐτός, subject of verb understood) 16.

Translation - "And a white robe was given to each of them and they were told that they should rest for a short time until the number of both their fellowservants and their brethren who were about to be killed as they in fact had been should be complete."

Comment: Often ἕκαστος (#1217) is followed by a partitive genitive, but here it is joined to αὐτοῖς, also in the dative of indirect object. The ἵνα clause is subfinal. It is used like ὅτι to introduce the object clause in indirect discourse. The martyrs are told to relax in glory for a short time (something less than 42 months) until other Christians who, at that time had escaped the Beast (Rev.13:7) and who were destined also to be killed as they in fact had been, should finish their work on earth and die for the faith (Rev.3:2; Eph.2:10; 2 Tim.4:6 *al*). The subjunctive in πληρωθῶσιν indicates the indefinite temporal clause. The time of the second coming is definite. Thus it is not in view, but we are not told the precise time when other Christians would be martyred. Not all of the Christians on earth at that time or those of the elect, still unsaved but destined to be effectually called are included in the number of martyrs still to die. There will be those who "are alive and remain unto the coming of the Lord" (1 Thess.4:15) who will not be raptured until those who are dead have been resurrected. But martyrdom still awaits some of them, as Satan, through the Antichrist and the False Prophet, knowing that he has but a short time (Rev.12:12) will vent his most intense fury against God (Psalm 2:1-3). All of the tribulation saints will have white robes (Rev.7:14).

The Revelation has now taken us through the entire seven years of Daniel's 70th week (Dan.9:27), as our Lord has opened the first five seals and is about to open the sixth. The first four presented the three kings (riders) and the fourth, a return of the first, who appears in the middle of the week will remain in power for the last half of the week (Rev.13:5). Revelation 13 gives us the details of his rule. It will extend until the last day (Rev.19:20) when he and the False Prophet will be thrown headlong into the lake of fire. The fifth seal is descriptive of a heavenly scene contemporary with the Antichrist's reign on earth. The sixth seal describes the second coming of our Lord on the last day and the seventh seal (Rev.8:1) only observes that there is a quiet time in heaven after the storm on earth is over. Let us then look at the last day of the last month of the last year of the 490 years marked out for Daniel in Dan.9:24-27. At the close of the last day, everything in Daniel 9:24 will have been accomplished. That the seventh trumpet (Rev.11:15-18) and the seventh vial (Rev.16:17-21) are two other descriptions of the same events on the same day should be obvious to those who study the charts on pp.60 and 64. If they are not descriptive of the same event but are separated by months, weeks or even days, then we have three great cataclysms of earth shaking proportions, all within the space of 3 1/2 years, in the second of which Jesus Christ takes His place upon the throne of David (Rev.11:15-18), judges the saints for their works and destroys His enemies upon the earth. Further that "the great day of His wrath" when none shall be able to stand occurs at some point in time, even prior to the seventh trumpet (Rev.16:17). All of this confusion is the mischief that results when commentators determine to make the text conform to their own prejudicial ideas. It will be apparent to the reader that this writer has no special authorization from heaven to interpret in any symbolic, figurative or allegorical sense language which is written in plain and clear Greek and which makes sense as it stands. "When the plain statements of Scripture makes sense, seek no other sense." If the Bible does not mean what it says why does it not say what it means?

The grand finale of this fascinating contest between Jesus Christ, to whom all power has been given, and Satan, the universal upstart and his pigmies of earth is about to begin. The sixth seal is ripped from the cover of the scroll in

Verse 12 - "And I beheld when he had opened the sixth seal, and lo, there was a great earthquake, and the sun became black as sackcloth of hair, and the moon became as blood;"

Καὶ εἶδον ὅτε ἤνοιξεν τὴν σφραγῖδα τὴν ἔκτην, καὶ σεισμὸς μέγας ἐγένετο, καὶ ὁ ἥλιος ἐγένετο μέλας ὡς σάκκος τρίχινος, καὶ ἡ σελήνη ὅλη ἐγένετο ὡς αἷμα,

"When he opened the sixth seal, I looked, and behold, there was a great earthquake; and the sun became black as sackcloth, the full moon became like blood, . . . " . . . RSV

καὶ (continuative conjunction) 14.
εἶδον (1st.per.sing.aor.act.ind.of ὁράω, constative) 144.
ὅτε (conjunction introducing the indicative in a definite temporal clause) 703.
ἤνοιξεν (3d.per.sing.aor.act.ind.of ἀνοίγω, constative) 188.
τὴν (acc.sing.fem.of the article in agreement with σφραγῖδα) 9.
σφραγῖδα (acc.sing.fem.of σφραγίς, direct object of ἤνοιξεν) 3886.
τὴν (acc.sing.fem.of the article in agreement with ἔκτην) 9.
ἔκτην (acc.sing.fem.of ἔκτος, in agreement with σφραγῖδα) 1317.
καὶ (continuative conjunction) 14.

σεισμὸς (nom.sing.masc.of σεισμός, subject of ἐγένετο) 751.

μέγας (nom.sing.masc.of μέγας, in agreement with σεισμὸς) 184.

ἐγένετο (3d.per.sing.aor.ind.of γίνομαι, ingressive) 113.

καὶ (continuative conjunction) 14.

ὁ (nom.sing.masc.of the article in agreement with ἥλιος) 9.

ἥλιος (nom.sing.masc.of ἥλιος, subject of ἐγένετο) 546.

ἐγένετο (3d.per.sing.aor.ind.of γίνομαι, ingressive) 113.

μέλας (nom.sing.masc.of μέλας, predicate adjective) 523.

ὡς (comparative particle) 128.

σάκκος (nom.sing.masc.of σάκκος, subject of ἐστιν understood) 942.

#5354 τρίχινος (nom.sing.masc.of τρίχονος, in agreement with σάκκος).

King James Version

of hair - Rev.6:12.

Revised Standard Version

(not translated).

Meaning: Made of hair. *Cf.* θρίξ (#261) - Rev.6:12.

καὶ (continuative conjunction) 14.

ἡ (nom.sing.fem.of the article in agreement with σελήνη) 9.

σελήνη (nom.sing.fem.of σελήνη, subject of ἐγένετο) 1505.

ὅλη (nom.sing.fem.of ὅλος, in agreement with σελήνη) 112.

ἐγένετο (3d.per.sing.aor.ind.of γίνομαι, ingressive) 113.

ὡς (comparative particle) 128.

αἷμα (nom.sing.neut.of αἷμα, subject of ἐστιν understood) 1203.

Translation - "And I watched as He opened the sixth seal, and a great earthquake began and the sun turned as black as hairy sackcloth and the entire moon became as blood."

Comment: The student should compare this verse with Mt.24:29; Mk.13:24; Lk.21:25; Joel 2:30-32; Acts 2:20 and decide whether or not the passages all refer to the same event. In Acts 2:16-21 Peter said in reference to the Pentecost scene, "This is that . . . " He did not say, "This is *all* of that. . . " The Joel prophecy had a partial fulfillment at Pentecost and will have a total fulfillment at the second coming of our Lord. This is another example of double imagery. *Cf.* our comment on Acts 2:16.

Note that this event described under the sixth seal is immediately *after* the tribulation of the days described by Jesus, which began with the Man of Sin in the middle of the week (Mt.24:15-29). Note especially Mt.24:15 and Mt.24:29, which is parallel to Rev.6:12,13. This is the second coming (Mt.24:30). This is also rapture time (Mt.24:31).

The sun failed when He died (Mt.27:45) and it will fail again when He returns in glory. On that great day who needs the sun? (Rev.1:16), We will have the Son!

Note that ἡ σελήνη is modified by ὅλη. Three and one half years before, at the time of the fourth trumpet judgment (Rev.8:12) one third of the moon was smitten. Now the destruction of the moon is total. This small but precise detail with reference to the moon supports our hypothesis that the fourth trumpet comes before the sixth seal. The view that vials must follow trumpets and that trumpets must follow seals is wrong.

The description of the scene on the day when our Lord returns to earth continues in

Verse 13 - "And the stars of heaven fell unto the earth, even as a fig tree casteth her untimely figs, when she is shaken of a mighty wind."

καὶ οἱ ἀστέρες τοῦ οὐρανοῦ ἔπεσαν εἰς τὴν γῆν, ὡς συκῆ βάλλει τοὺς ὀλύνθους αὐτῆς ὑπὸ ἀνέμου μεγάλου σειομένη,

"and the stars of the sky fell to the earth as the fig tree sheds its winter fruit when shaken by a gale; . . ." . . . RSV

καὶ (continuative conjunction) 14.
οἱ (nom.pl.masc.of the article in agreement with ἀστέρες) 9.
ἀστέρες (nom.pl.masc.of ἀστήρ, subject of ἔπεσαν) 145.
τοῦ (gen.sing.masc.of the article in agreement with οὐρανοῦ) 9.
οὐρανοῦ (gen.sing.masc.of οὐρανός, description) 254.
ἔπεσαν (3d.per.pl.aor.act.ind.of πίπτω, ingressive) 187.
εἰς (preposition with the accusative, extent) 140.
τὴν (acc.sing.fem.of the article in agreement with γῆν) 9.
γῆν (acc.sing.fem.of γῆ, extent) 157.
ὡς (comparative particle) 128.
συκῆ (nom.sing.fem.of συκῆ, subject of βάλλει, contra.for συκέα) 1366.
βάλλει (3d.per.sing.pres.act.ind.of βάλλω, customary) 299.
τοὺς (acc.pl.masc.of the article in agreement with ὀλύνθους) 9.

#5355 ὀλύνθους (acc.pl.masc.of ὄλυνθος, direct object of βάλλει).

King James Version

untimely fig - Rev.6:13.

Revised Standard Version

winter fruit - Rev.6:13.

Meaning: An unripe fig, which grows during the winter but is not ripe until summer, and falls off in the spring - Rev.6:13.

αὐτῆς (gen.sing.fem.of αὐτός, possession) 16.
ὑπὸ (preposition with the ablative, agent) 117.
ἀνέμου (abl.sing.masc.of ἄνεμος, agent) 698.
μεγάλου (abl.sing.masc.of μέγας, in agreement with ἀνέμου) 184.

σειομένη (pres.pass.part.nom.sing.fem.of σείω, adjectival, predicate position, restrictive, in agreement with συκῆ) 1354.

Translation - "And the stars of the sky fell unto the earth as a fig tree shaken by a great wind casts its unripe figs."

Comment: οὐρανοῦ here in the sense of the stellar heavens. *Cf.*#254. The participle σειομένη is adjectival, in modification of συκῆ. The reference to σείω here is only illustrative, but *cf.*#1354 (Mt.27:51; Heb.12:26). The description continues to parallel Mt.24:29, etc.

Verse 14 - "And the heavens departed as a scroll when it is rolled together: and every mountain and island were moved out of their places."

καὶ ὁ οὐρανὸς ἀπεχωρίσθη ὡς βιβλίον ἑλισσόμενον, καὶ πᾶν ὄρος καὶ νῆσος ἐκ τῶν τόπων αὐτῶν ἐκινήθησαν.

"the sky vanished like a scroll that is rolled up, and every mountain and island was removed from its place." . . . RSV

καὶ (continuative conjunction) 14.
ὁ (nom.sing.masc.of the article in agreement with οὐρανὸς) 9.
οὐρανὸς (nom.sing.masc.of οὐρανός, subject of ἀπεχωρίσθη) 254.
ἀπεχωρίσθη (3d.per.sing.aor.pass.ind.of ἀποχωρίζομαι) 3351.
ὡς (comparative particle) 128.
βιβλίον (nom.sing.neut.of βιβλίον) 1292.
ἑλισσόμενον (pres.pass.part.nom.sing.neut.of ἑλίσσω, adjectival, predicate position, restrictive, in agreement with βιβλίον) 4923.
καὶ (continuative conjunction) 14.
πᾶν (nom.sing.neut.of πᾶς, in agreement with ὄρος) 67.
ὄρος (nom.sing.neut.of ὄρος, subject of ἐκινήθησαν) 357.
καὶ (adjunctive conjunction joining nouns) 14.
νῆσος (nom.sing.masc.of νῆσος, subject of ἐκινήθησαν) 3277.
ἐκ (preposition with the ablative, separation) 19.
τῶν (abl.pl.masc.of the article in agreement with τόπων) 9.
τόπων (abl.pl.masc.of τόπος, separation) 1019.
αὐτῶν (gen.pl.masc.of αὐτός, possession) 16.
ἐκινήθησαν (3d.per.pl.aor.pass.ind.of κινέω, constative) 1435.

Translation - "And the sky was torn apart like a rolled up scroll, and every mountain and island was moved out of its place."

Comment: *Cf.* Heb.1:12; Rev.16:20. The worldwide earthquake that will move every mountain and island will certainly devastate every city on earth. The opening of the firmament will reveal to men on earth the coming King and His heavenly armies. Mt.24:30; Lk.21:25-27. Verses 15 and 16 describe the reaction of the unregenerate upon the earth.

Verse 15 - "And the kings of the earth, and the great men, and the rich men, and the chief captains, and the mighty men, and every bondman, and every free man, hid themselves in the dens and in the rocks of the mountains;"

καὶ οἱ βασιλεῖς τῆς γῆς καὶ οἱ μεγιστᾶνες καὶ οἱ χιλίαρχοι καὶ οἱ πλούσιοι
καὶ οἱ ἰσχυροὶ καὶ πᾶς δοῦλος καὶ ἐλεύθερος ἔκρυφαν ἑαυτοὺς εἰς τὰ σπήλαια
καὶ τὰς πέτρας τῶν ὀρέων,

*"Then the kings of the earth and the great men and the generals and the rich
and the strong, and every one, slave and free hid in the caves and among the
rocks of the mountains, . . . " . . . RSV*

καὶ (continuative conjunction) 14.

οἱ (nom.pl.masc.of the article in agreement with βασιλεῖς) 9.

βασιλεῖς (nom.pl.masc.of βασιλεύς, subject of ἔκρυφαν and λέγουσιν) 31.

τῆς (gen.sing.fem.of the article in agreement with γῆς) 9.

γῆς (gen.sing.fem.of γῆ, description) 157.

καὶ (adjunctive conjunction) 14.

οἱ (nom.pl.masc.of the article in agreement with μεγιστᾶνες) 9.

μεγιστᾶνες (nom.pl.masc.of μεγιστάν, subject of ἔκρυφαν and λέγουσιν)
2257.

καὶ (adjunctive conjunction joining nouns) 14.

οἱ (nom.pl.masc.of the article in agreement with χιλίαρχοι) 9.

χιλίαρχοι (nom.pl.masc.of χιλίαρχος, subject of ἔκρυφαν and λέγουσιν)
2258.

καὶ (adjunctive conjunction joining nouns) 14.

οἱ (nom.pl.masc.of the article in agreement with πλούσιος) 9.

πλούσιοι (nom.pl.masc.of πλούσιος, subject of ἔκρυφαν and λέγουσιν) 1306.

καὶ (adjunctive conjunction joining nouns) 14.

οἱ (nom.pl.masc.of the article in agreement with ἰσχυροὶ) 9.

ἰσχυροὶ (nom.pl.masc.of ἰσχυρός, subject of ἔκρυφαν and λέγουσιν) 303.

καὶ (adjunctive conjunction joining nouns) 14.

πᾶς (nom.sing.masc.of πᾶς, in agreement with δοῦλος) 67.

δοῦλος (nom.sing.masc.of δοῦλος, subject of ἔκρυφαν and λέγουσιν) 725.

καὶ (adjunctive conjunction joining nouns) 14.

ἐλεύθερος (nom.sing.masc.of ἐλεύθερος, subject of ἔκρυφαν and λέγουσιν)
1245.

ἔκρυφαν (3d.per.pl.aor.act.ind.of κρύπτω, ingressive) 451.

ἑαυτοὺς (acc.pl.masc.of ἑαυτοῦ, direct object of ἔκρυφαν) 288.

εἰς (preposition with the accusative, static locative use) 140.

τὰ (acc.pl.neut.of the article in agreement with σπήλαια) 9.

σπήλαια (acc.pl.neut.of σπήλαιον, locative of place) 1358.

καὶ (adjunctive conjunction joining prepositional phrases) 14.

εἰς (preposition with the accusative, static locative use) 140.

τὰς (acc.pl.fem.of the article in agreement with πέτρας) 9.

πέτρας (acc.pl.fem.of πέτρα, locative of place) 695.

τῶν (gen.pl.neut.of the article in agreement with ὀρέων) 9.

ὀρέων (gen.pl.neut.of ὄρος, description) 357.

Translation - "And the kings of the earth and the great men and the army officials and the plutocrats and the mighty men and every slave and freeman began to hide themselves in the caves and among the boulders of the mountains, . . ."

Comment: Note the original static use of εἰς and the accusative in the sense of ἐν with the locative. μεγιστᾶνες may mean "nobles" as opposed to "kings" or "politicians" or any other type of person who has distinguished himself, legitimately or otherwise (!). The point is that all men of all classes, sociologically, politically, culturally or economically, who are alike in that they are unregenerate, are going to be terrified when they see the Lord whom they have ignored or rejected. The rocks and mountains are going to be falling as a result of the worldwide earthquake described in verses 12 and 14. At that same time, our Lord, with the help of His angels will be rapturing his elect family, the saints who are members of His Body, the Church (Mt.24:31; 1 Thess.4:13-18; 1 Cor.15:51-58; Psalm 91:11-12). Lest we dash our foot against the falling stones to which the unregenerate will be praying for protection against the Judge, He will send His angels to "bear us up in their hands." Note that angels are used in the rapture - Mt.24:31; Psalm 91:11-12; Mt.18:10; Heb.1:14. That is a part of their duty to us. Rev.19:11-21 will help us appreciate why the unsaved will be so frightened when He comes.

The view that some members of the Body of Christ die in infancy has been advanced in these pages. Indeed if far more than half of the human race were not in this category, population pressure would long since have wiped out the race on this planet. *Cf.* the discussion of this matter *supra*, pp.47-50. With the recent widespread practice of abortion much controversy has resulted with regard to the status of the miscarried or aborted fetus. There is no doubt that under the present Constitution (April, 1984) the unborn fetus is not a citizen of the United States nor of the state in which he was aborted, but there can be no doubt that he is a human being into whom God has breathed the miraculous gift of life and therefore he enjoys the same status as he does after he is born. The only difference between the unborn fetus and the child after he is born is the degree of development. This development began at the moment of conception and is carried on both before and after birth, through infancy and youth until the maturation process is complete and we have the onset of senility. To argue therefore that the fetus is not a human being and that abortion is not murder is to be forced to admit that the killing of the child, after he is born is not murder. At what point in the maturation process does the fertilized ovum become human, if not at conception? At three months when the nervous system is in place? At six months? At birth? When the child is three months old? A year? Thirty years? If he is a human being, at what point in his development does he become accountable to God? When he has reached the age of discretion. And when is that? No one can tell, since the answer is different in every case. Idiots and imbeciles cannot discern the difference between right and wrong, although it is probable that morons are accountable. They graduate from high school and are admitted to college! But if babies, including the unborn, who die in infancy are *safe* and thus members of the Body of Christ it follows that they will be included in the rapture and resurrection. Which raises an interesting question. At what stage in their development will they be resurrected from the grave and/or raptured from the earth? This is a thornier question than perhaps some may realize and it would be presumptuous to offer more than a guarded opinion. Presumably when Paul said, "It is sown a natural body; it is raised a spiritual body. There is a natural body, and there is a spiritual body," (1 Cor.15:44) where there is no doubt that the spiritual body which is raised is the same in identity as the natural body which was buried, the meaning is that the body will be resurrected/raptured at the stage of development which it had reached at death or at the time of the rapture. Without being more dogmatic about this, we can raise this question — If infants, born and/or unborn are raptured/resurrected as infants, who will care for them in the kingdom age until they grow up? If the Scripture justifies the student in asking the question, we may be sure that the Scripture will give the answer. Legitimate questions find legitimate answers. Jesus warned us not to despise "one of these little ones" and added that "in heaven their angels do always behold the face of my Father which is in heaven." (Mt.18:10). Thus the concept of the "guardian angel" has become famous in song, in story and in art. We have even a stronger statement in Heb.1:14 to the effect that one of the functions of the angels is that of caring for them "who shall be heirs of salvation." Thus every little baby in the Kingdom of the Heavens will have the care, not only of parents and friends, but of his own guardian angel, who, we may be sure is an expert in pediatrics.

This thought is not directly related to the text in verse 15, but it is suggested by the reference to the falling rocks and mountains, which will hold no fears for the saints, thanks to the upward sweep of angelic power as our angels obey the summons of the King in Mt.24:31.

There is something intensely democratic about the judgment upon the unsaved at the second coming. There will be no special privilege, such as is offered in human society now for kings, nobles, politicians, Pentagon establishmentarians, professional athletes, movie stars or Chamber of Commerce presidents. The rich, the mighty and the free will cry out to the rocks as loud as the slaves, for the merciful obliteration which, they imagine, will hide them from the face of the Judge. At the foot of the cross of Christ the ground is level. It is also level at the foot of the judgment throne.

We hear their futile cry in

Verse 16 - "And said to the mountains and rocks, Fall on us and hide us from the face of him that sitteth on the throne, and from the wrath of the Lamb."

καὶ λέγουσιν τοῖς ὄρεσιν καὶ ταῖς πέτραις, Πέσετε ἐφ' ἡμᾶς καί κρύφατε ἡμᾶς ἀπὸ προσώπου τοῦ καθημένου ἐπὶ τοῦ θρόνου καὶ ἀπὸ τῆς ὀργῆς τοῦ ἀρνίου,

"calling to the mountains and rocks, 'Fall on us and hide us from the face of him who is seated on the throne, and from the wrath of the Lamb; . . . ". . . RSV

καί (adjunctive conjunction joining verbs) 14.

λέγουσιν (3d.per.pl.pres.act.ind.of λέγω, iterative) 66.

τοῖς (dat.pl.neut.of the article in agreement with ὄρεσιν) 9.

ὄρεσιν (dat.pl.neut.of ὄρος, indirect object of λέγουσιν) 357.

καί (adjunctive conjunction joining nouns) 14.

πέτραις (dat.pl.fem.of πέτρα, indirect object of λέγουσιν) 695.

Πέσετε (2d.per.pl.aor.act.impv.of πίπτω, entreaty) 187.

ἐφ' (preposition with the accusative, extent) 47.

ἡμᾶς (acc.pl.masc.of ἐγώ, extent) 123.

καί (adjunctive conjunction joining verbs) 14.

κρύψατε (2d.per.pl.aor.act.impv.of κρύπτω, entreaty) 451.

ἡμᾶς (acc.pl.masc.of ἐγώ, direct object of κρύψατε) 123.

ἀπό (preposition with the ablative of separation) 70.

προσώπου (abl.sing.neut.of πρόσωπον, separation) 588.

τοῦ (gen.sing.masc.of the article in agreement with καθημένου) 9.

καθημένου (pres.mid.part.gen.sing.masc.of κάθημαι, possession) 377.

ἐπί (preposition with the genitive of place description) 47.

τοῦ (gen.sing.masc.of the article in agreement with θρόνου) 9.

θρόνου (gen.sing.masc.of θρόνος, place description) 579.

καί (adjunctive conjunction joining prepositional phrases) 14.

ἀπό (preposition with the ablative of separation) 70.

τῆς (abl.sing.fem.of the article in agreement with ὀργῆς) 9.

ὀργῆς (abl.sing.fem.of ὀργή, separation) 283.

τοῦ (gen.sing.neut.of the article in agreement with ἀρνίου) 9.

ἀρνίου (gen.sing.neut.of ἀρνίον, possession) 2923.

Translation - *"and they continue to say to the mountains and the rocks, 'Fall upon us and hide us from the face of the One sitting upon the throne and from the wrath of the Lamb.' "*

Comment: We expect unregenerates to be irrational at all times, especially when they are seized with terror. The request made to mountains and boulders in avalanche to hide them from the sight of God and Christ is indeed singular! As though they could hide under a mountain from the Creator of the mountain! (Psalm 139:7; Isa.2:19). Those who feared nothing a moment before are now repeating in frantic intensity their request to mountains and rocks, "Cover us. Maybe He won't find us." They who with tough minded sophistication have insisted that they believed nothing except upon the basis of empirical evidence, now have the evidence that God exists and that He is angry. Driven by terror to total irrationality they employ the only method of problem solving they have ever known - trial and error. Note that both God who still sits upon the throne and His Son, the Lamb, are angry.

Verse 17 - *"For the great day of his wrath is come; and who shall be able to stand?"*

ὅτι ἦλθεν ἡ ἡμέρα ἡ μεγάλη τῆς ὀργῆς αὐτῶν, καὶ τίς δύναται σταθῆναι;

"for the great day of their wrath has come, and who can stand before it?" ...
RSV

ὅτι (conjunction introducing a subordinate causal clause) 211.

ἦλθεν (3d.per.sing.aor.ind.of ἔρχομαι, culminative) 146.

ἡ (nom.sing.fem.of the article in agreement with ἡμέρα) 9.

ἡμέρα (nom.sing.fem.of ἡμέρα, subject of ἦλθεν) 135.

ἡ (nom.sing.fem.of the article in agreement with μεγάλη) 9.

μεγάλη (nom.sing.fem.of μέγας, in agreement with ἡμέρα) 184.

τῆς (gen.sing.fem.of the article in agreement with ὀργῆς) 9.

ὀργῆς (gen.sing.fem.of ὀργή, description) 283.

αὐτῶν (gen.pl.masc.of αὐτός, possession) 16.

καὶ (inferential conjunction) 14.

τίς (nom.sing.masc.of τίς, interrogative pronoun, subject of δύναται, rhetorical question) 281.

δύναται (3d.per.sing.pres.ind.of δύναμαι, customary) 289.

σταθῆναι (aor.pass.inf.of ἵστημι, complementary) 180.

Translation - *"because the great day of their wrath has come, so who is able to be left standing?"*

Comment: "Although the reading αὐτοῦ is supported by A P 046 almost all minuscules cop_{sa,bo} arm eth,*al*, it appears to be the easier reading, having been introduced to avoid the ambiguity of αὐτῶν (which is strongly supported by Sinaiticus C 1611 1854 2053 2344 it_{gig,61} vg syr_{ph,h},*al)* and to carry on the reference to τῆς ὀργῆς τοῦ ἀρνίου of the preceding verse." (Metzger, *A Textual Commentary on the Greek New Testament*, 741, 742). *Cf.* Mal.3:2; Nahum 1:6; Joel 2:11; Rev.19:11-21.

Thus the book is at last unsealed and Daniel (Dan.12:49) and John (Rev.5:4) are to have their hopes realized, both as a nationalistic Jew looking for a Messiah, and as a Christian looking for a Saviour and King. All of God's promises to Abraham and David are fulfilled in Christ. Man's miserable "day" is over (1 Cor.4:3) and the "day of the Lord" is ushered in. World rulers Babylon, Media-Persia, Greece, Rome, then, in the gap, the chaos of Feudalism, nationalism, whether ruled by monarchs, oligarchs or by representative democrats are the political systems in which man seeks freedom and the good life. After the gap we will have the White Horse Rider of false diplomacy, the Red Horse of war, the Black Horse of famine and the Antichrist for 42 months. Each will have "strut(ted) and fret(ted) his hour upon the stage" but, thank God, will be "heard no more" (Macbeth, V, 5,25) after the last cry of terror has died away.

Plato's Philosopher King, the Lord Jesus Christ, Who loves us too much to inflict injury, is too intelligent to make a mistake, and big enough to rule, will be forever King of Kings and Lord of Lords. (Plato, *The Republic*, V, 473D).

In Chapter VII God's clock is not running as two necessary bits of information are given us to fit into the moving picture at their proper places.

The 144,000 of Israel Sealed

(Revelation 7:1-8)

Revelation 7:1 - "And after these things I saw four angels standing on the four corners of the earth, holding the four winds of the earth that the wind should not blow upon the earth, nor on the sea, nor on any tree."

Μετα τοῦτο : εἶδον τέσσαρας ἀγγέλους ἑστῶτας ἐπὶ τὰς τέσσαρας γωνίας τῆς γῆς, κρατοῦντας τοὺς τέσσαρας ἀνέμους τῆς γῆς, ἵνα μὴ πνέῃ ἄνεμος ἐπὶ τῆς γῆς μήτε ἐπὶ τῆς θαλάσσης μήτε ἐπὶ πᾶν δένδρον.

"After this I saw four angels standing at the four corners of the earth, holding back the four winds of the earth, that no wind might blow on earth or sea or against any tree." . . . RSV

Μετὰ (preposition with the accusative, in a time expression) 50.

τοῦτο (acc.sing.neut.of οὗτος, time expression) 93.

εἶδον (1st.per.sing.aor.act.ind.of ὁράω, constative) 144.

τέσσαρας (acc.pl.masc.of τέσσαρες, in agreement with ἀγγέλους) 1508.

ἀγγέλους (acc.pl.masc.of ἄγγελος, direct object of εἶδον) 96.

ἑστῶτας (perf.act.part.acc.pl.masc.of ἵστημι, adjectival, predicate position, restrictive, in agreement with ἀγγέλους) 180.

ἐπὶ (preposition with the accusative, rest) 47.

τὰς (acc.pl.fem.of the article in agreement with γωνίας) 9.

τέσσαρας (acc.pl.fem.of τέσσαρες, in agreement with γνωίας) 1508.

γωνίας (acc.pl.fem.of γωνία, rest) 567.

τῆς (gen.sing.fem.of the article in agreement with γῆς) 9.

γῆς (gen.sing.fem.of γῆ, description) 157.

κρατοῦντας (pres.act.part.acc.pl.masc.of κρατέω, adjectival, predicate position, restrictive, in agreement with ἀγγέλους) 828.

τοὺς (acc.pl.masc.of the article in agreement with ἀνέμους) 9.

τέσσαρας (acc.pl.masc.of τέσσαρες, in agreement with ἀνέμους) 1508.

ἀνέμους (acc.pl.masc.of ἄνεμος, direct object of κρατοῦντας) 698.

τῆς (gen.sing.fem.of the article in agreement with γῆς) 9.

γῆς (gen.sing.fem.of γῆ, description) 157.

ἵνα (conjunction with the subjunctive, negative purpose) 114.

μὴ (negative conjunction with the subjunctive, negative purpose) 87.

πνέῃ (3d.per.sing.pres.act.subj.of πνέω, negative purpose) 697.

ἄνεμος (nom.sing.masc.of ἄνεμος, subject of πνέῃ) 698.

ἐπὶ (preposition with the genitive of place description) 47.

τῆς (gen.sing.fem.of the article in agreement with γῆς) 9.

γῆς (gen.sing.fem.of γῆ, place description) 157.

μήτε (disjunctive) 518.

ἐπὶ (preposition with the genitive of place description) 47.

τῆς (gen.sing.fem.of the article in agreement with θαλάσσης) 9.

θαλάσσης (gen.sing.fem.of θάλασσα, place description) 374.

μήτε (disjunctive) 518.

ἐπὶ (preposition with the accusative of extent) 47.

πᾶν (acc.sing.neut.of πᾶς, in agreement with δένδρον) 67.

δένδρον (acc.sing.neut.of δένδρον, extent) 294.

Translation - "After this I saw four angels who had been standing upon the four corners of the earth, holding the four winds of the earth so that no wind would blow upon the earth, nor upon the sea nor upon any tree."

Comment: Μετὰ τοῦτο refers to the order in which the material is shown to John and therefore the order in which he is telling it to us, and it does not indicate that the material of chapter seven comes chronologically after that of chapter six. The Lord could not show it all to John at once nor could John tell it all to us at once. Internal evidence alone allows us to know where in the seven year program of events, any given event occurs. This simple fact, which is so obvious, has been overlooked by some and thus the plan of the book is confused. We are back at the beginning of the week — at the same time point where we stood in chapters 4 and 5. The sounding of the trumpets, each in its turn will trigger the events described under each of them, just as the letters to the seven churches revealed religious conditions in Christendom and the removal of the seals revealed the political history of the week, and the deeds of Antichrist.

The first three verses indicate that the four angels with the four winds are the angels who will sound the first four trumpets with the judgments upon earth, trees and sea (Rev.8:7-13). These first four trumpets occupy the time during the first half of the week, as we have seen. But now, before that action begins, John tells us that these angels are ordered to wait until God has put His own seal of ownership upon 144,000 elect Jews, who are to have a place in His kingdom.

Verse 2 - "And I saw another angel ascending from the east, having the seal of the living God: and he cried with a loud voice to the four angels to whom it was given to hurt the earth and the sea."

καὶ εἶδον ἄλλον ἄγγελον ἀναβαίνοντα ἀπὸ ἀνατολῆς ἡλίου, ἔχοντα σφραγῖδα θεοῦ ζῶντος, καὶ ἔκραξεν φωνῇ μεγάλῃ τοῖς τέσσαρσιν ἀγγέλοις οἷς ἐδόθη αὐτοῖς ἀδικῆσαι τὴν γῆν καὶ τὴν θάλασσαν,

"Then I saw another angel ascend from the rising of the sun, with the seal of the living God, and he called with a loud voice to the four angels who had been given power to harm earth and sea, . . . " . . . RSV

καὶ (continuative conjunction) 14.

εἶδον (1st.per.sing.aor.act.ind.of ὁράω, constative) 144.

ἄλλον (acc.sing.masc.of ἄλλος, in agreement with ἄγγελον) 198.

ἄγγελον (acc.sing.masc.of ἄγγελος, direct object of εἶδον) 96.

ἀναβαίνοντα (pres.act.part.acc.sing.masc.of ἀναβαίνω, adjectival, predicate position, restrictive, in agreement with ἄγγελον) 323.

ἀπὸ (preposition with the ablative of separation) 70.

ἀνατολῆς (abl.sing.fem.of ἀνατολή, separation) 138.

ἡλίου (gen.sing.masc.of ἥλιος, description) 546.

ἔχοντα (pres.act.part.acc.sing.masc.of ἔχω, adjectival, predicate position, restrictive, in agreement with ἄγγελον) 82.

σφραγῖδα (acc.sing.fem.of σφραγίς, direct object of ἔχοντα) 3886.

θεοῦ (gen.sing.masc.of θεός, possession) 124.

ζῶντος (pres.act.part.gen.sing.masc.of ζάω, adjectival, predicate position, restrictive, in agreement with θεοῦ) 340.

καὶ (continuative conjunction) 14.

ἔκραξεν (3d.per.sing.aor.act.ind.of κράζω, ingressive) 765.

φωνῇ (instru.sing.fem.of φωνή, means) 222.

μεγάλη (instru.sing.fem.of μέγας, in agreement with φωνῇ) 184.

τοῖς (dat.pl.masc.of the article in agreement with ἀγγέλοις) 9.

τέσσαρσιν (dat.pl.masc.of τέσσαρες, in agreement with ἀγγέλοις) 1508.

ἀγγέλοις (dat.pl.masc.of ἄγγελος, indirect object of ἔκραξεν) 96.

οἷς (dat.pl.masc.of ὅς, relative pronoun, indirect object of ἐδόθη) 65.

ἐδόθη (3d.per.sing.aor.act.ind.of δίδωμι, culminative) 362.

αὐτοῖς (dat.pl.masc.of αὐτός, indirect object of ἐδόθη, pleonastic) 16.

ἀδικῆσαι (aor.act.inf.of ἀδικέω, complementary) 1327.

τὴν (acc.sing.fem.of the article in agreement with γῆν) 9.

γῆν (acc.sing.fem.of γῆ, direct object of ἀδικῆσαι) 157.

καὶ (adjunctive conjunction joining nouns) 14.

τὴν (acc.sing.fem.of the article in agreement with θάλασσαν) 9.

θαλασσαν (acc.sing.fem.of θάλασσα, direct object of ἀδικῆσαι) 374.

Translation - "And I saw another angel ascending from the sunrise with a seal of the living God, and he began to shout with a loud voice to the four angels to whom had been given power to hurt the earth and the sea."

Comment: ἀνατολῆς ἡλίου is an idiom meaning "the east," the area of the rising sun. We have another example of pleonasm in οἷς ἐδόθη αὐτοῖς ἀδικῆσαι. We do not need both the relative and the personal pronoun in the dative case. This occurs often in the Revelation — Rev.3:8; 7:2,9; 13:8; 20:8. Mt.3:12 is not a parallel instance, but see Mk.1:7; 7:25; 13:19. The solecism is not serious since the thought is never in doubt.

What the angel from the sunrise with the seal of the living God has to say to the first four trumpet angels follows in

Verse 3 - "Saying, Hurt not the earth, neither the sea, nor the trees, till we have sealed the servants of our God in their foreheads."

λέγων, Μὴ ἀδικήσητε τὴν γῆν μήτε τὴν θάλασσαν μήτε τὰ δένδρα ἄχρι σφραγίσωμεν τοὺς δούλους τοῦ θεοῦ ἡμῶν ἐπὶ τῶν μετώπων αὐτων.

"saying, 'Do not harm the earth or the sea or the trees, till we have sealed the servants of our God upon their foreheads.' " . . . RSV

λέγων (pres.act.part.nom.sing.masc.of λέγω, recitative) 66.
Μὴ (negative conjunction with the subjunctive in a prohibition) 87.
ἀδικήσητε (2d.per.pl.aor.act.subj.of ἀδικέω, prohibition) 1327.
τὴν (acc.sing.fem.of the article in agreement with γῆν) 9.
γῆν (acc.sing.fem.of γῆ, direct object of ἀδικήσητε) 157.
μήτε (disjunctive) 518.
τὴν (acc.sing.fem.of the article in agreement with θάλασσαν) 9.
θάλασσαν (acc.sing.fem.of θάλασσα, direct object of ἀδικήσητε) 374.
μήτε (disjunctive) 518.
τὰ (acc.pl.neut.of the article in agreement with δένδρα) 9.
δένδρα (acc.pl.neut.of δένδρον, direct object of ἀδικήσητε) 294.
ἄχρι (conjunction with the subjunctive in an indefinite temporal clause) 1517.
σφραγίσωμεν (1st.per.pl.aor.act.subj.of σφραγίζω, indefinite temporal clause) 1686.
τοὺς (acc.pl.masc.of the article in agreement with δούλους) 9.
δούλους (acc.pl.masc.of δοῦλος, direct object of σφραγίσωμεν) 725.
τοῦ (gen.sing.masc.of the article in agreement with θεοῦ) 9.
θεοῦ (gen.sing.masc.of θεός, relationship) 124.
ἡμῶν (gen.pl.masc.of ἐγώ, relationship) 123.
ἐπὶ (preposition with the genitive of place description) 47.
τῶν (gen.pl.neut.of the article in agreement with μετώπων) 9.

#5356 μετώπων (gen.pl.neut.of μέταπον, place description).

King James Version

forehead - Rev.7:3; 9:4; 13:16; 14:1,9; 17:5; 20:4; 22:4.

Revised Standard Version

forehead - Rev.7:3; 9:4; 13:16; 14:1,9; 17:5; 20:4; 22:4.

Meaning: A combination of μετά (#50) and ὤφ - "eye." Hence "between the eyes" — forehead - Rev.7:3; 9:4; 13:16; 14:1,9; 12:5; 20:4; 22:4.

αὐτῶν (gen.pl.masc.of αὐτός, possession) 16.

Translation - "saying, 'Do not hurt the earth nor the sea nor the trees until we have sealed the servants of our God upon their foreheads.' "

Comment: Μὴ with the subjunctive in a prohibition is common. *Cf.*#87. *Cf.*#1517 for ἄχρι and the subjunctive in an indefinite temporal clause. Thus we are told that at the beginning of the tribulation week, before the first seal is removed and the first trumpet is sounded, God is going to seal in their foreheads elect Jews. Once sealed, they will flee from Antichrist in the middle of the week and be secure for 1260 days (Rev.12:6). The fourth verse tells us how many, what tribes they represent and verses 5-8 specify the number and tribes.

Verse 4 - "And I heard the number of them which were sealed: and there were sealed an hundred and forty and four thousand of all the tribes of the children of Israel."

καὶ ἤκουσα τὸν ἀριθμὸν τῶν ἐσφραγισμένων, ἑκατὸν τεσσαράκοντα τέσσαρες χιλιάδες, ἐσφραγισμένοι ἐκ πάσης φυλῆς υἱῶν Ἰσραήλ.

"And I heard the number of the sealed, a hundred and forty-four thousand sealed, out of every tribe of the sons of Israel, . . ." . . . RSV

καὶ (continuative conjunction) 14.

ἤκουσα (1st.per.sing.aor.act.ind.of ἀκούω, constative) 148.

τὸν (acc.sing.masc.of the article in agreement with ἀριθμὸν) 9.

ἀριθμὸν (acc.sing.masc.of ἀριθμός, direct object of ἤκουσα) 2278.

τῶν (gen.pl.masc.of the article in agreement with ἐσφραγισμένων) 9.

ἐσφραγισμένων (perf.pass.part.gen.pl.masc.of σφραγίζω, substantival, description) 1686.

ἕκατον (numeral) 1035.

τεσσαράκοντα (numeral) 333.

τέσσαρες (numeral) 1508.

χιλιάδες (nom.pl.masc.of χιλιάς, nominative absolute) 2536.

ἐσφραγισμένοι (perf.pass.part.nom.pl.masc.of σφραγίζω, nominative absolute) 1686.

ἐκ (preposition with the partitive genitive) 19.

πάσης (gen.sing.fem.of πᾶς, in agreement with φυλῆς) 67.

φυλῆς (gen.sing.fem.of φυλή, partitive) 1313.

υἱῶν (gen.pl.masc.of υἱός, description) 5.

Ἰσραήλ (gen.sing.masc.of Ἰσραήλ, description) 165.

Translation - "And I heard the number of those sealed — one hundred, forty-four thousand, sealed of all the tribes of the sons of Israel."

Comment: Not all of the promises of God to Abraham, Isaac, Jacob and David are fulfilled in the Church. In a spiritual sense all who have Abraham's faith are the children of Abraham (Gal.3:9) and the genetic patriarch of the Jews has become the spiritual patriarch of all Gentiles and Jews who have believed as Abraham did before he was circumcised (Rom.4:4-14).

But God also promised Abraham that he and his seed would own and possess a definite piece of land forever. The promise was confirmed to Isaac and reconfirmed to Jacob and to David (2 Sam.7:10-17), who was also promised perpetuity for his Seed upon a throne. This seed of David who was to succeed him (not immediately) upon a permanent throne, was not Solomon, but Jesus, as Heb.1:5 makes clear when it quotes 2 Samuel 7:14 and applies it to Christ. The statement of the angel Gabriel to Mary (Luke 1:30-33) is in line with this, as the statement of the twenty-four elders in Rev.11:17. These promises for national

Israel are as yet unfulfilled.

Amillenialists, who teach that there is no future for Israel as a nation, and that all of God's covenant promises to the patriarchs are fulfilled in the Church, which is the Body of Christ, must show that the covenant promises to Abraham and his seed are conditioned upon their obedience. To be sure, many of the physical children of Abraham forfeited any claim to future blessing, but the disobedience of some who fell in the wilderness or who crucified their Messiah and rejected the story that He had risen again, does not relieve God of His obligation to remain true to His promise for those who have not been disobedient. In order for the argument that the Abrahamic covenant was conditional to be valid, it would be necessary to prove that neither Abraham or any of his posterity were faithful to God.

The history of the children of Abraham briefly runs like this: Jacob and his twelve sons and one daughter and their children went to Egypt numbering about seventy. In 200 years of Egyptian slavery they multiplied to about 3 1/2 million, who crossed the Red Sea, all of whom, twenty years old and older, except Joshua and Caleb fell in the wilderness in the next 38 years, while the next two generations were born to replace them.

The period of the Judges was hectic, while the kingly line from Judah ran its course until the tenth generation to David. *Cf.* comment on Mt.1:13. The Davidic covenant reconfirmed God's promise to the nation (2 Samuel 7), but Israel's population, greatest perhaps under Solomon at 25 million, declined while they served under Babylon, Media-Persia, Greece and Rome. In A.D. 70 they were scattered throughout the world until in 1948, when they again assumed national autonomy in Palestine - the first since the Babylonian captivity. Their number in 1939, approximately 16 million, was decimated by Hitler to about 12 million, one third of whom lived in New York city. Since 1948 their population has increased again, perhaps to 15 million. This is a long way from what God promised to Abraham.

The territory now held by Israel is much less than that promised by God to Abraham. The original grant reached the Indus River in the east, the Carpathians in the north and almost to the Nile on the southwest. Since 1948 many Jews have returned to the land in unbelief and are today chiefly atheistic or deistic, with scant faith, except among minority groups, in orthodox Judaism, with its expectation that Messiah must yet come. Yet God's promise is sure and in keeping with it He will select a nucleus who will become as numerous as "the sands of the sea." If 70 persons in Egyptian bondage can grow to 3 1/2 million in 200 years, what can 144,000 do in 1000 years of peace and prosperity under Messiah?

Thus before the first seal will be removed and the first trumpet sounded, God will mark out, in elective grace, His nation. These who are selected and sealed will "look upon Him whom they pierced" (Zech. 12:10; John 19:37) and ask how He received His wounds (Zech. 13:6). As all Gentile powers unite against the little band of Jews (Zech. 14:1-2) Messiah will return to rescue them (Zech. 14:3-4) and His kingdom will begin (Rev. 11:15), as He, King David's Greater Son, sits forever upon David's throne in keeping with His promise in 2 Samuel 7 and Luke 1:30-33. The second coming of Messiah, which, until then, they will look upon as

His first coming, will fulfill the Jeremiah 31:31-34 prophecy as the 144,000 Jews, sealed seven years before will be saved. Thus God, having called out from the Gentiles a people for His name (Acts 15:14-18; Amos 9:11,12) will now select from each of twelve tribes, 12,000 Jews. That these people are not Mormons or Jehovah's Witnesses or Eskimos or anyone else except Jews is perfectly clear since the text says that they are Jews. Genealogy records have long since been lost, with the result that no Jew today can know for certain from which tribe he comes, but God knows and He will select and seal them accordingly.

The Scriptures do not tell us much about the role of these people during the first half of the week. The following interesting questions can be raised: Will the Jewish temple be rebuilt as a part of the confirmation of the covenant by the White Horse Rider? (Dan.9:27a; Rev.6:1-2). If so will orthodox Jewish worship, complete with the Levitical sacrifices, be practised? Will the 144,000 Jews, sealed at the beginning of the week, participate in these services if indeed they are held? Since it seems clear that the 144,000 will not be saved until the end of the week, what view or views will they hold during the week? It is clear that they will flee for their lives from the Antichrist at mid-week, when the Beast will enter the Holy Places in the temple and demand worship as God (2 Thess.2:4). At that time his subterfuge will be exposed and the 144,000 will see him in his true light. The answers to these questions will be evident when the time comes. Meanwhile it is not necessary that we probe more deeply into them. This much is clear — at the beginning of the tribulation the nucleus of Messiah's administrative governmental unit will be selected and sealed. Three and one half years later they will flee into the wilderness to escape the Antichrist. Twelve hundred and sixty days after that they will be saved. We learn more about them in Revelation 14:1-7. They will be without sex experience. One wonders if one half of them will be girls, and, if so, do we not have 72,000 couples who will begin to raise their families under the ideal conditions of the kingdom and thus fulfill God's promise to Abraham that his seed would be as the sand of the sea and as the stars of the sky in number?

Verse 5 - "Of the tribe of Judah were sealed twelve thousand. Of the tribe of Reuben were sealed twelve thousand. Of the tribe of Gad were sealed twelve thousand."

ἐκ φυλῆς Ἰούδα δώδεκα χιλιάδες ἐσφραγισμένοι, ἐκ φυλῆς Ῥουβὴν δώδεκα χιλιάδες, ἐκ φυλῆς Γὰδ δώδεκα χιλιάδες,

"twelve thousand sealed out of the tribe of Judah, twelve thousand of the tribe of Reuben, twelve thousand of the tribe of Gad, . . . " . . . *RSV*

ἐκ (preposition with the partitive genitive) 19.
φυλῆς (gen.sing.fem.of φυλή, partitive) 1313.
Ἰούδα (gen.sing.masc.of Ἰούδα, description) 13.
δώδεκα (numeral) 820.
χιλιάδες (nom.pl.masc.of χιλιάς, in agreement with ἐσφραγισμένοι) 2536.
ἐσφραγισμένοι (perf.pass.part.nom.pl.masc.of σφραγίζω, substantival, nominative absolute) 1686.

ἐκ (preposition with the partitive genitive) 19.
φυλῆς (gen.sing.fem.of φυλή, partitive) 1313.

#5357 Ῥουβὴν (gen.sing.masc.of Ῥουβήν, description).

King James Version

Reuben - Rev.7:5.

Revised Standard Version

Reuben - Rev.7:5.

Meaning: Jacob's firstborn son of Leah - Rev.7:5.

δώδεκα (numeral) 820.
χιλιάδες (nom.pl.masc.of χιλιάς, in agreement with ἐσφραγισμένοι) 2536.
ἐκ (preposition with the partitive genitive) 19.
φυλῆς (gen.sing.fen..of φυλή, partitive) 1313.

#5358 Γάδ (gen.sing.masc.of Γάδ, description).

King James Version

Gad - Rev.7:5

Revised Standard Version

Gad - Rev.7:5.

Meaning: The 7th son of Jacob, by Zilpah - Rev.7:5.

δώδεκα (numeral) 820.
χιλιάδες (nom.pl.masc.of χιλιάς, in agreement with ἐσφραγισμένοι) 2536.

Translation - "Of the tribe of Judah were twelve thousand sealed; of the tribe of Reuben, twelve thousand; or the tribe of Gad, twelve thousand.

Comment: God in divine grace will not discriminate against the sons of Leah, Zilpah and Bilhah, Jacob's less favored wife and his two concubines, although He did discriminate against Dan and Ephraim on other grounds.

Verse 6 - "Of the tribe of Aser were sealed twelve thousand. Of the tribe of Nepthalim were sealed twelve thousand. Of the tribe of Manasses were sealed twelve thousand."

ἐκ φυλῆς Ἀσὴρ δώδεκα χιλιάδες, ἐκ φυλῆς Νεφθαλὶμ δώδεκα χιλιάδες, ἐκ φυλῆς Μανασσῆ δώδεκα χιλιάδες,

"twelve thousand of the tribe of Asher, twelve thousand of the tribe of Naphtali, twelve thousand of the tribe of Manasseh, . . . " . . . RSV

ἐκ (preposition with the partitive genitive) 19.

φυλῆς (gen.sing.fem.of φυλή, partitive) 1313.

'Ασὴρ (gen.sing.masc.of 'Ασήρ, description) 1908.

δώδεκα (numeral) 820.

χιλιάδες (nom.pl.masc.of χιλιάς, in agreement with ἐσφραγισμένοι) 2536.

ἐκ (preposition with the partitive genitive) 19.

φυλῆς (gen.sing.fem.of φυλή, partitive) 1313.

Νεφθαλὶμ (gen.sing.masc.of Νεφθαλίμ, description) 373.

δώδεκα (numeral) 820.

χιλιάδες (nom.pl.masc.of χιλιάς, in agreement with ἐσφραγισμένοι) 2536.

ἐκ (preposition with the partitive genitive) 19.

φυλῆς (gen.sing.fem.of φυλή, partitive) 1313.

Μανασσῆ (gen.sing.masc.of Μανασσή, description) 43.

δώδεκα (numeral) 820.

χιλιάδες (nom.pl.masc.of χιλιάς, in agreement with ἐσφραγισμένοι) 2536.

Translation - "Of the tribe of Asher twelve thousand; of the tribe of Nephthalim twelve thousand; of the tribe of Manassah twelve thousand."

Comment: Note that Dan, the son of Jacob and the head of one of the tribes, is omitted from the list, and that Manasses, one of the sons of Joseph and the grandson of Jacob is substituted. Why was Dan excluded and why was Manasses chosen in his stead and not Ephraim, the brother of Manasses? Jacob prophesied on his death bed that although Dan would judge his family and be the head of one of the tribes of Israel, in the early phase of their history, he was a "snake in the grass" who would cause his brothers to fall (Gen.49:16,17). *Cf.* also Judges 18:1-31; 1 Kings 12:29; 15:20 for the story of Dan's idolatry. As for Ephraim and his idolatry, *cf.* Hosea 4:17; 5:1-14:9 *et passim.* The stories of Dan, the son of Jacob and Ephraim, his grandson and their exclusion from participation in Messiah's kingdom serve to illustrate that the covenants which God made with Abraham, Isaac, Jacob and David are unconditional only for those who reject idolatry. The Danites and the tribesmen of Ephraim persisted in the worship of false gods, in violation of the first three commandments (Ex.20:1-7). Amillenialists would have us believe that all of the children of Abraham were as guilty as the Danites and that none of them repented. God, who cannot lie, is obligated to Abraham, to fulfill the conditions of the covenant, if only one of his children remained faithful. But there were many more than one. The exploits in faith of Abraham, Sara, Isaac, Jacob, Joseph, Moses' parents and their son, Rahab, who was not Jewish, Gideon, Barak, Samson, Jephthae, David, Samuel, the prophets and many more are listed in Hebrews 11:8-40. The membership in "Faith's Hall of Fame" has been deliberately left open in order to include in its total roster New Testament saints who exercised faith in the integrity of God. Will it include the amillenialists who find it difficult to believe that God can and will do literally what He has promised to the Patriarchs and who have therefore found it necessary to adopt the allegorical method of interpretation which Origin taught to the early church? After all, if God has wished to make one nation special among all of His redeemed nations, what is wrong with that? My own impression is that the Sovereign God will do that which seems right to Him without regard, either to the views of amillenialists or premillenialists.

Verse 7 - "Of the tribe of Simeon were sealed twelve thousand. Of the tribe of Levi were sealed twelve thousand. Of the tribe of Issachar were sealed twelve thousand."

ἐκ φυλῆς Συμεὼν δώδεκα χιλιάδες, ἐκ φυλῆς Λευὶ δώδεκα χιλιάδες, ἐκ φυλῆς Ἰσσαχὰρ δώδεκα χιλιάδες,

"twelve thousand of the tribe of Simeon, twelve thousand of the tribe of Levi, twelve thousand of the tribe of Issachar, . . . " . . . RSV

ἐκ (preposition with the partitive genitive) 19.
φυλῆς (gen.sing.fem.of φυλή, partitive) 1313.

#5359 Συμεὼν (gen.sing.masc.of Συμεών description).

King James Version

Simeon - Rev.7:7.

Revised Standard Version

Simeon - Rev.7:7.

Meaning: The second son of Jacob by Leah (Gen.29:33) - Rev.7:7.

δώδεκα (numeral) 820.
χιλιάδες (nom.pl.masc.of χιλιάς, in agreement with ἐσφραγισμένοι) 2536.
ἐκ (preposition with the partitive genitive) 19.
φυλῆς (gen.sing.fem.of φυλή, partitive) 1313.
Λευὶ (gen.sing.masc.of Λευί, description) 4981.
δώδεκα (numeral) 820.
χιλιάδες (nom.pl.masc.of χιλιάς, in agreement with ἐσφραγισμένοι) 2536.
ἐκ (preposition with the partitive genitive) 19.
φυλῆς (gen.sing.fem.of φυλή, partitive) 1313.

#5360 Ἰσσαχὰρ (gen.sing.masc.of Ἰσσαχάρ, description).

King James Version

Issachar - Rev.7:7.

Revised Standard Version

Issachar - Rev.7:7.

Meaning: The son of Jacob by Leah - (Gen.30:18) — Rev.7:7.
δώδεκα (numeral) 820.
χιλιάδες (nom.pl.masc.of χιλιάς, in agreement with ἐσφραγισμένοι) 2536.

Translation - "*Of the tribe of Simeon, twelve thousand; of the tribe of Levi twelve thousand; of the tribe of Issachar twelve thousand.*

Verse 8 - "*Of the tribe of Zebulon were sealed twelve thousand. Of the tribe of Joseph were sealed twelve thousand. Of the tribe of Benjamin were sealed twelve thousand.*"

ἐκ φυλῆς Ζαβουλὼν δώδεκα χιλιάδες, ἐκ φυλῆς Ἰωσὴφ δώδεκα χιλιάδες, ἐκ φυλῆς Βενιαμεὶν δώδεκα χιλιάδες ἐσφραγισμένοι.

"*twelve thousand of the tribe of Zebulunm, twelve thousand of the tribe of Joseph, twelve thousand were sealed out of the tribe of Benjamin.*" . . . RSV

ἐκ (preposition with the partitive genitive) 19.
φυλῆς (gen.sing.fem.of φυλή, partitive) 1313.
Ζαβουλὼν (gen.sing.masc.of Ζαβουλὼν, description) 372.
δώδεκα (numeral) 820.
χιλιάδες (nom.pl.masc.of χιλιάς, in agreement with ἐσφραγισμένοι) 2536.
ἐκ (preposition with the partitive genitive) 19.
φυλῆς (gen.sing.fem.of φυλή, partitive) 1313.
Ἰωσὴφ (gen.sing.masc.of Ἰωσήφ, description) 2000.
δώδεκα (numeral) 820.
χιλιάδες (nom.pl.masc.of χιλιάς, in agreement with ἐσφραγισμένοι) 2526.
ἐκ (preposition with the partitive genitive) 19.
φυλῆς (gen.sing.fem.of φυλή, partitive) 1313.
Βενιαμεὶν (gen.sing.masc.of Βενιαμείν, description) 3295.
δώδεκα (numeral) 820.
χιλιάδες (nom.pl.masc.of χιλιάς, in agreement with ἐσφραγισμένοι) 2536.
ἐσφραγισμένοι (perf.pass.part.nom.pl.masc.of σφραγίζω, substantival, nominative absolute) 1686.

Translation - "*Of the tribe of Zebulon twelve thousand; of the tribe of Joseph twelve thousand; of the tribe of Benjamin were sealed twelve thousand.*"

Comment: *Cf.* comment on Rev.7:6 (page 93) about the fact that Dan is excluded from this list and that Manasses, one of the sons of Joseph is chosen to replace Dan, while Ephraim is not. Thus 144,000 elect Jews, sealed as God's property and assured divine protection from the attack of the Antichrist, will accept our returning Lord as their Saviour and Messiah when He comes and they will form the nucleus of the nation which will become the mightiest of all nations during the kingdom age with King David's Greater Son, Jesus Christ as their King (2 Sam.7:1-17; Lk.1:30-33; Isa.11:1-9; Mich 4:1-8; 11-13).

Another group, made up of Gentiles, also appears in Rev.7:9-17. The purpose of this chapter is to show that while Christ is about to open the first seal and unleash heaven's warfare upon a world that rejects Him, He has also succeeded in saving out of that world two select groups: (1) Select Jews, the 144,000, will fulfill His promises to the Patriarchs in terms of nationalistic hopes for world leadership, and (2) select Gentiles to make up the family of God, His Body, His Bride and His Church. The Gentiles here described are all saved. Thus our Lord is not a failure in redemption, with no alternative policy but to destroy in holy wrath and frustration men because He cannot persuade them to love and accept Him. His purpose in grace will be accomplished. (Eph.1:4-5; Rom.11:1-2).

The Multitude from Every Nation

(Revelation 7:9-17)

Verse 9 - "After this I beheld, and lo, a great multitude, which no man could number of all nations, and kindreds, and people, and tongues, stood before the throne, and before the Lamb, clothed with white robes, and palms in their hands."

Μετὰ ταῦτα εἶδον, καὶ ἰδοὺ ὄχλος πολύς, ὃν ἀριθμῆσαι αὐτὸν οὐδεὶς ἐδύνατο, ἐκ παντὸς ἔθνους καὶ φυλῶν καὶ λαῶν καὶ γλωσσῶν, ἑστῶτες ἐνώπιον τοῦ θρόνου καὶ ἐνώπιον τοῦ ἀρνίου, περιβεβλημένους στολὰς λευκάς, καὶ φοίνικες ἐν ταῖς χερσὶν αὐτῶν,

"After this I looked, and behold, a great multitude which no man could number, from every nation, from all tribes and peoples and tongues, standing before the throne and before the Lamb, clothed in white robes, with palm branches in their hands, . . . " . . . RSV

Μετὰ (preposition with the accusative, in a time expression) 50.

ταῦτα (acc.pl.neut.of οὗτος, time expression) 93.

εἶδον (1st.per.sing.aor.act.ind.of ὁράω, constative) 144.

καὶ (continuative conjunction) 14.

ἰδοὺ (exclamation) 95.

ὄχλος (nom.sing.masc.of ὄχλος, nominative absolute) 418.

πολύς (nom.sing.masc.of πολύς, in agreement with ὄχλος) 228.

ὃν (acc.sing.masc.of ὅς, relative pronoun, direct object of ἀριθμῆσαι) 65.

ἀριθμῆσαι (aor.act.inf.of ἀριθμέω, complementary) 894.

αὐτὸν (acc.sing.masc.of αὐτός, direct object of ἀριθμῆσαι pleonasm) 16.

οὐδεὶς (nom.sing.masc.of οὐδείς, subject of ἐδύνατο) 446.

ἐδύνατο (3d.per.sing.imp.mid.ind.of δύναμαι, progressive description) 289.

ἐκ (preposition with the ablative of source) 19.

παντὸς (abl.sing.masc.of πᾶς, in agreement with ἔθνους) 67.

ἔθνους (abl.sing.masc.of ἔθνος, source) 376.

καὶ (adjunctive conjunction joining nouns) 14.

φυλῶν (abl.pl.fem.of φυλή, source) 1313.

καὶ (adjunctive conjunction joining nouns) 14.

λαῶν (abl.pl.masc.of λαός, source) 110.

καὶ (adjunctive conjunction joining nouns) 14.

γλωσσῶν (abl.pl.fem.of γλῶσσα, source) 1846.

ἑστῶτες (perf.part.nom.pl.masc.of ἵστημι, adjectival, predicate position, restrictive, in agreement with ὄχλος) 180.

ἐνώπιον (preposition with the genitive of place description) 1798.

τοῦ (gen.sing.masc.of the article in agreement with θρόνου) 9.

θρόνου (gen.sing.masc.of θρόνος, place description) 519.

καὶ (adjunctive conjunction joining prepositional phrases) 14.

ἐνώπιον (preposition with the genitive of place description) 1798.

τοῦ (gen.sing.neut.of the article in agreement with ἀρνίου) 9.

ἀρνίου (gen.sing.neut.of ἀρνίον, place description) 2923.

περιβεβλημένους (perf.pass.part.acc.pl.masc.of περιβάλλω, adjectival, predicate position, restrictive, in agreement with ὄχλους) 631.

στολὰς (acc.pl.fem.of στολή, after a transitive passive verb) 2552.

λευκάς (acc.pl.fem.of λευκός, in agreement with στολὰς) 522.

καὶ (continuative conjunction) 14.

φοίνικες (nom.pl.fem.of φοίνιξ, nominative absolute) 2673.

ἐν (preposition with the locative, place) 80.

ταῖς (loc.pl.fem.of the article in agreement with χερσὶν) 9.

χερσὶν (loc.pl.fem.of χείρ, place) 308.

αὐτῶν (gen.pl.masc.of αὐτός, possession) 16.

Translation - "And then, as I was watching, Look! A great crowd which no man was able to count, out of every nation and from all tribes and peoples and tongues, standing before the throne and before the Lamb, clothed in white robes and with palm branches in their hands."

Comment: Μετὰ ταῦτα does not mean "after" in the chronological order of events but in the order in which the material is being shown to John and in which he is relating it to us. After John saw and heard about the sealing of the 144,000 Jews, he was next shown the great Gentile multitude of saints described.

We are back at the beginning of the week as is clear from the fact that the 144,000 are to be sealed before the first trumpet judgments are to be announced.

Just as John has every creature singing Christ's praises in Rev.5:13,14, before the seals were loosed (*cf.* comment, *en loc.*) so here he sees the tribulation saints in heaven, before the trumpets sound to begin the week. There is no problem if we remember that chapter seven is giving us additional information to fit into the chronological scheme which moves the clock only during churches, seals, trumpets and vials.

There is some solecism in the verse. ἰδού introduces the nominative absolute in ὄχλος πολύς. αὐτόν is pleonastic. *Cf.* Rev.3:8; 7:2; 13:8; 20:8. The structure is heterogeneous with εἶδον and ἰδού followed by the nominative absolute and the nominative in ἑστῶτες, which should be accusative to agree with ὄχλους. Note the passive transitive verb περιβεβλημένους, followed by the accusative plural στολὰς λευκάς. "Some verbs which have *only one accusative* in the active or middle yet retain the accusative of the thing in the passive with the person in the nominative. This is a freedom not possessed by the Latin. The person in the active was generally in the dative. . . . περιβάλλομαι is frequently so employed, as περιβεβλημένος σινδόνα (Mk.14:51; cf. 16:5; and especially in Rev., as 7:9,13; 10:1; 11:3; 12:1; 17:4; 18:16; 19:13)." (Robertson, *Grammar*, 485).

Note also that there is no verb in the last clause, καὶ φοίνικες ἐν ταῖς χερσὶν αὐτῶν. Robertson suggests that when John saw or heard something which was exciting he forgot his Greek grammar! This may be the explanation. If, as we suggest, John wrote the Revelation thirty years before he wrote his gospel and epistles, it is likely that his command of Greek was not as great in A.D.65 as in A.D.95, since he spent the last 30 years of his life as pastor of the Ephesus church, in a sophisticated Greek speaking city.

Here we have a Gentile group of people as distinct from the Jewish group in verses 1-8. They come from the entire world. Dressed in white with palm branches in their hands, they stand before the throne of God and before the Lamb. John sees these people already in heaven although in verse 14 they are said to have come "out of the tribulation the great one" - ἐκ τῆς θλίφεως τῆς μεγάλης. Cf. comment on Rev.7:14. Does "the great tribulation" of verse 14 mean the last half of the week, during which time Antichrist will make war on the saints (Rev.13:5), or does it refer to tribulation generally, which has been the lot of Christians in all ages? The view that these saints are in heaven *before* the first seal and first trumpet judgments, is necessary for those who wish to establish a pretribulation rapture. It conflicts with what the martyred saints are told in Rev.6:11 and also with what the saints on earth are told in Rev.3:1-6. If we disregard the logical necessities of the pretribulation rapture position, there is no difficulty. That which must follow with logic from a false position need not be explained. There is nothing in Rev.7:9-17 to mandate the view that the appearance of the martyrs in heaven is contemporary with the sealing of the 144,000 Jews. It is more likely that Rev.7:9-17 is contemporary with Rev.6:9-11 which describes the fifth seal judgment with the souls of the martyrs under the altar, asking when their deaths were to be avenged.

The time cannot be after the second coming because the Bride of Christ will be with Him upon the earth, not in heaven.

Verse 10 - "And cried with a loud voice, saying, Salvation to our God which sitteth upon the throne, and unto the Lamb."

καὶ κράζουσιν φωνῇ μεγάλη λέγοντες, Ἡ σωτηρία τῷ θεῷ ἡμῶν τῷ καθημένῳ ἐπὶ τῷ θρόνῳ καὶ τῷ ἀρνίῳ.

"and crying with a loud voice, 'Salvation belongs to your God who sits upon the throne, and to the Lamb!'" . . . RSV

καὶ (continuative conjunction) 14.
κράζουσιν (3d.per.pl.pres.act.ind.of κράζω, iterative) 765.
φωνῇ (instru.sing.fem.of φωνή, means) 222.
μεγάλη (instru.sing.fem.of μέγας, in agreement with φωνῇ) 184.
λέγοντες (pres.act.part.nom.pl.masc.of λέγω, recitative) 66.
Ἡ (nom.sing.fem.of the article in agreement with σωτηρία) 9.
σωτηρία (nom.sing.fem.of σωτηρία, subject of ἔστω understood) 1852.
τῷ (dat.sing.masc.of the article in agreement with θεῷ) 9.
θεῷ (dat.sing.masc.of θεός, possession) 124.

ἡμῶν (gen.pl.masc.of ἐγώ, relationship) 123.
τῷ (dat.sing.masc.of the article in agreement with καθημένῳ) 9.
καθημένῳ (pres.mid.part.dat.sing.masc.of κάθημαι, substantival, apposition) 377.
ἐπὶ (preposition with the locative, place) 47.
τῷ (loc.sing.masc.of the article in agreement with θρόνῳ) 9.
θρόνῳ (loc.sing.masc.of θρόνος, place) 519.
καὶ (adjunctive conjunction joining nouns) 14.
τῷ (dat.sing.neut.of the article in agreement with ἀρνίῳ) 9.
ἀρνίῳ (dat.sing.masc.of ἀρνίον, possession) 2923.

Translation - "And with a loud voice they keep crying out, saying, 'Salvation to our God, the One who is sitting on the throne, and to the Lamb.' "

Comment: Since God is not in need of salvation, the dative in τῷ θεῷ ... καὶ τῷ ἀρνίῳ must refer to praise to God and to the Lamb for salvation. Note ἐπὶ τῷ θρόνῳ - "upon the throne," in Rev.7:10; 19:4; 21:5, ἐπὶ τὸν θρόνον - "upon the throne" in Rev.4:2,4 and ἐπὶ τοῦ θρόνου - "upon the throne" in Rev.4:9,10; 5:1,7,13; 6:16; 7:15 - the same preposition with the locative, accusative and genitive. The difference, if any, is the result of the case.

The angels join the saints in the song of praise to God and the Lamb in

Verse 11 - "And all the angels stood round about the throne, and about the elders and the four beasts, and fell before the throne on their faces, and worshipped God."

καὶ πάντες οἱ ἄγγελοι εἱστήκεισαν κύκλῳ τοῦ θρόνου καὶ τῶν πρεσβυτέρων καὶ τῶν τεσσάρων ζῴων, καὶ ἔπεσαν ἐνώπιον τοῦ θρόνου ἐπὶ τὰ πρόσωπα αὐτῶν καὶ προσεκύνησαν τῷ θεῷ.

"And all the angels stood round the throne and round the elders and the four living creatures, and they fell on their faces before the throne and worshipped God, . . . " . . . RSV

καὶ (continuative conjunction) 14.
πάντες (nom.pl.masc.of πᾶς, in agreement with ἄγγελοι) 67.
οἱ (nom.pl.masc.of the article in agreement with ἄγγελοι) 9.
ἄγγελοι (nom.pl.masc.of ἄγγελος, subject of εἱστήκεισαν, ἔπεσαν and προσεκύνησαν) 96.
εἱστήκεισαν (3d.per.pl.pluperfect act.ind.of ἵστημι, intensive) 180.
κύκλῳ (loc.sing.masc.of κύκλος, adverbial) 2183.
τοῦ (gen.sing.masc.of the article in agreement with θρόνου) 9.
θρόνου (gen.sing.masc.of θρόνος, place description) 519.
καὶ (adjunctive conjunction joining nouns) 14.
τῶν (gen.pl.masc.of the article in agreement with πρεσβυτέρων) 9.
πρεσβυτέρων (gen.pl.masc.of πρεσβύτερος, place description) 1141.
καὶ (adjunctive conjunction joining nouns) 14.
τῶν (gen.pl.neut.of the article in agreement with ζῴων) 9.

τεσσάρων (gen.pl.neut.of τέσσαρες, in agreement with ζώων) 1508.
ζώων (gen.pl.neut.of ζώον, place description) 5086.
καὶ (adjunctive conjunction joining verbs) 14.
ἔπεσαν (3d.per.pl.aor.act.ind.of πίπτω, constative) 187.
ἐνώπιον (presposition with the genitive of place description) 1798.
τοῦ (gen.sing.masc.of the article in agreement with θρόνου) 9.
θρόνου (gen.sing.masc.of θρόνος, place description) 519.
ἐπὶ (preposition with the accusative of extent) 47.
τὰ (acc.pl.neut.of the article in agreement with πρόσωπα) 9.
πρόσωπα (acc.pl.neut.of πρόσωπον, extent) 588.
αὐτῶν (gen.pl.masc.of αὐτός, possession) 16.
καὶ (adjunctive conjunction joining verbs) 14.
προσεκύνησαν (3d.per.pl.aor.act.ind.of προσκυνέω, ingressive) 147.
τῷ (dat.sing.masc.of the article in agreement with θεῷ) 9.
θεῷ (dat.sing.masc.of θεός, indirect object) 124.

Translation - *"And all of the angels had been standing in a circle around the throne and around the elders and the four living creatures, and they fell down before the throne on their faces and they began to worship God. . ."*

Comment: The angels join the song, which follows in

Verse 12 - *"Saying, Amen: Blessing, and glory, and wisdom, and thanksgiving, and honour, and power, and might, be unto our God for ever and ever. Amen."*

λέγοντες,᾽Αμήν. ἡ εὐλογία καὶ ἡ δόξα καὶ ἡ σοφία καὶ ἡ εὐχαριστία καὶ ἡ τιμὴ καὶ ἡ δύναμις καί ἡ ἰσχὺς τῷ θεῷ ἡμῶν εἰς τοὺς αἰῶνας τῶν αἰώνων. ἀμήν.

"saying, 'Amen! Blessing and glory and wisdom and thanksgiving and honor and power and might be to our God for ever and ever! Amen.' " . . . *RSV*

λέγοντες (pres.act.part.nom.pl.masc.of λέγω, recitative) 66.
᾽Αμήν (explicative) 466.
ἡ (nom.sing.fem.of the article in agreement with εὐλογία) 9.
εὐλογία, (nom.sing.fem.of εὐλογία, subject of ἔστω understood, and so with all nominative substantives in the verse) 4060.
καὶ (adjunctive conjunction joining nouns) 14.
ἡ (nom.sing.fem.of the article in agreement with δόξα) 9.
δόξα (nom.sing.fem.of δόξα) 361.
καὶ (adjunctive conjunction joining nouns) 14.
ἡ (nom.sing.fem.of the article in agreement with σοφία) 9.
σοφία (nom.sing.fem.of σοφία) 934.
καὶ (adjunctive conjunction joining nouns) 14.
ἡ (nom.sing.fem.of the article in agreement with εὐχαριστία) 9.
εὐχαριστία (nom.sing.fem.of εὐχαριστία) 3616.
καὶ (adjunctive conjunction joining nouns) 14.
ἡ (nom.sing.fem.of the article in agreement with τιμὴ) 9.
τιμὴ (nom.sing.fem.of τιμή) 1619.

καὶ (adjunctive conjunction joining nouns) 14.

ἡ (nom.sing.fem.of the article in agreement with δύναμις) 9.

δύναμις (nom.sing.fem.of δύναμις) 687.

καὶ (adjunctive conjunction joining nouns) 14.

ἡ (nom.sing.fem.of the article in agreement with ἰσχὺς) 9.

ἰσχὺς (nom.sing.fem.of ἰσχύς) 2419.

τῷ (dat.sing.masc.of the article in agreement with θεῷ) 9.

θεῷ (dat.sing.masc.of θεός, indirect object) 124.

ἡμῶν (gen.pl.masc.of ἐγώ, relationship) 123.

εἰς (preposition with the accusative, time extent) 140.

τοὺς (acc.pl.masc.of the article in agreement with αἰῶνας) 9.

αἰῶνας (acc.pl.masc.of αἰών, time extent) 1002.

τῶν (gen.pl.masc.of the article in agreement with αἰώνων) 9.

αἰώνων (gen.pl.masc.of αἰών, partitive) 1002.

ἀμήν (explicative) 466.

Translation - "saying, 'Amen. Blessing and glory and wisdom and thanksgiving and honor and power and strength be to our God into the ages of the ages. Amen.' "

Comment: *Cf.* Rev.5:12,13. When angels sing like that there is nothing for mortals to add.

Verse 13 - "And one of the elders answered, saying unto me. What are these which are arrayed in white robes? And whence come they?"

Καὶ ἀπεκρίθη εἷς ἐκ τῶν πρεσβυτέρων λέγων μοι, Οὗτοι οἱ περιβεβλημένοι τὰς στολὰς τὰς λευκὰς τίνες εἰσὶν καὶ πόθεν ἦλθον;

"Then one of the elders addressed me, saying, 'Who are these, clothed in white robes, and whence have they come?' " . . . RSV

Καὶ (continuative conjunction) 14.

ἀπεκρίθη (3d.per.sing.aor.mid.ind.of ἀποκρίνομαι, ingressive) 318.

εἷς (nom.sing.masc.of εἷς, subject of ἀπεκρίθη) 469.

ἐκ (preposition with the partitive genitive) 19.

τῶν (gen.pl.masc.of the article in agreement with πρεσβυτέρων) 9.

πρεσβυτέρων (gen.pl.masc.of πρεσβύτερος, partitive) 1141.

λέγων (pres.act.part.nom.sing.masc.of λέγω, adverbial, modal) 66.

μοι (dat.sing.masc.of ἐγώ, indirect object of λέγων) 123.

Οὗτοι (nom.pl.masc.of οὗτος, in agreement with περιβεβλημένοι) 93.

οἱ (nom.pl.masc.of the article in agreement with περιβεβλημένοι) 9.

περιβεβλημένοι (perf.pass.part.nom.pl.masc.of περιβάλλω, predicate nominative) 631.

τὰς (acc.pl.fem.of the article in agreement with στολὰς) 9.

στολὰς (acc.pl.fem.of στολάς, after a transitive passive verb) 2552.

τὰς (acc.pl.fem.of the article in agreement with λευκὰς) 9.

λευκὰς (acc.pl.fem.of λευκός, in agreement with στολὰς) 522.

τίνες (nom.pl.masc.of τίς, interrogative pronoun, subject of εἰσίν) 281.
εἰσὶν (3d.per.pl.pres.ind.of εἰμί, aoristic) 86.
καὶ (continuative conjunction) 14.
πόθεν (local adverb) 1061.
ἦλθον (3d.per.pl.aor.mid.ind.of ἔρχομαι, culminative) 146.

Translation - "And one of the elders, speaking to me, said, 'Who are these who are clothed in white robes, and from whence have they come?' "

Comment: We have here the idiom, so often seen in Matthew, in which ἀποκρίνομαι is joined with λέγω or εἶπον. *Cf.*Mt.3:15; 4:4; 8:8; 11:4,25, etc. Note that ἀποκρίνομαι (#318) is used most frequently in the Gospels and Acts (20 times in Acts; 1 each in Colossians and Revelation). The student may wish to survey the idiom as used by Matthew, Mark, Luke (Gospel and Acts), Paul and John. Research projects of this type, the data for which is provided in this work serve to help us draw conclusions about authorship, style, etc. A great many critical articles for the Journals can be prepared by those who are interested in this type of work.

The question of the elder, directed to John, is rhetorical. John doesn't know and he says so, and the elder provides the answer to his own question with a full explanation in verses 14-17.

Verse 14 - "And I said unto him, Sir, thou knowest. And he said to me, These are they which came out of great tribulation, and have washed their robes, and made them white in the blood of the Lamb."

καὶ εἴρηκα αὐτῷ, Κύριέ μου, σὺ οἶδας. καὶ εἶπέν μοι, Οὗτοί εἰσιν οἱ ἐρχόμενοι ἐκ τῆς θλίφεως τῆς μεγάλης, καὶ ἔπλυναν τὰς στολὰς αὐτῶν καὶ ἐλεύκαναν αὐτὰς ἐν τῷ αἵματι τοῦ ἀρνίου.

"I said to him, 'Sir, you know.' And he said to me, 'These are they who have come out of the great tribulation; they have washed their robes and made them white in the blood of the Lamb.' " ... RSV

καὶ (continuative conjunction) 14.
εἴρηκα (1st.per.sing.perf.ind. (Attic) of ῥέω, preterit) 116.
αὐτῷ (dat.sing.masc.of αὐτός, indirect object of εἴρηκα) 16.
Κύριέ (voc.sing.masc.of κύριος, address) 97.
μου (gen.sing.masc.of ἐγώ, relationship) 123.
σὺ (nom.sing.masc.of σύ, subject of οἶδας) 104.
οἶδας (2d.per.sing.perf.act.ind.of ὁράω, intensive) 144b.
καὶ (continuative conjunction) 14.
εἶπέν (3d.per.sing.aor.act.ind.of εἶπον, constative) 155.
μοι (dat.sing.masc.of ἐγώ, indirect object of εἶπεν) 123.
Οὗτοί (nom.pl.masc.of οὗτος, deictic, subject of εἰσιν) 93.
εἰσιν (3d.per.pl.pres.ind.of εἰμί, aoristic) 86.
οἱ (nom.pl.masc.of the article in agreement with ἐρχόμενοι) 9.
ἐρχόμενοι (pres.mid.part.nom.pl.masc.of ἔρχομαι, substantival, predicate nominative) 146.

ἐκ (preposition with the ablative, separation) 19.

τῆς (abl.sing.fem.of the article in agreement with θλίφεως) 9.

θλίφεως (abl.sing.fem.of θλίφις, separation) 1046.

τῆς (abl.sing.fem.of the article in agreement with μεγάλης) 9.

μεγάλης (abl.sing.fem.of μέγας, in agreement with θλίφεως) 184.

καὶ (continuative conjunction) 14.

ἔπλυναν (3d.per.pl.1st.aor.act.ind.of πλύνω, culminative) 2043.

τὰς (acc.pl.fem.of the article in agreement with στολὰς) 9.

στολὰς (acc.pl.fem.of στολή, direct object of ἔπλυναν) 2552.

αὐτῶν (gen.pl.masc.of αὐτός, possession) 16.

καὶ (adjunctive conjunction joining verbs) 14.

ἐλεύκαναν (3d.per.pl.1st.aor.act.ind.of λευκαίνω, culminative) 2322.

αὐτὰς (acc.pl.fem.of αὐτός, direct object of ἐλεύκαναν) 16.

ἐν (preposition with the instrumental, means) 80.

τῷ (instru.sing.neut.of the article in agreement with αἵματι) 9.

αἵματι (instru.sing.neut.of αἷμα, means) 1203.

τοῦ (gen.sing.neut.of the article in agreement with ἀρνίου) 9.

ἀρνίου (gen.sing.neut.of ἀρνίον, possession) 2923.

Translation - *"And I said to him, 'My Lord, you know.' And he said to me, 'These are the ones coming out of the great tribulation, and they have washed their robes and bleached them in the blood of the Lamb.' "*

Comment: The grammarians argue about whether or not the present perfect tense still retains its character or whether it blended into an "aoristic" punctiliar or preterit idea. What Robertson (*Grammar*, 896) calls the "Dramatic Historical Present Perfect" depicts a completed past action as present for the sake of vividness. Burton (*Moods and Tenses*, para.78, p.38) says, "of the Historical perfect in the sense of a Perfect which expresses a past completed action, the result of which the speaker conceives himself to be witnessing (as in the case of the Historical Present he conceives himself to be witnessing the action itself), there is no certain New Testament instance. Possible instances are Matt.13:46; Lk.9:36; 2 Cor.12:17; Jas.1:24 *cf*.Br.162. This idiom is perhaps rather rhetorical than strictly grammatic." John 1:15 (κέκραγεν) is a vivid historical tense. It is the tense used in oratory and dramatics. Robertson adds that Isocrates and Demosthenes thus use the present perfect more than Plato. Simcox (*Language of the New Testament*,104, as cited in *Ibid.*,899) says that εἴληφεν in Rev.5:7; 8:5 and εἴρηκα in Rev.7:14 are "mere preterits in sense" and accuses us who may see in them the dramatic historical present perfect of being "doctrinaire special pleaders." Robertson denies the charge and calls Rev.5:7; 8:5 "vivid dramatic colloquial historical perfect(s)" but adds (*Ibid.*, 902) that Rev.7:14 (where B reads εἶπον) and Rev.19:3 (εἴρηκαν) seems "more like a real preterit than any other examples in the N.T." He goes on to argue that John, in Revelation, would be more likely to confuse the tenses than in other writings due to the intense dramatic impact of the series of visions which he saw and was called upon to describe. The argument in indeed rhetorical, not exegetic, because the interpretation of the passage is the same whether e³rhka is preterit or historical present perfect. John did not know the answer to the elder's question of verse 13 and passed it back. The elder thus answers his own question. οὗτοι is deictic, as, pointing to the redeemed multitude, he says, "These are . . . "

Only here do we have τῆς θλίφεως τῆς μεγάλης. Cf. Mt.24:21, where θλῖφϑς νεγάκγ occurs. These two (Mt.24:21 and Rev.7:14) are the only two instances of the substantive and the adjective used together, hence nothing conclusive can be drawn about the emphatic attributive position in Rev.7:14. But see Mκ.ʔʔ; Mτ.ʔʔ ʂηερε θλῖφις is described in other terms to indicate its unusual intensity. That the last 3 1/2 years of the week, which is concurrent with the reign of Satan (Rev.12:12) and Antichrist (Rev.13:5) is meant seems clear. Thus we have a preview in Rev.7:14 of the martyred saints of the tribulation and the raptured saints who will join them in the air with the Lord (1 Thess.4:14-18). I say preview, because at the time when John sees this happy throng, the first seal (Rev.6:1) and the first trumpet judgments (Rev.7:1-3) have not yet been ordered by Christ. Chapters 4 and 5 and Chapter 7 are two different descriptions of the same heavenly scene at the same time. And they provide us with pertinent and indispensable information which we need to understand the action when God's clock is running. Just as John describes as present in Rev.5:13l, the universe praise offered to Christ at a time when the unsaved will actually be blaspheming Christ (*cf.* comment on Rev.5:13), so now we see in preview a throng of martyred and/or raptured Christians, as though they were already in heaven, at a time when they are still on the earth. If pretribulation rapturists call this special pleading we reply that a strict exegesis does not fit their scheme either, since there are said to have come out of the great tribulation (ἐκ τῆς θλίφεως τῆς μεγάλης), a period of time which in their view follows the rapture.

The difficulty is resolved for all of us when we remember that heaven's point of view is eternal and hence it need not conform to clocks, calendars and time sequences. As we have remarked before Chapter 7 assures us that before Christ begins Daniel's 70th week, He will have done His elective and redemptive work for all of His chosen ones, be they the physical seed of Abraham, to whom He is committed with a promise or to the spiritual seed of Abraham to whom He is also committed with a promise (Rom.4:9-13; 11:-2). We should not allow eschatalogical arguments to cloud this glorious fact.

The last two clauses speak of redemption and forgiveness for confessed and forsaken sins (1 Peter 1:19; 1 John 1:9). The results of redemption are eternal.

Verse 15 - "Therefore are they before the throne of God, and serve him day and night in his temple and he that sitteth on the throne shall dwell among them."

διὰ τοῦτό εἰσιν ἐνώπιον τοῦ θρόνου τοῦ θεοῦ, καὶ λατρεύουσιν αὐτῷ ἡμέρας καὶ νυκτὸς ἐν τῷ ναῷ αὐτοῦ, καὶ ὁ καθήμενος ἐπὶ τοῦ θρόνου σκηνώσει ἐπ' αὐτούς.

"Therefore are they before the throne of God, and seve him day and night within his temple; and he who sits upon the throne will shelter them with his presence." . . . RSV

διὰ (preposition with the accusative, causal, anaphoric) 118.

τοῦτο (acc.sing.neut.of οὗτος, causal, anaphoric) 93.

εἰσιν (3d.per.pl.pres.ind.of εἰμί, aoristic) 86.

ἐνώπιον (preposition with the genitive, place description) 1798.

τοῦ (gen.sing.masc.of the article in agreement with θρόνου) 9.

θρόνου (gen.sing.masc.of θρόνος, place description) 5 19.

τοῦ (gen.sing.masc.of the article in agreement with θεοῦ) 9.

θεοῦ (gen.sing.masc.of θεός, possession) 124.

καὶ (adjunctive conjunction joining verbs) 14.

λατρεύουσιν (3d.per.pl.pres.act.ind.of λατρεύω, progressive description) 366.

αὐτῷ (dat.sing.masc.of αὐτός, personal advantage) 16.

ἡμέρας (gen.sing.fem.of ἡμέρα, time description) 135.

καὶ (adjunctive conjunction joining nouns) 14.

νυκτὸς (gen.sing.fem.of νύξ, time description) 209.

ἐν (preposition with the locative of place) 80.

τῷ (loc.sing.masc.of the article in agreement with ναῷ) 9.

ναῷ (loc.sing.masc.of ναός, place) 1447.

αὐτοῦ (gen.sing.masc.of αὐτός, possession) 16.

καὶ (continuative conjunction) 14.

ὁ (nom.sing.masc.of the article in agreement with καθήμενος) 9.

καθήμενος (pres.mid.part.nom.sing.masc.of κάθημαι, substantival, subject of σκηνώσει) 377.

ἐπὶ (preposition with the genitive of place description) 47.

τοῦ (gen.sing.masc.of the article in agreement with θρόνου) 9.

θρόνου (gen.sing.masc.of θρόνος, place description) 519/

σκηνώσει (3d.per.sing.fut.act.ind.of σκηνόω, predictive) 1698.

ἐπ' (preposition with the accusative, extent) 47.

αὐτούς (acc.pl.masc.of αὐτός, extent) 16.

Translation - "*Therefore they are before the throne of God and they always serve him by day and night in His temple; and the One who sits upon the throne will shelter them.*"

Comment: διὰ τοῦτο is causal. The present tense in λατρεύουσιν indicates an eternal service. Note the genitive of description with ἡμέρας καὶ νυκτός, rather than the accusative of time extent. Their's is a day and night time service, while the temporal extension of the service is shown in the present tense in λατρεύουσιν. The figure means "in all times and circumstances" since there will be no night there (Rev.21:25). The service of these favored saints will be ἐν τῷ ναῷ αὐτοῦ). These are believer priests, redeemed (ἔπλυναν, verse 14) and kept clean (ἐλεύκαναν, verse 14). They are not only saved, (1 Peter 1:19) but they have also daily consecrated their lives in terms of 1 John 1:9. Unconfessed and unforsaken sin in the Christian life does not cost him his salvation, for that is a gift, but it can cost him this special privilege of service for God in the heavenly temple. Note #1698 - "under the tent." He who sits upon the throne will shelter them.

To say that the Body of Christ will be raptured before the great tribulation, a position in support of which there is not a scintilla of objective exegetical evidence, is to raise questions for which there are no answers. When one presupposes that a part of the Scriptural scenario is true, it is necessary to make all other parts conform to his presupposition or he must admit that the Scriptures are self-contradictory. And yet pretribulation rapture teachers insist, as they should, upon inerrancy. If all of the elect who came to Christ for salvation before the tribulation were caught up in a rapture/resurrection before the tribulation, where did the saints of Revelation 7:9-17 come from? It is clearly said that they came out of the great tribulation (verse 14). How did they get saved if the Holy Spirit and the Church, which is His temple (1 Cor.6:19) left the earth before they got saved? Who preached the gospel of Christ to them? Desperate for an answer to this question, some say that the gospel will be preached by the elect Jews of Revelation 7:1-8. Yet there is no Scripture to support this idea, while we learn that the 144,000 will flee into the wilderness to escape Antichrist and remain there during the last half of the tribulation period (Rev.12:14. Others, equally desperate for an answer resort to selective rapture and teach that backslidden saints will not be raptured, but that, after the rapture, they will return to the Lord, and that they are the saints in our passage. Others insist that only Landmark Baptists are in the Body of Christ who comprise His Bride and only they will be raptured to attend the marriage supper of the Lamb. If so then all other Christians, who, though not in the Church or the Body or Bride of Christ, are nevertheless in the "family" of God and who were so backslidden at the rapture that they were not caught up, are now given the most honored position in glory, as described in Rev.7:15-17.

All of this manipulation and eisegesis of Scripture is avoided when we reject pretribulation rapture, a doctrine which no one ever read in Scripture until the early 19th century. The reason why God did not reveal pretribulation rapture to the Church until the 19th century is that it is not taught in the New Testament. Charismatics who lay claim to a direct line of communication from the throne of God often say that the Holy Spirit has revealed to them that which is in direct contradiction to what the Holy Spirit revealed in the New Testament. Thus they accuse Him, the omniscient God, of contradicting Himself. Better that than to admit that they could be wrong!

If we reject selective rapture, the view that only a part of the Body of Christ will be taken and that the others will be left to endure the tribulation persecution, for whatever reason — either that they are backslidden or they have not been immersed in water, then we have a picture of millions of backsliders being suddenly snatched from saloons, dance halls, massage parlors, bawdy houses, football games, etc., despite the fact that Paul told the Thessalonian saints that that day would not overtake them as a thief, since they were the children of the light and of the day (1 Thess.5:4,5). Since there is no rapture at the beginning of the tribulation, Daniel 12:10 will apply and the Body of Christ will return to their first love, while unsaved church members will either be saved or take the mark of the Beast (Rev.13:16-18) and thus be lost (Rev.19:20). Thus end-time rapture will not interrupt any poker games of sex orgies. Events upon the earth, particularly in the last half of the week (Dan.9:27), will have separated the lost from the saints, all of the latter of whom will have washed their robes white. Of course Arminians have no problem with pretribualtion rapture since they believe that backsliders will have already forfeited their salvation.

Verses 14-17 describe special rewards for special saints who will have earned them. Heaven will be full of saints, formerly backslidden, and who died unrepentant and have only the rewards of wasted lives. There is no Christian who will not pay eternal opportunity costs for missed opportunities to serve God on earth while they were here. Witness the tithe dollar that should have gone into the offering plate at church but was spent for a theatre ticket or a dress or tie that we did not need. Those for whom Christ died will miss Hell, else He died in vain, but there is no saint who will not miss the blessings of reward because he ignored 1 John 1:9.

Note in Rev.13:6 that after the Beast has sent the saints home to live with God, he will curse them (Rev.21:3). If the Beast were not satanically insane, he would have kept the saints on earth!

It is delightful to listen to the scenarios of the pretribulation rapture teachers as they describe the scene on earth which according to them could happen at any moment. Cars in rush hour traffic suddenly bereft of Christian drivers and left unattended to crash and create massive traffic jams. This picture can be adorned with the profanity of the unsaved drivers who will be profanely wondering where the missing drivers went. Great commercial airliners will crash to earth and their unsaved passengers killed because the pilot was suddenly taken from the controls. A Christian golfer who has just stroked a long putt will never know whether the putt fell or not and whether or not he got his par. An unsaved waiter in a restaurant will wonder for seven years why the man ordered a sirloin steak and did not stay to eat it. With two men out in the last half of the ninth inning and the home team three runs behind, the unsaved fans will never know whether the Christian who hit the grand slam homer crossed the home plate since he disappeared as he rounded third!

Reject pretribulation rapture in favor of what the Scriptures teach and the ground for these thrilling stories that build television audiences and enhance financial receipts will disappear. No Christian will be driving his car when the Lord returns since he will not have been able to buy gasoline for it for the preceding three and one half years. We may be sure that those who have refused to worship the Beast and to receive his mark will not be flying airplanes, playing baseball, driving cars or ordering expensive steak dinners in high cost restaurants. Wherever they who have escaped martyrdom and survived to the last day are, they will be looking up and lifting up their heads for they will know that this is the day when their redemption has drawn nigh.

Verse 16 - "They shall hunger no more, neither thirst any more; neither shall the sun light on them, nor any heat."

οὐ πεινάσουσιν ἔτι οὐδὲ διψήσουσιν ἔτι, οὐδὲ μὴ πέσῃ ἐπ' αὐτοὺς ὁ ἥλιος οὐδὲ πᾶν καῦμα,

"They shall hunger no more, neither thirst any more; the sun shall not strike them, nor any scorching heat." . . . *RSV*

οὐ (negative conjunction with the indicative) 130.
πεινάσουσιν (3d.per.pl.fut.act.ind.of πεινάω, predictive) 335.
ἔτι (temporal adverb) 448.
οὐδὲ (disjunctive particle) 452.
διψήσουσιν (3d.per.pl.fut.act.ind.of διψάω, predictive) 427.
ἔτι (temporal adverb) 448.
οὐδὲ (disjunctive particle) 452.
μὴ (negative conjunction with the subjunctive, prohibition) 87.
πέσῃ (3d.per.sing.2d.aor.act.subj.of πίπτω, prohibition) 187.
ἐπ' (preposition with the accusative, extent) 47.
αὐτοὺς (acc.pl.masc.of αὐτός, extent) 16.
ὁ (nom.sing.masc.of the article in agreement with ἥλιος) 9.
ἥλιος (nom.sing.masc.of ἥλιος, subject of πέσῃ) 546.
οὐδὲ (disjunctive particle) 452.
πᾶν (nom.sing.neut.of πᾶς, in agreement with καῦμα) 67.

#5361 καῦμα (nom.sing.neut.of καῦμα, subject of πέσῃ).

King James Version

heat - Rev.7:16; 16:9.

Revised Standard Version

scorching heat - Rev.7:16.
heat - Rev.16:9.

Meaning: Cf. καίω (#453) plus μα the result suffic. Hence, the result of burning - heat. Revelation 7:16 with reference to the saints in heaven. In Rev.16:9, with reference to the sinners on earth who will suffer from it - Rev.16:9.

Translation - "*They will never again hunger nor thirst, neither shall the sun ever fall upon them or any scorching heat.*

Comment: Two interpretations of this passage are possible, both of which can be true. In the light of Mt.5:6, saints who hunger and thirst for righteousness will be filled when they get to heaven and will therefore never again hunger and thirst. Saints on the earth during the last half of the tribulation will be unable to buy food and drink and will therefore hunger and thirst in a physical sense. But not after they have been martyred and taken to heaven. Note that the last clause is an aorist tense prohibition with the subjunctive. The scorching rays of the sun will torment the unsaved (Rev.16:8,9), but not the saints (Psalm 91:3-10). *Cf.* John 4:13; 7:37-39.

Verse 17 - "For the Lamb which is in the midst of the throne shall feed them, and shall lead them unto living fountains of waters; and God shall wipe away all tears from their eyes."

ὅτι τὸ ἀρνίον τὸ ἀνὰ μέσον τοῦ θρόνου ποιμανεῖ αὐτούς, καὶ ὁδηγήσει αὐτοὺς ἐπὶ ζωῆς πηγὰς ὑδάτων, καὶ ἐξαλείφει ὁ θεὸς πᾶν δάκρυον ἐκ τῶν ὀφθαλμῶν αὐτῶν.

"For the Lamb in the midst of the throne will be their shepherd, and he will guide them to springs of living water; and God will wipe away every tear from their eyes." . . . RSV

ὅτι (conjunction introducing a subordinate causal clause) 211.

τὸ (nom.sing.neut.of the article in agreement with ἀρνίον) 9.

ἀρνίον (nom.sing.neut.of ἀρνίον, subject of ποιμανεῖ) 2923.

τὸ (nom.sing.neut.of the article in agreement with ἀρνίον) 9.

ἀνὰ (preposition with the accusative, rest, place description - "above") 1059.

μέσον (acc.sing.neut.of μέσος, place description) 873.

τοῦ (gen.sing.masc.of the article in agreement with θρόνου) 9.

θρόνου (gen.sing.masc.of θρόνος, place description) 519.

ποιμανεῖ (3d.per.sing.fut.act.ind.of ποιμαίνω, predictive) 164.

αὐτούς (acc.pl.masc.of αὐτός, direct object of ποιμανεῖ) 16.

καὶ (adjunctive conjunction joining verbs) 14.

ὁδηγήσει (3d.per.sing.fut.act.ind.of ὁδηγέω, predictive) 1156.

αὐτοὺς (acc.pl.masc.of αὐτός, direct object of ὁδηγήσει) 16.

ἐπὶ (preposition with the genitive of place description) 47.

ζωῆς (gen.sing.fem.of ζωή, description) 668.

πηγὰς (acc.pl.fem.of πηγή, extent) 2001.

ὑδάτων (gen.pl.neut.of ὕδωρ, description) 301.

καὶ (continuative conjunction) 14.

ἐξαλείφει (3d.per.sing.fut.act.ind.of ἐξαλείφω, predictive) 3017.

ὁ (nom.sing.masc.of the article in agreement with θεὸς) 9.

θεὸς (nom.sing.masc.of θεός, subject of ἐξαλείφει) 124.

πᾶν (acc.sing.neut.of πᾶς, in agreement with δάκρυον) 67.

δάκρυον (acc.sing.neut.of δάκρυον, direct object of ἐξαλείφει) 2166.

ἐκ (preposition with the ablative of separation) 19.

τῶν (abl.pl.masc.of the article in agreement with ὀφθαλμῶν) 9.

ὀφθαλμῶν (abl.pl.masc.of ὀφθαλμός, separation) 501.

αὐτῶν (gen.pl.masc.of αὐτός, possession) 16.

Translation - "*Because the Lamb above the center of the throne will shepherd them, and He will lead them unto fountains of the water of life, and God will wipe away every tear from their eyes.*"

Comment: *Cf.* Psalm 23:1-6; 1 Peter 2:25; John 10:11; Heb.13:20,21; 1 Peter 5:4; Isa.49:10; Jer.2:13; Isa.25:8. Not only the Gentile saints but Israel as well will have Him as a Shepherd (Mt.2:6). The water of life will be freely dispensed (Rev.21:6; John 4:10,14,14; 7:38; Rev.22:1,17). The tears will be forever gone (Rev.21:4).

The student should examine all passages where the words in this verse occur. It is indeed a rich passage. *Cf.*#1059 for ἀνὰ μέσον and the genitive case as we have it here.

The Seventh Seal and the Golden Censer

(Revelation 8:1-5)

Revelation 8:1 - *"And when he had opened the seventh seal, there was silence in heaven about the space of half an hour."*

Καὶ ὅταν ἤνοιξεν τὴν σφραγῖδα ἑβδόμην, ἐγένετο σιγὴ ἐν τῷ οὐρανῷ ὡς ἡμίωρον.

"When the Lamb opened the seventh seal, there was silence in heaven for about half an hour." . . . *RSV*

Καὶ (continuative conjunction) 14.
ὅταν (conjunction with the indicative in a definite temporal clause) 436.
ἤνοιξεν (3d.per.sing.aor.act.ind.of ἀνοίγω, constative, in a definite temporal clause) 188.
τὴν (acc.sing.fem.of the article in agreement with σφραγῖδα) 9.
σφραγῖδα (acc.sing.fem.of σφραγίς, direct object of ἤνοιξεν) 3886.
τὴν (acc.sing.fem.of the article in agreement with ἑβδόμην) 9.
ἑβδόμην (acc.sing.fem.of ἕβδομος, in agreement with σφραγῖδα) 2020.
ἐγένετο (3d.per.sing.aor.mid.ind.of γίνομαι, ingressive) 113.
σιγὴ (nom.sing.fem.of σιγή, subject of ἐγένετο) 3571.
ἐν (preposition with the locative of place) 80.
τῷ (loc.sing.masc.of the article in agreement with οὐρανῷ) 9.
οὐρανῷ (loc.sing.masc.of οὐρανός, place) 254.
ὡς (comparative particle) 128.

#5362 ἡμίωρον (temporal adverb).

King James Version

the space of half an hour - Rev.8:1.

Revised Standard Version

about half an hour - Rev.8:1.

Meaning: Cf. ἥμι - "half." Cf.#'s 2259, 2422 and ὥρα (#735). One half hour. Cf. the long list of words in Liddell & Scott, I, 771-774, with ἥμι as a prefix. Rev.8:1.

Translation - *"And when He opened the seventh seal, silence reigned in heaven for half an hour."*

Comment: ὅταν with the aorist indicative in a definite temporal clause is rare. Cf. Mk.11:19. The sixth seal brought the second coming of the Lord and the end of Daniel's 70th week. The silence in heaven is the silence after the storm.
      The letters to the seven churches (Rev.2-3) will apply in a special way to the

saints who live on earth during the seven years of tribulation, just as they have applied generally to the saints of all the ages. In Revelation 2-3 we travelled through the week in a study of the problems which the churches will have. In Revelation 6:1-17 we travelled across the seven years looking at the political picture. We now return to the beginning of the week to travel across the same period the third time. In Revelation 8:6-9:21; 11:15-19 we have a description of the cosmic judgments which will fall upon the earth during the same period, although none of these judgments will fall upon the elect saints. They have the promise of 1 Thess.5:9 and Psalm 91. Thus the sixth and seventh church letters, the sixth and seventh seals and the seventh trumpet come at the same time, *viz.* on the last day of the tribulation period, when our Lord returns to take His place on David's throne and to rapture and resurrect the members of His body. In Revelation 16 we shall travel this same route again, beginning at mid-week and come in Revelation 16:17-21 to the end of the week and the second coming. These passages which describe churches, seals, trumpets and vials are not to be arranged consecutively in a temporal sense, even though, of course they are arranged consecutively in the order of narration. The Lord could not show and tell it all to John at once, nor could he describe it all to us on the same page! I have dealt with this matter in some length in comment upon Revelation 6:1, *supra*, page 52*ff.*

Verse 2 - "And I saw the seven angels which stood before God: and to them were given seven trumpets."

καὶ εἶδον τοὺς ἑπτὰ ἀγγέλους οἳ ἐνώπιον τοῦ θεοῦ ἑστήκασιν, καὶ ἐδόθησαν αὐτοῖς ἑπτὰ σάλπιγγες.

"Then I saw the seven angels who stand before God, and seven trumpets were given to them." . . . RSV

καὶ (continuative conjunction) 14.
εἶδον (1st.per.sing.aor.act.ind.of ὁράω, constative) 144.
τοὺς (acc.pl.masc.of the article in agreement with ἀγγέλους) 9.
ἑπτὰ (numeral) 1024.
ἀγγέλους (acc.pl.masc.of ἄγγελος, direct object of εἶδον) 96.
οἳ (nom.pl.masc.of ὅς, relative pronoun, subject of ἑστήκασιν) 65.
ἐνώπιον (preposition with the genitive of place description) 1798.
τοῦ (gen.sing.masc.of the article in agreement with θεοῦ) 9.
θεοῦ (gen.sing.masc.of θεός, place description) 124.
ἑστήκασιν (3d.per.pl.perf.act.ind.of ἵστημι, dramatic) 180.
καὶ (continuative conjunction) 14.
ἐδόθησαν (3d.per.pl.aor.pass.ind.of δίδωμι, constative) 362.
αὐτοῖς (dat.pl.masc.of αὐτός, indirect object of ἐδόθησαν) 16.
ἑπτὰ (numeral) 1024.
σάλπιγγες (nom.pl.fem.of σάλπιγξ, subject of ἐδόθησαν) 1507.

Translation - "And I saw the seven angels who were standing before God, and seven trumpets were given to them."

Comment: Seven angels whom John says have been standing before God are introduced. Each is equipped with a trumpet. Thus the scene of Rev.5:1-14 is amplified. Added to the heavenly scene with its living creatures, elders, innumerable angels, the throne and its Occupant and the Lamb with Daniel's book, are seven angels with trumpets.

As the Lamb removes the seals, one at a time, the trumpets are sounded, one at a time. *Cf.*Rev.8:7,8,10,12; 9:1,13 and Rev.11:15. The accompanying trumpet judgments coincide in time with the messages to the seven churches and the events of the seals. The seventh trumpet (Rev.11:15-18), as we have seen (*supra*, p.64) and as we shall see again, fits in perfect correlation with the sixth seal (second coming of Christ) and the immediately following silent seventh seal (Rev.8:1) and also with the seventh vial judgment (Rev.16:17-21). All of these bring us to the end of Daniel's 70th week. God has sealed His Jewish remnant (Rev.7:1-8) and the Holy Spirit is in the last stages of His missionary enterprise to complete the Body of Christ, which is composed of the Gentile elect (Acts 15:14) and those Jews who also have been and will be called into the Church. The mystery, defined in Ephesians 3:3-7, will be completed in the days of the voice of the seventh angel (Rev.10:7).

Everything correlates as we have every right to expect it to do.

Verse 3 - "And another angel came and stood at the altar, having a golden censer; and there was given unto him much incense, that he should offer it with the prayers of all saints upon the golden altar which was before the throne."

Καὶ ἄλλος ἄγγελος ἦλθεν καὶ ἐστάθη ἐπὶ τοῦ θυσιαστηρίου ἔχων λιβανωτὸν χρυσοῦν, καὶ ἐδόθη αὐτῷ θυμιάματα πολλὰ ἵνα δώσει ταῖς προσευχαῖς τῶν ἁγίων πάντων ἐπὶ τὸ θυσιαστήριον τὸ χρυσοῦν τὸ ἐνώπιον τοῦ θρόνου.

"*And another angel came and stood at the altar with a golden censer; and he was given much incense to mingle with the prayers of all the saints upon the golden altar before the throne; . . .* " . . . RSV

Καὶ (continuative conjunction) 14.

ἄλλος (nom.sing.masc.of ἄλλος, in agreement with ἄγγελος) 198.

ἄγγελος (nom.sing.masc.of ἄγγελος, subject of ἦλθεν and ἐστάθη) 96.

ἦλθεν (3d.per.sing.aor.mid.ind.of ἔρχομαι, constative) 146.

καὶ (adjunctive conjunction joining verbs) 14.

ἐστάθη (3d.per.sing.aor.pass.ind.of ἵστημι, ingressive) 180.

ἐπὶ (preposition with the genitive of place description) 47.

τοῦ (gen.sing.neut.of the article in agreement with θυσιαστηρίου) 9.

θυσιαστηρίου (gen.sing.neut.of θυσιαστήριον, place description) 484.

ἔχων (pres.act.part.nom.sing.masc.of ἔχω, adverbial, circumstantial) 82.

#5363 λιβανωτὸν (acc.sing.masc.of λιβανωτός, direct object of ἔχων).

King James Version

censer - Rev.8:3,5.

Revised Standard Version

censer - Rev.8:3,5.

Meaning: Cf. λίβανος (#193). In profane Greek, a frankincense; a gum deriving from ἐκ τοῦ λιβάνου. In the New Testament, a censer (synonymous with ἡ λιβανωτρίς, in profane authors). Rev.8:3,5.

χρυσοῦν (acc.sing.masc.of χρύσεος, in agreement with λιβανωτόν) 4828.
καὶ (continuative conjunction) 14.
ἐδόθη (3d.per.sing.aor.pass.ind.of δίδωμι, constative) 362.
αὐτῷ (dat.sing.masc.of αὐτός, indirect object of ἐδόθη) 16.
θυμιάματα (nom.pl.neut.of θυμίαμα, subject of ἐδόθη) 1793.
πολλὰ (nom.pl.neut.of πολύς, in agreement with θυμιάματα) 228.
ἵνα (conjunction with the future indicative, purpose) 114.
δώσει (3d.per.sing.fut.act.ind.of δίδωμι, purpose) 362.
ταῖς (instru.pl.fem.of the article in agreement with προσευχαῖς) 9.
προσευχαῖς (instru.pl.fem.of προσευχή, association) 1238.
τῶν (gen.pl.masc.of the article in agreement with ἁγίων) 9.
ἁγίων (gen.pl.masc.of ἅγιος, possession) 84.
πάντων (gen.pl.masc.of πᾶς, in agreement with ἁγίων) 67.
ἐπὶ (preposition with the accusative, extent) 47.
τὸ (acc.sing.neut.of the article in agreement with θυσιαστήριον) 9.
θυσιαστήριον (acc.sing.neut.of θυσιαστήριον, extent) 484.
τὸ (acc.sing.neut.of the article in agreement with θυσιαστήριον) 9.
χρυσοῦν (acc.sing.neut.of χρύσεος, in agreement with θυσιαστήριον) 4828.
τὸ (acc.sing.neut.of the article in agreement with θυσιαστήριον) 9.
ἐνώπιον (preposition with the genitive of place description) 1798.
τοῦ (gen.sing.masc.of the article in agreement with θρόνου) 9.
θρόνου (gen.sing.masc.of θρόνος, place description) 519.

Translation - *"And another angel came and stood before the altar having a golden censer; and much incense was given to him that he might offer it with the prayers of all the saints upon the golden altar before the throne."*

Comment: Note ἵνα with the future indicative in δώσει in a purpose clause. Rare but not unknown. *Cf.* Revelation 6:4. Note the article τὸ in the emphatic attributive position, and also added to the prepositional adjunct - ἐπὶ τὸ θυσιαστήριον τὸ χρυσοῦν τὸ ἐνώπιον τοῦ θρόνου.
Here, in Rev.8:3-4, we have the prayers of the saints on file in heaven, for the Judge's attention before He executes judgment, just as we saw it in Rev.5:8 — a further evidence that Revelation 4-5 and Revelation 7:1-8:5 are two descriptions of the same scene at the same time — the one in relation to the seal judgments and the other in relation to the trumpet judgments, both of which are about to take place.

Verse 4 - "And the smoke of the incense which came with the prayers of the saints, ascended up before God out of the angel's hand."

καὶ ἀνέβη ὁ καπνὸς τῶν θυμιαμάτων ταῖς προσευχαῖς τῶν ἁγίων ἐκ χειρὸς τοῦ ἀγγέλου ἐνώπιον τοῦ θεοῦ.

"and the smoke of the incense rose with the prayers of the saints from the hand of the angel before God." . . . RSV

καὶ (continuative conjunction) 14.

ἀνέβη (3d.per.sing.aor.act.ind.of ἀναβαίνω, ingressive) 323.

ὁ (nom.sing.masc.of the article in agreement with καπνὸς) 9.

καπνὸς (nom.sing.masc.of καπνός, subject of ἀνέβη) 2986.

τῶν (gen.pl.neut.of the article in agreement with θυμιαμάτων) 9.

θυμιαμάτων (gen.pl.neut.of θυμίαμα, description) 1793.

ταῖς (instru.pl.fem.of the article in agreement with προσευχαῖς) 9.

προσευχαῖς (instru.pl.fem.of προσευχή, association) 1238.

τῶν (gen.pl.masc.of the article in agreement with ἁγίων) 9.

ἁγίων (gen.pl.masc.of ἅγιος, possession) 84.

ἐκ (preposition with the ablative of separation) 19.

χειρὸς (abl.sing.fem.of χείρ, separation) 308.

τοῦ (gen.sing.masc.of the article in agreement with ἀγγέλου) 9.

ἀγγέλου (gen.sing.masc.of ἄγγελος, possession) 96.

ἐνώπιον (preposition with the genitive of place description) 1798.

τοῦ (gen.sing.masc.of the article in agreement with θεοῦ) 9.

θεοῦ (gen.sing.masc.of θεός, place description) 124.

Translation - "And the smoke of the incense began to ascend with the prayers of the saints before God out of the hand of the angel."

Comment: Before judgment falls, the prayers of Christians, some of which have been offered in behalf of those upon earth who have not yet been saved, must be taken into account. God in judgment is not unmindful of the prayers of the saints. That these prayers will still be answered, even after the tribulation has run its course is clear from Revelation 10:7, for not until the seventh angel prepares to sound his trumpet will the Body of Christ be complete (Eph.3:1-8).

There is no further reference to the prayers of the Christian before heaven's throne before the vial judgments are poured out. If they existed we would expect to find them in Chapters 14 and 15 or the opening verses of Chapter 16.

Verse 5 - "And the angel took the censer and filled it with fire of the altar, and cast it into the earth: and there were voices, and thunderings, and lightnings, and an earthquake."

καὶ εἴληφεν ὁ ἄγγελος τὸν λιβανωτόν, καὶ ἐγέμισεν αὐτὸν ἐκ τοῦ πυρὸς τοῦ θυσιαστηρίου καὶ ἔβαλεν εἰς τὴν γῆν, καὶ ἐγένοντο βρονταὶ καὶ φωναὶ καὶ ἀστραπαὶ καὶ σεισμός.

"Then the angel took the censer and filled it with fire from the altar and threw it on the earth; and there were peals of thunder, loud noises, flashes of lightning, and an earthquake." . . . RSV

καὶ (continuative conjunction) 14.

εἴληφεν (3d.per.sing.perf.act.ind.of λαμβάνω) 533.

ὁ (nom.sing.masc.of the article in agreement with ἄγγελος) 9.

ἄγγελος (nom.sing.masc.of ἄγγελος, subject of εἴληφεν, ἐγέμισεν and ἔβαλεν) 96.

τὸν (acc.sing.masc.of the article in agreement with λιβανωτόν) 9.

λιβανωτόν (acc.sing.masc.of λιβανωτός, direct object of εἴληφεν) 5363.

καὶ (adjunctive conjunction joining verbs) 14.

ἐγέμισεν (3d.per.sing.aor.act.ind.of γεμίζω, constative) 1972.

αὐτὸν (acc.sing.masc.of αὐτός, direct object of ἐγέμισεν) 16.

ἐκ (preposition with the ablative, source) 19.

τοῦ (abl.sing.neut.of the article in agreement with πυρὸς) 9.

πυρὸς (abl.sing.neut.of πῦρ, source) 298.

τοῦ (abl.sing.neut.of the article in agreement with θυσιαστηρίου) 9.

θυσιαστηρίου (abl.sing.neut.of θυσιαστήριον, source) 484.

καὶ (adjunctive conjunction joining verbs) 14.

ἔβαλεν (3d.per.sing.aor.act.ind.of βάλλω, constative) 299.

εἰς (preposition with the accusative of extent) 140.

τὴν (acc.sing.fem.of the article in agreement with γῆν) 9.

γῆν (acc.sing.fem.of γῆ, extent) 157.

καὶ (continuative conjunction) 14.

ἐγένοντο (3d.per.pl.aor.ind.of γίνομαι, ingressive) 113.

βρονταὶ (nom.pl.fem.of βροντή, subject of ἐγένοντο) 2117.

καὶ (adjunctive conjunction joining nouns) 14.

φωναὶ (nom.pl.fem.of φωνή, subject of ἐγένοντο) 222.

καὶ (adjunctive conjunction joining nouns) 14.

ἀστραπαὶ (nom.pl.fem.of ἀστραπή, subject of ἐγένοντο) 1502.

καὶ (adjunctive conjunction joining nouns) 14.

σεισμός (nom.sing.masc.of σεισμός, subject of ἐγένοντο) 751.

Translation - "And the angel took the censer and filled it with the fire from the altar and cast it into the earth. And thunders began to roll; voices began to speak; lightnings began to flash and the earth began to quake."

Comment: In εἴληφεν we have another debateable perfect. Is it a dramatic historical present perfect or an aoristic preterite? The verse recalls Revelation 4:5.

With the angel's action of casting fire into the earth, the seven trumpet angels prepare to sound. We are at the beginning of the seven year tribulation period again. Conditions described in the Ephesian church letter apply; the White Horse Rider is about to appear and fulfill Daniel 9:27a; the judgments of the first trumpet are about to fall.

The Trumpets

(Revelation 8:6-9:21)

Verse 6 - "And the seven angels which had the seven trumpets prepared themselves to sound."

Καὶ οἱ ἑπτὰ ἄγγελοι οἱ ἔχοντες τὰς ἑπτὰ σάλπιγγας ἡτοίμασαν αὐτοὺς ἵνα σαλπίσωσιν.

"Now the seven angels who had the seven trumpets made ready to blow them."
. . . RSV

Καὶ (continuative conjunction) 14.

οἱ (nom.pl.masc.of the article in agreement with ἄγγελοι) 9.

ἑπτὰ (numeral) 1024.

ἄγγελοι (nom.pl.masc.of ἄγγελος, subject of ἡτοίμασαν) 96.

οἱ (nom.pl.masc.of the article in agreement with ἔχοντες) 9.

ἔχοντες (pres.act.part.nom.pl.masc.of ἔχω, substantival, in apposition) 82.

τὰς (acc.pl.fem.of the article in agreement with σάλπιγγας) 9.

ἑπτὰ (numeral) 1024.

σάλπιγγας (acc.pl.fem.of σάλπιγξ, direct object of ἔχοντες) 1507.

ἡτοίμασαν (3d.per.pl.aor.act.ind.of ἑτοιμάζω, constative) 257.

αὐτοὺς (acc.pl.masc.of ἑαυτοῦ, contr.of reciproal pronoun, direct object of ἡτοίμασαν) 288.

ἵνα (conjunction with the subjunctive, purpose) 114.

σαλπίσωσιν (3d.per.pl.aor.act.subj.of σαλπίζω, purpose) 559.

Translation - "And the seven angels who had the seven trumpets made ready to blow them."

Comment: αὐτοὺς is a contraction of ἑαυτου, the reciprocal. The angels prepared themselves, not the trumpets. We do not know how much time will elapse between the first and second seals and the first and second trumpets. The false peace of the first seal will be short as the second seal takes peace from the earth. The trumpet judgments, as a whole extend across the seven years. At this point the last trumpet (1 Cor.15:51; Rev.11:15) is seven years in the future. Only the first angel will blow his trumpet at this time (verse 7). As we have seen as we studied the seals, the trumpets and seals coincide chronologically. Thus the time of the first seal (Rev.6:1-2) is also the time of the first trumpet. The evidence for this is not textual but correlative. As false peace and a false promise to Israel (Rev.6:1-2; Dan.9:27a) are offered, hail, fire and blood will fall upon the earth, burning one third of the trees and all of the cover crops.

Students often ask how we can tell when the week begins and God's clock starts the last seven year countdown, if the covenant with Israel is a well kept diplomatic secret. It is difficult to believe that the media would fail to know about and report such an outstanding development in Middle East diplomacy, particularly in view of the long standing animosity between the sons of Ishmael and the sons of Isaac. But even if such an agreement were secret (how can one hide a rider on a white horse?), no one is going to keep secret the hail, fire and blood that will fall upon the earth at the same time and destroy one third of the trees and all of the crops.

When the first angel blows his trumpet the countdown will resume and there will be no more programmed holds. It will be T minus 2520 days and counting.

Verse 7 - "The first angel sounded, and there followed hail and fire mingled with blood, and they were cast upon the earth: and the third part of the trees were burnt up, and all green grass was burnt up."

Καὶ ὁ πρῶτος ἐσάλπισεν, καὶ ἐγένετο χάλαζα καὶ πῦρ μεμιγμένα ἐν αἵματι, καὶ ἐβλήθη εἰς τὴν γῆν, καὶ τὸ τρίτον τῆς γῆς κατεκάη, καὶ τὸ τρίτον τῶν δένδρων κατεκάη, καὶ πᾶς χόρτος χλωρὸς κατεκάη.

"The first angel blew his trumpet, and there followed hail and fire, mingled with blood, which fell on the earth, and a third of the earth was burnt up, and a third of the trees were burnt up, and all green grass was burnt up." . . . RSV

Καὶ (continuative conjunction) 14.

ὁ (nom.sing.masc.of the article in agreement with πρῶτος) 9.

πρῶτος (nom.sing.masc.of πρῶτος, subject of ἐσάλπισεν) 487.

ἐσάλπισεν (3d.per.sing.aor.act.ind.of σαλπίζω, constative) 559.

καὶ (continuative conjunction) 14.

ἐγένετο (3d.per.sing.aor.mid.ind.of γίνομαι, ingressive) 113.

#5364 χάλαζα (nom.sing.fem.of χάλαζα, subject of ἐγένετο).

   King James Version

hail - Rev.8:7; 11:19; 16:21,21.

   Revised Standard Version

hail - Rev.8:7; 11:19; 16:21b.
hail stones - Rev.16:21a.

Meaning: Cf. χαλάω (#2045), though some authorities doubt that there is a connection. Moulton & Milligan (p.682) cite it in Epicurus, *Epist.* II P 106,107 (ed. Bailey). Hail - Rev.8:7; 11:19; 16:21,21.

καὶ (adjunctive conjunction joining nouns) 14.

πῦρ (nom.sing.neut.of πῦρ, subject of ἐγένετο) 298.

μεμιγμένα (perf.pass.part.nom.sing.fem.of μίγνυμι, adjectival, predicate position, restrictive, in agreement with χάλαζα) 1646.

ἐν (preposition with the locative of place) 80.

αἵματι (loc.sing.neut.of αἷμα, place) 1203.

καὶ (continuative conjunction) 14.

ἐβλήθη (3d.per.sing.aor.pass.ind.of βάλλω, constative) 299.

εἰς (preposition with the accusative of extent) 140.

τὴν (acc.sing.fem.of the article in agreement with γῆν) 9.

γῆν (acc.sing.fem.of γῆ, extent) 157.

καὶ (continuative conjunction) 14.

τὸ (nom.sing.neut.of the article in agreement with τρίτον) 9.

τρίτον (nom.sing.neut.of τρίτος, subject of κατεκάη) 1209.

τῆς (gen.sing.fem.of the article in agreement with γῆς) 9.

γῆς (gen.sing.fem.of γῆ, partitive) 157.

κατεκάη (3d.per.sing.2d.aor.pass.ind.of κατακαίω, constative) 314.

καὶ (continuative conjunction) 14.

τὸ (nom.sing.neut.of the article in agreement with τρίτον) 9.

τρίτον (nom.sing.neut.of τρίτος, subject of κατεκάη) 1209.

τῶν (gen.pl.neut.of the article in agreement with δένδρων) 9.

δένδρων (gen.pl.neut.of δένδρον, partitive) 294.

κατεκάη (3d.per.sing.2d.aor.pass.ind.of κατακαίω, constative) 314.

καὶ (continuative conjunction) 14.

πᾶς (nom.sing.masc.of πᾶς, in agreement with χόρτος) 67.

χόρτος (nom.sing.masc.of χόρτος, subject of κατεκάη) 632.

χλωρὸς (nom.sing.masc.of χλωρός, in agreement with χόρτος) 2267.

κατεκάη (3d.per.sing.2d.aor.pass.ind.of κατακαίω, constative) 314.

Translation - "And the first angel blew his trumpet and hail and fire appeared mixed with blood, and it was thrown unto the earth; and a third of the earth was burned up; and a third of the trees were burned up and all green grass was burned up."

Comment: It would be presumptuous to try to describe this fire storm before the fact. Those who live to witness it will appreciate its ferocity. There is no reason why we should not take the description literally. There is every reason why we should. Isaiah tell us that "the mountains and the hills shall break forth before you into singing, and all the trees of the field shall clap their hands" (Isa.55:12). He does not intend that we should understand that mountains and hills sing like opera stars, while the trees clap their hands and shout, "Bravo!" Mountains and hills cannot sing and trees have no hands, nor any appreciation of good music. But there is nothing difficult about believing that the fire and blood can fall from the sky and burn up the earth.

The first trumpet judgment will have immediate and long run effects upon the world economy. Agricultural, fruit and lumber production will be reduced, with consequent price inflation which is described under the third seal (Rev.6:5,6). International trade will be disrupted as one third of the merchant marine will be destroyed with higher transport costs, which will be passed on to the consumer. The fire will destroy much of commercial and residential housing. The time lapse between the first trumpet and the third seal will be something less than 3 1/2 years.

The believer, of course, will be untouched by any and all of God's judgments upon the unregenerate (1 Thess.5:9; Psalm 91:3-10). We may ask at this point when, since it was written, has the 91st Psalm been literally fulfilled, in a situation in which the unsaved suffer and the saints are delivered? Saints and sinners alike have suffered side by side in catastrophes of nature. Christians have been wounded and killed in battle along with atheists. Indeed Christians have died in battle when the unsaved in the same fox hole or trench did not. But the Psalm must some day have its literal fulfillment. The only time in recorded Scripture that we have anything like Psalm 91:3-10 is Israel's experience in Egypt during the ten plagues (Ex.9:4,26; 10:23; 11:7, etc.). Then God demonstrated in advance His ability to separate His people from those who are not, protecting the former and showing His power in judgment upon the latter. Thus the pretribulation rapture argument that God must rapture the saints out of the world before the tribulation in order to protect them from the tribulation horrors is pointless. God took Israel out of Egypt *after* the ten plauges occurred, *not before.* Yet Israel did not suffer.

As the Red Horse Rider takes the false peace from the earth (Rev.6:3,4) and plunges the world into war, the second trumpet judgment falls upon the sea. It is described in verses 8 and 9.

Verse 8 - "And the second angel sounded, and as it were a great mountain burning with fire was cast into the sea: and a third part of the sea became blood."

Καὶ ὁ δεύτερος ἄγγελος ἐσάλπισεν, καὶ ὡς ὄρος μέγα πυρὶ καιόμενον ἐβλήθη εἰς τὴν θάλασσαν, καὶ ἐγένετο τὸ τρίτον τῆς θαλάσσης αἷμα,

"The second angel blew his trumpet, and something like a great mountain, burning with fire, was thrown into the sea; ..." ... RSV

Καὶ (continuative conjunction) 14.

ὁ (nom.sing.masc.of the article in agreement with ἄγγελος) 9.

δεύτερος (nom.sing.masc.of δεύτερος, in agreement with ἄγγελος) 1371.

ἄγγελος (nom.sing.masc.of ἄγγελος, subject of ἐσάλπισεν) 96.

ἐσάλπισεν (3d.per.sing.aor.act.ind.of σαλπίζω, constative) 559.

καὶ (continuative conjunction) 14.

ὡς (comparative particle) 128.

ὄρος (nom.sing.neut.of ὄρος, subject of ἐβλήθη) 357.

μέγα (nom.sing.neut.of μέγας, in agreement with ὄρος) 184.

πυρὶ (instrumental sing.neut.of πῦρ, means) 298.

καιόμενον (pres.mid.part.nom.sing.neut.of καίω, adjectival, predicate position, restrictive, in agreement with ὄρος) 453.

ἐβλήθη (3d.per.sing.2d.aor.pass.ind.of βάλλω, constative) 299.

εἰς (preposition with the accusative of extent) 140.

τὴν (acc.sing.fem.of the article in agreement with θάλασσαν) 9.

θάλασσαν (acc.sing.fem.of θάλασσα, extent) 374.

καὶ (continuative conjunction) 14.

ἐγένετο (3d.per.sing.aor.mid.ind.of γίνομαι, ingressive) 113.

τὸ (nom.sing.neut.of the article in agreement with τρίτον) 9.

τρίτον (nom.sing.neut.of τρίτος, subject of ἐγένετο) 1209.

τῆς (gen.sing.fem.of the article in agreement with θαλάσσης) 9.

θαλάσσης (gen.sing.fem.of θάλασσα, partitive) 374.

αἷμα (nom.sing.neut.of αἷμα, predicate nominative) 1203.

Translation - "And the second angel trumpeted, and something that resembled a great mountain burning with fire was thrown into the sea, and the third part of the sea turned to blood."

Comment: A giant meteor perhaps? As a result the sea is polluted, as one third of the sea water becomes blood. The results of this are described in verse 9.

As war returns to a world (Rev.6:3,4), temporarily deceived into believing that peace has been at last restored (Rev.6:1-2), the planet, only recently partially burned over (Rev.8:7) on the land, is now to see the oceans corrupted with blood. The message to the church of Smyrna (Rev.2:8-11) will be of special interest to the saints of earth during this period. *Cf.* our comment *en loc.*

The time point now (second church, second seal, second trumpet) is that of Rev.17:10b.

One third of marine life will die as a result of the second trumpet judgment and one third of the ships will be destroyed, as we see in

Verse 9 - "And the third part of the creatures which were in the sea and had life, died; and the third part of the ships were destroyed."

καὶ ἀπέθανεν τὸ τρίτον τῶν κτισμάτων τῶν ἐν τῇ θαλάσσῃ, τὰ ἔχοντα ψυχάς, καὶ τὸ τρίτον τῶν πλοίων διεφθάρησαν.

"and a third of the sea became blood, a third of the living creatures in the sea died, and a third of the ships were destroyed." . . . RSV

καὶ (continuative conjunction) 14.

ἀπέθανεν (3d.per.sing.aor.act.ind.of ἀποθνήσκω, constative) 774.

τὸ (nom.sing.neut.of the article in agreement with τρίτον) 9.

τρίτον (nom.sing.neut.of τρίτος, subject of ἀπέθανεν) 1209.

τῶν (gen.pl.neut.of the article in agreement with κτισμάτων) 9.

κτισμάτων (gen.pl.neut.of κτίσμα, partitive) 4748.

τῶν (gen.pl.neut.of the article in agreement with κτισμάτων) 9.

ἐν (preposition with the locative of place) 80.

τῇ (loc.sing.fem.of the article in agreement with θαλάσσῃ) 9.

θαλάσσῃ (loc.sing.fem.of θάλασσα, place) 374.

τὰ (nom.pl.neut.of the article in agreement with ἔχοντα) 9.

ἔχοντα (pres.act.part.nom.pl.neut.of ἔχω, substantival, in apposition) 82.

ψυχάς (acc.pl.fem.of ψυχή, direct object of ἔχοντα) 233.

καὶ (continuative conjunction) 14.

τὸ (nom.sing.neut.of the article in agreement with τρίτον) 9.

τρίτον (nom.sing.neut.of τρίτος, subject of διεφθάρησαν) 1209.
τῶν (gen.pl.neut.of the article in agreement with πλοίων) 9.
πλοίων (gen.pl.neut.of πλοῖον, partitive) 400.
διεφθάρησαν (3d.per.pl.aor.pass.ind.of διαφθείρω, constative) 2485.

Translation - *"And a third of the marine life died, and a third of the ships were destroyed."*

Comment: Marine life at that time not found in the ocean may have escaped. The prepositional phrase ἐν τῇ θαλάσσῃ confines the death to marine life in the sea, not necessarily that in museums, laboratories, etc. Thus the sea food market is restricted to two thirds of its former production and the merchant marine capability is reduced. This will further exacerbate the famine conditions which are to come under the third seal (Rev.6:5,6).

The third trumpet judgment falls upon the land based water resources, as we learn in

Verse 10 - *"And the third angel sounded, and there fell a great star from heaven, burning as it were a lamp, and it fell upon the third part of the rivers, and upon the fountains of waters;"*

Καὶ ὁ τρίτος ἄγγελος ἐσάλπισεν, καὶ ἔπεσεν ἐκ τοῦ οὐρανοῦ ἀστὴρ μέγας καιόμενος ὡς λαμπάς, καὶ ἔπεσεν ἐπὶ τὸ τρίτον τῶν ποταμῶν καὶ ἐπὶ τὰς πηγὰς τῶν ὑδάτων.

"The third angel blew his trumpet, and a great star fell from heaven, blazing like a torch, and it fell on a third of the rivers and on the fountains of water." . .
                                                                                          RSV

Καὶ (continuative conjunction) 14.
ὁ (nom.sing.masc.of the article in agreement with ἄγγελος) 9.
τρίτος (nom.sing.masc.of τρίτος, in agreement with ἄγγελος) 1209.
ἄγγελος (nom.sing.masc.of ἄγγελος, subject of ἐσάλπισεν) 96.
ἐσάλπισεν (3d.per.sing.aor.act.ind.of σαλπίζω, ingressive) 559.
καὶ (continuative conjunction) 14.
ἔπεσεν (3d.per.sing.aor.act.ind.of πίπτω, constative) 187.
ἐκ (preposition with the ablative, separation) 19.
τοῦ (abl.sing.masc.of the article in agreement with οὐρανοῦ) 9.
οὐρανοῦ (abl.sing.masc.of οὐρανός, separation) 254.
ἀστὴρ (nom.sing.masc.of ἀστήρ, subject of ἔπεσεν) 145.
μέγας (nom.sing.masc.of μέγας, in agreement with ἀστήρ) 184.
καιόμενος (pres.mid.part.nom.sing.masc.of καίω, adjectival, predicate position, restrictive, in agreement with ἀστὴρ) 453.
ὡς (comparative particle) 128.
λαμπάς (nom.sing.fem.of λαμπάς subject of καίει understood) 1529.
καὶ (adjunctive conjunction joining verbs) 14.
ἔπεσεν (3d.per.sing.aor.act.ind.of πίπτω, constative) 187.
ἐπὶ (preposition with the accusative, extent) 47.

τό (acc.sing.neut.of the article in agreement with τρίτον) 9.

τρίτον (acc.sing.neut.of τρίτος, extent) 1209.

τῶν (gen.pl.masc.of the article in agreement with ποταμῶν) 9.

ποταμῶν (gen.pl.masc.of ποταμός, partitive) 274.

καὶ (adjunctive conjunction joining prepositional phrases) 14.

ἐπὶ (preposition with the accusative of extent) 47.

τὰς (acc.pl.fem.of the article in agreement with πηγὰς) 9.

πηγὰς (acc.pl.fem.of πηγή, extent) 2001.

τῶν (gen.pl.neut.of the article in agreement with ὑδάτων) 9.

ὑδάτων (gen.pl.neut.of ὕδωρ, description) 301.

Translation - "And the third angel began to blow his trumpet; and there fell from the sky a great star, burning like a lamp; and it fell upon a third of the rivers and upon the springs of water."

Comment: Thus water pollution is added to all of the other distresses. Land and sea, plus inland rivers, creeks, brooks and springs of water are polluted to add to the famine and pestilential conditions described under the third and fourth seals (Rev.6:5-8). Nothing is said about underground streams of water which might remain pure, but they could be tapped only by mass drilling operations which would require much time and money. Huge cities which are dependent for water upon rivers (Washington, D.C. and New York, *e.g.*) would be helpless.

The pestilential results of the third trumpet judgment are seen in verse 11. Note that only one third of the earth is affected by these judgments. Our Lord knows the toleration limits which the earth can endure and remain viable. The tribulation period has already been shortened by the decree of God to prevent all life on earth from being destroyed. *Cf.* Mt.24:22 and comment. At the time point of the third church/seal/trumpet there remains a little more than 3 1/2 years until the second coming.

Note that when John is describing scenes of heaven's judgments and other exciting events he uses parataxis much as Mark always does. Note the greater use of continuative over adjunctive καί (#14).

Verse 11 - "And the name of the star is called Wormwood: and the third part of the waters became wormwood: and many men died of the waters because they were made bitter."

καὶ τὸ ὄνομα τοῦ ἀστέρος λέγεται ὁ Ἄφινθος. καὶ ἐγένετο τὸ τρίτον τῶν ὑδάτων εἰς ἄφιντον, καὶ πολλοὶ τῶν ἀνθρώπων ἀπέθανον ἐκ τῶν ὑδάτων, ὅτι ἐπικράνθησαν.

"The name of the star is Wormwood. A third of the waters became wormwood, and many men died of the water, because it was made bitter." . . .

RSV

καὶ (continuative conjunction) 14.

τὸ (nom.sing.neut.of the article in agreement with ὄνομα) 9.

ὄνομα (nom.sing.neut.of ὄνομα, subject of λέγεται) 108.

τοῦ (gen.sing.masc.of the article in agreement with ἀστέρος) 9.
ἀστέρος (gen.sing.masc.of ἀστήρ, possession) 145.
λέγεται (3d.per.sing.pres.pass.ind.of λέγω, customary) 66.

#5365"Αφινθος (nom.sing.masc.of"Αφινθος, predicate nominative).

King James Version

wormwood - Rev.8:11,11.

Revised Standard Version

wormwood - Rev.8:11,11.

Meaning: wormwood. Absinthe - *artemisia absinthium*. Its continuous use causes nervous derangement. The name of the star in Rev.8:11a, and the condition of the water in Rev.8:11b.

καὶ (inferential conjunction) 14.
ἐγένετο (3d.per.sing.aor.mid.ind.of γίνομαι, ingressive) 113.
τὸ (nom.sing.neut.of the article in agreement with τρίτον) 9.
τρίτον (nom.sing.neut.of τρίτος, subject of ἐγένετο) 1209.
τῶν (gen.pl.neut.of the article in agreement with ὑδάτων) 9.
ὑδάτων (gen.pl.neut.of ὕδωρ, partitive) 301.
εἰς (preposition with the accusative, predicate accusative) 140.
ἄφινθον (acc.sing.masc.of ἄφινθος, predicate adverb) 5365.
καὶ (inferential conjunction) 14.
πολλοὶ (nom.pl.masc.of πολύς, subject of ἀπέθανον) 228.
τῶν (gen.pl.masc.of the article in agreement with ἀνθρώπων) 9.
ἀνθρώπων (gen.pl.masc.of ἄνθρωπος, partitive) 341.
ἀπέθανον (3d.per.pl.aor.act.ind.of ἀποθνήσκω, constative) 774.
ἐκ (preposition with the ablative, cause) 19.
τῶν (abl.pl.neut.of the article in agreement with ὑδάτων) 9.
ὑδάτων (abl.pl.neut.of ὕδωρ, cause) 301.
ὅτι (conjunction introducing a subordinate causal clause) 211.
ἐπικράνθησαν (3d.per.pl.aor.pass.ind.of πικραίνω, culminative) 4637.

Translation - "And the name of the star is called 'Wormwood,' and one third of the water became wormwood, and many of the people died because of the water, because it was made bitter."

Comment: Other instances of ἐκ with the ablative to indicate cause or occasion are found in Rom.12:18; Rev.16:10; Rom.5:1 (which is also source); Gal.3:10; 1 Cor.9:14; 2 Cor.13:4; Lk.16:9; John 12:3; John 6:13; Mk.7:11; Rev.2:11; Rev.18:3; Rev.19:21; John 4:6; Rom.1:17; Rev.16:21.

Thus God has attacked the earth and hurt both it and the seas and all that is in view. *Cf.* Rev.7:2,3. The third of the land area of the planet is burned over; one third of the trees and all of the cover crops are gone; one third of the ocean water is blood and one third of all marine life is dead. One third of all of the ships are destroyed. One third of all rivers and smaller streams and springs are poisoned and polluted.

The fourth trumpeter unleashes the divine judgment upon the sun, moon and stars. Thus as Antichrist makes his appearance (4th seal), God strikes at the stellar heavens. War, famine and pestilence stalk the earth. Now comes Satan's Messiah, with power, signs and lying wonders and with military, political and economic control of the world. But he and Satan have only 42 months (Rev.13:5), a relatively short time (Rev.12:12).

Meanwhile God's elect are not deceived (Mt.24:22-24) but continue their works (Rev.3:1-22) and the nucleus of God's nation Israel, firmly sealed (Rev.7:1-8) and safely protected (Rev.12:6) await the coming of the true Messiah.

At this point in time, not all of the elect have been effectually called to salvation by the Holy Spirit. His mission, to complete the Body of Christ, will be finished "in the days of the voice of the seventh angel when he shall begin to sound" (Rev.10:7). Thus at the "last trump" (1 Cor.15:51; Rev.11:15-19) the resurrection and rapture will occur. If it occurred at any time previous, it would be a partial rapture. There is no need for the Body of Christ to remain upon the earth one minute after she has completed her work of carrying out the worldwide missionary enterprise. Perhaps by that time the Moral Majority will have reached the conclusion that the Church cannot employ the police power of the unregenerate State to force Christian ethics upon unsaved people.

Verse 12 - "And the fourth angel sounded and the third part of the sun was smitten, and the third part of the moon, and the third part of the stars: so as the third part of them was darkened, and the day shone not for a third part of it, and the night likewise."

Καὶ ὁ τέταρτος ἄγγελος ἐσάλπισεν. καὶ ἐπλήγη τὸ τρίτον τοῦ ἡλίου καὶ τὸ τρίτον τῆς σελήνης καὶ τὸ τρίτον τῶν ἀστέρων, ἵνα σκοτισθῇ τὸ τρίτον αὐτῶν καὶ ἡ ἡμέρα μὴ φάνῃ τὸ τρίτον αὐτῆς, καὶ ἡ νὺξ ὁμοίως.

"The fourth angel blew his trumpet, and a third of the sun was struck, and a third of the moon, and a third of the stars, so that a third of their light was darkened; a third of the day was kept from shining, and likewise a third of the night." . . . RSV

Καὶ (continuative conjunction) 14.

ὁ (nom.sing.masc.of the article in agreement with ἄγγελος) 9.

τέταρτος (nom.sing.masc.of τέταρτος, in agreement with ἄγγελος) 1129.

ἄγγελος (nom.sing.masc.of ἄγγελος, subject of ἐσάλπισεν) 96.

ἐσάλπισεν (3d.per.sing.aor.act.ind.of σαλπίζω, ingressive) 559.

καὶ (continuative conjunction) 14.

#5366 ἐπλήγη (3d.per.sing.2d.aor.pass.ind. (Attic) of πλήσσω, constative).

King James Version

smite - Rev.8:12.

Revised Standard Version

strike - Rev.8:12.

Meaning: Cf. πληγή (#2421). To strike; to smite. With reference to God's judgment upon sun, moon and stars - Rev.8:12.

τό (nom.sing.neut.of the article in agreement with τρίτον) 9.

τρίτον (nom.sing.neut.of τρίτος, subject of ἐπλήγη) 1209.

τοῦ (gen.sing.masc.of the article in agreement with ἡλίου) 9.

ἡλίου (gen.sing.masc.of ἥλιος, partitive) 546.

καί (adjunctive conjunction joining nouns) 14.

τό (nom.sing.neut.of the article in agreement with τρίτον) 9.

τρίτον (nom.sing.neut.of τρίτος, subject of ἐπλήγη) 1209.

τῆς (gen.sing.fem.of the article in agreement with σελήνης) 9.

σελήνης (gen.sing.fem.of σελήνη, partitive) 1505.

καί (adjunctive conjunction joining nouns) 14.

τό (nom.sing.neut.of the article in agreement with τρίτον) 9.

τρίτον (nom.sing.neut.of τρίτος, subject of ἐπλήγη) 1209.

τῶν (gen.pl.masc.of the article in agreement with ἀστέρων) 9.

ἀστέρων (gen.pl.masc.of ἀστήρ, partitive) 145.

ἵνα (conjunction with the subjunctive, result) 114.

σκοτισθῇ (3d.per.sing.aor.pass.subj.of σκοτίζω, result) 1504.

τό (nom.sing.neut.of the article in agreement with τρίτον) 9.

τρίτον (nom.sing.neut.of τρίτος, subject of σκοτισθῇ) 1209.

αὐτῶν (gen.pl.masc.of αὐτός, partitive) 16.

καί (inferential conjunction) 14.

ἡ (nom.sing.fem.of the article in agreement with ἡμέρα) 9.

ἡμέρα (nom.sing.fem.of ἡμέρα, subject of φάνῃ) 135.

μή (negative conjunction with the subjunctive) 87.

φάνῃ (3d.per.sing.aor.act.subj.of φαίνω, prohibition) 100.

τό (acc.sing.neut.of the article in agreement with τρίτον) 9.

τρίτον (acc.sing.neut.of τρίτος, time extent) 1209.

αὐτῆς (gen.sing.fem.of αὐτός, partitive) 16.

καί (adjunctive conjunction joining nouns) 14.

ἡ (nom.sing.fem.of the article in agreement with νύξ) 9.

νύξ (nom.sing.fem.of νύξ, suspended subject) 209.

ὁμοίως (adverbial) 1425.

Translation - "And the fourth angel began to blow his trumpet. And a third of the sun and a third of the moon and a third of the stars were blasted with the result that a third of them was blacked out; and the day did not shine for a third of it, and the night likewise."

Comment: As the true Messiah died the stellar lights refused to shine. As the false Messiah rises from the abyss to blaspheme God for 42 months (Rev.13:5) again the stellar bodies will go on strike. ἵνα with σκοτισθῇ . . . μὴ φάνῃ is consecutive. *Cf.* Rev.16:10.

There is nothing in Rev.8:6-13 to indicate a chronological spacing of the first four trumpets. *Contra* Rev.9:5 and 9:15 which indicate a time space for the 5th and 6th trumpets. It is clear that the 7th trumpet (Rev.11:15-18) can come only the last day of the tribulation week. It may be true that the first four trumpets sound at the same time in which case all of the results — damage to earth, sea and sky, with its terrible results, will prevail at all times from the beginning of the week. However, famine shows up only in the third seal and pestilence only in the fourth seal, which lends support to the contemporaneity of churches, seals and trumpets, with the vials joining them in the last half of the week.

Verse 13 - "And I beheld, and heard an angel flying through the midst of heaven, saying with a loud voice, Woe, woe, woe to the inhabiters of the earth by reason of the other voices of the trumpet of the three angels, which are yet to sound."

Καὶ εἶδον, καὶ ἤκουσα ἑνὸς ἀετοῦ πετομένου ἐν μεσουρανήματι λέγοντος φωνῇ μεγάλῃ, Οὐαὶ οὐαὶ οὐαὶ τοὺς κατοικοῦντας ἐπὶ τῆς γῆς ἐκ τῶν λοιπῶν φωνῶν τῆς σάλπιγγος τῶν τριῶν ἀγγέλων τῶν μελλόντων σαλπίζειν.

"Then I looked, and I heard an eagle crying with a loud voice, as it flew in midheaven, 'Woe, woe, woe to those who dwell on the earth, at the blasts of the other trumpets which the three angels are about to blow!' " . . . RSV

Καὶ (continuative conjunction) 14.

εἶδον (1st.per.sing.aor.ind.of ὁράω, constative) 144.

καὶ (adjunctive conjunction joining verbs) 14.

ἤκουσα (1st.per.sing.aor.act.ind.of ἀκούω, constative) 148.

ἑνὸς (gen.sing.masc.of εἷς, in agreement with ἀετοῦ) 469.

ἀετοῦ (gen.sing.masc.of ἀετός, objective genitive) 1503.

πετομένου (pres.mid.part.gen.sing.masc.of πέτομαι, adjectival, predicate position, restrictive, in agreement with ἀετοῦ) 5346.

ἐν (preposition with the locative of place) 80.

#5367 μεσουρανήματι (loc.sing.neut.of μεσουράνημα, place).

King James Version

midst of heaven - Rev.8:13; 14:6; 19:17.

Revised Standard Version

midheaven - Rev.8:13; 14:6; 19:17.

Meaning: A combination of μέσος (#873), οὐρανός (#254) and μα the result suffix. In the midst of heaven. *Cf.* μεσουρανέω - "at the highest point in the zodiac, when the sun is at its highest point. Hence, a position from which one can be seen and heard by all - Rev.8:13; 14:6; 19:17.

λέγοντος (pres.act.part.gen.sing.masc.of λέγω, adjectival, predicate position, restrictive, in agreement with ἀετοῦ) 66.

φωνῇ (instru.sing.fem.of φωνή, means) 222.

μεγάλη (instru.sing.fem.of μέγας, in agreement with φωνῇ) 184.

Οὐαὶ (interjection) 936.

οὐαὶ (interjection) 936.

οὐαὶ (interjection) 936.

τοὺς (acc.pl.masc.of the article in agreement with κατοικοῦντας) 9.

κατοικοῦντας (pres.act.part.acc.pl.masc.of κατοικέω, adverbial accusative) 242.

ἐπὶ (preposition with the genitive of place description) 47.

τῆς (gen.sing.fem.of the article in agreement with γῆς) 9.

γῆς (gen.sing.fem.of γῆ, place description) 157.

ἐκ (preposition with the ablative, cause or occasion) 19.

τῶν (abl.pl.fem.of the article in agreement with φωνῶν) 9.

λοιπῶν (abl.pl.fem.of λοιπός, in agreement with φωνῶν) 1402.

φωνῶν (abl.pl.fem.of φωνή, cause or occasion) 222.

τῆς (gen.sing.fem.of the article in agreement with σάλπιγγος) 9.

σάλπιγγος (gen.sing.fem.of σάλπιγξ, description) 1507.

τῶν (gen.pl.masc.of the article in agreement with ἀγγέλων) 9.

τριῶν (gen.pl.masc.of τρεῖς, in agreement with ἀγγέλων) 1010.

ἀγγέλων (gen.pl.masc.of ἄγγελος, possession) 96.

τῶν (gen.pl.masc.of the article in agreement with μελλόντων) 9.

μελλόντων (pres.act.part.gen.pl.masc.of μέλλω, substantival, in apposition with ἀγγέλων) 206.

σαλπίζειν (pres.act.inf.of σαλπίζω, complementary) 559.

Translation - "And I watched; and I heard an eagle flying in the middle of the sky, saying with a loud voice, 'Woe, woe, woe to those who are living on the earth, because of the other voices of the trumpets of the three angels who are about to blow their trumpets.' "

Comment: ἑνός here may be regarded as an indefinite article, joined to ἀετοῦ. *Cf.* Mt.8:19; 26:69; Mk.12:42; Mt.18:24; 21:19. *Cf.* Rev.12:12 for the other case of the accusative after οὐαί. *Cf.* Mt.18:7 where we have οὐαὶ τῷ κόσμῳ, as we would expect to see a dative of personal disadvantage. The accusative after οὐαί may be regarded as an adverbial accusative.

The three woes (Rev.9:12) are identified as the last three trumpet judgments. We have just pointed out that there is nothing in the description of the first four trumpet judgments that definitely places them at some specific point in time in relation to the seven year period of Dan.9:27, except that the first comes at the beginning and the second and third follow. The time intervals between them, if indeed time will intervene, is not revealed. The fifth trumpet has rather definite correlative evidence that it comes contemporaneously with the fourth and fifth seals in the middle of and immediately following the middle of the week.

Revelation 9:1 - "And the fifth angel sounded, and I saw a star fall from heaven unto the earth: and to him was given the key of the bottomless pit."

Καὶ ὁ πέμπτος ἄγγελος ἐσάλπισεν, καὶ εἶδον ἀστέρα ἐκ τοῦ οὐρανοῦ πεπτωκότα εἰς τὴν γῆν, καὶ ἐδόθη αὐτῷ ἡ κλεὶς τοῦ φρέατος τῆς ἀβύσσου.

"And the fifth angel blew his trumpet, and I saw a star fallen from heaven to earth, and he was given the key of the shaft of the bottomless pit; . . . " . . . RSV

Καὶ (continuative conjunction) 14.

ὁ (nom.sing.masc.of the article in agreement with ἄγγελος) 9.

πέμπτος (nom.sing.masc.of πέμπτος, in agreement with ἄγγελος) 5353.

ἄγγελος (nom.sing.masc.of ἄγγελος, subject of ἐσάλπισεν) 96.

ἐσάλπισεν (3d.per.sing.aor.act.ind.of σαλπίζω, ingressive) 559.

καὶ (continuative conjunction) 14.

εἶδον (1st.per.sing.aor.ind.of ὁράω, constative) 144.

ἀστέρα (acc.sing.masc.of ἀστήρ, direct object of εἶδον) 145.

ἐκ (preposition with the ablative of separation) 19.

τοῦ (abl.sing.masc.of the article in agreement with οὐρανοῦ) 9.

οὐρανοῦ (abl.sing.masc.of οὐρανός, separation) 254.

πεπτωκότα (perf.act.part.acc.sing.masc.of πίπτω, adjectival, predicate position, restrictive, in agreement with ἀστέρα) 187.

εἰς (preposition with the accusative of extent) 140.

τὴν (acc.sing.fem.of the article in agreement with γῆν) 9.

γῆν (acc.sing.fem.of γῆ, extent) 157.

καὶ (continuative conjunction) 14.

ἐδόθη (3d.per.sing.aor.pass.ind.of δίδωμι, constative) 362.

αὐτῷ (dat.sing.masc.of αὐτός, indirect object of ἐδόθη) 16.

ἡ (nom.sing.fem.of the article in agreement with κλεὶς) 9.

κλεὶς (nom.sing.fem.of κλείς, subject of ἐδόθη) 1206.

τοῦ (gen.sing.neut.of the article in agreement with φρέατος) 9.

φρέατος (gen.sing.neut.of φρέαρ, description) 2006.

τῆς (gen.sing.fem.of the article in agreement with ἀβύσσου) 9.

ἀβύσσου (gen.sing.fem.of ἄβυσσος, description) 2231.

Translation - "And the fifth angel began to blow his trumpet; and I saw a star which had fallen from heaven unto the earth; and the key of the entrance to the abyss was given to him."

Comment: Note the perfect participial adjective, πεπτωκότα, which modifies ἀστέρα. At the time that John saw it, it had already fallen from the heavens and was upon the earth. The star apparently refers to an angel, to whom is given the key that opens the shaft that leads to the bottomless pit. Cf.#2006 for the definition of φρέαρ.

In the next ten verses (Rev.9:2-11) we have the following information, much of which cannot be explained until the time comes and these things are experienced. The personalized "star" is given the key that he uses to open the air shaft that leads from the surface of the earth to the abyss. (Rev.9:2). Do geologists know of shafts that lead downward into the earth to holes that are, so far as they know, bottomless? How deep is this shaft? How hot is it at the bottom? A shaft drilled downward twenty-five kilometers (15.5 miles) reaches a temperature of 250 degrees centigrade. From this pit will emerge creatures which are really indescribable. They have a "king" (Rev.9:11) who is called the "Destroyer." Note that the Beast who murders the two witnessess is said to ahve ascended from the bottomless pit (Rev.11:7), and that he is the White Horse Rider of Rev.6:1,2, who is killed (Rev.13:3) but resurrected (Rev.17:8). When the White Horse Rider, who is the Beast, is killed, he goes to the bottomless pit, but comes out (Rev.11:7; 17:8) to kill the two witnesses. When does he emerge from the pit? In the middle of the week (Daniel 9:27b) to appear as "the eighth" who is one of the seven, namely the fifth (Rev.17:8-11). How does he get out of the pit? Satan, the "star" lets him out (Rev.9:1-11). We need only to place Satan's fall out of heaven in the middle of the week. This is clear from Rev.12:7-9. This is a clear mid-week point from Rev.12:6.

Thus correlative evidence establishes that: (a) the time of the fifth trumpet is mid-week; (b) that it is the same time as the 4th seal; (c) that the "star" is Satan who at this time is thrown out of heaven (Rev.12:7-9); (d) that Satan opens the shaft that leads to the abyss and frees the Beast (Rev.9:2); (e) that the Beast, thus freed reappears on earth (Rev.11:7; 17:8); (f) that he brings with him the scorpions described in Rev.9:7-11, who will torment the unsaved on earth for five months (Rev.9:5); (g) the "king of the scorpions" (Rev.9:11) will make war with the saints (Rev.13:7) and (h) thus the fifth seal reveals these martyred saints in heaven as souls under the altar (Rev.6:9-11) who are demanding judgment upon the Beast on earth who killed them and are told to wait a little while until the rest of the elect upon earth are saved and either martyred or raptured.

The student is reminded that no Scripture is of its own interpretation (2 Peter 1:20), and that the Holy Spirit has put together a divine *gestalt* (mosaic) made up of individual bits and pieces of information which fit together harmoniously, if we achieve the goal that Paul held before Timothy (2 Tim.2:15).

One wonders if "the snare of the folwer" — ὅτι αὐτὸς ῥύσεταί ἐκ παγίδος θηρευτῶν — of Psalm 91:3, from which the saints will be delivered, is "the mark of the Beast" of Rev.13:16-18? *Cf.#*'s 2838, 2472. The temptation for the exegete to dogmatize about those things which are not at this time clear, must be resisted. Things that are unclear now will be clear when the time comes.

Verse 2 - "And he opened the bottomless pit; and there arose a smoke out of the pit, as the smoke of a great furnace; and the sun and the air were darkned by reason of the smoke of the pit."

καὶ ἤνοιξεν τὸ φρέαρ τῆς ἀβύσσου καὶ ἀνέβη καπνὸς ἐκ τοῦ φρέατος ὡς καπνὸς καμίνου μεγάλης, καὶ ἐσκοτώθη ὁ ἥλιος καὶ ὁ ἀὴρ ἐκ τοῦ καπνοῦ τοῦ φρέατος.

"he opened the shaft of the bottomless pit, and from the shaft rose smoke like the smoke of a great furnace, and the sun and the air were darkened with the smoke from the shalft." . . . RSV

καὶ (continuative conjunction) 14.
ἤνοιξεν (3d.per.sing.aor.act.ind.of ἀνοίγω, constative) 188.
τὸ (acc.sing.neut.of the article in agreement with φρέαρ) 9.
φρέαρ (acc.sing.neut.of φρέαρ, direct object of ἤνοιξεν) 2006.
τῆς (gen.sing.fem.of the article in agreement with ἀβύσσου) 9.
ἀβύσσου (gen.sing.fem.of ἄβυσσος, description) 2231.
καὶ (continuative conjunction) 14.
ἀνέβη (3d.per.sing.2d.aor.act.ind.of ἀναβαίνω, ingressive) 323.
καπνὸς (nom.sing.masc.of καπνός, subject of ἀνέβη) 2986.
ἐκ (preposition with the ablative, source/separation) 19.
τοῦ (abl.sing.neut.of the article in agreement with φρέατος) 9.
φρέατος (abl.sing.neut.of φρέαρ, source/separation) 2006.
ὡς (comparative particle) 128.
καπνὸς (nom.sing.masc.of καπνός, subject of ἔστιν understood) 2986.
καμίνου (abl.sing.fem.of κάμινος, source) 1083.
μεγάλης (abl.sing.fem.of μέγας, in agreement with καμίνου) 184.
καὶ (continuative conjunction) 14.
ἐσκοτώθη (3d.per.sing.aor.pass.ind.of σκοτόω, constative) 4501.
ὁ (nom.sing.masc.of the article in agreement with ἥλιος) 9.
ἥλιος (nom.sing.masc.of ἥλιος, subject of ἐσκοτώθη) 546.
καὶ (adjunctive conjunction joining nouns) 14.
ὁ (nom.sing.masc.of the article in agreement with ἀήρ) 9.
ἀὴρ (nom.sing.masc.of ἀήρ, subject of ἐσκοτώθη) 3584.
ἐκ (preposition with the ablative, cause/occasion) 19.
τοῦ (abl.sing.masc.of the article in agreement with καπνοῦ) 9.
καπνοῦ (abl.sing.masc.of καπνός, cause/occasion) 2986.
τοῦ (abl.sing.neut.of the article in agreement with φρέατος) 9.
φρέατος (abl.sing.neut.of φρέαρ, source) 2006.

Translation - "And he opened the entrance to the abyss, and a smoke began to ascend out of the air shaft, like smoke from a great furnace, and the sun and the air was darkened because of the smoke from the air shaft."

Comment: The sky will be darkened as the black smoke begins to rise from the pit, which has just been opened by Satan, who has just been banished for the last time from access to heaven. He will now know that he has only a short time (Rev.12:12) — exactly 42 months/ 1260 days/ 3 1/2 years. Satan's rage will be intense. The smoke contains tormentors.

The key and the act of unlocking the shaft to the abyss may very well be figurative language. Geologists know about the pressures in the earth's crust that result in diastrophism. The language suggests volcanic action.

Verse 3 - "And there came out of the smoke locusts upon the earth: and unto them was given power, as the scorpions of the earth have power."

καὶ ἐκ τοῦ καπνοῦ ἐξῆλθον ἀκρίδες εἰς τὴν γῆν, καὶ ἐδόθη αὐτοῖς ἐξουσία ὡς ἔχουσιν ἐξουσίαν οἱ σκορπίοι τῆς γῆς.

"Then from the smoke came locunts on the earth, and they were given power like the power of scorpions on the earth;" . . . RSV

καὶ (continuative conjunction) 14.
ἐκ (preposition with the ablative of source/separation) 19.
τοῦ (abl.sing.masc.of the article in agreement with καπνοῦ) 9.
καπνοῦ (abl.sing.masc.of καπνός, source/separation) 2986.
ἐξῆλθον (3d.per.pl.aor.mid.ind.of ἐξέρχομαι, ingressive) 161.
ἀκρίδες (nom.pl.fem.of ἀκρίς, subject of ἐξῆλθον) 267.
εἰς (preposition with the accusative of extent) 140.
τὴν (acc.sing.fem.of the article in agreement with γῆν) 9.
γῆν (acc.sing.fem.of γῆ, extent) 157.
καὶ (continuative conjunction) 14.
ἐδόθη (3d.per.sing.aor.pass.ind.of δίδωμι, constative) 362.
αὐτοῖς (dat.pl.masc.of αὐτός, indirect object of ἐδόθη) 16.
ἐξουσία (nom.sing.fem.of ἐξουσία, subject of ἐδόθη) 707.
ὡς (comparative particle) 128.
ἔχουσιν (3d.per.pl.pres.act.ind.of ἔχω, customary) 82.
ἐξουσίαν (acc.sing.fem.of ἐξουσία, direct object of ἔχουσιν) 707.
οἱ (nom.pl.masc.of the article in agreement with σκορπίοι) 9.
σκορπίοι (nom.pl.masc.of σκορπίος, subject of ἔχουσιν) 2416.
τῆς (gen.sing.fem.of the article in agreement with γῆς) 9.
γῆς (gen.sing.fem.of γῆ, description) 157.

Translation - "And out of the smoke came locusts unto the earth, and power was given to them such as power which the skorpions of earth have."

Comment: Locusts from the pit, but more dangerous than those which provided John the Baptist with his diet (Mt.3:4; Mk.1:6). These are not ordinary locusts, as is clear from the description in verses 7-11. They are given their orders in

Verse 4 - "And it was commanded them that they should not hurt the grass of the earth, neither any green thing, neither any tree; but only those men which have not the seal of God in their foreheads."

καὶ ἐρρέθη αὐτοῖς ἵνα μὴ ἀδικήσουσιν τὸν χόρτον τῆς γῆς οὐδὲ πᾶν χλωρὸν οὐδὲ πᾶν δένδρον, εἰ μὴ τοὺς ἀνθρώπους οἵτινες οὐκ ἔχουσι τὴν σφραγίδα τοῦ θεοῦ ἐπὶ τῶν μετώπων.

"they were told not to harm the grass of the earth or any green growth or any tree, but only those of mankind who have not the seal of God upon their foreheads;" . . . RSV

καὶ (continuative conjunction) 14.
ἐρρέθη (3d.per.sing.aor.ind.of ῥέω, constative) 116.
αὐτοῖς (dat.pl.masc.of αὐτός, indirect object of ἐρρέθη) 16.
ἵνα (conjunction with the indicative, negative purpose) 114.
μὴ (negative conjunction with the future indicative, negative purpose) 87.

ἀδικήσουσιν (3d.per.pl.fut.act.ind.of ἀδικέω, negative purpose) 1327.

τὸν (acc.sing.masc.of the article in agreement with χόρτον) 9.

χόρτον (acc.sing.masc.of χόρτος, direct object of ἀδικήσουσιν) 632.

τῆς (gen.sing.fem.of the article in agreement with γῆς) 9.

γῆς (gen.sing.fem.of γῆ, description) 157.

οὐδὲ (disjunctive particle) 452.

πᾶν (acc.sing.masc.of πᾶς, in agreement with χλωρὸν) 67.

χλωρὸν (acc.sing.masc.of χλωρός, direct object of ἀδικήσουσιν) 2267.

οὐδὲ (disjunctive particle) 452.

πᾶν (acc.sing.neut.of πᾶς, in agreement with δένδρον) 67.

δένδρον (acc.sing.neut.of δένδρον, direct object of ἀδικήσουσιν) 294.

εἰ (conditional particle in an elliptical condition) 337.

μὴ (negative conjunction in an elliptical condition) 87.

τοὺς (acc.pl.masc.of the article in agreement with ἀνθρώπους) 9.

ἀνθρώπους (acc.pl.masc.of ἄνθρωπος, direct object of ἀδικήσουσιν) 341.

οἵτινες (nom.pl.masc.of ὅστις, definite relative pronoun, subject of ἔχουσι) 163.

οὐκ (negative conjunction with the indicative) 130.

ἔχουσι (3d.per.pl.pres.act.ind.of ἔχω, aoristic) 82.

τὴν (acc.sing.fem.of the article in agreement with σφραγῖδα) 9.

σφραγῖδα (acc.sing.fem.of σφραγίς, direct object of ἔχουσι) 3886.

τοῦ (gen.sing.masc.of the article in agreement with θεοῦ) 9.

θεοῦ (gen.sing.masc.of θεός, description) 124.

ἐπὶ (preposition with the genitive, place description) 47.

τῶν (gen.pl.neut.of the article in agreement with μετώπων) 9.

μετώπων (gen.pl.neut.of μέτωπων, place description) 5356.

Translation - "And they were ordered not to hurt the grass of the earth, nor any green thing, nor any tree; but only such men who do not have the seal of God upon their foreheads."

Comment: Three and one half years before the green cover crops of earth had been burned up by the judgment of the first trumpet (Rev.8:7). Now, some of it has grown again. One third of the trees were destroyed before, but two thirds escaped the first judgment. Cover crops and the trees that remain will not be touched by this judgment.   If they were destroyed, there would be no food grown during the last half of the week and the famine would wipe out the population of earth. The 144,000 Jews, sealed as God's elect nation, will escape this judgment, as they flee into the wilderness to escape the Beast (Rev.12:6). Gentile saints are also sealed by the Holy Spirit when they are saved (Eph.1:13), though this seal is not visible. It is not clear that the seal of the 144,000 will be visible. Christians are protected from God's judgments by other passages (1 Thess.5:9; Psalm 91:5-10). We may be sure that the temple of the Holy Spirit (1 Cor.6:19) will be protected from the varmints of hell.

Verse 5 - "And to them it was given that they should not kill them but that they should be tormented five months: and their torment was as the torment of a scorpion, when he striketh a man."

καὶ ἐδόθη αὐτοῖς ἵνα μὴ ἀποκτείνωσιν αὐτούς, ἀλλ' ἵνα βασανισθήσονται μῆνας πέντε. καὶ ὁ βασανισμὸς αὐτῶν ὡς βασανισμὸς σκορπίου, ὅταν παίσῃ ἄνθαρωποι.

"they were allowed to torture them for five months, but not to kill them, and their torture was like the torture of a scorpion, when it stings a man." . . . RSV

καὶ (continuative conjunction) 14.
ἐδόθη (3d.per.sing.aor.pass.ind.of δίδωμι, constative) 362.
αὐτοῖς (dat.pl.masc.of αὐτός, indirect object of ἐδόθη) 16.
ἵνα (conjunction with the subjuntive, negative purpose) 114.
μὴ (negative conjunction with the subjunctive, negative purpose) 87.
ἀποκτείνωσιν (3d.per.pl.pres.act.subj.of ἀποκτείνω, negative purpose) 889.
αὐτούς (acc.pl.masc.of αὐτός, direct object of ἀποκτείνωσιν) 16.
ἀλλ' (alternative conjunction) 342.
ἵνα (conjunction with the future indicative, purpose) 114.
βασανισθήσονται (3d.per.pl.fut.pass.ind.of βασανίζω, purpose) 719.
μῆνας (acc.pl.fem.of μήν, time extent) 1809.
πέντε (numeral) 1119.
καὶ (continuative conjunction) 14.
ὁ (nom.sing.masc.of the article in agreement with βασανισμὸς) 9.

#**5368** βασανισμὸς (nom.sing.masc.of βασανισμός, subject of ἔστι understood).

King James Version

torment - Rev.9:5,5; 14:11; 18:7,10,15.

Revised Standard Version

torture - Rev.9:5,5.
torment - Rev.14:11; 18:7,10,15.

Meaning: Cf. βασανίζω (#719); βασανιοτής (#1282); βάσανος (#413). A testing experience, by the touchstone, or by torture. The act of tormenting - Rev.9:5,5; the condition of those tortured - Rev.18:7,10,15; the torment which produces smoke - Rev.14:11.

αὐτῶν (gen.pl.masc.of αὐτός, possession) 16.
ὡς (comparative particle) 128.
βασανισμὸς (nom.sing.masc.of βασανισμός, subject of ἔστι understood) 5368.
σκορπίου (gen.sing.masc.of σκορπίος, description) 2416.
ὅταν (conjunction with the subjunctive in an indefinite temporal clause) 436.
παίσῃ (3d.per.sing.aor.act.subj.of παίω, indefinite temporal clause) 1608.
ἄνθρωπον (acc.sing.masc.of ἄνθρωπος, direct object of παίω) 341.

Translation - "And an order was given to them that they should not kill them, but that they should be tormented for five months, and their torture is like the torture of a scorpion when he stings a man."

Comment: The ἵνα μὴ clause is in apposition to ἐδόθη. The order to the locusts (the antecedent of αὐτοῖς is ἀκρίδες of verse 3) is not to kill but only to torture. αὐτούς has as its antecedent τοὺς ἀνθρώπους of verse 4. The comparative clause with ὡς describes the torture. The torture is so great that before the five months of torture have passed, those suffering would rather die.

When we add to the five months of the fifth trumpet, the year, month, day and hour (Rev.9:15) of the sixth, we have accounted for only 18 months of the last half of the week, since it is clear that the seventh trumpet brings us to the second coming of Christ (Rev.11:15-18). Rev.10:7 indicates that the seventh trumpet judgment begins at some indeterminate time before the final day.

Verse 6 - "And in those days shall men seek death, and shall not find it; and shall desire to die, and death shall flee from them."

καὶ ἐν ταῖς ἡμέραις ἐκείναις ζητήσουσιν οἱ ἄνθρωποι τὸν θάνατον καὶ οὐ μὴ εὑρήσουσιν αὐτόν, καὶ ἐπιθυμήσουσιν ἀποθανεῖν καὶ φεύγει ὁ θάνατος ἐπ᾽ αὐτῶν.

"And in those days men will seek death and will not find it; they will long to die, and death will fly from them." . . . RSV

καὶ (continuative conjunction) 14.
ἐν (preposition with the locative, time point) 80.
ταῖς (loc.pl.fem.of the article in agreement with ἡμέραις) 9.
ἡμέραις (loc.pl.fem.of ἡμέρα, time point) 135.
ἐκείναις (loc.pl.fem.of ἐκεῖνος, in agreement with ἡμέραις) 246.
ζητήσουσιν (3d.per.pl.fut.act.ind.of ζητέω,predictive) 207.
οἱ (nom.pl.masc.of the article in agreement with ἄνθρωποι) 9.
ἄνθρωποι (nom.pl.masc.of ἄνθρωπος, subject of ζητήσουσιν) 341.
τὸν (acc.sing.masc.of the article in agreement with θάνατον) 9.
θάνατον (acc.sing.masc.of θάνατος, direct object of ζητήσουσιν) 381.
καὶ (adversative conjunction) 14.
οὐ (negative conjunction with μὴ and the future indicative, emphatic negation) 130.
μὴ (negative conjunction with οὐ and the future indicative, emphatic negation) 87.
εὑρήσουσιν (3d.per.pl.fut.act.ind.of εὑρίσκω, emphatic negation, predictive) 79.
αὐτόν (acc.sing.masc.of αὐτός, direct object of εὑρήσουσιν) 16.
καὶ (adjunctive conjunction joining verbs) 14.
ἐπιθυμήσουσιν (3d.per.pl.fut.act.ind.of ἐπιθυμέω, predictive) 500.
ἀποθανεῖν (aor.act.inf.of ἀποθνήσκω, complementary) 774.
καὶ (adversative conjunction) 14.
φεύγει (3d.per.sing.pres.act.ind.of φεύγω, futuristic) 202.
ὁ (nom.sing.masc.of the article in agreement with θάνατος) 9.
θάνατος (nom.sing.masc.of θάνατος, subject of φεύγει) 381.

ἀπ' (preposition with the ablative of separation) 70.

αὐτῶν (abl.pl.masc.of αὐτός, separation) 16.

Translation - "And in those days the men shall seek death but they shall never find it; and they shall desire to die, but death will flee from them."

Comment: We have οὐ μὴ with the future indicative to express emphatic negation only very rarely, but we have it here. The futuristic present in φεύγει is for dramatic effect, in order to give certainty to the affirmation, not merely prediction. Tormented by the locusts the unsaved will attempt suicide only to fail in the attempt.

We can only follow the description of these creatures in verses 7-10 without an attempt to interpret. Those who live to see these dreadful creatures will be duly impressed. In the days of unidentified flying objects and coelacanthidae dredged up from the Indian Ocean who is to say what sort of varmints are and are not available in the universe?

Verse 7 - "And the shape of the locusts were like unto horses prepared unto battle: and on their heads were as it were crowns like gold, and their faces were as the faces of men."

Καὶ τὰ ὁμοιώματα τῶν ἀκρίδων ὅμοιοι ἵπποις ἡτοιμασμένοις εἰς πόλεμον, καὶ ἐπὶ τὰς κεφαλὰς αὐτῶν ὡς στέφανοι ὅμοιοι χρυσῷ, καὶ τὰ πρόσωπα αὐτῶν ὡς πρόσωπα ἀνθρώπων,

"In appearance the locusts were like horses arrayed for battle; on their heads were what looked like crowns of gold; their faces were like human faces, " ...
RSV

Καὶ (continuative conjunction) 14.

τὰ (nom.pl.neut.of the article in agreement with ὁμοιώματα) 9.

ὁμοιώματα (nom.pl.neut.of ὁμοίωμα, subject of ἦσαν understood) 3803.

τῶν (gen.pl.fem.of the article in agreement with ἀκρίδων) 9.

ἀκρίδων (gen.pl.fem.of ἀκρίς, possession) 267.

ὅμοιοι (nom.pl.masc.of ὅμοιος, predicate adjective) 923.

ἵπποις (dat.pl.masc.of ἵππος, comparison) 5121.

ἡτοιμασμένοις (perf.pass.part.dat.pl.masc.of ἑτοιμάζω, adjectival, predicate position, restrictive, in agreement with ἵπποις) 257.

εἰς (preposition with the accusative, predicate accusative) 140.

πόλεμον (acc.sing.masc.of πόλεμος, predicate accusative) 1483.

καὶ (continuative conjunction) 14.

ἐπὶ (preposition with the accusative, rest) 47.

τὰς (acc.pl.fem.of the article in agreement with κεφαλὰς) 9.

κεφαλὰς (acc.pl.fem.of κεφαλή, rest) 521.

αὐτῶν (gen.pl.masc.of αὐτός, possession) 16.

ὡς (comparative particle) 128.

στέφανοι (nom.pl.masc.of στέφανος, predicate nominative) 1640.

ὅμοιοι (nom.pl.masc.of ὅμοιος, in agreement with στέφανοι) 923.

χρυσῷ (dat.sing.masc.of χρυσός, comparison) 192.
καὶ (continuative conjunction) 14.
τὰ (nom.pl.neut.of the article in agreement with πρόσωπα) 9.
πρόσωπα (nom.pl.neut.of πρόσωπον, subject of ἦσαν understood) 588.
αὐτῶν (gen.pl.masc.of αὐτός, possession) 16.
ὡς (comparative particle) 128.
πρόσωπα (nom.pl.neut.of πρόσωπον, predicate nominative) 588.
ἀνθρώπων (gen.pl.masc.of ἄνθρωπος, definition) 341.

Translation - "And the locusts looked like horses prepared for battle, and upon their heads what looked like crowns of gold and their faces looked human."

Comment: *Cf.* Joel 2:4,5.

Verse 8 - "And they had hair as the hair of women, and their teeth were as the teeth of lions."

καὶ εἶχον τρίχας ὡς τρίχας γυναικῶν, καὶ οἱ ὀδόντες αὐτῶν ὡς λεόντων ἦσαν.

"their hair like women's hair, and their teeth like lions' teeth;..." ... RSV

καὶ (continuative conjunction) 14.
εἶχον (3d.per.pl.imp.act.ind.of ἔχω, progressive description) 82.
τρίχας (acc.pl.fem.of θρίξ, direct object of εἶχον) 261.
ὡς (comparative particle) 128.
τρίχας (acc.pl.fem.of θρίξ, predicate accusative) 261.
γυναικῶν (gen.pl.fem.of γυνή, description) 103.
καὶ (continuative conjunction) 14.
οἱ (nom.pl.masc.of the article in agreement with ὀδόντες) 9.
ὀδόντες (nom.pl.masc.of ὀδούς, subject of ἦσαν understood) 526.
αὐτῶν (gen.pl.masc.of αὐτός, possession) 16.
ὡς (comparative particle) 128.
λεόντων (abl.pl.masc.of λέων, comparison) 4872.
ἦσαν (3d.per.pl.imp.ind.of εἰμί, progressive description) 86.

Translation - "And they had hair like that of a woman, and their teeth were like those of lions."

Comment: *Cf.* Joel 1:6.

Verse 9 - "And they had breastplates, as it were breastplates of iron: and the sound of their wings was as the sound of chariots of many horses running to battle."

καὶ εἶχον θώρακας ὡς θώρακας σιδηροῦς, καὶ ἡ φωνὴ τῶν πτερύγων αὐτῶν ὡς φωνὴ ἁρμάτων ἵππων πολλῶν τρεχόντων εἰς πόλεμον.

"they had scales like iron breastplates, and the noise of their wings was like the

noise of many chariots with horses rushing into battle." . . . RSV

καὶ (continuative conjunction) 14.

εἶχον (3d.per.pl.imp.act.ind.of ἔχω, progressive description) 82.

θώρακας (acc.pl.fem.of θώραξ, direct object of εἶχον) 4533.

ὡς (comparative particle) 128.

θώρακας (acc.pl.fem.of θώραξ, predicate accusative) 4533.

σιδηροῦς (acc.pl.fem.of σιδήρεος in agreement with θώρακας) 3248.

καὶ (continuative conjunction) 14.

ἡ (nom.sing.fem.of the article in agreement with φωνὴ) 9.

φωνὴ (nom.sing.fem.of φωνή, subject of ἦν understood) 222.

τῶν (gen.pl.fem.of the article in agreement with πτερύγων) 9.

πτερύγων (gen.pl.fem.of πτέρυξ, description) 1480.

αὐτῶν (gen.pl.masc.of αὐτός, possession) 16.

ὡς (comparative particle) 128.

φωνὴ (nom.sing.fem.of φωνή, predicate nominative) 222.

ἀρμάτων (abl.pl.neut.of ἅρμα, comparison) 3173.

ἵππων (gen.pl.masc.of ἵππος, description) 5121.

πολλῶν (gen.pl.masc.of πολύς, in agreement with ἵππων) 228.

τρεχόντων (pres.act.part.gen.pl.masc.of τρέχω, adjectival, predicate position, restrictive, in agreement with ἵππων) 1655.

εἰς (preposition with the accusative, extent) 140.

πόλεμον (acc.sing.masc.of πόλεμος, extent) 1483.

Translation - "And they had breastplates that looked like they were made of iron, and the sound of their wings was like the sound of chariots of many horses running into battle."

Comment: *Cf.* Joel 2:5.

Verse 10 - "And they had tails like unto scorpions, and there were stings in their tails: and their power was to hurt men five months."

καὶ ἔχουσιν οὐρὰς ὁμοίας σκορπίοις καὶ κέντρα, καὶ ἐν ταῖς οὐραῖς αὐτῶν ἡ ἐξουσία αὐτῶν ἀδικῆσαι τοὺς ἀνθρώπους μῆνας πέντε.

"They have tails like scorpions, and stings, and their power of hurting men for five months lies in their tails." . . . RSV

καὶ (continuative conjunction) 14.

ἔχουσιν (3d.per.pl.pres.act.ind.of ἔχω, progressive description) 82.

#5369 οὐρὰς (acc.pl.fem.of οὐρά, direct object of ἔχουσιν).

King James Version

tail - Rev.9:10,10,19; 12:4.

Revised Standard Version

tail - Rev.9:10,10,19; 12:4.

Meaning: A tail. Of the locusts of Rev.9:10,10,19; of Satan - Rev.12:4.

ὁμοίας (acc.pl.fem.of ὅμοιος, in agreement with οὐρὰς) 923.
σκορπίοις (dat.pl.masc.of σκορπίος, comparison) 2416.
καὶ (adjunctive conjunction joining nouns) 14.
κέντρα (acc.pl.neut.of κέντρον, direct object of ἔχουσιν) 3662B.
καὶ (continuative conjunction) 14.
ἐν (preposition with the locative of place) 80.
ταῖς (loc.pl.fem.of the article in agreement with οὐραῖς) 9.
οὐραῖς (loc.pl.fem.of οὐρά, place) 5369.
αὐτῶν (gen.pl.masc.of αὐτός, possession) 16.
ἡ (nom.sing.fem.of the article in agreement with ἐξουσία) 9.
ἐξουσία (nom.sing.fem.of ἐξουσία, subject of ἔστιν understood) 707.
αὐτῶν (gen.pl.masc.of αὐτός, possession) 16.
ἀδικῆσαι (aor.act.inf.of ἀδικέω, apposition) 1327.
τοὺς (acc.pl.masc.of the article in agreement with ἀνθρώπους) 9.
ἀνθρώπους (acc.pl.masc.of ἄνθρωπος, direct object of ἀδικῆσαι) 341.
μῆνας (acc.pl.fem.of μήν, time extent) 1809.
πέντε (numeral) 1119.

Translation - "And they have tails like scorpion tails and stings; and their power to hurt men for five months is in their tails."

Comment: That the stings in the tails of the locusts here referred to were interpreted by some, during World War II, as tail gunners in fighter aircraft (!), some of whom were Christians, is an example of the erudition of self-styled "prophecy" preachers, who are too impatient to wait for events to interpret prophecy. These "locusts" of the fifth trumpet have not yet appeared, nor will they appear until the beginning of the last half of the seven year period. When they do appear we may be sure that those who see them will note the accuracy of John's description. Tail gunners in B—17's and B—52's did not have hair like women. If they had when they entered the Air Force, they would have been treated to tonsorial treatment in keeping with Air Force standards. Anyone who wears his hair like a woman is not going to be in the Air Force. As far as we know there is no Air Force rule against a fighter pilot having teeth like lions (!).

Some of the same prophecy preachers who identified tail gunners with locusts also identified Benito Mussolini with the Antichrist.

Verse 11 - "And they had a king over them, which is the angel of the bottomless pit, whose name in the Hebrew tongue is Abaddon, but in the Greek tongue hath his name Apollyon."

ἔχουσιν ἐπ' αὐτῶν βασιλέα τὸν ἄγγελον τῆς ἀβύσσου. ὄνομα αὐτῷ Ἑβραϊστὶ Ἀβαδδὼν καὶ ἐν τῇ Ἑλληνικῇ ὄνομα ἔχει Ἀπολλύων.

"They have as king over them the angel of the bottomless pit; his name in

Hebrew is Abaddon, and in Greek he is called Apollyon." . . . *RSV*

ἔχουσιν (3d.per.pl.pres.act.ind.of ἔχω, aoristic) 82.
ἐπ' (preposition with the genitive, authority) 47.
αὐτῶν (gen.pl.masc.of αὐτός, authority) 16.
βασιλέα (acc.sing.masc.of βασιλεύς, direct object of ἔχουσιν) 31.
τὸν (acc.sing.masc.of the article in agreement with ἄγγελον) 9.
ἄγγελον (acc.sing.masc.of ἄγγελος, apposition) 96.
τῆς (gen.sing.fem.of the article in agreement with ἀβύσσου) 9.
ἀβύσσου (gen.sing.fem.of ἄβυσσος, description) 2231.
ὄνομα (nom.sing.neut.of ὄνομα, nominative absolute) 108.
αὐτῷ (dat.sing.masc.of αὐτός, reference) 16.
Ἐβραϊστὶ (instrumental, adverbial) 2094.

#5370 Ἀβαδδὼν (indeclinable).

King James Version

Abaddon - Rev.9:11.

Revised Standard Version

Abaddon - Rev.9:11.

Meaning: Ruin; destruction. *Cf.* Job 26:6; Prov.15:11. The name given to the king of the locusts in Rev.9:11.

καὶ (continuative conjunction) 14.
ἐν (preposition with the locative of sphere) 80.
τῇ (loc.sing.fem.of the article in agreement with Ἑλληνικῇ) 9.
Ἑλληνικῇ (loc.sing.fem.of Ἑλληνιστί sphere) 2860.
ὄνομα (acc.sing.neut.of ὄνομα, direct object of ἔχει) 108.
ἔχει (3d.per.sing.pres.act.ind.of ἔχω, aoristic) 82.

#5371 Ἀπολλύων (nom.sing.masc.of Ἀπολλύων, appellation).

King James Version

Apollyon - Rev.9:11.

Revised Standard Version

Apollyon - Rev.9:11.

Meaning: The author's Greek translation of the Hebrew Ἀβαδδὼν in Rev.9:11 for the Beast.

Translation - "*They have over them a king, the messenger of the abyss. His name in Aramaic is Abaddon and in the Greek his name is Apollyon.*"

Comment: Ἑλληνικῇ is an example of an adjective used without a substantive, where the gender and number make the context clear. Robertson lists some examples: Lk.13:32, where the context demands ἡμέρα with τῇ τρίτῃ; Mt.6:34; 27:8; Lk.13:33; Acts 16:11; 21:1; 20:15. (Robertson, *Grammar,* 1202).

The evidence that Apollyon is the Beast of Rev.13 and the Pale Horse Rider of Rev.6:7-8 (who is the resurrected White Horse Rider of Rev.6:1-2) is circumstantial. There is no passage that says that he is, but when we examine Rev.11:7; 17:8 together with Rev.9:1-2 and note that Rev.9:1-2 is at the same time as Rev.12:9, it looks convincing. If he is not, he comes from the abyss at the same time as the Beast. Review it carefully. It is mid-week (Rev.12:6). Satan is cast out of heaven (Rev.12:9). The personalized "star" falls from heaven to earth (Rev.9:1, 5th trumpet). He opens the abyss (Rev.9:2). The "king of the locusts" who is Apollyon emerges to reappear on earth. He kills the two witnesses (Rev.11:7). He is the 8th, of the seven (Rev.17:9-11) who, after 42 months (Rev.13:5) goes into perdition (Rev.17:11).

In verse Rev.9:12; 11:14 we learn that the last three trumpet judgments are also called "woes."

Verse 12 - "One woe is past; and, behold, there come two woes more hereafter."

Ἡ οὐαὶ ἡ μία ἀπῆλθεν. ἰδοὺ ἔρχεται ἔτι δύο οὐαὶ μετὰ ταῦτα.

"The first woe has passed; behold, two woes are still to come." . . . RSV

Ἡ (nom.sing.fem.of the article in agreement with οὐαὶ) 9.
οὐαὶ (nom.sing.fem.of οὐαί, subject of ἀπῆλθεν) 936.
ἡ (nom.sing.fem.of the article in agreement with οὐαὶ) 9.
μία (nom.sing.fem.of εἷς, in agreement with οὐαὶ) 469.
ἀπῆλθεν (3d.per.sing.aor.mid.ind.of ἀπέρχομαι, culminative) 239.
ἰδοὺ (exclamation) 95.
ἔρχεται (3d.per.sing.pres.mid.ind.of ἔρχομαι, futuristic) 146.
ἔτι (temporal adverb) 448.
δύο (numeral) 385.
οὐαὶ (nom.sing.fem.of οὐαί, subject of ἔρχεται) 936.
μετὰ (preposition with the accusative, time extent) 50.
ταῦτα (acc.pl.neut.of οὗτος, time extent) 93.

Translation - "One woe is past; Look! Two woes are yet to come after this."

Comment: It seems clear that the three woes are identified with the last three trumpet judgments. *Cf.* Rev.8:13; 9:12; 11:14. The remainder of chapter 9 is devoted to the second woe, which is the sixth trumpet judgment. The seventh trumpet (1 Cor.15:51) which is the third woe is described after the parenthetical material of Revelation 10:1 — 11:14 in Revelation 11:15-19.

Verse 13 - "And the sixth angel sounded, and I heard a voice from the four horns of the golden altar which is before God."

Καὶ ὁ ἔκτος ἄγγελος ἐσάλπισεν, καὶ ἤκουσα φωνὴν μίαν ἐκ τῶν κεράτων τοῦ θυσιαστηρίου τοῦ χρυσοῦ τοῦ ἐνώπιον τοῦ θεοῦ.

"Then the sixth angel blew his trumpet, and I heard a voice from the four horns of the golden altar before God, . . . " . . . RSV

Καὶ (continuative conjunction) 14.
ὁ (nom.sing.masc.of the article in agreement with ἄγγελος) 9.
ἕκτος (nom.sing.masc.of ἕκτος, in agreement with ἄγγελος) 1317.
ἄγγελος (nom.sing.masc.of ἄγγελος, subject of ἐσάλπισεν) 96.
ἐσάλπισεν (3d.per.sing.aor.act.ind.of σαλπίζω, ingressive) 559.
καὶ (continuative conjunction) 14.
ἤκουσα (1st.per.sing.aor.act.ind.of ἀκούω, constative) 148.
φωνὴν (acc.sing.fem.of φωνή, direct object of ἤκουσα) 222.
μίαν (acc.sing.fem.of εἷς, in agreement with φωνὴν) 469.
ἐκ (preposition with the ablative of source) 19.
τῶν (abl.pl.neut.of the article in agreement with κεράτων) 9.
κεράτων (abl.pl.neut.of κέρας, source) 1851.
τοῦ (gen.sing.neut.of the article in agreement with θυσιαστηρίου) 9.
θυσιαστηρίου (gen.sing.neut.of θυσιαστήριον, description) 484.
τοῦ (gen.sing.neut.of the article in agreement with θυσιαστηρίου) 9.
χρυσοῦ (gen.sing.neut.of χρύσεος, in agreement with θυσιαστηρίου) 4828.
τοῦ (gen.sing.neut.of the article in agreement with θυσιαστηρίου) 9.
ἐνώπιον (preposition with the genitive of place description) 1798.
τοῦ (gen.sing.masc.of the article in agreement with θεοῦ) 9.
θεοῦ (gen.sing.masc.of θεός, description) 124.

Translation - "And the sixth angel began to blow his trumpet, and I heard one voice from the horns of the golden altar before God . . . "

Comment: *Cf.* Rev.8:3 where John has τὸ θυσιαστήριον τὸ χρυσοῦν τὸ ἐνώπιον τοῦ θεοῦ. The Aland Committee, since the publication of the second edition of their text, has decided to put τεσσάρων before κεράτων, though within brackets, since the weight of external evidence for the presence and for the absence of τεσσάρων is almost evenly balanced. (Metzger, *A Textual Commentary on the Greek New Testament*, 744). The exegesis is not changed by the variant reading of the manuscripts.

The voice from the altar gives instruction to the sixth angel in

Verse 14 - "Saying to the sixth angel which had the trumpet, Loose the four angels which are bound in the great river Euphrates."

λέγοντα τῷ ἕκτῳ ἀγγέλῳ, ὁ ἔχων τὴν σάλπιγγα, Λῦσον τοὺς τέσσαρας ἀγγέλους τοὺς δεδεμένους ἐπὶ τῷ ποταμῷ τῷ μεγάλῳ Εὐφράτῃ.

". . . saying to the sixth angel who had the trumpet, 'Release the four angels who are bound at the great river Euphrates.' " . . . RSV

λέγοντα (pres.act.part.acc.sing.masc.of λέγω, recitative) 66.

τῷ (dat.sing.masc.of the article in agreement with ἀγέλλῳ) 9.

ἕκτῳ (dat.sing.masc.of ἕκτος, in agreement with ἀγέλλῳ) 1317.

ἀγγέλῳ (dat.sing.masc.of ἄγγελος, indirect object of λέγοντα) 96.

ὁ (nom.sing.masc.of the article in agreement with ἔχων) 9.

ἔχων (pres.act.part.nom.sing.masc.of ἔχω, substantival, in apposition with ἀγγέλῳ) 82.

τὴν (acc.sing.fem.of the article in agreement with σάλπιγγα) 9.

σάλπιγγα (acc.sing.fem.of σάλπιγξ, direct object of ἔχων) 1507.

Λῦσον (2d.per.sing.aor.act.impv.of λύω, command, ingressive) 471.

τοὺς (acc.pl.masc.of the article in agreement with ἀγγέλους) 9.

τέσσαρας (acc.pl.masc.of τέσσαρες, in agreement with ἀγγέλους) 1508.

ἀγγέλους (acc.pl.masc.of ἄγγελος, direct object of λῦσον) 96.

τοὺς (acc.pl.masc.of the article in agreement with ἀγγέλους) 9.

δεδεμένους (perf.pass.part.acc.pl.masc.of δέω, constative, in apposition with ἀγγέλους) 998.

ἐπὶ (preposition with the locative of sphere) 47.

τῷ (loc.sing.masc.of the article in agreement with ποταμῷ) 9.

ποταμῷ (loc.sing.masc.of ποταμός, sphere) 274.

τῷ (loc.sing.masc.of the article in agreement with ποταμῷ) 9.

μεγάλῳ (loc.sing.masc.of μέγας, in agreement with ποταμῷ) 184.

#5372 Εὐφράτῃ (loc.sing.masc.of Εὐφράτης, in apposition).

King James Version

Euphrates - Rev.9:14; 16:12.

Revised Standard Version

Euphrates - REv.9:14; 16:12.

Meaning: The river rising in the southern slopes of the mountain range at the southeastern edge of the Black Sea, in central Turkey and flowing south and east, through Syria and Iraq to join the Tigris at Basra, at the head of the Persian Gulf. It enters the triangle (formed by Batum, Baku and Kuwait within which lies the bulk of the mid-eastern oil reserves) at its southern point. This area will figure largely in the international struggle for economic and political power - Rev.9:14; 16:12.

Translation - "saying to the sixth angel, who has the trumpet, 'Release the four angels who have been assigned to the great river Euphrates.' "

Comment: We have the wrong gender in λέγοντα (whether it is accusative singular or nominative plural neuter) since it is joined to φωνὴν which is feminine). We also have the wrong case in ὁ ἔχων which is in apposition to τῷ ἕκτῳ ἀγγέλῳ. The participle λέγοντα is to be construed κατὰ σύνεσιν.

Comparison of the sixth trumpet with the sixth vial judgment (Rev.16:12) gives further evidence of the contemporaneity and co-terminality of seals, trumpets and vials. At the sixth stage we are approaching the last days of the tribulation period and the second coming of our Lord. As a result of the release of the four angels at the Euphrates, a great army is revealed (Rev.9:15-19). See the similarity in Rev.16:12-14.

Verse 15 - "And the four angels were loosed, which were prepared for an hour, and a day, and a month, and a year, for to slay the third part of men."

καὶ ἐλύθησαν οἱ τέσσαρες ἄγγελοι οἱ ἡτοιμασμένοι εἰς τὴν ὥραν καὶ ἡμέραν καὶ μῆνα καὶ ἐνιαυτόν, ἵνα ἀποκτείνωσιν τὸ τρίτον τῶν ἀνθρώπων.

"So the four angels were released, who had been held ready for the hour, the day, the month, and the year, to kill a third of mankind." . . . RSV

καὶ (continuative conjunction) 14.

ἐλύθησαν (3d.per.pl.aor.pass.ind.of λύω, culminative) 471.

οἱ (nom.pl.masc.of the article in agreement with ἄγγελοι) 9.

τέσσαρες (nom.pl.masc.of τέσσαρες, in agreement with ἄγγελοι) 1508.

ἄγγελοι (nom.pl.masc.of ἄγγελος, subject of ἐλύθησαν) 96.

οἱ (nom.pl.masc.of the article in agreement with ἄγγελοι) 9.

ἡτοιμασμένοι (perf.pass.part.nom.pl.masc.of ἐτοιμάζω, adjectival, emphatic attributive position, ascriptive, in agreement with ἄγγελοι) 257.

εἰς (preposition with the accusative, time limitation) 140.

τὴν (acc.sing.fem.of the article in agreement with ὥραν) 9.

ὥραν (acc.sing.fem.of ὥρα, time limitation) 735.

καὶ (adjunctive conjunction joining nouns) 14.

ἡμέραν (acc.sing.fem.of ἡμέρα, time limitation) 135.

καὶ (adjunctive conjunction joining nouns) 14.

μῆνα (acc.sing.fem.of μήν, time limitation) 1809.

καὶ (adjunctive conjunction joining nouns) 14.

ἐνιαυτόν (acc.sing.masc.of ἐνιαυτός, time limitation) 2025.

ἵνα (conjunction with the subjunctive, purpose) 114.

ἀποκτείνωσιν (3d.per.pl.pres.act.subj.of ἀποκτείνω, purpose) 889.

τὸ (acc.sing.neut.of the article in agreement with τρίτον) 9.

τρίτον (acc.sing.neut.of τρίτος, direct object of ἀποκτείνωσιν) 1209.

τῶν (gen.pl.masc.of the article in agreement with ἀνθρώπων) 9.

ἀνθρώπων (gen.pl.masc.of ἄνθρωπος, partitive) 341.

Translation - "And the four angels who had been assigned duty at the specific hour and day and month and year were released in order that they might kill one third of the human race."

Comment: These four angels had been given a specific part to play in the scenario. They were under orders not to act until the proper time. No good actor walks on stage and performs his part until his cue is given. The cue here is specific - a given hour of a given day of a given month of a given year. We have here an interesting use of εἰς with the accusative of time limitation. Extension always involves limitation. The divine purpose is the slaughter of one third of the remaining population of earth. Thus the pestilence of the fourth seal (Rev.6:8) is augmented by the slaughter of one third of those remaining. Having been tormented for five months (Rev.9:5,10) with the privilege of dying withheld (Rev.9:6) they now will die. This hellish army numbers two hundred million.

Verse 16 - "And the number of the army of the horsemen were two hundred thousand thousand; and I heard the number of them."

καὶ ὁ ἀριθμὸς τῶν στρατευμάτων τοῦ ἱππικοῦ δισμυριάδες μυριάδων. ἤκουσα τὸν ἀριθμὸν αὐτῶν.

"The number of the troops of cavalry was twice ten thousand times ten thousand; I heard their number." . . . RSV

καὶ (continuative conjunction) 14.
ὁ (nom.sing.masc.of the article in agreement with ἀριθμὸς) 9.
ἀριθμὸς (nom.sing.masc.of ἀριθμός, subject of ἦν understood) 2278.
τῶν (gen.pl.neut.of the article in agreement with στρατευμάτων) 9.
στρατευμάτων (gen.pl.neut.of στράτευμα, description) 1404.
τοῦ (gen.sing.masc.of the article in agreement with ἱππικοῦ) 9.

#5373 ἱππικοῦ (gen.sing.masc.of ἱππικός, description).

   King James Version

horsemen - Rev.9:16.

   Revised Standard Version

cavalry - Rev.9:16.

Meaning: equestrian; pertaining to a horse. An adjective, used like a substantive - Rev.9:16.

#5374 δισμυριάδες (nom.pl.fem.of δισμυρίας, predicate nominative).

   King James Version

two hundred thousand - Rev.9:16.

   Revised Standard Version

twice ten thousand - Rev.9:16.

Meaning: twice ten thousand. Two myriads. Followed by μυριάδων - Rev.9:16.

μυριάδων (gen.pl.fem.of μυρίας, description) 2473.
ἤκουσα (1st.per.sing.aor.act.ind.of ἀκούω, constative) 148.
τὸν (acc.sing.masc.of the article in agreement with ἀριθμὸν) 9.
ἀριθμὸν (acc.sing.masc.of ἀριθμός, direct object of ἤκουσα) 2278.
αὐτῶν (gen.pl.masc.of αὐτός, description) 16.

Translation - "And the number of the army of horsemen was two hundred million."

Comment: It is really difficult to say what διαμυριάδες μυριάδων means. The KJV says, "two hundred thousand thousand" while the RSV has "twice ten thousand times ten thousand" which computes to the same figure. Weymouth says, "two hundred million." If μυριάς means exactly 10,000, this is correct. The point is not lost whether we know or do not know exactly how many horsemen will be involved, though it is a large number. John's statement in the last clause seems to indicate that he understood the exact number.

Verse 17 - "And thus I saw the horses in the vision, and them that sat on them having breastplates of fire, and of jacinth, and brimstone: and the heads of the horses were as the heads of lions; and out of their mouths issued fire and smoke and brimstone."

καὶ οὕτως εἶδον τοὺς ἵππους ἐν τῇ ὁράσει καὶ τοὺς καθημένους ἐπ' αὐτῶν, ἔχοντας θώρακας πυρίνους καὶ ὑακινθίνους καὶ θειώδεις καὶ αἱ κεφαλαὶ τῶν ἵππων ὡς κεφαλαὶ λεόντων, καὶ ἐκ τῶν στομάτων αὐτῶν ἐκπορεύεται πῦρ καὶ καπνὸς καὶ θεῖον.

"And this was how I saw the horses in my vision: the riders wore breatplates the color of fire and of sapphire and of sulphur, and the heads of the horses were like lions' heads, and fire and smoke and sulphur issued from their mouths." . . . *RSV*

καὶ (continuative conjunction) 14.

οὕτως (adverbial) 74.

εἶδον (1st.per.sing.aor.act.ind.of ὁράω, constative) 144.

τοὺς (acc.pl.masc.of the article in agreement with ἵππους) 9.

ἵππους (acc.pl.masc.of ἵππος, direct object of εἶδον) 5121.

ἐν (preposition with the instrumental, means) 80.

τῇ (instru.sing.fem.of the article in agreement with ὁράσει) 9.

ὁράσει (instru.sing.fem.of ὅρασις, means) 2982.

καὶ (adjunctive conjunction joining substantives) 14.

τοὺς (acc.pl.masc.of the article in agreement with καθημένους) 9.

καθημένους (pres.mid.part.acc.pl.masc.of κάθημαι, substantival, direct object of εἶδον) 377.

ἐπ' (preposition with the genitive, rest) 47.

αὐτῶν (gen.pl.masc.of αὐτός, place description, rest) 16.

ἔχοντας (pres.act.part.acc.pl.masc.of ἔχω, adverbial, circumstantial) 82.

θώρακας (acc.pl.fem.of θώραξ, direct object of ἔχοντας) 4533.

#5375 πυρίνους (acc.pl.fem.of πύρινος, in agreement with θώρακας).

King James Version

of fire - Rev.9:17.

Revised Standard Version

the color of fire - Rev.9:17.

Meaning: Cf. πῦρ (#298) and related words, #'s 3757, 737, 738, 4158, 5210, 491, 5350. Shining like fire - Rev.9:17; *Cf.* Ezek.28:14,16.

καὶ (adjunctive conjunction joining adjectives) 14.

#5376 ὑακινθίνους (acc.pl.fem.of ὑακίνθινος, in agreement with θώρακας).

King James Version

of jacinth - Rev.9:17.

Revised Standard Version

sapphire - Rev.9:17.

Meaning: Cf. ὑάκινθος in Rev.21:20. Of the color of the hyacinth. Of a red color bordering on black. The ὑάκινθος (#5438) is not a flower but a stone, composed of zirconium silicate. The ὑάκινθος is a yellow, orange, red or brown variety of zircon. The mineral is found in Ceylon, but also occurs in various igneous and crystalline rocks in Bohemia, Norway, Greenland, Germany and the Ural Mountains. Not to be confused with the flower, hyacinth, which is a species of iris. (*American Peoples' Encyclopedia*, X, 800). Rev.9:17.

καὶ (adjunctive conjunction joining nouns) 14.

#5377 θειώδεις (acc.pl.fem.of θειώδης, in agreement with θώρακας).

King James Version

of brimstone - Rev.9:17.

Revised Standard Version

of sulphur - Rev.9:17.

Meaning: Cf. θεῖον (#2619). Like brimstone; of sulphurous quality - Rev.9:17.

καὶ (continuative conjunction) 14.
αἱ (nom.pl.fem.of the article in agreement with κεφαλαὶ) 9.
κεφαλαὶ (nom.pl.fem.of κεφαλή, subject of ἦν understood) 521.
τῶν (gen.pl.masc.of the article in agreement with ἵππων) 9.
ἵππων (gen.pl.masc.of ἵππος, description) 5121.
ὡς (comparative particle) 128.
κεφαλαὶ (nom.pl.fem.of κεφαλή, predicate nominative) 521.
λεόντων (gen.pl.masc.of λέων, description) 4872.
καὶ (continuative conjunction) 14.
ἐκ (preposition with the ablative of separation) 19.
τῶν (abl.pl.neut.of the article in agreement with στομάτων) 9.
στομάτων (abl.pl.neut.of στόμα, separation) 344.
αὐτῶν (gen.pl.masc.of αὐτός, possession) 16.
ἐκπορεύεται (3d.per.sing.pres.mid.ind.of ἐκπορεύομαι, historical) 270.

πῦρ (nom.sing.neut.of πῦρ, subject of ἐκπορεύεται) 298.

καὶ (adjunctive conjunction joining nouns) 14.

καπνὸς (nom.sing.masc.of καπνός, subject of ἐκπορεύεται) 2986.

καὶ (adjunctive conjunction joining nouns) 14.

θεῖον (nom.sing.neut.of θεῖον, subject of ἐκπορεύεται) 2619.

Translation - "And this is how I saw the horses and those sitting upon them, in the vision: as having breastplates that looked fiery red and like a sapphire and sulphurous; and the heads of the horses looked like lions' heads and from their mouths poured forth fire and smoke and sulphurous fumes."

Comment: Fiery red, dark blue and yellow - this is how the breastplates of the horses looked to John - lions' heads with fire, smoke and sulphur coming from their mouths. Obviously this will be no human cavalry unit, though they will be accompanied by a human army composed of soldiers of all nations (Rev. 16:12-14). This hellish horde of creatures will kill one third of all of the unregenerates who will remain upon the earth at that time.

Interpreters who speak of symbolism offer their opinions about what is symbolized, and thus the Word of God is subjected to the subjective views of all, and thus it becomes the objective revelation of nothing. There is no objection to saying that something is symbolic if we do not seek to interpret the symbol. It seems far better to take obscure passages literally and to await the time when the events in question will occur. All that we can say at present is that what John saw on this occasion was a destructive force that killed one third of the people. What these horses will be and who their riders with their breastplates will be we do not know. We learn in verse 18 how the slaughter will be done.

Verse 18 - "By these three was the third part of men killed, by the fire and by the smoke, and by the brimstone, which issued out of their mouths."

ἀπὸ τῶν τριῶν πληγῶν τούτων ἀπεκτάνθησαν τὸ τρίτον τῶν ἀνθρώπων, ἐκ τοῦ πυρὸς καὶ τοῦ καπνοῦ καὶ τοῦ θείου τοῦ ἐκπορευομένου ἐκ τῶν στομάτων αὐτῶν.

"By these three plagues a third of mankind was killed, by the fire and smoke and sulphur issuing from their mouths." . . . RSV

ἀπὸ (preposition with the ablative, means) 70.

τῶν (abl.pl.fem.of the article in agreement with πληγῶν) 9.

τριῶν (abl.pl.fem.of τρεῖς, in agreement with πληγῶν) 1010.

πληγῶν (abl.pl.fem.of πληγή, means) 2421.

τούτων (abl.pl.fem.of οὗτος, in agreement with πληγῶν) 93.

ἀπεκτάνθησαν (3d.per.pl.aor.pass.ind.of ἀποκτείνω, constative) 889.

τὸ (nom.sing.neut.of the article in agreement with τρίτον) 9.

τρίτον (nom.sing.neut.of τρίτος, subject of ἀπεκτάνθησαν) 1209.

τῶν (gen.pl.masc.of the article in agreement with ἀνθρώπων) 9.

ἀνθρώπων (gen.pl.masc.of ἄνθρωπος, partitive) 341.

ἐκ (preposition with the ablative, source) 19.

τοῦ (abl.sing.neut.of the article in agreement with πυρὸς) 9.
πυρὸς (abl.sing.neut.of πῦρ, source) 298.
καὶ (adjunctive conjunction joining nouns) 14.
τοῦ (abl.sing.masc.of the article in agreement with καπνοῦ) 9.
καπνοῦ (abl.sing.masc.of καπνός, source) 2986.
καὶ (adjunctive conjunction joining nouns) 14.
τοῦ (abl.sing.neut.of the article in agreement with θείου) 9.
θείου (abl.sing.neut.of θεῖον, source) 2619.
τοῦ (abl.sing.neut.of the article in agreement with ἐκπορευομένου) 9.
ἐκπορευομένου (pres.mid.part.abl.sing.neut.of ἐκπορεύομαι, adjectival, emphatic attributive position, in agreement with πυρὸς, καπνοῦ and θείου) 270.
ἐκ (preposition with the ablative of separation) 19.
τῶν (abl.pl.neut.of the article in agreement with στομάτων) 9.
στομάτων (abl.pl.neut.of στόμα, separation) 344.
αὐτῶν (gen.pl.masc.of αὐτός, possession) 16.

Translation - *"By these three, a third of the remaining population was killed - by the fire and the smoke and the sulphur that poured from their mouths."*

Comment: Note the ablative of means with ἀπό and the ablative of source with ἐκ. τούτων is deictic.

Keep in mind that the time of the sixth trumpet is a short time before the last great day. The sixth vial judgment calls the armies of the world together to Jerusalem for the battle of Armageddon (Rev.16:12-14). This hellish horde described under the sixth trumpet seems to come from the Euphrates River valley, the site of ancient Babylon, Israel's old enemy.

Verse 19 - *"For their power is in their mouth, and in their tails: for their tails were like unto serpents, and had heads, and with them they do hurt."*

ἡ γὰρ ἐξουσία τῶν ἵππων ἐν τῷ στόματι αὐτῶν ἐστιν καὶ ἐν ταῖς οὐραῖς αὐτῶν. αἱ γὰρ οὐραὶ αὐτῶν ὅμοιαι ὄφεσιν, ἔχουσαι κεφαλάς, καὶ ἐν αὐταῖς ἀδικοῦσιν.

"For the power of the horses is in their mouths and in their tails; their tails are like serpents, with heads, and by means of them they wound." ... RSV

ἡ (nom.sing.fem.of the article in agreement with ἐξουσία) 9.
γὰρ (causal conjunction) 105.
ἐξουσία (nom.sing.fem.of ἐξουσία, subject of ἐστιν) 707.
τῶν (gen.pl.masc.of the article in agreement with ἵππων) 9.
ἵππων (gen.pl.masc.of ἵππος, possession) 5121.
ἐν (preposition with the locative of place) 80.
τῷ (loc.sing.neut.of the article in agreement with στόματι) 9.
στόματι (loc.sing.neut.of στόμα, place) 344.
αὐτῶν (gen.pl.masc.of αὐτός, possession) 16.
ἐστιν (3d.per.sing.pres.ind.of εἰμί, aoristic) 86.

καὶ (adjunctive conjunction joining prepositional phrases) 14.

ἐν (preposition with the locative of place) 80.

ταῖς (loc.pl.fem.of the article in agreement with οὐραῖς) 9.

οὐραῖς (loc.pl.fem.of οὐρά, place) 5369.

αὐτῶν (gen.pl.masc.of αὐτός, possession) 16.

αἱ (nom.pl.fem.of the article in agreement with οὐραὶ) 9.

γὰρ (causal conjunction) 105.

οὐραὶ (nom.pl.fem.of οὐρά, subject of ἦσαν understood) 5369.

αὐτῶν (gen.pl.masc.of αὐτός, possession) 16.

ὅμοιαι (nom.pl.fem.of ὅμοιος, predicate adjective) 923.

ὄφεσιν (dat.pl.masc.of ὄφις, comparison) 658.

ἔχουσαι (pres.act.part.nom.pl.fem.of ἔχω, adverbial, complementary) 82.

κεφαλάς (acc.pl.fem.of κεφαλή, direct object of ἔχουσαι) 521.

καὶ (continuative conjunction) 14.

ἐν (preposition with the instrumental, means) 80.

αὐταῖς (instru.pl.fem.of αὐτός, means) 16.

ἀδικοῦσιν (3d.per.pl.pres.act.ind.of ἀδικέω, customary) 1327.

Translation - "For the power of the horses is in their mouth, and in their tails; for their tails are like snakes, having heads, and with them they inflict injury."

Comment: No comment is necessary. The reader's imagination is as good as mine. I only warn again that we do not try to make something out of this description other than what is says. Zoologists, if they are scientists with open minds, should be the last to say that they have seen, described and classified all of the creatures in existence. That no one except John (and he only with supernatural help) has ever seen one of these horses is obvious. But this does not mean that they do not exist. The real question is whether or not we believe the Book of the Revelation. Is it the Word of God or not? The assumption of this study is that it is.

The reaction of the unregenerate to this second woe (Rev.11:14) is precisely what any Calvinist would expect. We see it in

Verse 20 - "And the rest of the men which were not killed by these plagues yet repented not of the works of their hands, that they should not worship devils, and idols of gold, and silver, and brass and stone, and of wood: which neither can see, nor hear, nor walk."

Καὶ οἱ λοιποὶ τῶν ἀνθρώπων, οἳ οὐκ ἀπεκτάνθησαν ἐν ταῖς πληγαῖς ταύταις, οὐδὲ μετενόησαν ἐκ τῶν ἔργων τῶν χειρῶν αὐτῶν, ἵνα μὴ προσκυνήσουσιν τὰ δαιμόνια καὶ τὰ εἴδωλα τὰ χρυσᾶ καὶ τὰ ἀργυρᾶ καὶ τὰ χαλκᾶ καὶ τὰ λίθινα καὶ τὰ ξύλινα, ἃ οὔτε βλέπειν δύναται οὔτε ἀκούειν οὔτε περιπατεῖν.

"The rest of mankind, who were not killed by these plagues, did not repent of their works of their hands nor give up worshipping demons and idols of gold and silver and bronze and stone and wood, which cannot either see or hear or walk;". . . RSV

Καὶ (continuative conjunction) 14.

οἱ (nom.pl.masc.of the article in agreement with λοιποὶ) 9.

λοιποὶ (nom.pl.masc.of λοιπός, subject of μετενόησαν) 1402.

τῶν (gen.pl.masc.of the article in agreement with ἀνθρώπων) 9.

ἀνθρώπων (gen.pl.masc.of ἄνθρωπος, partitive) 341.

οἳ (nom.pl.masc.of ὅς, relative pronoun, subject of ἀπεκτάνθησαν) 65.

οὐκ (negative conjunction with the indicative) 130.

ἀπεκτάνθησαν (3d.per.pl.aor.pass.ind.of ἀποκτείνω, constative) 889.

ἐν (preposition with the instrumental, means) 80.

ταῖς (instru.pl.fem.of the article in agreement with πληγαῖς) 9.

πληγαῖς (instru.pl.fem.of πληγή, means) 2421.

ταύταις (instru.pl.fem.of οὗτος, in agreement with πληγαῖς, deictic) 93.

οὐδὲ (disjunctive particle) 452.

μετενόησαν (3d.per.pl.aor.act.ind.of μετανοέω, ingressive) 251.

ἐκ (preposition with the ablative of separation) 19.

τῶν (abl.pl.neut.of the article in agreement with ἔργων) 9.

ἔργων (abl.pl.neut.of ἔργον, separation) 460.

τῶν (gen.pl.fem.of the article in agreement with χειρῶν) 9.

χειρῶν (gen.pl.fem.of χείρ, description) 308.

αὐτῶν (gen.pl.masc.of αὐτός, possession) 16.

ἵνα (conjunction with the future indicative in a negative ecbatic clause) 114.

μὴ (negative conjunction with the indicative) 87.

προσκυνήσουσιν (3d.per.pl.fut.act.ind.of προσκυνέω, negative ecbatic clause) 147.

τὰ (acc.pl.neut.of the article in agreement with δαιμονία) 9.

δαιμονία (acc.pl.neut.of δαιμόνιον, direct object of προσκυνήσουσιν) 686.

καὶ (adjunctive conjunction joining nouns) 14.

τὰ (acc.pl.neut.of the article in agreement with εἴδωλα) 9.

εἴδωλα (acc.pl.neut.of εἴδωλον, direct object of προσκυνήσουσιν) 3138.

τὰ (acc.pl.neut.of the article in agreement with χρυσᾶ) 9.

χρυσᾶ (acc.pl.neut.of χρύσος, in agreement with εἴδωλα) 192.

καὶ (adjunctive conjunction joining adjectives) 14.

τὰ (acc.pl.neut.of the article in agreement with ἀργυρᾶ) 9.

ἀργυρᾶ (acc.pl.neut.of ἄργυρος, in agreement with εἴδωλα) 860.

καὶ (adjunctive conjunction joining adjectives) 14.

τὰ (acc.pl.neut.of the article in agreement with χαλκᾶ) 9.

#5378 χαλκᾶ (acc.pl.neut.of χάλκεος, in agreement with εἴδωλα).

King James Version

of brass - Rev.9:20.

Revised Standard Version

of bronze - Rev.9:20.

Meaning: Cf. χαλκός (#861) and #'s 5326, 2300 and 5430. Bronze; made of brass - Rev.9:20.

καὶ (adjunctive conjunction joining adjectives) 14.
τὰ (acc.pl.neut.of the article in agreement with λίθινα) 9.
λίθινα (acc.pl.neut.of λίθινος, in agreement with εἴδωλα) 1969.
καὶ (adjunctive conjunction joining adjectives) 14.
τὰ (acc.pl.neut.of the article in agreement with ξύλινα) 9.
ξύλινα (acc.pl.neut.of ξύλινος, in agreement with εἴδωλα) 4829.
ἃ (nom.pl.neut.of ὅς, relative pronoun, subject of δύνανται) 65.
οὔτε (negative copulative conjunction) 598.
βλέπειν (pres.act.inf.of βλέπω, complementary) 499.
δύνανται (3d.per.pl.pres.mid.ind.of δύναμαι, aoristic) 289.
οὔτε (negative copulative conjunction) 598.
ἀκούειν (pres.act.inf.of ἀκούω, complementary) 148.
οὔτε (negative copulative conjunction) 598.
περιπατεῖν (pres.act.inf.of περιπατέω, complementary) 384.

Translation - "And the rest of the people, those who were not killed by these plagues did not begin to repent of the works of their hands, so as no longer to worship the demons and the idols of gold and of silver and of bronze and of stone and of wood, which are able neither to see, nor to hear nor to walk about."

Comment: By introducing οὐδὲ, without a correlative clause, John has created a difficulty. It would have been better if he had said οὐ. Thus scribes of "many minuscules *arm al* substitute(d) οὐ (or καὶ οὐ 2329 *al*). As between οὐδέ (p47 Sinaiticus 046 69 1778 2020 2053txt *al*) and οὔτε (A P I 1611 2053comm 2065 2081 2432 *al*), the Committee preferred the former, since copyists were likely to alter it to οὔτε by assimilation to the correlative οὔτε . . . οὔτε later in the verse." (Metzger, *A Textual Commentary on the Greek New Testament*, 744).

The first relative clause, οἳ . . . ταύταις is in apposition to οἱ λοιποί. Note the ecbatic use of ἵνα μή and the future indicative. It expresses the result of their repentance if indeed they had repented, which they did not. Unregenerate men do not repent under the scourge of punishment. Esau did not repent (μετανοέω). He was sorry that he lost his birthright but his tears did not produce repentance (Heb.12:16,17) just as sinners are sorry that they are punished. But emotion does not produce repentance, which is a change of the mind, not a change of our feelings. Only God, the Holy Spirit can grant repentance to the elect (Acts 11:18) and no man can call Jesus the Lord of his life without the motivation of the Holy Spirit (1 Cor.12:3).

That idol worship on the Euphrates (typical Moslem country) will be reinstituted in the last days, is clear from this verse. Man is "incurably religious" and if he will not worship Christ he will fashion with his own hands those gods which he will worship.

Idol worship leads to all of the other sins mentioned in

Verse 21 - "Neither repented they of their murders, nor of their sorceries, nor of their fornication, nor of their thefts."

καὶ οὐ μετενόησαν ἐκ τῶν φόνων αὐτῶν οὔτε ἐκ τῶν φαρμάκων αὐτῶν οὔτε ἐκ
τῆς πορνείας αὐτῶν οὔτε ἐκ τῶν κλεμμάτων αὐτῶν.

*"nor did they repent of their murders or their sorceries or their immorality or
their thefts." . . . RSV*

καὶ (continuative conjunction) 14.
οὐ (negative conjunction with the indicative) 130.
μετενόησαν (3d.per.pl.aor.act.ind.of μετανοέω, ingressive) 251.
ἐκ (preposition with the ablative of separation) 19.
τῶν (abl.pl.masc.of the article in agreement with φόνων) 9.
φόνων (abl.pl.masc.of φόνος, separation) 1166.
αὐτῶν (gen.pl.masc.of αὐτός, possession) 16.
οὔτε (negative copulative conjunction) 598.
ἐκ (preposition with the ablative of separation) 19.
τῶν (abl.pl.fem.of the article in agreement with φαρμάκων) 9.
φαρμάκων (abl.pl.fem.of φαρμακεία, separation) 4451.
αὐτῶν (gen.pl.masc.of αὐτός, possession) 16.
οὔτε (negative copulative conjunction) 598.
ἐκ (preposition with the ablative of separation) 19.
τῆς (abl.sing.fem.of the article in agreement with πορνείας) 9.
πορνείας (abl.sing.fem.of πορνεία, separation) 511.
αὐτῶν (gen.pl.masc.of αὐτός, possession) 16.
οὔτε (negative copulative conjunction) 598.
ἐκ (preposition with the ablative of separation) 19.
τῶν (abl.pl.neut.of the article in agreement with κλεμμάτων) 9.

#5379 κλεμμάτων (abl.pl.neut.of κλέμμα, separation).

King James Version

theft - Rev.9:21.

Revised Standard Version

theft - Rev.9:21.

Meaning: Cf. κλέπτω (#597), κλέπτης (#595). Theft - Rev.9:21.

αὐτῶν (gen.pl.masc.of αὐτός, possession) 16.

Translation - "Nor did they begin to repent of their murders, nor of their
sorceries, nor of their immorality nor of their thefts."

Comment: Note that black magic (sorcery) is listed among the prominent sins of
the last days - another evidence of demonism. A mystic from the Middle East
visits a state university in the United States and bends car keys by stroking them
with his hand, and Ph.D's in physics and chemistry become believers (!) while a
Christian Ph.D. in History who is a student of the Greek New Testament taunts

them for their "faith." Jesus came in His Father's name and men received Him not. If another comes in his own name, him they will receive. (John 5:43).

The Revelation interrupts the picture of the clock count-down just before the end to give us information essential to our understanding of the rest of the story. This information is found in the parenthesis in Revelation 10:1-11:14.

The Angel and the Little Scroll

(Revelation 10:1-11)

Revelation 10:1 - "And I saw another mighty angel come down from heaven, clothed with a cloud; and a rainbow was upon his head, and his face was as it were the sun, and his feet as pillars of fire."

Καὶ εἶδον ἄλλον ἄγγελον ἰσχυρὸν καταβαίνοντα ἐκ τοῦ οὐρανοῦ, περιβεβλημένον νεφέλην, καὶ ἡ ἶρις ἐπὶ τὴν κεφαλὴν αὐτοῦ, καὶ τὸ πρόσωπον αὐτοῦ ὡς ὁ ἥλιος, καὶ οἱ πόδες αὐτοῦ ὡς στῦλοι πυρός,

"Then I saw another mighty angel coming down from heaven, wrapped in a cloud, with a rainbow over his head, and his face was like the sun, and his legs like pillars of fire." . . . RSV

Καὶ (continuative conjunction) 14.

εἶδον (1st.per.sing.aor.act.ind.of ὁράω, constative) 144.

ἄλλον (acc.sing.masc.of ἄλλος, in agreement with ἄγγελος) 198.

ἄγγελον (acc.sing.masc.of ἄγγελος, direct object of εἶδον)

ἰσχυρὸν (acc.sing.masc.of ἰσχυρός, in agreement with ἄγγελον) 303.

καταβαίνοντα (pres.act.part.acc.sing.masc.of καταβαίνω, adjectival, predicate position, restrictive, in agreement with ἄγγελον) 324.

ἐκ (preposition with the ablative of separation) 19.

τοῦ (abl.sing.masc.of the article in agreement with οὐρανοῦ) 9.

οὐρανοῦ (abl.sing.masc.of οὐρανός, separation) 254.

περιβεβλημένον (perf.pass.part.acc.sing.masc.of περιβάλλω, adjectival, predicate position, restrictive, in agreement with ἄγγελον) 631.

νεφέλην (acc.sing.fem.of νεφέλη, adverbial accusative) 1225.

καὶ (continuative conjunction) 14.

ἡ (nom.sing.fem.of the article in agreement with ἶρις) 9.

ἶρις (nom.sing.fem.of ἶρις, subject of ἦν understood) 5341.

ἐπὶ (preposition with the accusative, rest) 47.

τὴν (acc.sing.fem.of the article in agreement with κεφαλὴν) 9.

κεφαλὴν (acc.sing.fem.of κεφαλή, rest) 521.

αὐτοῦ (gen.sing.masc.of αὐτός, possession) 16.

καὶ (continuative conjunction) 14.

τὸ (nom.sing.neut.of the article in agreement with πρόσωπον) 9.

πρόσωπον (nom.sing.neut.of πρόσωπον, subject of ἦν understood) 588.

αὐτοῦ (gen.sing.masc.of αὐτός, possession) 16.
ὡς (comparative particle) 128.
ὁ (nom.sing.masc.of the article in agreement with ἥλιος) 9.
ἥλιος (nom.sing.masc.of ἥλιος, subject of ἔστιν understood) 546.
καὶ (continuative conjunction) 14.
οἱ (nom.pl.masc.of the article in agreement with πόδες) 9.
πόδες (nom.pl.masc.of πούς, subject of ἦν understood) 353.
αὐτοῦ (gen.sing.masc.of αὐτός, possession) 16.
ὡς (comparative particle) 128.
στῦλοι (nom.pl.masc.of στῦλος, subject of εἰσίν understood) 4422.
πυρός (gen.sing.neut.of πῦρ, description) 298.

Translation - "And I saw another mighty angel coming down from heaven, clothed with a cloud, and the rainbow upon his head, and his face looked like the sun, and his feet were like fiery pillars."

Comment: Here again, as in Rev.7:9,13; 11:3; 12:1; 17:4; 18:16 and 19:13 we have περιβάλλω as a perfect passive participle followed by the accusative case. *Cf.* comment on Rev.7:9. *Cf.* also Rev.1:15,16; 4:3. The accoutrements suggest that this angel is our Lord Himself, but the context seems to have no conclusive evidence.

Verse 2 - "And he had in his hand a little book open: and he set his right foot upon the sea, and his left foot on the earth."

καὶ ἔχων ἐν τῇ χειρὶ αὐτοῦ βιβλαρίδιον ἠνεῳγμένον. καὶ ἔθηκεν τὸν πόδα αὐτοῦ τὸν δεξιὸν ἐπὶ τῆς θαλάσσης, τὸν δὲ εὐώνυμον ἐπὶ τῆς γῆς,

"He had a little scroll open in his hand. And he set his right foot on the sea, and his left foot on the land, . . . " . . . RSV

καὶ (adjunctive conjunction joining participles) 14.
ἔχων (pres.act.part.nom.sing.masc.of ἔχω, adverbial, circumstantial) 82.
ἐν (preposition with the locative of place) 80.
τῇ (loc.sing.fem.of the article in agreement with χειρὶ) 9.
χειρὶ (loc.sing.fem.of χείρ, place) 308.
αὐτοῦ (gen.sing.masc.of αὐτός, possession) 16.

#5380 βιβλαρίδιον (acc.sing.neut.of βιβλαρίδιον, direct object of ἔχων).

King James Version

little book - Rev.10:2,9,10.

Revised Standard Version

little scroll - Rev.10:2,9,10.

Meaning: dimin.of βίβλιον. Little book; little scroll - Rev.10:2,9,10.

ἠνεῳγμένον (perf.pass.part.acc.sing.neut.of ἀνοίγω, adjectival, predicate position, restrictive, in agreement with βιβλαρίδιον) 188.

καὶ (continuative conjunction) 14.

ἔθνκεν (3d.per.sing.aor.act.ind.of τίθημι, ingressive) 455.

τὸν (acc.sing.masc.of the article in agreement with πόδα) 9.

πόδα (acc.sing.masc.of πούς, direct object of ἔθηκεν) 353.

αὐτοῦ (gen.sing.masc.of αὐτός, possession) 16.

τὸν (acc.sing.masc.of the article in agreement with πόδα) 9.

δεξιὸν (acc.sing.masc.of δεξιός, in agreement with πόδα) 502.

ἐπὶ (preposition with the genitive, place description) 47.

τῆς (gen.sing.fem.of the article in agreement with θαλάσσης) 9.

θαλάσσης (gen.sing.fem.of θάλασσα, place description) 374.

τὸν (acc.sing.masc.of the article in agreement with εὐώνυμον) 9.

εὐώνυμον (acc.sing.masc.of εὐώνυμος, direct object of ἔθηκεν) 1329.

ἐπὶ (preposition with the genitive, place description) 47.

τῆς (gen.sing.fem.of the article in agreement with γῆς) 9.

γῆς (gen.sing.fem.of γῆ, place description) 157.

Translation - "And having in his hand a little open book. And he set his right foot upon the sea and his left upon the land. . . "

Comment: Note the two adjectival participles describing ἄγγελον of verse 1, and the circumstantial adverbial participle ἔχων of verse 2. The angel which John saw was "descending" and "clothed" and he had in his hand the little scroll. Moulton (Robertson, *Grammar*, 1135) explains ἔχων as an "indicative" participle, *i.e.* serving like ἔχει. We need not go to such extremes. ἔχων is a circumstantial adverb.

Just as we had parenthetical material between the sixth and seventh seals (Rev.7:1-17) so here, between the sixth and seventh trumpets we have another parenthesis (Rev.10:1-11:14). Under the fifth seal, which comes immediately after the mid-week point, the martyred souls in heaven were told to be patient and rest ἔτι χρόνον μικρόν until others were also martyred (Rev.6:11). Now in Rev.10:6, just before the seventh trumpet, we learn that the waiting period is over - ὅτι χρόνος οὐκέτι ἔσται. Thus it is clear that in chapter 10 we are in the brief period just before the seventh trumpet. Chapter 11:1-14 contains information about the two witnesses. It is not necessary to identify the strong angel of verses 1-2. He may represent our Lord Himself. He claims both sea and land as His domain.

Verse 3 - "And cried with a loud voice, as when a lion roareth: and when he had cried, seven thunders uttered their voices."

καὶ ἔκραξεν φωνῇ μεγάλῃ ὥσπερ λέων μυκᾶται. καὶ ὅτε ἔκραξεν, ἐλάλησαν αἱ ἑπτὰ βρονταὶ τὰς ἑαυτῶν φωνάς.

"and called out with a loud voice, like lion roaring; when he called out, the seven thunders sounded." . . . RSV

καὶ (adjunctive conjunction joining verbs) 14.
ἔκραξεν (3d.per.sing.aor.act.ind.of κράζω, ingressive) 765.
φωνῇ (instru.sing.fem.of φωνή, means) 222.
μεγάλῃ (instru.sing.fem.of μέγας, in agreement with φωνῇ) 184.
ὥσπερ (intensive comparative adverb) 560.
λέων (nom.sing.masc.of λέων, subject of μυκᾶται) 4872.

#5381 μυκᾶται (3d.per.sing.pres.mid.ind.of μυκάομαι, customary).

King James Version

roar - Rev.10:3.

Revised Standard Version

roaring - Rev.10:3.

Meaning: Cf. μύ or μῦ - the sound of a cow lowing. A roar (when joined with λέων) - Rev.10:3.

καὶ (continuative conjunction) 14.
ὅτε (adverb with the indicative in a definite temporal clause) 703.
ἔκραξεν (3d.per.sing.aor.act.ind.of κράζω, ingressive) 765.
ἐλάλησαν (3d.per.sing.aor.act.ind.of λαλέω, ingressive) 815.
αἱ (nom.pl.fem.of the article in agreement with βρονταὶ) 9.
ἑπτὰ (numeral) 1024.
βρονταὶ (nom.pl.fem.of βροντή, subject of ἐλάλησαν) 2117.
τὰς (acc.pl.fem.of the article in agreement with φωνάς) 9.
ἑαυτῶν (gen.pl.fem.of ἑαυτοῦ, possession) 288.
φωνάς (acc.pl.fem.of φωνή, direct object of ἐλάλησαν) 222.

Translation - "And he began to cry with a loud voice, precisely as a lion roars, and when he began to cry out the seven thunders began to raise their own voices."

Comment: Note ἑαυτῶν as a possessive pronoun used like an adjective in the attributive position. The voice of the mighty angel, like everything else about John, was impressive. As he began to speak with a voice that sounded like the roar of a lion, the seven thunders also began to speak. John prepared to write down what the thunders said, but was forbidden to do so in

Verse 4 - "And when the seven thunders had uttered their voices, I was about to write: and I heard a voice from heaven saying unto me, Seal up those things which the seven thunders uttered, and write them not."

καὶ ὅτε ἐλάλησαν αἱ ἑπτὰ βρονταί, ἔμελλον γράφειν, καὶ ἤκουσα φωνὴν ἐκ τοῦ οὐρανοῦ λέγουσαν, Σφράγισον ἃ ἐλάλησαν αἱ ἑπτὰ βρονταί, καὶ μὴ αὐτὰ γράφῃς.

"And when the seven thunders had sounded, I was about to write, but I heard a voice from heaven saying, 'Seal up what the seven thunders have said, and do not write it down.' " . . . RSV

καὶ (continuative conjunction) 14.
ὅτε (adverb with the indicative in a definite temporal clause) 703.
ἐλάλησαν (3d.per.pl.aor.act.ind.of λαλέω, ingressive) 815.
αἱ (nom.pl.fem.of the article in agreement with βρονταὶ) 9.
ἑπτὰ (numeral) 1024.
βρονταὶ (nom.pl.fem.of βροντή, subject of ἐλάλησαν) 2117.
ἔμελλον (1st.per.sing.imp.act.ind.of μέλλω, inceptive) 206.
γράφειν (pres.act.inf.of γράφω, complementary) 156.
καὶ (adversative conjunction) 14.
ἤκουσα (1st.per.sing.aor.act.ind.of ἀκούω, ingressive) 148.
φωνὴν (acc.sing.fem.of φωνή, direct object of ἤκουσα) 222.
ἐκ (preposition with the ablative, source) 19.
τοῦ (abl.sing.masc.of the article in agreement with οὐρανοῦ) 9.
οὐρανοῦ (abl.sing.masc.of οὐρανός, source) 254.
λέγουσαν (pres.act.part.acc.sing.fem.of λέγω, adjectival, predicate position, restrictive, in agreement with φωνὴν) 66.
Σφράγισον (2d.per.sing.aor.act.impv.of σφραγίζω, command) 1686.
ἃ (acc.pl.neut.of ὅς, relative pronoun, direct object of σφράγισον) 65.
ἐλάλησαν (3d.per.pl.aor.act.ind.of λαλέω, culminative) 815.
αἱ (nom.pl.fem.of the article in agreement with βρονταί) 9.
ἑπτὰ (numeral) 1024.
βρονταί (nom.pl.fem.of βροντή, subject of ἐλάλησαν) 2117.
καὶ (adjunctive conjunction joining verbs) 14.
μὴ (negative conjunction with the subjunctive, prohibition) 87.
αὐτὰ (acc.pl.neut.of αὐτός, direct object of γράφῃς) 16.
γράφῃς (2d.per.sing.aor.act.subj.of γράφω, prohibition) 156.

Translation - "And when the seven thunders began to speak I was about to write, but I began to hear a voice from the heaven saying, 'Seal up that which the seven thunders have said, and do not begin to write them.' "

Comment: μὴ with the aorist subjunctive in a prohibition means, "do not begin to write" *i.e.* "do not write even one word." It goes naturally with ἔμελλον γράφειν - "I was in the process of making preparations to write." Unless there is some deductive evidence which at this point escapes us, like the evidence that tells us what Jesus wrote upon the ground (John 8:6,8, *cf.* comment), we will never know what the seven thunders said since John was forbidden to record it. We are told, however what the great angel said in verses 5-7.

Verse 5 - "And the angel which I saw stand upon the sea and upon the earth lifted up his hand to heaven,"

Καὶ ὁ ἄγγελος ὃν εἶδον ἑστῶτα ἐπὶ τῆς θαλάσσης καὶ ἐπὶ τῆς γῆς ἦρεν τὴν χεῖρα αὐτοῦ τὴν δεξιὰν εἰς τὸν οὐρανὸν

"And the angel whom I saw standing on sea and land lifted up his right hand to heaven . . . " . . . RSV

καὶ (continuative conjunction) 14.

ὁ (nom.sing.masc.of the article in agreement with ἄγγελος) 9.

ἄγγελος (nom.sing.masc.of ἄγγελος, subject of ἦρεν and ὤμοσεν) 96.

ὃν (acc.sing.masc.of ὅς, relative pronoun, direct object of εἶδον) 65.

εἶδον (1st.per.sing.aor.act.ind.of ὁράω, constative) 144.

ἑστῶτα (perf. act.part.acc.sing.masc.of ἵστημι, adjectival, predicate position, restrictive, in agreement with ὃν) 180.

ἐπὶ (preposition with the genitive of place description) 47.

τῆς (gen.sing.fem.of the article in agreement with θαλάσσης) 9.

θαλάσσης (gen.sing.fem.of θάλασσα, place description) 374.

καὶ (adjunctive conjunction joining prepositional phrases) 14.

ἐπὶ (preposition with the genitive of place description) 47.

τῆς (gen.sing.fem.of the article in agreement with γῆς) 9.

γῆς (gen.sing.fem.of γῆ, place description) 157.

ἦρεν (3d.per.sing.aor.act.ind.of αἴρω, constative) 350.

τὴν (acc.sing.fem.of the article in agreement with χεῖρα) 9.

χεῖρα (acc.sing.fem.of χείρ, direct object of ἦρεν) 308.

αὐτοῦ (gen.sing.masc.of αὐτός, possession) 16.

τὴν (acc.sing.fem.of the article in agreement with χεῖρα) 9.

δεξιὰν (acc.sing.fem.of δεξιός, in agreement with χεῖρα) 502.

εἰς (preposition with the accusative of extent) 140.

τὸν (acc.sing.masc.of the article in agreement with οὐρανόν) 9.

οὐρανόν (acc.sing.masc.of οὐρανός, extent) 254.

Translation - "And the angel whom I had seen standing upon the sea and upon the land raised his right hand unto heaven . . . "

Comment: While the action of verses 3 and 4 was taking place, John's attention was diverted from the first angel of verses 1-2. Now the angel whom John had seen (perfect participle in ἑστῶτα) upon sea and land again takes the center of the stage.

Verse 6 - "And swore by him that liveth forever and ever, who created heaven and the things that therein are, and the earth, and the things that therein are, and the sea, and the things which are therein, that there should be time no longer."

καὶ ὤμοσεν ἐν τῷ ζῶντι εἰς τοὺς αἰῶνας τῶν αἰώνων, ὃς ἔκτισεν τὸν οὐρανὸν καὶ τὰ ἐν αὐτῷ καὶ τὴν γῆν καὶ τὰ ἐν αὐτῇ καὶ τὴν θάλασσαν καὶ τὰ ἐν αὐτῇ, ὅτι χρόνος οὐκέτι ἔσται,

"and swore by him who lives for ever and ever, who created heaven and what is in it, the earth and what is in it, and the sea and what is in it, that there should be no more delay, . . . " . . . RSV

καὶ (adjunctive conjunction joining verbs) 14.

ὤμοσεν (3d.per.sing.aor.act.ind.of ὄμνυμι, constative) 516.

ἐν (preposition with the instrumental, association) 80.

τῷ (instru.sing.masc.of the article in agreement with ζῶντι) 9.

ζῶντι (pres.act.part.instru.sing.masc.of ζάω, substantival, association) 340.

εἰς (preposition with the accusative, time extent) 140.

τοὺς (acc.pl.masc.of the article in agreement with αἰῶνας) 9.

αἰῶνας (acc.pl.masc.of αἰών, time extent) 1002.

τῶν (gen.pl.masc.of the article in agreement with αἰώνων) 9.

αἰώνων (gen.pl.masc.of αἰών, partitive) 1002.

ὃς (nom.sing.masc.of ὅς, relative pronoun, subject of ἔκτισεν) 65.

ἔκτισεν (3d.per.sing.aor.act.ind.of κτίζω, constative) 1284.

τὸν (acc.sing.masc.of the article in agreement with οὐρανὸν) 9.

οὐρανὸν (acc.sing.masc.of οὐρανός, direct object of ἔκτισεν) 254.

καὶ (adjunctive conjunction joining substantives) 14.

τὰ (acc.pl.neut.of the article, direct object of ἔκτισεν) 9.

ἐν (preposition with the locative of place) 80.

αὐτῷ (loc.sing.masc.of αὐτός, place) 16.

καὶ (adjunctive conjunction joining nouns) 14.

τὴν (acc.sing.fem.of the article in agreement with γῆν) 9.

γῆν (acc.sing.fem.of γῆ, direct object of ἔκτισεν) 157.

καὶ (adjunctive conjunction joining substantives) 14.

τὰ (acc.pl.neut.of the article, direct object of ἔκτισεν) 9.

ἐν (preposition with the locative of place) 80.

αὐτῇ (loc.sing.fem.of αὐτός, place) 16.

καὶ (adjunctive conjunction joining nouns) 14.

τὴν (acc.sing.fem.of the article in agreement with θάλασσαν) 9.

θάλασσαν (acc.sing.fem.of θάλασσα, direct object of ἔκτισεν) 374.

καὶ (adjunctive conjunction joining substantives) 14.

τὰ (acc.pl.neut.of the article, direct object of ἔκτισεν) 9.

ἐν (preposition with the locative of place) 80.

αὐτῇ (loc.sing.fem.of αὐτός, place) 16.

ὅτι (conjunction introducing an object clause in indirect discourse) 211.

χρόνος (nom.sing.masc.of χρόνος, subject of ἔσται) 168.

οὐκέτι (temporal adverb) 1289.

ἔσται (3d.per.sing.fut.ind.of εἰμί, predictive) 86.

Translation - "... *and he swore by Him Who lives into the ages of the ages, Who created the heaven and that which is in it, and the earth and that which is in it, and the sea and that which is in it, that no more time remained.*"

Comment: This oath sworn on the authority of the Creator is to be construed in the light of Rev.6:9-11. There the martyred saints asked God for vengeance upon their murderer, the Beast who had made war against them (Rev.13:7), and were told to wait for a short time - ἔτι χρόνον μικρόν. Now that "little time" is past. God will ask the martyred saints to wait no longer. In the interim period other

Christians, not included in the first martyrdom, will have died for their faith, as did those of the fifth seal. Also, in the interim period (the last half of the week) the evangelistic ministry of the saints on earth will have been finished, when the last elect soul for whom Christ died, and who is therefore an elect member of His Body will be saved. This he says in verse 7.

This analysis is not understood by those who insist upon viewing 2 Peter 3:9 out of context. There Peter is talking about the scoffers who ridicule the doctrine of the second coming of Christ and advance their own evolutionary view of uniformitarianism. (2 Peter 3:3,4). They do this because they choose to ignore the story of the flood (2 Peter 3:5-7). They must deny that there was a flood in Noah's day because the flood provides a plausible alternative explanation for the fossil record upon which evolutionists depend to prove their theory. The next verse (2 Peter 3:8) lays down the principle that God is eternal and therefore not a creature of time, and thus that with Him one day is of no greater import than a thousand years, nor a thousand years of greater import than a day. The rest of the chapter (2 Peter 3:9-18) is directed to the believer. Indeed the entire chapter is written to the believer. Peter is not writing to the unsaved but to the saved *about* the unsaved. Christians may become impatient since they, unlike God, are creatures of time and space, and may tend to accuse the Lord of slackness concerning His promise to return to earth. Peter denies that the Lord is slack concerning His promise, in the sense that some regard slackness, and goes on to reveal the rationale of God's program. He has not forgotten His promise, but He is longsuffering to Christians. He is not willing that any Christian should perish but has decreed that every one of His elect shall come to repentance. How often have we heard the Arminians, as well as others who call themselves Calvinists (!) quote 2 Peter 3:9 and apply it to the entire human race. God selected the personnel of the Body of Christ before the foundation of the world (Eph.1:4-6; Romans 8:29,30; 1 Peter 1:2 *et al*), and thus He could not return to earth until the last elect soul whom He has chosen is born and called by the Holy Spirit to salvation. The second coming of Christ must await the "days of the voice of the seventh angel, for when he begins to blow his trumpet, the mystery of God (Eph.3:1-11) will be complete, and there will be no reason for any further delay. Our Lord must sit at the Father's right hand "until His enemies are made His footstool" (Psalm 110:1). Pre/mid tribulation rapture teachers would have Christ return and rapture an incomplete Body, since they teach that after the rapture of the church, others will be saved during the tribulation, though they do not explain how anyone can be saved after the Holy Spirit and the Body of Christ have left the earth.

Verse 7 - "But in the days of the voice of the seventh angel, when he shall begin to sound, the mystery of God should be finished, as he hath declared to his servants the prophets."

ἀλλ' ἐν ταῖς ἡμέραις τῆς φωνῆς τοῦ ἑβδόμου ἀγγέλου, ὅταν μέλλῃ σαλπίζειν, καὶ ἐτελέσθη τὸ μυστήριον τοῦ θεοῦ, ὡς εὐηγγέλισεν τοὺς ἑαυτοῦ δούλους τοὺς προφήτας.

"... *but that in the days of the trumpet call to be sounded by the seventh angel, the mystery of God, as he announced to his servants the prophets, should be fulfilled."* ... *RSV*

ἀλλ' (adversative conjunction) 342.

ἐν (preposition with the locative of time point) 80.

ταῖς (loc.pl.fem.of the article in agreement with ἡμέραις) 9.

ἡμέραις (loc.pl.fem.of ἡμέρα, time point) 135.

τῆς (gen.sing.fem.of the article in agreement with φωνῆς) 9.

φωνῆς (gen.sing.fem.of φωνή, description) 222.

τοῦ (gen.sing.masc.of the article in agreement with ἀγγέλου) 9.

ἑβδόμου (gen.sing.masc.of ἕβδομος, in agreement with ἀγγέλου) 2020.

ἀγγέλου (gen.sing.masc.of ἄγγελος, description) 96.

ὅταν (conjunction with the subjunctive in an indefinite temporal clause) 436.

μέλλῃ (3d.per.sing.pres.act.subj.of μέλλω, indefinite temporal clause) 206.

σαλπίζειν (pres.act.inf.of σαλπίζω, complementary) 559.

καὶ (emphatic conjunction) 14.

ἐτελέσθη (3d.per.sing.aor.pass.ind.of τελέω, culminative) 704.

τὸ (nom.sing.neut.of the article in agreement with μυστήριον) 9.

μυστήριον (nom.sing.neut.of μυστήριον, subject of ἐτελέσθη) 1038.

τοῦ (gen.sing.masc.of the article in agreement with θεοῦ) 9.

θεοῦ (gen.sing.masc.of θεός, description) 124.

ὡς (comparative particle) 128.

εὐηγγέλισεν (3d.per.sing.aor.act.ind.of εὐαγγελίζω, constative) 909.

τοὺς (acc.pl.masc.of the article in agreement with δούλους) 9.

ἑαυτοῦ (gen.sing.masc.of ἑαυτοῦ, possession) 288.

δούλους (acc.pl.masc.of δοῦλος, direct object of εὐηηέλισεν) 725.

τοὺς (acc.pl.masc.of the article in agreement with προφήτους) 9.

προφήτους (acc.pl.masc.of προφήτης, apposition) 119.

Translation - "But in the days of the voice of the seventh angel, when he is about to blow his trumpet the mystery of God will in fact have been finished, in keeping with how He promised His own servants the prophets."

Comment: The problem in interpretation here, of course, is the reference to the mystery of God. *Cf.*#1038 and examine Paul's use of the word.

Pretribulation rapture teachers must deny that the "mystery" here means what Paul meant in Eph.3:3,4,9, since the seventh trumpet comes at the end of the week. But their problem arises from their assumption that the rapture is at the beginning, rather than at the end of the tribulation week. If the mystery of Ephesians 3:3,4-9 is the mystery referred to in Rev.10:7 then the Gentile Body of Christ will be complete and the rapture will follow immediately.

There is really no reason why Christ should delay His coming after His Body is complete. The Holy Spirit, working through His churches on earth, will have completed the missionary enterprise. When the mystery is complete the great commission will have been completed and there will be no further reason for the churches to remain on earth.

This analysis comports with 1 Cor.15:52, which places the rapture and resurrection at the "last trump." Meyer objects to this on the ground that the "last trump" of 1 Cor.15:52 is not necessarily the seventh trumpet of Revelation 11:15-19. Who says that it is? But it should be clear that if it is not then it must come *after* the seventh trumpet. There may indeed be two trumpet sounds on that day - the one blown by the seventh angel and "the trumpet of God" (1 Thess.4:16) which will be heard as the Lord descends from heaven. All that can be said with certainty is that the rapture trumpet is the "last trump" (1 Cor.15:52).

The seventh trumpet of Rev.11:15-19 clearly brings in Christ's eternal kingdom (Rev.11:15-17), His wrath against the unsaved world (Rev.11:18) and the judgment seat of Christ (Rev.11:18, middle clauses of the verse). This comports with Luke 14:14, upon which *cf.* comment.

If the rapture can occur before Rev.10:7, then it will be incomplete, or, if not, the mystery of Rev.10:7 has no reference to Eph.3:3,4-9.

The mystery of Rom.11:25; 16:25 also fits the time schedule of the seventh trumpet. Certainly partial blindness will be Israel's lot until that day when the 144,000 Jews see Christ. If the "fullness of the Gentiles" (Rom.11:25) means the completion of the mystery (Rev.10:7) then the pattern of events fits perfectly.

Because there is other clear evidence for the rapture at the seventh trumpet, it is consistent to say that the mystery of Rev.10:7 comports both with Rom.11:25 and the Pauline passages in which he uses the word $\mu\nu\sigma\tau\acute{\eta}\rho\iota o\nu$ to mean that the Gentiles shall be fellow heirs and of the same body with believing Jews (Eph.3:3,4-9).

At the risk of being unnecessarily repetitious I urge that when the last elect soul for whom Christ died is saved, there will be no further reason for waiting. There was a need to wait when Rev.6:11 was spoken three and one half years before. It may be true that the mystery will become complete, not when the last discrete soul makes his concious decision to accede to the conviction of the Holy Spirit, but when the last elect soul is conceived or born, since it is our view that babies, born or as yet unborn, who die in infancy are as *safe* as though they had reached the age of accountability and were *saved*. If this is not true then the vast majority of the human race will spend eternity in hell.

The Arminian denial of election makes God's decision to save indeterminate, since it is contingent upon free will. We may interpret "free will" as the absence of coercion, but when Arminians interpret it as the absence of motivation, they make it impossible for even God to set a definite time for the "last trump." If God is not willing that any of Adam's fallen race to perish, then He is destined to disappointment, or we must accept universalism. Suppose some lost sinner "freely" decides to be saved after the last trump? God would always need to wait another day to see what the sinner's decision was. If the personnel of the family of God is known to Him, then the period of time that will be needed before the "fullness of the Gentiles" is complete is also known to Him and can then be announced with finality. Only Calvinism comports with a definite time schedule for the program of God's eschatology. Rev.11:2 supports the view that the mystery of Rev.10:7 is the same as that of Rom.11:25.

Verse 8 - "And the voice which I heard from heaven spake unto me again, and said, Go and take the little book which is open in the hand of the angel which standeth upon the sea and upon the earth."

Καὶ ἡ φωνὴ ἣν ἤκουσα ἐκ τοῦ οὐρανοῦ, πάλιν λαλοῦσαν μετ ' ἐμοῦ καὶ λέγουσαν, Ὕπαγε λάβε τὸ βιβλίον τὸ ἠνεῳγμένον ἐν τῇ χειρὶ τοῦ ἀγγέλου τοῦ ἑστῶτος ἐπὶ τῆς θαλάσσης καὶ ἐπὶ τῆς γῆς.

"Then the voice which I heard from heaven spoke to me again, saying, 'Go, take the scroll which is open in the hand of the angel who is standing on the sea and on the land.' " . . . RSV

Καὶ (continuative conjunction) 14.

ἡ (nom.sing.fem.of the article in agreement with φωνή) 9.

φωνή (nom.sing.fem.of φωνή, suspended subject) 222.

ἥν (acc.sing.fem.of ὅς, direct object of ἤκουσα) 65.

ἤκουσα (1st.per.sing.aor.act.ind.of ἀκούω, constative) 148.

ἐκ (preposition with the ablative of source) 19.

τοῦ (abl.sing.masc.of the article in agreement with οὐρανοῦ) 9.

οὐρανοῦ (abl.sing.masc.of οὐρανός, source) 254.

πάλιν (temporal adverb) 355.

λαλοῦσαν (pres.act.part.acc.sing.fem.of λαλέω, adjectival, predicate position, restrictive, in agreement with ἥν) 815.

μετ᾽ (preposition with the genitive, accompaniment) 50.

ἐμοῦ (gen.sing.masc.of ἐμός, accompaniment) 1267.

καὶ (adjunctive conjunction joining participles) 14.

λέγουσαν (pres.act.part.acc.sing.fem.of λέγω, adjectival, predicate position, restrictive, in agreement with ἥν) 66.

Ὕπαγε (2d.per.sing.pres.act.impv.of ἤπάγω, command) 364.

λάβε (2d.per.sing.2d.aor.act.impv.of λαμβάνω, command) 533.

τὸ (acc.sing.neut.of the article in agreement with βιβλίον) 9.

βιβλίον (acc.sing.neut.of βίβλιον, direct object of λάβε) 1292.

τὸ (acc.sing.neut.of the article in agreement with ἠνεῳγμένον) 9.

ἠνεῳγμένον (perf.pass.part.acc.sing.neut.of ἀνοίγω, adjectival, emphatic attributive position, ascriptive, in agreement with βίβλιον) 188.

ἐν (preposition with the locative of place) 80.

τῇ (loc.sing.fem.of the article in agreement with χειρὶ) 9.

χειρὶ (loc.sing.fem.of χείρ, place) 308.

τοῦ (gen.sing.masc.of the article in agreement with ἀγγέλου) 9.

ἀγγέλου (gen.sing.masc.of ἄγγελος, possession) 96.

τοῦ (gen.sing.masc.of the article in agreement with ἑστῶτος) 9.

ἑστῶτος (perf.part.gen.sing.masc.of ἵστημι, adjectival, emphatic attributive position, ascriptive, in agreement with ἀγγέλου) 180.

ἐπὶ (preposition with the genitive of place description) 47.

τῆς (gen.sing.fem.of the article in agreement with θαλάσσης) 9.

θαλάσσης (gen.sing.fem.of θάλασσα, place description) 374.

καὶ (adjunctive conjunction, joining prepositional phrases) 14.

ἐπὶ (preposition with the genitive of place description) 47.

τῆς (gen.sing.fem.of the article in agreement with γῆς) 9.
γῆς (gen.sing.fem.of γῆ, place description) 157.

Translation - "And the voice which I heard from heaven again speaking with me and saying, 'Go. Take the little open book in the hand of the angel standing upon the sea and the land.' "

Comment: ἡ φωνή, the subject is suspended - left without a verb. The two participles λαλοῦσαν and λέγουσαν are adjectives. The voice was the speaking and saying voice. The meaning is clear. John gets an order to approach the mighty angel and take the little book from his hand. He complies in

Verse 9 - "And I went unto the angel and said unto him, Give me the little book. And he said unto me, Take it, and eat it up; and it shall make thy belly bitter, but it shall be in thy mouth sweet as honey."

καὶ ἀπῆλθα πρὸς τὸν ἄγγελον λέγων αὐτῷ δοῦναί μοι τὸ βιβλαρίδιον. καὶ λέγει μοι, Λάβε καὶ κατάφαγε αὐτό, καὶ πικρανεῖ σου τὴν κοιλίαν, ἀλλ᾽ ἐν τῷ στόματί σου ἔσται γλυκὺ ὡς μέλι.

"So I went to the angel and told him to give me the little scroll; and he said to me, 'Take it and eat; it will be bitter to your stomach, but sweet as honey in your mouth.' " . . . RSV

καὶ (inferential conjunction) 14.
ἀπῆλθα (1st.per.sing.aor.mid.ind.of ἀπέρχομαι, constative) 239.
πρὸς (preposition with the accusative of extent) 197.
τὸν (acc.sing.masc.of the article in agreement with ἄγγελον) 9.
ἄγγελον (acc.sing.masc.of ἄγγελος, extent) 96.
λέγων (pres.act.part.nom.sing.masc.of λέγω, adverbial, complementary) 66.
αὐτῷ (dat.sing.masc.of αὐτός, indirect object of λέγων) 16.
δοῦναί (2d.aor.act.inf.of δίδωμι, complementary) 362.
μοι (dat.sing.masc.of ἐγώ, indirect object of δοῦναί) 123.
τὸ (acc.sing.neut.of the article in agreement with βιβλαρίδιον) 9.
βιβλαρίδιον (acc.sing.neut.of βιβλαρίδιον, direct object of δοῦναί) 5380.
καὶ (inferential conjunction) 14.
λέγει (3d.per.sing.pres.act.ind.of λέγω, historical) 66.
μοι (dat.sing.masc.of ἐγώ, indirect object of λέγει) 123.
Λάβε (2d.per.sing.aor.act.impv.of λαμβάνω, command) 533.
καὶ (adjunctive conjunction joining verbs) 14.
κατάφαγε (2d.per.sing.aor.act.impv.of κατεσθίω, command) 1028.
αὐτό (acc.sing.neut.of αὐτός, direct object of κατάφαγε) 16.
καὶ (continuative conjunction) 14.
πικρανεῖ (3d.per.sing.fut.act.ind.of πικραίνω, predictive) 4637.
σου (gen.sing.masc.of σύ, possession) 104.
τὴν (acc.sing.fem.of the article in agreement with κοιλίαν) 9.
κοιλίαν (acc.sing.fem.of κοιλία, direct object of πικρανεῖ) 1008.
ἀλλ᾽ (adversative conjunction) 342.

ἐν (preposition with the locative of place) 80.

τῷ (loc.sing.neut.of the article in agreement with στόματί) 9.

στόματί (loc.sing.neut.of στόμα, place) 344.

σου (gen.sing.masc.of σύ, possession) 104.

ἔσται (3d.per.sing.fut.ind.of εἰμί, predictive) 86.

γλυκὶ (nom.sing.neut.of γλυκύς, predicate adjective) 5134.

ὡς (comparative particle) 128.

μέλι (nom.sing.neut.of μέλι, subject of ἔστι understood) 268.

Translation - "So I went to the angel and asked him to give me the little book. So he said to me, 'Take and eat it up, and it will upset your stomach, but in your mouth it will be as sweet as honey."

Comment: Our rule in Revelation is to confess ignorance when we encounter material that, in the absence of clarification from the text itself, is obscure. It is probable that the little book which John loved to eat but which made him sick, has something to do with his commission to further service. We learn in verse 11 that he was still to prophesy again to a wide audience. If we are correct in assuming that the Revelation was written either in the seventh or eighth decade of the first century, John was still at the time to write his epistles and gospels.

Ezekiel's commission to preach was in terms of a book (Ezek.2:1-10), the contents of which was "lamentations and mourning and woe." *Cf.* Psalm 19:10; 40:8; 119:103.

Verse 10 - "And I took the little book out of the angel's hand, and ate it up: and it was in my mouth sweet as honey, and as soon as I had eaten it, my belly was bitter."

καὶ ἔλαβον τὸ βιβλαρίδιον ἐκ τῆς χειρὸς τοῦ ἀγγέλου καὶ κατέφαγον αὐτό, καὶ ἦν ἐν τῷ στόματί μου ὡς μέλι γλυκύ, καὶ ὅτε ἔφαγον αὐτό, ἐπικράνθη ἡ κοιλία μου.

"And I took the little scroll from the hand of the angel and ate it; it was sweet as honey in my mouth, but when I had eaten it my stomach was made bitter." ... RSV

καὶ (inferential conjunction) 14.

ἔλαβον (1st.per.sing.aor.act.ind.of λαμβάνω, constative) 533.

τὸ (acc.sing.neut.of the article in agreement with βιβλαρίδιον) 9.

βιβλαρίδιον (acc.sing.neut.of βιβλαρίδιον, direct object of ἔλαβον) 5380.

ἐκ (preposition with the ablative of separation) 19.

τῆς (abl.sing.fem.of the article in agreement with χειρὸς) 9.

χειρὸς (abl.sing.fem.of χείρ, separation) 308.

τοῦ (gen.sing.masc.of the article in agreement with ἀγγέλου) 9.

ἀγγέλου (gen.sing.masc.of ἄγγελος, possession) 96.

καὶ (adjunctive conjunction joining verbs) 14.

κατέφαγον (1st.per.sing.aor.act.ind.of κατεσθίω, ingressive) 1028.

αὐτό (acc.sing.neut.of αὐτός, direct object of κατέφαγον) 16.

καὶ (continuative conjunction) 14.
ἦν (3d.per.sing.imp.ind.of εἰμί, progressive description) 86.
ἐν (preposition with the locative of place) 80.
τῷ (loc.sing.neut.of the article in agreement with στόματί) 9.
στόματί (loc.sing.neut.of στόμα, place) 344.
μου (gen.sing.masc.of ἐγώ, possession) 123.
ὡς (comparative particle) 128.
μέλι (nom.sing.neut.of μέλι, subject of ἔστι understood) 268.
γλυκύ (nom.sing.neut.of γλυκός, in agreement with μέλι) 5134.
καὶ (adversative conjunction) 14.
ὅτε (conjunction with the indicative in a definite temporal clause) 703.
ἔφαγον (1st.per.sing.aor.act.ind.of ἐσθίω, culminative) 610.
αὐτό (acc.sing.neut.of αὐτός, direct object of ἔφαγον) 16.
ἐπικράνθη (3d.per.sing.aor.pass.ind.of πικραίνω, constative) 4637.
ἡ (nom.sing.fem.of the article in agreement with κοιλία) 9.
κοιλία (nom.sing.fem.of κοιλία, subject of ἐπικράνθη) 1008.
μου (gen.sing.masc.of ἐγώ, possession) 123.

Translation - "So I took the little book from the hand of the angel and I ate it up; and it was as sweet as honey in my mouth, but after I ate it, my stomach was upset."

Comment: καὶ (1st use) is inferential. John was following orders (verses 8,9). Note that the prepositional prefix is dropped from ἔφαγον in its second use. ὅτε here, the temporal conjunction means "after" only because of the demand of the context. John likes the idea of eating the book but its contents are not agreeable to him. So it is with all of God's prophets. It is an honor to be commissioned to preach, despite the fact that if we follow the guidance of the Holy Spirit we may find outselves compelled to bring a message of woe.

Verse 11 - "And he said unto me, Thou must prophesy again before many peoples, and nations, and tongues, and kings."

καὶ λέγουσίν μοι, Δεῖ σε πάλιν προφητεῦσαι ἐπὶ λαοῖς καὶ ἔθνεσιν καὶ γλώσσαις καὶ βασιλεῦσιν πολλοῖς.

"And I was told, 'You must again prophesy about many peoples and nations and tongues and kings.' " . . . RSV

καὶ (continuative conjunction) 14.
λέγουσίν (3d.per.pl.pres.act.ind.of λέγω, historical) 66.
μοι (dat.sing.masc.of ἐγώ, indirect object of λέγουσίν) 123.
Δεῖ (3d.per.sing.pres.ind.of δεῖ, impersonal) 1207.
σε (acc.sing.masc.of σύ, general reference) 104.
πάλιν (temporal adverb) 355.
προφητεῦσαι (aor.act.inf.of προφητεύω, complementary) 685.
ἐπὶ (preposition with the dative of reference) 47.
λαοῖς (dat.pl.masc.of λαός, reference) 110.

καὶ (adjunctive conjunction joining nouns) 14.

ἔθνεσιν (dat.pl.masc.of ἔθνος, reference) 376.

καὶ (adjunctive conjunction joining nouns) 14.

γλώσσαις (dat.pl.fem.of γλῶσσα, reference) 1846.

καὶ (adjunctive conjunction joining nouns) 14.

βασιλεῦσιν (dat.pl.masc.of βασιλεύς, reference) 31.

πολλοῖς (dat.pl.masc.of πολύς, in agreement with the foregoing substantives) 228.

Translation - "And they said to me, 'You must prophesy again about many peoples and nations and tongues and kings.' "

Comment: Note the historical present in λέγουσίν. We have it also in λέγει in verse 9.

ἐπί here with the dative. It can be either reference, as I have taken it or the dative of personal advantage and disadvantage. It is not locative and cannot be translated as the KJV has it.

The remainder of the Revelation concerns the fortunes and misfortunes of the human race, described here as "peoples and nations and tongues and kings." His message will be "about" them and it will be for the advantage for some and for the disadvantage of others.

The Two Witnesses

(Revelation 11:1-14)

Revelation 11:1 - "And there was given me a reed like unto a rod: and the angel stood, saying, Rise, and measure the temple of God, and the altar, and them that worship therein."

Καὶ ἐδόθη μοι κάλαμος ὅμοιος ῥάβδῳ, λέγων, Ἔγειρε καὶ μέτρησον τὸν ναὸν τοῦ θεοῦ καὶ τὸ θυσιαστήριον καὶ τοὺς προσκυνοῦντας ἐν αὐτῷ.

"Then I was given a measuring rod like a staff, and I was told: 'Rise and measure the temple of God and the altar and those who worship there, . . . " . . . RSV

Καὶ (continuative conjunction) 14.

ἐδόθη (3d.per.sing.aor.pass.ind.of δίδωμι, constative) 362.

μοι (dat.sing.masc.of ἐγώ, indirect object of ἐδόθη) 123.

κάλαμος (nom.sing.masc.of κάλαμος, subject of ἐδόθη) 910.

ὅμοιος (nom.sing.masc.of ὅμοιος, in agreement with κάλαμος) 923.

ῥάβδῳ (dat.sing.masc.of ῥάβδος, comparison) 863.

λέγων (pres.act.part.nom.sing.masc.of λέγω, adverbial, circumstantial) 66.

Ἔγειρε (2d.per.sing.pres.act.impv.of ἐγείρω, command) 125.

καὶ (adjunctive conjunction joining verbs) 14.

μέτρησον (2d.per.sing.aor.act.impv.of μετρέω, command) 644.

τὸν (acc.sing.masc.of the article in agreement with ναὸν) 9.

ναὸν (acc.sing.masc.of ναός, direct object of μέτρησον) 1447.

τοῦ (gen.sing.masc.of the article in agreement with θεοῦ) 9.

θεοῦ (gen.sing.masc.of θεός, possession) 124.

καὶ (adjunctive conjunction joining nouns) 14.

τὸ (acc.sing.neut.of the article in agreement with θυσιαστήριον) 9.

θυσιαστήριον (acc.sing.neut.of θυσιαστήριον, direct object of μέτρησον) 484.

καὶ (adjunctive conjunction joining substantives) 14.

τοὺς (acc.pl.masc.of the article in agreement with προσκυνοῦντας) 9.

προσκυνοῦντας (pres.act.part.acc.pl.masc.of προσκυνέω, substantival, direct object of μέτρησον) 147.

ἐν (preposition with the locative of place) 80.

αὐτῷ (loc.sing.masc.of αὐτός, place) 16.

Translation - "And a measuring rod like a staff was given to me as he said, 'Rise and measure the temple of God and   the altar and count those who are worshipping in it.' "

Comment: The participle λέγων is another of John's peculiarities in the Revelation. I have called it adverbial and circumstantial, but it does not fit the passive ἐδόθη which has as its subject κάλαμος. The rod was given to John, but it did not speak to him. The angel spoke to him, but ὁ ἄγγελος does not occur in the verse. Naturally the Holy Spirit, Who writes good Greek, noticed John's error but did not choose to correct it, since He knew that good Greek exegetes would understand what is being said. Those who teach a dictation theory of plenary verbal inspiration should be embarrassed by these cases in which bad grammar and/or syntax nevertheless does not hide the plenary and inerrant concept which is being revealed. Those who oppose a dictation theory do not reject a plenary and inerrant inspiration. Indeed our view is more supernatural than the dictation theory. No honest and scholarly Greek exegete has ever been misled by a solecism, a case of asyndeton or an example of anacoluthon. If we could be the Holy Spirit at that point would have dictated the form in order to avoid confusion. His divine superintendance is all that is required and it was always available.

As the angel gave the rod to John he told him what to measure and who to count. In verse two he is told what not to measure. Thus the point is that there is a fundamental difference between the temple of God and its worshippers and the court that surrounds the temple.

Verse 2 - "But the court which is without the temple leave out, and measure it not: for it is given unto the Gentiles: and the holy city shall they tread under foot forty and two months."

καὶ τὴν αὐλὴν τὴν ἔξωθεν τοῦ ναοῦ ἔκβαλε ἔξωθεν καὶ μὴ αὐτὴν μετρήσῃς, ὅτι ἐδόθη τοῖς ἔθνεσιν, καὶ τὴν πόλιν τὴν ἁγίαν πατήσουσιν μῆνας τεσσαράκοντα δύο.

"but do not measure the court outside the temple; leave that out, for it is given over to the nations, and they will trample over the holy city for forty-two months." . . . RSV

καὶ (adversative conjunction) 14.
τὴν (acc.sing.fem.of the article in agreement with αὐλὴν) 9.
αὐλὴν (acc.sing.fem.of αὐλή, direct object of ἔκβαλε) 1554.
τὴν (acc.sing.fem.of the article in agreement with αὐλὴν) 9.
ἔξωθεν (adverbial of ἔξω, used here like an attributive adjective, in agreement with αὐλὴν) 1455.
τοῦ (abl.sing.masc.of the article in agreement with ναοῦ) 9.
ναοῦ (abl.sing.masc.of ναός, separation) 1447.
ἔκβαλε (2d.per.sing.aor.act.impv.of ἐκβάλλω, command) 649.
ἔξωθεν (adverbial) 1455.
καὶ (adjunctive conjunction joining verbs) 14.
μὴ (negative conjunction with the subjunctive in a prohibition) 87.
αὐτὴν (acc.sing.fem.of αὐτός, direct object of μετρήσῃς) 16.
μετρήσῃς (2d.per.sing.aor.act.subj.of μετρέω, prohibition) 644.
ὅτι (conjunction introducing a subordinate causal clause) 211.
ἐδόθη (3d.per.sing.aor.pass.ind.of δίδωμι, culminative) 362.
τοῖς (dat.pl.masc.of the article in agreement with ἔθνεσιν) 9.
ἔθνεσιν (dat.pl.masc.of ἔθνος, indirect object of ἐδόθη) 376.
καὶ (inferential conjunction) 14.
τὴν (acc.sing.fem.of the article in agreement with πόλιν) 9.
πόλιν (acc.sing.fem.of πόλις, direct object of πατήσουσιν) 243.
τὴν (acc.sing.fem.of the article in agreement with ἁγίαν) 9.
ἁγίαν (acc.sing.fem.of ἅγιος, in agreement with πόλιν) 84.
πατήσουσιν (3d.per.pl.fut.act.ind.of πατέω, predictive) 2415.
μῆνας (acc.pl.masc.of μήν, time extension) 1809.
τεσσαράκοντα (numeral) 333.
δύο (numeral) 385.

Translation - "But the outer court of the temple leave out and do not measure it, because it has been given to the Gentiles; so they will overrun the holy city for forty-two months."

Comment: Note ἔξωθεν, first used like a preposition to define τὴν αὐλὴν and in its second use as an adverb.

If this temple and its outer court is the one in Jerusalem, we have a bit of internal evidence that the Revelation was written before A.D.70, when the city was destroyed. Certainly the outer court of the heavenly temple will not be profaned by the Beast and Antichrist and their legions. This passage appears to parallel Luke 21:24. John is told to include God's property, which is the temple area itself and the altar, but to omit the outer court, as if the measurements would be needed in order to rebuild the temple and place the altar in precisely the right spot after the second coming of Messiah. Of course there is nothing here to say that the temple will be used in the Kingdom Age for the Levitical sacrifices which were ordered under the Mosaic covenant. Amillenialists are correct in saying that the Church, the Body of Christ is the fulfillment of the prophecy of Amos 9:11 which James cites in Acts 15:13-18. They are incorrect, in my view, as they read τὸν θρόνον Δαυὶδ for τὴν σκηνὴν Δαυὶδ. To be sure the tabernacle of David, where animal sacrifices were offered daily under the old covenant, will see no blood of bulls and goats, nor the ashes of the heifer (Heb.9:13) during the Kingdom Ages. Messiah will dwell with His Body in the tabernacle which John is here ordered to measure. But the Church is not the throne. Our Lord is a King forever as well as a Priest and He will occupy the throne of David forever (Luke 1:31-33).

John is told to secure the precise locations of the four corners of the tabernacle and the spot within the temple where the altar will be placed. But he is also told not to be concerned about the measurement of the area outside the temple. The causal clause tells us why. For the last half of the tribulation week (Dan.9:27; Rev.13:5) Antichrist will blaspheme the temple of God. He will enter it, sit in it and demand that he be worshipped as God (2 Thess.2:4). But his blasphemous tenure will extend for only forty-two months, a time period with which Rev.13:5 agrees. Thus we have a chronological key as to the time of this conversation in Rev.11:1-14. It is sometime just before the beginning of the last half of the week. The Beast's violation of the covenant which he will have made with Israel forty-two months before (Dan.9:27a,b; Mt.24:15; 2 Thess.2:4; Rev.13:1-18) is yet future at the time of the angel's order to John to meausre. The "times of the Gentiles" are identified as the period when Jerusalem will be politically dominated by Gentile powers (Lk.21:24). Thus the last half of the week is the final phase of "the times of the Gentiles." It is also in this same period that the "fullness of the Gentiles" will be made complete (Rom.11:25) and the "mystery" which God gave to Paul (Eph.3:1-8) will be complete (Rev.10:7). Immediately after this Israel's partial blindness will be healed and she will see clearly as 144,000 Jews (Rev.7:1-8) will be saved at the second coming of their Messiah. The family of God, called out from among the Gentiles (Acts 15:14) will be completed at the end of the period also (Rev.10:7).

This last three and one half year period of Daniel's 70th week (here called 42 months) is the final phase of the "times of the Gentiles" which began with the Babylonian captivity in Daniel's day. Not since then, except for the current brief period since A.D.1948, has Israel as a nation been in control of any part of the covenanted land which God gave to Abraham. Since 1948 she has exercised hegemony over only a small part of her territory. During the great tribulation (the last half of the week) Antichrist and the Beast will dominate Jerusalem. This is the period during which elect Israel, the 144,000 Jews, will be protected from the onslaught of the Beast (Rev.12:13-16), ready to be saved at the end of the period. These chronological terms ("in the midst of the week," "forty-two months," "twelve hundred and sixty days," and "time, times and half a time") all measure the same amount of time and refer to the same period. Were it not for them we should not be able to piece the scenario together, and that is precisely why we have them.

This is the same period that will see the ministry of the two witnesses, the description of which follows in verses 3-14. Thus we see the beautiful correlation of the descriptive material in the Revelation.

Verse 3 - "And I will give power unto my two witnesses and they shall prophesy a thousand two hundred and threescore days, clothed in sackcloth."

καὶ δώσω τοῖς δυσὶν μάρτυσίν μου, καὶ προφητεύσουσιν ἡμέρας χιλίας διακοσίας ἑξήκοντα περιβεβλημένοι σάκκους.

"And I will grant my two witnesses power to prophesy for one thousand two hundred and sixty days, clothed in sackcloth." . . . RSV

καὶ (continuative conjunction) 14.

δώσω (1st.per.sing.fut.act.ind.of δίδωμι, predictive) 362.

τοῖς (dat.pl.masc.of the article in agreement with μάρτυσίν) 9.

δυσὶν (dat.pl.masc.of δύο, in agreement with μάρτυσίν) 385.

μάρτυσίν (dat.pl.masc.of μάρτυς, indirect object of δώσω) 1263.

μου (gen.sing.masc.of ἐγώ, relationship) 123.

καὶ (continuative conjunction) 14.

προφητεύσουσιν (3d.per.pl.fut.act.ind.of προφητεύω, predictive) 685.

ἡμέρας (acc.pl.fem.of ἡμέρα, time extent) 135.

χιλίας (acc.pl.fem.of χίλιος, in agreement with ἡμέρας) 5278.

διακοσίας (acc.pl.fem.of διακόσιοι, in agreement with ἡμέρας) 2265.

ἑξήκοντα (acc.pl.fem.of ἑξήκοντα, in agreement with ἡμέρας) 1036.

περιβεβλημένοι (perf.pass.part.nom.pl.masc.of περιβάλλω, adverbial, modal) 631.

σάκκους (acc.pl.masc.of σάκκος, adverbial accusative, manner) 942.

Translation - "And I will appoint my two witnesses, and they will prophesy one thousand two hundred and sixty days, clothed in sackcloth."

Comment: We may supply ἐξουσίαν προφητεύειν or some other appropriate object after δώσω. The two witnesses will be given a ministry that will continue throughout the latter half of the tribulation week. If we wish to be precise about the number of days, it is necessary to place the beginning of their ministry three and one half days before the middle of the week, since they will lie dead in the streets three and one half days before they are raptured. Or does their ministry extend to the end of the period? If not, they begin to witness at some earlier time than the reappearance of the Beast. Perhaps they appear a short time before he does in order to acquaint the saints still upon the earth, who are about to enter into a period of persecution with the coming events, thus to forewarn them. The seventh trumpet judgment, which is the third woe, brings us clearly to the end of the week and the second coming of Messiah.

We have another instance of περιβεβλημένος, the passive participle, followed by the accusative case. *Cf.* Rev.7:9 for comment. *Cf.* also Rev.7:13; 10:1; 11:3; 17:4; 18:16; 19:13, where the same construction occurs.

The ministry of the two witnesses is described in verses 4-13.

Verse 4 - "These are the two olive trees, and the two candlesticks standing before the God of the earth."

οὗτοί εἰσιν αἱ δύο ἐλαῖαι καὶ αἱ δύο λυχνίαι αἱ ἐνώπιον τοῦ κυρίου τῆς γῆς ἑστῶτες.

"These are the two olive trees and the two lampstands which stand before the Lord of the earth." . . . RSV

οὗτοί (nom.pl.masc.of οὗτος, subject of εἰσιν, deictic) 93.
εἰσιν (3d.per.pl.pres.ind.of εἰμί, aoristic) 86.
αἱ (nom.pl.fem.of the article in agreement with ἐλαῖαι) 9.
δύο (numeral) 385.
ἐλαῖαι (nom.pl.fem.of ἐλαία, predicate nominative) 1341.
καὶ (adjunctive conjunction joining nouns) 14.
αἱ (nom.pl.fem.of the article in agreement with λυχνίαι) 9.
δύο (numeral) 385.
λυχνίαι (nom.pl.fem.of λυχνία, predicate nominative) 457.
αἱ (nom.pl.fem.of the article in agreement with ἑστῶτες) 9.
ἐνώπιον (preposition with the genitive of place description) 1798.
τοῦ (gen.sing.masc.of the article in agreement with κυρίου) 9.
κυρίου (gen.sing.masc.of κύριος, place description) 97.
τῆς (gen.sing.fem.of the article in agreement with γῆς) 9.
γῆς (gen.sing.fem.of γῆ, place description) 157.
ἑστῶτες (perf.act.part.nom.pl.fem.of ἵστημι, adjectival, emphatic attributive position, ascriptive, in agreement with ἐλαῖαι and λυχνίαι) 180.

Translation - "These are the two olive trees and the two candlesticks that have been standing before the Lord of the earth."

Comment: This is an obvious reference to Zechariah 4:3, 11-14, which brings our interpretation of Zechariah into the last week of Daniel's prophecy. These two witnesses will preach against the Beast, the Antichrist and their deceptions throughout the last half of the week. Possibly through their ministry the last of the elect will be saved (Rev.10:7). They will have ample power to protect themselves during their period of ministry, which will extend for 1260 days. At the last they will be killed by the Beast and after three and one half days, raptured. They illustrate the fact that God's yielded servants are immortal until their appointed tasks on earth are done. No weapon employed by the enemy against the yielded child of God shall prosper (Isa.54:17).

There is some evidence that these two witnesses may be Elijah the Prophet and Moses the Lawgiver.

During their ministry the war of the Beast against the Christians will be going on and there will be many martyrs (Rev.6:11).

Verse 5 - "And if any man will hurt them, fire proceedeth out of their mouth, and devoureth their enemies: and if any man will hurt them, he must in this manner be killed."

καὶ εἴ τις αὐτοὺς θέλει ἀδικῆσαι, πῦρ ἐκπορεύεται ἐκ τοῦ στόματος αὐτῶν καὶ κατεσθίει τοὺς ἐχθροὺς αὐτῶν. καὶ εἴ τις θελήσει αὐτοὺς ἀδικῆσαι, οὕτως δεῖ αὐτὸν ἀποκτανθῆναι.

"And if any one would harm them, fire pours from their mouth and consumes their foes; if any one would harm them, thus he is doomed to be killed."... RSV

καὶ (continuative conjunction) 14.

εἴ (conditional particle with the indicative in a first-class condition) 337.

τις (nom.sing.masc.of τις, indefinite pronoun, subject of θέλει, in a first-class condition) 486.

αὐτοὺς (acc.pl.masc.of αὐτός, direct object of ἀδικῆσαι) 16.

θέλει (3d.per.sing.pres.act.ind.of θέλω, in a first-class condition) 88.

ἀδικῆσαι (aor.act.inf.of ἀδικέω, complementary) 1327.

πῦρ (nom.sing.neut.of πῦρ, subject of ἐκπορεύεται and κατεσθίει) 298.

ἐκπορεύεται (3d.per.sing.pres.mid.ind.of ἐκπορεύομαι, futuristic) 270.

ἐκ (preposition with the ablative of source) 19.

τοῦ (abl.sing.neut.of the article in agreement with στόματος) 9.

στόματος (abl.sing.neut.of στόμα, source) 344.

αὐτῶν (gen.pl.masc.of αὐτός, possession) 16.

καὶ (adjunctive conjunction joining verbs) 14.

κατεσθίει (3d.per.sing.pres.act.ind.of κατεσθίω, futuristic) 1028.

τοὺς (acc.pl.masc.of the article in agreement with ἐχθροὺς) 9.

ἐχθροὺς (acc.pl.masc.of ἐχθρός, direct object of κατεσθίει) 543.

αὐτῶν (gen.pl.masc.of αὐτός, relationship) 16.

καὶ (inferential conjunction) 14.

εἴ (conditional particle with the indicative in a first-class condition) 337.

τις (nom.sing.masc.of τις, indefinite pronoun, subject of θελήσει in a first-class condition) 486.

θελήσει (3d.per.sing.fut.act.ind.of θέλω, predictive, in a first-class condition) 88.

αὐτοὺς (acc.pl.masc.of αὐτός, direct object of ἀδικῆσαι) 16.

ἀδικῆσαι (aor.act.inf.of ἀδικέω, complementary) 1327.

οὕτως (adverbial) 74.

δεῖ (3d.per.sing.pres.ind.of δεῖ, impersonal, aoristic) 1207.

αὐτὸν (acc.sing.masc.of αὐτός, general reference) 16.

ἀποκτανθῆναι (aor.pass.inf.of ἀποκτείνω, complementary, direct object of δεῖ) 889.

Translation - "And if anyone wishes to harm them, fire will issue from their mouth and it will consume their enemies; and if anyone wishes to harm them, thus it is necessary for him to be killed."

Comment: Note εἴ with the present indicative where the assumption may be considered true or untrue, but is assumed to be true. I have taken θελει as a futuristic present tense, since John uses the future in θελήσει as he repeats the first-class condition. Of course it is necessary that the enemies of God who otherwise would interfere with the ministry of the two witnesses, for them to be killed, if the alternative is that they would kill the witnesses, since God had decreed that the witnesses will carry on their ministry for exactly 1260 days, after which they will be killed, to lie dead in the streets for 3 and 1/2 days before they are raptured. These witnesses are men, not heavenly beings, since they can be killed and raised from the dead. Bible commentators have long thought that Elijah is one of these witnesses, on the basis of Malachi 4:5-6. Verse 6 sounds as if Moses might possibly be the other.

At a time when the Beast and the Antichrist will be displaying supernatural powers of demonism (Rev.13:11-18), by which they will influence the non-elect, it will be encouraging to the saints, as well as those who will yet be brought into the Body of Christ (Rev.10:7) to see the manifestations of divine power in the works of the two witnesses.

Verse 6 - "These have power to shut heaven, that it rain not in the days of their prophecy; and power over waters to turn them to blood, and to smite the earth with all plagues, as often as they will."

οὗτοι ἔχουσιν τὴν ἐξουσίαν κλεῖσαι τὸν οὐρανόν, ἵνα μὴ ὑετὸς βρέχῃ τὰς ἡμέρας τῆς προφητείας αὐτῶν, καὶ ἐξουσίαν ἔχουσιν ἐπὶ τῶν ὑδάτων στέφειν αὐτὰ εἰς αἷμα καὶ πατάξαι τὴν γῆν ἐν πάσῃ πληγῇ ὁσάκις ἐὰν θελήσωσιν.
"

"They have power to shut the sky, that no rain may fall during the days of their prophesying, and they have power over the waters to turn them into blood, and to smite the earth with every plague, as often as they desire." . . . RSV

οὗτοι (nom.pl.masc.of οὗτος, subject of ἔχουσιν) 93.
ἔχουσιν (3d.per.pl.pres.act.ind.of ἔχω, futuristic) 82.
τὴν (acc.sing.fem.of the article in agreement with ἐξουσίαν) 9.
ἐξουσίαν (acc.sing.fem.of ἐξουσία, direct object of ἔχουσιν) 707.
κλεῖσαι (aor.act.inf.of κλείω, in apposition with ἐξουσίαν) 570.
τὸν (acc.sing.masc.of the article in agreement with οὐρανόν) 9.
οὐρανόν (acc.sing.masc.of οὐρανός, direct object of κλεῖσαι) 254.
ἵνα (conjunction with the subjunctive, negative result) 114.
μὴ (negative conjunction with the subjuntive, result) 87.
ὑετὸς (nom.sing.masc.of ὑετός, subject of βρέχῃ) 3327.
βρέχῃ (3d.per.sing.pres.act.subj.of βρέχω, negative result) 548.
τὰς (acc.pl.fem.of the article in agreement with ἡμέρας) 9.
ἡμέρας (acc.pl.fem.of ἡμέρα, time extent) 135.
τῆς (gen.sing.fem.of the article in agreement with προφητείας) 9.
προφητείας (gen.sing.fem.of προφητεία, description) 1041.
αὐτῶν (gen.pl.masc.of αὐτός, description) 16.
καὶ (adjunctive conjunction joining verbs) 14.
ἐξουσίαν (acc.sing.fem.of ἐξουσία, direct object of ἔχυσιν) 707.
ἔχουσιν (3d.per.pl.pres.act.ind.of ἔχω, futuristic) 82.
ἐπὶ (preposition with the genitive, metaphorical "over") 47.

τῶν (gen.pl.neut.of the article in agreement with ὑδάτων) 9.

ὑδάτων (gen.pl.neut.of ὕδωρ, metaphorical, "over") 301.

στρέφειν (pres.act.inf.of στρέφω, in apposition with ἐξουσίαν) 530.

αὐτὰ (acc.pl.neut.of αὐτός, direct object of στρέφειν) 16.

εἰς (preposition with the accusative, predicate use) 140.

αἷμα (acc.sing.neut.of αἷμα, predicate accusative) 1203.

καὶ (adjunctive conjunction joining infinitives) 14.

πατάξαι (aor.act.inf.of πατάσσω, in apposition with ἐξουσίαν) 1579.

τὴν (acc.sing.fem.of the article in agreement with γῆν) 9.

γῆν (acc.sing.fem.of γῆ, direct object of πατάξαι) 157.

ἐν (preposition with the instrumental, means) 80.

πάσῃ (instru.sing.fem.of πᾶς, in agreement with πληγῇ) 67.

πληγῇ (instru.sing.fem.of πληγή, means) 2421.

ὁσάκις (temporal adverb) 4210.

ἐὰν (conditional particle with the subjunctive in a third-class condition) 363.

θελήσωσιν (3d.per.pl.aor.act.subj.of θέλω, third-class condition) 88.

Translation - *"These have the authority to shut up the heaven, so that no rain falls during the days of their prophecy, and they have power over waters to turn them to blood, and to strike the earth with any plague as they wish."*

Comment:　　The infinitives κλεῖσαι and στρέφειν are in apposition with ἐξουσίαν. Power to stop the rain reminds us of Elijah (Lk.4:25; James 5:17,17; 1 Kings 17:1), and Moses (Exodus 7:19-21). ἐπὶ τῶν ὑδάτων - a metaphorical use of ἐπί. Note εἰς αἷμα, the predicate use of εἰ. *Cf.* 1 Cor.11:25,26 for the indefinite ὁσάκις with ἐάν and the subjunctive. ἐν πάσῃ πληγῇ - the singular forbids "with all plagues" and means "with any one of all of the plagues" in keeping with their whim.

Thus these men will be very powerful - capable of defending themselves against murder for the duration of the 1260 days and also able to inflict great damage to the earth (verse 10).

Their function will be to warn all that the Beast and the False Prophet are Satanic, and that their wonders and signs are designed only to deceive. Elijah with his power on Mount Carmel was able to show that Baal was powerless to respond to the prayers of his priests.

The elect will derive great benefit from the ministry of the two witnesses during the last half of the week (*Cf.* Mt.24:24; 2 Thess.2:9-12; Rev.13:16; 19:20). No Christian will receive the mark of the Beast, possibly because of the two witnesses and their clear-cut message of warning. They will also have an evangelistic appeal, since the "fullness of the Gentiles" is not complete until the close of their ministry (Rev.10:7). Just as Satan's emissaries in Pharaoh's court in Egypt kept the non-elect in spiritual darkness (2 Cor.4:4) while God's servants, Moses and Aaron, were given power to smite Egypt and rescue His elect, so God will have His two witnesses on earth in the tribulation period to counter the influence of Antichrist.

The story has a dramatic ending as we see in verses 7-12.

Verse 7 - "And when they shall have finished their testimony, the beast that ascendeth out of the bottomless pit shall make war against them, and shall overcome them, and kill them."

καὶ ὅταν τελέσωσιν τὴν μαρτυρίαν αὐτῶν, τὸ θηρίον τὸ ἀναβαῖνον ἐκ τῆς ἀβύσσου ποιήσει μετ' αὐτῶν πόλεμον καὶ νικήσει αὐτοὺς καὶ ἀποκτενεῖ αὐτούς.

"And when they have finished their testimony, the beast that ascends from the bottomless pit will make war upon them and conquer them and kill them." . . . RSV

καὶ (continuative conjunction) 14.

ὅταν (temporal conjunction with the subjunctive in an indefinite temporal clause) 436.

τελέσωσιν (3d.per.pl.1st.aor.act.subj.of τελέω, indefinite temporal clause) 704.

τὴν (acc.sing.fem.of the article in agreement with μαρτυρίαν) 9.

μαρτυρίαν (acc.sing.fem.of μαρτυρία, direct object of τελέσωσιν) 1695.

αὐτῶν (gen.pl.masc.of αὐτός, possession) 16.

τὸ (nom.sing.neut.of the article in agreement with θηρίον) 9.

θηρίον (nom.sing.neut.of θηρίον, subject of ποιήσιε, νικήσει and ἀπολκτενεῖ) 1951.

τὸ (nom.sing.neut.of the article in agreement with ἀναβαῖνον) 9.

ἀναβαῖνον (pres.part.part.nom.sing.neut.of ἀναβαίνω, adjectival, emphatic attribute position, ascriptive, in agreement with θηρίον) 323.

ἐκ (preposition with the ablative of separation) 19.

τῆς (abl.sing.fem.of the article in agreement with ἀβύσσου) 9.

ἀβύσσου (abl.sing.fem.of ἄβυσσος, separation) 2231.

ποιήσει (3d.per.sing.fut.act.ind.of ποιέω, predictive) 127.

μετ' (preposition with the genitive, opposition) 50.

αὐτῶν (gen.pl.masc.of αὐτός, opposition) 16.

πόλεμον (acc.sing.masc.of πόλεμος, direct object of ποιήσει) 1483.

καὶ (adjunctive conjunction joining verbs) 14.

νικήσει (3d.per.sing.fut.act.ind.of νικάω, predictive) 2454.

αὐτοὺς (acc.pl.masc.of αὐτός, direct object of νικήσει) 16.

καὶ (adjunctive conjunction joining verbs) 14.

ἀποκτενεῖ (3d.per.sing.fut.act.ind.of ἀποκτείνω, predictive) 889.

αὐτούς (acc.pl.masc.of αὐτός, direct object of ἀποκτενεῖ) 16.

Translation - "And when they have finished their testimony the beast who is coming out of the abyss will make war against them and capture them and kill them."

Comment: Only when (ὅταν) and not until when the witnesses have finished their ministry on earth (Eph.2:10; Phil.1:6; 2 Tim.4:7; Rev.3:2) will the Beast be able to overcome and kill them (1 John 4:4). The Beast, who first appeared as the

White Horse Rider (Rev.6:1-2), who will at that time confirm the covenant with Israel for seven years (Dan.9:27a), to resume the countdown on God's clock of the "times of the Gentiles" (Lk.21:24), the "fifth" (Rev.17:10), who, along with the first four (Babylon, Media-Persia, Greece, Rome) had fallen, who also is the eighth (Rev.17:11), after his resurrection (Rev.13:3), who   came out of the abyss (Rev.11:7; 9:1-11) in the middle of the week, to rule 42 more months (Rev.13:5), and to make war with the saints (Rev.13:7), now, at the close of the 1260 days of witnessing by God's prophets,   kills them. What is so difficult about understanding Revelation? Examine this correlative evidence carefully. Keep 2 Peter 1:20 in mind. The two witnesses will have finished their work. The family of God will have become complete (Rev.10:7). The "times of the Gentiles" will have been finished (Lk.21:24). The "fullness of the Gentiles" will have been accomplished (Acts 15:14), the "mystery" will have become complete (Eph.3:3,4,9; Rev.10:7). Satan and his blasphemy and lawlessness will have reached his highest development for the time being, until he makes his final and futile attempt one thousand years later. Nothing will remain but judgment. Hell, Satan and his demons and his victims will have one last fling. See the description in verses 8-10. We shall hear "the laughter of the fool" as the "crackling of thorns under a pot. This also is vanity" (Eccles.7:6).

Verse 8 - "And their dead bodies shall lie in the street of the great city, which spiritually is called Sodom and Egypt, where also our Lord was crucified."

καὶ τὸ πτῶμα αὐτῶν ἐπὶ τῆς πλατείας τῆς πόλεως τῆς μεγάλης, ἥτις καλεῖται πνευματικῶς Σόδομα καὶ Αἴγυπτος, ὅπου καὶ ὁ κύριος αὐτῶν ἐσταυρώθη.

"and their dead bodies will lie in the street of the great city which is allegorically called Sodom and Egypt, where their Lord was crucified." ... RSV

καὶ (continuative conjunction) 14.

τὸ (nom.sing.neut.of the article in agreement with πτῶμα) 9.

πτῶμα (nom.sing.neut.of πτῶμα, suspended subject) 1115.

αὐτῶν (gen.pl.masc.of αὐτός, possession) 16.

ἐπὶ (preposition with the genitive of place description) 47.

τῆς (gen.sing.fem.of the article in agreement with πλατείας) 9.

πλατείας (gen.sing.fem.of πλατεῖα, place description) 568.

τῆς (gen.sing.fem.of the article in agreement with πόλεως) 9.

πόλεως (gen.sing.fem.of πόλις, description) 243.

τῆς (gen.sing.fem.of the article in agreement with μεγάλης) 9.

μεγάλης (gen.sing.fem.of μέγας, in agreement with πόλεως) 184.

ἥτις (nom.sing.fem.of ὅστις, subject of καλεῖται) 163.

καλεῖται (3d.per.sing.pres.pass.ind.of καλέω, customary) 107.

πνευματικῶς (adverbial) 4113.

Σόδομα (nom.sing.neut.of Σόδομος, predicate nominative) 871.

καὶ (adjunctive conjunction joining nouns) 14.

Αἴγυπτος (nom.sing.masc.of Αἴγυπτος, predicate nominative) 203.

ὅπου (local adverb) 592.

καί (emphatic conjunction) 14.

ὁ (nom.sing.masc.of the article in agreement with κύριος) 9.

κύριος (nom.sing.masc.of κύριος, subject of ἐσταυρώθη) 97.

αὐτῶν (gen.pl.masc.of αὐτός, relationship) 16.

ἐσταυρώθη (3d.per.sing.aor.pass.ind.of σταυρόω, constative) 1328.

Translation - "And their bodies will lie upon the street of the great city, which is known allegorically as Sodom and Egypt, where in fact their Lord was crucified."

Comment: πλατεῖα (#568) means "broadway." Hence we take τῆς μεγάλης with τῆς πόλεως, though it agrees with πλατείας in gender also. ἥτις here is definite and agrees in gender with its antecedent, πόλεως. It is explanatory.

The two witnesses will die in Jerusalem, the same city in which their Lord died. The last καί is emphatic. It is fitting that the two witnesses should should finish their ministry and meet their death in Jerusalem, since that is where the Beast will have his headquarters - within the inner veil of the restored sanctuary, which he will have rebuilt seven years before. There he will demand that he be worshipped as God (2 Thess.2:4). The witnesses will be crying out against him, as they explain to the elect who are as yet not called and also as they warn the saints not to believe and worship him.

The death of these two witnesses, who, for the past 1260 days (Rev.11:3) will have been invincible, as they visited God's judgments upon the world, will trigger three and one half days of high carnival among the lost who will not be aware that they are indulging their last hurrah. The scene is described further in

Verse 9 - "And they of the people and kindreds and tongues and nations shall see their dead bodies three days and a half, and shall not suffer their dead bodies to be put in graves."

καὶ βλέπουσιν ἐκ τῶν λαῶν καὶ φυλῶν καὶ γλωσσῶν καὶ ἐθνῶν τὸ πτῶμα αὐτῶν ἡμέρας τρεῖς καὶ ἥμισυ, καὶ τὰ πτώματα αὐτῶν οὐκ ἀφίουσιν τεθῆναι εἰς μνῆμα.

"For three days and a half men from the peoples and tribes and tongues and nations gaze at their dead bodies and refuse to let them be placed in a tomb, ... ".
. . RSV

καί (continuative conjunction) 14.

βλέπουσιν (3d.per.pl.pres.act.ind.of βλέπω, futuristic) 499.

ἐκ (preposition with the partitive ablative) 19.

τῶν (abl.pl.masc.of the article in agreement with λαῶν) 9.

λαῶν (abl.pl.masc.of λαός, partitive) 110.

καί (adjunctive conjunction joining nouns) 14.

φυλῶν (abl.pl.fem.of φυλή, partitive) 1313.

καί (adjunctive conjunction joining nouns) 14.

γλωσσῶν (abl.pl.fem.of γλῶσσα, partitive) 1846.

καί (adjunctive conjunction joining nouns) 14.

ἐθνῶν (abl.pl.masc.of ἔθνος, partitive) 376.
τὸ (acc.sing.neut.of the article in agreement with πτῶμα) 9.
πτῶμα (acc.sing.neut.of πτῶμα, direct object of βλέπουσιν) 1115.
αὐτῶν (gen.pl.masc.of αὐτός, possession) 16.
ἡμέρας (acc.pl.fem.of ἡμέρα, time extent) 135.
τρεῖς (numeral) 1010.
καὶ (adjunctive conjunction joining substantives) 14.
ἥμισυ (acc.sing.neut.of ἥμισυς, time extent) 2259.
καὶ (adversative conjunction) 14.
τὰ (acc.pl.neut.of the article in agreement with πτώματα) 9.
πτώματα (acc.pl.neut.of πτῶμα, general reference) 1115.
αὐτῶν (gen.pl.masc.of αὐτός, possession) 16.
οὐκ (negative conjunction with the indicative) 130
ἀφίουσιν (3d.per.pl.pres.act.ind.of ἀφίημι, futuris ᵓ) 319.
τεθῆναι (aor.pass.inf.of τίθημι, complementary, object of ἀφίουσιν) 455.
εἰς (preposition with the accusative, extent) 140.
μνῆμα (acc.sing.neut.of μνῆμα, extent) 2876.

Translation - "And some of the peoples and tribes and tongues and nations will see their corpses for three and a half days, but they will not permit their dead bodies to be placed into a grave."

Comment: Note the futuristic present tenses in βλέπουσιν and ἀφίουσιν. The absence of a noun with βλέπουσιν contributes to the partitive construction.

Apparently there will be an attempt to bury the bodies of the two witnesses, but it will not be permitted. τεθῆναι with τὰ πτώματα, joined in general reference, is the object infinitive of ἀφίουσιν. The unsaved will not wish to be deprived of the privilege of gazing upon the dead bodies of their former tormentors whom they hate. Italians in the street in Milan violated the body of Benito Mussolini and that of his mistress in 1945. People from all over the world saw the pictures of their bodies suspended by their feet, as Italians kicked their faces off.

The description of the party continues in

Verse 10 - "And they that dwell upon the earth shall rejoice over them and make merry, and shall send gifts one to another; because these two prophets tormented them that dwell on the earth."

καὶ οἱ κατοικοῦντες ἐπὶ τῆς γῆς χαίρουσιν ἐπ' αὐτοῖς καὶ εὐφραίνονται, καὶ δῶρα πέμφουσιν ἀλλήλοις, ὅτι οὗτοι οἱ δύο προφῆται ἐβασάνισαν τοὺς κατοικοῦντας ἐπὶ τῆς γῆς.

"and those who dwell on the earth will rejoice over them and make merry and exchange presents, because these two prophets had been a torment to those who dwell on the earth." . . . RSV

καὶ (continuative conjunction) 14.
οἱ (nom.pl.masc.of the article in agreement with κατοικοῦντες) 9.
κατοικοῦντες (pres.act.part.nom.pl.masc.of κατοικέω, substantival, subject of χαίρουσιν, εὐφραίνονται and πέμφουσιν) 242.

ἐπὶ (preposition with the genitive, place description) 47.

τῆς (gen.sing.fem.of the article in agreement with γῆς) 9.

γῆς (gen.sing.fem.of γῆ, place description) 157.

χαίρουσιν (3d.per.pl.pres.act.ind.of χαίρω, futuristic) 182.

ἐπὶ (preposition with the instrumental, cause) 47.

αὐτοῖς (instru.pl.masc.of αὐτός, cause) 16.

καὶ (adjunctive conjunction joining verbs) 14.

εὐφραίνονται (3d.per.pl.pres.mid.ind.of εὐφραίνομαι, futuristic) 2479.

καὶ (adjunctive conjunction joining verbs) 14.

δῶρα (acc.pl.neut.of δῶρον, direct object of πέμφουσιν) 191.

πέμφουσιν (3d.per.pl.fut.act.ind.of πέμπω, predictive) 169.

ἀλλήλοις (dat.pl.masc.of ἀλλήλων, indirect object of πέμφουσιν) 1487.

ὅτι (conjunction introducing an subordinate causal clause) 211.

οἱ (nom.pl.masc.of the article in agreement with προφῆται) 9.

δύο (numeral) 385.

προφῆται (nom.pl.masc.of προφήτης, subject of ἐβασάνισαν) 119.

ἐβασάνισαν (3d.per.pl.aor.act.ind.of βασανίζω, culminative) 719.

τοὺς (acc.pl.masc.of the article in agreement with κατοικοῦντας) 9.

κατοικοῦντας (pres.act.part.acc.pl.masc.of κατοικέω, substantival, direct object of ἐβασάνισαν) 242.

ἐπὶ (preposition with the genitive of place description) 47.

τῆς (gen.sing.fem.of the article in agreement with γῆς) 9.

γῆς (gen.sing.fem.of γῆ, place description) 157.

Translation - "And those dwelling on the earth will rejoice because of them and they will celebrate and they will send gifts to each other, because these two prophets had tormented them who dwell on the earth."

Comment: Note that John uses the futuristic present tense with the first two verbs, yet shifts to the future in πέμφουσιν. His reason for referring to the people as οἱ κατοικοῦντες and τοὺς κατοικοῦντας probably is that, at this late date (three and one half days before the second coming) not many are left alive. Note the killing, famine and pestilence throughout the seven year period in Rev.6:4,8,9,11; 8:5,8,9-11; 9:18; 11:5. The ranks of the unregenerate population of earth will have been greatly decimated by this time. But those who will survive will have learned nothing (2 Tim.3:7). Antichrist's victory over the two witnesses will be interpreted as his ultimate success in building a world society without Christ.

Let us concentrate on an appreciation of the *zeitgeist* by imagining ourselves as unsaved and yet alive at that time. For the past seven years world events have been as described in the Revelation. Widespread desolation and death has just devastated the earth. Earthquake, fire, blood, visitation of hitherto unknown varmints and universal pollution of the environment have reduced the world and its society to chaos. Two preachers have for the past three and one half years warned all and sundry that Antichrist and the Beast are satanic and scheduled for hell. Now the Beast has killed them and their bodies lie rotting in the street.

They had been preaching for three and one half years that the Kingdom of Christ would soon prevail over the kingdom of Antichrist. It is no wonder that the world will rejoice when they see them dead, and send gifts and get drunk! But their glee will be short-lived, as we see in

Verse 11 - "And after three days and an half the spirit of life from God entered into them, and they stood upon their feet; and great fear fell upon them which saw them."

καὶ μετὰ τὰς τρεῖς ἡμέρας καὶ ἥμισυ πνεῦμα ζωῆς ἐκ τοῦ θεοῦ εἰσῆλθεν ἐν αὐτοῖς, καὶ ἔστησαν ἐπὶ τοὺς πόδας αὐτῶν, καὶ φόβος μέγας ἐπέπεσεν ἐπὶ τοὺς θεωροῦντας αὐτούς.

"But after the three and a half days a breath of life from God entered them, and they stood up on their feet, and great fear fell on those who saw them." . . . RSV

καὶ (continuative conjunction) 14.

μετὰ (preposition with the accusative of time extent) 50.

τὰς (acc.pl.fem.of the article in agreement with ἡμέρας) 9.

τρεῖς (numeral) 1010.

ἡμέρας (acc.pl.fem.of ἡμέρα, time extent) 135.

καὶ (adjunctive conjunction joining substantives) 14.

ἥμισυ (acc.sing.neut.of ἥμισυς, time extent) 2259.

πνεῦμα (nom.sing.neut.of πνεῦμα, subject of εἰσῆλθεν) 83.

ζωῆς (gen.sing.fem.of ζωή, description) 668.

ἐκ (preposition with the ablative of source) 19.

τοῦ (abl.sing.masc.of the article in agreement with θεοῦ) 9.

θεοῦ (abl.sing.masc.of θεός, source) 124.

εἰσῆλθεν (3d.per.sing.aor.ind.of εἰσέρχομαι, constative) 234.

ἐν (preposition with the locative of place) 80.

αὐτοῖς (loc.pl.masc.of αὐτός, place) 16.

καὶ (continuative conjunction) 14.

ἔστησαν (3d.per.pl.aor.act.ind.of ἵστημι, constative) 180.

ἐπὶ (preposition with the accusative, adverbial accusative) 47.

τοὺς (acc.pl.masc.of the article in agreement with πόδας) 9.

πόδας (acc.pl.masc.of πούς, adverbial accusative) 353.

αὐτῶν (gen.pl.masc.of αὐτός, possession) 16.

καὶ (continuative conjunction) 14.

φόβος (nom.sing.masc.of φόβος, subject of ἐπέπεσεν) 1131.

μέγας (nom.sing.masc.of μέγας, in agreement with φόβος) 184.

ἐπέπεσεν (3d.per.sing.2d.aor.act.ind.of ἐπιπίπτω, ingressive) 1794.

ἐπὶ (preposition with the accusative, adverbial accusative) 47.

τοὺς (acc.pl.masc.of the article in agreement with θεωροῦντας) 9.

θεωροῦντας (pres.act.part.acc.pl.masc.of θεωρέω, substantival, adverbial accusative) 1667.

αὐτούς (acc.pl.masc.of αὐτός, direct object of θεωροῦντας) 16.

Translation - "And after the three days and a half a living spirit from God came into them; and they stood upon their feet; therefore great fear seized upon those who saw them."

Comment: This apparently is a special resurrection and rapture for the two witnesses, since a little time seems to elapse before the seventh trumpet is sounded, at which time all of the saints are resurrected and/or translated. Note ἐν αὐτοῖς after εἰς in composition, and ἐπί after ἐπί in composition. The life giving Spirit from God raises the witnesses from the dead.

The reaction of the mob to this resurrection can be imagined. Delighted beyond expression that the preachers are dead, and holding high carnival over their violated corpses, they suddenly witness their resurrection. The text does not tell us who will hear the voice out of heaven which will speak to them, in

Verse 12 - "And they heard a great voice from heaven saying unto them, Come up hither. And they ascended up to heaven in a cloud; and their enemies beheld them."

καὶ ἤκουσαν φωνῆς μεγάλης ἐκ τοῦ οὐρανοῦ λεγούσης αὐτοῖς, Ἀνάβατε ὧδε. καὶ ἀνέβησαν εἰς τὸν οὐρανὸν ἐν τῇ νεφέλῃ, καὶ ἐθεώρησαν αὐτοὺς οἱ ἐχθροὶ αὐτῶν.

"Then they heard a loud voice from heaven saying to them, 'Come up hither!' And in the sight of their foes they went up to heaven in a cloud." ... RSV

καὶ (continuative conjunction) 14.
ἤκουσαν (3d.per.pl.aor.act.ind.of ἀκούω, constative) 148.
φωνῆς (gen.sing.fem.of φωνή, direct object of ἤκουσαν) 222.
μεγάλης (gen.sing.fem.of μέγας, in agreement with φωνῆς) 184.
ἐκ (preposition with the ablative of source) 19.
τοῦ (abl.sing.masc.of the article in agreement with οὐρανοῦ) 9.
οὐρανοῦ (abl.sing.masc.of οὐρανός, source) 254.
λεγούσης (pres.act.part.gen.sing.fem.of λέγω, recitative) 66.
αὐτοῖς (dat.pl.masc.of αὐτός, indirect object of λεγούσης) 16.
Ἀνάβατε (2d.per.pl.aor.act.impv.of ἀναβαίνω, command) 323.
ὧδε (local adverb) 766.
καὶ (inferential conjunction) 14.
ἀνέβησαν (3d.per.pl.aor.act.ind.of ἀναβαίνω, ingressive) 323.
εἰς (preposition with the accusative of extent) 140.
τὸν (acc.sing.masc.of the article in agreement with οὐρανὸν) 9.
οὐρανὸν (acc.sing.masc.of οὐρανός, extent) 254.
ἐν (preposition with the locative of place) 80.
τῇ (loc.sing.fem.of the article in agreement with νεφέλῃ) 9.
νεφέλῃ (loc.sing.fem.of νεφέλη, place) 1225.
καὶ (continuative conjunction) 14.
ἐθεώρησαν (3d.per.pl.aor.act.ind.of θεωρέω, constative) 1667.
αὐτοὺς (acc.pl.masc.of αὐτός, direct object of ἐθεώρησαν) 16.

οἱ (nom.pl.masc.of the article in agreement with ἐχϑροὶ) 9.
ἐχϑροὶ (nom.pl.masc.of ἐχϑρός, subject of ἐϑεώρησαν) 543.
αὐτῶν (gen.pl.masc.of αὐτός, relationship) 16.

Translation - "And they heard a loud voice out of heaven saying to them, 'Come up here!' So they ascended into heaven in the cloud, and their enemies watched them."

Comment: Note the variant spelling of the 2d.per.pl.aor.act.impv. ἀνάβατε. *Cf.* John 7:8.
The two witnesses followed our Lord's example:

Three and one half years of faithful witnessing —
They witnessed against the World Establishment —
They died on time at the hands of the Establishment —
They were dead three days —
They were resurrected from the dead —
They ascended to heaven.

Verse 13 - "And the same hour was there a great earthquake, and the tenth part of the city fell, and in the earthquake were slain of men seven thousand: and the remnant were affrighted, and gave glory to the God of heaven."

Καὶ ἐν ἐκείνῃ τῇ ὥρᾳ ἐγένετο σεισμὸς μέγας, καὶ τὸ δέκατον τῆς πόλεως ἔπεσεν, καὶ ἀπεκτάνϑησαν ἐν τῷ σεισμῷ ὀνόματα ἀνϑρώπων χιλιάδες ἑπτά, καὶ οἱ λοιποὶ ἔμφοβοι ἐγένοντο καὶ ἔδωκαν δόξαν τῷ ϑεῷ τοῦ οὐρανοῦ.

"And at that hour there was a great earthquake, and a tenth of the city fell; seven thousand people were killed in the earthquake, and the rest were terrified and gave glory to the God of heaven."

Καὶ (continuative conjunction) 14.
ἐν (preposition with the locative of time point) 80.
ἐκείνῃ (loc.sing.fem.of ἐκεῖνος, in agreement with ὥρᾳ) 246.
τῇ (loc.sing.fem.of the article in agreement with ὥρᾳ) 9.
ὥρᾳ (loc.sing.fem.of ὥρα, time point) 735.
ἐγένετο (3d.per.sing.aor.ind.of γίνομαι, ingressive) 113.
σεισμὸς (nom.sing.masc.of σεισμός, subject of ἐγένετο) 751.
μέγας (nom.sing.masc.of μέγας, in agreement with σεισμὸς) 184.
καὶ (continuative conjunction) 14.
τὸ (nom.sing.neut.of the article in agreement with δέκατον) 9.
δέκατον (nom.sing.neut.of δέκατος, subject of ἔπεσεν) 1961.
τῆς (gen.sing.fem.of the article in agreement with πόλεως) 9.
πόλεως (gen.sing.fem.of πόλις, partitive) 243.
ἔπεσεν (3d.per.sing.aor.act.ind.of πίπτω, ingressive) 187.
καὶ (continuative conjunction) 14.
ἀπεκτάνϑησαν (3d.per.pl.aor.pass.ind.of ἀποκτείνω, constative) 889.
ἐν (preposition with the instrumental, means) 80.

τῷ (instru.sing.masc.of the article in agreement with σεισμῷ) 9.
σεισμῷ (instru.sing.masc.of σεισμός, means) 751.
ὀνόματα (nom.pl.neut.of ὄνομα, subject of ἦιν ϑνδερστοοδ)*.
ἀνϑρώπων (gen.pl.masc.of ἄνϑρωπος, description) 341.
χιλιάδες (nom.pl.neut.of χιλιάς, predicate nominative) 2536.
ἑπτά (numeral) 1024.
καὶ (continuative conjunction) 14.
οἱ (nom.pl.masc.of the article in agreement with λοιποὶ) 9.
λοιποὶ (nom.pl.masc.of λοιπός, subject of ἐγένετο and ἔδωκαν) 1402.
ἔμφοβοι (nom.pl.masc.of ἔμφοβος, predicate adjective) 2890.
ἐγένοντο (3d.per.pl.aor.mid.ind.of γίνομαι, ingressive) 113.
καὶ (adjunctive conjunction joining verbs) 14.
ἔδωκαν (3d.per.pl.aor.act.ind.of δίδωμι, ingressive) 362.
δόξαν (acc.sing.fem.of δόξα, direct object of ἔδωκαν) 361.
τῷ (dat.sing.masc.of the article in agreement with ϑεῷ) 9.
ϑεῷ (dat.sing.masc.of ϑεός, indirect object of ἔδωκαν) 124.
τοῦ (gen.sing.masc.of the article in agreement with οὐρανοῦ) 9.
οὐρανοῦ (gen.sing.masc.of οὐρανός, description) 254.

Translation - "And in that hour a great earthquake began and the tenth part of the city began to fall, and the names of the men who were willed by the earthquake came to seven thousand, and the others were seized with terror and began to give glory to the God of heaven."

Comment: On the use of ὀνόματα here *cf.* Rev.3:4.

This earthquake is the last judgment before those under the sixth seal (Rev.6:12-18), the seventh trumpet (Rev.11:15-19) and the seventh vial (Rev.16:17-21). The destruction in Jerusalem covers one tenth of the city and seven thousand people are killed. The others are seized with terror (ingressive aorist in ἐγένοντο) and begin to give glory to God. It is not clear that ἔδωκαν δόξαν τῷ ϑεῷ τοῦ οὐρανοῦ means regeneration. *Cf.* Phil.2:10-11 and Rev.5:13. God makes even the wrath of man to praise Him (Psalm 76:10).

Two of the "woes" (Rev.8:13; 9:12) have been visited upon the earth. They were the fifth and sixth trumpet judgments. The third is the last trumpet, which will come without further delay. The time point is the end of the tribulation period.

Verse 14 - "The second woe is past; and, the third woe cometh quickly."

Ἡ οὐαὶ ἡ δευτέρα ἀπῆλθεν, ἰδοὺ ἡ οὐαὶ ἡ τρίτη ἔρχεται ταχύ.

"The second woe has passed; behold, the third woe is soon to come." ... RSV

Ἡ (nom.sing.fem.of the article in agreement with οὐαὶ) 9.
οὐαὶ (nom.sing.fem.of οὐαί, subject of ἀπῆλθεν) 936.
ἡ (nom.sing.fem.of the article in agreement with δευτέρα) 9.
δευτέρα (nom.sing.fem.of δεύτερος, in agreement with οὐαὶ) 1371.
ἀπῆλθεν (3d.per.sing.aor.ind.of ἀπέρχομαι, culminative) 239.

ἰδού (exclamation) 95.

ἡ (nom.sing.fem.of the article in agreement with οὐαὶ) 9.

οὐαὶ (nom.sing.fem.of οὐαί, subject of ἔρχεται) 936.

ἡ (nom.sing.fem.of the article in agreement with τρίτη) 9.

τρίτη (nom.sing.fem.of τρίτος, in agreement with οὐαὶ) 1209.

ἔρχεται (3d.per.sing.pres.ind.of ἔρχομαι, predictive) 146.

ταχύ (temporal adverb) 491.

Translation - "The second woe has passed; look out! the third woe is coming quickly."

Comment: *Cf.* Rev.8:13; 9:12 and 11:14. Thus we see that the last three trumpet judgments are also referred to as οὐαί. They will be particulary destructive to Satan, unsaved man and his world society. The locusts from the abyss (Rev.9:11) and the hellish cavalry on the Euphrates (Rev.9:13-21) are the first two. The third is the last trumpet judgment, which occurs simultaneously with the sixth and seventh seals and the seventh vial. These events terminate the tribulation period with Messiah's return, the resurrection of the righteous and the rapture of those who are still alive on earth (1 Cor.15:52).

The Seventh Trumpet

(Revelation 11:15-19)

Verse 15 - "And the seventh angel sounded: and there were great voices in heaven, saying, The kingdoms of this world are become the kingdoms of our Lord, and of his Christ; and he shall reign forever and ever."

Καὶ ὁ ἕβδομος ἄγγελος ἐσάλπισιν, καὶ ἐγένοντο φωναὶ μεγάλαι ἐν τῷ οὐρανῷ λέγοντες, Ἐγένετο ἡ βασιλεία τοῦ κόσμου τοῦ κυρίου ἡμῶν καὶ τοῦ Χριστοῦ αὐτοῦ, καὶ βασιλεύσει εἰς τοὺς αἰῶνας τῶν αἰώνων.

"Then the seventh angel blew his trumpet, and there were loud voices in heaven, saying, 'The kingdom of the world has become the kingdom of our Lord and of his Christ, and he shall reign for ever and ever.' " . . . RSV

Καὶ (continuative conjunction) 14.

ὁ (nom.sing.masc.of the article in agreement with ἄγγελος) 9.

ἕβδομος (nom.sing.masc.of ἕβδομος, in agreement with ἄγγελος) 2020.

ἄγγελος (nom.sing.masc.of ἄγγελος, subject of ἐσάλπισεν) 96.

ἐσάλπισεν (3d.per.sing.aor.act.ind.of σαλπίζω, ingressive) 559.

καὶ (continuative conjunction) 14.

ἐγένοντο (3d.per.pl.aor.ind.of γίνομαι, ingressive) 113.

φωναὶ (nom.pl.fem.of φωνή, subject of ἐγένοντο) 222.

μεγάλαι (nom.pl.fem.of μέγας, in agreement with φωναὶ) 184.

ἐν (preposition with the locative of place) 80.

τῷ (loc.sing.masc.of the article in agreement with οὐρανῷ) 9.

οὐρανῷ (loc.sing.masc.of οὐρανός, place) 254.

λέγοντες (pres.act.part.nom.pl.masc.of λέγω, recitative) 66.

Ἐγένετο (3d.per.sing.aor.ind.of γίνομαι, ingressive) 113.

ἡ (nom.sing.masc.of the article in agreement with βασιλεία) 9.

βασιλεία (nom.sing.masc.of βασιλεία, subject of Ἐγένετο) 253.

τοῦ (gen.sing.masc.of the article in agreement with κόσμου) 9.

κόσμου (gen.sing.masc.of κόσμος, description) 360.

τοῦ (gen.sing.masc.of the article in agreement with κυρίου) 9.

κυρίου (gen.sing.masc.of κύριος, possession) 97.

ἡμῶν (gen.pl.masc.of ἐγώ, relationship) 123.

καὶ (adjunctive conjunction joining nouns) 14.

τοῦ (gen.sing.masc.of the article in agreement with Χριστοῦ) 9.

Χριστοῦ (gen.sing.masc.of Χριστός, possession) 4.

αὐτοῦ (gen.sing.masc.of αὐτός, relationship) 16.

καὶ (continuative conjunction) 14.

βασιλεύσει (3d.per.sing.fut.act.ind.of βασιλεύω, predictive) 236.

εἰς (preposition with the accusative of time extent) 140.

τοὺς (acc.pl.masc.of the article in agreement with αἰῶνας) 9.

τῶν (gen.pl.masc.of the article in agreement with αἰώνων) 9.

αἰώνων (gen.pl.masc.of αἰών, partitive genitive) 1002.

Translation - "And the seventh angel began to blow his trumpet; and there were loud voices in heaving, saying, 'The hegemony of our Lord and of His Messiah over the world has begun, and He shall reign into the ages of the ages.' "

Comment: The King James Version has taken unwarranted liberties with the text. It is obvious that the world political system throughout history, until the last three and one half years, has been divided between many and varied poles of political power. During the great tribulation it will be one kingdom, dominated by Antichrist. That one world system, over which Antichrist will rule for forty-two months (Rev.13:5) will be a political unit, upon which God will make relentless war, and in which His only concern will be the work of the Holy Spirit in finishing the ministry of calling out His Body. When our Lord returns the world system will not be divided into kingdoms, but will have been merged into one satanic kingdom with the Beast in control. That world system will become the kingdom (singular) of God and His Messiah.

    Not all of the unregenerate will be killed and sent to hell at the beginning of this kingdom age of divine righteousness. Some will survive and become subject to Him Who will rule "with a rod of iron" (Rev.19:15). They will enjoy the political and economic peace of the Kingdom Age; they will live to much longer ages than formerly (Isa.65:2) and they will have children, some of whom will be saved during the kingdom age. But Messiah will need political administrators in His Kingdom and will appoint deserving saints to rule over the cities (Mt.25:21,23). The twelve Apostles will occupy the twelve benches of the divine judicial system over the nation Israel. Where will Messiah recruit these administrators? From the graves throughout the earth where they will have been in decay, some of them for centuries and others perhaps for only a few minutes. The dead in Christ will rise first (1 Thess.4:16), and they will be joined by those who are alive and remain.

For at this time the "last trumpet" (1 Cor.15:52) will sound. If the trumpet of Rev.11:15 is not the last, then "the trumpet of God" (1 Thess.4:16) must follow it (this comment for those who delight in indulging in exegetical hair-splitting!), and this last trump calls the saints in resurrection from the graves and in rapture from the earth, in the case of those saints who will still be alive and who will remain upon the earth until the end. The last elect member of the Body of Christ will have only recently been baptized into His Body (1 Cor.12:13; Rev.10:7).

For those who insist that Paul's "last trump" of 1 Cor.15:52 is not the seventh trumpet of Rev.11:15, we point out that the noun σάλπιγξ (#1507) does not occur in the New Testament after Rev.9:14 and the verb σαλπίζω (#559), which means "to blow on a horn" occurs last in Rev.11:15. If Paul's "last trump" is not the seventh trumpet, then the rapture and resurrection must occur *after* our Lord has returned to earth. But 1 Thess.4:17 says that we will be caught together to meet Him "in the air" after which we shall always be with the Lord. This is said in verse 18 to be a source of comfort for us.

Pretribulation rapture teachers want to blow this horn seven years before the world kingdom becomes "the kingdom of our Lord and of His Christ."

We had a boy in the high school band who never could learn when to blow his horn!

Jesus said that at the resurrection of the just, rewards would be given to the saints (Mt.16:27; Lk.14:12-14) and Paul said that the resurrection of the just would be at "the last trump" (1 Cor.15:52). Hence we have every legitimate expectation to find the judgment seat of Christ, when the saints are judged for their works and rewarded at the last trump and so we do in Rev.11:18. If things equal to the same things are equal to each other, then events that are scheduled to happen simultaneously must be simultaneous.

The rapture and resurrection occur at the same time - the resurrection first and that immediately followed by the rapture. The dead in Christ will rise first because they have six feet further to go. (1 Thess.4:16,17). At that same time the saints will be rewarded for their "gold, silver and precious stones" (1 Cor.3:11-14; Lk.14:12-14). The judgment seat of Christ will occur at the seventh (last) trumpet of Rev.11:15-19. *Cf.* verse 18. Hence the rapture and resurrection will occur at that time.

When, in relation to Daniel's 70th week, with its great tribulation during the last half, will this last trumpet be blown? On the last day. How can we discern this? What the heavenly voices say (Rev.11:15-16) could not be truthfully said one day before Messiah's second coming. Until that very moment Antichrist will be king of the world. Satan will be the world's god as they celebrate the death of God's two witnesses, who will be lying unburied in the street. Only when He comes to reign does the world kingdom, united under Satan and the Beast become "the united kingdom of our Lord and of His Messiah."

Once He has taken to Him His great power and has begun to reign, for how long will He exercise this sovereignty over a united world kingdom? βασιλεύσει εἰς τοὺς αἰῶνας τῶν αἰώνων. *Cf.* Lk.1:33. Gabriel's promise to Mary will be fulfilled completely at the last trumpet. *Cf.* 1 Tim.6:15; Rev.11:17; 19:6; 20:4,6; 1 Cor.15:25. Five of his promises were fulfilled in our Lord's first coming. She conceived, bore a son and called His name Jesus. He was great and He was called the Son of the Highest. In His second coming He will begin a reign over the house of Jacob on the throne of His father David and of His kingdom there will be no end.

The kingdoms of this world (note the plural) once belonged to Satan (Mt.4:8; Lk.4:5) and were offered to Jesus on a tradeoff if He would forget Calvary. Jesus rejected Satan's offer because He was looking forward to Rev.11:15, when they would be His forever.

Under Satan's rule kingdoms have always fought against kingdoms because Satan is a killer (Mt.24:7; Mk.13:8; Lk.21:10). Christians, by faith, have exercised some direction over world politics (Heb.11:33), under the direction of the Holy Spirit Who has always been transcendant above and yet immanent in history. This was in keeping with His purpose of calling out the elect. For a short time this world will be under the control of the Beast (Rev.16:10) and his subordinates (Rev.17:12,17) and the Harlot of Babylon (Rev.17:18). The basis for this temporary control will be economic as the Beast will monopolize international trade and thus the internal economies of each nation.

The kingdom once owned by Herod will be incorporated into that of our Lord Messiah at the last trumpet (Rev.11:15).

Note the ingressive aorist in ἐγένετο. At the time that they speak Messiah will have just assumed power. What they say could not be said one day before the end of the week. What the twenty-four elders add in verses 16 and 17 accentuates the point that Jesus, the Messiah at that time will actually be sitting upon David's throne, in keeping with the promise of God to David in 2 Sam.7:10-17.

Verse 16 - "And the four and twenty elders, which sat before God on their seats, fell upon their faces, and worshipped God."

καὶ οἱ εἴκοσι τέσσαρες πρεσβύτεροι οἱ ἐνώπιον τοῦ θεοῦ κάθηνται ἐπὶ τοὺς θρόνους αὐτῶν ἔπεσαν ἐπὶ τὰ πρόσωπα αὐτῶν καὶ προσεκύνησαν τῷ θεῷ

"And the twenty-four elders who sit on their thrones before God fell on their faces and worshipped God, . . . " . . . RSV

καὶ (continuative conjunction) 14.

οἱ (nom.pl.masc.of the article in agreement with πρεσβύτεροι) 9.

εἴκοσι (numeral) 2283.

τέσσαρες (numeral) 1508.

πρεσβύτεροι (nom.pl.masc.of πρεσβύτερος, subject of ἔπεσαν and προσεκύνησαν) 1141.

οἵ (nom.pl.masc.of ὅς, relative pronoun, subject of κάθηνται) 65.

ἐνώπιον (preposition with the genitive of place description) 1798.

τοῦ (gen.sing.masc.of the article in agreement with θεοῦ) 9.

θεοῦ (gen.sing.masc.of θεός, place description) 124.

κάθηνται (3d.per.pl.pres.mid.ind.of κάθημαι, customary) 377.

ἐπὶ (preposition with the accusative, rest) 47.
τοὺς (acc.pl.masc.of the article in agreement with θρόνους) 9.
θρόνους (acc.pl.masc.of θρόνος, rest) 519.
αὐτῶν (gen.pl.masc.of αὐτός, possession) 16.
ἔπεσαν (3d.per.pl.aor.act.ind.of πίπτω, constative) 187.
ἐπὶ (preposition with the accusative, metaphorical place) 47.
τὰ (acc.pl.neut.of the article in agreement with πρόσωπα) 9.
πρόσωπα (acc.pl.neut.of πρόσωπον, metaphorical) 588.
αὐτῶν (gen.pl.masc.of αὐτός, possession) 16.
καὶ (adjunctive conjunction joining verbs) 14.
προσεκύνησαν (3d.per.pl.aor.act.ind.of προσκυνέω, ingressive) 147.
τῷ (dat.sing.masc.of the article in agreement with θεῷ) 9.
θεῷ (dat.sing.masc.of θεός, personal interest) 124.

Translation - "And the twenty four elders who were sitting before God on their thrones fell upon their faces and worshipped God. . . "

Comment: The relative clause οἵ . . . θρόνους αὐτῶν is descriptive. We saw these heavenly creatures in chapters 4,5 and 7. They appear again in chapters 14 and 19. What they have to say in verse 17 supports the view that the time of the last trumpet is the closing moments of the tribulation week.

Verse 17 - "Saying, We give thee thanks, O Lord God Almighty, which art, and wast, and art to come; because thou hast taken to thee thy great power, and hast reigned."

λέγοντες, Εὐχαριστοῦμέν σοι, κύριες ὁ θεὸς ὁ παντοκράτωρ, ὁ ὢν καὶ ὁ ἦν, ὅτι εἴληφας τὴν δύναμίν σου τὴν μεγάλην καὶ ἐβασίλευσας.

"saying, 'We give thanks to thee, Lord God Almighty, who art and who wast, that thou hast taken thy great power and begun to reign.' " . . . RSV

λέγοντες (pres.act.part.nom.pl.masc.of λέγω, recitative) 66.
Εὐχαριστοῦμέν (1st.per.pl.pres.act.ind.of εὐχαριστέω, aoristic) 1185.
σοι (dat.sing.masc.of σύ, indirect object of εὐχαριστοῦμέν) 104.
κύριε (voc.sing.masc.of κύριος, address) 97.
ὁ (nom.sing.masc.of the article in agreement with θεὸς) 9.
θεὸς (nom.sing.masc.of θεός, for θεέ, address) 124.
ὁ (nom.sing.masc.of the article in agreement with παντοκράτωρ) 9.
παντοκράτωρ (nom.sing.masc.of παντοκράτωρ, apposition) 4325.
ὁ (nom.sing.masc.of the article in agreement with ὢν) 9.
ὢν (pres.part.nom.sing.masc.of εἰμί, appellation) 86.
καὶ (adjunctive conjunction joining substantives) 14.
ὁ (nom.sing.masc.of the article, in apposition) 9.
ἦν (3d.per.sing.imp.ind.of εἰμί, appelation) 86.
ὅτι (conjunction introducing a subordinate causal clause) 211.
εἴληφας (2d.per.sing.perf.act.ind.of λαμβάνω, intensive) 533.
τὴν (acc.sing.fem.of the article in agreement with δύναμίν) 9.

δύναμίν (acc.sing.fem.of δύναμις, direct object of εἴληφας) 687.
σου (gen.sing.masc.of σύ, possession) 104.
τὴν (acc.sing.fem.of the article in agreement with μεγάλην) 9.
μεγάλην (acc.sing.fem.of μέγας, in agreement with δύναμίν) 184.
καὶ (adjunctive conjunction joining verbs) 14.
ἐβασίλευσας (2d.per.sing.aor.act.ind.of βασιλεύω, ingressive) 236.

Translation - "saying, 'We give thanks to you, Lord God, the Sovereign One, the One Who is and Who has always been, because you have taken for yourself your great power and you have begun to reign.' "

Comment: *Cf.* Rev.1:8; 4:8; 11:17 and 16:5. This formula speaks of the unchangeable character of God. He claimed sovereignty after His resurrection (Mt.28:18) but ascended to heaven to await the moment when He would actually take to Himself this power (Psalm 110:1). His work was finished (Heb.1:3), but, due to the division of labor in the Godhead, the work of the Holy Spirit was not. Now, at the end of the church age, the Holy Spirit has finished His work and has called out from among the Gentiles a people for His name (Acts 15:14) in keeping with Amos 9:11-12; Isa.45:21,22; Rev.10:7.

God the Father chose His elect (Eph.1:3,4); God the incarnate Son reconciled them unto the Father and God the Holy Spirit will have effactually called them into the intimate personal relationship described by Jesus in John 17:21. There is nothing further to be done, except to assert the divine prerogative, which Messiah has ample power to do.

Note the punctiliar action in past time that yields the duration situation in the eternal present in the second perfect εἴληφας - "you have received your power and hence now you have it." Note also the ingressive aorist in ἐβασίλευσας, which accents the action at its beginning and thus supports the notion that the elders speak of Messiah as having already assumed power.

Man's day (1 Cor.4:3) when "no man can work" (John 9:4) is over. Satan will be no longer "the god of this world" (2 Cor.4:4). Messiah is King (Lk.1:30-33; 2 Sam.7). "Everlasting righteousness has been brought in" (Dan.9:24). Since Gentile fulless is complete (Eph.3:3,4,9; Rev.10:7; Rom.11:25) the Body of Christ has been raptured (1 Cor.15:52; 1 Thess.4:14-18). We have just been caught up to meet Him in the air as He descended to His place on the Mount of Olives (Zech.14:1-4), after which He will procede to the spot where David's throne stood and where it will stand again. The partial blindness of the 144,000 Jews (Rom.11:25; Rev.7:1-8) has been removed and replaced with spiritual understanding. Our Lord Messiah will have the nucleus of the great nation that He promised to Abraham and to his seed.

Those who try to place the trumpet judgments earlier in the tribulation week, or indeed in some historic past time, are confronted with the fact that at this last trumpet Messiah is said already to have become King and to have taken His power. Thus they are forced into an allegorical interpretation of the language or into an existential position of agnosticism. Was Christ the King when Hitler murdered 600,000 Jews or when thousands starved in Bangledesh?! Or when Jim

Jones seduced 900 holy roller fanatics to commit suicide?

Two more elements in the picture are found in verse 18. Angry sinners, divine wrath and divine destruction visited upon those who destroy the earth, and, in the middle clauses of the verses, the judgment seat of Christ.

Verse 18 - "And the nations were angry, and thy wrath is come, and the time of the dead, that they should be judged, and that thou shouldst give reward unto thy servants the prophets, and to the saints, and them that fear thy name, small and great; and should destroy them which destroy the earth."

καὶ τὰ ἔθνη ὠργίσθησαν, καὶ ἦλθεν ἡ ὀργή σου καὶ ὁ καιρὸς τῶν νεκρῶν κριθῆναι καὶ δοῦναι τὸν μισθὸν τοῖς δούλοις σου τοῖς προφήταις καὶ τοῖς ἁγίοις καὶ τοῖς φοβουμένοις τὸ ὄνομά σου, τοὺς μικροὺς καὶ τοὺς μεγάλους, καὶ διαφθεῖραι τοὺς διαφθείροντας τὴν γῆν.

"The nations raged, but thy wrath came, and the time for the dead to be judged, for rewarding thy servants, the prophets and saints, and those who fear thy name, both small and great, and for destroying the destroyers of the earth.'".
. . RSV

καὶ (continuative conjunction) 14.

τὰ (nom.pl.neut.of the article in agreement with ἔθνη) 9.

ἔθνη (nom.pl.neut.of ἔθνος, subject of ὠργίσθησαν) 376.

ὠργίσθησαν (3d.per.pl.aor.pass.ind.of ὀργίζω, constative) 479.

καὶ (continuative conjunction) 14.

ἦλθεν (3d.per.sing.aor.ind.of ἔρχομαι, constative) 146.

ἡ (nom.sing.fem.of the article in agreement with ὀργή) 9.

ὀργή (nom.sing.fem.of ὀργή, subject of ἦλθεν) 283.

σου (gen.sing.masc.of σύ, possession) 104.

καὶ (adjunctive conjunction joining nouns) 14.

ὁ (nom.sing.masc.of the article in agreement with καιρὸς) 9.

καιρὸς (nom.sing.masc.of καιρός, subject of ἦλθεν) 767.

τῶν (gen.pl.masc.of the article in agreement with νεκρῶν) 9.

νεκρῶν (gen.pl.masc.of νεκρός, description) 749.

κριθῆναι (aor.pass.inf.of κρίνω, in apposition with καιρὸς) 531.

καὶ (adjunctive conjunction joining infinitives) 14.

δοῦναι (aor.act.inf.of δίδωμι, in apposition with καιρὸς) 362.

τὸν (acc.sing.masc.of the article in agreement with μισθὸν) 9.

μισθὸν (acc.sing.masc.of μισθός, direct object of δοῦναι) 441.

τοῖς (dat.pl.masc.of the article in agreement with δούλοις) 9.

δούλοις (dat.pl.masc.of δοῦλος, indirect object of δοῦναι) 725.

σου (gen.sing.masc.of σύ, relationship) 104.

τοῖς (dat.pl.masc.of the article in agreement with προφήταις) 9.

προφήταις (dat.pl.masc.of προφήτης, in apposition with δούλοις) 119.

καὶ (adjunctive conjunction joining nouns) 14.

τοῖς (dat.pl.masc.of the article in agreement with ἁγίοις) 9.

ἁγίοις (dat.pl.masc.of ἅγιος, indirect object of δοῦναι) 84.

καὶ (adjunctive conjunction joining substantives) 14.

τοῖς (dat.pl.masc.of the article in agreement with φοβουμένοις) 9.

φοβουμένοις (pres.mid.part.dat.pl.masc.of φοβέομαι, substantival, indirect object of δοῦναι) 101.

τὸ (acc.sing.neut.of the article in agreement with ὄνομά) 9.

ὄνομά (acc.sing.neut.of ὄνομα, direct object of φοβουμένοις) 108.

σου (gen.sing.masc.of σύ, possession) 104.

τοὺς (acc.pl.masc.of the article in agreement with μικροὺς) 9.

μικροὺς (acc.pl.masc.of μικρός, direct object of κριθῆναι) 901.

καὶ (adjuntive conjunction joining adjectival nouns) 14.

τοὺς (acc.pl.masc.of the article in agreement with μεγάλους) 9.

μεγάλους (acc.pl.masc.of μέγας, direct object of κριθῆναι) 184.

καὶ (adjunctive conjunction joining infinitives) 14.

διαφθεῖραι (1st.aor.act.inf.of διαφθείρω, in apposition with καιρὸς) 2485.

τοὺς (acc.pl.masc.of the article in agreement with διαφθείροντας) 9.

διαφθείροντας (pres.act.part.acc.pl.masc.of διαφθείρω, substantival, direct object of διαφθεῖραι) 2985.

τὴν (acc.sing.fem.of the article in agreement with γῆν) 9.

γῆν (acc.sing.fem.of γῆ, direct object of διαφθείροντας) 157.

Translation - "And the nations have become angry, and your anger has come, and the time has come that the dead should be judged, the small and the great, and that you should give the reward to your servants, the prophets, and to the saints, to those who revere your name, and that you should destroy those who are destroying the earth."

Comment: The first two clauses remind us of Psalm 2. It is the time for the wrath of God to be felt. It is the occasion (καιρὸς) for three events. ὁ καιρὸς has in apposition the three infinitives κριθῆναι, δοῦναι and διαφθεῖραι. He will judge "small and great" - τοὺς μικροὺς καὶ τοὺς μεγάλους. He will also give rewards to the categories of Christians mentioned. He will also destroy those who will at that time be destroying the earth.

The nations of earth, motivated by the three evil spirits of Rev.16:12-14, will mobilize their forces at Armageddon (Zech.14:1-4). It will be all of the Gentile power against God's chosen people Israel, huddled like sheep in the desert.

The resurrected dead and the raptured saints who will have survived martyrdom to the end will be judged at the judgment seat of Christ (1 Cor.3:13-15; 2 Cor.5:10; Mt.16:27; Lk.14:12-14, *et al.*). It is only thus that the language can be construed. That this is not the judgment of the Great White Throne of Revelation 20:11*ff* is clear. That judgment is postmillenial. This one is premillenial. A thousand years separates them.

The earth is the Lord's (Psalm 24:1) and those who destroy it will be destroyed by Him who owns it. This last clause could refer to the widespread industrial pollution of the earth by the aggravated industrialization which is scene in Babylon (Rev.18:1-24). During the last half of the tribulation international trade will thrive as the Antichrist with his mark monopolizes world markets.

The student should arrange the detailed events in vertical parallel columns that he finds under the sixth seal (Rev.6:12-18), the seventh trumpet (Rev.11:15-19) and the seventh vial (Rev.16:17-21). These events occur at the same time, *viz.*on the day of the second coming of Christ. They are three different descriptions of events that will occur simultaneously. The correlative evidence is overwhelming. Reject it and we must have these events occurring again and again and again, with time elapsing between each set of events. *Cf.* the chart on page 64 *supra.*

Verse 19 - "And the temple of God was opened in heaven, and there was seen in his temple the ark of his testamont: and there were lightnings, and voices, and thunderings, and an earthquake, and great hail."

καὶ ἠνοίγη ὁ ναὸς τοῦ θεοῦ (ὁ) ἐν τῷ οὐρανῷ, καὶ ὤφθη ἡ κιβωτὸς τῆς διαθήκης αὐτοῦ ἐν τῷ ναῷ αὐτοῦ, καὶ ἐγένοντο ἀστραπαὶ καὶ φωναὶ καὶ βρονταὶ καὶ σεισμὸς καὶ χάλαζα μεγάλη.

"Then God's temple in heaven was opened, and the ark of his covenant was seen within his temple; and there were flashes of lightning, loud noises, peals of thunder, an earthquake, and heavy hail." . . . RSV

καὶ (continuative conjunction) 14.
ἠνοίγη (3d.per.sing.2d.aor.pass.ind.of ἀνοίγω, ingressive) 188.
ὁ (nom.sing.masc.of the article in agreement with ναὸς) 9.
ναὸς (nom.sing.masc.of ναός, subject of ἠνοίγη) 1447.
τοῦ (gen.sing.masc.of the article in agreement with θεοῦ) 9.
θεοῦ (gen.sing.masc.of θεός, possession) 124.
ὁ (nom.sing.masc.of the article in agreement with ναὸς) 9.
ἐν (preposition with the locative of place) 80.
τῷ (loc.sing.masc.of the article in agreement with οὐρανῷ) 9.
οὐρανῷ (loc.sing.masc.of οὐρανός, place) 254.
καὶ (continuative conjunction) 14.
ὤφθη (3d.per.sing.aor.pass.ind.of ὁράω, constative) 144.
ἡ (nom.sing.fem.of the article in agreement with κιβωτὸς) 9.
κιβωτὸς (nom.sing.fem.of κιβωτός, subject of ὤφθη) 1518.
τῆς (gen.sing.fem.of the article in agreement with διαθήκης) 9.
διαθήκης (gen.sing.fem.of διαθήκη, description) 1575.
αὐτοῦ (gen.sing.masc.of αὐτός, possession) 16.
ἐν (preposition with the locative of place) 80.
τῷ (loc.sing.masc.of the article in agreement with ναῷ) 9.
ναῷ (loc.sing.masc.of ναός, place) 1447.
αὐτοῦ (gen.sing.masc.of αὐτός, possession) 16.
καὶ (continuative conjunction) 14.
ἐγένοντο (3d.per.pl.aor.ind.of γίνομαι, ingressive) 113.
ἀστραπαὶ (nom.pl.fem.of ἀστραπή, subject of ἐγένοντο) 1502.
καὶ (adjunctive conjunction joining nouns) 14.
φωναὶ (nom.pl.fem.of φωνή, subject of ἐγένοντο) 222.

καὶ (adjunctive conjunction joining nouns) 14.
βρονταὶ (nom.pl.fem.of βροντή, subject of ἐγένοντο) 2117.
καὶ (adjunctive conjunction joining nouns) 14.
σεισμὸς (nom.sing.masc.of σεισμός, subject of ἐγένοντο) 751.
καὶ (adjunctive conjunction joining nouns) 14.
χάλαζα (nom.sing.fem.of χάλαζα, subject of ἐγένοντο) 5364.
μεγάλη (nom.sing.fem.of μέγας, in agreement with χάλαζα) 184.

Translation - "And the temple of God in heaven was opened, and the ark of His covenant was seen in His temple. And there were lightnings and voices and thunders and an earthquake and great hail."

Comment: *Cf.* Rev.6:14. Thus the temple in heaven could be seen. Events described in the following passages occur at this time: Zech.14:1-4; Mt.24:29-31; 1 Thess.4:13-18; 1 Cor.15:51-55; 2 Thess.1:7-10; Mt.16:27; Phil.3:20,21; 1 John 3:1-3; 1 Cor.3:11-15; 2 Cor.5:10; Rev.19:11-16; Dan.2:34-35, 44, etc.

Once again we have come to the end of the tribulation week as we did in Rev.6:17. We shall come to this point again at Rev.16:21.

Chapters 12-15 are vignettes that provide essential information as we study the movement of God's clock. At Rev.16:1 we shall begin at the second half of the week and travel with the seven vials, across the last half of the week.

The Woman and the Dragon

(Revelation 12:1-18)

Revelation 12:1 - "And there appeared a great wonder in heaven; a woman clothed with the sun, and the moon under her feet, and upon her head a crown of twelve stars."

Καὶ σημεῖον μέγα ὤφθη ἐν τῷ οὐρανῷ, γυνὴ περιβεβλημένη τὸν ἥλιον, καὶ ἡ σελήνη ὑποκάτω τῶν ποδῶν αὐτῆς, καὶ ἐπὶ τῆς κεφαλῆς αὐτῆς στεφανος ἀστέρων δώδεκα,

"And a great portent appeared in heaven, a woman clothed with the sun, with the moon under her feet, and on her head a crown of twelve stars; ..." ... RSV

Καὶ (continuative conjunction) 14.
σημεῖον (nom.sing.neut.of σημεῖον, subject of ὤφθη) 1005.
μέγα (nom.sing.neut.of μέγας, in agreement with σημεῖον) 184.
ὤφθη (3d.per.sing.aor.pass.ind.of ὁράω, constative) 144.
ἐν (preposition with the locative of place) 80.
τῷ (loc.sing.masc.of the article in agreement with οὐρανῷ) 9.
οὐρανῷ (loc.sing.masc.of οὐρανός, place) 254.
γυνὴ (nom.sing.fem.of γυνή, in apposition with σημεῖον) 103.
περιβεβλημένη (perf.pass.part.nom.sing.fem.of περιβάλλω, adjectival, predicate position, restrictive, in agreement with γυνή) 631.

τὸν (acc.sing.masc.of the article in agreement with ἥλιον) 9.

ἥλιον (acc.sing.masc.of ἥλιος, adverbial accusative) 546.

καὶ (continuative conjunction) 14.

ἡ (nom.sing.fem.of the article in agreement with σελήνη) 9.

σελήνη (nom.sing.fem.of σελήνη, subject of ἦν understood) 1505.

ὑποκάτω (preposition with the ablative of separation) 1429.

τῶν (abl.pl.masc.of the article in agreement with ποδῶν) 9.

ποδῶν (abl.pl.masc.of πούς, separation) 353.

αὐτῆς (gen.sing.fem.of αὐτός, possession) 16.

καὶ (continuative conjunction) 14.

ἐπὶ (preposition with the genitive, place description) 47.

τῆς (gen.sing.fem.of the article in agreement with κεφαλῆς) 9.

κεφαλῆς (gen.sing.fem.of κεφαλή, place description) 521.

αὐτῆς (gen.sing.fem.of αὐτους, possession) 16.

στέφανος (nom.sing.masc.of στέφανος, subject of ἦν understood) 1640.

ἀστέρων (gen.pl.masc.of ἀστήρ, description) 145.

δώδεκα (numeral) 820.

Translation - "And a great symbol was seen in heaven — a woman clothed with the sun and the moon (was) under her feet and a crown of twelve stars (was) upon her head."

Comment: John omitted the verb in the last two clauses. Chapter twelve is devoted to Israel and her age-long conflict with Satan. Enough of the details seem clear to allow us to deduce the significance of those less clear symbols from other correlative Scriptures.

We seem to have a historical *potpourri* — a picture of Satan's original fall from heaven and his opposition to Messiah as soon as the baby was born. Then we move to the middle of the tribulation week of Daniel's prophecy to see Satan again attempting to destroy the 144,000 Jews who have been sealed as God's property — the nucleus of the nation in the Kingdom age. Israel's flight for refuge is pictured. Satan's final fall from heaven and his wrath at having fallen is pictured.

These bits and pieces of information are helpful in portraying the moving scene of Israel's history as it relates to the divine plan of the ages. That the woman is Israel seems clear from verses 4,5 and 6. That she was clothed with the sun, with a cloud under her feet and a crown of twelve stars on her head are symbolic details that need not concern us. The twelve stars in her crown may indicate the twelve tribes of Israel, to be ruled by the twelve Apostles. (Mt.19:28; Lk.22:30).

Verse 2 - "And she being with child cried, travailing in birth, and pained to be delivered."

καὶ ἐν γαστρὶ ἔχουσα, καὶ κράζει ὠδίνουσα καὶ βασανιζομένη τεκεῖν.

"she was with child and she cried out in her pangs of birth, in anguish for deliverance." . . . RSV

καὶ (continuative conjunction) 14.

ἐν (preposition with the locative of place) 80.

γαστρὶ (loc.sing.fem.of γαστήρ, place) 81.

ἔχουσα (pres.act.part.nom.sing.fem.of ἔχω, adverbial, causal) 82.

καὶ (inferential conjunction) 14.

κράζει (3d.per.sing.pres.act.ind.of κράζω, aoristic) 765.

ὠδίνουσα (pres.act.part.nom.sing.fem.of ὠδίνω, adverbial, causal) 4444.

καὶ (adjunctive conjunction joining participles) 14.

βασανιζομένη (pres.pass.part.nom.sing.fem.of βασανίζω, adverbial, causal) 719.

τεκεῖν (2d.aor.act.inf.of τίκτω, purpose) 106.

Translation - "And because she was pregnant she cried out for she was in travail and in pain to be delivered."

Comment: *Cf.*Mt.1:18 for another use of this idiom. The participles are causal and the infinitive is purpose.

Israel was promised a King and a kingdom, under whose reign and in whose kingdom they would rule the world forever. That was God's pledge to Abraham, Isaac, Jacob, Judah and David. She has had only one legitimate king who ruled for a short time on a throne, temporary to him and the nation, but permanent, because of the promise of God to David in 2 Samuel 7:10-17. Jacob, on his deathbed in Egypt (Gen.49:10) properly vested the throne rights of Israel in his son Judah, who promptly forfeited them by his adultery with his daughter-in-law, Tamar (Gen.38; Deur.23:2). Thus he cast the curse of God upon his line for ten generations. David, the son of Jesse, and the first of Judah's line to be free from the curse of Deut.23:2 promptly forfeited his right to a permanent place on the throne, first by his marriage to Michael, Saul's daughter, who was a Benjamite (1 Sam.14:49; 18:20,27; 19:12; 25:44; 2 Sam. 3:13; 6:16,23; 21:8; 1 Chron.15:29) and later to miscellaneous other women (1 Samuel 25:3 *et al*), one of whom, though from his own tribe, Judah, was the wife of another man. Bathsheba's bastard, born of David, died in infancy, but she promptly bore him two more, Solomon and Nathan, both of whom were banned from the throne by the same law that banned Pharez, the bastard son of Judah (Deut.23:2).

In a political court intrigue, the queen mother of Solomon, succeeded in placing her bastard son on the throne, at a time when David, decrepit with senility was unaware of what was going on. Nathan, her other bastard never had a chance to rule Israel, and would not have been permitted to do so, even if given the chance because his line was also cursed for ten generations. God, in patient wisdom, allowed the Solomonic line to carry on its charade until the eve of the Babylonian captivity, when He ordered Jeremiah, the Prophet, to record in the register of the kings that Jeconiah, who in fact had six sons, died without issue (Jer.22:28-30). Thus the Solomonic line, with never a claim to the throne for the first ten generations was terminated. What happened to the Tudors when Elizabeth I died in 1603 without issue (at least none that were legitimate!) happened to the Solomonics. Meanwhile the Nathanic line was forgotten, buried in remote obscurity in the genealogy of Luke 3:23-38. The first man in the Nathanic line who could have ruled in Israel on the throne of Judah and David, was Jorim (Lk.3:29), but by the time he was born, Israel had passed under the hegemony of Gentile powers (Babylon, Media-Persia, Greece and Rome), and Jerusalem was destined to be overrun by the Gentiles until the times of the Gentiles be fulfilled (Lk.21:24).

We have pointed out (*The Renaissance New Testament*, 1, 4) that Mary, the virgin mother of Jesus, was of the Nathanic line, safely beyond the ten generation limit, and was therefore the only human being in Israel who had a right to the eternal throne of David, but she could not exercise that right because she was a woman. But she did retain the right to convey it to her first-born son, Jesus, with the provision only that she gave her hand in marriage to a man of her own tribe (Numbers 27,36). This she did, for Joseph, the carpenter, was not only from the tribe of Judah, but also from the Davidic family, being descended in the Solonomic line, while Mary was from the Nathanic line.

The result of all of this is that Jesus was the only man in Israel who had the legal right to take the throne of David, as Israel's Messiah, and rule His people and the rest of the world forever, as God had promised to the patriarchs and to David. Israel chose to murder Him. Had God not raised Him from the dead, the divine promise to Abraham and David would have failed and Israel today would have no hope for the future. Meanwhile, for four thousand years (since Abraham) Israel has wandered throughout the world, tortured by pogroms, discrimianted against by bigotry, incinerated by Hitler and his Nazis thugs and now, though with restored   nationalism in a small portion of the land which is rightfully hers under the Abrahamic covenant (Gen.15), beset by her Arab and Persian enemies.

Israel, clothed with the sun, with the moon under her feet and crowned with twelve stars, nevertheless has nothing in her eternal account, except her Messiah, Jesus Christ of Nazareth, whom she crucified and whom she now rejects. This is the story, sad from Israel's point of view, but gloriously revelatory of the manifest wisdom of the sovereign God who does everything after the counsel of His own will (Eph.1:11). Israel's "partial blindess' (Rom.11:25) is destined to be healed, when 144,000 of her sons and daughters, pursued by Satan and the Antichrist for 1260 days will look upon Him whom their fathers pierced, as He descends from the clouds to rescue them at Armageddon, and a nation will be born in a day. Then the nucleus of the nation, ruled by the King of Kings, will become the great nation which God promised to Abraham, Isaac, Jacob and David.

Israel has agonized for 4000 years. She had a brief period of glory in the sun under David and Solomon, but, because God had a redemptive plan to atone for the sins of the elect and include in the number a people for His name from among the Gentiles, her national hopes have not yet been realized. But they will be, in God's own good time.

Before John goes on with the account of the birth to Israel, the agonizing woman, he must introduce her ancient enemy, Satan. This he does in verses 3 and 4.

Verse 3- "And there appeared another wonder in heaven; and behold a great red dragon, having seven heads and ten horns, and seven crowns upon his head."

καὶ ὤφθη ἄλλο σημεῖον ἐν τῷ οὐρανῷ, καὶ ἰδοὺ δράκων πυρρὸς μέγας, ἔχων κεφαλὰς ἑπτὰ καὶ κέρατα δέκα καὶ ἐπὶ τὰς κεφαλὰς αὐτοῦ ἑπτὰ διαδήματα,

"And another portent appeared in heaven; behold, a great red dragon, with seven heads and ten horns, and seven diadems upon his heads." . . . RSV

καὶ (continuative conjunction) 14.
ὤφθη (3d.per.sing.aor.pass.ind.of ὁράω, constative) 144.
ἄλλο (nom.sing.neut.of ἄλλος, in agreement with σημεῖον) 198.
σημεῖον (nom.sing.neut.of σημεῖον, subject of ὤφθη) 1005.
ἐν (preposition with the locative of place) 80.
τῷ (loc.sing.masc.of the article in agreement with οὐρανῷ) 9.
οὐρανῷ (loc.sing.masc.of οὐρανός, place) 254.
καὶ (consecutive conjunction) 14.
ἰδοὺ (exclamation) 95.

#5382 δράκων (nom.sing.masc.of δράκων, nominative absolute).

King James Version

dragon - Rev.12:3,4,7,7,9,13,16,17; 13:2,4,11; 16:13; 20:2.

Revised Standard Version

dragon - Rev.12:3,4,7,7,9,13,16,17; 13:2,4,11; 16:13; 20:2.

Meaning: Cf. δέρκομαι, of which ἔδρακον is the 2d.aorist. Equivalent to ὀξὺ βλέπων - "one looking sharp" or "of terrible aspect." Hence, since Homer, a dragon; a fabulous animal; a hideous beast. Since in Gen.3:1, Satan is described as a beast, the word came to mean Satan. So used in all passages in Revelation. The enemy of Israel and Messiah (Rev.12:3,4,7,7,9,13,16,17). Motivation of Antichrist (Rev.13:2,4,11). He incites to war (Rev.16:3); he is to be bound in the abyss - Rev.20:2.

πυρρὸς (gen.sing.masc.of πυρρός, description) 5350.
μέγας (nom.sing.masc.of μέγας, in agreement with δράχων) 184.
ἔχων (pres.act.part.nom.sing.masc.of ἔχω, adverbial, circumstantial) 82.
κεφαλὰς (acc.pl.fem.of κεφαλή, direct object of ἔχων) 521.
ἑπτὰ (numeral) 1024.
καὶ (adjunctive conjunction joining nouns) 14.
κέρατα (acc.pl.neut.of κέρας, direct object of ἔχων) 1851.
δέκα (numeral) 1330.
καὶ (adjunctive conjunction joining nouns) 14.
ἐπὶ (preposition with the accusative, place, rest) 47.
τὰς (acc.pl.fem.of the article in agreement with κεφαλὰς) 9.
κεφαλὰς (acc.pl.fem.of κεφαλή, place) 521.
αὐτοῦ (gen.sing.masc.of αὐτός, possession) 16.

ἑπτὰ (numeral) 1024.

#5383 διαδήματα (acc.pl.neut.of διάδημα, direct object of εχων).

King James Version

crown - Rev.12:3; 13:1; 19:12.

Revised Standard Version

diadems - Rev.12:3; 13:1; 19:12.

Meaning: Cf. διαδέω - "to bind around." Hence, the blue band, marked with white with which Persians kings used to bind on the turban or tiara. The kingly ornament for the head. στέφανος (#1640), like the Latin *corona* is a crown in the sense of a chaplet, wreath or garland - the badge of "victory in the games, of civic worth, of military valor, of festal gladness." διάδημα is a crown as a badge of royalty. Satan assumes these - Rev.12:3; Antichrist wears them - Rev.13;1. Only Messiah merits them - Rev.19:12.

Translation - "And another symbol was seen in heaven; and Look! A great fiery dragon with seven heads and ten horns and upon his heads seven diadems."

Comment: The second portent in heaven is presented for John's consideration and for ours. Satan is introduced (Rev.20:2). The seven heads and ten horns are symbolic, and, following the rule of hermeneutics for symbols, we must wait for the text to identify them or remain silent as to their meaning. Rev.17:9 identifies the heads as seven mountains where the whore of Rev.17 sits. This may or may not refer to Rome which is known in history as the "city of the seven hills." The horns seem to be symbols of political and military power (*cf.*#1851). For the fact that there are ten, *cf.* Dan.7:7. Personally I see great danger in the attempt to be too certain about the specific interpretations of these details before the fact. That they have something to do with the political, police and economic power of the Beast in the last half of the tribulation week, empowered as he will be by Satan, and working in cooperation with the Harlot of Revelation 17:18, is obvious. This is enough for us to know in order to get the general outline of the Revelation. An attempt to identify these "horns" as the European Common Market, or any other diplomatic regional arrangement is premature and almost certain to end in embarrassment for the commentator.

Verse 4 - "And his tail drew the third part of the stars of heaven, and did cast them to the earth; and the dragon stood before the woman which was ready to be delivered, for to devour her child as soon as it was born."

καὶ ἡ οὐρὰ αὐτοῦ σύρει τὸ τρίτον τῶν ἀστέρων τοῦ οὐρανοῦ καὶ ἔβαλεν αὐτοὺς εἰς τὴν γῆν. καὶ ὁ δράκων ἔστηκεν ἐνώπιον τῆς γυναικὸς τῆς μελλούσης τεκεῖν, ἵνα ὅταν τέκῃ τὸ τέκνον αὐτῆς καταφάγῃ.

"His tail swept down a third of the stars of heaven, and cast them to the earth.

And the dragon stood before the woman who was about to bear a child, that he might devour her child when she brought it forth." . . . RSV

καὶ (continuative conjunction) 14.
ἥ (nom.sing.fem.of the article in agreement with οὐρά) 9.
οὐρά (nom.sing.fem.of οὐρά, subject of σύρει) 5369.
αὐτοῦ (gen.sing.masc.of αὐτός, possession) 16.
σύρει (3d.per.sing.pres.act.ind.of σύρω, historical) 2911.
τὸ (acc.sing.neut.of the article in agreement with τρίτον) 9.
τρίτον (acc.sing.neut.of τρίτος, direct object of σύρει) 1209.
τῶν (gen.pl.masc.of the article in agreement with ἀστέρων) 9.
ἀστέρων (gen.pl.masc.of ἀστήρ, partitive) 145.
τοῦ (gen.sing.masc.of the article in agreement with οὐρανοῦ) 9.
οὐρανοῦ (gen.sing.masc.of οὐρανός, description) 254.
καὶ (continuative conjunction) 14.
ἔβαλεν (3d.per.sing.aor.act.ind.of βάλλω, constative) 299.
αὐτὸν (acc.pl.masc.of αὐτός, direct object of ἔβαλεν) 16.
εἰς (preposition with the accusative of extent) 140.
τὴν (acc.sing.fem.of the article in agreement with γῆν) 9.
γῆν (acc.sing.fem.of γῆ, extent) 157.
καὶ (continuative conjunction) 14.
ὁ (nom.sing.masc.of the article in agreement with δράκων) 9.
δράκων (nom.sing.masc.of δράκων, subject of ἔστηκεν) 5382.
ἔστηκεν (3d.per.sing.perf.act.ind.of ἵστημι, intensive) 180.
ἐνώπιον (preposition with the genitive of place description) 1798.
τῆς (gen.sing.fem.of the article in agreement with γυναικὸς) 9.
γυναικὸς (gen.sing.fem.of γυνή, place description) 103.
τῆς (gen.sing.fem.of the article in agreement with μελλούσης) 9.
μελλούσης (pres.act.part.gen.sing.fem.of μέλλω, adjectival, emphatic attributive position, ascriptive, in agreement with γυναικὸς) 206.
τεκεῖν (2d.aor.inf.of τίκτω, complementary) 106.
ἵνα (conjunction with the subjunctive, purpose) 114.
ὅταν (temporal conjunction with the subjunctive in an indefinite temporal clause) 436.
τέκῃ (3d.per.sing.2d.aor.subj.of τίκτω, indefinite temporal clause) 106.
τὸ (nom.sing.neut.of the article in agreement with τέκνον) 9.
τέκνον (nom.sing.neut.of τέκνον, subject of τέκῃ) 229.
αὐτῆς (gen.sing.fem.of αὐτός, relationship) 16.
καταφάγῃ (3d.per.sing.aor.act.subj.of κατεσθίω, purpose) 1028.

Translation - "And his tail drew the third of the stars of heaven and threw them into the earth; and the dragon stood before the woman who was about to give birth, in order that when her child was born, he might devour it."

Comment: The action of Satan in drawing the third of the stars and casting them down is difficult and calls for caution in comment. *Cf.* Dan.8:10.
The usual interpretation is that Lucifer, one of the three archangels (Gabriel

and Michael being the others) had one third of the angels under his control, and that, following his unsuccessful *coup d' etat* (Ezek.28:11-19; Isa.14:12-17), when he was cast out of heaven to the earth (Lk.10:18) he dragged down one third of the angels, who, as fallen angels, became demons. We offer this with caution, since we have no better explanation. Satan did indeed oppose all of God's redemptive program, having understood from the beginning, after Adam's fall (Gen.3:15) that God's redemptive program and his own downfall (Heb.2:14) depended upon the birth of Messiah, the Seed of the Woman. Thus Satan had been long standing before the woman, Israel, throughout her long history from Abraham to the Virgin Mary, seeking to prevent the fulfillment of God's promises to Adam, Abraham, David and to Mary.

Pharaoh's order that all of the infant males should be thrown into the Nile River was only one of Satan's attempt to eliminate Israel as God's chosen nation. The Red Sea deliverance, the miraculous support for Israel in the wilderness wanderings and God's support for Jews, scattered throughout the world in the diaspora for centuries are indications of God's determination to fulfill His promise to Abraham.

Satan's program to prevent the incarnation may be termed anti-Messianity, and involves a long list of incidents, any one of which, had it been successful, would have prevented Jesus from having been born. That Israel did in fact finally produce the incarnate Messiah- Redeemer (Gal.4:4), despite Satan's opposition only proves God's sovereign control of history (1 John 4:4). Herod's effort to kill Jesus as soon as He was born (Mt.2:1-23) is the event referred to here in Rev.12:4.

Note the two subjunctives. καταφάγῃ belongs in the ἵνα clause of purpose and τέκῃ is joined with ὅταν, the temporal relative in an indefinite temporal clause. - "In order that, when she had the baby, he might devour it."

Verse 5 brings the story forward in time to the birth of Christ.

Verse 5 - "And she brought forth a manchild, who was to rule all nations with a rod of iron: and her child was caught up unto God, and to his throne."

καὶ ἔτεκεν υἱόν, ἄρσεν, ὅς μέλλει ποιμαίνειν πάντα τὰ ἔθνη ἐν ῥάβδῳ σιδηρᾷ. καὶ ἡρπάσθη τὸ τέκνον αὐτῆς πρὸς τὸν θεὸν καὶ πρὸς τὸν θρόνον αὐτοῦ.

"she brought forth a male child, one who is to rule all the nations with a rod of iron, but her child was caught up to God and to his throne." . . . RSV

καὶ (continuative conjunction) 14.

ἔτεκεν (3d.per.sing.aor.act.ind.of τίκτω, constative) 106.

υἱὸν (acc.sing.masc.of υἱός, direct object of ἔτεκεν) 5.

ἄρσεν (acc.sing.masc.of ἄρσην, in apposition with υἱὸν) 1286.

ὅς (nom.sing.masc.of ὅς, relative pronoun, subject of μέλλει) 65.

μέλλει (3d.per.sing.pres.act.ind.of μέλλω, aoristic) 206.

ποιμαίνειν (pres.act.inf.of ποιμαίνω, complementary) 164.

πάντα (acc.pl.neut.of πᾶς, in agreement with ἔθνη) 67.

τὰ (acc.pl.neut.of the article in agreement with ἔθνη) 9.

ἔθνη (acc.pl.neut.of ἔθνος, direct object of ποιμαίνειν) 376.

ἐν (preposition with the instrumental, means) 80.

ῥάβδῳ (instru.sing.masc.of ῥάβδος, means) 863.

σιδηρᾷ (instru.sing.masc.of σίδηρος, in agreement with ῥάβδῳ) 3248.

καὶ (continuative conjunction) 14.

ἡρπάσθη (3d.per.sing.(Attic) aor.pass.ind.of ἁρπάζω, constative) 920.

τὸ (nom.sing.neut.of the article in agreement with τέκνον) 9.

τέκνον (nom.sing.neut.of τέκνον, subject of ἡρπάσθη) 229.

αὐτῆς (gen.sing.fem.of αὐτός, relationship) 16.

πρὸς (preposition with the accusative of extent) 197.

τὸν (acc.sing.masc.of the article in agreement with θεὸν) 9.

θεὸν (acc.sing.masc.of θεός, extent) 124.

καὶ (adjunctive conjunction joining prepositional phrases) 14.

πρὸς (preposition with the accusative of extent) 197.

τὸν (acc.sing.masc.of the article in agreement with θρόνον) 9.

θρόνον (acc.sing.masc.of θρόνος, extent) 519.

αὐτοῦ (gen.sing.masc.of αὐτός, possession) 16.

Translation - "And she bore a male heir who is destined to shepherd the nations with an iron rod, and her child was taken up to God and to His throne."

Comment: *Cf.* Gal.4:4. The Christ child is destined to rule the world. It is no wonder that Satan wanted to prevent His birth, or, failing that, to kill Him as soon as He was born (Mt.2). But again he failed, and we add to the long list of evidences of anti-Messianity before Messiah was born, the long list of attempts by Satan, after He was born, to disqualify Him for redemption purposes (Mt.4) or to prevent Him from going to the cross. (*Cf.* Mt.16:22,23; 17:4; Lk.9:33; 22:49,50 *et al*). He went to the cross to destroy Satan's power forever (Heb.2:14) and from the grave He arose to ratify what He did at Calvary, after which He was taken up to God and to His throne (Acts 1:9-11; Psalm 110:1; Heb.12:2, *et al.*). When He comes again it will be to take all of the kingdoms of the present world, now ruled by Satan (2 Cor.4:4) and blend them into one great spiritual kingdom (Rev.11:15,16) over which He will rule with a rod of iron (Rev.2:27; Mt.2:6; Rev.19:15).

Thus in verses 1-5 we have two antagonists introduced — Israel and Satan. She will produce the Saviour-King and Satan will do all possible to prevent His birth, kill Him when He is born, or cause Him to sin after He is born, or kill Him in some manner that does not involve His heel-bruising death of Gen.3:15.

The history of Israel can be told in terms of the time periods when she has had hegemony over the land which God promised to Abraham (Gen.15) and when she has been in bondage to Gentile powers. Israel, out of the land, or in the land but under the jurisdiction of a Gentile power is known as "the times of the Gentiles" (Lk.21:24). God called Abraham, the progenitor of Israel out of a pagan land into Canaan, which he defined geographically (Gen.15) in far more extensive terms (Gen.15) than those which have defined it since, and promised him that though he would not control the Promised Land personally, his children would and that one of them, the Lord Jesus Christ, would redeem and rule, not only the genetic children of Abraham, but also the spiritual children who would be called out from among the Gentiles (Gal.3:7; Eph.3:1-8; Acts 15:14) and known as the Body of Christ. Abraham lived in the land of promise (Heb.1 I·:13) as a guest of the natives, never owning a square foot of it except for a burial place for his wife, for which he paid a full market price. Nor did Isaac, his son control Canaan. Nor did Jacob, although he became wealthy. He and his family went to Egypt, became slaves to a Gentile power, were delivered from bondage, wandered in the wilderness forty years and finally entered Canaan, the Promised Land, which they conquered only partially and in which, thanks to their social contacts with the pagan natives, they backslid, forsook their monotheism, with its social, economic and political ethics system, and bowed before the local gods.

They had throne rights vested in one of their number - Judah (Gen.49:10), but his family was cursed for ten generations by his adultery (Gen.38; Deut.23:2) and could not assume the kingly role. In a mistaken zeal for nationalism, they demanded a king, at a time when Samuel could not place Jesse on the throne, because he was still under the curse of Deut.23:2 and God, in weary disgust for their ignorance and intransigence, gave them a Benjamite, until such time as a little shepherd boy, named David, the son of Jesse and the first of Judah's line who was not under the curse, could serve. David married Saul's daughter and thus corrupted his family, insofar as throne rights were concerned, and later he married many others, including Bathsheba in an adulterous union, after which he arranged for the death of her husband. She was from the proper tribe, but none of her sons by David, (the first of whom died in infancy and Solomon and Nathan) could sit upon the throne. The law of Deut.23:2 applied to David as well as to Judah.

We have already told the story of the charade that placed Solomon on the throne, despite the fact that he had no right to sit there, and the added story of the continued corruption of Israel's morals, as she sacrificed her monotheism, and the ethics of the Mosaic code, to the idol worship of her pagan neighbours, while maintaining an empty form of Levitical worship, in keeping with the Aaronic priesthood - a bit of hypocrisy which God hated (Hosea 4; Malachi 1). Among their many transgressions was their failure to keep the Mosaic law of the Sabbath. Every seventh day, every seventh year and the forty-ninth, fiftieth, ninety-ninth and one hundreth years of every century were to have been periods of rest. During these sabbath periods the land would be permitted to lie fallow and recover its fertility. In the jubilee years, which were scheduled twice each century, land titles were to be restored to their original owners, the law thus providing a remedy for monopoly of the nation's assets in a few hands. All of this Israel ignored until she was in debt to the Lord for seventy years of sabbatical disobedience, which He collected during the seventy years of captivity to Babylon and the Medes and Persians. With the Babylonian invasion of Nebuchadnezzar "the times of the Gentiles" began, and have not run their course until this day, for even though Israel regained her national sovereignty in 1948 she controls only a small part of the original grant under the Abrahamic covenant and yields jurisdiction for the greater part of the territory to her Arab and Persian neighbours who hate her and are destined eventually to seek to push her into the Mediterranean Sea.

Seventy years of bondage in Babylon, under the reign of the Babylonians, Medes and Persians (Nebuchadnezzar, Belshazzar, Cyrus and Xerxes), they later returned to Jerusalem, as political slaves of the Greeks (Alexander the Great and others) and continued in the land as slaves of the Romans (Pompeys, Caesars) until Vespasian and Titus in A.D.70, sacked the city of Jerusalem, took the temple of Herod apart piece by piece, crucified the Jews on the tottering walls that surrounded the city and drove the survivors to the ends of the earth. The diaspora has continued since, as the children of Abraham have yielded obedience to the Gentiles in every nation of earth.

This will continue under the Antichrist and the False Prophet (Rev.13) until the second coming of Messiah. Then the "times of the Gentiles" will be fulfilled and the holy city will cease to be overrun by Gentile powers, as Messiah, the Lord Jesus, the only Son of Abraham, Isaac, Jacob, Judah and David who has a legal right to sit upon David's throne will take His place. For a thousand years and then, after the final unsuccessful attempt at *coup d'etat* of Satan and his deluded hordes, forever and ever in keeping with the promise of God to David (2 Sam.7) and of the angel Gabriel to Mary (Luke 1:30-33).

Meanwhile, with Israel out of the land or, as now, since 1948, only partially in control of it, the Holy Spirit has been busy through His Body, the Church in pursuing the missionary enterprise which Jesus commanded (Mt.28:18-20) and, as He effectually calls those for whom Christ died, "calling out from the Gentiles a people for His name" (Acts 15:14). The Body of Christ, complete at the rapture at the end of the tribulation (Rev.10:7) will be the spiritual "tabernacle of David" in which our Lord, Melchizedek, the High Priest, will offer, not the blood of bulls and of goats, nor the ashes of a heifer, but His own precious blood in eternal expiation for the sins of those whom He has chosen.

But the temple is only a part of the eternal kingdom government. There is also a throne. James did not say that the Body of Christ is the fulfillment of God's promise to restore the throne, but that she is the symbolic restoration of the temple (Acts 15:16), as the Epistle to the Hebrews abundantly attests. This is in keeping with the prophecy of Amos (Amos 9:11-12).

With this sketch of Jewish history, we return to the Revelation which now leaps across time from the end of Daniel's 69th week, when Israel's male child was caught up to the throne of God (Psalm 110:1) there to sit until His enemies are made His footstool, to the middle of Daniel's 70th week. Israel's son, the Messiah sits triumphantly at the right hand of the throne of God, awaiting the moment when the last elect soul for whom He died on the cross is called by the Holy Spirit into His Body. Then He will return. But His mother is still being pursued by the Gentiles.

Verse 6 - "And the woman fled into the wilderness, where she hath a place prepared of God, that they should feed her there a thousand and two hundred and three-score days."

καὶ ἡ γυνὴ ἔφυγεν εἰς τὴν ἔρημον, ὅπου ἔχει ἐκεῖ τόπον ἡτοιμασμένον ἀπὸ τοῦ θεοῦ, ἵνα ἐκεῖ τρέφωσιν αὐτὴν ἡμέρας χιλίας διακοσίας ἑξήκοντα.

"and the woman fled into the wilderness, where she has a place prepared by God, in which to be nourished for one thousand two hundred and sixty days." . . . RSV

καὶ (continuative conjunction) 14.

ἡ (nom.sing.fem.of the article in agreement with γυνὴ) 9.

γυνὴ (nom.sing.fem.of γυνή, subject of ἔφυγεν and ἔχει) 103.

ἔφυγεν (3d.per.sing.aor.act.ind.of φεύγω, constative) 202.

εἰς (preposition with the accusative of extent) 140.

τὴν (acc.sing.fem.of the article in agreement with ἔρημον) 9.

ἔρημον (acc.sing.fem.of ἔρημος, extent) 250.

ὅπου (local adverb with the indicative in a definite local clause) 592.

ἔχει (3d.per.sing.pres.act.ind.of ἔχω, futuristic) 82.

ἐκεῖ (local adverb) 204.

τόπον (acc.sing.masc.of τόπος, direct object of ἔχει) 1019.

ἡτοιμασμένον (perf.pass.part.acc.sing.masc.of ἐτοιμάζω, adjectival, predicate position, restrictive, in agreement with τόπον) 257.

ἀπὸ (preposition with the ablative of agent) 70.

τοῦ (abl.sing.masc.of the article in agreement with θεοῦ) 9.

θεοῦ (abl.sing.masc.of θεός, agent) 124.

ἵνα (conjunction with the subjunctive, purpose) 114.

ἐκεῖ (local adverb) 204.

τρέφωσιν (3d.per.pl.pres.act.subj.of τρέφω, purpose) 618.

αὐτὴν (acc.sing.fem.of αὐτός, direct object of τρέφωσιν) 16.

ἡμέρας (acc.pl.fem.of ἡμέρα, time extent) 135.

χιλίας (acc.pl.fem.of χιλίοι, in agreement with ἡμέρας) 5278.

διακοσίας (acc.pl.fem.of διακόσιοι, in agreement with ἡμέρας) 2265.

ἑξήκοντα (numeral) 1036.

Translation - "*And the woman fled into the wilderness where she has there a place prepared by God, so that they will feed her there one thousand, two hundred and sixty days.*"

Comment: The time clue definitely fixes the woman's flight into the desert to escape the attack of Antichrist at the middle of the week. This is what Jesus referred to in Mt.24:15-22. The time point is the middle of Dan.9:27. Other passages referring to events at the same time are Revelation 13; 2 Thess.2:4; Rev.9:1-11 *et al.*

The 144,000 Jews who were chosen of God (Rev.7:1-8) will flee. Where the prepared place is the text does not say. It is widely speculated that it is Petra. The text does not tell us who will feed this nucleus of Messiah's kingdom during this period. The 1260 days brings us to the second coming when the 144,000 will fulfill Zech.13:6 and Isa.66:8. Another phase of the story is unfolded beginning in

Verse 7 - "And there was war in heaven: Michael and his angels fought against the dragon; and the dragon fought and his angels."

Καὶ ἐγένετο πόλεμος ἐν τῷ οὐρανῷ, ὁ Μιχαὴλ καὶ οἱ ἄγγελοι αὐτοῦ τοῦ πολεμῆσαι μετὰ τοῦ δράκοντος, καὶ ὁ δράκων ἐπολέμησεν καὶ οἱ ἄγγελοι αὐτοῦ.

"Now war arose in heaven, Michael and his angels fighting against the dragon; and the dragon and his angels fought, . . . " . . . RSV

Καὶ (explanatory conjunction) 14.
ἐγένετο (3d.per.sing.aor.ind.of γίνομαι, ingressive) 113.
πόλεμος (nom.sing.masc.of πόλεμος, subject of ἐγένετο) 1483.
ἐν (preposition with the locative of place) 80.
τῷ (loc.sing.masc.of the article in agreement with οὐρανῷ) 9.
οὐρανῷ (loc.sing.masc.of οὐρανός, place) 254.
ὁ (nom.sing.masc.of the article in agreement with Μιχαὴλ) 9.
Μιχαὴλ (nom.sing.masc.of Μιχαήλ, nominative absolute) 5306.
καὶ (adjunctive conjunction joining nouns) 14.
οἱ (nom.pl.masc.of the article in agreement with ἄγγελοι) 9.
ἄγγελοι (nom.pl.masc.of ἄγγελος, nominative absolute) 96.
αὐτοῦ (gen.sing.masc.of ἄγγελος, relationship) 16.
τοῦ (gen.sing.masc.of the article in agreement with πολεμῆσαι) 9.
πολεμῆσαι (1st.aor.act.inf.of πολεμέω, in apposition with πόλεμος) 5140.
μετὰ (preposition with the genitive, accompaniment) 50.
τοῦ (gen.sing.masc.of the article in agreement with δράκοντος) 9.
δράκοντος (gen.sing.masc.of δράκων, accompaniment) 5382.
καὶ (continuative conjunction) 14.
ὁ (nom.sing.masc.of the article in agreement with δράκων) 9.
δράκων (nom.sing.masc.of δράκων, subject of ἐπολέμησεν) 5382.
ἐπολέμησεν (3d.per.sing.aor.act.ind.of πολεμέω, ingressive) 5140.
καὶ (adjunctive conjunction joining nouns) 14.
οἱ (nom.pl.masc.of the article in agreement with ἄγγελοι) 9.
ἄγγελοι (nom.pl.masc.of ἄγγελος, subject of ἐπολέμησεν) 96.
αὐτοῦ (gen.sing.masc.of αὐτός, relationship) 16.

Translation - "Now a war began in heaven — Michael and his angels in a fight with the dragon; and the dragon and his angels fought."

Comment: τοῦ πολεμῆσαι is "an independent parenthesis" (Robertson, *Grammar*, 1093). The articular infinitive in the genitive, τοῦ πολεμῆσαι "is a loose construction of which the most extreme instance is seen in Rev.12:7. . . . This inf. (note the nom.with it) is in explanatory apposition with πόλεμος" (*Ibid.*, 1066). Moulton illustrates it with, "There will be a cricket match — the champions to play the rest." (J.H. Moulton, *A Grammar of New Testament Greek*, Vol.I, *Prolegomena*, 218) as cited in *Ibid*).

It is most unusual to find a genitive infinitive in apposition with a noun in the nominative. It serves to describe the war of the first clause. It is a conflict between Michael and Satan, each angel supported by his subordinate angels, a view which sheds light on the "stars" of the dragon in verse 4.

The time point is mid-week. *Cf.* Rev.9:1, where the star falling from heaven is Satan of Rev.12:9. Satan's original fall from heaven (Luke 10:18; Ezek.28; Isa.14) was not a permanent banishment. Though his *coup d' etat* failed he has had access to heaven since. *Cf.* Job 1:6; 2:1 and Rev.12:10. Now at mid-week his final fight with Michael and the holy host of warriors occurs, as a result of which he is forever banished.

Verse 8 - "And prevailed not: neither was their place found any more in heaven."

καὶ οὐκ ἴσχυσεν, οὐδὲ τόπος εὑρέθη αὐτῶν ἔτι ἐν τῷ οὐρανῷ.

"but they were defeated and there was no longer any place for them in heaven." . . . RSV

καὶ (adversative conjunction) 14.

οὐκ (negative conjunction with the indicative) 130.

ἴσχυσεν (3d.per.sing.aor.act.ind.of ἰσχύω, constative) 447.

οὐδὲ (disjunctive particle) 452.

τόπος (nom.sing.masc.of τόπος, subject of εὑρέθη) 1019.

εὑρέθη (3d.per.sing.aor.pass.ind.of εὑρίσκω, constative) 79.

αὐτῶν (gen.pl.masc.of αὐτός, possession) 16.

ἔτι (temporal adverb) 448.

ἐν (preposition with the locative of place) 80.

τῷ (loc.sing.masc.of the article in agreement with οὐρανῷ) 9.

οὐρανῷ (loc.sing.masc.of οὐρανός, place) 254.

Translation - "... but he did not win, nor was there found for them a place in heaven from that time on."

Comment: The fight is finished. Michael and his heavenly hosts are victorious. Satan and his demons are defeated and, as a result, he and his demons must leave heaven permanently.

This mid-week fight in heaven rids the courts of glory of the pest, but unloads him upon the earth, from which he goes immediately to the abyss to release the Beast (Rev.9:1-11) and his locusts. *Cf.* comment on Rev.9:1-11. The Beast, now resurrected, breaks the covenant relationship which he had made with Israel three and one half years before (Daniel 9:27a,b), blasphemes God (2 Thess.2:4; Mt.24:15) and prepares to attack the 144,000 (Rev.12;13) who flee into the desert for 1260 days (Rev.12:6). Satan will know at this time that his days are numbered and will visit his hellish vengeance upon the saints (Rev.12:12; 13:7).

Verse 9 - "And the great dragon was cast out, that old serpent, called the Devil and Satan, which deceiveth the whole world: he was cast out into the earth, and his angels were cast out with him."

καὶ ἐβλήθη ὁ δράκων ὁ μέγας, ὁ ὄφις ὁ ἀρχαῖος, ὁ καλούμενος Διάβολος καὶ ὁ Σατανᾶς, ὁ πλανῶν τὴν οἰκουμένην ὅλην — ἐβλήθη εἰς τὴν γῆν, καὶ οἱ ἄγγελοι αὐτοῦ μετ' αὐτοῦ ἐβλήθησαν.

"And the great dragon was thrown down, that ancient serpent, who is called the Devil and Satan, the deceiver of the whole world — he was thrown down to the earth, and his angels were thrown down with him." . . . RSV

καὶ (continuative conjunction) 14.

ἐβλήθη (3d.per.sing.aor.pass.ind.of βάλλω, constative) 299.

ὁ (nom.sing.masc.of the article in agreement with δράκων) 9.

δράκων (nom.sing.masc.of δράκων, subject of ἐβλήθη) 5382.

ὁ (nom.sing.masc.of the article in agreement with δράκων) 9.

μέγας (nom.sing.masc.of μέγας, in agreement with δράκων) 184.

ὁ (nom.sing.masc.of the article in agreement with ὄφις) 9.

ὄφις (nom.sing.masc.of ὄφις, in apposition with δράκων) 658.

ὁ (nom.sing.masc.of the article in agreement with ὄφις) 9.

ἀρχαῖος (nom.sing.masc.of ἀρχαῖος, in agreement with ὄφις) 475.

ὁ (nom.sing.masc.of the article in agreement with καλούμενος) 9.

καλούμενος (pres.pass.part.nom.sing.masc.of καλέω, substantival, in apposition with δράκων) 107.

Διάβολος (nom.sing.masc.of διάβολος, appelation) 331.

καὶ (adjunctive conjunction joining nouns) 14.

ὁ (nom.sing.masc.of the article in agreement with Σατανᾶς) 9.

Σατανᾶς (nom.sing.masc.of Σατανᾶς, appelation) 365.

ὁ (nom.sing.masc.of the article in agreement with πλανῶν) 9.

πλανῶν (pres.act.part.nom.sing.masc.of πλανάω, substantival, in apposition with Σατανᾶς) 1257.

τὴν (acc.sing.fem.of the article in agreement with οἰκουμένην) 9.

οἰκουμένην (acc.sing.fem.of οἰκουμένη, direct object of πλανῶν) 1491.

ὅλην (acc.sing.fem.of ὅλος, in agreement with οἰκουμένην) 112.

ἐβλήθη (3d.per.sing.aor.pass.ind.of βάλλω, constative) 299.

εἰς (preposition with the accusative of extent) 140.

τὴν (acc.sing.fem.of the article in agreement with γῆν) 9.

γῆν (acc.sing.fem.of γῆ, extent) 157.

καὶ (continuative conjunction) 14.

οἱ (nom.pl.masc.of the article in agreement with ἄγγελοι) 9.

ἄγγελοι (nom.pl.masc.of ἄγγελος, subject of ἐβλήθησαν) 96.

αὐτοῦ (gen.sing.masc.of αὐτός, relationship) 16.

μετ' (preposition with the genitive of accompaniment) 50.

αὐτοῦ (gen.sing.masc.of αὐτός, accompaniment) 16.

ἐβλήθησαν (3d.per.pl.aor.pass.ind.of βάλλω, constative) 299.

Translation - "And the great dragon was thrown out — the old serpent, the one called Devil and Satan, the one who deceives the entire inhabited earth — he was hurled down unto the earth, and his angels were thrown out with him."

Comment: As a result of the fight in heaven, Satan and his demons, who previously had been permitted there in the role of "accuser of the brethren" (verse 10), but only up to the precise moment that our sovereign Lord has decreed, will be cast down to the earth. The time point, in relation to the countdown of the prophetic clock is precise. Satan will have only 1260 days to deceive the world and visit his wrath upon the saints before he is judged at the second coming of Messiah and consigned to the abyss for one thousand years. Thus hell's forces, both Satan and all of the demons will be concentrated on this planet. They will persecute the saints, but at the same time God's plagues will be falling upon Satan's unregenerates. *Cf.*the fifth, sixth and seven trumpets and all of the seven vials (Rev.16).

The judgments of God upon the unsaved will not touch those Christians who are still upon the earth. This is clear from Psalm 91 and 1 Thess.5:9. Pretribulation rapture teachers assume that God cannot protect His saints amid His judgments upon sinners on earth, and thus that He must rapture them from the earth before His judgments fall. God has already abundantly demonstrated His ability to distinguish between saints and sinners by His policy during the contest between Moses and Pharaoh in Egypt. He did not remove Israel from Egypt until after the ten plagues had fallen upon the Egyptians. Yet His plagues did not fall upon His chosen people.

It is proper to ask when, since Psalm 91 was written has it seen a literal fulfillment? Is this language figurative? Or was David mistaken?

Verse 10 - "And I heard a loud voice saying in heaven, Now is come salvation, and strength and the kingdom of our God, and the power of his Christ: for the accuser of our brethren is cast down, which accused them before our God day and night."

καὶ ἤκουσα φωνὴν μεγάλην ἐν τῷ οὐρανῷ λέγουσαν, Ἄρτι ἐγένετο ἡ σωτηρία καὶ ἡ δύναμις καὶ ἡ βασιλεία τοῦ θεοῦ ἡμῶν καὶ ἡ ἐξουσία τοῦ Χριστοῦ αὐτοῦ, ὅτι ἐβλήθη ὁ κατήγωρ τῶν ἀδελφῶν ἡμῶν, ὁ καρηγορῶν αὐτοὺς ἐνώπιον τοῦ θεοῦ ἡμῶν ἡμέρας καὶ νυκτός.

"And I heard a loud voice in heaven, saying, 'Now the salvation and the power and the kingdom of our God and the authority of his Christ have come, for the accuser of our brethren has been thrown down, who accuses them day and night before our God.' " . . . RSV

καὶ (continuative conjunction) 14.

ἤκουσα (1st.per.sing.aor.act.ind.of ἀκούω, constative) 148.

φωνὴν (acc.sing.fem.of φωνή, direct object of ἤκουσα) 222.

μεγάλην (acc.sing.fem.of μέγας, in agreement with φωνὴν) 184.

ἐν (preposition with the locative of place) 80.

τῷ (loc.sing.masc.of the article in agreement with οὐρανῷ) 9.

οὐρανῷ (loc.sing.masc.of οὐρανός, place) 254.

λέγουσαν (pres.act.part.acc.sing.fem.of λέγω, recitative) 66.

Ἄρτι (temporal adverb) 320.

ἐγένετο (3d.per.sing.aor.ind.of γίνομαι, ingressive) 113.

ἡ (nom.sing.fem.of the article in agreement with σωτηρία) 9.

σωτηρία (nom.sing.fem.of σωτηρία, subject of ἐγένετο) 1852.

καὶ (adjunctive conjunction joining nouns) 14.

ἡ (nom.sing.fem.of the article in agreement with δύναμις) 9.

δύναμις (nom.sing.fem.of δύναμις, subject of ἐγένετο) 687.

καὶ (adjunctive conjunction joining nouns) 14.

ἡ (nom.sing.fem.of the article in agreement with βασιλεία) 9.

βασιλεία (nom.sing.fem.of βασιλεία, subject of ἐγένετο) 253.

τοῦ (gen.sing.masc.of the article in agreement with θεοῦ) 9.

θεοῦ (gen.sing.masc.of θεός, possession) 124.

ἡμῶν (gen.pl.masc.of ἐγώ, relationship) 123.

καὶ (adjunctive conjunction joining nouns) 14.

ἡ (nom.sing.fem.of the article in agreement with ἐξουσία) 9.

ἐξουσία (nom.sing.fem.of ἐξουσία, subject of ἐγένετο) 707.

τοῦ (gen.sing.masc.of the article in agreement with Χριστοῦ) 9.

Χριστοῦ (gen.sing.masc.of Χριστός, possession) 4.

αὐτοῦ (gen.sing.masc.of αὐτός, relationship) 16.

ὅτι (conjunction introducing a subordinate causal clause) 211.

ἐβλήθη (3d.per.sing.aor.pass.ind.of βάλλω, culminative) 299.

ὁ (nom.sing.masc.of the article in agreement with κατήγωρ) 9.

κατήγωρ (nom.sing.masc.of κατήγωρ, subject of ἐβλήθη) 3606.

τῶν (gen.pl.masc.of the article in agreement with ἀδελφῶν) 9.

ἀδελφῶν (gen.pl.masc.of ἀδελφός, relationship) 15.

ἡμῶν (gen.pl.masc.of ἐγώ, relationship) 123.

ὁ (nom.sing.masc.of the article in agreement with κατηγορῶν) 9.

κατηγορῶν (pres.act.part.nom.sing.masc.of κατηγορέω, substantival, in apposition with κατήγωρ) 974.

αὐτοὺς (acc.pl.masc.of αὐτός, direct object of κατηγορῶν) 16.

ἐνώπιον (preposition with the genitive of place description) 1798.

τοῦ (gen.sing.masc.of the article in agreement with θεοῦ) 9.

θεοῦ (gen.sing.masc.of θεός, place description) 124.

ἡμῶν (gen.pl.masc.of ἐγώ, relationship) 123.

ἡμέρας (gen.sing.fem.of ἡμέρα, time description) 135.

καὶ (adjunctive conjunction joining nouns) 14.

νυκτός (gen.sing.fem.of νύξ, time description) 209.

Translation - "And I heard a loud voice in heaven saying, ' Now has come salvation and might and the kingdom of God and the authority of His Messiah, because the accuser of our brothers has been thrown out, the one who accuses them before our God day and night."

Comment: The banishment of Satan and his demonic angels is heralded in heaven as the evidence and advent of God's kingdom, despite the fact that Messiah's return to earth, to take David's throne, is still three and one half years in the future. But our Lord's authority, asserted when He rose from the dead (Mt.28:18), has now been demonstrated and it is only a matter of time, something that interests heaven, with its eternal point of view, not at all.

Satan is cast in the role of the universal prosecuting attorney, who had spent his time and effort bringing charges against the saints, many of which were true charges, though some were false, since Satan is a "liar and the father of lies" (John 8:44), but, whether true or false, he had always lost his case, since we have an Advocate with the Father, "Jesus Christ the Righteous" (1 John 2:1).

Satan learned in the Garden of Eden that if Jesus died the heel bruising death of the cross, his own power would be destroyed (Heb.2:14), and he tried without success to block God's covenanted program of redemption, which produced the Messiah of Israel and the Saviour of the elect. Unable to prevent Jesus' birth, he tried to kill him when He was two years old; he tried to throw Him down a cliff at Nazareth (Luke 4:29); he tried to drown Him when He was asleep on a pillow in a boat (Mk.4:38); he tried to trade Him out of it (Mt.4:8-10); he tried to talk Him out of it (Mt.16:22); he used Peter to suggest that they forget the cross in Jerusalem and remain in transfiguration glory on the mountain (Luke 9:33) and he used Peter again in the Garden of Gethsemane in an attempt to prevent his arrest (Lk.22:50). The Big Fisherman, motivated by forces which he little understood, would have put to flight the entire Roman army that night if Jesus had not rebuked him.

Satan understood, far better than many theologians, that the basis of God's redemption was the death of His Son on the cross, and that the entire divine plan of the ages would come to nothing if Jesus did not pay the debt in full. It was when He cried, Τετέλεσται (John 19:30) that Satan's power over his subjects was eternally broken.

Unable to challenge the efficacy of Jesus' sacrifice for sin, Satan is soon to feel the intensity of His wrath.

Verse 11 - "And they overcame him by the blood of the Lamb, and by the word of their testimony; and they loved not their lives unto the death."

καὶ αὐτοὶ ἐνίκησαν αὐτὸν διὰ τὸ αἷμα τοῦ ἀρνίου καὶ διὰ τὸν λόγον τῆς μαρτυρίας αὐτῶν, καὶ οὐκ ἠγάπησαν τὴν ψυχὴν αὐτῶν ἄρχι θανάτου.

"And they have conquered him by the blood of the Lamb and by the word of their testimony, for they loved not their lives even unto death." . . . RSV

καὶ (continuative conjunction) 14.

αὐτοὶ (nom.pl.masc.of αὐτός, subject of ἐνίκησαν) 16.

αὐτὸν (acc.sing.masc.of αὐτός, direct object of ἐνίκησαν) 16.

διὰ (preposition with the accusative, cause) 118.

τὸ (acc.sing.neut.of the article in agreement with αἷμα) 9.

αἷμα (acc.sing.neut.of αἷμα, cause) 1203.

τοῦ (gen.sing.neut.of the article in agreement with ἀρνίου) 9.

ἀρνίου (gen.sing.neut.of ἀρνίου, description) 2923.

καὶ (adjunctive conjunction joining prepositional phrases) 14.

διὰ (preposition with the accusative, cause) 118.

τὸν (acc.sing.masc.of the article in agreement with λόγον) 9.

λόγον (acc.sing.masc.of λόγος, cause) 510.

τῆς (gen.sing.fem.of the article in agreement with μαρτυρίας) 9.

μαρτυρίας (gen.sing.fem.of μαρτυρία, description) 1695.

αὐτῶν (gen.pl.masc.of αὐτός, possession) 16.
καὶ (adjunctive conjunction joining verbs) 14.
οὐκ (negative conjunction with the indicative) 130.
ἠγάπησαν (3d.per.pl.aor.act.ind.of ἀγαπάω, constative) 540.
τὴν (acc.sing.fem.of the article in agreement with ψυχήν) 9.
ψυχὴν (acc.sing.fem.of ψυχή, direct object of ἠγάπησαν) 233.
αὐτῶν (gen.pl.masc.of αὐτός, possession) 16.
ἄχρι (preposition with the genitive in a time expression) 1517.
θανάτου (gen.sing.masc.of θάνατος, time expression) 381.

Translation - "And they overcame him because of the blood of the Lamb, and because of the message of their testimony and they loved not their lives unto death."

Comment: The antecedent of αὐτοὶ is αὐτός in verse 11, which in turn refers to ἀδελφῶν of verse 11. They, the Christian brethren whom Satan had accused day and night, won their case against Satan and his accusations, even though, in many cases, the charges brought against them were true. The defense was not that they were innocent, but rather that they were guilty as charged, but that they had already paid the debt, in the person of their substitute, the Lamb and therefore that the full demands of the transgressed law had been met. There can be no double jeopardy in heaven's court. The blood of the Lamb speaks of expiation (1 John 2:1). We have our Lord's promise (Mt.10:32) that He will represent all who give their testimony of faith in Him. The blood of the Lamb and their confession of faith in Him is the twofold reason why Satan's accusations against the saints are of no avail. These brethren paid with their lives for their faith. All of this is ground for rejoicing as we see in

Verse 12 - "Therefore rejoice, ye heavens, and ye that dwell in them. Woe to the inhabiters of the earth and of the sea! For the devil is come down unto you, having great wrath, because he knoweth that he hath but a short time."

διὰ τοῦτο εὐφραίνεσθε, οὐρανοὶ, καὶ οἱ ἐν αὐτοῖς σκηνοῦντες, οὐαὶ τὴν γῆν καὶ τὴν θάλασσαν, ὅτι κατέβη διάβολος πρὸς ὑμᾶς ἔχων θυμὸν μέγαν, εἰδὼς ὅτι ὀλίγον καιρὸν ἔχει.

"Rejoice then, O heaven and you that dwell therein! But woe to you, O earth and sea, for the devil has come down to you in great wrath, because he knows that his time is short!" " . . . RSV

διὰ (preposition with the accusative, cause) 118.
τοῦτο (acc.sing.neut.of οὗτος, cause) 93.
εὐφραίνεσθε (2d.per.pl.pres.mid.impv.of εὐφραίνω, command) 2479.
οὐρανοὶ (voc.pl.masc.of οὐρανός, address) 254.
καὶ (adjunctive conjunction joining substantives) 14.
οἱ (voc.pl.masc.of the article in agreement with σκηνοῦντες) 9.
ἐν (preposition with the locative of place) 80.
αὐτοῖς (loc.pl.masc.of αὐτός, place) 16.

σκηνοῦντες (pres.act.part.voc.pl.masc.of σκηνόω, substantival, address) 1698.

οὐαὶ (exclamation) 936.

τὴν (acc.sing.fem.of the article in agreement with γῆν) 9.

γῆν (acc.sing.fem.of γῆ, adverbial accusative) 157.

καὶ (adjunctive conjunction joining nouns) 14.

τὴν (acc.sing.fem.of the article in agreement with θάλασσαν) 9.

θάλασσαν (acc.sing.fem.of θάλασσα, adverbial accusative) 374.

ὅτι (conjunction introducing a subordinate causal clause) 211.

κατέβη (3d.per.sing.2d.aor.act.ind.of καταβαίνω, culminative) 324.

ὁ (nom.sing.masc.of the article in agreement with διάβολος) 9.

διάβολος (nom.sing.masc.of διάβολος, subject of κατέβυ and ἔχει) 331.

πρὸς (preposition with the accusative of extent) 197.

ὑμᾶς (acc.pl.masc.of σύ, extent) 104.

ἔχων (pres.act.part.nom.sing.masc.of ἔχω, adverbial, circumstantial) 82.

θυμὸν (acc.sing.masc.of θυμός, direct object of ἔχων) 2034.

μέγαν (acc.sing.masc.of μέγας, in agreement with θυμὸν) 184.

εἰδὼς (perf.part.nom.sing.masc.of ὁράω, adverbial, causal) 144b.

ὅτι (conjunction introducing an object clause in indirect discourse) 211.

ὀλίγον (acc.sing.masc.of ὀλίγος, in agreement with καιρὸν) 669.

καιρὸν (acc.sing.masc.of καιρός, direct object of ἔχει) 767.

ἔχει (3d.per.sing.pres.act.ind.of ἔχω, aoristic) 82.

Translation - "Therefore rejoice, you heavens and those who live in them. Woe to the earth and the sea, because the Devil has come down to you in great rage because he has found out that he has only a little time left."

Comment: The διὰ τοῦτο phrase, which prompts the imperative εὐφραίνεσθε is because of the fact that Satan has been expelled from heaven. Those who dwell there need not endure his presence and his silly accusations any longer. Then woe is pronounced upon the earth and sea for the same reason. Satan, expelled from heaven, has now fallen to earth where he will concentrate his wrath upon its inhabitants, particularly so, since now he has discovered and therefore knows (perfect intensive in εἰδὼς) that his time is short. He has only three and one half years to be the "god of this world" (2 Cor.4:4), after which he will spend 1000 years in the abyss (Rev.20:1-2) at the end of which, following his last short rebellion (Rev.20:3,7-10) he will be cast forever into the lake of fire. Thus what will be heaven's gain, as Satan is expelled, will become earth's loss, but only for a short time since this is the beginning of the end for Satan. Note that when he falls to earth his first attack is upon the nation Israel, who produced Messiah, the Serpent Bruiser (Gen.3:15).

Verse 13 - "And when the dragon saw that he was cast into the earth, he persecuted the woman which brought forth the man child."

Καὶ ὅτε εἶδεν ὁ δράκων ὅτι ἐβλήθη εἰς τὴν γῆν, ἐδίωξεν τὴν γυναῖκα ἥτις ἔτεκεν τὸν ἄρσενα.

"And when the dragon saw that he had been thrown down to the earth, he pursued the woman who had borne the male child." . . . RSV

Καὶ (continuative conjunction) 14.

ὅτε (conjunction with the indicative in a definite temporal clause) 703.

εἶδεν (3d.per.sing.aor.act.ind.of ὁράω, culminative) 144.

ὁ (nom.sing.masc.of the article in agreement with δράκων) 9.

δράκων (nom.sing.masc.of δράκων, subject of εἶδεν and ἐδίωξεν) 5382.

ὅτι (conjunction introducing an object clause in indirect discourse) 211.

ἐβλήθη (3d.per.sing.aor.pass.ind.of βάλλω, culminative) 299.

εἰς (preposition with the accusative, extent) 140.

τὴν (acc.sing.fem.of the article in agreement with γῆν) 9.

γῆν (acc.sing.fem.of γῆ, extent) 157.

ἐδίωξεν (3d.per.sing.aor.act.ind.of διώκω, ingressive) 434.

τὴν (acc.sing.fem.of the article in agreement with γυναῖκα) 9.

γυναῖκα (acc.sing.fem.of γυνή, direct object of ἐδίωξεν) 103.

ἥτις (nom.sing.fem.of ὅστις, relative pronoun, subject of ἔτεκεν) 163.

ἔτεκεν (3d.per.sing.aor.act.ind.of τίκτω, culminative) 106.

τὸν (acc.sing.masc.of the article in agreement with ἄρσενα) 9.

ἄρσενα (acc.sing.masc.of ἄρσην, direct object of ἔτεκεν) 1286.

Translation - "And when the dragon realized that he had been thrown out unto the earth, he began to pursue the woman who had borne the male child."

Comment: The ὅτε clause is temporal and definite. Note εἶδεν followed by the objective ὅτι clause in indirect discourse.

The story returns to its main theme — the conflict between Satan and the nation Israel. Satan hates all nations, but he fears as well as hates Israel because she is the only nation of earth who has the covenant relationship with God by which she produced the Messiah, destined first to die the heel brusing death of Gen.3:15, in order to "destroy him that has the power of death, that is the devil" (Heb.2:14) and then, after resurrection, to sit at the Father's right hand until the Holy Spirit has made His enemies His footstool (Psalm 110:1). Then He will return to bruise Satan under the feet of the Body of Christ (Rom.16:20) and send him to hell. Thus Satan, since he first heard the promise of Gen.3:15 to Adam, has hated the human race and, after God had selected Abraham, as the progenitor of the chosen nation which would produce the Serpent Bruiser, especially he has hated Israel. He can control the Ayrans, the Orientals, the Indians, the Eskimos, the Irish, the English, the Americans and all of the other Gentile peoples, for he is the "god of this world" (2 Cor.4:4) but he struggled unsuccessfully to prevent Israel from producing the Messiah, and stood helplessly by when "in the fullness of time, God sent forth His Son, made of a woman, made under the law, in order that He might redeem those who are under the law in order that we might receive the adoption of sons" (Gal.4:4,5). Once our Lord was born, Satan hoped, there was still a chance that he could kill Him in some other way before He had the chance to go to the cross and die the death that would "bruise the serpent's head." But those plans also failed and Messiah having plumbed the awful depths of the despair and degradation of hell upon the cross, triumphantly announced Τετέλεσται — "it has been finished" (John 19:30), after which, in the most sovereign act of His life, He calmly laid down His physical life in order to prove that He was big enough to take it up again (John 10:15-18). Thus the Lord Jesus broke the power of spiritual death for the elect and demonstrated that He had nothing to fear from the power of physical death.

Satan had been the "god of this world" (2 Cor.4:4) and the strong man who thought that his house with its possessions was safe from the stronger Man Who would break, enter, bind and steal (Luke 11:21-22). Since Calvary and an empty tomb, Satan realizes that he has been robbed. The members of the Body of Christ, known but to the God who chose them (Eph.1:4) were redeemed and reconciled by the death of our Lord, and the sin debt of every one, from Adam, Eve and righteous Abel to the last one to be conceived, born and/or born again had been or would be effectually called by the Holy Spriti to repentance and faith. In the case of the vast majority of the human race, these elect members of the Body of Christ died in infancy or were aborted and thus were safely in the fold. Others who lived to the age of discretion were convinced by the Holy Spirit of "sin, and of righteousness and of judgment" (John 16:7-11) and "baptized into the Body" (1 Cor.12:13). They were "sealed with that Holy Spirit of promise" (Eph.1:13) "unto the day of redemption" (Eph.4:30). And each is assured of resurrection/rapture and the deliverance from the bondage of corruption "into the liberty of the glory of the children of God" (Rom.8:21).

Satan, the strong man who secured his house with its hellish possessions against the robber, has been overcome by the stronger Man, Christ Jesus, because Christ is greater than he that is in the world (1 John 4:4). Hell's domination over God's creation is over. Satan has lost his domain. Once determined to be the king of the universe (Isa.14:12-14) he was hurled to the earth by Him Who watched him fall, head over heels, all the way down until the sickening impact — *splat!* - probably somewhere in Texas! Dallas, perhaps. (Luke 10:18). He continued his deception, this time with great success, as the woman was deceived (1 Tim.2:14), and her husband opted for sex instead of holiness. If Satan could not be "like the Most High" at least he could seduce the human race into being "like Elohim" (Gen.3:5). Adam's deliberate decision (he was not deceived) to step down to Eve's sordid level was permitted by the sovereign God in His wisdom, and thus the human family was started, most of whom were destined to be redeemed at the cross. If Adam had not sinned, there would have been no human family, for Eve, banished from the garden, with the curse of death, spiritual and physical, upon her, would have wandered throughout the earth until she died and went to hell, while Adam would have remained in Eden, playing with the animals, birds and fish, each of whom had a mate, though he had none and tilling the soil, uncursed by thorns, weeds and briers, smelling the flowers in a lonely life that would have gone on forever and ever. The reader should reflect upon the fact that if God had not permitted the fall, he, the reader, would never have been born and God's eternal purpose to create man in His image and then redeem him could never have been accomplished.

God was not surprized when Eve, in her ineffable stupidity, believed the devil's lie and made her futile bid for omniscience; nor was He when Adam, with eyes wide open to the truth and its consequences chose living death with the woman he loved and to whom he was sexually attracted, for 930 years, instead of eternal but lonely bliss in a garden. A bit of philosophical reflection is apt to convince us that it is impossible to surprize God. He was not surprized, but He was ready with the next step in the redemptive scenario which He has planned in history. His announcement to the devil struck fear and consternation to the satanic heart. "You have used this stupid woman to bring about the downfall of the human race. I will use her to bring about its redemption. The seed of the woman will bruise your head. He will put you out of the business of dragging human beings down to hell. In the process He must die a death in which you will nail His heel to a cross and bruise it. But He will be God incarnate and He will rise again." (Gen.3:15).

All of these divine plans for history and the eternal ages will have been carried out by the point in time when the Revelation has begun, except one. The Messiah has come, lived, died and risen again. God has promised Abraham and his seed permanent hegemony over a choice piece of real estate between the Tigris-Euphrates river valley and the river of Egypt. This is where the oil is. Israel, dispersed for centuries throughout the globe has been called back to the land of her fathers. The "times of the Gentiles" when Jerusalem is overrun by pagan nations will be coming to an end (Lk.21:24). The "fullness of the Gentiles" (Rom.11:25) will be near   completion (Rev.10:7). Messiah, at the right hand of God (Psalm 110:1) will be about to return to earth to claim His throne. But one thing will be lacking. Messiah will have a throne and a national territory over which to rule and from which He will rule all the nations of earth, but He will have no nation. How can the King of the Jews be king when there are no Jews? He thought of that, of course, and, at the beginning of the tribulation week He sealed 144,000 in their foreheads as His property, destined to be saved when he returns and to become the nucleus of the new nation. If seventy Jews who went to Egypt with Jacob could multiply to three and one half million in two hundred fifty years, under conditions of slavery, how great will be the population of God's chosen people when 144,000 Jews, 72,000 men and their brides, have lived under ideal Kingdom conditions for one thousand years?

But when the dragon is thrown out of heaven in the middle of the tribulation week these 144,000 Jews, though sealed by God and marked for salvation, are not yet saved. Maybe Satan can kill them and thus, at this late date, frustrate the divine purpose by depriving the King of His earthly kingdom people.

Satan has always hated the woman. She produced the Messiah who destroyed his power to damn the entire human race. He still hates her because she has produced 144,000 glorious young people who will become Messiah's administrative nation through whose law He will rule the world. This is why Satan, who will have only 1260 days to acceomplish it, must kill these people.

Verse 14 - "And to the woman were given two wings of a great eagle, that she might fly into the wilderness, into her place, where she is nourished for a time, and times, and half a time, from the face of the serpent."

καὶ ἐδόθησαν τῇ γυναικὶ αἱ δύο πτέρυγες τοῦ ἀετοῦ τοῦ μεγάλου, ἵνα πέτηται εἰς τὴν ἔρημον εἰς τὸν τόπον αὐτῆς, ὅπου τρέφεται ἐκεῖ καιρὸν καὶ καιροὺς καὶ ἥμισυ καιροῦ ἀπὸ προσώπου τοῦ ὄφεως.

"But the woman was given the two wings of the great eagle that she might fly from the serpent into the wilderness, to the place where she is to be nourished for a time, and times, and half a time." . . . RSV

καὶ (continuative conjunction) 14.
ἐδόθησαν (3d.per.pl.aor.pass.ind.of δίδωμι, constative) 362.
τῇ (dat.sing.fem.of the article in agreement with γυναικὶ) 9.
γυναικὶ (dat.sing.fem.of γυνή, indirect object of ἐδόθησαν) 103.
αἱ (nom.pl.fem.of the article in agreement with πτέρυγες) 9.
δύο (numeral) 385.
πτέρυγες (nom.pl.fem.of πτέρυξ, subject of ἐδόθησαν) 1480.
τοῦ (gen.sing.masc.of the article in agreement with ἀετοῦ) 9.
ἀετοῦ (gen.sing.masc.of ἀετός, possession) 1503.
τοῦ (gen.sing.masc.of the article in agreement with ἀετοῦ) 9.
μεγάλου (gen.sing.masc.of μέγας, in agreement with ἀετοῦ) 184.
ἵνα (conjunction with the subjunctive, sub-final) 114.

#**5384** πέτηται (3d.per.sing.pres.subj.of πέτομαι, purpose/result).

King James Version

fly - Rev.12:14.

Revised Standard Version

fly - Rev.12:14.

Meaning: Cf. πετάομαι (#5346), πετεινόν (#615). To fly - Rev.12:14.

εἰς (preposition with the accusative of extent) 140.
τὴν (acc.sing.fem.of the article in agreement with ἔρημον) 9.
ἔρημον (acc.sing.fem.of ἔρημος, extent) 250.
εἰς (preposition with the accusative of extent) 140.
τὸν (acc.sing.masc.of the article in agreement with τόπον) 9.
τόπον (acc.sing.masc.of τόπος, extent) 1019.
αὐτῆς (gen.sing.fem.of αὐτός, possession) 16.
ὅπου (local adverb with the indicative in a definite local clause) 592.
τρέφεται (3d.per.sing.pres.pass.ind.of τρέφω, futuristic) 618.
ἐκεῖ (local adverb) 204.
καιρὸν (acc.sing.masc.of καιρός, time extent) 767.
καὶ (adjunctive conjunction joining nouns) 14.
καιροὺς (acc.pl.masc.of καιρός, time extent) 767.
καὶ (adjunctive conjunction joining substantives) 14.
ἥμισυ (acc.sing.neut.of ἥμισυς, time extent) 2259.
καιροῦ (gen.sing.masc.of καιρός, partitive) 767.

ἀπὸ (preposition with the ablative of separation) 70.
προσώπου (abl.sing.neut.of πρόσωπον, separation) 588.
τοῦ (gen.sing.masc.of the article in agreement with ὄφεως) 9.
ὄφεως (gen.sing.masc.of ὄφις, description) 658.

Translation - "And the two wings of the great eagle were given to the woman, in order (and with the result) that she may fly into the desert into her place where she will be nourished there for a time, and times and a half time from the presence of the serpent."

Comment: There is little need to comment on this verse and great wisdom in restraint. This writer has no idea what the wings of the eagle mean nor who or what the eagle is. Those skilled in eisegesis will see in the passage a commercial for United Air Lines. In some way the eagle will help the Jewish nucleus of the kingdom nation, sealed as God's property three and one half years before (Rev.7:1-8) to escape from Satan who will be trying to kill them. That he will fail is obvious, since God has already sealed them as His own. In this desert hideaway the 144,000 will be fed for the next 1260 days (42 months; 3 1/2 years). Elijah was fed by the ravens during a previous drought period of three and one half years (James 5:17).

Israel will make her escape despite Satan's frantic attempts to overtake her, as we learn in

Verse 15 - "And the serpent cast out of his mouth water as a flood after the woman, that he might cause her to be carried away of the flood."

καὶ ἔβαλεν ὁ ὄφις ἐκ τοῦ στόματος αὐτοῦ ὀπίσω τῆς γυναικὸς ὕδωρ ὡς ποταμόν, ἵνα αὐτὴν ποταμοφόρητον ποιήσῃ.

"The serpent poured water like a river out of his mouth after the woman, to sweep her away with the flood. . . . RSV

καὶ (inferential conjunction) 14.
ἔβαλεν (3d.per.sing.aor.act.ind.of βάλλω, ingressive) 299.
ὁ (nom.sing.masc.of the article in agreement with ὄφις) 9.
ὄφις (nom.sing.masc.of ὄφις, subject of ἔβαλεν) 658.
ἐκ (preposition with the ablative of source) 19.
τοῦ (abl.sing.neut.of the article in agreement with στόματος) 9.
στόματος (abl.sing.neut.of στόμα, source) 344.
αὐτοῦ (gen.sing.masc.of αὐτός, possession) 16.
ὀπίσω, (preposition with the ablative of separation, with persons) 302.
τῆς (abl.sing.fem.of the article in agreement with γυναικὸς) 9.
γυναικὸς (abl.sing.fem.of γυνή, separation) 103.
ὕδωρ (acc.sing.fem.of ὕδωρ, direct object of ἔβαλεν) 301.
ὡς (comparative particle) 128.
ποταμόν (acc.sing.masc.of ποταμός, adverbial accusative) 274.
ἵνα (conjunction with the subjunctive, purpose) 114.
αὐτὴν (acc.sing.fem.of αὐτός, direct object of ποιήσῃ) 16.

#**5385** ποταμοφόρητον (acc.sing.fem.of ποταμοφόρητος, predicate adjective, in agreement with ποταμόν).

King James Version

carried away of the flood - Rev.12:15.

Revised Standard Version

sweep away with the flood - Rev.12:15.

Meaning: A combination of ποταμός (#274) and φέρω (#683). Hence, borne away or swept away in a flood. *Cf.* φορέω (#913). To be overwhelmed with water. With reference to Satan's attempt to destroy Israel in Rev.12:15.

ποιήσῃ (3d.per.sing.aor.act.subj.of ποιέω, purpose) 127.

Translation - "And the serpent spewed water like a river out of his mouth after the woman in order to drown her."

Comment: Again we advise caution. No one now (1984) really knows precisely what this language means, if we are not to take it literally. Some things are clear. Satan, cast out of heaven (Rev.12:7-9) in the middle of the week, open the abyss (Rev.9:1-2) and releases the Beast (Rev.9:11; Rev.6:7-8) who breaks his promise to Israel (Dan.9:27b) and invades the temple (2 Thess.2:4). This event, predicted by Jesus who advised flight (Mt.24:15-22) will precipitate the flight of the Jews (Rev.12:6, 13-17) into the desert and Satan's wet pursuit. Does the flood of water mean a literal flood, which the sands of the desert absorb? (Rev.12:16). In which direction will the 144,000 flee? Petra has been suggested. *Cf. Encyclopedia Britannica* on Petra. Located at 35 degrees, 19 minutes East and 30 degrees, 19 minutes north, it is east of the Jordan, but in the edge of the Jordan valley. However it lies south of the Dead Sea. Could an earthquake in the area break up the surface structure and pour the waters of the Dead Sea in the direction that the woman has chosen in flight? Or does Satan, who is "the prince of the power of the air" (Eph.2:2) and hence has some control over the weather, generate a rain storm that results in a flash flood? Is it possible that the desert sands could absorb such a flood and render it harmless? The Revelation mentions no earthquake in the middle of the week. *Cf.* Rev.6:12; 8:5; 11:13,13,19; 16:18,18. These occur, either at the beginning of the week (Rev.8:5) or at the end.

The overall idea is clear. Israel will flee to the desert to escape Satan's murderous attack, and she will escape and be fed somewhere during the last half of the week, until her Messiah comes to save her.

Verse 16 describes the manner in which Satan's attempt to drown the woman is frustrated.

Verse 16 - "And the earth helped the woman, and the earth opened her mouth, and swallowed up the flood, which the dragon cast out of his mouth."

καὶ ἐβοήθησεν ἡ γῆ τῇ γυναικί, καὶ ἤνοιξεν ἡ γῆ τὸ στόμα αὐτῆς καὶ κατέπιεν τὸν ποταμὸν ὃν ἔβαλεν ὁ δράκων ἐκ τοῦ στόματος αὐτοῦ.

"But the earth came to help the woman, and the earth opened its mouth and swallowed the river which the dragon had poured from his mouth." . . . RSV

καὶ (adversative conjunction) 14.
ἐβοήθησεν (3d.per.sing.aor.act.ind.of βοηθέω, constative) 1173.
ἡ (nom.sing.fem.of the article in agreement with γῇ) 9.
γῆ (nom.sing.fem.of γῆ, subject of ἐβοήθησαν) 157.
τῇ (dat.sing.fem.of the article in agreement with γυναικί) 9.
γυναικί (dat.sing.fem.of γυνή, personal advantage) 103.
καὶ (adjunctive conjunction joining verbs) 14.
ἤνοιξεν (3d.per.sing.aor.act.ind.of ἀνοίγω, constative) 188.
ἡ (nom.sing.fem.of the article in agreement with γῇ) 9.
γῆ (nom.sing.fem.of γῆ, subject of ἤνοιξεν and κατέπιεν) 157.
τὸ (acc.sing.neut.of the article in agreement with στόμα) 9.
στόμα (acc.sing.neut.of στόμα, direct object of ἤνοιξεν) 344.
αὐτῆς (gen.sing.fem.of αὐτός, possession) 16.
καὶ (adjunctive conjunction joining verbs) 14.
κατέπιεν (3d.per.sing.2d.aor.act.ind.of καταπίνω, constative) 1454.
τὸν (acc.sing.masc.of the article in agreement with ποταμὸν) 9.
ποταμὸν (acc.sing.masc.of ποταμός, direct object of κατέπιεν) 274.
ὃν (acc.sing.masc.of ὅς, relative pronoun, direct object of ἔβαλεν) 65.
ἔβαλεν (3d.per.sing.aor.act.ind.of βάλλω, constative) 299.
ὁ (nom.sing.masc.of the article in agreement with δράκων) 9.
δράκων (nom.sing.masc.of δράκων, subject of ἔβαλεν) 5382.
ἐκ (preposition with the ablative of source) 19.
τοῦ (abl.sing.neut.of the article in agreement with στόματος) 9.
στόματος (abl.sing.neut.of στόμα, source) 344.
αὐτοῦ (gen.sing.masc.of αὐτός, possession) 16.

Translation - "But the earth came to the rescue of the woman, and the earth opened her mouth and swallowed the river which the dragon cast out of his mouth."

Comment: Check our translation "came to the rescue" against the meaning of #1173. Weymouth has "came to the woman's help." The choice of the verb presents us with a dramatic picture of the 144,000 Jews fleeing   fearfully across a desert with a turbulent flood of water in pursuit. The cries of the people reverberate among the rocks and echo across the desert. The earth hears and helps. The desert sands absorb the water. Satan, in frustration, mobilizes the Gentile armies against the Hebrew Christians in the world. This is the message of

Verse 17 - "And the dragon was wroth with the woman, and went to make war with the remnant of her seed, which keep the commandments of God, and have the testimony of Jesus Christ."

καὶ ὠργίσθη ὁ δράκων ἐπὶ τῇ γυναικί, καὶ ἀπῆλθεν ποιῆσαι πόλεμον μετὰ τῶν λοιπῶν τοῦ στέρματος αὐτῆς, τῶν τηρούντων τὰς ἐντολὰς τοῦ θεοῦ καὶ ἐχόντων τὴν μαρτυρίαν Ἰησοῦ.

"Then the dragon was angry with the woman, and went off to make war onthe rest of her offspring, on those who keep the commandments of God and bear testimony to Jesus. And he stood on the sand of the sea." . . . RSV

καὶ (inferential conjunction) 14.

ὠργίσθη (3d.per.sing.aor.pass.ind.of ὀργίζω, ingressive) 479.

ὁ (nom.sing.masc.of the article in agreement with δράκων) 9.

δράκων (nom.sing.masc.of δράκων, subject of ὠρίσθη and ἀπῆλθεν) 5382.

ἐπὶ (preposition with the dative, hostility) 47.

τῇ (dat.sing.fem.of the article in agreement with γυναικί) 9.

γυναικί (dat.sing.fem.of γυνή, hostility) 103.

καὶ (adjunctive conjunction joining verbs) 14.

ἀπῆλθεν (3d.per.sing.aor.mid.ind.of ἀπέρχομαι, ingressive) 239.

ποιῆσαι (aor.act.inf.of ποιέω, telic) 127.

πόλεμον (acc.sing.masc.of πόλεμος, direct object of ποιῆσαι) 1483.

μετὰ (preposition with the genitive, accompaniment, hostility) 50.

τῶν (gen.pl.masc.of the article in agreement with λοιπῶν) 9.

λοιπῶν (gen.pl.masc.of λοιπός, hostility) 1402.

τοῦ (gen.sing.neut.of the article in agreement with σπέρματος) 9.

σπέρματος (gen.sing.neut.of σπέρμα, partitive genitive) 1056.

αὐτῆς (gen.sing.fem.of αὐτός, relationship) 16.

τῶν (gen.pl.masc.of the article in agreement with τηρούντων and ἐχόντων) 9.

τηρούντων (pres.act.part.gen.pl.masc.of τηρέω, adjectival, emphatic attributive position, ascriptive, in agreement with λοιπῶν) 1297.

τὰς (acc.pl.fem.of the article in agreement with ἐντολὰς) 9.

ἐντολὰς (acc.pl.fem.of ἐντολή, direct object of τηρούντω) 472.

τοῦ (gen.sing.masc.of the article in agreement with θεοῦ) 9.

θεοῦ (gen.sing.masc.of θεός, description) 124.

καὶ (adjunctive conjunction joining participles) 14.

ἐχόντων (pres.act.part.gen.pl.masc.of ἔχω, adjectival, emphatic attributive position, ascriptive, in agreement with λοιπῶν) 82.

τὴν (acc.sing.fem.of the article in agreement with μαρτυρίαν) 9.

μαρτυρίαν (acc.sing.fem.of μαρτυρία, direct object of ἐχόντων) 1695.

Ἰησοῦ (gen.sing.masc.of Ἰησοῦς, description) 3.

Translation - "So the dragon became angry with the woman, and he went away in order to wage war against the rest of her children, who keep the commandments of God and have the testimony of Jesus."

Comment: καὶ is inferential. Satan will be frustrated because his attempt to drown the fleeing Jews will have failed. If he succeeded, the Messiah, now about to leave His throne in the glory and return to take His place of David's throne on earth, would be a King of the Jews without a kingdom people. It is therefore inevitable that the attack upon the 144,000 will fail. Satan, unable to destroy the woman, will go away in frustration to other hellish activity. He will now make war against a group identified as the physical descendants of Israel who are further described by the two adjectival participles. They will be Jews who have an orthodox Jewish attitude toward God's commands as promulgated by Moses, and who also adhere to the message (testimony, cnfession) of Jesus. This seems to indicate that these people are Hebrew Christians. They will feel the brunt of the satanic attack. Of course Satan will also attack all of the Gentiles saints, members of the Body of Christ, who are still alive at the time (Rev.13:7).

(Note: The next sentence is written in W-H, Tregelles and the United Bible Societies' Committee text as verse 18 of chapter 12. However, since we are following the English King James Version, which erroneously puts it into the first verse of the 13th chapter, we will do so also. The sentence refers to Satan, not to John as the King James Version indicates.)

The Two Beasts

Revelation 13:1 - "And I stood upon the sand of the sea, and saw a beast rise up out of the sea, having seven heads and ten horns and upon his horns ten crowns, and upon his heads the name of blasphemy."

Καὶ εἶδον ἐκ τῆς θαλάσσης θηρίον ἀναβαῖνον, ἔχον κέρατα δέκα καὶ κεφαλὰς ἑπτά, καὶ ἐπὶ τῶν κεράτων αὐτοῦ δέκα διαδήματα, καί ἐπὶ τὰς κεφαλὰς αὐτου ὄνομα βλασφημίας.

"And I saw a beast rising out of the sea, with ten horns and seven heads, with ten diadems upon its horns and a blasphemous name upon its heads." ... *RSV*

Καὶ (continuative conjunction) 14.
ἐστάθη (3d.per.sing.1st.aor.ind.of ἵστημι, ingressive) 180.
ἐπὶ (preposition with the accusative of extent, rest) 47.
τὴν (acc.sing.fem.of the article in agreement with ἄμμον) 9.
ἄμμον (acc.sing.fem.of ἄμμος, extent, rest) 701.
τῆς (gen.sing .fem.of the article in agreement with θαλάσσης) 9.
θαλάσσης (gen.sing.fem.of θάλασσα, description) 374.
καὶ (continuative conjunction) 14.
εἶδον (1st.per.sing.aor.act.ind.of ὁράω, constative) 144.
ἐκ (preposition with the ablative of separation) 19.
τῆς (abl.sing.fem.of the article in agreement with θαλάσσης) 9.
θαλάσσης (abl.sing.fem.of θάλασσα, separation) 374.
θηρίον (acc.sing.neut.of θηρίον, direct object of εἶδον) 1951.
ἀναβαῖνον (pres.act.part.acc.sing.neut.of ἀναβαίνω, adjectival, predicate position, restrictive, in agreement with θηρίον) 323.
ἔχον (pres.act.part.acc.sing.neut.of ἔχω, adjectival, predicate position, restrictive, in agreement with θηρίον) 82.
κέρατα (acc.pl.neut.of κέρας, direct object of ἔχον) 1851.

δέκα (numeral) 1330.

καὶ (adjunctive conjunction joining nouns) 14.

κεφαλὰς (acc.pl.fem.of κεφαλή, direct object of ἔχον) 521.

ἑπτά (numeral) 1024.

καὶ (adjunctive conjunction joining nouns) 14.

ἐπὶ (preposition with the genitive of place description) 47.

τῶν (gen.pl.neut.of the article in agreement with κεράτων) 9.

κεράτων (gen.pl.neut.of κέρας, place description) 1851.

αὐτοῦ (gen.sing.masc.of αὐτός, possession) 16.

δέκα (numeral) 1330.

διαδήματα (acc.pl.neut.of διάδημα, direct object of ἔχον) 5383.

καὶ (adjunctive conjunction joining nouns) 14.

ἐπὶ (preposition with the accusative of extent, rest) 47.

τὰς (acc.pl.fem.of the article in agreement with κεφαλὰς) 9.

κεφαλὰς (acc.pl.fem.of κεφαλή, extent, rest) 521.

αὐτοῦ (gen.sing.masc.of αὐτός, possession) 16.

ὀνόματα (acc.pl.neut.of ὄνομα, direct object of ἔχον) 108.

βλασφημίας (gen.sing.fem.of βλασφημία, description) 1001.

Translation - "And he (Satan) stood upon the sand of the sea. And I saw a beast coming up out of the sea having ten horns and seven heads and upon his horns ten diadems and upon his heads blasphemous names."

Comment: Should we read ἐστάθη ("he stood") or ἐστάθην ("I stood")? Who stood? Satan (Rev.12:17) or John (Rev.13:1). Metzger says, "Instead of καὶ ἐστάθη which is well supported by p47 Sinaiticus A C about 25 minuscules (including 1854 2344) and itgig,61 vg syrh arm eth *al*, the Textus Receptus, following P 046 051 most minuscules syrph copsa, bo *al*, reads καὶ ἐστάθην (preceded by a full stop). The latter reading appears to have arisen when copyists accommodated ἐστάθη to the first person of the following εἶδον." (*A Textual Commentary on the Greek New Testament*, 748).

There is also doubt as to whether we should read ὄνομα or ὀνόματα (plural). "On the one hand, the reading ὄνομα may have arisen from ὀνόματα through the accidental omission of τα after μα; on the other hand, however, after the plural κεφαλὰς copyists may have tended to alter ὄνομα to ὀνόματα. On the strength of the two most important witnesses (A 2053) a majority of the Committee preferred to print ὀνόματα in the text, but to enclose the last two letters within square brackets, in order to represent the opposing evidence." (*Ibid.*)

As in so many other cases of variant readings, the essential exegesis of the passage remains unaffected. The point is that the beast came out of the sea, whether it was Satan or John standing upon the shore, and whether his heads had one or many blasphemous names, does not affect the fact that the Beast is a blasphemer. We know that from other passages.

Some commentators have noted the difference between the origin of the first Beast from the sea (Rev.13:1) and the second (Rev.13:11) coming from the earth.

Eisegetes need vivid imaginations since their game is to make the text teach what they have already decided is true. Is the sea a type of Gentile humanity? If so, where does the Bible say so? If so, we might say that by analogy the earth ($\gamma\tilde{\eta}$) is a type of the Jew. Why is it necessary for us to know that now? Will it not be clear to those who live then?

The beasts of Rev.13:1,11 are the two riders of the fourth seal (Rev.6:7-8). Since their role is to deceive the entire unregenerate world (except those elect members of the Body of Christ who are at that time as yet unsaved), they will be more effective perhaps, if one is a Jew and the other a Gentile. But we warn against an imagined typology for which there is no specific scriptural warrant. Some will protest that there need be no scriptural warrant for what we believe, since we have special lines of communication with the Holy Spirit who is still in the business of calling prophets, apostles and miracle workers and who is now completing the task of inspiring the New Testament message. Thus the "holy rollers" have scant interest in New Testament exegesis because they regard their insights as more authoritative than those which exegetes can gain from reading what the New Testament says. Joseph Smith, Mary Baker Eddy, the charismatic girl in Scotland who first "understood" pretribulation rapture and Jim Jones all had their special lines of communication with the Lord — sources of truth not open to any others. Therefore these "prophets" feel called to tell us ordinary mortals, to whom the Lord has not chosen to speak, what the good word is!

The fact that the Beast came from the sea suggests Daniel 7:3 and his heads, horns and names suggest Rev.17:3, 7-12, while his leonine aspect connects him with Dan.7:4-6.

We have already alluded to the fact that the Beast of Rev.13:1 is the eighth in the series of Gentile dictators who have ruled or will have ruled over Palestine during the "times of the Gentiles" (Lk.21:24), in the period covered by Daniel's seventy weeks of years (Dan.9:24-27). The eight are: (a) in the first 69 weeks, Ancient Babylon, Ancient Media-Persia, Ancient Greece and Ancient Rome, and (b) in the 70th week, yet future to us now (22 May 1984) the White Horse Rider (Rev.6:1-2), the Red Horse Rider (Rev.6:3-4), the Black Horse Rider (Rev.6:5-6) and the Pale Horse Rider (Rev.6:7-8), who is also the Beast out of the Sea (Rev.13:1-10). He is the eighth and he is one of the preceding seven, namely the 5th (Rev.17:10,11). Before his death and descent into the abyss he was the fifth. In the middle of the week, after his rescue from the abyss (Rev.9:1-11) he will be the eighth and last. He will continue for 42 months (Rev.13:5) and be cast into the lake of fire at the second coming of our Lord (Rev.19:20). It all correlates perfectly.

That the Beast's heads, horns, diadems and blasphemous name(s) refer in some way to his political organization may be true. It is a point, unclear to us before the fact and hence something about which wise exegetes will be cautious, but we may be sure that it will all be clear to those who live to see it.

Verse 2 - "And the beast which I saw was like a leopard, and his feet were as the feet of a bear, and his mouth as the mouth of a lion: and the dragon gave him his power, and his seat, and great authortiy."

καὶ τὸ θηρίον ὃ εἶδον ἦν ὅμοιον παρδάλει, καὶ οἱ πόδες αὐτοῦ ὡς ἄρκου, καὶ τὸ στόμα αὐτοῦ ὡς στόμα λέοντος. καὶ ἔδωκεν αὐτῷ ὁ δράκων τὴν δύναμιν αὐτοῦ καὶ τὸν θρόνον αὐτοῦ καὶ ἐξουσίαν μεγάλην.

"And the beast that I saw was like a leopard, its feet were like a bear's, and its mouth was like a lion's mouth. And to it the dragon gave his power and his throne and great authority." . . . RSV

καὶ (continuative conjunction) 14.
τὸ (nom.sing.neut.of the article in agreement with θηρίον) 9.
θηρίον (nom.sing.neut.of θηρίον, subject of ἦν) 1951.
ὃ (acc.sing.neut.of ὅς, relative pronoun, direct object of εἶδον) 65.
εἶδον (1st.per.sing.aor.ind.of ὁράω, ingressive) 144.
ἦν (3d.per.sing.imp.ind.of εἰμί, progressive description) 86.
ὅμοιον (nom.sing.neut.of ὅμοιος, predicate adjective in agreement with θηρίον) 923.

#5386 παρδάλει (dat.sing.fem.of πάρδαλις, comparison).

King James Version

leopard - Rev.13:2.

Revised Standard Version

leopard - Rev.13:2.

Meaning: An Asiatic and African animal with a tawny skin marked with large black spots. Panther, leopard; pard (*cf.* Shakespeare, *As You Like It*, II, 7, 150). One of the characteristics of the Beast - Rev.13:2.

καὶ (continuative conjunction) 14.
οἱ (nom.pl.masc.of the article in agreement with πόδες) 9.
πόδες (nom.pl.masc.of πούς, subject of ἦν understood) 353.
αὐτοῦ (gen.sing.masc.of αὐτός, possession) 16.
ὡς (comparative particle) 128.

#5387 ἄρκου (gen.sing.masc.of ἄρκος, description).

King James Version

bear - Rev.13:2.

Revised Standard Version

bear's - Rev.13:2.

Meaning: A bear - Rev.13:2.

καὶ (continuative conjunction) 14.
τὸ (nom.sing.neut.of the article in agreement with στόμα) 9.
στόμα (nom.sing.neut.of στόμα, subject of ἦν understood) 344.

αὐτοῦ (gen.sing.masc.of αὐτός, possession) 16.

ὡς (comparative particle) 128.

στόμα (nom.sing.neut.of στόμα, subject of ἔστι, understood) 344.

λέοντος (gen.sing.masc.of λέων, possession) 4872.

καὶ (continuative conjunction) 14.

ἔδωκεν (3d.per.sing.aor.act.ind.of δίδωμι, constative) 362.

αὐτῷ (dat.sing.masc.of αὐτός, indirect object of ἔδωκεν) 16.

ὁ (nom.sing.masc.of the article in agreement with δράκων) 9.

δράκων (nom.sing.masc.of δράκων, subject of ἔδωκεν) 5382.

τὴν (acc.sing.fem.of the article in agreement with δύναμιν) 9.

δύναμιν (acc.sing.fem.of δύναμις, direct object of ἔδωκεν) 687.

αὐτοῦ (gen.sing.masc.of αὐτός, possession) 16.

καὶ (adjunctive conjunction joining nouns) 14.

τὸν (acc.sing.masc.of the article in agreement with θρόνον) 9.

θρόνον (acc.sing.masc.of θρόνος, direct object of ἔδωκεν) 519.

αὐτοῦ (gen.sing.masc.of αὐτό, possession) 16.

καὶ (adjunctive conjunction joining nouns) 14.

ἐξουσίαν (acc.sing.fem.of ἐξουσία, direct object of ἔδωκεν) 707.

μεγάλην (acc.sing.fem.of μέγας, in agreement with ἐξουσίαν) 184.

Translation - "And the beast which I saw was like a leopard, and his feet were like those of a bear, and his mouth was like the mouth of a lion, and the dragon gave to him his power and his throne and great authority."

Comment: This composite description connects the Beast with the Daniel image (Daniel 7:1-8). Note that Daniel describes them separately in the chronological order in which they will appear - lion, bear, leopard and the nondescript terror of Dan.7:8, which has the ten horns, has a colleague ("another little horn") and speaks great things. In Revelation 13:2, this nondescript beast is in view. His description contains those of the preceding three in reverse order (leopard, bear and lion). The "little horn" is probably identified as the False Prophet of Rev.13:11-18.

The important point, and the only one that need concern us now who at this point are not seeing the fulfillment of these things, is that both of these men are mouthpieces of Satan, who has given to them his power, his throne and his great authority. This Beast and the False Prophet will continue forty-two months and be cast into hell at the second coming. The ten horns, three of which will be destroyed by the "little horn" may represent the political allies of the Beast during the first half of the week. It is not essential to identify them with the revived Roman Empire, the European Common Market, the North Atlantic Treaty Organization or any other political and economic bloc. This much seems clear. The Beast and his allies will be enemies of Soviet Russia, the Warsaw Pact and other powers within the sphere of Communist influence.

Satan has been the "god of this world" (2 Cor.4:4) since Adam's fall. He will now transfer his power, his throne and his authority to the Beast and, vicariously, in Antichrist receive the worship of the unsaved world, something

that he has wanted since the beginning of his recorded career (Isa.14:12-14).
The way in which the Beast and his hellish colleague, the False Prophet, will exploit this satanic power is the subject of the remainder of the 13th chapter.

Verse 3 - "And I saw one of his heads as it were wounded to death; and his deadly wound was healed: and all the world wondered after the beast."

καὶ μίαν ἐκ τῶν κεφαλῶν αὐτοῦ ὡς ἐσφαγμένην εἰς θάνατον, καὶ ἡ πληγὴ τοῦ θανάτου αὐτοῦ ἐθεραπεύθη. καὶ ἐθαυμάσθη ὅλη ἡ γῆ ὀπίσω τοῦ θηρίου,

"One of its heads seemed to have a mortal wound, but its mortal wound was healed, and the whole earth followed the beast with wonder." . . . RSV

καὶ (continuative conjunction) 14.

μίαν (acc.sing.fem.of εἷς, direct object of εἶδον understood) 469.

ἐκ (preposition with the partitive genitive) 19.

τῶν (gen.pl.fem.of the article in agreement with κεφαλῶν) 9.

κεφαλῶν (gen.pl.fem.of κεφαλή, partitive) 521.

αὐτοῦ (gen.sing.masc.of αὐτός, possession) 16.

ὡς (comparative particle) 128.

ἐσφαγμένην (perf.pass.part.acc.sing.fem.of σφάζω, adjectival, predicate position, restrictive, in agreement with μίαν) 5292.

εἰς (preposition with the predicate accusative) 140.

θάνατον (acc.sing.masc.of θάνατος, adverbial accusative) 381.

καὶ (adversative conjunction) 14.

ἡ (nom.sing.fem.of the article in agreement with πληγή) 9.

πληγή (nom.sing.fem.of πληγή, subject of ἐθεραπεύθη) 2421.

τοῦ (gen.sing.masc.of the article in agreement with θανάτου) 9.

θανάτου (gen.sing.masc.of θάνατος, description) 381.

αὐτοῦ (gen.sing.masc.of αὐτός, possession) 16.

ἐθεραπεύθη (3d.per.sing.aor.pass.ind.of θεραπεύω, culminative) 406.

καὶ (inferential conjunction) 14.

ἐθαυμάσθη (3d.per.sing.aor.pass.ind.of θαυμάζω, ingressive) 726.

ὅλη (nom.sing.fem.of ὅλος, in agreement with γῆ) 112.

ἡ (nom.sing.fem.of the article in agreement with γῆ) 9.

γῆ (nom.sing.fem.of γῆ, subject of ἐθαυμάσθη) 157.

ὀπίσω (preposition with the ablative, with persons) 302.

τοῦ (abl.sing.neut.of the article in agreement with θηρίου) 9.

θηρίου (abl.sing.neut.of θηρίον) 1951.

Translation - "And I saw one of his heads which appeared to have been mortally wounded, but the deadly wound was now healed; therefore the entire earth began to marvel at the Beast."

Comment: We must supply εἶδον in the first clause, since the sentence containing εἶδον in verse 1 ends with βλασφημίας. Verse two contains two paratactic sentences. Hence we cannot carry εἶδον over from verse 1. Note that the adjectival participle is in the perfect tense - a present condition as a result of a past completed action. At the time John saw the Beast he noted that he had in the past been mortally wounded, but (adversative καὶ) the wound had since been healed (culminative aorist in ἐθεραπεύθη). The wounded head and its subsequent healing involves us in detail where we could only conjecture. The main point is that a notable miracle had occurred with reference to this man, as a result of which the entire unregenerate world will begin to marvel (ingressive aorist in ἐθαυμάσθη). The text does not tell us how the Beast, at the end of his first rule, as Rider on the White Horse (Rev.6:1-2) received this deadly wound, who inflicted it upon him or whether or not it resulted in his death, though εἰς θάνατον would seem to say that it did. Because of it he goes to the abyss, from which he is liberated at the beginning of the second half of the week as we learned in Rev.9:1-11.

It will be helpful if the student at this point will review the events which will have taken place during the three and one half years which comprise the first half of the week. Religious conditions in the Body of Christ can be studied in the first four churches (Rev.2:1-2:28). Political conditions are described in the first four seals (Rev.6:1-8) and cosmic and environmental conditions on earth are described in the first four trumpets (Rev.8:1-13). Special attention should be given to the widespread death and devastation which will occur during this first half of the period. Thus we can put ourselves in a position to appreciate the psychological condition of the unsaved who, having suffered under the blows which have fallen from heaven, have nevertheless survived. The miracles which the Beast and the False Prophet will be empowered by Satan to perform will convince all but the elect that the Beast is the saviour of the world. They will worship him and will not hesitate to take his mark, without which they will be excluded from the market. Only those Christians alive at the time and those other elect who have not yet been effectually called by the Holy Spirit will understand that the Beast is Satan's man, scheduled for damnation after 42 months. Meanwhile wickedness will engulf world society as Daniel prophesied - "Many shall be purified, and made white, and tried; but the wicked shall do wickedly: and none of the wicked shall understand: but the wise shall understand." (Dan.12:10).

None of this analysis can be made to fit logically into the scenario which the teachers of pretribulation rapture have invented, every part of which is the result of eisegesis. When will Christians cease trying to make the Bible teach what they have already determined to be the truth? If pretribulation rapture is taught in the New Testament why was it never discovered until the beginning of the 19th century, and then by an overly emotional holy roller? Was there not a single exegete until 1800 who was able to understand the Bible?

Verse 4 - "And they worshipped the dragon which gave power unto the beast: and they worshipped the beast, saying, Who is like unto the beast? Who is able to make war with him?"

καὶ προσεκύνησαν τῷ δράκοντι ὅτι ἔδωκεν τὴν ἐξουσίαν τῷ θηρίῳ, καὶ προσεκύνησαν τῷ θηρίῳ λέγοντες, Τίς ὅμοιος τῷ θηρίῳ, καί τίς δύναται πολεμῆσαι μετ' αὐτοῦ;

"Men worshipped the dragon, for he had given his authority to the beast, and they worshipped the beast, saying, 'Who is like the beast, and who can fight against it?' " . . . RSV

καὶ (continuative conjunction) 14.
προσεκύνησαν (3d.per.pl.aor.act.ind.of προσκυνέω, ingressive) 147.
τῷ (dat.sing.masc.of the article in agreement with δράκοντι) 9.
δράκοντι (dat.sing.masc.of δράκων, personal advantage) 5382.
ὅτι (conjunction introducing a subordinate causal clause) 211.
ἔδωκεν (3d.per.sing.aor.act.ind.of δίδωμι, culminative) 362.
τὴν (acc.sing.fem.of the article in agreement with ἐξουσίαν) 9.
ἐξουσίαν (acc.sing.fem.of ἐξουσία, direct object of ἔδωκεν) 707.
τῷ (dat.sing.neut.of the article in agreement with θηρίῳ) 9.
θηρίῳ (dat.sing.neut.of θηρίον, indirect object of ἔδωκεν) 1951.
καὶ (adjunctive conjunction joining verbs) 14.
προσεκύνησαν (3d.per.pl.aor.act.ind.of προσκυνέω, ingressive) 147.
τῷ (dat.sing.neut.of the article in agreement with θηρίῳ) 9.
θηρίῳ (dat.sing.neut.of θηρίον, personal advantage) 1951.
λέγοντες (pres.act.part.nom.pl.masc.of λέγω, recitative) 66.
Τίς (nom.sing.masc.of τίς, interrogative pronoun, subject of ἔστιν, in direct question) 281.
ὅμοιος (nom.sing.masc.of ὅμοιος, predicate adjective) 923.
τῷ (dat.sing.neut.of the article in agreement with θηρίῳ) 9.
θηρίῳ (dat.sing.neut.of θηρίον, comparison) 1951.
καὶ (adjunctive conjunction joining direct questions) 14.
τίς (nom.sing.masc.of τίς, interrogative pronoun, subject of δύναται, direct question) 281.
δύναται (3d.per.sing.pres.ind.of δύναμαι, aoristic) 289.
πολεμῆσαι (aor.act.inf.of πολεμέω, complementary) 5140.
μετ' (preposition with the genitive of accompaniment, hostility) 50.
αὐτοῦ (gen.sing.masc.of αὐτός, accompaniment, hostility) 16.

Translation - "So they began to worship the dragon because he had given the power to the Beast, and they began to worship the Beast, saying, 'Who is like the Beast and who is able to wage war against him?' "

Comment: The ὅτι subordinate clause is causal. The unsaved of earth began to worship Satan (ingressive aorist in προσεκύνσαν) and the Beast whom the dragon inspired. Thus Satan's desire to be worshipped is fulfilled. *Cf.* Mt.9:8, where men worshipped God because he gave power to Christ to heal the palsied man. Now men will worship Satan for the same reason — that he empowers his agents to perform miracles. The incurably religious nature of unregenerate man is here seen. They will have rejected Christ, the heavenly miracle. But man must worship something. The Beast and the False Prophet, with Satan's help, will be real miracle workers, for deceptive purposes (2 Thess.2:9-12; Rev.13:12-15). Note the litany of their worship. John gives it to us in direct discourse, introduced by λέγοντες. The questions, though rhetorical, have a good answer.

The devil was like the Beast and the Beast was like the devil. God became incarnate in a man at the beginning of the age. Satan became incarnate in a man at its close. Who was able to make war with the Beast? The answer will be, "The two witnesses" (Rev. 11:5). That is why there will be such celebration when at last the Beast will succeed in killing them (Rev. 11:7-10). Then the hymn of praise to Satan will finally appear to be true.

But though the Beast cannot harm the two witnesses during the term of their ministry, he can kill other saints (Rev. 13:7).

Verse 5 - "And there was given unto him a mouth speaking great things and blasphemies; and power was given unto him to continue forty and two months."

Καὶ ἐδόθη αὐτῷ στόμα λαλοῦν μεγάλα καὶ βλασφημίας, καὶ ἐδόθη αὐτῷ ἐξουσία ποιῆσαι μῆνας τεσσαράκοντα δύο.

"And the beast was given a mouth uttering haughty and blasphemous words, and it was allowed to exercise authority for forty-two months." . . . RSV

Καὶ (continuative conjunction) 14.
ἐδόθη (3d.per.sing.aor.pass.ind.of δίδωμι, constative) 352.
αὐτῷ (dat.sing.masc.of αὐτός, indirect object of ἐδόθη) 16.
στόμα (nom.sing.neut.of στόμα, subject of ἐδόθη) 344.
λαλοῦν (pres.act.part.nom.sing.neut.of λαλέω, adjectival, predicate position, restrictive, in agreement with στόμα) 815.
μεγάλα (acc.pl.neut.of μέγας, direct object of λαλοῦν) 184.
καὶ (adjunctive conjunction joining substantives) 14.
βλασφημίας (acc.pl.fem.of βλασφημία, direct object of λαλοῦν) 1001.
καὶ (continuative conjunction) 14.
ἐδόθη (3d.per.sing.aor.pass.ind.of δίδωμι, constative) 362.
αὐτῷ (dat.sing.masc.of αὐτός, indirect object of ἐδόθη) 16.
ἐξουσία (nom.sing.fem.of ἐξουσία, subject of ἐδόθη) 707.
ποιῆσαι (aor.act.inf.of ποιέω, in apposition with ἐξουσία) 127.
μῆνας (acc.pl.masc.of μήν, time extent) 1809.
τεσσαράκοντα (numeral) 333.
δύο (numeral) 385.

Translation - "And eloquence was given to him to speak grandiose and blasphemous things, and power was given to him to continue forty-two months."

Comment: An eloquent orator; a braggart; a blasphemer. (2 Thess. 2:4). Dan. 7:8 which seems to identify the "little horn" with the Beast of our passage. If so, the three "first horns" would be the first, second and third seal individuals. *Cf.* also Dan. 7:20,25. As prophecy becomes history, events of the time will do much to help us relate Daniel 7 to Revelation 13.

Verse 6 - "And he opened his mouth in blasphemy against God, to blaspheme his name, and his tabernacle, and them that dwell in heaven."

καὶ ἤνοιξεν τὸ στόμα αὐτοῦ εἰς βλασφημίας πρὸς τὸν θεόν, βλασφημῆσαι τὸ ὄνομα αὐτοῦ καὶ τὴν σκηνὴν αὐτοῦ, τοὺς ἐν τῷ οὐρανῷ σκηνοῦντας.

"it opened its mouth to utter blasphemies against God, blaspheming his name and his dwelling, that is, those who dwell in heaven." . . . RSV

καὶ (continuative conjunction) 14.

ἤνοιξεν (3d.per.sing.aor.act.ind.of ἀνοίγω, ingressive) 188.

τὸ (acc.sing.neut.of the article in agreement with στόμα) 9.

στόμα (acc.sing.neut.of στόμα, direct object of ἤνοιξεν) 344.

αὐτοῦ (gen.sing.masc.of αὐτός, possession) 16.

εἰς (preposition with the accusative, purpose) 140.

βλασφημίας (acc.sing.fem.of βλασφημία, purpose) 1001.

πρὸς (preposition with the accusative, extent, opposition) 197.

τὸν (acc.sing.masc.of the article in agreement with θεόν) 9.

θεόν (acc.sing.masc.of θεός, opposition) 124.

βλασφημῆσαι (aor.act.inf.of βλασφημῆσαι, purpose) 781.

τὸ (acc.sing.neut.of the article in agreement with ὄνομα) 9.

ὄνομα (acc.sing.neut.of ὄνομα, direct object of βλασφημῆσαι) 108.

αὐτοῦ (gen.sing.masc.of αὐτός, possession) 16.

καὶ (adjunctive conjunction joining nouns) 14.

τὴν (acc.sing.fem.of the article in agreement with σκηνὴν) 9.

σκηνὴν (acc.sing.fem.of σκηνή, direct object of βλασφημῆσαι) 1224.

αὐτοῦ (gen.sing.masc.of αὐτός, possession) 16.

τοὺς (acc.pl.masc.of the article in agreement with σκηνοῦντας) 9.

ἐν (preposition with the locative of place) 80.

τῷ (loc.sing.masc.of the article in agreement with οὐρανῷ) 9.

οὐρανῷ (loc.sing.masc.of οὐρανός, place) 254.

σκηνοῦντας (pres.act.part.acc.pl.masc.of σκηνόω, substantival, direct object of βλασφημῆσαι) 1698.

Translation - "And he began to open his mouth in blasphemy against God, in order to blaspheme His name and His tabernacle, namely those who dwell in heaven."

Comment: Note that the Beast, inspired by Satan, is not an atheist. He does not deny that God exists. His attack is upon God - His name, His tabernacle, which means those who dwell in heaven. *Cf.* Rev.21:3. God's tabernacle consists of those with whom He lives.

There are several variant readings. "Among the several readings a majority of the Committee preferred τοὺς . . . σκηνοῦντας on the grounds of its superior external support (it is read by (Sinaiticus *) A C (1006) 1611 2053comm 2344 *al*) and its being the more difficult reading. The presence of καί before τοὺς (in Sinaiticusc P 046* 051 most minuscules and early versions) appears to be due to copyists who wished to alleviate the strained syntax. In view of occasional omissions in p47 the Committee regarded its reading ἐν τῷ οὐρανῷ as a secondary modification introduced probably because of the syntactical difficulty. The

singular reading of syr_ph is probably due to the freedom of the translator."
(Metzger, *A Textual Commentary on the Greek New Testament*, 748, 749). Thus
the last phrase is in apposition with σκηνήν.

*Verse 7 - "And it was given unto him to make war with the saints, and to
overcome them: and power was given unto him over all kindreds, and tongues,
and nations."*

καὶ ἐδόθη αὐτῷ ποιῆσαι πόλεμον μετὰ τῶν ἁγίων καὶ νικῆσαι αὐτούς, καὶ
ἐδόθη αὐτῷ ἐξουσία ἐπὶ πᾶσαν φυλὴν καὶ λαὸν καὶ γλῶσσαν καὶ ἔθνος.

*"Also it was allowed to make war on the saints and to conquer them. And
authority was given it over every tribe and people and tongue and nation," . . .
RSV*

καὶ (continuative conjunction) 14.
ἐδόθη (3d.per.sing.aor.pass.ind.of δίδωμι, constative) 362.
αὐτῷ (dat.sing.masc.of αὐτός, indirect object of ἐδόθη) 16.
ποιῆσαι (aor.act.inf.of ποιέω, noun use, subject of ἐδόθη) 127.
πόλεμον (acc.sing.masc.of πόλεμος, direct object of ποιῆσαι) 1483.
μετὰ (preposition with the genitive, hostility) 50.
τῶν (gen.pl.masc.of the article in agreement with ἁγίων) 9.
ἁγίων (gen.pl.masc.of ἅγιος, hostility) 84.
καὶ (adjunctive conjunction joining infinitives) 14.
νικῆσαι (aor.act.inf.of νικάω, noun use, subject of ἐδόθη) 2454.
αὐτούς (acc.pl.masc.of αὐτός, direct object of νικῆσαι) 16.
καὶ (continuative conjunction) 14.
ἐδόθη (3d.per.sing.aor.pass.ind.of δίδωμι, constative) 362.
αὐτῷ (dat.sing.masc.of αὐτός, indirect object of ἐδόθη) 16.
ἐξουσία (nom.sing.fem.of ἐξουσία, subject of ἐδόθη) 707.
ἐπὶ (preposition with the accusative, metaphorial, place) 47.
πᾶσαν (acc.sing.fem.of πᾶς, in agreement with φυλήν, λαὸν, γλῶσσαν and
ἔθνος) 67.
φυλὴν (acc.sing.fem.of φυλή, metaphorical place) 1313.
καὶ (adjunctive conjunction joining nouns) 14.
λαὸν (acc.sing.masc.of λαός, metaphorical place) 110.
καὶ (adjunctive conjunction joining nouns) 14.
γλῶσσαν (acc.sing.fem.of γλῶσσα, metaphorical place) 1846.
καὶ (adjunctive conjunction joining nouns) 14.
ἔθνος (acc.sing.neut.of ἔθνος, metaphorical place) 376.

*Translation - "And freedom to make war with the saints was given to him and to
overcome them: and authority was given to him over every tribe and people and
tongue and nation."*

Comment: The infinitives ποιῆσαι and νικῆσαι, in their noun use, are the
subjects of ἐδόθη. Liberty to attack and power to overcome the Christians and
world-wide authority will be given to the Beast for 42 months. Only the two

witnesses will be able to withstand him. There will be many martyrs for the Christian faith. *Cf.* Rev.7:9-17. Some of the Beast's first victims are seen in the fifth seal (Rev.6:9-11).

Pretribulation rapture teachers often cite 1 Thess.5:9 as support for their view on the ground that God has not appointed us unto wrath. If the last generation of saints in the Body of Christ must spend the last seven years on the earth, subject to the wrath of the Beast, is there not a conflict? The Scripture no where promises the Christian immunity from the wrath of unsaved man. Indeed many passages point to the fact that Christians will be persecuted (Mt.5:10-12; John 15:18,19; 1 Peter 4:12-16). Church history abundantly supports these predictions. *Cf.* Fox, *Book of Martyrs* and many others. John and Betty Stam were murdered by the Chinese communists; four Catholic sisters were recently murdered in El Salvador; "the three Freds," missionaries in the jungles of South America were killed by the natives; many Christians languish in prisons behind the Iron Curtain.

It is somewhat less than honest for Christians in America and Western Europe to view the sufferings of other Christians for their faith and then look forward to a sudden translation into heaven before persecution in our part of the world begins. Such teaching also overlooks the honor and special reward that is connected with dying for the faith. Christians alive on earth on the last day of the tribulation will have "kept the word of (His) patience" and He will "also keep (them) from the hour of temptation, which shall come upon all the world, to try them that dwell upon the earth" (Rev.3:11). In the next verse, He says, "Behold, I come quickly." This is the promise of rapture for the Philadelphian Church. He promises to keep them from the "hour" not the last seven years of temptation. Jesus counselled that Christians "Watch therefore: for ye know not what hour your Lord doth come." (Mt.24:42). Of course. To know the day of the second coming in advance, as those privileged to live at that time watch the countdown of the prophetic clock, is not to be told the hour of the great day. The earth, rotating toward the east, is divided into twenty-four time zones. Will the Lord descend on the appointed day as that day is determined in Jerusalem, Greenwich, Tokyo or on which side of the International Date Line? It is difficult to imagine a Christian on that day doing anything else than watching the skies to imagine a Christian on that day doing anything other than watch the sky, as he listens for the shout, the voice of the archangel and the last trump of God. that at that time He did not even know. He did not say that no man would ever know. On the contrary Paul has written that Christians are not in darkness "that that day should overtake us as a thief" (1 Thess.5:4). The unsaved, busy with eating, drinking, marrying and giving in marriage will not know. That day will overtake them as a thief (1 Thess.5:2,3). They will have been worshipping the Devil, the Antichrist and the False Prophet for the past three and one half years and they will be saying, "Peace and safety." Then "sudden destruction (will come) upon them, . . . and they shall not escape." Paul then adds "But ye, brethren, are not in darkness, that that day should overtake you as a thief. Ye are all the children of light, and the children of the day: we are not of night, nor of darkness" (1 Thess.5:4,5). Noah knew that the flood would come in his lifetime and seven days before it came he was told the precise day when the rain would begin to fall. It was on that day that he and his family entered the ark (Gen.7:1-13). Jesus said, "As the day of Noah — so shall also the coming of the Son of man be." (Mt.24:37). The eating, drinking, sex and unawareness of the coming flood of the next two verses applies to Noah's unsaved neighbours — not to Noah and his family. This is in line with 1 Thess.5:1-5. Exegesis demands that we take note of the context.

The distinction must be made between the wrath of unsaved men, immunity from which has never been promised to the Christian, and the wrath of God, under the blows of which the child of God is forever immune. This is what 1 Thess.5:9 says. God need not rapture His children out of the world in order to protect them from His wrath which will be falling upon the unsaved in the same areas. Psalm 91 clearly predicts safety for the child of God in the same areas where the unsaved will be set upon by the divine judgments. Israel, in Egypt during the period of the ten plagues illustrates the point. God did not lead Israel out of Egypt before He visited the plagues upon the Egyptians. In fact, He used Moses and Aaron as agents of delivery of His miseries upon His enemies, just as He will use the two witnesses during the tribulation period. (Rev.11:6).

Our passage tells us that the Beast will dominate the unsaved world. His authority will extend to every tribe, people, tongue and nation. All of the world will worship and obey him, because "the wicked shall do wickedly and none of the wicked shall understand; but the wise shall understand" (Dan.12:10). All military, political, cultural, intellectual and social control depends upon economic control. Karl Marx, arguing from his materialistic presupposition, was not wrong. Basic to international stress today is the competition and conflict that characterizes international trade. The internal economy, and thus the standard of living of the people within it, depends, in part, upon import/export balance/imbalance. For example Japan suffers currently from her excessive imports over exports. The interest rate in the United States, the result of fiscal policy which demands more defense than we can pay for, as we insist upon a nuclear arsenal with capability of overkill, overvalues the American dollar *vis a vis* other currencies. Why should a Frenchman surrender more francs than he used to give for an American dollar in order to buy American goods, increase our imports and provide employment for American workers in American factories, when he can buy the American dollar, albeit at a price too high in relation to francs, and spend the dollar, not in the goods and servies market but in the American money market, where high interest rates insure high returns on the investment? This problem has been with us ever since the rise of nation states, and it will continue to be with us until the Beast seizes control of the world money market with his mark and dictates that no one shall participate in the market without first yielding to his dictation. For three and one half years we will have a coordinated world market and the law of comparative advantage, which economists have extolled as heaven on earth for two hundred years will apply. As a result the picture of flourishing internatinal trade, with Babylon as the economic capital of the Beast, is described in Revelation 18.

Cf. Daniel 7:21, 22-25 as Daniel moves out of the tribulation to the second coming.

Verse 8 - "And all that dwell upon the earth shall worship him, whose names are not written in the book of life of the Lamb slain from the foundation of the world."

καὶ προσκυνήσουσιν αὐτὸν πάντες οἱ κατοικοῦντες ἐπὶ τῆς γῆς, οὗ οὐ γέγραπται τὸ ὄνομα αὐτοῦ ἐν τῷ βιβλίῳ τῆς ζωῆς τοῦ ἀρνίου τοῦ ἐσφαγμένου ἀπὸ καταβολῆς κόσμου.

"and all who dwell on earth will worship it, every one whose name has not been written before the foundation of the world in the book of life of the Lamb that was slain." . . . *RSV*

καὶ (continuative conjunction) 14.

προσκυνήσουσιν (3d.per.pl.fut.act.ind.of προσκυνέω, predictive) 147.

αὐτὸν (acc.sing.masc.of αὐτός, direct object of προσκυνήσουσιν) 16.

πάντες (nom.pl.masc.of πᾶς, in agreement with κατοικοῦντες) 67.

οἱ (nom.pl.masc.of the article in agreement with κατοικοῦντες) 9.

κατοικοῦντες (pres.act.part.nom.pl.masc.of κατοικέω, substantival, subject of προσκυνήσουσιν) 242.

ἐπὶ (preposition with the genitive of place description) 47.

τῆς (gen.sing.fem.of the article in agreement with γῆς) 9.

γῆς (gen.sing.fem.of γῆ, place description) 157.

οὗ (gen.sing.masc.of ὅς, relative pronoun, possession) 65.

οὐ (negative conjunction with the indicative) 130.

γέγραπται (3d.per.sing.perf.pass.ind.of γράφω, intensive) 156.

τὸ (nom.sing.neut.of the article in agreement with ὄνομα) 9.

ὄνομα (nom.sing.neut.of ὄνομα, subject of γέγραπται) 108.

αὐτοῦ (gen.sing.masc.of αὐτός, possession, pleonastic) 16.

ἐν (preposition with the locative of place) 80.

τῷ (loc.sing.neut.of the article in agreement with βιβλίῳ) 9.

βιβλίῳ (loc.sing.neut.of βιβλίον, place) 1292.

τῆς (gen.sing.fem.of the article in agreement with ζωῆς) 9.

ζωῆς (gen.sing.fem.of ζωή, description) 668.

τοῦ (gen.sing.neut.of the article in agreement with ἀρνίου) 9.

ἀρνίου (gen.sing.neut.of ἀρνίον, possession) 2923.

τοῦ (gen.sing.neut.of the article in agreement with ἐσφαγμένου) 9.

ἐσφαγμένου (perf.pass.part.gen.sing.neut.of σφάζω, adjectival, emphatic attributive position, ascriptive, in agreement with ἀρνίου) 5292.

ἀπὸ (preposition with the ablative of time separation) 70.

καταβολῆς (abl.sing.fem.of καταβολή, time separation) 1079.

κόσμου (gen.sing.masc.of κόσμος, description) 360.

Translation - "And all those dwelling upon the earth will worship him, every one the name of whom has not been written in the book of life of the Lamb, Who has been slain from the foundation of the world."

Comment: We have here another example of pleonasm. John did not need αὐτοῦ after ὄνομα. *Cf.*Rev.3:8; 7:2,9; 20:8; Mk.1:7; Lk.3:16; 7:25; Mk.13:19 and a few others. Not everyone on earth will worship the Beast and his hellish superior. Only those who are unregenerate and destined to stay that way. Christians will not be deceived (Mt.24:24), nor will those elect members of the Body of Christ who have not yet been effectually called by the Holy Spirit. He Who first called the believer to repentance and faith (John 16:7-11), then baptizes him into the Body of Christ (1 Cor.12:13), seals him unto the day of redemption (Eph.1:13) and guarantees his rapture/resurrection (Rom.8:11). He also witnesses with the spirit of the believer and assures Sonship with God and Heirship with Jesus Christ. His teaching is a safeguard against Satan and his deceptions (1 John 4:4 *contra* 2 Thess.2:10,11; Ps.91:4b). *Cf.* Rev.17:8 where John makes the statement parallel to Rev.13:8.

The name of the believer in the Lamb's Book of Life is good insurance. Note the intensive perfect tense in γέγραπται. The names of the elect were written into the book before the fall of Satan (Isa.14:12-14), Adam (Genesis 3) and of each of those whom He has chosen in Him before the foundation of the world (Eph.1:4).

The fact that one is intellectually humble enough to accept this doctrine of divine determinism, which is totally repugnant to the unregenerate mind, is the evidence that one is indeed chosen in him. Those who will worship the Beast and accept his mark will never have the "ear" to "hear."

Verse 9 - "If any man have an ear, let him hear."

Εἴ τις ἔχει οὖς ἀκουσάτω.

"If any one has an ear, let him hear:" . . . *RSV*

εἴ (conditional particle with the indicative in a first-class condition) 337.

τις (nom.sing.masc.of τις, indefinite pronoun, subject of ἔχει, in a first-class condition) 486.

ἔχει (3d.per.sing.pres.act.ind.of ἔχω, first-class condition) 82.

οὖς (acc.sing.neut.of οὖς, direct object of ἔχει) 887.

ἀκούσατω (3rd.per.sing.aor.act.impv.of ἀκούω, command) 148.

Translation - "If any one has the capacity to understand, let him take note."

Comment: This formula — a challenge to the listener and reader, was used in Rev.2:7 ,11,17,29; 3:6,13,22. *Cf.*# 887 for others.

Verse 10 - "He that leadeth into captivity shall go into captivity: he that killeth with the sword must be killed with the sword. Here is the patience and the faith of the saints."

εἴ τις εἰς αἰχμαλωσίαν, εἰς αἰχμαλωσίαν ὑπάγει. εἴ τις ἐν μαχαίρῃ ἀποκτανθῆναι, αὐτὸν ἐν μαχαίρῃ ἀποκτανθῆναι.ʹΩδέ ἐστιν ἡ ὑπομονὴ καὶ ἡ πίστις τῶν ἁγίων.

"If any one is to be taken captive, to captivity he goes; if any one slays with the

sword, with the sword must he be slain. Here is a call for the endurance and faith of the saints." . . . RSV

εἴ (conditional particle in a first-class condition) 337.

τις (nom.sing.masc.of τις, indefinite pronoun, subject of αἰχμαλωτίζει, understood) 486.

εἰς (preposition with the accusative, extent) 140.

αἰχμαλωσίαν (acc.sing.fem.of αἰχμαλωσία, extent) 4492.

εἰς (preposition with the accusative of extent) 140.

αἰχμαλωσίαν (acc.sing.fem.of αἰχμαλωσία, extent) 4492.

ὑπάγει (3d.per.sing.pres.act.ind.of ὑπάγω, futuristic) 364.

εἴ (conditional particle in a first-class condition) 337.

τις (nom.sing.masc.of τις, indefinite pronoun) 486.

ἐν (preposition with the instrumental, means) 80.

μαχαίρῃ (instru.sing.fem.of μάχαιρα (for μαχαίρᾳ) 896.

ἀποκτανθῆναι (aor.pass.inf.of ἀποκτείνω) 889.

αὐτὸν (acc.sing.masc.of αὐτός, general reference) 16.

ἐν (preposition with the instrumental, means) 80.

μαχαίρῃ (instru.sing.fem.of μάχαιρα, for μαχαίρᾳ) 896.

ἀποκτανθῆναι (aor.pass.inf.of ἀποκτείνω) 880.

Ὧδέ (local adverb) 766.

ἐστιν (3d.per.sing.pres.ind.of εἰμί, aoristic) 86.

ἡ (nom.sing.fem.of the article in agreement with ὑπομονὴ) 9.

ὑπομονὴ (nom.sing.fem.of ὑπομονή, subject of ἐστιν) 2204.

καὶ (adjunctive conjunction joining nouns) 14.

ἡ (nom.sing.fem.of the article in agreement with πίστις) 9.

πίστις (nom.sing.fem.of πίστις, subject of ἐστιν) 728.

τῶν (gen.pl.masc.of the article in agreement with ἁγίων) 9.

ἁγίων (gen.pl.masc.of ἅγιος, possession) 84.

Translation - "If any one is destined for captivity he leads into captivity. If any one kills with the sword he shall with the sword be killed. The patience and the faith of the saints is based upon this principle."

Comment: "The epigrammatic style of the saying has perplexed the scribes. The reading εἰς αἰχμαλωσίαν, εἰς αἰχμαλωσίαν ὑπάγει (A vg Ps-Ambrose) best accounts for the origin of the others. The absence of one of the two instances of εἰς αἰχμαλωσίαν, although rather widespread (p47 Sinaiticus C P 046 1006 1611 2053 *al*), appears to be the result of accidental oversight in transcription. The absence of a verb with the first clause prompted various copyists to attempt to improve the text by adding either ἀπάγει (616 1828 1854 1862 1888 2322 itgig,(61) vgmss syrph,h *al*) or συνάγει (2059 2 081 Arethas, followed by the Textus Receptus), or by altering the construction to αἰχμαλωτίζιε (94 104 459 2019). The reading ἔχει αἰχμαλωσίαν ὑπάγει (051 and about 130 minuscules), which can scarcely be translated, must be regarded as a scribal blunder (ἔχει being written instead of εἰς); it is thus a further development of the second reading mentioned above (p47 *al*)." *(Metzger, A Textual Commentary on the Greek New*

Testament, 749,750).

Metzger adds that there are a dozen variant readings of the second clause. "...
the least unsatisfactory appears to be ἀποκτανϑῆναι, αὐτόν supported by codex
Alexandrinus. As in the first two lines of the verse, the third and fourth lines
teach (as does also Jeremiah 15:2, on which the saying rests) the duty of
endurance and the fulfillment of the will of God. Perhaps under the influence of
such sayings as Mt.26:52 (πάντες γὰρ οἱ λαβόντες μάχαιραν ἐν μαχαίρῃ ἀπὸ
λοῦνται) copyists modified in various ways the different Greek constructions
(which, as Charles points out, seems to be a literal rendering of a distinctively
Hebrew idiom . . . "if anyone is to be slain with the sword, he is to be slain with
the sword") and introduced the idea of retribution (persecutors will be requited
in strict accord with the *lex talonis)"* (Metzger, *Ibid.,* 750).

The last clause adds that the principle of *lex talonis* will be the basis upon
which Christians in the tribulation, who are killed by the Beast, will be able to
endure martyrdom. Their faith will assure them that the days of the Beast are
numbered and that divine judgment upon him is certain. Jesus reminded Peter of
this principle in Mt.26:52.

We saw in Revelation 6:7-8 that when the Pale Horse Rider of the fourth seal
appeared, he had an accomplice named ὁ ἅδης. Since Rev.13:1-10 is a picture of
the Pale Horse Rider, we naturally expect a description of his hellish partner.
This we have in Rev.13:11-18.

The principle of *lex talonis* is seen everywhere in the natural, physical and
social sciences as well as in the field of ethics. Classical physics teaches that for
every action there is an equal and opposite reaction. Living organisms, whether
plant or animal, through photosynthesis maintain a chemical equilibrium with
their environment. At death they lose radioactive carbon 14 at a rate that can be
measured. The same is true of the magnetism of the core of the earth. It has a
definite half life period. Alfred Marshall discovered the principle of equilibrium
in a free market economy by observing the rise and fall of sea waves. Waves rise
only so high before they fall to give rise to other waves. God's "eye for an eye and
tooth for a tooth" principle of Exodus 21:23-25 is a principle of eternal law,
which Jesus came, not to destroy but to fulfill. Paul stated it by saying that
"Whatsoever a man soweth that shall he also reap," and "the wages of sin is
death" — a penalty which someone must pay - if not the sinner his substitute
upon the cross. Economists often say that "There is no such thing as a free lunch"
and that "One cannot eat onions and keep it a secret."

*Verse 11 - "And I beheld another beast coming up out of the earth: and he had
two horns like a lamb, and he spake as a dragon."*

Καὶ εἶδον ἄλλο θηρίον ἀναβαῖνον ἐκ τῆς γῆς, καὶ εἶχεν κέρατα δύο ὅμοια
ἀρνίῳ, καὶ ἐλάλει ὡς δράκων.

*"Then I saw another beast which rose out of the earth; it had two horns like a
lamb and it spoke like a dragon." . . . RSV*

Καὶ (continuative conjunction) 14.

εἶδον (1st.per.sing.aor.act.ind.of ὁράω, constative) 144.

ἄλλο (acc.sing.neut.of ἄλλος, in agreement with θηρίον) 198.

θηρίον (acc.sing.neut.of θηρίον, direct object of εἶδον) 1951.

ἀναβαῖνον (pres.act.part.acc.sing.neut.of ἀναβαίνω, adjectival, predicate position, restrictive, in agreement with θηρίον) 323.

ἐκ (preposition with the ablative of source) 19.

τῆς (abl.sing.fem.of the article in agreement with γῆς) 9.

γῆς (abl.sing.fem.of γῆ, source) 157.

καὶ (continuative conjunction) 14.

εἶχεν (3d.per.sing.imp.act.ind.of ἔχω, progressive description) 82.

κέρατα (acc.pl.neut.of κέρας, direct object of εἶχεν) 1851.

δύο (numeral) 385.

ὅμοια (acc.pl.neut.of ὅμοις, predicate adjective) 923.

ἀρνίῳ (dat.sing.neut.of ἀρνίον, comparison) 2923.

καὶ (adjunctive conjunction joining verbs) 14.

ἐλάλει (3d.per.sing.imp.act.ind.of λαλέω, progressive duration) 815.

ὡς (comparative particle) 128.

δράκων (nom.sing.masc.of δράκων, subject of λάλει understood) 5382.

Translation - *"And I watched another beast coming up out of the earth, and he had two horns like a lamb but he was talking like a dragon."*

Comment: The earth is the source of the False Prophet as the sea was the source of the Beast. *Cf.* comment on Rev.13:1. The reference to the lamb is not to Christ the Lamb of God. εἶχεν κέρατα δύο ὅμοια ἀρνίῳ means "like the horns of a lamb." This character looks peaceful but he comes up talking like the devil, and, we may add, acting by Satan's power.

Verse 12 - *"And he exerciseth all the power of the first beast before him, and causeth the earth and them that dwell therein to worship the first beast, whose deadly wound was healed."*

καὶ τὴν ἐξουσίαν τοῦ πρώτου θηρίου πᾶσαν ποιεῖ ἐνώπιον αὐτοῦ. καὶ ποιεῖ τὴν γῆν καὶ τοὺς ἐν αὐτῇ κατοικοῦντας ἵνα προσκυνήσουσιν τὸ θηρίον τὸ πρῶτον, οὗ ἐθεραπεύθη ἡ πληγὴ τοῦ θανάτου αὐτοῦ.

"It exercises all the authority of the first beast in its presence, and makes the earth and its inhabitants worship the first beast, whose mortal wound was healed." . . . *RSV*

καὶ (adjunctive conjunction joining verbs) 14.

τὴν (acc.sing.fem.of the article in agreement with ἐξουσίαν) 9.

ἐξουσίαν (acc.sing.fem.of ἐξουσία, direct object of ποιεῖ) 707.

τοῦ (gen.sing.neut.of the article in agreement with θηρίου) 9.

πρώτου (gen.sing.neut.of πρῶτος, in agreement with θηρίου) 487.

θηρίου (gen.sing.neut.of θηρίον, description) 1951.

πᾶσαν (acc.sing.fem.of πᾶς, in agreement with ἐξουσίαν) 67.

ποιεῖ (3d.per.sing.pres.act.ind.of ποιέω, customary) 127.

ἐνώπιον (preposition with the genitive of place description) 1798.

αὐτοῦ (gen.sing.masc.of αὐτός, place description) 16.

καὶ (adjunctive conjunction joining verbs) 14.

ποιεῖ (3d.per.sing.pres.act.ind.of ποιέω, customary) 127.

τὴν (acc.sing.fem.of the article in agreement with γῆν) 9.

γῆν (acc.sing.fem.of γῆ, direct object of ποιεῖ) 157.

καὶ (adjunctive conjunction joining substantives) 14.

τοὺς (acc.pl.masc.of the article in agreement with κατοικοῦντας) 9.

ἐν (preposition with the locative of place) 80.

αὐτῇ (loc.sing.fem.of αὐτός, place) 16.

κατοικοῦντας (pres.act.part.acc.pl.masc.of κατοικέω, substantival, direct object of ποιεῖ) 242.

ἵνα (conjunction with the future indicative, purpose) 114.

προσκυνήσουσιν (3d.per.pl.fut.act.ind.of προσκυνέω, purpose) 147.

τὸ (acc.sing.neut.of the article in agreement with θηρίον) 9.

θηρίον (acc.sing.neut.of θηρίον, direct object of προσκυνήσουσιν) 1951.

τὸ (acc.sing.neut.of the article in agreement with πρῶτον) 9.

πρῶτον (acc.sing.neut.of πρῶτος, in agreement with θηρίον) 487.

οὗ (gen.sing.neut.of ὅς, relative pronoun, possession) 65.

ἐθεραπεύθη (3d.per.sing.aor.pass.ind.of θεραπεύω, culminative) 406.

ἡ (nom.sing.fem.of the article in agreement with πληγή) 9.

πληγὴ (nom.sing.fem.of πληγή, subject of ἐθεραπεύθη) 2421.

τοῦ (gen.sing.masc.of the article in agreement with θανάτου) 9.

θανάτου (gen.sing.masc.of θάνατος, description) 381.

αὐτοῦ (gen.sing.masc.of αὐτός, possession, pleonasm) 16.

Translation - "And he exercises all the power of the first beast and he influences the earth and those dwelling in it so that they will worship the first Beast, the mortal wound of whom was healed."

Comment: ἐνώπιον αὐτοῦ seems here to mean "in the presence of" the first beast. The False Prophet (*Cf.* Deut.18:15; John 1:21) receives his power from Satan, much as does the Beast and hence is powerful as he. He uses his power to cause the earth dwellers to worship the Beast. Note the purpose clause with ἵνα, and the future indicative, rare, but not unknown in the New Testament.

Verse 12 is qualified by verse 8 which excludes Christians. They will not worship the Beast and many of them will be martyred (verse 15).

It may be remarked that the liberalism of democracy, so proudly defended as a bed rock foundation stone of democratic freedom, will not be in vogue under Antichrist and the Beast. Here is dictatorship of the most absolute sort. Those who bow and worship will be spared and made the victims of future exploitation. Those who do not bow and worship will be killed. First amendment freedoms, such as modern constitutional systems provide, will not be available. And liberals who now, before the time, prate about their enthusiasm for the religious liberty which permits, but does not enforce worship of anything or any body, will worship the Beast, whether they wish to do so or not, or they will die.

Whether ποιεῖ of verse 12, second clause, means coercion or motivation is an interesting point that grammar or etymology cannot settle. Other passages, however, indicate that the unregenerate, be he "liberal" or "conservative" will not need coercion. He will worship Satan and his Beasts of his own free will. An evil and adulterous generation seeks a sign and the Beast and the False Prophet will provide all the signs and portents that they may require (Mt.12:38-42; Rev.13:13,14). Men who reject the "sign of the Prophet Jonah" will accept Satan's signs without question — a fact which proves that the so-called and self-styled "liberals" are not as tough minded and objective as they say they are. For their naive gullibility they will find the Queen of Sheba and the Ninevites rising up in the judgment to condemn them. The interest that the modern unregenerate world has in Edgar Cacey, Jeanne Dixon, extra sensory perception specialists, television preachers, gurus and three headed calves indicates that the world will be a willing subject for Satan's deceptions when the tribulation period begins.

Verse 13 - "And he doeth great wonders, so that he maketh fire come down from heaven on the earth in the sight of men."

καὶ ποιεῖ σημεῖα μεγάλα, ἵνα καὶ πῦρ ποιῇ ἐκ τοῦ οὐρανοῦ καταβαίνειν εἰς τὴν γῆν ἐνώπιον τῶν ἀνθρώπων.

"It works great signs, even making fire come down from heaven to earth in the sight of men; . . . " . . . RSV

κα‌ὶ (continuative conjunction) 14.

ποιεῖ (3d.per.sing.pres.act.ind.of ποιέω, customary) 127.

σημεῖα (acc.pl.neut.of σημεῖον, direct object of ποιεῖ) 1005.

μεγάλα (acc.pl.neut.of μέγας, in agreement with σημεῖα) 184.

ἵνα (conjunction with the subjunctive, ecbatic) 114.

καὶ (ascensive conjunction) 14.

πῦρ (acc.sing.neut.of πῦρ, general reference) 298.

ποιῇ (3d.per.sing.pres.act.subj.of ποιέω, ecbatic) 127.

ἐκ (preposition with the ablative, source) 19.

τοῦ (abl.sing.masc.of the article in agreement with οὐρανοῦ) 9.

οὐρανοῦ (abl.sing.masc.of οὐρανός, source) 254.

καταβαίνειν (pres.act.inf.of καταβαίνω, object of ποιῇ) 324.

εἰς (preposition with the accusative of extent) 140.

τὴν (acc.sing.fem.of the article in agreement with γῆν) 9.

γῆν (acc.sing.fem.of γῆ, extent) 157.

ἐνώπιον (preposition with the genitive of place description) 1798.

τῶν (gen.pl.masc.of the article in agreement with ἀνθρώπων) 9.

ἀνθρώπων (gen.pl.masc.of ἄνθρωπος, place description) 341.

Translation - "And he performs great miracles so that he even makes fire descend out of the sky to the earth in the sight of men."

Comment: Burton (*Moods and Tenses*, 94) thinks that "Rev.13:13 is the most probable instance of ἵνα denoting actual result." He adds that ἵνα . . . ποιῇ is probably equivalent to ὥστε ποιεῖν and "is epexegetic of μεγάλω." (*Ibid.*). The result clause explains how great his miracles are. Thus καὶ is ascensive. We recall that Elijah (if indeed he is to be one of the two witnesses) who will be upon the earth withstanding Antichrist at this time, will be defending himself in this same fashion (Rev.11:5) as once he called down fire at Mt. Carmel (1 Kings 18:30-39). Just as Jannes and Jambres (2 Tim.3:8; Exod.7:11-13) came in in second place in their contest with Moses, so Antichrist will try to duplicate the miracles of the two witnesses. But Antichrist's miracles will deceive no one except the non-elect.

Verse 14 - "And deceiveth them that dwell on the earth by the means of those miracles which he had power to do in the sight of the beast; saying to them that dwell on the earth that they should make an image to the beast, which had the wound by a sword, and did live."

καὶ πλανᾷ τοὺς κατοικοῦντας ἐπὶ τῆς γῆς διὰ τὰ σημεῖα ἃ ἐδόθη αὐτῷ ποιῆσαι ἐνώπιον τοῦ θηρίου, λέγων τοῖς κατοικοῦσιν ἐπὶ τῆς γῆς ποιῆσαι εἰκόνα τῷ θηρίῳ ὃς ἔχει τὴν πληγὴν τῆς μαχαίρης καὶ ἔζησεν.

"and by the signs which it is allowed to work in the presence of the beast, it deceives those who dwell on earth, bidding them make an image for the beast which was wounded by the sword and yet lived; . . . " . . . RSV

καὶ (continuative conjunction) 14.

πλανᾷ (3d.per.sing.pres.act.ind.of πλανάω, customary) 1257.

τοὺς (acc.pl.masc.of the article in agreement with κατοικοῦντας) 9.

κατοικοῦντας (pres.act.part.acc.pl.masc.of κατοικέω, substantival, direct object of πλανᾷ) 242.

ἐπὶ (preposition with the genitive, place description) 47.

τῆς (gen.sing.fem.of the article in agreement with γῆς) 9.

γῆς (gen.sing.fem.of γῆ, place description) 157.

διὰ (preposition with the accusative, cause) 118.

τὰ (acc.pl.neut.of the article in agreement with σημεῖα) 9.

σημεῖα (acc.pl.neut.of σημεῖον, cause) 1005.

ἃ (nom.pl.neut.of ὅς, relative pronoun, subject of ἐδόθη) 65.

αὐτῷ (dat.sing.masc.of αὐτός, indirect object of ἐδόθη) 16.

ποιῆσαι (aor.act.inf.of ποιέω, purpose) 127.

ἐνώπιον (preposition with the genitive of place description) 1798.

τοῦ (gen.sing.neut.of the article in agreement with θηρίου) 9.

θηρίου (gen.sing.neut.of θηρίον, place description) 1951.

λέγων (pres.act.part.nom.sing.masc.of λέγω, adverbial, modal) 66.

τοῖς (dat.pl.masc.of the article in agreement with κατοικοῦσιν) 9.

κατοικοῦσιν (pres.act.part.dat.pl.masc.of κατοικέω, substantival, indirect object of λέγων) 242.

ἐπὶ (preposition with the genitive of place description) 47.

τῆς (gen.sing.fem.of the article in agreement with γῆς) 9.

γῆς (gen.sing.fem.of γῆ, place description) 157.

ποιῆσαι (aor.act.inf.of ποιέω, object of λέγων) 127.

εἰκόνα (acc.sing.fem.of εἰκών, direct object of ποιῆσαι) 1421.

τῷ (dat.sing.neut.of the article in agreement with θηρίῳ) 9.

θηρίῳ (dat.sing.neut.of θηρίον, comparison) 1951.

ὅς (nom.sing.masc.of ὅς, relative pronoun, subject of ἔχει) 65.

ἔχει (3d.per.sing.pres.act.ind.of ἔχω, aoristic) 82.

τὴν (acc.sing.fem.of the article in agreement with πληγὴν) 9.

πληγὴν (acc.sing.fem.of πληγή, direct object of ἔχει) 2421.

τῆς (abl.sing.fem.of the article in agreement with μαχαίρης) 9.

μαχαίρης (abl.sing.fem.of μάχαιρα, means) 896.

καὶ (adversative conjunction) 14.

ἔζησεν (3d.per.sing.aor.act.ind.of ζάω, ingressive) 340.

Translation - "And he deceives those who live upon the earth because of the miracles, power to perform which in the presence of the Beast, has been given to him, by telling the earth dwellers to build a statue to the Beast who had the wound by the sword and yet lives."

Comment: John mixes his aorists and historical presents. Antichrist deceives (πλανᾷ) and the Beast has (ἔχει). διά with the accusative of cause. In the relative clause ἅ is the subject of ἐδόθη. The ὅς relative clause is explanatory or appositive.

We learn from this verse how the Beast was killed — by a sword, (or in battle) — (Rev.6:3-4). Thus in the tribulation period, ungodly men, unwilling to worship the God-Man, Christ Jesus, will erect a statue to the Devil-Man (Rom.1:23). Paul's analysis is accurate.

An illustration of the impatient unwillingness of some prophecy students arose in World War II. It was reported that a large statue of Benito Mussolini had been erected and equipped with a tape recorder, with the result that the image appeared to speak. This fact (if true) was widely hailed at prophetic Bible (!) conferences as evidence that Mussolini was the Beast. Disneyland has a talking image of Abraham Lincoln giving the Gettysburg Address. The miracle which the Antichrist will perform in giving life and power to speak to the Beast's image, will not be achieved by modern technology. The demons do not need modern science.

Verse 15 - "And he had power to give life unto the image of the beast, that the image of the beast should both speak and cause that as many as would not worship the image of the beast should be killed."

καὶ ἐδόθη αὐτῷ δοῦναι πνεῦμα τῇ εἰκόνι τοῦ θηρίου, ἵνα καὶ λαλήσῃ ἡ εἰκὼν τοῦ θηρίου καὶ ποιήσῃ ἵνα ὅσοι ἐὰν μὴ προσκυνήσωσιν τῇ εἰκόνι τοῦ θηρίου ἀποκτανθῶσιν.

"and it was allowed to give breath to the image of the beast so that the image of the beast should even speak, and to cause those who would not worship the image of the beast should be slain." . . . . . . *RSV*

καί (continuative conjunction) 14.

ἐδόθη (3d.per.sing.aor.pass.ind.of δίδωμι, constative) 362.

αὐτῷ (dat.sing.masc.of αὐτός, indirect object of ἐδόθη) 16.

δοῦναι (aor.act.inf.of δίδωμι, noun use, subject of ἐδόθη) 362.

πνεῦμα (acc.sing.neut.of πνεῦμα, direct object of δοῦναι) 83.

τῇ (dat.sing.fem.of the article in agreement with εἰκόνι) 9.

εἰκόνι (dat.sing.fem.of εἰκων, indirect object of δοῦναι) 1421.

τοῦ (gen.sing.neut.of the article in agreement with θηρίου) 9.

θηρίου (gen.sing.neut.of θηρίον, description) 1951.

ἵνα (conjunction with the subjunctive, ecbatic) 114.

καί (ascensive conjunction) 14.

λαλήσῃ (3d.per.sing.aor.act.subj.of λαλέω, ecbatic) 815.

ἡ (nom.sing.fem.of the article in agreement with εἰκων) 9.

εἰκων (nom.sing.fem.of εἰκών, subject of λαλήσῃ and ποιήσῃ) 1421.

τοῦ (gen.sing.neut.of the article in agreement with θηρίου) 9.

θηρίου (gen.sing.neut.of θηρίον, description) 1951.

καί (adjunctive conjunction joining verbs) 14.

ποιήσῃ (3d.per.sing.aor.act.subj.of ποιέω, ecbatic) 127.

ἵνα (conjunction with the subjunctive, ecbatic) 114.

ὅσοι (nom.pl.masc.of ὅσος, subject of ἀποκτανθῶσιν) 660.

ἐάν (conditional particle with the subjuntive in a third-class condition) 363.

μή (negative conjunction with the subjunctive) 87.

προσκυνήσωσιν (3d.per.pl.aor.act.subj.of προσκυνέω, third-class condition) 147.

τῇ (dat.sing.fem.of the article in agreement with εἰκόνι) 9.

εἰκόνι (dat.sing.fem.of εἰκων, personal advantage) 1421.

τοῦ (gen.sing.neut.of the article in agreement with θηρίου) 9.

θηρίου (gen.sing.neut.of θηρίον, description) 1951.

ἀποκτανθῶσιν (3d.per.pl.aor.pass.subj.of ἀποκτείνω, ecbatic) 889.

Translation - "And power to give life to the image of the Beast was given to him, so that the image of the Beast even spoke and decreed that as many as did not worship the image of the Beast should be killed."

Comment: The subject of ἐδόθη is the infinitive δοῦναι. To give life to the statue was the privilege given to Antichrist. The result is two-fold: (1) the image even speaks (ascensive καί) and (2) it decrees that men either worship the statue or die. Thus we have a result clause within a result clause. ὅσοι introduces the indefinite relative clause.

Satan, on his last three and one half year fling, will be extending himself in giving power to his two hellish emissaries who will make the most of it. But their time is short — so very short in comparison with eternity (Rev.12:12; 20:10).

The United Bible Societies' Committee, between the 2d. and 3d. edition of their text,has had second thoughts about ἵνα after ποιήσῃ."The word ἵνα, which seems to be indispensable with ἀποκτανθῶσιν, stands after ποιήσῃ in A P 1006 2065 *al*, and before ἀποκτανθῶσιν in 1511 1854 2073 and the Textus Receptus.

The latter reading, which is supported by inferior external witnesses, is an obvious scribal amelioration of the difficulty occasioned by ἵνα... ἐὰν followed by two verbs in the subjunctive. The omission of ἵνα in Sinaiticus 046 1611 1859 *al* appears to be accidental, resulting in a shift of subject ("that even the image of the beast should speak; and he shall cause that as many as . . . should be killed." ASVmg). In view of the multiplicity of readings, no one of which clearly explains the origin of the others, a majority of the Committee thought it best to include ἵνα in the text, but to enclose the word within square brackets." (Metzger, *A Textual Commentary on the Greek New Testament*, 750, 751).

Verse 16 - "And he causeth all, both small and great, rich and poor, free and bond, to receive a mark in their right hand, or in their foreheads."

καὶ ποιεῖ πάντας, τοὺς μικροὺς καὶ τοὺς μεγάλους, καὶ τοὺς πλουσίους καὶ τοὺς πτωχούς, καὶ τοὺς ἐλευθέρους καὶ τοὺς δούλους, ἵνα δῶσιν αὐτοῖς χάραγμα ἐπὶ τῆς χειρὸς αὐτῶν τῆς δεξιᾶς ἢ ἐπὶ τὸ μέτωπον αὐτῶν,

"Also it causes all, both small and great, both rich and poor, both free and slave, to be marked on the right hand or the forehead, . . . " . . . RSV

καὶ (continuative conjunction) 14.
ποιεῖ (3d.per.sing.pres.act.ind.of ποιέω, futuristic) 127.
πάντας (acc.pl.masc.of πᾶς, direct object of ποιεῖ) 67.
τοὺς (acc.pl.masc.of the article in agreement with μικροὺς) 9.
μικροὺς (acc.pl.masc.of μικρός, apposition) 901.
καὶ (adjunctive conjunction joining nouns) 14.
τοὺς (acc.pl.masc.of the article in agreement with μεγάλους) 9.
μεγάλους (acc.pl.masc.of μέγας, apposition) 184.
καὶ (adjunctive conjunction joining nouns) 14.
τοὺς (acc.pl.masc.of the article in agreement with πλουσίους) 9.
πλουσίους (acc.pl.masc.of πλούσιος, apposition) 1306.
καὶ (adjunctive conjunction joining nouns) 14.
τοὺς (acc.pl.masc.of the article in agreement with πτωχοὺς) 9.
πτωχούς (acc.pl.masc.of πτωχός, apposition) 423.
καὶ (adjunctive conjunction joining nouns) 14.
τοὺς (acc.pl.masc.of the article in agreement with ἐλευθέρους) 9.
ἐλευθέρους (acc.pl.masc.of ἐλεύθερος, apposition) 1245.
καὶ (adjunctive conjunction joining nouns) 14.
τοὺς (acc.pl.masc.of the article in agreement with δούλους) 9.
δούλους (acc.pl.masc.of δοῦλος, apposition) 725.
ἵνα (conjunction with the subjunctive, sub-final) 114.
δῶσιν (3d.per.pl.aor.act.subj.of δίδωμι, purpose/result) 362.
αὐτοῖς (dat.pl.masc.of αὐτός, indirect object of δῶσιν) 16.
χάραγμα (acc.sing.neut.of χάραγμα, direct object of δῶσιν) 3420.
ἐπὶ (preposition with the genitive, place description) 47.
τῆς (gen.sing.fem.of the article in agreement with χειρὸς) 9.
χειρὸς (gen.sing.fem.of χείρ, place description) 308.

αὐτῶν (gen.pl.masc.of αὐτός, possession) 16.
τῆς (gen.sing.fem.of the article in agreement with δεξιᾶς) 9.
δεξιᾶς (gen.sing.fem.of δεξιός, in agreement with χειρὸς) 502.
ἤ (disjunctive particle) 465.
ἐπὶ (preposition with the accusative, extent, rest) 47.
τό (acc.sing.neut.of the article in agreement with μέτωπον) 9.
μέτωπον (acc.sing.neut.of μέταπον, extent, rest) 5356.
αὐτῶν (gen.pl.masc.of αὐτός, possession) 16.

Translation - *"And he will decree that all, the small and the great and the rich and the poor and the free and the slaves be given a mark upon their right hand or upon their forehead."*

Comment: The syntax is tangled here. We need an object infinitive such as λαβεῖν with πάντας as an accusative of general reference. "He will decree that all should receive . . . κ.τ.λ." As it is, παντὰς is the object of ποιεῖ and the substantives, tied together by adjunctive καὶ, are in apposition. Thus all — small, great, rich, poor, free and bond must receive the mark. αὐτοῖς refers to μικροὺς, μεγάλους, etc., but it does not conform in case. Literally, as written, it translates "he will decree that all should give to them, the rich, poor, etc., a mark . . . κ.τ.λ." All who? The result of the decree of the Antichrist is that all unregenerates will be marked with his mark. The purpose of the mark is stated in verse 17. Note ἐπὶ τῆς χειρὸς and ἐπὶ τὸ μέτωπον, with little reason to distinguish between the genitive and the accusative. *Cf.*#3420 for the nature of the mark. Will it be stamped, printed, engraved, burned or by what method imposed upon those who have it?

Of course the elect will not receive it, either because they are aware of the consequences of receiving it (Rev.19:20) or because in some other way they are delivered from receiving it. No doubt the two witnesses will warn all who are about to receive it of the eternal consequences. The immediate consequences of rejecting the mark is exclusion from the market.

Verse 17 - *"And that no man might buy or sell save he that had the mark, or the name of the beast, or the number of his name."*

καὶ ἵνα μή τις δύνηται ἀγοράσαι ἤ πωλῆσαι εἰ μὴ ὁ ἔχων τὸ χάραγμα, τὸ ὄνομα τοῦ θηρίου ἤ τὸν ἀριθμὸν τοῦ ὀνόματος αὐτοῦ.

"so that no one can buy or sell unless he has the mark, that is, the name of the beast or the number of his name." . . . RSV

καὶ (adjunctive conjunction joining ἵνα clauses) 14.
ἵνα (conjunction with the subjunctive, sub-final) 114.
μή (negative conjunction with the subjunctive) 87.
τις (nom.sing.masc.of τις, indefinite pronoun, subject of δύνηται) 486.
δύνηται (3d.per.sing.pres.act.subj.of δύναμαι, purpose/result) 289.
ἀγοράσαι (aor.act.inf.of ἀγοράζω, complementary) 1085.

ἤ (disjunctive particle) 465.

πωλῆσαι (aor.act.inf.of πωλέω, complementary) 892.

εἰ (conditional particle in an elliptical condition) 337.

μὴ (negative conjunction in an elliptical condition) 87.

ὁ (nom.sing.masc.of the article in agreement with ἔχων) 9.

ἔχων (pres.act.part.nom.sing.masc.of ἔχω, substantival, in an elliptical condition) 82.

τὸ (acc.sing.neut.of the article in agreement with χάραγμα) 9.

χάραγμα (acc.sing.neut.of χάραγμα, direct object of ἔχων) 3420.

τὸ (acc.sing.neut.of the article in agreement with ὄνομα) 9.

ὄνομα (acc.sing.neut.of ὄνομα, direct object of ἔχων) 108.

τοῦ (gen.sing.neut.of the article in agreement with θηρίου) 9.

θηρίου (gen.sing.neut.of θηρίον, description) 1951.

ἤ (disjunctive particle) 465.

τὸν (acc.sing.masc.of the article in agreement with ἀριθμὸν) 9.

ἀριθμὸν (acc.sing.masc.of ἀριθμός, direct object of ἔχων) 2278.

τοῦ (gen.sing.neut.of the article in agreement with ὀνόματος) 9.

ὀνόματος (gen.sing.neut.of ὄνομα, description) 108.

αὐτοῦ (gen.sing.masc.of αὐτός, possession) 16.

Translation - "and that no one should be permitted to buy or to sell except the one who has the mark, the name of the Beast or the number of his name."

Comment: The ἵνα μὴ clause depends upon ποιεῖ (verse 16) and is coordinate with the ἵνα δῶσιν clause. The Beast's decree is two-fold: (1) everyone must take his mark and (2) no one shall be permitted to buy or sell unless he does take the mark. Thus Christians and those elect who, at the middle of the tribulation week, have not yet been saved (Rev.10:7) will be excluded from all market transactions.

Mt.6:11 will have special significance then, since no Christian will be able to buy food.

This dictatorial control of the world's economy is consistent with the picture of internal and international trade in chapters 17 and 18, which represent the Beast in control of world commerce. In the light of these passages Mt.6:19-21 becomes exceptionally good advice.

The recent decontrol of the banking industry in the United States has made bankers careless about making high risk and high interest loans, particularly to third world countries, with the up-front assumption that they will not be repaid. As a result American banks, which may be in trouble, must turn to the federal government for rescue from bankruptcy. In order to protect the Amerian dollar in foreign exchange markets, thus to support American exports, and through them, full employment at home, our government must comply. This financial chaos — chaos which always results when any industry is allowed to resort to social darwinism, sets the stage for the kind of problem in the international banking industry that will make it easy for Antichrist to take control with his mark. Thus economists who are knowledgeable in the field of international economics are not surprized at the prediction of Revelation 13; indeed those economists who are unsaved and destined to remain so may look forward in hope to the day when global control of economics will be the rule. Thus it is not difficult to understand why the Beast will be so universally received, except by God's elect. The wisdom that will allow the saints to understand is spelled out in

Verse 18 - "Here is wisdom. Let him that hath understanding count the number of the beast; for it is the number of a man: and his number is six hundred, threescore and six."

Ὧδε ἡ σοφία ἐστίν. ὁ ἔχων νοῦν φηφισάτω τὸν ἀριθμὸν τοῦ θηρίου, ἀριυμὸς γὰρ ἀνθρώπου ἐστίν, καὶ ὁ ἀριθμὸς αὐτοῦ ἑξακόσιοι ἑξήκοντα ἕξ.

"This calls for wisdom: let him who has understanding reckon the number of the beast, for it is a human number, its number is six hundred and sixty-six."... RSV

Ὧδε (local adverb) 766.
ἡ (nom.sing.fem.of the article in agreement with σοφία) 9.
σοφία (nom.sing.fem.of σοφία, subject of ἐστίν) 934.
ἐστίν (3d.per.sing.pres.ind.of εἰμί, aoristic) 86.
ὁ (nom.sing.masc.of the article in agreement with ἔχων) 9.
ἔχων (pres.act.part.nom.sing.masc.of ἔχω, substantival, subject of φηφισάτω) 82.
νοῦν (acc.sing.masc.of νοῦς, direct object of ἔχων) 2928.
φηφισάτω (3d.per.sing.aor.act.impv.of φηφίζω, command) 2532.
τὸν (acc.sing.masc.of the article in agreement with ἀριθμὸν) 9.
ἀριθμὸν (acc.sing.masc.of ἀριθμός, direct object of φηφισάτω) 2278.
τοῦ (gen.sing.neut.of the article in agreement with θηρίου) 9.
θηρίου (gen.sing.neut.of θηρίον, description) 1951.
ἀριθμὸς (nom.sing.masc.of ἀριθμός, predicate nominative) 2278.
γὰρ (causal conjunction) 105.
ἀνθρώπου (gen.sing.masc.of ἄνθρωπος, designation) 341.
ἐστίν (3d.per.sing.pres.ind.of εἰμί, aoristic) 86.
καὶ (continuative conjunction) 14.
ὁ (nom.sing.masc.of the article in agreement with ἀριθμὸς) 9.
ἀριθμὸς (nom.sing.masc.of ἀριθμός, subject of ἐστίν understood) 2278.
αὐτοῦ (gen.sing.masc.of αὐτός, possession) 16.

#5388 ἑξακόσια (numeral).

King James Version

six hundred - Rev.13:18; 14:20.

Revised Standard Version

six hundred - Rev.13:18; 14:20.

Meaning: Six hundred. The number of the Beast - 666 - Rev.13:18; in the distance measurement of Rev.14:20.

ἐξήκοντα (numeral) 1036.
ἕξ (numeral) 1220.

Translation - *"Here is the test of your ingenuity. The one with a capacity to understand must compute the number of the Beast; because it is a human number; and his number is six hundred and sixty six."*

Comment: John gives end-time Christians a hint that will help them to identify the Beast, as though his other characteristics were insufficient to identify him. The shrewd thinker will be able to solve the problem. His number is a human number. ἀνθρώπου, without the article is a descriptive genitive. The number 666 is one digit short of 777. For numeralologists (and this writer has often thought that Biblical numeralology is probably overplayed), seven is the number of perfection. Hence six is a human number. The culmination of "man's day" (1 Cor.4:3) will be the "Man of Sin" (2 Thess.2:3) whose number indicates that like all unregenerate men, he is a braggart and an ultimate loser.

The United Bible Societies' Committee supports the 666 number with a B degree of certitude. "Instead of ἐξήκοντα which is strongly supported by p47 Sinaiticus A P 046 051 all extant minuscules itgig vg syrph,h cop sa,bo arm *al* δέκα is read by C some manuscripts known to Irenaeus (who, however, says that 666 is found "in all good and ancient copies" and is "attested by those who had themselves seen John face to face") and Tyconius pt. According to Tischendorf's 8th ed., the numeral 616 was also read by two minuscule manuscripts which unfortunately are no longer extant (nos. 5 and 11: *Cf.* C.R.Gregory, *Prolegomena,* p.676). When Greek letters are used as numerals the difference between 666 and 616 is merely a change from ξ to ι (666 equals χξς and 616 equals χιζ). Perhaps the change was intentional, seeing that the Greek form Neron Caesaw written in Hebrew characters . . . is equivalent to 666, whereas the Latin form Nero Caesar . . . is equivalent to 616." Metzger, *A Textual Commentary on the Greek New Testament,* 751, 752).

With all of the other characteristics of the Beast there is small doubt that any Christian who sees him would fail to recognize him, with or without the number.

Chapter XIV does not describe the countdown of God's clock in the closing week of "the times of the Gentiles." Like Rev.1:1-20; 4:1-5:14; 7:1-8:1; 8:2-6; 10:1-11:14; 12:1-15:8, Chapter 14 1:1-16:1; 17:1-20:15 all contain valuable information which we need to complete the detailed picture of the action in the passages omitted from the above list where God's clock is running. The last two chapters describe the heavenly scene after the millenium, except for Rev.22:6-21 which comprise the epilogue.

The Song of the 144,000

(Revelation 14:1-5)

Revelation 14:1 - "And I looked and, lo, a Lamb stood on the mount Sion, and with him an hundred forty and four thousand, having his Father's name written in their foreheads."

Καὶ εἶδον, καὶ ἰδοὺ τὸ ἀρνίον ἑστὸς ἐπὶ τὸ ὄρος Σιών, καὶ μετ᾽ αὐτοῦ ἑκατὸν τεσσαράκοντα τέσσαρες χιλιάδες ἔχουσαι τὸ ὄνομα αὐτοῦ καὶ τὸ ὄνομα τοῦ πατρὸς αὐτοῦ γεγραμμένον ἐπὶ τῶν μετώπων αὐτῶν.

"Then I looked, and lo, on Mount Zion stood the Lamb, and with him a hundred and forty-four thousand who had his name and his Father's name written on their foreheads." . . . RSV

Καὶ (continuative conjunction) 14.

εἶδον (1st.per.sing.aor.act.ind.of ὁράω, constative) 144.

καὶ (continuative conjunction) 14.

ἰδοὺ (exclamation) 95.

τὸ (nom.sing.neut.of the article in agreement with ἀρνίον) 9.

ἀρνίον (nom.sing.neut.of ἀρνίον, nominative absolute) 2923.

ἑστὸς (perf.act.part.nom.sing.neut.of ἵστημι, adjectival, predicate position, restrictive, in agreement with ἀρνίον) 180.

ἐπὶ (preposition with the accusative, rest) 47.

τὸ (acc.sing.neut.of the article in agreement with ὄρος) 9.

ὄρος (acc.sing.neut.of ὄρος, extent, rest) 357.

Σιών (acc.sing.neut.of Σιών, apposition) 1345.

καὶ (adjunctive conjunction joining prepositional phrases) 14.

μετ᾽ (preposition with the genitive, accompaniment) 50.

αὐτοῦ (gen.sing.masc.of αὐτός, accompaniment) 16.

ἑκατὸν (numeral) 1035.

τεσσαράκοντα (numeral) 333.

τέσσαρες (numeral) 1508.

χιλιάδες (nom.pl.fem.of χιλιάς) 2536.

ἔχουσαι (pres.act.part.nom.pl.fem.of ἔχω, adverbial, circumstantial) 82.

τὸ (acc.sing.neut.of the article in agreement with ὄνομα) 9.

ὄνομα (acc.sing.neut.of ὄνομα, direct object of ἔχουσαι) 108.

αὐτοῦ (gen.sing.masc.of αὐτός, possession) 16.

καὶ (adjunctive conjunction joining nouns) 14.

τὸ (acc.sing.neut.of the article in agreement with ὄνομα) 9.

ὄνομα (acc.sing.neut.of ὄνομα, direct object of ἔχουσαι) 108.

τοῦ (gen.sing.masc.of the article in agreement with πατρὸς) 9.

πατρὸς (gen.sing.masc.of πατήρ, description) 238.

αὐτοῦ (gen.sing.masc.of αὐτός, relationship) 16.

γεγραμμένον (perf.pass.part.acc.sing.neut.of γράφω, adjectival, predicate position, restrictive, in agreement with ὄνομα) 156.

ἐπὶ (preposition with the genitive of place description) 47.

τῶν (gen.pl.neut.of the article in agreement with μετώπων) 9.

μετώπων (gen.pl.neut.of μέτωπον, place description) 5356.

αὐτῶν (gen.pl.masc.of αὐτός, possession) 16.

Translation - "And I watched, and look! The Lamb standing upon Mount Zion, and with Him one hundred forty-four thousand, having His name and the name of His Father written upon their foreheads."

Comment: The time point is immediately after the second coming of Messiah. (Zech.14:1-4*ff*). This is the third time that we have met the 144,000. They were selected and sealed as God's property in Rev.7:1-8. They fled from the Beast to the desert to be fed for 1260 days in Rev.12:6. Now they have been rescued from the Gentile armies which will be determined to wipe out the Jews and they stand upon Mount Zion in Jerusalem, as Messiah takes His throne (2 Sam.7:10-17; Luke 1:30-33).

Also Babylon is said to have fallen (Rev.14:8). We have a more detailed picture of this in Rev.18:1-24. Messiah's nation, 12,000 out of each of twelve tribes, were sealed seven years before. They will be the nucleus of the nation which God promised to Abraham.

Verse 2 - "And I heard a voice from heaven, as the voice of many waters, and as the voice of a great thunder: and I heard the voice of harpers harping with their harps."

καὶ ἤκουσα φωνὴν ἐκ τοῦ οὐρανοῦ ὡς φωνὴν ὑδάτων πολλῶν καὶ ὡς φωνὴν βροντῆς μεγάλης, καὶ ἡ φωνὴ ἣν ἤκουσα ὡς κιθαρῳδῶν κιθαριζόντων ἐν ταῖς κιθάραις αὐτῶν.

"And I heard a voice from heaven like the sound of many waters and like the sound of loud thunder; the voice I heard was like the sound of harpers playing on their harps, . . . " . . . RSV

καὶ (continuative conjunction) 14.

ἤκουσα (1st.per.sing.aor.act.ind.of ἀκούω, ingressive) 148.

φωνὴν (acc.sing.fem.of φωνή, direct object of ἤκουσα) 222.

ἐκ (preposition with the ablative, source) 19.

τοῦ (abl.sing.masc.of the article in agreement with οὐρανοῦ) 9.

οὐρανοῦ (abl.sing.masc.of οὐρανός, source) 254.

ὡς (comparative particle) 128.

φωνὴν (acc.sing.fem.of φωνή, adverbial accusative) 222.

ὑδάτων (gen.pl.neut.of ὕδωρ, description) 301.

πολλῶν (gen.pl.neut.of πολύς, in agreement with ὑδάτων) 228.

καὶ (adjunctive conjunction joining comparative phrases) 14.

ὡς (comparative particle) 128.

βροντῆς (gen.sing.fem.of βροντή, description) 2117.

μεγάλης (gen.sing.fem.of μέγας, in agreement with βροντῆς) 184.

καὶ (continuative conjunction) 14.
ἡ (nom.sing.fem.of the article in agreement with φωνή) 9.
φωνή (nom.sing.fem.of φωνή, subject of ἦν understood) 222.
ἦν (acc.sing.fem.of ὅς, relative pronoun, direct object of ἤκουσα) 65.
ἤκουσα (1st.per.sing.aor.act.ind.of ἀκούω, constative) 148.
ὡς (comparative particle) 128.

#5389 κιθαρῳδῶν (abl.pl.masc.of κιθαρωδός, comparison).

King James Version

harper - Rev.14:2; 18:22.

Revised Standard Version

harper - Rev.14:2; 18:22.

Meaning: Cf. κιθάρα (#4232), κιθαρίζω (#4233). κιθάρα plus ᾠδό, a contraction from αἰαδός - "a singer." Hence, κιθαρῳδός is one who sings and accompanies himself on a harp - Rev.14:2; 18:22. In an ablative of comparison in Rev.14:2; used with other musicians playing other instruments in Rev.18:22.

κιθαριζόντων (pres.act.part.abl.pl.masc.of κιθαρίζω, adjectival, predicate position, restrictive, in agreement with κιθαρῳδῶν). 4233.
ἐν (preposition with the instrumental, means) 80.
ταῖς (instru.pl.fem.of the article in agreement with κιθάραις) 9.
κιθάραις (instru.pl.fem.of κιθάρα, means) 4232.
αὐτῶν (gen.pl.masc.of αὐτός, possession) 16.

Translation - "And I began to hear a voice from heaven that sounded like a roar of many waters, and like the crash of mighty thunder, and the sound which I heard sounded like singers accompanying themselves on their harps."

Comment: This is one of the most beautiful sound descriptions in the Revelation. Harmony, mighty volume, crashing detonation of heavenly artillery; the majestic roar of a heavenly Niagra. *Cf.* Rev.1;15, with which John introduced us to the Ancient of Days and Rev.19:6, which pictures Him as the King Who has returned. Rev.19:6 seems clearly parallel to Rev.14:2 and places the time at the second coming of Messiah.

Verse 3 - "And they sung as it were a new song before the throne, and before the four beasts, and the elders: and no man could learn that song but the hundred and forty four thousand, which were redeemed from the earth."

καὶ ᾄδουσιν (ὡς) ᾠδὴν καινὴν ἐνώπιον τοῦ θρόνου καὶ ἐνώπιον τῶν τεσσάρων ζῴων καὶ τῶν πρεσβυτέρων. καὶ οὐδεὶς ἐδύνατο μαθεῖν τὴν ᾠδὴν εἰ μὴ αἱ ἑκατὸν τεσσαράκοντα τέσσαρες χιλιάδες, οἱ ἠγορασμένοι ἀπὸ τῆς γῆς.

"and they sing a new song before the throne and before the four living creatures and before the elders. No one could learn that song except the hundred

and forty-four thousand who had been redeemed from the earth." . . . RSV

καὶ (continuative conjunction) 14.

ᾄδουσιν (3d.per.pl.pres.act.ind.of ᾄδω, historical) 4519.

ὡς (comparative particle) 128.

ᾠδὴν (acc.sing.fem.of ᾠδή, direct object of ᾄδουσιν) 4518.

καινὴν (acc.sing.fem.of καινός, in agreement with ᾠδὴν) 812.

ἐνώπιον (preposition with the genitive of place description) 1798.

τοῦ (gen.sing.masc.of the article in agreement with θρόνου) 9.

θρόνου (gen.sing.masc.of θρόνος, place description) 519.

καὶ (adjunctive conjunction joining prepositional phrases) 14.

ἐνώπιον (preposition with the genitive of place description) 1798.

τῶν (gen.pl.neut.of the article in agreement with ζῴων) 9.

τεσσάρων (gen.pl.neut.of τέσσαρες, in agreement with ζῴων) 1508.

ζῴων (gen.pl.neut.of ζῷον, place description) 5086.

καὶ (adjunctive conjunction joining nouns) 14.

τῶν (gen.pl.masc.of the article in agreement with πρεσβυτέρων) 9.

πρεσβυτέρων (gen.pl.masc.of πρεσβύτερος, place description) 1141.

καὶ (continuative conjunction) 14.

οὐδεὶς (nom.sing.masc.of οὐδείς, subject of ἐδύνατο) 446.

ἐδύνατο (3d.per.sing.imp.mid.ind.of δύναμαι, progressive description) 289.

μαθεῖν (aor.act.inf.of μανθάνω, complementary) 794.

τὴν (acc.sing.fem.of the article in agreement with ᾠδὴν) 9.

ᾠδὴν (acc.sing.fem.of ᾠδή, direct object of μαθεῖν) 4518.

εἰ (conditional particle in an elliptical condition) 337.

μὴ (negative conjunction in an elliptical condition) 87.

οἱ (nom.pl.masc.of the article in agreement with χιλιάδες) 9.

ἑκατὸν (numeral) 1035.

τεσσαράκοντα (numeral) 333.

τέσσαρες (numeral) 1508.

χιλιάδες (nom.pl.masc.of χιλιάς, subject of ellided verb) 2536.

οἱ (nom.pl.masc.of the article in agreement with ἠγορασμένοι) 9.

ἠγορασμένοι (perf.pass.part.nom.pl.masc.of ἀγοράζω, adjectival, emphatic attributive position, ascriptive, in agreement with χιλιάδες) 1085.

ἀπὸ (preposition with the ablative of separation) 70.

τῆς (abl.sing.fem.of the article in agreement with γῆς) 9.

γῆς (abl.sing.fem.of γῆ, separation) 157.

Translation - "And they sing what sounds like a new song before the throne and in the presence of the four living creatures and the elders; but no man was ever able to learn the song except the hundred and forty-four thousand who had been redeemed from the earth."

Comment: Apparently the singers of verse 2 teach the song to the 144,000 Jews who alone are able to learn it. It is their song. Another group of the redeemed in Chapter 15 sing the song of Moses and the song of the Lamb. *Cf.* comment. This song of Rev.14:3 is not the song of Moses, which is not a new song. *Cf.*

Exodus 15:1. This song is for the exclusive use of redeemed Israel in the Kingdom Age which is about to begin.

Verse 4 - "These are they which were not defiled with women; for they are virgins. These are they which follow the Lamb whithersoever he goeth. These were redeemed from among men, being the first fruits unto God and to the Lamb."

οὗτοί εἰσιν οἱ μετὰ γυναικῶν οὐκ ἐμολύνθησαν παρθένοι γάρ εἰσιν. οὗτοι οἱ ἀκολουθοῦντες τῷ ἀρνίῳ ὅπου ἂν ὑπάγῃ. οὗτοι ἠγοράσθησαν ἀπὸ τῶν ἀνθρώπων ἀπαρχὴ τῷ θεῷ καὶ τῷ ἀρνίῳ,

"It is these who have not defiled themselves with women, for they are chaste; it is these who follow the Lamb wherever he goes; these have been redeemed from mankind as first fruits for God and the Lamb, . . . RSV

οὗτοὶ (nom.pl.masc.of οὗτος, subject of εἰσιν) 93.

εἰσιν (3d.per.pl.pres.ind.of εἰμί, aoristic) 86.

οἱ (nom.pl.masc.of ὅς, relative pronoun, subject of ἐμολύνθησαν) 65.

μετὰ (preposition with the genitive of accompaniment) 50.

γυναικῶν (gen.pl.fem.of γυνή, accompaniment) 103.

οὐκ (negative conjunction with the indicative) 130.

ἐμολύνθησαν (3d.per.pl.aor.pass.ind.of μολύνω, culminative) 4171.

παρθένοι (nom.pl.masc.of παρθένος, predicate nominative) 120.

γάρ (causal conjunction) 105.

εἰσιν (3d.per.pl.pres.ind.of εἰμί, aoristic) 86.

οὗτοι (nom.pl.masc.of οὗτος, subject of εἰσιν understood) 93.

οἱ (nom.pl.masc.of the article in agreement with ἀκολουθοῦντες) 9.

ἀκολουθοῦντες (pres.act.part.nom.pl.masc.of ἀκολουθέω, substantival, predicate nominative) 394.

τῷ (dat.sing.neut.of the article in agreement with ἀρνίῳ) 9.

ἀρνίῳ (dat.sing.neut.of ἀρνίον, personal advantage) 2923.

ὅπου (loc.adverb with the subjunctive in an indefinite local clause, future action) 592.

ἂν (contingent particle with the subjunctive in an indefinite local clause) 205.

ὑπάγῃ (3d.per.sing.pres.act.subj.of ὑπάγω, indefinite local clause) 364.

οὗτοι (nom.pl.masc.of οὗτος, subject of ἠγοράσθησαν) 93.

ἠγοράσθησαν (3d.per.pl.aor.pass.ind.of ἀγοράζω, culminative) 1085.

ἀπὸ (preposition with the ablative, source) 70.

τῶν (abl.pl.masc.of the article in agreement with ἀνρθώπων) 9.

ἀνθρώπων (abl.pl.masc.of ἄνθρωπος, source) 341.

ἀπαρχὴ (nom.sing.fem.of ἀπαρχή, apposition) 3946.

τῷ (dat.sing.masc.of the article in agreement with θεῷ) 9.

θεῷ (dat.sing.masc.of θεός, personal advantage) 124.

καὶ (adjunctive conjunction joining nouns) 14.

τῷ (dat.sing.neut.of the article in agreement with ἀρνίῳ) 9.

ἀρνίῳ (dat.sing.neut.of ἀρνίον, personal advantage) 2923.

Translation - "These are those who were not defiled with women; for they are virgins. These are they who always follow the Lamb wherever He may go. These have been redeemed from men as firstfruits to God and to the Lamb."

Comment: οὗτοί is deictic in all instances. The text is pointing specifically to this special group of 144,000 Jews, selected in Rev.7:1-8 at the beginning of the week, protected during the last half of the week (Rev.12:6) and now saved at the end of the tribulation week. They are the nucleus for national Israel during the new Kingdom age.

The view which has been suggested in these pages (*supra*, p.91), that half of these people are women and thus that we have 72,000 couples who will marry and produce the new generation of Jews, is clouded by the language of this verse. These are said not to have defiled themselves with women (μετὰ γυναικῶν). Does this statement refer only to the men in the group? Or are they all men? If so, where will they find wives to produce the next generation? This is not clear. Nor need it be, since we can trust the promise of God to Abraham to make his seed as numerous as the sands of the sea and the stars of the heavens. The fact that the 144,000 will not have sex experience guarantees a pure blood stream. They will enter into the Kingdom without death or subsequent glorification, and they will populate the land of Israel during the millenium.

Some premillenialists have taught that the Levitical offerings will be resumed in the Kingdom age — a monstrous thought in view of Hebrews 5-10, which has brought undeserved reproach upon premillenialism. Of course the Levitical offerings will never again be resumed. These people will follow the Lamb. They are the first fruits to God and Christ in the new nation Israel, under their Messiah King. In them God will fulfill all of the covenant promises which He made to Abraham, Isaac, Jacob and David. Their children and children's children will be saved in the Kingdom age. This is what the everlasting gospel (verse 6) is for.

Verse 5 - "And in their mouth was found no guile: for they are without fault before the throne of God."

καὶ ἐν τῷ στόματι αὐτῶν οὐχ εὑρέθη ψεῦδος, ἄμωμοί εἰσιν.

"and in their mouth no lie was found, for they are spotless." . . . *RSV*

καὶ (continuative conjunction) 14.
ἐν (preposition with the locative, place) 80.
τῷ (loc.sing.neut.of the article in agreement with στόματι) 9.
στόματι (loc.sing.neut.of στόμα, place) 344.
αὐτῶν (gen.pl.masc.of αὐτός, possession) 16.
οὐχ (negative conjunction with the indicative) 130.
εὑρέθη (3d.per.sing.aor.pass.ind.of εὑρίσκω, constative) 79.
ψεῦδος (nom.sing.neut.of ψεῦδος, subject of εὑρέθη) 2388.
ἄμωμοί (nom.pl.masc.of ἄμωμος, predicate adjective) 4460.
εἰσιν (3d.per.pl.pres.ind.of εἰμί, aoristic) 86.

Translation - "And in their mouth was found no lie; they are spotless."

Comment: This small nucleus which will become a mighty nation under the rule of Messiah has kept God's laws. No adultery; no falsehood; they are faultless. *Cf.* Jer.24:7; Zeph.3:13; Jer.31:31-34. The law of God, in the hand of Moses, so disastrously transgressed by Israel when it was first given, will be obeyed by the new Israeli mucleus.

The Messages of the Three Angels

(Revelation 14:6-13)

Verse 6 - "And I saw another angel fly in the midst of heaven, having the everlasting gospel to preach unto them that dwell on the earth, and to every nation, and kindred, and tongue and people."

Καὶ εἶδον ἄλλον ἄγγελον πετόμενον ἐν μεσουρανήματι, ἔχοντα εὐαγγέλιον αἰώνιον εὐαγγελίσαι ἐπὶ τοὺς καθημένους ἐπὶ τῆς γῆς καὶ ἐπὶ πᾶν ἔθνος καὶ φυλὴν καὶ γλῶσσαν καὶ λαόν,

"Then I saw another angel flying in midheaven, with an eternal gospel to proclaim to those who dwell on earth, to every nation and tribe and tongue and people;" . . . RSV

Καὶ (continuative conjunction) 14.

εἶδον (1st.per.sing.aor.act.ind.of ὁράω constative) 144.

ἄλλον (acc.sing.masc.of ἄλλος in agreement with ἄγγελον) 198.

ἄγγελον (acc.sing.masc.of ἄγγελος, direct object of εἶδον) 96.

πετόμενον (pres.mid.part.acc.sing.masc.of πετάομαι, adjectival, predicate position, restrictive, in agreement with ἄγγελον) 5346.

ἐν (preposition with the locative of place) 80.

μεσουρανήματι (loc.sing.neut.of μεσουράνημα, place)5367.

ἔχοντα (pres.act.part.acc.sing.masc.of ἔχω, adjectival, predicate position, restrictive, in agreement with ἄγγελον) 82.

εὐαγγέλιον (acc.sing.neut.of εὐαγγέλιον, direct object of ἔχοντα) 405.

αἰώνιον (acc.sing.neut.of αἰώνιος, in agreement with εὐαγγέλιον) 1255.

εὐαγγελίσαι (aor.act.inf.of εὐαγγελίζω, purpose) 909.

ἐπὶ (preposition with the accusative, extent) 47.

τοὺς (acc.pl.masc.of the article in agreement with καθημένους) 9.

καθημένους (pres.mid.part.acc.pl.masc.of κάθημαι, substantival, direct object of εὐαγγελίσαι) 377.

ἐπὶ (preposition with the genitive of place description) 47.

τῆς (gen.sing.fem.of the article in agreement with γῆς) 9.

γῆς (gen.sing.fem.of γῆ, place description) 157.

καὶ (adjunctive conjunction joining prepositional phrases) 14.

ἐπὶ (preposition with the accusative of extent) 47.

πᾶν (acc.sing.neut.of πᾶς, in agreement with ἔθνος, φυλὴν, γλῶσσαν and λαόν) 67

ἔθνος (acc.sing.neut.of ἔθνος, extent) 376.
καὶ (adjunctive conjunction joining nouns) 14.
φυλὴν (acc.sing.fem.of φυλή, extent) 1313.
καὶ (adjunctive conjunction joining nouns) 14.
γλῶσσαν (acc.sing.fem.of γλῶσσα, extent) 1846.
καὶ (adjunctive conjunction joining nouns) 14.
λαόν (acc.sing.masc.of λαός, extent) 110.

Translation - "And I saw another angel flying in the vault of heaven having an everlasting gospel in order to evangelize those who dwell on the earth and to preach to every nation and tribe and tongue and people."

Comment: Robertson (*Grammar*, 892) points to Rev.10:1; 13:1,11; 14:6; 18:1; 20:1; Acts 19:35 *al*, where the present participle follows εἶδον. The participle is adjectival, defining the object of the verb of sensation. John saw the angel (direct object) flying (πετόμενον) and having (ἔχοντα) the the gospel to preach.

This eternal gospel which the angel has is to be preached to the earth dwellers who will survive the Battle of Armageddon and the judgments upon the earth which will accompany it. They will beget children and children's children in every nation, tribe, tongue and people. Not all of these Gentiles will be saved as Rev.20:7-15 makes clear, but many will. It is unlikely that the infant mortality rate will be as high as it has been in the past, when the earth was under the curse. Those who accepted the mark of the Beast before the second coming, who are not killed at the second coming, and who thus may survive to live into the millenium will not accept this everlasting gospel. There will be no second chance for them. But their children may be saved. The picture of the Great White Throne judgment at the end of the millenium indicates that some who appear before the Judge upon the throne will have been saved. During the course of the Kingdom Age the blessed story of Calvary will still be told and the Holy Spirit will still be effectually calling the elect.

We learn what the angel is saying in

Verse 7 - "Saying with a loud voice, Fear God, and give glory to him: for the hour of his judgment is come: and worship him that made heaven and earth, and the sea, and the fountains of waters."

λέγων ἐν φωνῇ μεγάλῃ, Φοβήθητε τὸν θεὸν καὶ δότε αὐτῷ δόξαν, ὅτι ἦλθεν ἡ ὥρα τῆς κρίσεως αὐτοῦ, καὶ προσκυνήσατε τῷ ποιήσαντι τὸν οὐρανὸν καὶ τὴν γῆν καὶ θάλασσαν καὶ πηγὰς ὑδάτων.

"and he said with a loud voice, 'Fear God and give him glory, for the hour of his judgment has come; and worship him who made heaven and earth, the sea and the fountains of waters.' " . . . RSV

λέγων (pres.act.part.nom.sing.masc.of λέγω, recitative) 66.
ἐν (preposition with the instrumental, means) 80.
φωνῇ (instru.sing.fem.of φωνή, means) 222.
μεγάλῃ (instru.sing.fem.of μέγας, in agreement with φωνῇ) 184.

Φοβήθητε (2d.per.pl.aor.mid.impv.of φοβέομαι, command) 101.

τὸν (acc.sing.masc.of the article in agreement with θεὸν) 9.

θεὸν (acc.sing.masc.of θεός, direct object of φοβήθητε) 124.

καὶ (adjunctive conjunction joining verbs) 14.

δότε (2d.per.pl.2d.aor.act.impv.of δίδωμι, command) 362.

αὐτῷ (dat.sing.masc.of αὐτός, indirect object of δότε) 16.

δόξαν (acc.sing.fem.of δόξα, direct object of δότε) 361.

ὅτι (conjunction introducing a subordinate causal clause) 211.

ἦλθεν (3d.per.sing.aor.mid.ind.of ἔρχομαι, culminative) 146.

ἡ (nom.sing.fem.of the article in agreement with ὥρα) 9.

ὥρα (nom.sing.fem.of ὥρα, subject of ἦλθεν) 735.

τῆς (gen.sing.fem.of the article in agreement with κρίσεως) 9.

κρίσεως (gen.sing.fem.of κρίσις, description) 478.

αὐτοῦ (gen.sing.masc.of αὐτός, possession)

καὶ (adjunctive conjunction joining verbs) 14.

προσκυνήσατε (2d.per.pl.aor.act.impv.of προσκυνέω, command) 147.

τῷ (dat.sing.masc.of the article in agreement with ποιήσαντι) 9.

ποιήσαντι (aor.act.part.dat.sing.masc.of ποιέω, substantival, indirect object of προσκυνήσατε) 127.

τὸν (acc.sing.masc.of the article in agreement with οὐρανὸν) 9.

οὐρανὸν (acc.sing.masc.of οὐρανός, direct object of ποιήσαντι) 254.

καὶ (adjunctive conjunction joining nouns) 14.

τὴν (acc.sing.fem.of the article in agreement with γῆν) 9.

γῆν (acc.sing.fem.of γῆ, direct object of ποιήσαντι) 157.

καὶ (adjunctive conjunction joining nouns) 14.

θάλασσαν (acc.sing.fem.of θάλασσα, direct object of ποιήσαντι) 374.

καὶ (adjunctive conjunction joining nouns) 14.

πηγὰς (acc.pl.fem.of πηγή, direct object of ποιήσαντι) 2001.

ὑδάτων (gen.pl.neut.of ὕδωρ, description) 301.

Translation - "Crying with a loud voice, 'Fear God and give glory to Him because the hour of His discrimination is here: and worship the One Who made the heaven and the earth with its sea and wells of water.' "

Comment: λέγων is nominative, unlike the accusative participles in verse 6, and is not adjectival, as are they, but recitative, introducing the direct discourse. The imperatives Φοβήθητε and δότε depend upon the ὅτι subordinate causal clause. Men should fear God and give Him glory *because* the hour of judgment is here (culminative aorist in ἦλθεν). This pin points the time at the end of the tribulation week. The hour of divine judgment cannot be said to have come one day before the second coming of Messiah. The third imperative demands worship because Christ is the creator of heaven and earth. *Cf.* Rev.4:8-11. Note John's careful use of the article. οὐρανὸν and γῆν are to be distinguished; hence each has the article, but θάλασσαν and πηγὰς are parts of the earth and need not to be distinguished from it. Hence they are anarthrous.

The first angel is an evangelist, announcing judgment and urging fear, worship

and the giving of glory to God.
The second angel announces the fall of Babylon.

Verse 8 - "And there followed another angel, saying, Babylon is fallen, is fallen, that great city, because she made all nations drink of the wine of the wrath of her fornication."

Καὶ ἄλλος δεύτερος (ἄγγελος) ἠκολούθησεν λέγων, Ἔπεσεν, ἔπεσεν Βαβυλὼν ἡ μεγάλη, ἣ ἐκ τοῦ οἴνου τοῦ θυμοῦ τῆς πορνείας αὐτῆς πεπότικεν πάντα τὰ ἔθνη.

"And another angel, a second, followed, saying, 'Fallen, fallen is Babylon the great, she who made all nations drink the wine of her impure passion.'"... RSV

Καὶ (continuative conjunction) 14.
ἄλλος (nom.sing.masc.of ἄλλος, in agreement with ἄγγελος) 198.
δεύτερος (nom.sing.masc.of δεύτερος, in agreement with ἄγγελος) 1371.
(ἄγγελος) (nom.sing.masc.of ἄγγελος, subject of ἠκολούθησεν) 96.
ἠκολούθησεν (3d.per.sing.aor.act.ind.of ἀκολουθέω, constative) 394.
λέγων (pres.act.part.nom.sing.masc.of λέγω, recitative) 66.
Ἔπεσεν (3d.per.sing.aor.act.ind.of πίπτω, dramatic) 187.
ἔπεσεν (3d.per.sing.aor.act.ind.of πίπτω, dramatic) 187.
Βαβυλὼν (nom.sing.fem.of Βαβυλών, subject of ἔπεσεν) 49.
ἡ (nom.sing.fem.of the article in agreement with μεγάλη) 9.
μεγάλη (nom.sing.fem.of μέγας, in agreement with Βαβυλὼν) 184.
ἣ (instru.sing.fem.of ὅς, relative pronoun, cause) 65.
ἐκ (preposition with the ablative of source) 19.
τοῦ (abl.sing.masc.of the article in agreement with οἴνου) 9.
οἴνου (abl.sing.masc.of οἶνος, source) 808.
τοῦ (abl.sing.masc.of the article in agreement with θυμοῦ) 9.
θυμοῦ (abl.sing.masc.of θυμός, source) 2034.
τῆς (abl.sing.fem.of the article in agreement with πορνείας) 9.
πορνείας (abl.sing.fem.of πορνεία, source) 511.
αὐτῆς (gen.sing.fem.of αὐτός, possession) 16.
πεπότικεν (3d.per.sing.perf.act.ind.of ποτίζω, culminative) 900.
πάντα (nom.pl.neut.of πᾶς, in agreement with ἔθνη) 67.
τὰ (nom.pl.neut.of the article in agreement with ἔθνη) 9.
ἔθνη (nom.pl.neut.of ἔθνος, subject of πεπότικεν) 376.

Translation - "And another second angel followed, saying, 'She has fallen! She has fallen! Babylon the great! Because of which city all the nations have been drinking of the wine of the passion of her immorality.'"

Comment: ἔπεσεν (repeated for emphasis) is a dramatic aorist, used to speak of an event which has just happened. There are many instances in the New Testament. Robertson (*Grammar*, 842) calls attention to Mt.9:18; 5:28; 14:15; 17:12; 6:12; 12:28; 14:2; 16:17; 18:15; 20:12, etc. These can all be translated by the English "have." So here in Rev.14:8 and again in Rev.18:2.

The relative clause with ἣ is causal. "Because of the great city of commerce

(Rev.18) all of the nations will become passionately (τοῦ θυμοῦ τῆς πορνείας αὐτῆς) involved with her." Actually they will have no other choice, since Babylon will be the commercial capital of the world with the Beast in control of the market through the use of his mark.

Revelation 18 is a picture of economic and commercial frenzy that will surround this mighty end-time city. Modern students of economics and Bible prophecy are inclined to relate Babylon with the Arab oil producing countries. Ancient Babylon, on the Euphrates, near the head of the Persian Gulf is in the area recently dominated by OPEC (Organization of Petroleum Exporting Countries). With modern industry power shortages and great dependence upon petroleum, it is not difficult to see that the great industrial nations, may opt to deal with the Arab world for the sake of petroleum supplies, even though the Arabs control production to administer a high price. This high price may include the Arab demand that the nations which have supported Israel forsake her.

Verse 9 - "And the third angel followed them, saying with a loud voice, If any man worship the beast and his image, and receive his mark in his forehead or in his hand, . . . "

Καὶ ἄλλος ἄγγελος τρίτος ἠκολούθησεν αὐτοῖς λέγων ἐν φωνῇ μεγάλῃ, Εἴ τις προσκυνεῖ τὸ θηρίον καὶ τὴν εἰκόνα αὐτοῦ, καὶ λαμβάνει χάραγμα ἐπὶ τοῦ μετώπου αὐτοῦ ἢ ἐπὶ τὴν χεῖρα αὐτοῦ,

"And another angel, a third, followed them, saying with a loud voice, 'If any one worships the beast and its image, and receives a mark on his forehead or on his hand, . . . " . . . RSV

Καὶ (continuative conjunction) 14.

ἄλλος (nom.sing.masc.of ἄλλος, in agreement with ἄγγελος) 198.

ἄγγελος (nom.sing.masc.of ἄγγελος, subject of ἠκολούθησεν) 96.

τρίτος (nom.sing.masc.of τρίτος, in agreement with ἄγγελος) 1209.

ἠκολούθησεν (3d.per.sing.aor.act.ind.of ἀκολουθέω, constative) 394.

αὐτοῖς (dat.pl.masc.of αὐτός, with persons) 16.

λέγων (pres.act.part.nom.sing.masc.of λέγω, recitative) 66.

ἐν (preposition with the instrumental, means) 80.

φωνῇ (instru.sing.fem.of φωνή, means) 222.

μεγάλῃ (instru.sing.fem.of μέγας, in agreement with φωνῇ) 184.

Εἴ (conditional particle in a first-class condition) 337.

τις (nom.sing.masc.of τις, indefinite pronoun, subject of προσκυνεῖ) 486.

προσκυνεῖ (3d.per.sing.pres.act.ind.of προσκυνέω, first-class condition) 147.

τὸ (acc.sing.neut.of the article in agreement with θηρίον) 9.

θηρίον (acc.sing.neut.of θηρίον, direct object of προσκυνεῖ) 1951.

καὶ (adjunctive conjunction joining nouns) 14.

τὴν (acc.sing.fem.of the article in agreement with εἰκόνα) 9.

εἰκόνα (acc.sing.fem.of εἰκών, direct object of προσκυνεῖ) 1421.

αὐτοῦ (gen.sing.masc.of αὐτός, possession) 16.

καὶ (adjunctive conjunction joining verbs) 14.

λαμβάνει (3d.per.sing.pres.act.ind.of λαμβάνω, first-class condition) 533.
χάραγμα (acc.sing.neut.of χάραγμα, direct object of λαμβάνει) 3420.
ἐπὶ (preposition with the genitive of place description) 47.
τοῦ (gen.sing.neut.of the article in agreement with μετώπου) 9.
μετώπου (gen.sing.neut.of μέτωπον, place description) 5356.
αὐτοῦ (gen.sing.masc.of αὐτός, possession) 16.
ἢ (disjunctive) 465.
ἐπὶ (preposition with the accusative, extent) 47.
τὴν (acc.sing.fem.of the article in agreement with χεῖρα) 9.
χεῖρα (acc.sing.fem.of χείρ, extent) 308.
αὐτοῦ (gen.sing.masc.of αὐτός, possession) 16.

Translation - "And another angel, a third, followed them saying with a loud voice, 'If any one worships the Beast and his image and receives a mark upon his forehead or in his hand, . . . "

Comment: εἰ with the present indicative in προσκυνεῖ and λαμβάνει is a first-class condition where the premise may be considered true, but there is some doubt since τις in indefinite. Indeed the entire non-elect world population will take the mark of the Beast (Rev.13:8) but there is reasonable doubt that any specific person would do so. The apodosis of the condition follows in

Verse 10 - "The same shall drink of the wine of the wrath of God, which is poured out without mixture into the cup of his indignation, and he shall be tormented with fire and brimstone in the presence of the holy angels, and in the presence of the Lamb."

καὶ αὐτὸς πίεται ἐκ τοῦ οἴνου τοῦ θυμοῦ τοῦ θεοῦ τοῦ κεκερασμένου ἀκράτου ἐν τῷ ποτηρίῳ τῆς ὀργῆς αὐτοῦ, καὶ βασανισθήσεται ἐν πυρὶ καὶ θείῳ ἐνώπιον ἀγγέλων ἁγίων καὶ ἐνώπιον τοῦ ἀρνίου.

"he also shall drink the wine of God's wrath, poured unmixed into the cup of his anger, and he shall be tormented with fire and brimstone in the presence of the holy angels and in the presence of the Lamb." . . . RSV

καὶ (adjunctive conjunction joining verbs) 14.
αὐτὸς (nom.sing.masc.of αὐτός, subject of πίεται and βασανισθήσεται) 16.
πίεται (3d.per.sing.fut.ind.act.of πίνω, predictive) 611.
ἐκ (preposition with the ablative of source) 19.
τοῦ (abl.sing.masc.of the article in agreement with οἴνου) 9.
οἴνου (abl.sing.masc.of οἶνος, source) 808.
τοῦ (gen.sing.masc.of the article in agreement with θυμοῦ) 9.
θυμοῦ (gen.sing.masc.of θυμός, description) 2034.
τοῦ (gen.sing.masc.of the article in agreement with θεοῦ) 9.
θεοῦ (gen.sing.masc.of θεός, description) 124.
τοῦ (gen.sing.masc.of the article in agreement with κεκερασμένου) 9.

#5390 κεκερασμένου (perf.pass.part.gen.sing.masc.of κεράννυμι, adjectival, emphatic attributive position in agreement with οἴνου).

King James Version

fill - Rev.18:6,6.
pour out - Rev.14:10.

Revised Standard Version

mix - Rev.18:6,6.
pour - Rev.14:10.

Meaning: Cf. κεραννύω - "to mix." To mix a drink; to combine two elements so as to produce a new mixture. *Contra* μίγνυμι (#1646), which means to mingle mechanically - a promiscuous mixing without the purpose of chemical blend. Followed by the genitive ἀκράτου in Rev.14:10. Metaphorically, of the mixture of sin and depravity of Babylon and of God's mixture of wrath - Rev.18:6,6.

#5391 ἀκράτου (gen.sing.masc.of ἄκρατος, in agreement with οἴνου).

King James Version

without mixture - Rev.14:10.

Revised Standard Version

unmixed - Rev.14:10.

Meaning: α privative plus κεράννυμι (#5390). Unmixed; undiluted. With reference to God's wrath - Rev.14:10.

ἐν (preposition with the locative of place) 80.
τῷ (loc.sing.neut.of the article in agreement with ποτηρίῳ) 9.
ποτηρίῳ (loc.sing.neut.of ποτήριον, place) 902.
τῆς (gen.sing.fe m.of the article in agreement with ὀργῆς) 9.
ὀργῆς (gen.sing.fem.of ὀργή, description) 283.
αὐτοῦ (gen.sing.masc.of αὐτός, possession) 16.
καὶ (adjunctive conjunction joining verbs) 14.
βασανισθήσεται (3d.per.sing.fut.pass.ind.of βασανίζω, predictive) 719.
ἐν (preposition with the instrumental, means) 80.
πυρὶ (instru.sing.neut.of πύρ, means) 298.
καὶ (adjunctive conjunction joining nouns) 14.
θείῳ (instru.sing.neut.of θεῖον, means) 2619.
ἐνώπιον (preposition with the genitive, place description) 1798.
ἀγγέλων (gen.pl.masc.of ἄγγελος, place description) 96.
ἁγίων (gen.pl.masc.of ἅγιος, in agreement with ἀγγέλων) 84.
καὶ (adjunctive conjunction joining prepositional phrases) 1798.
ἐνώπιον (preposition with the genitive of place description) 1798.
τοῦ (gen.sing.neut.of the article in agreement with ἀνίου) 9.
ἀρνίου (gen.sing.neut.of ἀρνίον, place description) 2923.

Translation - "... he shall also drink of the wine of the undiluted wrath of God, poured out into the cup of His wrath, and he shall be tormented with fire and brimstone in the presence of holy   angels and before the Lamb."

Comment: Adjunctive καὶ goes back to verse 8. Just as nations will drink of the wine of Babylon's commercialization, also those who, in order to do business with the Beast in Babylon, take his mark shall drink of a different kind of wine. The wine of passion (ἐκ τοῦ οἴνου τοῦ θυμοῦ τῆς πορνείας) is balanced against the wine of God's wrath (ἐκ τοῦ οἴνου τοῦ θυμοῦ τοῦ θεοῦ). Note that the Babylon whore had her cup (Rev.18:6) as God has His (Rev.14:10). Divine retribution will be certain and eternal.

Verse 11 - "And the smoke of their torment ascendeth up for ever and ever: and they have no rest, day nor night, who worship the beast and his image, and whosoever receiveth the mark of his name."

καὶ ὁ καπνὸς τοῦ βασανισμοῦ αὐτῶν εἰς αἰῶνας αἰώνων ἀναβαίνει, καὶ οὐκ ἔχουσιν ἀνάπαυσιν ἡμέρας καὶ νυκτός, οἱ προσκυνοῦντες τὸ θηρίον καὶ τὴν εἰκόνα αὐτοῦ, καὶ εἴ τις λαμβάνει τὸ χάραγμα τοῦ ὀνόματος αὐτοῦ.

"And the smoke of their torment goes up for ever and ever; and they have no rest, day or night, these worshippers of the beast and its image, and whoever receives the mark of its name.' " . . . RSV

καὶ (continuative conjunction) 14.

ὁ (nom.sing.masc.of the article in agreement with καπνὸς) 9.

καπνὸς (nom.sing.masc.of καπνός, subject of ἀναβαίνει) 2986.

τοῦ (gen.sing.masc.of the article in agreement with βασανισμοῦ) 9.

βασανισμοῦ (gen.sing.masc.of βασανισμός, description) 5368.

αὐτῶν (gen.pl.masc.of αὐτός, description) 16.

εἰς (preposition with the accusative of time extent) 140.

αἰῶνας (acc.pl.masc.of αἰών, time extent) 1002.

αἰώνων (gen.pl.masc.of αἰών, partitive) 1002.

ἀναβαίνει (3d.per.sing.pres.act.ind.of ἀναβαίνω, futuristic) 323.

καὶ (continuative conjunction) 14.

οὐκ (negative conjunction with the indicative) 130.

ἔχουσιν (3d.per.pl.pres.act.ind.of ἔχω, futuristic) 82.

ἀνάπαυσιν (acc.sing.fem.of ἀνάπαυσις, direct object of ἔχουσιν) 958.

ἡμέρας (gen.sing.fem.of ἡμέρα, description) 135.

καὶ (adjunctive conjunction joining nouns) 14.

νυκτός (gen.sing.fem.of νύξ, time description) 209.

οἱ (nom.pl.masc.of the article in agreement with προσκυνοῦντες) 9.

προσκυνοῦντες (pres.act.part.nom.pl.masc.of προσκυνέω, substantival, subject of ἔχουσιν) 147.

τὸ (acc.sing.neut.of the article in agreement with θηρίον) 9.

θηρίον (acc.sing.neut.of θηρίον, direct object of προσκυνοῦντες) 1951.

καὶ (adjunctive conjunction joining nouns) 14.

τὴν (acc.sing.fem.of the article in agreement with εἰκόνα) 9.

εἰκόνα (acc.sing.fem.of εἰκών, direct object of προσκυνοῦντες) 1421.

αὐτοῦ (gen.sing.masc.of αὐτός, possession) 16.
καὶ (continuative conjunction) 14.
εἰ (conditional particle in an elliptical condition) 337.
τις (nom.sing.masc.of τις, indefinite pronoun, subject of λαμβάνει) 486.
λαμβάνει (3d.per.sing.pres.act.ind.of λαμβάνω, futuristic) 533.
τὸ (acc.sing.neut.of the article in agreement with χάραγμα) 9.
χάραγμα (acc.sing.neut.of χάραγμα, direct object of λαμβάνει) 3420.
τοῦ (gen.sing.neut.of the article in agreement with ὀνόματος) 9.
ὀνόματος (gen.sing.neut.of ὄνομα, description) 108.
αὐτοῦ (gen.sing.masc.of αὐτός, possession) 16.

Translation - "And the smoke of their torment will rise into ages of ages, and those who worship the Beast and his statue will have no rest by day or by night, nor will any who receive the mark of his name."

Comment: Note the elliptical conditional clause at the end of the verse. There is no rest for the wicked (Isa.57:20,21; Mt.12:43; Lk.11:24; Rev.14:11) but *Cf.* Mt.11:29!

Verse 12 - "Here is the patience of the saints: here are they that keep the commandments of God, and the faith of Jesus."

Ὧδε ἡ ὑπομονὴ τῶν ἁγίων ἐστίν, οἱ τηροῦντες τὰς ἐντολὰς τοῦ θεοῦ καὶ τὴν πίστιν Ἰησοῦ.

"Here is a call for the endurance of the saints, those who keep the commandments of God and the faith of Jesus." . . . RSV

Ὧδε (local adverb) 766.
ἡ (nom.sing.fem.of the article in agreement with ὑπομονὴ) 9.
ὑπομονὴ (nom.sing.fem.of ὑπομονή, subject of ἐστίν) 2204.
τῶν (gen.pl.masc.of the article in agreement with ἁγίων) 9.
ἁγίων (gen.pl.masc.of ἅγιος, possession) 84.
ἐστίν (3d.per.sing.pres.ind.of εἰμί, aoristic) 86.
οἱ (nom.pl.masc.of the article in agreement with τηροῦντες) 9.
τηροῦντες (pres.act.part.nom.pl.masc.of τηρέω, substantival, subject of εἰσίν understood) 1297.
τὰς (acc.pl.fem.of the article in agreement with ἐντολὰς) 9.
ἐντολὰς (acc.pl.fem.of ἐντολή, direct object of τηροῦντες) 472.
τοῦ (gen.sing.masc.of the article in agreement with θεοῦ) 9.
θεοῦ (gen.sing.masc.of θεός, description) 124.
καὶ (adjunctive conjunction joining nouns) 14.
τὴν (acc.sing.fem.of the article in agreement with πίστιν) 9.
πίστιν (acc.sing.fem.of πίστις, direct object of τηροῦντες) 728.
Ἰησοῦ (gen.sing.masc.of Ἰησοῦς, description) 3.

Translation - "Here is ground for the patience of the saints, those who are keeping the commandments of God and the faith of Jesus."

Comment: οἱ τηροῦντες . . .'Ιησοῦ is tacked on loosely. *Cf.* ἡ καταβαίνουσα . . . . θεοῦ μου in Rev.3:12. We may consider οἱ τηροῦντες as appositive to τῶν ἁγίων, though the concord in case in missing, or we can supply the missing verb.

The saints who have suffered at the hands of the Beast and have kept the faith may derive comfort from knowing that had they denied Christ and worshipped the Beast, their fate would have been much worse. On the contrary, since they have kept the faith they have the promise of

Verse 13 - "And I heard a voice from heaven saying unto me, Write, Blessed are the dead which die in the Lord from henceforth: yea, saith the Spirit, that they may rest from their labours, and their works do follow them."

Καὶ ἤκουσα φωνῆς ἐκ τοῦ οὐρανοῦ λεγούσης, Γράφον. Μακάριοι οἱ νεκροὶ οἱ ἐν κυρίῳ ἀποθνῄσκοντες ἀπ' ἄρτι. ναί, λέγει τὸ πνεῦμα, ἵνα ἀναπαήσονται ἐκ τῶν κόπων αὐτῶν, τὰ γὰρ ἔργα αὐτῶν ἀκολουθεῖ μετ' αὐτῶν.

"And I heard a voice from heaven saying, 'Write this: Blessed are the dead who die in the Lord henceforth.' 'Blessed indeed,' says the Spirit, 'that they may rest from their labors, for their deeds follow them!' " . . . RSV

Καὶ (continuative conjunction) 14.

ἤκουσα (1st.per.sing.aor.act.ind.of ἀκούω, ingressive) 148.

φωνῆς (gen.sing.fem.of φωνή, objective genitive) 222.

ἐκ (preposition with the ablative of source) 19.

τοῦ (abl.sing.masc.of the article in agreement with οὐρανοῦ) 9.

οὐρανοῦ (abl.sing.masc.of οὐρανός, source) 254.

λεγούσης (pres.act.part.abl.sing.fem.of λέγω, recitative) 66.

Γράφον (2d.per.sing.aor.act.impv.of γράφω, command) 156.

Μακάριοι (nom.pl.masc.of μακάριος, predicate adjective) 422.

οἱ (nom.pl.masc.of the article in agreement with νεκροὶ) 9.

νεκροὶ (nom.pl.masc.of νεκρός, subject of εἰσι understood) 749.

οἱ (nom.pl.masc.of the article in agreement with ἀποθνῄσκοντες) 9.

ἐν (preposition with the instrumental, association) 80.

κυρίῳ (instru.sing.masc.of κύριος, association) 97.

ἀποθνῄσκοντες (pres.act.part.nom.pl.masc.of ἀποινῄσκω, adjectival, emphatic attributive position, ascriptive, in agreement with νεκροὶ) 774.

ἀπ' (preposition with the temporal adverb) 70.

ἄρτι (temporal adverb) 320.

ναί (particle of affirmation) 524.

λέγει (3d.per.sing.pres.act.ind.of λέγω, aoristic) 66.

τὸ (nom.sing.neut.of the article in agreement with πνεῦμα) 9.

πνεῦμα (nom.sing.neut.of πνεῦμα, subject of λέγει) 83.

ἵνα (conjunction with the subjunctive, result) 114.

ἀναπαήσονται (3d.per.pl.pres.mid.subj.of ἀναπαύω, result) 955.

ἐκ (preposition with the ablative of separation) 19.

τῶν (abl.pl.masc.of the article in agreement with κόπων) 9.

κόπων (abl.pl.masc.of κόπος, separation) 1565.

αὐτῶν (gen.pl.masc.of αὐτός, possession) 16.
τὰ (nom.pl.neut.of the article in agreement with ἔργα) 9.
γὰρ (adversative conjunction) 105.
ἔργα (nom.pl.neut.of ἔργον, subject of ἀκολουθεῖ) 460.
αὐτῶν (gen.pl.masc.of αὐτός, possession) 16.
ἀκολουθεῖ (3d.per.sing.pres.act.ind.of ἀκολουθέω, futuristic) 394.
μετ' (preposition with the genitive of accompaniment) 50.
αὐτῶν (gen.pl.masc.of αὐτός, accompaniment) 16.

Translation - "And I began to hear a voice from heaven saying, 'Write: Blessed are the dead who die in association with the Lord from now on. Yes! the Spirit agrees, so that they will be relieved of their toils, but their activities will follow with them.' "

Comment: The blessedness of the Christian dead is what is defined by ἀπ ἄρτι. The time of this saying is at the second coming. There will be no more Christians die after this date, except those who will be saved during the Kingdom age. Those who were born into the Body of Christ during the Church Age will be resurrected or raptured without death when Messiah returns. Thus ἀπ ἄρτι points forward to the blessedness, not to the fact of death.

The Holy Spirit agrees with the statement uttered by the voice from heaven and cites the result. They will be relieved from their trials and toils — the unpleasant features of human existence as a Christian in an unfriendly world. This is what is terminated. *Cf.* #1565 for meaning. Their ἔργα (#460) will still be a glorious part of their eternal experience. The fallacious notion that heaven will be a place of idleness is thus exposed. We will "rest" from κόπων, not from ἔργα. Who wants to rest when he is not tired? Note γὰρ here in an adversative sense.

The last clause may also suggest that the ἔργα of the Christian in life will follow with him to the Judgment seat of Christ, where he will be rewarded. But the greater meaning is that eternity will open up to us as a period of Holy Spirit inspired achievement. *Cf.* Eph.4:13.

The remainder of the chapter deals with judgment. God's chosen Israel is standing with their King Messiah in Zion (Rev.14:1-5). The raptured family of God is also there (Rev.14:6-7). Babylon is judged and utterly destroyed (Rev.14:8). The worshippers of the Beast are condemned (Rev.14:9-12). The saints are comforted (Rev.14:12-13). And now — Armageddon (Rev.14:14-20).

The Harvest of the Earth

(Revelation 14:14-20)

Verse 14 - "And I looked, and behold a white cloud, and upon the cloud one sat like unto the Son of Man, having on his head a golden crown, and in his hand a sharp sickle."

Καὶ εἶδον, καὶ ἰδοὺ νεφέλη λευκή, καὶ ἐπὶ τὴν νεφέλην καθήμενον ὅμοιον υἱὸν ἀνθρώπου, ἔχων ἐπὶ τῆς κεφαλῆς αὐτοῦ στέφανον χρυσοῦν καὶ ἐν τῇ χειρὶ αὐτοῦ δρέπανον ὀξύ.

"Then I looked, and lo, a white cloud, and seated on the cloud one like a son of man, with a golden crown on his head, and a sharp sickle in his hand." . . . RSV

Καὶ (continuative conjunction) 14.

εἶδον (1st.per.sing.aor.act.ind.of ὁράω, constative) 144.

καὶ (continuative conjunction) 14.

ἰδοὺ (exclamation) 95.

νεφέλη (nom.sing.fem.of νεφέλη, nominative absolute) 1225.

λευκή (nom.sing.fem.of λευκός, in agreement with νεφέλη) 522.

καὶ (adjunctive conjunction joining nouns) 14.

ἐπὶ (preposition with the accusative, extent, rest) 47.

τὴν (acc.sing.fem.of the article in agreement with νεφέλην) 9.

νεφέλην (acc.sing.fem.of νεφέλη, extent, rest) 1225.

καθήμενον (pres.mid.part.acc.sing.masc.of κάθημαι, substantival, direct object of εἶδον) 377.

ὅμοιον (acc.sing.masc.of ὅμοιος, in agreement with καθήμενον) 923.

υἱὸν (acc.sing.masc.of υἱός, for υἱῷ, comparison) 5.

ἀνθρώπου (gen.sing.masc.of ἄνθρωπος, description) 341.

ἔχων (pres.act.part.nom.sing.masc.of ἔχω, adverbial, circumstantial) 82.

ἐπὶ (preposition with the genitive of place description) 47.

τῆς (gen.sing.fem.of the article in agreement with κεφαλῆς) 9.

κεφαλῆς (gen.sing.fem.of κεφαλή, place description) 521.

αὐτοῦ (gen.sing.masc.of αὐτός, possession) 16.

στέφανον (acc.sing.masc.of στέφανος, direct object of εἶδον) 1640.

χρυσοῦν (acc.sing.masc.of χρύσεος, in agreement with στέφανον) 4828.

καὶ (adjunctive conjunction joining nouns) 14.

ἐν (preposition with the locative of place) 80.

τῇ (loc.sing.fem.of the article in agreement with χειρὶ) 9.

χειρὶ (loc.sing.fem.of χείρ, place) 308.

αὐτοῦ (gen.sing.masc.of αὐτός, possession) 16.

δρέπανον (acc.sing.neut.of δρέπανον, direct object of ἔχων) 2192.

ὀξύ (acc.sing.neut.of ὀξύς, in agreement with δρέπανον) 3867.

Translation - "And I watched, and Look! A white cloud and one sitting upon the cloud like a son of man, having upon his head a golden crown and in his hand a sharp scythe."

Comment: I have elected to be strictly literal with the text and translate υἱὸν ἀνθρώπου, since it is without the article as "a son of man" or "a human son." The context surely suggests τὸν υἱὸν τοῦ ἀνρώπου - "the Son of Man" our Lord Jesus Christ. Note that another, an angel (verse 17) also has a sythe. υἱὸν (accusative) after ὅμοιον is a solecism (should be υἱῷ). Also there is a lack of case concord in ἔχων (should be ἔχον to agree with υἱόν). This is a picture of the second coming of Christ (Rev.1:7; 19:11-18; 1 Thess.4:17). Note νεφέλη (#1225) and its association with our Lord's ascension and return and the rapture. This event is chronologically parallel to Rev.6:12-17; 11:15-19 and 16:17-21.

Verse 15 - "And another angel came out of the temple, crying with a loud voice to him that sat on the cloud, Thrust in thy sickle, and reap: for the time is come for thee to reap; for the harvest of the earth is ripe."

καὶ ἄλλος ἄγγελος ἐξῆλθεν ἐκ τοῦ ναοῦ, κράζων ἐν φωνῇ μεγάλῃ τῷ καθημένῳ ἐπὶ τῆς νεφέλης, Πέμφον τὸ δρέπανόν σου καὶ θέρισον, ὅτι ἦλθεν ἡ ὥρα θερίσαι, ὅτι ἐξηράνθη ὁ θερισμὸς τῆς γῆς.

"And another angel came out of the temple, calling with a loud voice to him who sat upon the cloud, 'Put in your sickle, and reap, for the hour to reap has come, for the harvest of the earth is fully ripe.' " . . . *RSV*

καὶ (continuative conjunction) 14.
ἄλλος (nom.sing.masc.of ἄλλος, in agreement with ἄγγελος) 198.
ἄγγελος (nom.sing.masc.of ἄγγελος, subject of ἐξῆλθεν) 96.
ἐξῆλθεν (3d.per.sing.aor.ind.of ἐξέρχομαι, ingressive) 161.
ἐκ (preposition with the ablative of separation) 19.
τοῦ (abl.sing.masc.of the article in agreement with ναοῦ) 9.
ναοῦ (abl.sing.masc.of ναός, separation) 1447.
κράζων (pres.act.part.nom.sing.masc.of κράζω, adverbial, modal) 765.
ἐν (preposition with the instrumental, means) 80.
φωνῇ (instru.sing.fem.of φωνή, means) 222.
μεγάλῃ (instru.sing.fem.of μέγας, in agreement with φωνῇ) 184.
τῷ (dat.sing.masc.of the article in agreement with καθημένῳ) 9.
καθημένῳ (pres.mid.part.dat.sing.masc.of κάθημαι, substantival, indirect object of κράζων) 377.
ἐπὶ (preposition with the genitive of place description) 47.
τῆς (gen.sing.fem.of the article in agreement with νεφέλης) 9.
νεφέλης (gen.sing.fem.of νεφέλη, place description) 1225.
Πέμφον (2d.per.sing.aor.act.impv.of πέμπω, entreaty) 169.
τὸ (acc.sing.neut.of the article in agreement with δρέπανον) 9.
δρέπανόν (acc.sing.neut.of δρέπανον, direct object of Πέμφον) 2192.
σου (gen.sing.masc.of σύ, possession) 104.
καὶ (adjunctive conjunction joining verbs) 14.
θέρισον (2d.per.sing.aor.act.impv.of θερίζω, entreaty) 617.
ὅτι (conjunction introducing a subordinate causal clause) 211.
ἦλθεν (3d.per.sing.aor.ind.of ἔρχομαι, culminative) 146.
ἡ (nom.sing.fem.of the article in agreement with ὥρα) 9.
ὥρα (nom.sing.fem.of ὥρα subject of ἦλθεν) 735.
θερίσαι (aor.act.inf.of θερίζω, in apposition with ὥρα) 617.
ὅτι (conjunction introducing a subordinate causal clause) 211.
ἐξηράνθη (3d.per.sing.aor.pass.ind.of ξηραίνω, culminative) 1033.
ὁ (nom.sing.masc.of the article in agreement with θερισμὸς) 9.
θερισμὸς (nom.sing.masc.of θερισμός, subject of ἐξηξράνθη) 839.

τῆς (gen.sing.fem.of the article in agreement with γῆς) 9.

γῆς (gen.sing.fem.of γῆ, description) 157.

Translation - "And another angel emerged from the temple, crying with a loud voice to him who sat upon the cloud, Plunge in your scythe and reap, because the hour to reap has come because the harvest of the earth is ripe."

Comment: *Cf.* Mt.13:30,39-40. The time for judgment upon the unregenerate world cannot come before the last elect soul has been saved. Thus the seventh trumpet pictures both events (Rev.10:7; 11:15-19). At this time tares and wheat will be distinguished and separated. The tares will be gathered and burned *first* (Mt.13:30), after which the wheat will be gathered into God's barn. The pretribulation rapture teachers have this order reversed. The unsaved, with their hands and/or foreheads marked (Rev.13:16,17; 14:9,11; 19:20; 20:4) will be judged and the saints will be raptured (1 Cor.15:52).

Verse 16 - "And he that sat on the cloud thrust in his sickle on the earth; and the earth was reaped."

καὶ ἔβαλεν ὁ καθήμενος ἐπὶ τῆς νεφέλης τὸ δρέπανον αὐτοῦ ἐπὶ τὴν γῆν, καὶ ἐθερίσθη ἡ γῆ.

"So he who sat upon the cloud swung his sickle on the earth, and the earth was reaped." . . . RSV

καὶ (inferential conjunction) 14.

ἔβαλεν (3d.per.sing.aor.act.ind.of βάλλω, ingressive) 299.

ὁ (nom.sing.masc.of the article in agreement with καθήμενος) 9.

καθήμενος (pres.mid.part.nom.sing.masc.of κάθημαι, substantival, subject of ἔβαλεν) 377.

ἐπὶ (preposition with the genitive of place description) 47.

τῆς (gen.sing.fem.of the article in agreement with νεφέλης) 9.

νεφέλης (gen.sing.fem.of νεφέλη, place description) 1225.

τὸ (acc.sing.neut.of the article in agreement with δρέπανον) 9.

δρέπανον (acc.sing.neut.of δρέπανον, direct object of ἔβαλεν) 2192.

αὐτοῦ (gen.sing.masc.of αὐτός, possession) 16.

ἐπὶ (preposition with the accusative, extent) 47.

τὴν (acc.sing.fem.of the article in agreement with γῆν) 9.

γῆν (acc.sing.fem.of γῆ, extent) 157.

καὶ (continuative conjunction) 14.

ἐθερίσθη (3d.per.sing.aor.pass.ind.of θερίζω, constative) 617.

ἡ (nom.sing.fem.of the article in agreement with γῆ) 9.

γῆ (nom.sing.fem.of γῆ, subject of ἐθξερίσθη) 157.

Translation - "And he that sat upon the cloud swung his scythe upon the earth, and the earth was harvested."

Comment: This is a world wide judgment. *Cf.* Mt.24:26-28.

Verse 17 - "And another angel came out of the temple which is in heaven, he also having a sharp sickle."

Καὶ ἄλλος ἄγγελος ἐξῆλθεν ἐκ τοῦ ναοῦ τοῦ ἐν τῷ οὐρανῷ, ἔχων καὶ αὐτὸς δρέπανον ὀξύ.

"And another angel came out of the temple in heaven, and he too had a sharp sickle." . . . RSV

Καὶ (continuative conjunction) 14.
ἄλλος (nom.sing.masc.of ἄλλος, in agreement with ἄγγελος) 198.
ἄγγελος (nom.sing.masc.of ἄγγελος, subject of ἐξῆλθεν) 96.
ἐξῆλθεν (3d.per.sing.aor.ind.of ἐξέρχομαι, ingressive) 161.
ἐκ (preposition with the ablative of separation) 19.
τοῦ (abl.sing.masc.of the article in agreement with ναοῦ) 9.
ναοῦ (abl.sing.masc.of ναός, separation) 1447.
τοῦ (abl.sing.masc.of the article in agreement with ναοῦ) 9.
ἐν (preposition with the locative of place) 80.
τῷ (loc.sing.masc.of the article in agreement with οὐρανῷ) 9.
οὐρανῷ (loc.sing.masc.of οὐρανός, place) 254.
ἔχων (pres.act.part.nom.sing.masc.of ἔχω, adverbial, modal) 82.
καὶ (adjunctive conjunction) 14.
αὐτὸς (nom.sing.masc.of αὐτός, intensive) 16.
δρέπανον (acc.sing.neut.of δρέπανον, direct object of ἔχων) 2192.
ὀξύ (acc.sing.neut.of ὀξύς, in agreement with δρέπανον) 3867.

Translation - "And another angel emerged from the temple in heaven, he also himself having a sharp scythe."

Comment: Another heavenly angel gets into the heavenly warfare upon a Christ rejecting earth.

Verse 18 - "And another angel came out from the altar, which had power over fire; and cried with a loud cry to him that had the sharp sickle saying, Thrust in thy sharp sickle, and gather the clusters of the vine of the earth; for her grapes are fully ripe."

Καὶ ἄλλος ἄγγελος ἐκ τοῦ θυσιαστηρίου, ἔχων ἐξουσίαν ἐπὶ τοῦ πυρός, καὶ ἐφώνησεν φωνῇ μεγάλῃ τῷ ἔχοντι τὸ δρέπανον τὸ ὀξὺ λέγων, Πέμφον σου τὸ δρέπανον τὸ ὀξὺ καὶ τρύγησον τοὺς βότρυας τῆς ἀμπέλου τῆς γῆς, ὅτι ἤκμασαν αἱ σταφυλαὶ αὐτῆς.

"Then another angel came out from the altar, the angel who has power over fire, and he called with a loud voice to him who had the sharp sickle, 'Put in your sickle, and gather the clusters of the vine of the earth, for its grapes are ripe.'" . . . RSV

Καὶ (continuative conjunction) 14.
ἄλλος (nom.sing.masc.of ἄλλος, in agreement with ἄγγελος) 198.

ἄγγελος (nom.sing.masc.of ἄγγελος, subject of ἦλθεν understood) 96.

ἐκ (preposition with the ablative of separation) 19.

τοῦ (abl.sing.neut.of the article in agreement with θυσιαστηρίου) 9.

θυσιαστηρίου (abl.sing.neut.of θυσιαστήριον, separation) 484.

ἔχων (pres.act.part.nom.sing.masc.of ἔχω, adverbial, modal) 82.

ἐξουσίαν (acc.sing.fem.of ἐξουσία, direct object of ἔχων) 707.

ἐπὶ (preposition with the genitive, adverbial reference) 47.

τοῦ (gen.sing.neut.of the article in agreement with πυρός) 9.

πυρός (gen.sing.neut.of πῦρ, adverbial reference) 298.

καὶ (adjunctive conjunction joining verbs) 14.

ἐφώνησεν (3d.per.sing.aor.act.ind.of φωνέω, ingressive) 1338.

φωνῇ (instru.sing.fem.of φωνή, means) 222.

μεγάλῃ (instru.sing.fem.of μέγας, in agreement with φωνῇ) 184.

τῷ (dat.sing.masc.of the article in agreement with ἔχοντι) 9.

ἔχοντι (pres.act.part.dat.sing.masc.of ἔχω, indirect object of ἐφώνησεν) 82.

τὸ (acc.sing.neut.of the article in agreement with δρέπανον) 9.

δρέπανον (acc.sing.neut.of δρέπανον, direct object of ἔχοντι) 2192.

τὸ (acc.sing.neut.of the article in agreement with ὀξὺ) 9.

ὀξὺ (acc.sing.neut.of ὀξύς, in agreement with δρέπανον) 3867.

λέγων (pres.act.part.nom.sing.masc.of λέγω, recitatitve) 66.

Πέμψον (2d.per.sing.aor.act.impv.of πέμπω, entreaty) 169.

σου (gen.sing.masc.of σύ, possession) 104.

τὸ (acc.sing.neut.of the article in agreement with δρέπανον) 9.

δρέπανον (acc.sing.neut.of δρέπανον, direct object of Πέμψον) 2192.

τὸ (acc.sing.neut.of the article in agreement with ὀξὺ) 9.

ὀξὺ (acc.sing.neut.of ὀξύς, in agreement with δρέπανον) 3867.

καὶ (adjunctive conjunction joining verbs) 14.

τρύγησον (2d.per.sing.aor.act.impv.of τρυγάω, entreaty) 2139.

τοὺς (acc.pl.masc.of the article in agreement with βότρυας) 9.

#5392 βότρυας (acc.pl.masc.of βότρυς, direct object of τρύγησον).

King James Version

cluster - Rev.14:18.

Revised Standard Version

cluster - Rev.14:18.

Meaning: bunch of grapes. *Cf.* Gen.40:10; Numbers 13:24; Rev.14:18.

τῆς (gen.sing.fem.of the article in agreement with ἀμπέλου) 9.

ἀμπέλου (gen.sing.fem.of ἄμπελος, description) 1577.

τῆς (gen.sing.fem.of the article in agreement with γῆς) 9.

γῆς (gen.sing.fem.of γῆ, description) 157.

ὅτι (conjunction introducing a subordinate causal clause) 211.

#5393 ἤκμασαν (3d.per.pl.aor.act.ind.of ἀκμάζω, culminative).

King James Version

be fully ripe - Rev.14:18.

Revised Standard Version

be ripe - Rev.14:18.

Meaning: Cf. ἀκμή - "the highest point of development of anything." The acme. Hence, in a context with αἱ σταφυλαί, ripe. Fully developed grapes. Ready for harvest. Illustratively of the full development of sin - Rev.14:18.

αἱ (nom.pl.fem.of the article in agreement with σταφυλαὶ) 9.
σταφυλαὶ (nom.pl.fem.of σταφυλή, subject of ἤκμασαν) 679.
αὐτῆς (gen.sing.fem.of αὐτός, possession) 16.

Translation - "And another angel emerged from the altar, having authority over the fire and he began to shout with a loud voice, to the one having the sharp scythe, saying, 'Plunge in your sharp scythe and gather the clusters of the grapes of the earth because her grapes are fully developed.' "

Comment: John has omitted ἦλθεν in the first clause, though variant readings have it. There is no exegetical problem as Metzger explains, "On the one hand, it can be argued that ἐξῆλθεν was inserted by scribes from ver.17, sometimes after ἄγγελος (Sinaiticus C P 046 most minuscules ith syrph,h copsa,bo arm *al*) and sometimes after θυσιαστηρίου (051 1854 2073). On the other hand, repetition is characteristic of the author of the Apocalypse, and the absence of the verb in p47 1611 2053 *al* may be due to either accidental omission or deliberate excision by scribes who considered it unnecessary in view of its presence in the preceding verse. Because of the balance of such considerations, a majority of the Committee preferred to follow Sinaiticus A 1006 *al* and to include the word in the text, but to enclose it within square brackets, thus reflecting considerable doubt that it belongs there." (*A Textual Commentary on the Greek New Testament*, 754). Since we have been following the United Bible Societies' second edition, which omits ἐξῆλθεν, we do not have it in the text. Either ἦλθεν or ἐξῆλθεν meets the need, since the preposition ἐκ follows, both in verses 17 and 18.

The element of fire is introduced into the second coming judgment. *Cf.* 2 Thess.1:7.

Verse 19 - "And the angel thrust in his sickle into the earth, and gathered the vine of the earth, and cast it into the winepress of the wrath of God."

καὶ ἔβαλεν ὁ ἄγγελος τὸ δρέπανον αὐτοῦ εἰς τὴν γῆν, καὶ ἐτρύγησεν τὴν ἄμπελον τῆς γῆς καὶ ἔβαλεν εἰς τὴν ληνὸν τοῦ θυμοῦ τοῦ θεοῦ τὸν μέγαν.

"So the angel swung his sickle on the earth and gathered the vintage of the

earth, and threw it into the great wine press of the wrath of God." . . . *RSV*

καὶ (inferential conjunction) 14.

ἔβαλεν (3d.per.sing.aor.act.ind.of βάλλω, ingressive) 299.

ὁ (nom.sing.masc.of the article in agreement with ἄγγελος) 9.

ἄγγελος (nom.sing.masc.of ἄγγελος, subject of ἔβαλεν) 96.

τὸ (acc.sing.neut.of the article in agreement with δρέπανον) 9.

δρέπανον (acc.sing.neut.of δρέπανον, direct object of ἔβαλεν) 2192.

αὐτοῦ (gen.sing.masc.of αὐτός, possession) 16.

εἰς (preposition with the accusative of extent) 140.

τὴν (acc.sing.fem.of the article in agreement with γῆν) 9.

γῆν (acc.sing.fem.of γῆ, extent) 157.

καὶ (adjunctive conjunction joining verbs) 14.

ἐτρύγησεν (3d.per.sing.aor.act.ind.of τρυγάω, ingressive) 2139.

τὴν (acc.sing.fem.of the article in agreement with ἄμπελον) 9.

ἄμπελον (acc.sing.fem.of ἄμπελος, direct object of ἐτρύγησεν) 1577.

τῆς (gen.sing.fem.of the article in agreement with γῆς) 9.

γῆς (gen.sing.fem.of γῆ, description) 157.

καὶ (adjunctive conjunction joining verbs) 14.

ἔβαλεν (3d.per.sing.aor.act.ind.of βάλλω, ingressive) 299.

εἰς (preposition with the accusative of extent) 140.

τὴν (acc.sing.fem.of the article in agreement with ληνὸν) 9.

ληνὸν (acc.sing.fem.of ληνός, extent) 1378.

τοῦ (gen.sing.masc.of the article in agreement with θυμοῦ) 9.

θυμοῦ (gen.sing.masc.of θυμός, description) 2034.

τοῦ (gen.sing.masc.of the article in agreement with θεοῦ) 9.

θεοῦ (gen.sing.masc.of θεός, description) 124.

τὸν (acc.sing.masc.of the article in agreement with μέγαν) 9.

μέγαν (acc.sing.masc.of μέγας, in agreement with ληνὸν) 184.

Translation - *"So the angel began to swing his scythe into the earth and he began to harvest the vine of the earth and he began to throw it into the great wine vat of the wrath of God."*

Comment: Here we have both feminine and masculine genders (εἰς τὴν ληνὸν .. . τὸν μέγαν) found with the same word. The vine is cut and the grapes are cast into the great wine press. This is figurative language speaking of the battle of Armageddon between God and His army of angels and Satan, the Beast, the Antichrist, the demons and godless men.

Verse 20 - "And the winepress was trodden without the city, and blood came out of the winepress, even unto the horse bridles, by the space of a thousand and six hundred furlongs."

καὶ ἐπατήθη ἡ ληνὸς ἔξωθεν τῆς πόλεως, καὶ ἐξῆλθεν αἷμα ἐκ τῆς ληνοῦ ἄχρι τῶν χαλινῶν τῶν ἵππων ἀπὸ σταδίων χιλίων ἑξακοσίων.

"and the wine press was trodden outside the city, and blood flowed from the

wine press, as high as a horse's bridle, for one thousand six hundred stadia." . . .
RSV

καὶ (continuative conjunction) 14.
ἐπατήθη (3rd.per.sing.aor.pass.ind.of πατέω, cosntative) 2415.
ἡ (nom.sing.fem.of the article in agreement with ληνὸς) 9.
ληνὸς (nom.sing.fem.of ληνός, subject of ἐπατήθη) 1378.
ἔξωθεν (preposition with the ablative of separation) 1455.
τῆς (abl.sing.fem.of the article in agreement with πόλεως) 9.
πόλεως (abl.sing.fem.of πόλις, separation) 243.
καὶ (inferential conjunction) 14.
ἐξῆλθεν (3d.per.sing.aor.ind.of ἐξέρχομαι, ingressive) 161.
αἷμα (nom.sing.neut.of αἷμα, subject of ἐξῆλθεν) 1203.
ἐκ (preposition with the ablative of separation) 19.
τῆς (abl.sing.fem.of the article in agreement with ληνοῦ) 9.
ληνοῦ (abl.sing.fem.of ληνός, separation) 1378.
ἄχρι (preposition with the genitive, extent, with places) 1517.
τῶν (gen.pl.masc.of the article in agreement with χαλινῶν) 9.
χαλινῶν (gen.pl.masc.of χαλινός, description, extent of space) 5122.
τῶν (gen.pl.masc.of the article in agreement with ἵππων) 9.
ἵππων (gen.pl.masc.of ἵππος, description) 5121.
ἀπὸ (preposition with the ablative of separation) 70.
σταδίων (abl.pl.masc.of στάδιος, separation) 1127.
χιλίων (abl.pl.masc.of χίλιοι, in agreement with σταδίων) 5278.
ἑξακοσίων (abl.pl.masc.of ἑξακόσιοι, in agreement with σταδίων) 5388.

Translation - *"And the wine press was trodden outside the city, and blood began to pour out of the winepress until it reached the depth of the bridles of the horses for a distance of 183.86 miles."*

Comment: The computed length of the river of blood, four to four and one half feet deep is 183.86 English miles. It will extend south of Jerusalem beyond the Dead Sea and deep into the Arabian desert. *Cf.* Isa.63:3; Lam.1:15; Rev.19:15. This is a phenomenon difficult to imagine, until we remember that all of the Gentile nations will have assembled their armies against Jerusalem in Satan's penultimate and unsuccessful attempt to destroy the people to whom God is obligated in an eternal because unconditional covenant.

The Angels with the Last Plagues

(Revelation 15:1-8)

Revelation 15:1 - *"And I saw another sign in heaven, great and marvellous, seven angels having the seven last plagues: for in them is filled up the wrath of God."*

Καὶ εἶδον ἄλλο σημεῖον ἐν τῷ οὐρανῷ μέγα καὶ θαυμαστόν, ἀγγέλους ἑπτὰ ἔχοντας πληγὰς ἑπτὰ τὰς ἐσχάτας, ὅτι ἐν αὐταῖς ἐτελέσθη ὁ θυμὸς τοῦ θεοῦ.

"Then I saw another portent in heaven, great and wonderful, seven angels with seven plagues, which are the last, for with them the wrath of God is ended." . . . RSV

Καὶ (continuative conjunction) 14.

εἶδον (1st.per.sing.aor.act.ind.of ὁράω, constative) 144.

ἄλλο (acc.sing.neut.of ἄλλος, in agreement with σημεῖον) 198.

σημεῖον (acc.sing.neut.of σημεῖον, direct object of εἶδον) 1005.

ἐν (preposition with the locative of place) 80.

τῷ (loc.sing.masc.of the article in agreement with οὐρανῷ) 9.

οὐρανῷ (loc.sing.masc.of οὐρανός, place) 254.

μέγα (acc.sing.neut.of μέγας, in agreement with σημεῖον) 184.

καὶ (adjunctive conjunction joining adjectives) 14.

θαυμαστόν (acc.sing.neut.of θαυμαστός, in agreement with σημεῖον) 1391.

ἀγγέλους (acc.pl.masc.of ἄγγελος, in apposition with σημεῖον) 96.

ἑπτὰ (numeral) 1024.

ἔχοντας (pres.act.part.acc.pl.masc.of ἔχω, adverbial, modal) 82.

πληγὰς (acc.pl.fem.of πληγή, direct object of ἔχοντας) 2421.

ἑπτὰ (numeral) 1024.

τὰς (acc.pl.fem.of the article in agreement with ἐσχάτας) 9.

ἐσχάτας (acc.pl.fem.of ἔσχατος, in agreement with πληγὰς) 496.

ὅτι (conjunction introducing a subordinate causal clause) 211.

ἐν (preposition with the locative of time point) 80.

αὐταῖς (loc.pl.fem.of αὐτός, time point) 16.

ἐτελέσθη (3d.per.sing.aor.pass.ind.of τελέω, culminative) 704.

ὁ (nom.sing.masc.of the article in agreement with θυμὸς) 9.

θυμὸς (nom.sing.masc.of θυμός, subject of ἐτελέσθη) 2034.

τοῦ (gen.sing.masc.of the article in agreement with θεοῦ) 9.

θεοῦ (gen.sing.masc.of θεός, description) 124.

Translation - "And I saw another great and marvellous sign in the heaven — seven angels having the seven last plagues, because when they are poured out the wrath of God will have been exhausted."

Comment: I have pointed out before, in the text and in the charts, that the seven vial judgments are confined to the last half of the period known as Daniel's 70th week. This is clear from the fact that the first is poured out upon those who have already received the mark of the Beast (Rev.16:2). This mark is not imposed until the last half of the week (Rev.13:5, 16-18). I assumed, and so stated, that the vials would be contemporaneous with the last three churches, seals and trumpets. The seventh vial is indeed simultaneous with the sixth and seventh seal and the seventh trumpet, but it appears, in closer study of Revelation 15 that the seven vials may be poured out in quick succession at the close of the week (perhaps within the last day or two). Note that there is nothing in the description of the seven vials to indicate the passage of long periods of time, as in the case of the fifth trumpet with its five months long torment (Rev.9:5). The vials fall upon the earth (Rev.16:2), the sea (Rev.16:3), the rivers and fountains of waters (Rev.16:4), the sun (Rev.16:8), the throne of the Beast (Rev.16:10) and the Euphrates river (Rev.16:12). This sixth vial judgment brings the three foul spirits, like frogs which go throughout the earth to mobilize the armies of the world at the battle of Armageddon (Rev.16:12-16). Here there is an indication of a short lapse of time. How long does it take to fly an army from any point on earth to Jerusalem? The seventh vial (Rev.16:17-21) is obviously at the same time as the seventh trumpet and the sixth and seventh seals. Note the promise of blessing to the saints who have survived on earth and who will be raptured.

With the pouring out of the seven vials the divine wrath will have been exhausted.

Verse 2 - "And I saw as it were a sea of glass mingled with fire: and them that had gotten the victory over the beast, and over his image, and over his mark, and over the number of his name, stand on the sea of glass, having the harps of God."

Καὶ εἶδον ὡς θάλασσαν ὑαλίνην μεμιγμένην πυρί, καὶ τοὺς νικῶντας ἐκ τοῦ θηρίου καὶ ἐκ τῆς εἰκόνος αὐτοῦ καὶ ἐκ τοῦ ἀριθμοῦ τοῦ ὀνόματος αὐτοῦ ἑστῶτας ἐπὶ τὴν θάλασσαν τὴν ὑαλίνην, ἔχοντας κιθάρας τοῦ θεοῦ.

"And I saw what appeared to be a sea of glass mingled with fire, and those who had conquered the beast and its image and the number of its name, standing beside the sea of glass with harps of God in their hands." . . . RSV

Καὶ (continuative conjunction) 14.
εἶδον (1st.per.sing.aor.act.ind.of ὁράω, ingressive) 144.
ὡς (comparative particle) 128.
θάλασσαν (acc.sing.fem.of θάλασσαν, direct object of εἶδον) 374.
ὑαλίνην (acc.sing.fem.of ὑάλινός, in agreement with θάλασσαν) 5344.
μεμιγμένην (perf.pass.part.acc.sing.fem.of μίγνυμι, adjectival, predicate position, restrictive, in agreement with θάλασσαν) 1646.
πυρί (instru.sing.neut.of πῦρ, association) 298.
καὶ (adjunctive conjunction joining substantives) 14.
τοὺς (acc.pl.masc.of the article in agreement with νικῶντας) 9.
νικῶντας (pres.act.part.acc.pl.masc.of νικάω, substantival, direct object of εἶδον) 2454.
ἐκ (preposition with the ablative of separation) 19.
τοῦ (abl.sing.neut.of the article in agreement with θηρίου) 9.
θηρίου (abl.sing.neut.of θηρίον, separation) 1951.
καὶ (adjunctive conjunction joining prepositional phrases) 14.
ἐκ (preposition with the ablative of separation) 19.
τῆς (abl.sing.fem.of the article in agreement with εἰκόνος) 9.
εἰκόνος (abl.sing.fem.of εἰκών, separation) 1421.
αὐτοῦ (gen.sing.masc.of αὐτός, possession) 16.
καὶ (adjunctive conjunction joining prepositional phrases) 14.

ἐκ (preposition with the ablative of separation) 19.

τοῦ (abl.sing.masc.of the article in agreement with ἀριθμοῦ) 9.

ἀριθμοῦ (abl.sing.masc.of ἀριθμός, separation) 2278.

τοῦ (gen.sing.neut.of the article in agreement with ὀνόματος) 9.

ὀνόματος (gen.sing.neut.of ὄνομα, description) 108.

αὐτοῦ (gen.sing.masc.of αὐτός, possession) 16.

ἑστῶτας (perf.act.part.acc.pl.masc.of ἵστημι, adjectival, predicate position, restrictive, in agreement with νικῶντας) 180.

ἐπὶ (preposition with the accusative of extent, rest) 47.

τὴν (acc.sing.fem.of the article in agreement with θάλασσαν) 9.

θάλασσαν (acc.sing.fem.of θάλασσα, rest) 374.

τὴν (acc.sing.fem.of the article, in agreement with ὑαλίνην) 9.

ὑαλίνην (acc.sing.fem.of ὑάλινος, in agreement with θάλασσαν) 5344.

ἔχοντας (pres.act.part.acc.pl.masc.of ἔχω, adjectival, predicate position, restrictive, in agreement with νικῶντας) 82.

κιθάρας (acc.pl.fem.of κιθάρα, direct object of ἔχοντας) 4232.

τοῦ (gen.sing.masc.of the article in agreement with θεοῦ) 9.

θεοῦ (gen.sing.masc.of θεός, possesion) 124.

Translation - "And I began to watch what looked like a glass sea mingled with fire, and those who were victorious over the Beast and over his statue and over the number of his name standing on the sea of glass and holding the harps of God."

Comment: This imagery must wait for interpretation until we see what John saw. Note ἐκ and the ablative of separation after νικάω. Victory over the Beast and escape from his clutches, whether they died of natural causes or were murdered by him and his goons — in either case they were forever free from him now. Now they rejoice in heaven. The harps of God will be used to accompany the singers as they sing the song of Moses and the Lamb of

Verse 3 - "And they sing the song of Moses, the servant of God, and the song of the Lamb, saying, Great and marvellous are thy works, Lord God Almighty; just and true are thy ways, thou King of saints."

καὶ ᾄδουσιν τὴν ᾠδὴν Μωϋσέως τοῦ δούλου τοῦ θεοῦ καὶ τὴν ᾠδὴν τοῦ ἀρνίου λέγοντες, Μεγάλα καὶ θαυμαστὰ τὰ ἔργα σου, κύριε ὁ θεὸς ὁ παντοκράτωρ, δίκαιαι καὶ ἀληθιναὶ αἱ ὁδοί σου, ὁ βασιλεὺς τῶν ἐθνῶν.

"And they sing the song of Moses, the servant of God, and the song of the Lamb, saying, 'Great and wonderful are thy deeds, O Lord God the Almighty! Just and true are thy ways, O King of the ages!' " . . . RSV

καὶ (continuative conjunction) 14.

ᾄδουσιν (3d.per.pl.pres.act.ind.of ᾄδω, aoristic) 4519.

τὴν (acc.sing.fem.of the article in agreement with ᾠδὴν) 9.

ᾠδὴν (acc.sing.fem.of ᾠδή, direct object of ᾄδουσιν) 4518.

Μωϋσέως (gen.sing.masc.of Μωϋσῆς, description) 715.

τοῦ (gen.sing.masc.of the article in agreement with δούλου) 9.

δούλου (gen.sing.masc.of δοῦλος, apposition) 725.

τοῦ (gen.sing.masc.of the article in agreement with θεοῦ) 9.

θεοῦ (gen.sing.masc.of θεός, relationship) 124.

καὶ (adjunctive conjunction joining nouns) 14.

τὴν (acc.sing.fem.of the article in agreement with ᾠδὴν) 9.

ᾠδὴν (acc.sing.fem.of ᾠδή, direct object of ἄδουσιν) 4518.

τοῦ (gen.sing.neut.of the article in agreement with ἀρνίου) 9.

ἀρνίου (gen.sing.neut.of ἀρνίον, description) 2923.

λέγοντες (pres.act.part.nom.pl.masc.of λέγω, recitative) 66.

Μεγάλα (nom.pl.neut.of μέγας, in agreement with ἔργα) 184.

καὶ (adjunctive conjunction joining adjectives) 14.

θαυμαστὰ (nom.pl.neut.of θαυμαστός, in agreement with ἔργα) 1391.

τὰ (nom.pl.neut.of the article in agreement with ἔργα) 9.

ἔργα (nom.pl.neut.of ἔργον, subject of ἐστίν, understood) 460.

σου (gen.sing.masc.of σύ, possession) 104.

κύριε (voc.sing.masc.of κύριος, address) 97.

ὁ (nom.sing.masc.of the article in agreement with θεὸς) 9.

θεὸς (nom.sing.masc.of θεός, apposition) 124.

ὁ (nom.sing.masc.of the article in agreement with παντοκράτωρ) 9.

παντοκράτωρ (nom.sing.masc.of παντοκράτωρ, apposition) 4325.

δίκαιαι (nom.pl.fem.of δίκαιος, predicate adjective) 85.

καὶ (adjunctive conjunction joining adjectives) 14.

ἀληθιναὶ (nom.pl.fem.of ἀληθινός, predicate adjective) 1696.

αἱ (nom.pl.fem.of the article in agreement with ὁδοί) 9.

ὁδοί (nom.pl.fem.of ὁδός, subject of ἐστίν understood) 199.

σου (gen.sing.masc.of σύ, possession) 104.

ὁ (nom.sing.masc.of the article in agreement with βασιλεὺς) 9.

βασιλεὺς (nom.sing.masc.of βασιλεύς, for the vocative, address) 31.

τῶν (gen.pl.neut.of the article in agreement with ἐθνῶν) 9.

ἐθνῶν (gen.pl.neut.of ἔθνος, description) 376.

Translation - "And they sing the song of Moses, the servant of God, and the song of the Lamb, saying, 'Great and marvellous are your works, Lord, God, the Almighty; righteous and true are thy ways, O King of the nations.' "

Comment: The Song of Moses (Exodus 15:1), sung appropriately enough to celebrate God's judgment upon a Gentile power, which power, if successful, would have wiped out Israel and brought the divine redemptive program to a standstill, is now sung again as the seven angels with the last seven bowls of divine wrath prepare to pour out God's wrath upon all of the Gentile powers, headed up by the Beast, and soon to be seduced to their death at the Battle of Armageddon.

The Beast, like Pharoah, the Egyptian, if successful, would reign over the nations; Israel would be pushed into the Mediterranean and destroyed and King Messiah would be forever without a throne. But, of course, such hellish frustration of the divine purpose is not going to be.

The tribulation saints, speaking from a heavenly viewpoint, will know this and thus they will sing. They will also sing the song of the Lamb of Rev.5:9-10. God's works are great and amazing; His ways are just and truthful (Rev.16:7). He is the Omnipotent One and is not only the King of the Jews, but now King of all nations (Micah 4:1-7).

The MSS differ on the last word in the verse. Some have αἰώνων instead of ἐθνῶν, while 296 2049 Victorinus-Pettau Tyconius Apringius Cassiodorus have ἁγίων. "The weight of external evidence supporting the reading ἐθνῶν (Sinaiticusₐ A P 046 051 most minuscules itᵍᵢᵍ,ₕ copᵇᵒ arm eth Cyprian *al*) is nearly the same as that supporting αἰώνων (p47 Sinaiticus*,c C 94 469 1006 1611 1841 2040 2065 2073ₘg 2076 2254 2258 2344ᵥᵢd 2432 it61 vg syrₚₕ,ₕ copₛₐ *al*). The former reading was preferred by a majority of the Committee on the grounds that (a) αἰώνων was introduced by copyists who recollected 1 Tim.1:17 (*cf.* Enoch 9.4 and Tobit 13.4), and (b) the reading ἐθνῶν is more in accord with the context (ver.4). In order to enhance the meaning a few witnesses add πάντων (itₕ arm eth Primasius). The reading of the Textus Receptus (ἁγίων), which has only the slenderest support in Greek witnesses (296 2049 neither of which was available when the Textus Receptus was formed) appears to have arisen from confusion of the Latin compendia for *sanctorus (sctorum)* and *saeculorum (sclorum (*equals αἰώνων); "saint" is also read by severanl Latin writers, including Victorinus-Pettau, Tyconius, Apringius and Cassiodorus." (Metzger, *A Textual Commentary on the Greek New Testament*, 755, 756).

There need be no conflict among the three concepts since Christ is King (or He will be) of all nations, all saints and in all the ages (1 Cor.15:25,26). The song goes on in

Verse 4 - "Who shall not fear thee, O Lord, and glorify thy name? For thou only art holy: for all nations shall come and worship before thee; for thy judgments are made manifest."

τίς οὐ μὴ φοβηθῇ, κύριε, καὶ δοξάσει τὸ ὄνομά σου; ὅτι μόνος ὅσιος, ὅτι πάντα τὰ ἔθνη ἥξουσιν καὶ προσκυνήσουσιν ἐνώπιόν σου, ὅτι τὰ δικαιώματά σου ἐφανερώθησαν.

"Who shall not fear and glorify thy name, O Lord? For thou alone art holy. All nations shall come and worship thee, for thy judgments have been revealed." ... *RSV*

τίς (nom.sing.masc.of τίς, interrogative pronoun, in a negative rhetorical question) 281.

οὐ (negative conjunction with μὴ with the subjunctive in a rhetorical question) 130.

μὴ (negative conjunction with οὐ and the subjunctive in a rhetorical question) 87.

φοβηθῇ (3d.per.sing.1st.aor.mid.subj.of φοβέομαι, rhetorical question) 101.

κύριε (voc.sing.masc.of κύριος, address) 97.

καὶ (adjunctive conjunction joining verbs) 14.
δοξάσει (3d.per.sing.fut.act.ind.of δοξάζω, rhetorical question) 461.
τὸ (acc.sing.neut.of the article in agreement with ὄνομά) 9.
ὄνομά (acc.sing.neut.of ὄνομα, direct object of δοξάσει) 108.
σου (gen.sing.masc.of σύ, possession) 104.
ὅτι (conjunction introducing a subordinate causal clause, εἰ supplied) 211.
μόνος (nom.sing.masc.of μόνος, adverbial) 339.
ὅσιος (nom.sing.masc.of ὅσιος, predicate adjective) 2995.
ὅτι (conjunction introducing two subordinate causal clauses) 211.
πάντα (nom.pl.neut.of πᾶς, in agreement with ἔθνη) 67.
τὰ (nom.pl.neut.of the article in agreement with ἔθνη) 9.
ἔθνη (nom.pl.neut.of ἔθνος, subject of ἥξουσιν and προσκυνήσουσιν) 376.
ἥξουσιν (3d.per.pl.fut.act.ind.of ἥκω, predictive) 730.
καὶ (adjunctive conjunction joining verbs) 14.
προσκυνήσουσιν (3d.per.pl.fut.act.ind.of προσκυνέω, predictive) 147.
ἐνώπιόν (preposition with the genitive of place description) 1798.
σου (gen.sing.masc.of σύ, place description) 104.
ὅτι (conjunction introducing a subordinate causal clause) 211.
τὰ (nom.pl.neut.of the article in agreement with δικαιώματά) 9.
δικαιώματά (nom.pl.neut.of δικαίωμα, subject of ἐφανερώθησαν) 1781.
σου (gen.sing.masc.of σύ, possession) 104.
ἐφανερώθησαν (3d.per.pl.aor.pass.ind.of φανερόω, culminative) 1960.

Translation - "Who indeed shall not fear, O Lord, and glorify your name, because You alone are adequate, because all the nations shall come and worship before You, because Your judgments have been made apparent."

Comment: τίς introduces a rhetorical question in the negative. Note that in it we have, side by side, a deliberative aorist subjunctive and a future indicative. Note the emphatic double negative with φοβηθῇ. A similar double negative in a rhetorical question is found in Luke 18:7. We supply εἰ in the first ὅτι clause.

Universal respect and glorification is predicted on the basis of three ὅτι causal clauses: (1) God alone is adequate as a problem solver; (2) all nations will recognize this fact and come to worship, because (3) at long last they will recognize the empirical evidence that divine judgments are valid. The modern world, in its rebellion against Renaissance metaphysics and epistemology, has exchewed deduction and opted for a radical inductive empiricism that has resulted in agnostic existentialism. No one believes anything anymore. The human mind, conceived as being incapable of logic, is victimized totally by stimulii over which it is alleged that it has no control. This verse declares that if it is empirical evidence that they want, this is what they are going to get. Christ's precepts are going to be demonstrated to be valid. The phrase μόνος εἰ ὅσιος - "You alone are complete" is the goal of gestalt psychology. In Messiah world society will find closure. He is totality. He lacks nothing. He puts it all together. Hence, He alone should be the King. This, finally, the nations are going to come to understand. And when they do they will come to Him and worship. (Micah

4:1-2). Thus He indeed is ὁ βασιλεὺς τῶν ἐθνῶν (verse 3).

He is Plato's Philosopher-King (*Republic*, V, 473, D). That the elect are able to come to this conclusion before the time when the non-elect can see it only after the fact — that we know by faith (deduction) what they will know only by sight (induction) is not to our credit, but only because of God's grace. The elect before salvation were no different from the non-elect. We are all "dead in trespasses and sins" (Eph.2:1). *Cf.* Rom.1:32. Once unsaved man did know of God's judgments and chose to ignore them.

Verse 5 - "And after that I looked, and behold the temple of the tabernacle of the testimony in heaven was opened."

Καὶ μετὰ ταῦτα εἶδον, καὶ ἠνοίγη ὁ ναὸς τῆς σκηνῆς τοῦ μαρτυρίου ἐν τῷ οὐρανῷ,

"After this I looked, and the temple of the tent of witness in heaven was opened," . . . RSV

Καὶ (continuative conjunction) 14.

μετὰ (preposition with the accusative, time extent) 50.

ταῦτα (acc.pl.neut.of οὗτος, time extent) 93.

εἶδον (1st.per.sing.aor.act.ind.of ὁράω, constative) 144.

καὶ (continuative conjunction) 14.

ἠνοίγη (3d.per.sing.2d.aor.pass.ind.of ἀνοίγω, constative) 188.

ὁ (nom.sing.masc.of the article in agreement with ναὸς) 9.

ναὸς (nom.sing.masc.of ναός, subject of ἠνοίγη) 1447.

τῆς (gen.sing.fem.of the article in agreement with σκηνῆς) 9.

σκηνῆς (gen.sing.fem.of σκηνή, description) 1224.

τοῦ (gen.sing.neut.of the article in agreement with μαρτυρίου) 9.

μαρτυρίου (gen.sing.neut.of μαρτύριον, description) 716.

ἐν (preposition with the locative of place) 80.

τῷ (loc.sing.masc.of the article in agreement with οὐρανῷ) 9.

οὐρανῷ (loc.sing.masc.of οὐρανός, place) 254.

Translation - "And after this I looked! And the temple of the tabernacle of the testimony was opened in heaven."

Comment: μετὰ ταῦτα only in the order of the narration to John. The overcoming saints out of the tribulation have sung their songs. Now John sees heaven opened to reveal the heavenly tabernacle (Heb.8:2,5,11). This is the tabernacle in heaven that the Beast has been blaspheming (Rev.13:6) as well he might in view of what is about to come out of it (Rev.15:6). Moses saw it once and built his tabernacle at Sinai after its pattern. Now John sees it and from it come the seven angels with the bowls of the seven final plagues.

Verse 6 - "And the seven angels came out of the temple, having the seven plagues, clothed in pure and white linen, and having their breasts girded with golden girdles."

καὶ ἐξῆλθον οἱ ἑπτὰ ἄγγελοι (οἱ) ἔχοντες τὰς ἑπτὰ πληγὰς ἐκ τοῦ ναοῦ, ἐνδεδυμένοι λίνον καθαρὸν λαμπρὸν καὶ περιεζωσμένοι περὶ τὰ στήθη ζώνας χρυσᾶς.

"... and out of the temple came the seven angels with the seven plagues, robed in pure bright linen, and their breasts girded with golden girdles." ... RSV

καὶ (continuative conjunction) 14.

ἐξῆλθον (3d.per.pl.aor.mid.ind.of ἐξέρχομαι, ingressive) 161.

οἱ (nom.pl.masc.of the article in agreement with ἄγγελοι) 9.

ἑπτά (numeral) 1024.

ἄγγελοι (nom.pl.masc.of ἄγγελος, subject of ἐξῆλθον) 96.

οἱ (nom.pl.masc.of the article in agreement with ἔχοντες) 9.

ἔχοντες (pres.act.part.nom.pl.masc.of ἔχω, adjectival, emphatic attributive position, ascriptive, in agreement with ἄγγελοι) 82.

τὰς (acc.pl.fem.of the article in agreement with πληγὰς) 9.

ἑπτά (numeral) 1024.

πληγὰς (acc.pl.fem.of πληγή, direct object of ἔχοντες) 2421.

ἐκ (preposition with the ablative of separation) 19.

τοῦ (abl.sing.masc.of the article in agreement with ναοῦ) 9.

ναοῦ (abl.sing.masc.of ναός, separation) 1447.

ἐνδεδυμένοι (perf.pass.part.nom.pl.masc.of ἐνδύω, adjectival, predicate position, restrictive, in agreement with ἄγγελοι) 613.

λίνον (acc.sing.neut.of λίνον, adverbial accusative, manner) 987.

καθαρὸν (acc.sing.neut.of καθαρός, in agreement with λίνον) 431.

λαμπρὸν (acc.sing.neut.of λαμπρός, in agreement with λίνον) 2832.

καὶ (adjunctive conjunction joining participles) 14.

περιεζωσμένοι (perf.pass.part.nom.pl.masc.of περιζώννυμι, adjectival, predicate position, restrictive, in agreement with ἄγγελοι) 2486.

περὶ (preposition with the accusative of extent) 173.

τὰ (acc.pl.neut.of the article in agreement with στήθη) 9.

στήθη (acc.pl.neut.of στῆθος, extent) 2631.

ζώνας (acc.pl.fem.of ζώνη, extent) 263.

χρυσᾶς (acc.pl.fem.of χρύσεος, in agreement with ζώνας) 4828.

Translation - "And the seven angels who had the seven plagues came out of the temple clothed in sparkling clean linen and girded about the breasts with golden belts."

Comment: Verbs that have two accusatives in the active voice may carry the accusative also in the true passive form. Robertson (*Grammar*, 485) cites Acts 18;25; 2 Thess.2:15; Mt.22:11; Mk.1:6; Rev.1:13; 19:14 as other examples. There are others. The action of the seven angels is preparatory to the pouring out of the last seven vials of wrath upon the earth.

Verse 7 - "And one of the four beasts gave unto the seven angels seven golden vials full of the wrath of God, who liveth forever and ever."

καὶ ἓν ἐκ τῶν τεσσάρων ζῴων ἔδωκεν τοῖς ἑπτὰ ἀγγέλοις ἑπτὰ φιάλας χρυσᾶς γεμούσας τοῦ θυμοῦ τοῦ θεοῦ τοῦ ζῶντος εἰς τοὺς αἰῶνας τῶν αἰώνων.

"And one of the four living creatures gave the seven angels seven golden bowls full of the wrath of God who lives forever and ever;" . . . RSV

καὶ (continuative conjunction) 14.

ἓν (nom.sing.neut.of εἷς, subject of ἔδωκεν) 469.

ἐκ (preposition with the partitive genitive) 19.

τῶν (gen.pl.neut.of the article in agreement with ζῴων) 9.

τεσσάρων (gen.pl.neut.of τέσσαρες, in agreement with ζῴων) 1508.

ζῴων (gen.pl.neut.of ζῷον, partitive) 5086.

ἔδωκεν (3d.per.sing.aor.act.ind.of δίδωμι, constative) 362.

τοῖς (dat.pl.masc.of the article in agreement with ἀγγέλοις) 9.

ἑπτὰ (numeral) 1024.

ἀγγέλοις (dat.pl.masc.of ἄγγελος, indirect object of ἔδωκεν) 96.

ἑπτὰ (numeral) 1024.

φιάλας (acc.pl.fem.of φιάλη, direct object of ἔδωκεν) 5348.

χρυσᾶς (acc.pl.fem.of χρύσεος, in agreement with φιάλας) 4828.

γεμούσας (aor.act.part.acc.pl.fem.of γέμω, adjectival, predicate position, restrictive, in agreement with φιάλας) 1457.

τοῦ (gen.sing.masc.of the article in agreement with θυμοῦ) 9.

θυμοῦ (gen.sing.masc.of θυμός, adverbial) 2034.

τοῦ (gen.sing.masc.of the article in agreement with θεοῦ) 9.

θεοῦ (gen.sing.masc.of θεός, description) 124.

τοῦ (gen.sing.masc.of the article in agreement with ζῶντος) 9.

ζῶντος (pres.act.part.gen.sing.masc.of ζάω, adjectival, emphatic attributive position, ascriptive, in agreement with θεοῦ) 340.

εἰς (preposition with the accusative, time extent) 140.

τοὺς (acc.pl.masc.of the article in agreement with αἰῶνας) 9.

αἰῶνας (acc.pl.masc.of αἰών, time extention) 1002.

τῶν (gen.pl.masc.of the article in agreement with αἰώνων) 9.

αἰώνων (gen.pl.masc.of αἰών, partitive) 1002.

Translation - "And one of the four living creatures gave to the seven angels seven golden bowls which had been filled with the wrath of God, who lives into the ages of the ages."

Comment: Another heavenly action preparatory to God's final action on the earth prior to the second coming.

Verse 8 - "And the temple was filled with smoke from the glory of God, and from his power; and no man was able to enter into the temple till the seven plagues of the seven angels were fulfilled."

καὶ ἐγεμίσθη ὁ ναὸς καπνοῦ ἐκ τῆς δόξης τοῦ θεοῦ καὶ ἐκ τῆς δυνάμεως αὐτοῦ, καὶ οὐδεὶς ἐδύνατο εἰσελθεῖν εἰς τὸν ναὸν ἄχρι τελεσθῶσιν αἱ ἑπτὰ πληγαὶ τῶν ἑπτὰ ἀγγέλων.

"and the temple was filled with smoke from the glory of God and from his power, and no one could enter the temple until the seven plagues of the seven angels were ended." . . . RSV

καὶ (continuative conjunction) 14.

ἐμεμίσθη (3d.per.sing.aor.pass.ind.of γέμω, constative) 1457.

ὁ (nom.sing.masc.of the article in agreement with ναὸς) 9.

ναὸς (nom.sing.masc.of ναός, subject of ἐγεμίσθη) 1447.

καπνοῦ (gen.sing.masc.of καπνός, subjective genitive) 2986.

ἐκ (preposition with the ablative of source) 19.

τῆς (abl.sing.fem.of the article in agreement with δόξης) 9.

δόξης (abl.sing.fem.of δόξα, source) 361.

τοῦ (gen.sing.masc.of the article in agreement with θεοῦ) 9.

θεοῦ (gen.sing.masc.of θεός, description) 124.

καὶ (adjunctive conjunction joining prepositional phrases) 14.

ἐκ (preposition with the ablative of source) 19.

τῆς (abl.sing.fem.of the article in agreement with δυνάμεως) 9.

δυνάμεως (abl.sing.fem.of δύναμις, source) 687.

αὐτοῦ (gen.sing.masc.of αὐτός, description) 16.

καὶ (continuative conjunction) 14.

οὐδεὶς (nom.sing.masc.of οὐδείς, subject of ἐδύνατο) 446.

ἐδύνατο (3d.per.sing.imp.mid.ind.of δύναμαι, progressive description) 289.

εἰσελθεῖν (aor.mid.inf.of εἰσέρχομαι, complementary) 234.

εἰς (preposition with the accusative of extent) 140.

τὸν (acc.sing.masc.of the article in agreement with ναὸν) 9.

ναὸν (acc.sing.masc.of ναός, extent) 1447.

ἄχρι (conjunction with the subjunctive in an indefinite temporal clause) 1517.

τελεσθῶσιν (3d.per.pl.aor.pass.subj.of τελέω, indefinite temporal clause) 704.

αἱ (nom.pl.fem.of the article in agreement with πληγαὶ) 9.

ἑπτὰ (numeral) 1024.

πληγαὶ (nom.pl.fem.of πληγή, subject of τελεσθῶσιν) 2421.

τῶν (gen.pl.masc.of the article in agreement with ἀγγέλων) 9.

ἑπτὰ (numeral) 1024.

ἀγγέλων (gen.pl.masc.of ἄγγελος, description) 96.

Translation - "And the temple was filled with smoke from the glory of God and from His power, and no one was able to enter the temple until the seven plagues of the seven angels were finished."

Comment: ἐκ and the ablative of source in τῆς δόξης and τῆς δυνάμεως after καπνοῦ, the subjective genitive. The smoke was the result of God's glory and power and it (καπνοῦ) filled the temple. The last clause comports with Rev.11:19. It is as He comes in glory that the heaven is rolled away like a scroll and the temple of thrown open (Rev.19;11; 6:14).

The Bowls of God's Wrath

(Revelation 16:1-21)

Revelation 16:1 - "And I heard a great voice out of the temple saying to the seven angels, Go your ways, and pour out the vials of the wrath of God upon the earth."

Καὶ ἤκουσα μεγάλης φωνῆς ἐκ τοῦ ναοῦ λεγούσης τοῖς ἑπτὰ ἀγγέλοις, Ὑπάγετε καὶ ἐκχέετε τὰς ἑπτὰ φιάλας τοῦ θυμοῦ τοῦ θεοῦ εἰς τὴν γῆν.

"Then I heard a loud voice from the temple telling the seven angels, 'Go and pour out on the earth the seven bowls of the wrath of God.' " . . . RSV

Καὶ (continuative conjunction) 14.

ἤκουσα (1st.per.sing.aor.act.ind.of ἀκούω, ingressive) 148.

μεγάλης (gen.sing.fem.of μέγας in agreement with φωνῆς) 184.

φωνῆς (gen.sing.fem.of φωνή, objective genitive) 222.

ἐκ (preposition with the ablative of source) 19.

τοῦ (abl.sing.masc.of the article in agreement with ναοῦ) 9.

ναοῦ (abl.sing.masc.of ναός, source) 1447.

λεγούσης (pres.act.part.gen.sing.fem.of λέγω, adjectival, predicate position, restrictive, in agreement with φωνῆς) 66.

τοῖς (dat.pl.masc.of the article in agreement with ἀγγέλοις) 9.

ἑπτὰ (numeral) 1024.

ἀγγέλοις (dat.pl.masc.of ἄγγελος, indirect object of λεγούσης) 96.

Ὑπάγετε (2d.per.pl.pres.act.impv.of ὑπάγω, command) 364.

καὶ (adjunctive conjunction joining verbs) 14.

ἐκχέετε (2d.per.pl.pres.act.impv.of ἐκχέω, command) 811.

τὰς (acc.pl.fem.of the article in agreement with φιάλας) 9.

ἑπτὰ (numeral) 1024.

φιάλας (acc.pl.fem.of φιάλη, direct object of ἐκχέετε) 5348.

τοῦ (gen.sing.masc.of the article in agreement with θυμοῦ) 9.

θυμοῦ (gen.sing.masc.of θυμός, description) 2034.

τοῦ (gen.sing.masc.of the article in agreement with θεοῦ) 9.

θεοῦ (gen.sing.masc.of θεός, description) 124.

εἰς (preposition with the accusative of extent) 140.

τὴν (acc.sing.fem.of the article in agreement with γῆν) 9.

γῆν (acc.sing.fem.of γῆ, extent) 157.

Translation - "And I began to hear a loud voice out of the temple saying to the seven angels, 'Go and pour out the seven bowls of the wrath of God into the earth.' "

Comment: Once again in Revelation we come to a point on God's clock when the final day of the tribulation and the second coming of our Lord is at hand.

There is nothing in the descriptions of the last bowls of wrath to indicate precisely when the first one begins, except that it cannot come before the middle of the week, when the mark of the Beast is imposed. The first six could come in quick succession or even simultaneously. The sixth bowl requires time to mobilize the armies of the Gentile powers of the world at Jerusalem against Israel — a matter of a few days or weeks. The last bowl is poured out on the last day of the week. The language is not symbolic and the results must be taken literally.

Note that the wrath of God does not fall upon the saints, even though the remnant of the Body of Christ is still upon the earth (1 Thess.5:9; Psalm 91)

Verse 2 - "And the first went and poured out his vial upon the earth; and there fell a noisome and grievous sore upon the men which had the mark of the beast, and upon them which worshipped his image."

Καὶ ἀπῆλθεν ὁ πρῶτος καὶ ἐξέχεεν τὴν φιάλην αὐτοῦ εἰς τὴν γῆν, καὶ ἐγένετο ἕλκος κακὸν καὶ πονηρὸν ἐπὶ τοὺς ἀνθρώπους τοὺς ἔχοντας τὸ χάραγμα τοῦ θηρίου καὶ τοὺς προσκυνοῦντας τῇ εἰκόνι αὐτοῦ.

"So the first angel went and poured his bowl on the earth, and foul and evil sores came upon the men who bore the mark of the beast and worshiped its image." . . . RSV

Καὶ (inferential conjunction) 14.

ἀπῆλθεν (3d.per.sing.aor.ind.of ἀπέρχομαι, constative) 239.

ὁ (nom.sing.masc.of the article in agreement with πρῶτος) 9.

πρῶτος (nom.sing.masc.of πρῶτος, subject of ἀπῆλθεν and ἐξέχεεν) 487.

καὶ (adjunctive conjunction joining verbs) 14.

ἐξέχεεν (3d.per.sing.aor.act.ind.of ἐκχεω, constative) 811.

τὴν (acc.sing.fem.of the article in agreement with φιάλην) 9.

φιάλην (acc.sing.fem.of φιάλη, direct object of ἐξέχεεν) 5348.

αὐτοῦ (gen.sing.masc.of αὐτός, possession) 16.

εἰς (preposition with the accusative of extent) 140.

τὴν (acc.sing.fem.of the article in agreement with γῆν) 9.

γῆν (acc.sing.fem.of γῆ, extent) 157.

καὶ (inferential conjunction) 14.

ἐγένετο (3d.per.sing.aor.ind.of γίνομαι, ingressive) 113.

ἕλκος (nom.sing.neut.of ἕλκος, subject of ἐγένετο) 2582.

κακὸν (nom.sing.neut.of κακός, in agreement with ἕλκος) 1388.

καὶ (adjunctive conjunction joining adjectives) 14.

πονηρὸν (nom.sing.neut.of πονηρός, in agreement with ἕλκος) 438.

ἐπὶ (preposition with the accusative of extent) 47.

τοὺς (acc.pl.masc.of the article in agreement with ἀνθρώπους) 9.

ἀνθρώπους (acc.pl.masc.of ἄνθρωπος, extent) 341.

τοὺς (acc.pl.masc.of the article in agreement with ἔχοντας) 9.

ἔχοντας (pres.act.part.acc.pl.masc.of ἔχω, adjectival, emphatic attributive position, ascriptive, in agreement with ἀνθρώπυς) 82.

τὸ (acc.sing.neut.of the article in agreement with χάραγμα) 9.

χάραγμα (acc.sing.neut.of χάραγμα, direct object of ἔχοντας) 3420.
τοῦ (gen.sing.neut.of the article in agreement with θηρίου) 9.
θηρίου (gen.sing.neut.of θηρίον, description) 1951.
καὶ (adjunctive conjunction joining participles) 14.
τοὺς (acc.pl.masc.of the article in agreement with προσκυνοῦντας) 9.
προσκυνοῦντας (pres.act.part.acc.pl.masc.of προσκυνέω, adjectival, emphatic attributive position, ascriptive, in agreement with ἀνθρώπους) 147.
τῇ (dat.sing.fem.of the article in agreement with εἰκόνι) 9.
εἰκόνι (dat.sing.fem.of εἰκών, reference) 1421.
αὐτοῦ (gen.sing.masc.of αὐτός, description) 16.

Translation - "So the first went away and poured out his bowl into the earth. And an excruciating and loathsome sore developed upon the people who had the mark of the Beast and who worshiipped his statue."

Comment: It is difficult to know just what English adjective, as descriptive of a sore (ἕλκος), should be used to translate κακὸν and πονηρόν. Evil in a physical sense is what is meant. Loathsome, repugnant, repelling, vile, painful, *al.* Note that the victims are the unsaved (Psalm 91:3-10; 1 Thess.5:9). God's wrath can never fall upon one for whom Christ died.

Verse 3 - "And the second angel poured out his vial upon the sea; and it became as the blood of a dead man: and every living soul died in the sea."

Καὶ ὁ δεύτερος ἐξέχεεν τὴν φιάλην αὐτοῦ εἰς τὴν θάλασσαν, καὶ ἐγένετο αἷμα ὡς νεκροῦ, καὶ πᾶσα ψυχὴ ζωῆς ἀπέθανεν, τὰ ἐν τῇ θαλάσσῃ.

"The second angel poured his bowl into the sea, and it became like the blood of a dead man, and every living thing died that was in the sea." . . . RSV

Καὶ (continuative conjunction) 14.
ὁ (nom.sing.masc.of the article in agreement with δεύτερος) 9.
δεύτερος (nom.sing.masc.of δεύτερος, subject of ἐξέχεεν) 1371.
ἐξέχεεν (3d.per.sing.sing.aor.act.ind.of ἐκχέω, constative) 811.
τὴν (acc.sing.fem.of the article in agreement with φιάλην) 9.
φιάλην (acc.sing.fem.of φιάλη, direct object of ἐξέχεεν) 5348.
αὐτοῦ (gen.sing.masc.of αὐτός, possession) 16.
εἰς (preposition with the accusative of extent) 140.
τὴν (acc.sing.fem.of the article in agreement with θάλασσαν) 9.
θάλασσαν (acc.sing.fem.of θάλασσα, extent) 374.
καὶ (continuative conjunction) 14.
ἐγένετο (3d.per.sing.aor.ind.of γίνομαι, ingressive) 113.
αἷμα (nom.sing.neut.of αἷμα, predicate nominative) 1203.
ὡς (comparative particle) 128.
νεκροῦ (abl.sing.masc.of νεκρός, comparison) 749.
καὶ (continuative conjunction) 14.
πᾶσα (nom.sing.fem.of πᾶς, in agreement with ψυχὴ) 67.
ψυχὴ (nom.sing.fem.of ψυχή, subject of ἀπέθανεν) 233.

ζωῆς (gen.sing.fem.of ζωή, description) 668.
ἀπέθανεν (3d.per.sing.aor.act.ind.of ἀποινήσκω, constative) 774.
τὰ (nom.pl.neut.of the article, apposition) 9.
ἐν (preposition with the locative of place) 80.
τῇ (loc.sing.fem.of the article in agreement with θαλάσσῃ) 9.
θαλάσσῃ (loc.sing.fem.of θάλασσα, place) 374.

Translation - *"And the second poured out his bowl into the sea and it became blood like that of the dead, and every living thing such as are in the sea died."*

Comment: The phrase τὰ ἐν τῇ θαλάσσῃ is tacked on loosely to define πᾶσα φυχή. John means that all marine life died as a result of the blood in the sea. In the second trumpet judgment (Rev.8:8), which occurred during the first half of the tribulation week, perhaps five or six years before, only one third of the sea became blood and one third of marine life died. Here the entire sea is turned to blood and all marine life dies. One can scarce imagine the stench.

Verse 4 - "And the third angel poured out his vial upon the rivers and fountains of waters; and they became blood."

Καὶ ὁ τρίτος ἐξέχεεν τὴν φιάλην αὐτοῦ εἰς τοὺς ποταμοὺς καὶ τὰς πηγὰς τῶν ὑδάτων. καὶ ἐγένετο αἷμα.

"The third angel poured his bowl into the rivers and the fountains of water, and they became blood." . . . RSV

Καὶ (continuative conjunction) 14.
ὁ (nom.sing.masc.of the article in agreement with τρίτος) 9.
τρίτος (nom.sing.masc.of τρίτος subject of ἐξέχεεν) 1209.
ἐξέχεεν (3d.per.sing.aor.act.ind.of ἐκχέω, constative) 811.
τὴν (acc.sing.fem.of the article in agreement with φιάλην) 9.
φιάλην (acc.sing.fem.of φιάλη, direct object of ἐξέχεεν) 5348.
αὐτοῦ (gen.sing.masc.of αὐτός, possession) 16.
εἰς (preposition with the accusative of extent) 140.
τοὺς (acc.pl.masc.of the article in agreement with ποταμοὺς) 9.
ποταμοὺς (acc.pl.masc.of ποταμός, extent) 274.
καὶ (adjunctive conjunction joining nouns) 14.
τὰς (acc.pl.fem.of the article in agreement with πηγὰς) 9.
πηγὰς (acc.pl.fem.of πηγή, extent) 2001.
τῶν (gen.pl.neut.of the article in agreement with ὑδάτων) 9.
ὑδάτων (gen.pl.neut.of ὕδωρ, description) 301.
καὶ (inferential conjunction) 14.
ἐγένετο (3d.per.sing.aor.ind.of γίνομαι, ingressive) 113.
αἷμα (nom.sing.neut.of αἷμα, predicate nominative) 1203.

Translation - *"And the third emptied his bowl into the rivers and the water fountains, and they turned to blood."*

Comment: The verb should be ἐγένοντο, to conform in number to the preceding plurals, τοὺς ποταμοὺς καὶ τὰς πηγὰς, but, although several important witnesses have ἐγένοντο, "the more difficult reading ἐγένετο is adequately supported by Sinaiticus C P 046 051 most minuscules it₆₁ vg arm *al."* (Metzger, *A Textual Commentary on the Greek New Testament,* 757).

This plague recalls the plagues of the two witnesses (Rev.11:6) and of Moses in Egypt, except this is much worse. It triggers a comment from the angel of the waters, in verses 5 and 6, with an added word in verse 7.

Verse 5 - "And I heard the angel of the waters say, Thou art righteous, O Lord, which art, and wast, and shalt be, because thou has judged thus."

καὶ ἤκουσα τοῦ ἀγγέλου τῶν ὑδάτων λέγοντος, Δίκαιος εἶ, ὁ ὢν καὶ ὁ ἦν, ὁ ὅσιος, ὅτι ταῦτα ἔκρινας,

"And I heard the angel of water say, 'Just art thou in these thy judgments, thou who art and wast, O Holy One. . ." . . . *RSV*

καὶ (continuative conjunction) 14.
ἤκουσα (1st.per.sing.aor.act.ind.of ἀκούω, ingressive) 148.
τοῦ (gen.sing.masc.of the article in agreement with ἀγγέλου) 9.
ἀγγέλου (gen.sing.masc.of ἄγγελος, objective genitive) 96.
τῶν (gen.pl.neut.of the article in agreement with ὑδάτων) 9.
ὑδάτων (gen.pl.neut.of ὕδωρ, description) 301.
λέγοντος (pres.act.part.gen.sing.masc.of λέγω, recitative) 66.
Δίκαιος (nom.sing.masc.of δίκαιος, predicate adjective) 85.
εἶ (2d.per.sing.pres.ind.of εἰμί, aoristic) 86.
ὁ (nom.sing.masc.of the article in agreement with ὢν) 9.
ὢν (pres.act.part.nom.sing.masc.of εἰμί, apposition) 86.
καὶ (adjunctive conjunction joining substantives) 14.
ὁ (nom.sing.masc.of the article in agreement with ἦν) 9.
ἦν (3d.per.sing.imp.ind.of εἰμί) 86.
ὁ (nom.sing.masc.of the article in agreement with ὅσιος) 9.
ὅσιος (nom.sing.masc.of ὅσιος, apposition) 2995.
ὅτι (conjunction introducing a subordinate causal clause) 211.
ταῦτα (acc.pl.neut.of οὗτος, direct object of ἔκρινας) 93.
ἔκρινας (2d.per.sing.1st.aor.act.ind.of κρίνω, culminative) 531.

Translation - "And I heard the angel of the waters saying, 'You are Just, the One Who is, and Who has always been, the Holy One, because you have decreed these things . . ."

Comment: The remainder of the reason is given in

Verse 6 - "For they have shed the blood of saints and prophets and thou hast given them blood to drink; for they are worthy."

ὅτι αἷμα ἁγίων καὶ προφητῶν ἐξέχεαν, καὶ αἷμα αὐτοῖς δέδωκας πιεῖν. ἄξιοί εἰσιν.

"For men have shed the blood of saints and prophets, and thou hast given them blood to drink. It is their due!' " . . . RSV

ὅτι (conjunction introducing a subordinate causal clause) 211.

αἷμα (acc.sing.neut.of αἷμα, direct object of ἐξέχεαν) 1203.

ἁγίων (gen.pl.masc.of ἅγιος, possession) 84.

καὶ (adjunctive conjunction joining nouns) 14.

προφητῶν (gen.pl.masc.of προφήτης, possession) 119.

ἐξέχεαν (3d.per.pl.aor.act.ind.of ἐκχέω, culminative) 811.

καὶ (inferential conjunction) 14.

αἷμα (acc.sing.fem.of αἷμα, direct object of δέδωκας) 1203.

αὐτοῖς (dat.pl.masc.of αὐτός, indirect object of δέδωκας) 16.

δέδωκας (2d.per.sing.perf.act.ind.of δίδωμι, consummative) 362.

πιεῖν (aor.act.inf.of πίνω, purpose) 611.

ἄξιοί (nom.pl.masc.of ἄξιος, predicate adjective) 285.

εἰσιν (3d.per.pl.pres.ind.of εἰμί, aoristic) 86.

Translation - ". . . *because they have shed the blood of saints and prophets; therefore you have given them blood to drink. They deserve it."*

Comment: It is another example of *lex talonis. Cf.* Rev.13:10.

God's immanent attributes are absolute. They are those attributes which are His which have nothing to do with His connection with the universe which He has created. "By Absolute or Immanent Attributes, we mean attributes which respect the inner being of God, which are involved in God's relations to himself, and which belong to his nature independently of his connection with the universe." (A.H. Strong, *Systematic Theology*, I, 247).

God also has Relative or Transitive Attributes "which respect the outward revelation of God's being, which are involved in God's relations to the creation, and which are exercised in consequence of the existence of the universe and its dependence upon him." (*Ibid.*). These Relative or Transitive Attributes relate to (1) time and space, (2) creation and (3) moral beings. The observation of "the angel of the waters" (verses 4-6) that God is just because He has decreed that those who have shed blood shall some day drink it, is a commentary on His relative and transitive attributes that relate to moral beings. There are three of them: (1) His veracity and faithfulness is transitive truth; (1) His mercy and goodness is transitive love and (3) His justice is transitive holiness. God's immanent attributes reveal Him as Infinite and Perfect Spirit. His transitive attributes reveal Him as the Source, Support and End of all things. (*Ibid.* 248). It is His justice which concerns us in the matter of the application of the *lex talonis* of Exodus 21:24,25. Principles of His moral law are reflected in and consistent with the principles of His natural law. Classical physics teaches us that force in the universe tends always to equilibrium. Newton's second law says that "for every action there is an equal and opposite reaction." When physical objects are moved about they tend to remain where they are put, not only because of Newton's first law that, "every particle of matter is attracted to every other particle with a force which is directly proportional to the product of their masses, and inversely proportional to the square of the distance between them" but also because of his third principle of inertia which says that bodies in motion tend to remain in motion and that bodies at rest tend to remain at rest, unless acted upon by outside superior force.

The amount of carbon fourteen in living bodies (plants and animals) is always in equilibrium with the amount of carbon fourteen in the environment of the living plant and/or animal. When the plant or animal dies the process of photo synthesis ceases and the radio activity of the remains begins. This is the principle of equilibrium.

Matter disintegrates to produce energy and to increase entropy, but the energy of the sun is translated by photosynthesis into matter. Thus, though entropy decreases the amount of available energy, photosynthesis counters the tendency. This again is equilibrium.

Alfred Marshall the British economist is said to have grasped the concept of equilibrium in a *laissez faire* market by watching the rise and fall of the ocean waves. Waves arose, but they also fell, as the principle of equilibrium maintained the level of the ocean water at a proper height. Similarly in a perfectly competitive market, in which homogeneous products are sold without advertizing by an infinite number of sellers to an infinite number of buyers, no one of which, either sellers or buyers are big enough to affect the market price, the law of supply and demand will equilibrate a market price, that will clear the market. There will be neither gluts nor shortages as sellers must take what the market price dictates and buyers must pay that market price. There are few perfect markets, therefore equilibrium in the market is seldom found, but the principle is sound.

The God Who in creation ordained the laws of equilibrium in the natural and social sciences, is the God Who has also ordained the laws that apply in the moral world. That is why He told Moses to say that eye shall be paid for eye, and tooth for tooth. God's justice dictates that in the end injustice will be requited. The sower will reap what he sowed (Gal.6:7). The wages of sin is death (Rom.6:23) and the debt must be paid, if not upon the Cross by our Reconciling Substitute, then by us in the lake of fire. The *lex talonis* principle dictates that the eleventh commandment, "Thou shalt get by with it" is not valid. No one transgresses God's law, either in the physical or moral world, without suffering the consequences. One cannot eat onions and keep it a secret and the TANSTAAFL principle ("There ain't no such thing as a free lunch") is sound.

These truths are self-evident. If this were not true there could be no permanence in a moral universe in which, for reasons sufficient unto Himself, God has chosen to permit evil. God's justice is transitive holiness.

Verse 7 - "And I heard another out of the altar say, Even so, Lord God Almighty, true and righteous are thy judgments."

καὶ ἤκουσα τοῦ θυσιαστηρίου λέγοντος, Ναί, κύριε ὁ θεὸς ὁ παντοκράτωρ, ἀληθιναὶ καὶ δίκαιαι αἱ κρίσεις σου.

"And I heard the altar cry, 'Yea, Lord God the Almighty, true and just are thy judgments!'" . . . *RSV*

καὶ (continuative conjunction) 14.
ἤκουσα (1st.per.sing.aor.act.ind.of ἀκούω, ingressive) 148.
τοῦ (abl.sing.neut.of the article in agreement with θυσιαστηρίου) 9.
θυσιαστηρίου (abl.sing.neut.of θυσιαστήριον, source) 484.
λέγοντος (pres.act.part.gen.sing.masc.of λέγω, recitative) 66.
Ναί (particle of affirmation) 524.
κύριε (voc.sing.masc.of κύριος, address) 97.
ὁ (nom.sing.masc.of the article in agreement with θεὸς) 9.
θεὸς (nom.sing.masc.of θεός, for θεέ, address) 124.
παντοκράτωρ (nom.sing.masc.of παντοκράτωρ, address) 4325.
ἀληθιναὶ (nom.pl.fem.of ἀληθινός, predicate adjective) 1696.
καὶ (adjunctive conjunction joining adjectives) 14.
δίκαιαι (nom.pl.fem.of δίκαιος, predicate adjective) 85.
αἱ (nom.pl.fem.of the article in agreement with κρίσεις) 9.
κρίσεις (nom.pl.fem.of κρίσις, subject of εἰσιν understood) 478.
σου (gen.sing.masc.of σύ, description) 104.

Translation - *"And I heard one from the altar saying, 'Yes, Lord God, the Almighty! Your judgments are true and just.' "*

Comment: *Cf*.Amos 4:13; Rev.1:8; 4:8; 11:17; 15:3; 16:14; 19:6,15; 21:22; Ps.19:9; 119:137; Rev.19:2.

Verse 8 - *"And the fourth angel poured out his vial upon the sun; and power was given unto him to scorch men with fire."*

Καὶ ὁ τέταρτος ἐξέχεεν τὴν φιάλην αὐτοῦ ἐπὶ τὸν ἥλιον, καὶ ἐδόθη αὐτῷ καυματίσαι τοὺς ἀνθρώπους ἐν πυρί.

"The fourth angel poured his bowl on the sun, and it was allowed to scorch men with fire;" . . . RSV

Καὶ (continuative conjunction) 14.
ὁ (nom.sing.masc.of the article in agreement with τέταρτος) 9.
τέταρτος (nom.sing.masc.of τέταρτος, subject of ἐξέχεεν) 1129.
ἐξέχεεν (3d.per.sing.1st.aor.act.ind.of ἐκχέω, constative) 811.
τὴν (acc.sing.fem.of the article in agreement with φιάλην) 9.
φιάλην (acc.sing.fem.of φιάλη, direct object of ἐξέχεεν) 5348.
αὐτοῦ (gen.sing.masc.of αὐτός, possession) 16.
ἐπὶ (preposition with the accusative of extent) 47.
τὸν (acc.sing.masc.of the article in agreement with ἥλιον) 9.
ἥλιον (acc.sing.masc.of ἥλιος, extent) 546.
καὶ (continuative conjunction) 14.
ἐδόθη (3d.per.sing.aor.pass.ind.of δίδωμι, constative) 362.
αὐτῷ (dat.sing.masc.of αὐτός, indirect object of ἐδόθη) 16.
καυματίσαι (aor.act.inf.of καυματίζω, in apposition with δύναμιν understood) 1032.
τοὺς (acc.pl.masc.of the article in agreement with ἀνθρώπους) 9.

ἀνθρώπους (acc.pl.masc.of ἄνθρωπος, direct object of καυματίσαι) 341.
ἐν (preposition with the instrumental, means) 80.
πυρί (instrumental sing.neut.of πῦρ, means) 298.

Translation - "And the fourth emptied his bowl upon the sun. And power was given to him to scorch the people with fire."

Comment: Sores, blood in the ocean, blood to drink and now intense heat! In all of this there is no repentance as we learn in

Verse 9 - "And men were scorched with great heat, and blasphemed the name of God, which hath power over these plagues: and they repented not to give him glory."

καὶ ἐκαυματίσθησαν οἱ ἄνθρωποι καῦμα μέγα, καὶ ἐβλασφήμησαν τὸ ὄνομα τοῦ θεοῦ τοῦ ἔχοντος τὴν ἐξουσίαν ἐπὶ τὰς πληγὰς ταύτας, καὶ οὐ μετενόησαν δοῦναι αὐτῷ δόξαν.

"men were scorched by the fierce heat, and they cursed the name of God who had power over these plagues, and they did not repent and give him glory." . . . RSV

καὶ (continuative conjunction) 14.
ἐκαυματίσθησαν (3d.per.pl.aor.pass.ind.of καυματίζω, ingressive) 1032.
οἱ (nom.pl.masc.of the article in agreement with ἄνθρωποι) 9.
ἄνθρωποι (nom.pl.masc.of ἄνθρωπος, subject of ἐκαυματίσθησαν) 341.
καῦμα (acc.sing.neut.of καῦμα, cognate accusative, inner content) 5361.
μέγα (acc.sing.neut.of μέγας, in agreement with καῦμα) 184.
καὶ (inferential conjunction) 14.
ἐβλασφήμασαν (3d.per.pl.aor.act.ind.of βλασφημέω, ingressive) 781.
τὸ (acc.sing.neut.of the article in agreement with ὄνομα) 9.
ὄνομα (acc.sing.neut.of ὄνομα, direct object of ἐβλασφήμησαν) 108.
τοῦ (gen.sing.masc.of the article in agreement with θεοῦ) 9.
θεοῦ (gen.sing.masc.of θεός, possession) 124.
τοῦ (gen.sing.masc.of the article in agreement with ἔχοντος) 9.
ἔχοντος (pres.act.part.gen.sing.masc.of ἔχω, adjectival, emphatic attributive position, ascriptive, in agreement with θεοῦ) 82.
τὴν (acc.sing.fem.of the article in agreement with ἐξουσίαν) 9.
ἐξουσίαν (acc.sing.fem.of ἐξουσία, direct object of ἔχοντος) 707.
ἐπὶ (preposition with the accusative, metaphorical, "over") 47.
τὰς (acc.pl.fem.of the article in agreement with πληγὰς) 9.
πληγὰς (acc.pl.fem.of πληγή, "over") 2421.
ταύτας (acc.pl.fem.of οὗτος, in agreement with πληγὰς) 93.
καὶ (continuative conjunction) 14.
οὐ (negative conjunction with the indicative) 130.
μετενόησαν (3d.per.pl.aor.act.ind.of μετανοέω, constative) 251.
δοῦναι (aor.act.inf.of δίδωμι, result) 362.
αὐτῷ (dat.sing.masc.of αὐτός, indirect object of δοῦναι) 16.

δόξαν (acc.sing.fem.of δόξα, direct object of δοῦναι) 361.

Translation - "And the people began to be scorched with intense heat; therefore they began to revile the name of God Who had the authority over these plagues, and they did not repent to give Him glory."

Comment: Note the cognate accusative of inner content in ἐκαυματ ίσθησαν ... καῦμα μέγα — "scorched with great scorching. Others are found in John 7:24; 1 Pet.3:14; Col.2:19; 1 Tim.1;18; 6:12; Rev.17:6; Mk.10:38. (Robertson, *Grammar*, 478). The first καὶ can be considered inferential as well as continuative. We should not expect the people to do other than blaspheme God's name under the heat of judgment. These are the people who have already taken the mark of the Beast and have offered worship to his image. If they had been elect they would have refused his mark and by this time they would have been called by the Holy Spirit into the Body of Christ (Rev.10:7). The non-elect can only rebel against God's judgments.

Is δοῦναι, the anarthrous infinitive after μετενόησαν purpose or result? Is it, or not like ἀνοῖξαι of Rev.5:5? Robertson thinks it is, and we have already agreed with his view that they are both result. *Cf.* comment on Rev.5:5. Indeed, Robertson himself is confused since he says that δοῦναι is result (*Grammar*, 1001) and then says that it is purpose (*Ibid.*, 1088, 1089), but admits (*Ibid.*, 1090) that the "kinship (of result) with purpose is so strong." I believe that ἀνοῖξαι in Rev.5:5 is consecutive, for reasons given *en loc* and that it is also consecutive in Rev.16:9. If the unsaved, suffering under intense heat did in fact repent, the result would be to give glory to God. Of course it can be argued that if one were thinking about repenting it would be for the purpose of giving glory to God. No grammarian should be condemned for his view on these border line cases. Only the context can give the final answer. With millions of cross references in a large work, it is likely that the grammarian will be contradicting himself through oversight. Therefore no censure is intended when disagreement occurs. The point of the passage is that another bowl of wrath, this time resulting in great heat, was poured out and that the victims were driven into agonized rage against God. Unimpressed by the message of the cross (2 Cor.4:4) they are impressed by the judgment of God, only to curse.

The writer recalls a man in a hospital whose legs had been horribly burned by a gasoline fire, who drove us from his bedside with curses, when we tried to tell him of the love of God in Christ. Such is human depravity.

Verse 10 - "And the fifth angel poured out his vial upon the seat of the beast: and his kingdom was full of darkness; and they gnawed their tongues for pain,"

Καὶ ὁ πέμπτος ἐξέχεεν τὴν φιάλην αὐτοῦ ἐπὶ τὸν θρόνον τοῦ θηρίου, καὶ ἐγένετο ἡ βασιλεία αὐτοῦ ἐσκοτωμένη, καὶ ἐμασῶντο τὰς γλώσσας αὐτῶν ἐκ τοῦ πόνου,

"The fifth angel poured his bowl on the throne of the beast, and its kingdom was in darkness; men gnawed their tongues in anguish . . . " . . . RSV

Καὶ (continuative conjunction) 14.

ὁ (nom.sing.masc.of the article in agreement with πέμπτος) 9.
πέμπτος (nom.sing.masc.of πέμπτος, subject of ἐξέχεεν) 5353.
ἐξέχεεν (3d.per.sing.aor.act.ind.of ἐκχέω, constative) 811.
τὴν (acc.sing.fem.of the article in agreement with φιάλην) 9.
φιάλην (acc.sing.fem.of φιάλη, direct object of ἐξέκεεν) 5348.
αὐτοῦ (gen.sing.masc.of αὐτός, possession) 16.
ἐπὶ (preposition with the accusative of extent) 47.
τὸν (acc.sing.masc.of the article in agreement with θρόνον) 9.
θρόνον (acc.sing.masc.of θρόνος, extent) 519.
τοῦ (gen.sing.neut.of the article in agreement with θηρίου) 9.
θηρίου (gen.sing.neut.of θηρίον, possession) 1951.
καὶ (inferential conjunction) 14.
ἐγένετο (3d.per.sing.aor.ind.of γίνομαι, constative) 113.
ἡ (nom.sing.fem.of the article in agreement with βασιλεία) 9.
βασιλεία (nom.sing.fem.of βασιλεία, subject of ἐγένετο) 253.
αὐτοῦ (gen.sing.masc.of αὐτός, possession) 16.
ἐσκοτωμένη (perf.pass.part.nom.sing.fem.of σκοτέω, perfect periphrastic. *Cf.*
Comment, *infra*) 4501.
καὶ (continuative conjunction) 14.

#5394 ἐμασῶντο (3d.per.pl.imp.mid.ind.of μασσάομαι, inceptive).

King James Version

gnaw - Rev.16:10.

Revised Standard Version

gnaw - Rev.16:10.

Meaning: prop.to chew, masticate. In the context of Rev.16:10 with τῆς γλώσσας as object and in the imperfect (inceptive) tense - "to begin to gnaw" or "chew upon their tongues because of pain" - Rev.16:10.

τὰς (acc.pl.fem.of the article in agreement with γλώσσας) 9.
γλώσσας (acc.pl.fem.of γλῶσσα, direct object of ἐμασῶντο) 1846.
αὐτῶν (gen.pl.masc.of αὐτός, possession) 16.
ἐκ (preposition with the ablative, cause) 19.
τοῦ (abl.sing.masc.of the article in agreement with πόνου) 9.
πόνου (abl.sing.masc.of πόνος, cause) 4643.

Translation - "And the fifth emptied his bowl upon the throne of the Beast. Whereupon his kingdom was blacked out, and they began to gnaw their tongues because of the anguish."

Comment: πόνου here (#4643) means psychical as well as physical pain. In addition to the pain there will be the enraged agony of frustration as the brilliantly lighted kingdom of the Beast, in all of its commercial and cultural glory (Rev.18) will suddenly be plunged in darkness. Note that the judgment falls upon the throne of the Beast, not upon the sun or the moon. Thus it could be explained as a gigantic power failure on earth. ἐγένετο . . . ἐσκοτωμένη is a perfect periphrastic construction with ἐγένετο and the perfect participle in ἐσκοτωμένη, instead of γίνομαι. Robertson calls this a case of "a mixture of tenses." (Grammar, 902, 903). The imperfect tense in ἐμασῶντο is dramatic. One does not continue to chew upon his own tongue unless he is driven to insane rage and intense agony. ἐκ with the ablative to express cause is unusual. Just as they did not repent because of the heat (verses 8,9), so they will not repent because of darkness of the fifth bowl judgment. Repentance is a gift of God's grace (Acts 11:18).

Verse 11 - "And blasphemed the God of heaven, because of their pains and their sores, and repented not of the deeds."

καὶ ἐβλασφήμησαν τὸν θεὸν τοῦ οὐρανοῦ ἐκ τῶν πόνων αὐτῶν καὶ ἐκ τῶν ἑλκῶν αὐτῶν, καὶ οὐ μετενόησαν ἐκ τῶν ἔργων αὐτῶν.

". . . and cursed the God of heaven for their pain and sores, and did not repent of their deeds." . . . RSV

καὶ (adjunctive conjunction joining verbs) 14.
ἐβλασθήμησαν (3d.per.pl.aor.act.ind.of βλασφημέω, ingressive) 781.
τὸν (acc.sing.masc.of the article in agreement with θεὸν) 9.
θεὸν (acc.sing.masc.of θεός, direct object of ἐβλασθήμησαν) 124.
τοῦ (gen.sing.masc.of the article in agreement with οὐρανοῦ) 9.
οὐρανοῦ (gen.sing.masc.of οὐρανός, description) 254.
ἐκ (preposition with the ablative, cause) 19.
τῶν (abl.pl.masc.of the article in agreement with πόνων) 9.
πόνων (abl.pl.masc.of πόνος, cause) 4643.
αὐτῶν (gen.pl.masc.of αὐτός, possession) 16.
καὶ (adjunctive conjunction joining prepositional phrases) 14.
ἐκ (preposition with the ablative of cause) 19.
τῶν (abl..pl.neut.of the article in agreement with ἑλκῶν) 9.
ἑλκῶν (abl.pl.neut.of ἕλκος, cause) 2582.
αὐτῶν (gen.pl.masc.of αὐτός, possession) 16.
καὶ (adjunctive conjunction joining verbs) 14.
οὐ (negative conjunction with the indicative) 130.
μετενόησαν (3d.per.pl.aor.act.ind.of μετανοέω, constative) 251.
ἐκ (preposition with the ablative, separation) 19.
τῶν (abl.pl.neut.of the article in agreement with ἔργων) 9.
ἔργων (abl.pl.neut.of ἔργον, separation) 460.
αὐτῶν (gen.pl.masc.of αὐτός, possession) 16.

Translation - ". . . and they began to revile the God of heaven because of their pains and because of their sores, and they did not repent of their deeds."

Comment: ἐκ with the ablative of separation after μετενόησαν is a clear example of what true repentance is — a change of the mind that results in a separation from and a forsaking of sin. This is further evidence of the total unregenerate character of human nature. To blaspheme natural law is insanity.

The sixth bowl, unlike the first five which brought physical suffering and mental anguish to the unsaved inhabitants of earth, brings a hellish seduction and a physical preparation for compliance with it.

Verse 12 - "And the sixth angel poured out his vial upon the great river Euphrates: and the water thereof was dried up, that the way of the kings of the east might be prepared."

Καὶ ὁ ἕκτος ἐξέχεεν τὴν φιάλην αὐτοῦ ἐπὶ τὸν ποταμὸν τὸν μέγαν τὸν Εὐφράτην, καὶ ἐξηράνθη τὸ ὕδωρ αὐτοῦ, ἵνα ἑτοιμασθῇ ἡ ὁδὸς τῶν βασιλέων τῶν ἀπὸ ἀνατολῆς ἡλίου.

"The sixth angel poured his bowl on the great river Euphrates, and its water was dried up, to prepare the way for the kings of the east." . . . RSV

Καὶ (continuative conjunction) 14.

ὁ (nom.sing.masc.of the article in agreement with ἕκτος) 9.

ἕκτος (nom.sing.masc.of ἕκτος, subject of ἐξέχεεν) 1317.

ἐξέχεεν (3d.per.sing.aor.act.ind.of ἐκχέω, constative) 811.

τὴν (acc.sing.fem.of the article in agreement with φιάλην) 9.

φιάλην (acc.sing.fem.of φιάλη, direct object of ἐξέχεεν) 5348.

αὐτοῦ (gen.sing.masc.of αὐτός, possession) 16.

ἐπὶ (preposition with the accusative of extent) 47.

τὸν (acc.sing.masc.of the article in agreement with ποταμὸν) 9.

ποταμὸν (acc.sing.masc.of ποταμός, extent) 274.

τὸν (acc.sing.masc.of the article in agreement with μέγαν) 9.

μέγαν (acc.sing.masc.of μέγας, in agreement with ποταμὸν) 184.

τὸν (acc.sing.masc.of the article in agreement with Εὐφράτην) 9.

Εὐφράτην (acc.sing.masc.of Εὐφράτης, apposition) 5372.

καὶ (consecutive conjunction) 14.

ἐξηράνθη (3d.per.sing.aor.pass.ind.of ζηραίνω, constative) 1033.

τὸ (nom.sing.neut.of the article in agreement with ὕδωρ) 9.

ὕδωρ (nom.sing.neut.of ὕδωρ, subject of ἐξηράνθη) 301.

αὐτοῦ (gen.sing.masc.of αὐτός, description) 16.

ἵνα (conjunction with the subjunctive, purpose) 114.

ἑτοιμασθῇ (3d.per.sing.aor.pass.subj.of ἑτοιμάζω, purpose) 257.

ἡ (nom.sing.fem.of the article in agreement with ὁδὸς) 9.

ὁδὸς (nom.sing.fem.of ὁδός, subject of ἑτοιμάσθη) 199.

τῶν (gen.pl.masc.of the article in agreement with βασιλέων) 9.

βασιλέων (gen.pl.masc.of βασιλεύς, description) 31.

τῶν (gen.pl.masc.of the article in agreement with βασιλέων) 9.

ἀπὸ (preposition with the ablative, separation) 70.

ἀνατολῆς (abl.sing.fem.of ἀνατολή, separation) 138.

ἡλίου (gen.sing.masc.of ἥλιος, description) 546.

Translation - *"And the sixth emptied his bowl upon the great river, the Euphrates, with the result that its flow was stopped, in order that the road of the kings from the rising sun might be made available."*

Comment: Note the article with a proper name in apposition. John wishes us to know precisely which river he has in mind. The flow of the Euphrates, which lies athwart the path of oriental armies soon to be on the march to Jerusalem is stopped, thus obviating the necessity for army engineers to build bridges. This suggests that millions of men and much ordnance and logistic equipment — too much for existing bridges to accommodate, will soon be on the move westward, which is precisely what verses 13 and 14 describe. ἐξηράνϑη (# 1033) suggests, not an evaporation of water so much as an interruption in the flow of water from the northwestern reaches of the great river. The Euphrates rises in northeastern Turkey and flows in a southeasterly direction to join the Tigris perhaps 50-100 miles north of its mouth at the north end of the Persian Gulf. After its confluence with the Tigris, it is much larger than the Ohio at Louisville, Kentucky. North of the confluence point it is about the size of the Ohio. In the spring its banks are full, due to winter rains and the melting of winter snows to the north, in the watershed which it drains. In mid and late summer its volume is reduced. Both In World Wars I and II eastern armies marching westward had problems in crossing it, but nothing like the problem to be faced by vast movements of Oriental troops from India, China, Japan and other Oriental countries, which will be marching to Jerusalem to attack Israel and her Messiah.

Why will they be marching westward? And why at the same time will all of the armed forces of the Gentile nations be hastening to Jerusalem? We learn the reason in verses 13 and 14.

Verse 13 - *"And I saw three unclean spirits like frogs come out of the mouth of the dragon, and out of the mouth of the beast, and out of the mouth of the false prophet."*

Καὶ εἶδον ἐκ τοῦ στόματος τοῦ δράκοντος καὶ ἐκ τοῦ στόματος τοῦ θηρίου καὶ ἐκ τοῦ στόματος τοῦ ψευδοπροφήτου πνεύματα τρία ἀκάθαρτα ὡς βάτραχοι.

"And I saw, issuing from the mouth of the dragon and from the mouth of the beast and from the mouth of the false prophet, three foul spirits like frogs;" . . . RSV

Καὶ (continuative conjunction) 14.
εἶδον (1st.per.sing.aor.act.ind.of ὁράω, constative) 144.
ἐκ (preposition with the ablative of separation) 19.
τοῦ (abl.sing.neut.of the article in agreement with στόματος) 9.
στόματος (abl.sing.neut.of στόμα, separation) 344.
τοῦ (gen.sing.masc.of the article in agreement with δράκοντος) 9.
δράκοντος (gen.sing.masc.of δράκων, possession) 5382.
καὶ (adjunctive conjunction joining prepositional phrases) 14.

ἐκ (preposition with the ablative of separation) 19.

τοῦ (abl.sing.neut.of the article in agreement with στόματος) 9.

στόματος (abl.sing.neut.of στόμα, separation) 344.

τοῦ (gen.sing.neut.of the article in agreement with θηρίου) 9.

θηρίου (gen.sing.neut.of θηρίον, possession) 1951.

καὶ (adjunctive conjunction joining prepositional phrases) 14.

ἐκ (preposition with the ablative of separation) 19.

τοῦ (abl.sing.neut.of the article in agreement with στόματος) 9.

στόματος (abl.sing.neut.of στόμα, separation) 344.

τοῦ (gen.sing.masc.of the article in agreement with ψευδοπροφήτου) 9.

ψευδοπροφήτου (gen.sing.masc.of ψευδοπροφήτης, possession) 670.

πνεύματα (acc.pl.neut.of πνεῦμα, direct object of εἶδον) 83.

τρία (acc.pl.neut.of τρεῖς, in agreement with πνεύματα) 1010.

ἀκάθαρτα (acc.pl.neut.of ἀκάθαρτος, in agreement with πνεύματα) 843.

ὡς (comparative particle) 128.

#5395 βάτραχοι (nom.pl.masc.of βάτρακος, subject of εἰσίν understood).

King James Version

frog - Rev.16:13.

Revised Standard Version

frog - Rev.16:13.

Meaning: a frog - Rev.16:13.

Translation - "And I saw out of the mouth of the dragon, and out of the mouth of the Beast and out of the mouth of the false prophet, three unclean spirits that looked like frogs."

Comment: As a result of the sixth bowl the Euprhates river bed is dry, and thus it offers no barrier to an advancing army. Satan needs only to mobilize his armies to drive Israel into the Mediterranean Sea forever and put a permanent stop to the claims of Messiah as King of the Jews. He produces a foul spirit, as do also the Beast and the False Prophet. We need not speculate about who or what these three unclean spirits are. The text does not tell us how they look, except that it is clear to John that they are evil. Text does not tell us how they do it, but verse 14 tells us what they do.

Verse 14 - "For they are the spirits of devils, working miracles, which go forth unto the kings of the earth and of the whole world, gather them to the battle of that great day of God Almighty."

εἰσὶν γὰρ πνεύματα δαιμονίων ποιοῦντα σημεῖα, ἃ ἐκπορεύεται ἐπὶ τοὺς βασιλεῖς τῆς οἰκουμένης ὅλης, συναγαγεῖν αὐτοὺς εἰς τὸν πόλεμον τῆς μεγάλης ἡμέρας τοῦ θεοῦ τοῦ παντοκράτορος.

"for they are demonic spirits, performing signs, who go abroad to the kings of the whole world, to assemble them for battle on the great day of God the Almighty." . . . RSV

εἰσὶν (3d.per.pl.pres.ind.of εἰμί, aoristic) 86.

γὰρ (explanatory conjunction) 105.

πνεύματα (nom.pl.neut.of πνεῦμα, predicate nominative) 83.

δαιμονίων (gen.pl.neut.of δαιμόνιον, description) 686.

ποιοῦντα (pres.act.part.acc.pl.neut.of ποιέω, adjectival, predicate position, restrictive, in agreement with πνεύματα) 127.

σημεῖα (acc.pl.neut.of σημεῖον, direct object of ποιοῦντα) 1005.

ἃ (nom.pl.neut.of ὅς, relative pronoun, subject of ἐκπορεύεται) 65.

ἐκπορεύεται (3d.per.sing.pres.mid.ind.of ἐκπορεύομαι, futuristic) 270.

ἐπὶ (preposition with the accusative of extent) 47.

τοὺς (acc.pl.masc.of the article in agreement with βασιλεῖς) 9.

βασιλεῖς (acc.pl.masc.of βασιλεύς, extent) 31.

τῆς (gen.sing.fem.of the article in agreement with οἰκουμένη) 9.

οἰκουμένης (gen.sing.fem.of οἰκουμένη, description) 1491.

ὅλης (gen.sing.fem.of ὅλος in agreement with οἰκουμένης) 112.

συναγαγεῖν (2d.aor.act.inf.of συνάγω, purpose) 150.

αὐτοὺς (acc.pl.masc.of αὐτός, direct object of συναγαγεῖν) 16.

εἰς (preposition with the accusative of extent) 140.

τὸν (acc.sing.masc.of the article in agreement with πόλεμον) 9.

πόλεμον (acc.sing.masc.of πόλεμος, extent) 1483.

τῆς (gen.sing.fem.of the article in agreement with ἡμέρας) 9.

μεγάλης (gen.sing.fem.of μέγας, in agreement with ἡμέρας) 184.

ἡμέρας (gen.sing.fem.of ἡμέρα, description) 135.

τοῦ (gen.sing.masc.of the article in agreement with θεοῦ) 9.

θεοῦ (gen.sing.masc.of θεός, description) 124.

τοῦ (gen.sing.masc.of the article in agreement with παντοκράτορος) 9.

παντοκράτορος (gen.sing.masc.of παντοκράτωρ, in agreement with θεοῦ) 4325.

Translation - "*Now they are demonic spirits who perform miracles, who will be going out to the kings of the entire inhabited world in order to mobilize them at the battle of the great day of God, the Almighty."*

Comment: *Cf.* Zech.14:1-4, which says that God will gather the nations to Armageddon. Now we learn that He will use the unclean spirits to do this work of mobilization. What miracles they will perform in order to convince the leaders of Gentile world governments to unite in the attack against Jerusalem we are not told, but they will be successful. Every Gentile politician will be convinced that the world's problems will never be solved until we get rid of the Jews. Every nation will have its army there to fight against Israel and her Messiah, the Lord Jesus. *Cf.* Psalm 2. The heathen (Gentiles) will rage and the people will indulge an insane ambition — that mortal man, with his hordes of soldiers and his scientific technology can conquer Almighty God. "He that sitteth in the heavens shall laugh!" The Great Day is Armageddon (Rev.6:17). *Cf.* Mt.24:28.

Verse 15 - "Behold, I come as a thief. Blessed is he that watcheth, and keepeth his garments, lest he walk naked, and they see his shame."

Ἰδοὺ ἔρχομαι ὡς κλέπτης. μακάριος ὁ γρηγορῶν καὶ τηρῶν τὰ ἱμάτια αὐτοῦ, ἵνα μὴ γυμνὸς περιπατῇ καὶ βλέπωσιν τὴν ἀσχημοσύνην αὐτοῦ.

("Lo, I am coming like a thief! Blessed is he who is awake, keeping his garments that he may not go naked and be seen exposed!") . . . RSV

Ἰδοὺ (exclamation) 95.

ἔρχομαι (1st.per.sing.pres.ind.of ἔρχομαι aoristic) 146.

ὡς (comparative particle) 128.

κλέπτης (nom.sing.masc.of κλέπτης, subject of ἔρχεται, understood) 595.

μακάριος (nom.sing.masc.of μακάριος, predicate adjective) 422.

ὁ (nom.sing.masc.of the article in agreement with γρηγορῶν and τηρῶν) 9.

γρηγορῶν (pres.act.part.nom.sing.masc.of γρηγορέω, substantival, subject of ἐστί understood) 1520.

καὶ (adjunctive conjunction joining participles) 14.

τηρῶν (pres.act.part.nom.sing.masc.of τηρέω, substantival, subject of ἐστι understood) 1297.

τὰ (acc.pl.neut.of the article in agreement with ἱμάτια) 9.

ἱμάτια (acc.pl.neut.of ἱμάτιον, direct object of τηρῶν) 534.

αὐτοῦ (gen.sing.masc.of αὐτός, possession) 16.

ἵνα (conjunction with the subjunctive, negative purpose) 114.

μὴ (negative conjunction with the subjunctive) 87.

γυμνὸς (nom.sing.masc.of γυμνός, adverbial) 1548.

περιπατῇ (3d.per.sing.pres.act.subj.of περιπατέω, negative purpose) 384.

καὶ (adjunctive conjunction joining verbs) 14.

βλέπωσιν (3d.per.pl.pres.act.subj.of βλέπω, negative purpose) 499.

τὴν (acc.sing.fem.of the article in agreement with ἀσχημοσύνην) 9.

ἀσχημοσύνην (acc.sing.fem.of ἀσχημοσύνη, direct object of βλέπωσιν) 3814.

αὐτοῦ (gen.sing.masc.of αὐτός, possession) 16.

Translation - "Attention! I am coming as a thief. Happy is the one who is watching and keeping his clothing, lest he walk naked and they see him indecently exposed."

Comment: *Cf.* 1 Thess.5:2,4; 2 Pet.3:10; Rev.3:3, in which passages the "thief like" (unexpected) coming of Christ is a warning given to the unsaved, or to the backslidden Christian (Rev.3:3). He will not come as a thief to the alert Christian (1 Thess.5:4). *Cf.* comment on each of these passages.

Note that the admonition to watch (Mt.24:42; 25:13; Mk.13:35,37; Lk.12:37; 1 Thess.5:6; Rev.3:2,3; 16:15) is given in order to make Christians alert to the signs of the times in the sense of Lk.21:28. The end-time Christian (the time of Rev.16:15 is *immediately* before the second coming) will no doubt be watching, since world events which scarcely can be ignored, will herald the coming of Messiah. But the unsaved will not know until they see Him (Mt.24:30; Rev.1:7).

Just as Noah's neighbours did not know of the approaching flood, even though they had been told (Mt.24:37-39), so shall it be in the days of the coming of the Son of Man. During the tribulation period "Many shall be purified, and made white, and tried; but the wicked shall do wickedly: and none of the wicked shall understand; but the wise shall understand." (Dan.12:10).

Those who teach a rapture before the seven year tribulation period are faced with a problem for which there are four possible solutions: (1) they can deny the eternal security of the believer, as Arminians do, and teach that Christians who are living defeated lives are lost; (2) they can teach that defeated Christians are nevertheless saved, as Calvinists teach, but that they will be raptured unexpectedly while engaged in sinful practices — illicit sex, intoxication, gambling, profanity, etc., etc. (3) Or they can teach a selective rapture which will take only the Christians who are living the victorious life and who at the precise moment of the rapture are looking for the Lord. (4) Or they can abandon their pretribualtion rapture position. Those who teach that the rapture is simultaneous with the revelation and that it comes on the last day of the tribulation week, have no difficulty in showing that all of the children of God will have had three and one half years (in the case of Bible taught Christians, seven years) in which to prepare for the coming of the Lord. There is nothing in Scripture to tell us the hour of His coming, but those who are "alive and (who) remain unto the coming of the Lord" will know the day, just as Noah knew, seven days before the flood, on which day the judgment would fall upon the antediluvians (Gen.7:1-13).

The Holy Scriptures are so perfectly coordinated by the Holy Spirit into a self-consistent gestalt, that to misinterpret any part of the inerrant story is to create the necessity of facing contradictions in other parts. Jig saw puzzles go together harmoniously only when every piece in the puzzle is placed where it belongs - in perfect harmony with all of the other parts.

Verse 16 - "And he gathered them together into a place called in the Hebrew tongue Armageddon."

καὶ συνήγαγεν αὐτοὺς εἰς τὸν τόπον τὸν καλούμενον Ἑβραϊστὶ Ἀρμαγεδών.

"And they assembled them at the place which is called in Hebrew Armageddon." . . . RSV

καὶ (continuative conjunction) 14.

συνήγαγεν (3d.per.sing.aor.act.ind.of συνάγω, constative) 150.

αὐτοὺς (acc.pl.masc.of αὐτός, direct object of συνήγαγεν) 16.

εἰς (preposition with the accusative of extent) 140.

τὸν (acc.sing.masc.of the article in agreement with τόπον) 9.

τόπον (acc.sing.masc.of τόπος, extent) 1019.

τὸν (acc.sing.masc.of the article in agreement with καλούμενον) 9.

καλούμενον (perf.pass.part.acc.sing.masc.of καλέω, adjectival, emphatic attributive position, ascriptive, in agreement with τόπον) 107.

Ἑβραϊστὶ (loc.sing.fem.of Ἑβραΐς, sphere) 3572.

#5396 Ἁρμαγεδών (predicate nominative).

King James Version

Armageddon - Rev.16:16.

Revised Standard Version

Armageddon - Rev.16:16.

Meaning: Cf. Judges 5:19; 2 Kings 9:27; 23:29 and Zech.12:11, which tend to associate the place with the Valley of Megiddo. Megoddio is northwest of Jerusalem on the coast, near the modern city of Haifa. The valley of Megiddo lies down the slope from Mt. Carmel. The student should read Zechariah 12 carefully. Verse 9 predicts the divine destruction of nations which will have assembled armies against Jerusalem. *Cf.* Zech.14:1-3. Since the Lord will return to Jerusalem (Rev.14:1; Zech.14:1-3) and since all nations will mobilize their troops against Israel, and since Haifi is the outstanding seaport on the Mediterranean coast, it is logical to expect troops coming from the European and American continents to disembark at Haifa and assemble for battle in Megiddo near by, preparatory to an attack on Tel Aviv and Jerusalem. Thus the river of blood, 200 miles in length (Rev.14:20) would extend from Haifa, southeastward to engulf the low lands around Jerusalem and on to the Dead Sea and beyond.

Verses 17-21 depict the outpouring of the last bowl of wrath, which is contemporary to the time of the raptured sixth church, the sixth and seventh seals and the seventh trumpet, and which brings us once again (Rev.6:12-17; 11:15-19; 16:17-21) to the last day of the "times of the Gentiles" (Dan.9:24-27; Lk.21:24). Rev.16:16.

Translation - "And he brought them together to a place called in Hebrew, 'Armageddon.' "

Comment: *Cf.* discussion *supra* under #5396.

Verse 17 - "And the seventh angel poured out his vial into the air; and there came a great voice out of the temple of heaven, from the throne, saying, It is done."

Καὶ ὁ ἕβδομος ἐξέχεεν τὴν φιάλην αὐτοῦ ἐπὶ τὸν ἀέρα, καὶ ἐξῆλθεν φωνὴ μεγάλη ἐκ τοῦ ναοῦ ἀπὸ τοῦ θρόνου λέγουσα, Γέγονεν.

"The seventh angel poured his bowl into the air, and a great voice came out of the temple, from the throne, saying, 'It is done!' " . . . *RSV*

Καὶ (continuative conjunction) 14.

ὁ (nom.sing.masc.of the article in agreement with ἕβδομος) 9.

ἔβδομος (nom.sing.masc.of ἔβδομος, subject of ἐξέχεεν) 2020.

ἐξέχεεν (3d.per.sing.aor.act.ind.of ἐκχέω, constative) 811.

τὴν (acc.sing.fem.of the article in agreement with φιάλην) 9.

φιάλην (acc.sing.fem.of φιάλη, direct object of ἐξέχεεν) 5348.

αὐτοῦ (gen.sing.masc.of αὐτός, possession) 16.

ἐπὶ (preposition with the accusative of extent) 47.

τὸν (acc.sing.masc.of the article in agreement with ἀέρα) 9.

ἀέρα (acc.sing.masc.of ἀήρ, extent) 3584.

καὶ (continuative conjunction) 14.

ἐξῆλθεν (3d.per.sing.aor.ind.of ἐξέρχομαι, ingressive) 161.

φωνὴ (nom.sing.fem.of φωνή, subject of ἐξῆλθεν) 222.

μεγάλη (nom.sing.fem.of μέγας, in agreement with φωνῇ) 184.

ἐκ (preposition with the ablative of source) 19.

τοῦ (abl.sing.masc.of the article in agreement with ναοῦ) 9.

ναοῦ (abl.sing.masc.of ναός, source) 1447.

ἀπὸ (preposition with the ablative, separation) 70.

τοῦ (abl.sing.masc.of the article in agreement with θρόνου) 9.

θρόνου (abl.sing.masc.of θρόνος, separation) 519.

λέγουσα (pres.act.part.nom.sing.fem.of λέγω, recitative) 66.

Γέγονεν (3d.per.sing.2d.perf.ind.of γίνομαι, dramatic) 113.

Translation - "And the seventh poured out his bowl into the air, and a great voice came out of the temple from the throne saying, 'It has been done!' "

Comment: Contrast John 19:30 — Τετέλεσται. Redemption was complete at Calvary and now God's judgment has been accomplished — Γέγονεν. The pouring of the contents of the last bowl will precipitate the events which follow in verses 18-21.

We have stated repeatedly that correlative evidence shows clearly the contemporaneity and coterminality of the sixth and seventh seals, the seventh trumpet and the seventh bowl. This chart has been presented before but we present it again for emphasis. The student should remember that the alternative to acceptance of this view is that the same type of events collectively must occur on three separate and chronologically distinct occasions with measureable time spans intervening.

Other correlative scriptures link other events into this pattern: 1 Cor.15:52 with Rev.11:15; Luke 14:14 with 1 Cor.15:52 and Rev.11:15; Rev.10:7 with Rev.11:15; Mt.24:29 with Rev.6:12-14; Mt.24:30 with Rev.6:15,16,17; Mt.24:31 with 1 Cor.15:52 and Rev.11:15, etc. Deeper reseach will reveal many more correlatives. (2 Tim.2:15).

6th and 7th Seals	7th Trumpet	7th Bowl
(Rev.6:12-17; 8:1)	(Rev.11:15-19)	(Rev.16:17-21)

earthquake (6:12) —— —— —— earthquake (11:19) —— —— —— —— earthquake (16:18)
sun becomes black (6:12)
moon like blood (6:12)
stars fall (6:13)
heavens rolled back (6:14) —— temple of God open (11:19)
mts.and is. moved (6:14) —— —— —— —— —— —— —— —— —— —— mts.and is. moved (16:19)
great men hide (6:15) —— —— —— —— —— —— —— —— —— —— mountains fall (16:19)
face of God revealed (6:16)
great day of wrath (6:17)

wrath (11:18)
voices in heaven (11:15) —— —— —— voices (16:18)
Christ's kingdoms (11:15)
beginning of reign (11:15)
angry nations (11:18)
judgment on lost (11:18)
saints' rewards (11:18)
destruction (11:18)
lightnings (11:19) —— —— —— —— —— lightnings (16:18)
thunder (11:19) —— —— —— —— —— thunder (16:18)
hail (11:19) —— —— —— —— —— hail (16:19)
Jerusalem divided (16:19)
cities fall (16:19)
Babylon destroyed (16:19)

Silence in Heaven
after the storm (Rev.8:1)

Verse 18 - "And there were voices, and thunders, and lightnings: and there was a great earthquake, such as was not since men were upon the earth, so mighty an earthquake, and so great."

καὶ ἐγένοντο ἀστραπαὶ καὶ φωναὶ καὶ βρονταί, καὶ σεισμὸς ἐγένετο μέγας οἷος οὐκ ἐγένετο ἀφ' οὗ ἄνθρωπος ἐγένετο ἐπὶ τῆς γῆς πηλικοῦτος σεισμὸς οὕτω μέγας

"And there were flashes of lightning, loud noises, peals of thunders, and a great earthquake such as had never been since men were on the earth, so great was that earthquake." . . . RSV

καί (continuative conjunction) 14.

ἐγένοντο (3d.per.pl.aor.ind.of γίνομαι, ingressive) 113.

ἀστραπαί (nom.pl.fem.of ἀστραπή, subject of ἐγένοντο) 1502.

καί (adjunctive conjunction joining nouns) 14.

φωναί (nom.pl.fem.of φωνή, subject of ἐγένοντο) 222.

καί (adjunctive conjunction joining nouns) 14.

. βρονταί (nom.pl.fem.of βροντή, subject of ἐγένοντο) 2117.

καί (continuative conjunction) 14.

σεισμός (nom.sing.masc.of σεισμός, subject of ἐγένετο) 751.

ἐγένετο (3d.per.sing.aor.ind.of γίνομαι, ingressive) 113.

μέγας (nom.sing.masc.of μέγας, in agreement with σεισμός) 184.

οἷος (nom.sing.masc.of οἷος, subject of ἐγένετο) 1496.

οὐκ (negative conjunction with the indicative) 130.

ἐγένετο (3d.per.sing.aor.ind.of γίνομαι, constative) 113.

ἀφ' (preposition with the ablative of time separation) 70.

οὗ (abl.sing.neut.of ὅς, relative pronoun, time separation) 65.

ἄνθρωπος (nom.sing.masc.of ἄνθρωπος, subject of ἐγένετο) 113.

ἐγένετο (3d.per.sing.aor.ind.of γίνομαι, ingressive) 113.

ἐπί (preposition with the genitive of place description) 47.

τῆς (gen.sing.fem.of the article in agreement with γῆς) 9.

γῆς (gen.sing.fem.of γῆ, place description) 157.

τηλικοῦτος (nom.sing.masc.of τηλικοῦτος , in agreement with σεισμός, explanatory apposition, redundant) 4267.

σεισμός (nom.sing.masc.of σεισμός, nominative absolute) 751.

οὕτω (demonstrative adverb) 74.

μέγας (nom.sing.masc.of μέγας, in agreement with σεισμός) 184.

Translation - *"And lightnings and voices and thunders began, and a great earthquake occurred, the like of which had never occurred from the time man first existed upon the earth, it was so great."*

Comment: Note οὕτω μέγας - an adverb and an adjective together. The last phrase τηλικοῦτος . . . μέγας is an explanatory apposition which helps out οἷος. It is really redundant, added for emphasis. ἀφ' οὗ is equivalent to ἀπὸ τούτου ὅτε - "from the time when." Some MSS read ἄνθρωποι ἐγένοντο or οἱ ἄνθρωποι ἐγένοντο. No change in the exegesis is involved.

The thrust of the passage is that this last day earthquake transcends all previous disturbances in intensity. Its results are described in verse 19. An earthquake that levels all cities on earth is indeed the greatest. *Cf.* Ex.19:16-19. Similar phenomena — thunders, lightnings and an earthquake of lesser intensity will occur at the beginning of the trumpet judgments (Rev.8:5) seven years before. *Cf.* Rev.11:19 for the last trumpet description. *Cf.* Daniel 12:1.

Verse 19 - "And the great city was divided into three parts, and the cities of the nations fell: and great Babylon came in remembrance before God, to give unto her the cup of the wine of the fierceness of his wrath."

καὶ ἐγένετο ἡ πόλις ἡ μεγάλη εἰς τρία μέρη, καὶ αἱ πόλεις τῶν ἐθνῶν ἔπεσαν. καὶ Βαβυλὼν ἡ μεγάλη ἐμνήσθη ἐνώπιον τοῦ θεοῦ δοῦναι αὐτῇ τὸ ποτήριον τοῦ οἴνου τοῦ θυμοῦ τῆς ὀργῆς αὐτοῦ.

"The great city was split into three parts, and the cities of the nations fell, and God remembered great Babylon, to make her drain the cup of the fury of his wrath." . . . RSV

καὶ (continuative conjunction) 14.
ἐγένετο (3d.per.sing.aor.ind.of γίνομαι, ingressive) 113.
ἡ (nom.sing.fem.of the article in agreement with πόλις) 9.
πόλις (nom.sing.fem.of πόλις, subject of ἐγένετο) 243.
ἡ (nom.sing.fem.of the article in agreement with μεγάλη) 9.
μεγάλη (nom.sing.fem.of μέγας, in agreement with πόλις) 184.
εἰς (preposition with the accusative, predicate use, adverbial accusative) 140.
τρία (acc.pl.neut.of τρεῖς, in agreement with μέρη) 1010.
μέρη (acc.pl.neut.of μέρος, adverbial accusative) 240.
καὶ (continuative conjunction) 14.
αἱ (nom.pl.fem.of the article in agreement with πόλεις) 9.
πόλεις (nom.pl.fem.of πόλις, subject of ἔπεσαν) 243.
τῶν (gen.pl.neut.of the article in agreement with ἐθνῶν) 9.
ἐθνῶν (gen.pl.neut.of ἔθνος, description) 376.
ἔπεσαν (3d.per.pl.aor.act.ind.of πίπτω, ingressive) 187.
καὶ (continuative conjunction) 14.
Βαβυλὼν (nom.sing.fem.of Βαβυλών, subject of ἐμνήσθη) 49.
ἡ (nom.sing.fem.of the article in agreement with μεγάλη) 9.
μεγάλη (nom.sing.fem.of μέγας, in agreement with Βαβύλων) 184.
ἐμνήσθη (3d.per.sing.aor.pass.ind.of μιμνήσκω, constative) 485.
ἐνώπιον (preposition with the genitive of place description) 1798.
τοῦ (gen.sing.masc.of the article in agreement with θεοῦ) 9.
θεοῦ (gen.sing.masc.of θεός, place description) 124.
δοῦναι (aor.act.inf.of δίδωμι, purpose) 362.
αὐτῇ (dat.sing.fem.of αὐτός, indirect object of δοῦναι) 16.
τὸ (acc.sing.neut.of the article in agreement with ποτήριον) 9.
ποτήριον (acc.sing.neut.of ποτήριον, direct object of δοῦναι) 902.
τοῦ (gen.sing.masc.of the article in agreement with οἴνου) 9.
οἴνου (gen.sing.masc.of οἶνος, description) 808.
τοῦ (gen.sing.masc.of the article in agreement with θυμοῦ) 9.
θυμοῦ (gen.sing.masc.of θυμός, description) 2034.
τῆς (gen.sing.fem.of the article in agreement with ὀργῆς) 9.
ὀργῆς (gen.sing.fem.of ὀργή, description) 283.
αὐτοῦ (gen.sing.masc.of αὐτός, possession) 16.

Translation - "And the great city began to break up into three parts; and the cities of the nations fell; and Babylon the great was remembered before God that to her should be given the cup of the wine of the intensity of His anger."

Comment: We assume that the "great city" is Jerusalem, the city of the great King (Mt.5:35). Geologists have reported that faults in the rocks around Jerusalem indicate the possibility of earthquake results. *Cf.* Zech.14:4 which speaks of a two-fold division of the Mount of Olives.

All Gentile cities will fall — London, Paris, Berlin, New York, Tokyo *et al.*

Babylon (Revelation 17-18) will come in for the worst treatment, a description of which we have in Revelation 18. Rev.17:9 is sometimes cited as evidence that "Babylon" means Rome, the "city of the seven hills." Protestants are more eager to accept this view than Catholics. There is no evidence that Christians in the first century referred to Rome as "Babylon." This development came later when dissident groups of Christians began to look upon the Papacy as evil. Babylon's commercial prominence (Revelation 18) argues more for a city in closer connection with petroleum interests. Rome is situated about 20 miles inland from the Tyrrhenian Sea, and it is doubtful that the Tiber River, which connects her to the coast is navigable for a large volume of international shipping, nor does she have port facilities. Revelation 18:9-15 tells us of sea captains standing "afar off" and watching the smoke of the city's destruction. An ocean going vessel, standing off-shore, twenty miles to the west, would be close enough for her captain to see the smoke, but it is unlikely that he could bring his ship up the Tiber for trading. Babylon, however, if rebuilt on its ancient site, would lie fifty miles or less upstream on the Tigris-Euphrates River. Such a city would probably extend to the north end of the Persian Gulf.

It is not necessry for exegetes to decide the point in advance. Certainly, wherever it is, Babylon will be a great city, in terms of sin and blasphemy and also one of great commercial and financial influence. End-time Christians will have no difficulty in identifying her.

This world-wide earthquake reminds us of Isaiah 2:1-22, where we have Isaiah's prophecy of the same event pictured under the seventh bowl, seventh trumpet and sixth seal.

Verse 20 - "And every island fled away, and the mountains were not found.

καί πᾶσα νῆσος ἔφυγεν, καὶ ὄρη οὐχ εὑρέθησαν.

"And every island fled away, and no mountains were to be found;" . . . *RSV*

καὶ (continuative conjunction) 14.
πᾶσα (nom.sing.fem.of πᾶς, in agreement with νῆσος) 67.
νῆσος (nom.sing.fem.of νῆσος, subject of ἔφυγεν) 3277.
ἔφυγεν (3d.per.sing.aor.act.ind.of ἔφευγω, ingressive) 202.
καὶ (continuative conjunction) 14.
ὄρη (nom.pl.neut.of ὄρος, subject of εὑρέθησαν) 357.
οὐχ (negative conjunction with the indicative) 130.
εὑρέθησαν (3d.per.pl.aor.pass.ind.of εὑρίσκω, culminative) 79.

Translation - "And every island fled and mountains disappeared."

Comment: Dramatic evidence of the intensity and universality of the earthquake. We have not translated literally in order to intensify the dramatic effect. Literally it says, "mountains were not found." Weymouth says, "there was not a mountain anywhere to be seen." Goodspeed has, "the mountains disappeared."

Verse 21 - "And there fell upon men a great hail out of heaven, every stone about the weight of a talent: and men blasphemed God because of the hail; for the plague thereof was exceeding great."

καὶ χάλαζα μεγάλη ὡς ταλαντιαία καταβαίνει ἐκ τοῦ οὐρανοῦ ἐπὶ τοὺς ἀνθρώπους, καὶ ἐβλασφήμησαν οἱ ἄνθρωποι τὸν θεὸν ἐκ τῆς πληγῆς τῆς χαλάζης, ὅτι μεγάλη ἐστὶν ἡ πληγὴ αὐτῆς σφόδρα.

"and great hailstones, heavy as a hundred-weight, dropped on men from heaven, till men cursed God for the plague of the hail, so fearful was that plague." . . . *RSV*

καὶ (continuative conjunction) 14.
χάλαζα (nom.sing.fem.of χάλαζα, subject of καταβαίνει) 5364.
μεγάλη (nom.sing.fem.of μέγας, in agreement with χάλαζα) 184.
ὡς (comparative particle) 128.

#5397 ταλαντιαία (nom.sing.fem.of ταλαντιαῖος, in agreement with χάλαζα).

King James Version

the weight of a talent - Rev.16:21.

Revised Standard Version

heavy as a hundred weight - Rev.16:21.

Meaning: Cf. τάλαντος (#1273). Equal in weight to a talent - Rev.16:21. ". . . any of several ancient units of weight (as a unit of Palestine and Syria equal to 3000 shekels or a Greek unit equal to 6000 drachmas). *b.* a unit of value equal to the value of talent of gold or silver." (*Webster's Seventh New Collegiate Dictionary*).

καταβαίνει (3d.per.sing.pres.act.ind.of καταβαίνω, aoristic) 324.
ἐκ (preposition with the ablative of source) 19.
τοῦ (abl.sing.masc.of the article in agreement with οὐρανοῦ) 9.
οὐρανοῦ (abl.sing.masc.of οὐρανός, source) 254.
ἐπὶ (preposition with the accusative of extent) 47.
τοὺς (acc.pl.masc.of the article in agreement with ἀνρθώπους) 9.
ἀνθρώπους (acc.pl.masc.of ἄνθρωπος, extent) 341.
καὶ (continuative conjunction) 14.
ἐβλασφήμησαν (3d.per.pl.aor.act.ind.of βλασφημέω, ingressive) 781.
οἱ (nom.pl.masc.of the article in agreement with ἄνθρωποι) 9.

ἄνθρωποι (nom.pl.masc.of ἄνθρωπος, subject of ἐβλασφήμησαν) 341.
τὸν (acc.sing.masc.of the article in agreement with θεὸν) 9.
θεὸν (acc.sing.masc.of θεός, direct object of ἐβλασφήμησαν) 124.
ἐκ (preposition with the ablative, cause) 19.
τῆς (abl.sing.fem.of the article in agreement with πληγῆς) 9.
πληγῆς (abl.sing.fem.of πληγή, cause) 2421.
τῆς (gen.sing.fem.of the article in agreement with χαλάζης) 9.
χαλάζης (gen.sing.fem.of χάλαζα, description) 5364.
ὅτι (conjunction introducing a subordinate causal clause) 211.
μεγάλη (nom.sing.fem.of μέγας, predicate adjective) 184.
ἐστὶν (3d.per.sing.pres.ind.of εἰμί, aoristic) 86.
ἡ (nom.sing.fem.of the article in agreement with πληγή) 9.
πληγὴ (nom.sing.fem.of πληγή, subject of ἐστίν) 2421.
αὐτῆς (gen.sing.fem.of αὐτός, description) 16.
σφόδρα (adverbial) 185.

Translation - *"And huge hailstones of immense weight fall out of heaven upon the people. And the people begin to blaspheme God, because of the plague of the hail, because the plague of it is very great."*

Comment: Hail also accompanied the first trumpet judgment (Rev.8:7). We cannot be sure of the exact weight of the talent. Moulton and Milligan describe it as ranging from 108 to 130 pounds. Such hailstones would wreak terrible vengeance. City residents fleeing to the open country to escape falling buildings in the earthquake will be struck down by the hail.

Thus we are brought again as in Rev.6:12-17 and Rev.11:15-19 to the great day of the Lord and the second coming of Christ. God's clock, having run the course of seven years three times, first to describe religious conditions in the Body of Christ, second to describe political conditions with the seals and third, to describe cosmic conditions with the trumpets, has now come to the end of the week again with the bowls of divine wrath which are concentrated at the end of the week. The remainder of the material in the Revelation is descriptive of various scenes, persons and events which occur either during or at the end of the week, after the millenium or of heaven throughout the eternal ages.

Chapters 17 and 18 give us a closeup of Babylon and her position in the world and in chapter 18 of her fate.

The Great Harlot and the Beast

(Revelation 17:1-18)

Revelation 17:1 - "And there came one of the seven angels which had the seven vials and talked with me, saying unto me, Come hither: I will shew unto thee the judgment of the great whore that sitteth upon many waters."

Καὶ ἦλθεν εἰς ἐκ τῶν ἑπτὰ ἀγγέλων τῶν ἐχόντων τὰς ἑπτὰ φιάλας, καὶ ἐλάησεν μετ' ἐμοῦ λέγων, Δεῦρο, δείξω σοι τὸ κρίμα τῆς πόρνης τῆς μεγάλης τῆς καθημένης ἐπὶ ὑδάτων πολλῶν,

"Then one of the seven angels who had the seven bowls came and said to me,
'Come, I will show you the judgment of the great harlot who is seated upon many
waters, . . . " . . . RSV

Καὶ (continuative conjunction) 14.
ἦλθεν (3d.per.sing.aor.ind.of ἔρχομαι, constative) 146.
εἷς (nom.sing.masc.of εἷς, subject of ἦλθεν and ἐλάλησεν) 469.
ἐκ (preposition with the partitive ablative) 19.
τῶν (abl.pl.masc.of the article in agreement with ἀγγέλων) 9.
ἑπτὰ (numeral) 1024.
ἀγγέλων (abl.pl.masc.of ἄγγελος, partitive) 96.
ἑπτὰ (numeral 1024.
ἀγγέλων (abl.pl.masc.of ἄγγελος, partitive) 96.
τῶν (abl.pl.masc.of the article in agreement with ἐχόντων) 9.
ἐχόντων (pres.act.part.abl.pl.masc.of ἔχω, adjectival, emphatic attributive
position, ascriptive, in agreement with ἀγγέλων) 82.
τὰς (acc.pl.fem.of the article in agreement with φιάλας) 9.
ἑπτὰ (numeral) 1024.
φιάλας (acc.pl.fem.of φιάλη, direct object of ἐχόντων) 5348.
καὶ (adjunctive conjunction joining verbs) 14.
ἐλάλησεν (3d.per.sing.aor.act.ind.of λαλέω, ingressive) 815.
μετ' (preposition with the genitive of accompaniment) 50.
ἐμοῦ (gen.sing.masc.of ἐμός, accompaniment) 1267.
λέγων (pres.act.part.nom.sing.masc.of λέγω, recitative) 66.
Δεῦρο (imperatival interjection) 1304.
δείξω (1st.per.sing.fut.act.ind.of δείξω, predictive) 359.
σοι (dat.sing.masc.of σύ, indirect object of δείξω) 104.
τὸ (acc.sing.neut.of the article in agreement with κρίμα) 9.
κρίμα (acc.sing .neut.of κρίμα, direct object of δείξω) 642.
τῆς (gen.sing.fem.of the article in agreement with πόρνης) 9.
πόρνης (gen.sing.fem.of πόρνη, description) 1374.
τῆς (gen.sing.fem.of the article in agreement with μεγάλης) 9.
μεγάλης (gen.sing.fem.of μέγας, in agreement with πόρνης) 184.
τῆς (gen.sing.fem.of the article in agreement with καθημένης) 9.
καθημένης (pres.mid.part.gen.sing.fem.of κάθημαι, adjectival, emphatic
attributive position, ascriptive, in agreement with πόρνης) 377.
ἐπὶ (preposition with the genitive of place description) 47.
ὑδάτων (gen.pl.neut.of ὕδωρ, place description) 301.
πολλῶν (gen.pl.neut.of πολύς, in agreement with ὑδάτων) 228.

Translation - "And one of the seven angels having the seven bowls approached
and began to talk to me, saying, 'Come, I will show you the judgment of the great
harlot who is sitting upon many waters. . . . "

Comment: A hint as to what ἐπὶ ὑδάτων πολλῶν means may be found in verse two. This woman is in illicit relations with the peoples of all of the earth. Just as the Beast of Rev.13:1-10 came out of the sea (Rev.13:1), so this woman sits upon the many waters of the earth (Rev.18:17). She is destined for divine judgment. We learn the nature of her "fornication" in

Verse 2 - ". . . with whom the kings of the earth have committed fornication, and the inhabitants of the earth have been made drunk with the wine of her fornication."

μεθ' ἧς ἐπόρνευσαν οἱ βασιλεῖς τῆς γῆς, καὶ ἐμεθύσθησαν οἱ κατοικοῦντες τὴν γῆν ἐκ τοῦ οἴνου τῆς πορνείας αὐτῆς.

". . . with whom the kings of the earth have committed fornication, and with the wine of whose fornication the dwellers on earth have become drunk.' " . . . RSV

μεθ' (preposition with the genitive of association) 50.
ἧς (gen.sing.fem.of ὅς, relative pronoun, association) 65.
ἐπόρνευσαν (3d.per.pl.aor.act.ind.of πορνεύω, constative) 4152.
οἱ (nom.pl.masc.of the article in agreement with βασιλεῖς) 9.
βασιλεῖς (nom.pl.masc.of βασιλεύς, subject of ἐπόρνευσαν) 31.
τῆς (gen.sing.fem.of the article in agreement with γῆς) 9.
γῆς (gen.sing.fem.of γῆ, description) 157.
καὶ (continuative conjunction) 14.
ἐμεθύσθησαν (3d.per.pl.aor.pass.ind.of μεθύω, culminative) 1527.
οἱ (nom.pl.masc.of the article in agreement with κατοικοῦντες) 9.
κατοικοῦντες (pres.act.part.nom.pl.masc.of κατοικέω, substantival, subject of ἐμεθύσθησαν) 242.
τὴν (acc.sing.fem.of the article in agreement with γῆν) 9.
γῆν (acc.sing.fem.of γῆ, distribution, after κατά in composition) 157.
ἐκ (preposition with the ablative of means) 19.
τοῦ (abl.sing.masc.of the article in agreement with οἴνου) 9.
οἴνου (abl.sing.masc.of οἶνος, means) 808.
τῆς (gen.sing.fem.of the article in agreement with πορνείας) 9.
πορνείας (gen.sing.fem.of πορνεία, description) 511.
αὐτῆς (gen.sing.fem.of αὐτός, description) 16.

Translation - ". . . with whom the kings of the earth consorted, while the inhabitants throughout the world became intoxicated with the wine of her immorality.' "

Comment: κατά, in composition with the accusative in τὴν γῆν is distributive. The inhabitants throughout the entire earth as well as the political leaders have all been involved with Babylon. When we see the character of the woman, it becomes apparent that to deal with her in any way is to accept her anti-God philosophy. That those who will deal with Babylon are unsaved is clear from the fact that no one can buy or sell without the mark of the Beast. The picture in chapter 18 is one of great commercialism. Since no one can participate in the market without the mark and without having worshipped the Beast, it is clear that no one already saved or those elect destined to be saved before the "days of the voice of the seventh angel" (Rev.10:7) will be doing business in Babylon. Her market places will be filled with those who worship the Beast and proudly display his mark. That there will also be harlotry in Babylon in the physical sense, of course, is evident as one of the many "works of the flesh" (Gal.5:17 21).

Verse 3 - "So he carried me away in the spirit into the wilderness: and I saw a woman sit upon a scarlet coloured beast, full of names of blasphemy, having seven heads and ten horns."

καὶ ἀπήνεγκέν με εἰς ἔρημον ἐν πνεύματι. καὶ εἶδον γυναῖκα καθημένην ἐπὶ θηρίον κόκκινον, γέμοντα ὀνόματα βλασφημίας, ἔχων κεφαλὰς ἑπτὰ καὶ κέρατα δέκα.

"And he carried me away in the Spirit into a wilderness, and I saw a woman sitting on a scarlet beast which was full of blasphemous names, and it had seven heads and ten horns." . . . RSV

καὶ (continuative conjunction) 14.

ἀπήνεγκέν (3d.per.sing.aor.act.ind.of ἀποφέρω, constative) 2583.

με (acc.sing.masc.of ἐγώ, direct object of ἀπήνεγκέν) 123.

εἰς (preposition with the accusative of extent) 140.

ἔρημον (acc.sing.fem.of ἔρημος, extent) 250.

ἐν (preposition with the instrumental, association) 80.

πνεύματι (instru.sing.neut.of πνεῦμα, association) 83.

καὶ (continuative conjunction) 14.

εἶδον (1st.per.sing.aor.ind.of ὁράω, ingressive) 144.

γυναῖκα (acc.sing.fem.of γυνή, direct object of εἶδον) 103.

καθημένην (pres.mid.part.acc.sing.fem.of κάθημαι, adjectival, predicate position, restrictive, in agreement with γυναῖκα) 377.

ἐπὶ (preposition with the accusative, extent, rest) 47.

θηρίον (acc.sing.neut.of θηρίον, extent, rest) 1951.

κόκκινον (acc.sing.neut.of κόκκινος, in agreement with θηρίον) 1638.

γέμοντα (pres.act.part.acc.sing.neut.of γέμν, adjectival, predicate position, restrictive, in agreement with θηρίον) 1457.

ὀνόματα (acc.pl.neut.of ὄνομα, adverbial) 108.

βλασφημίας (gen.sing.fem.of βλασφημία, description) 1001.

ἔχων (pres.act.part.nom.sing.masc.of ἔχω, adverbial, circumstantial) 82.

κεφαλὰς (acc.pl.fem.of κεφαλή, direct object of ἔχων) 521.

ἑπτὰ (numeral) 1024.

καὶ (adjunctive conjunction joining nouns) 14.

κέρατα (acc.pl.neut.of κέρας, direct object of ἔχων) 1851.

δέκα (numeral) 1330.

Translation - "And he carried me away in Spirit unto a wilderness and I saw a woman seated upon a red beast which was full of blasphemous names, having seven heads and ten horns."

Comment: Note ἔχων which should read ἔχοντα (neut.acc.instead of masc.nom.) to agree with θηρίον. Note also γέμοντα, followed by ὀνόματα (accusative) instead of ὀνομάτων (genitive). ἔχων is a solecism, but after a verb of filling the accusative, especially in later Greek, made inroads upon the genitive. *Cf.* Phil.1:11, where we have πεπληρωμένοι καρπόν. The student can find others by running references on γέμω (#1457) and πληρόω (#115). Originally there was only the accusative. The other cases have evolved in the Attic period. In modern Greek again the accusative is dominate.

The women, Babylon (verse 5) is here associated with the Beast of Rev.13:1-10, in terms of world politics, commerce and godless philosophy and worship. Her description and her activities are covered in chapters 17 and 18. The time of this vision is prior to the middle of the week since the resurrection of the Beast from the abyss (Rev.9:1-11) is seen as a future event (Rev.17:8), but after his deadly wound (Rev.7:10). Indeed Rev.17:10 places the time as being during the second seal, the sixth and before the seventh. Thus John gets a little preview of the godless alliance which the Beast will make with this whorish institution the middle of the week when he reappears. Again we warn against being too eager to associate this woman with Roman Catholicism. Even if verse 9 points to Rome, as a city, the text does not identify the city of Rome with the Papacy. I have no wish to unduly approbate Catholicism, but I have an intense desire to avoid associating the Catholic system with Satan. Whatever the city of the seven hills turns out to be, it will be the capital city of the Beast and a center of great commercial activity (Rev.18). The woman will be very rich and very wicked as verses 4-6 point out.

Verse 4 - "And the woman was arrayed in purple and scarlet colour, and decked with gold and precious stones and pearls, having a golden cup in her hand full of abominations and filthiness of her fornication."

καὶ ἡ γυνὴ ἦν περιβεβλημένη πορφυροῦν καὶ κόκκινον, καὶ κεχρυσωμένη χρυσίῳ καὶ λίθῳ τιμίῳ καὶ μαργαρίταις, ἔχουσα ποτήριον χρυσοῦν ἐν τῇ χειρὶ αὐτῆς γέμον βδελυγμάτων καὶ τὰ ἀκάθαρτα τῆς πορνείας αὐτῆς,

"The woman was arrayed in purple and scarlet, and bedecked with gold and jewels and pearls, holding in her hand a golden cup full of abominations and the impurities of her fornication;" . . . RSV

καὶ (continuative conjunction) 14.
ἡ (nom.sing.fem.of the article in agreement with γυνή) 9.
γυνὴ (nom.sing.fem.of γυνή, subject of ἦν) 103.
περιβεβλημένη (perf.pass.part.nom.sing.fem.of περιβάλλβ, pluperfect periphrastic) 631.
πορφυροῦν (acc.sing.neut.of πορφύρεος, adverbial accusative) 2844.
καὶ (adjunctive conjunction joining nouns) 14.
καὶ (adjunctive conjunction joining participles) 14.
κόκκινον (acc.sing.neut.of κόκκινος, adverbial accusative) 1638
καὶ (adjunctive conjunction joining participles) 14.

#5398 κεχρυσωμένη (perf.pass.part.nom.sing.fem.of χρυσόω, pluperfect periphrastic).

#5398 κεχρυσωμένη (perf.pass.part.nom.sing.fem.of χρυσόω, pluperfect periphrastic).

King James Version

deck - Rev.17:14; 18:16.

Revised Standard Version

bedeck - Rev.17:4; 18:16.

Meaning: To adorn with gold; to gild; to cover with gold as with a veneer. The woman of Rev.17:4; 18:16 wears so much gold that she appears to be covered with it. Moulton and Milligan use the word "overlay." Followed by χρυσίῳ καὶ λίθῳ τιμίῳ καὶ μαργαρίταις in Rev.17:4 and 18:16 (μαργαρίτῃ). It is a picture of gaudy and vulgar display of great wealth.

χρυσίῳ (instru.sing.neut.of χρυσίον, means) 3006.
καὶ (adjunctive conjunction joining nouns) 14.
λίθῳ (instru.sing.masc.of λίθος, means) 290.
τιμίῳ (instru.sing.masc.of τίμιος, in agreement with λίθῳ) 3070.
καὶ (adjunctive conjunction joining nouns) 14.
μαργαρίταις (instru.pl.masc.of μαργαρίτης, means) 652.
ἔχουσα (pres.act.part.nom.sing.fem.of ἔχω, adjectival, predicate position, in agreement with γυνή) 82.
ποτήριον (acc.sing.neut.of ποτήριον, direct object of ἔχουσα) 902.
χρυσοῦν (acc.sing.neut.of χρύσεος, in agreement with ποτήριον) 4828.
ἐν (preposition with the locative of place) 80.
τῃ (loc.sing.fem.of the article in agreement with χειρὶ) 9.
χειρὶ (loc.sing.fem.of χείρ, place) 308.
αὐτῆς (gen.sing.fem.of αὐτός, possession) 16.
γέμον (pres.act.part.acc.sing.neut.of γέμω, adjectival, predicate position, restrictive, in agreement with ποτήριον) 1457.
βδελυγμάτων (abl.pl.neut.of βδέλυγμα, source) 1492.
καὶ (adjunctive conjunction joining nouns) 14.
τὰ (acc.pl.neut.of the article in agreement with ἀκάθαρτα) 9.
ἀκάθαρτα (acc.pl.neut.of ἀκαθαρτός, adverbial accusative) 843.
τῆς (gen.sing.fem.of the article in agreement with πορνείας) 9.
πορνείας (gen.sing.fem.of πορνεία, description) 511.
αὐτῆς (gen.sing.fem.of αὐτός, possession) 16.

Translation - "And the woman had been clothed in purple and scarlet and dressed up with gold and costly stones and pearls, with a golden cup in her hand filled with abominations and the filth of her immorality."

Comment: Note the translation reflecting the pluperfect periphrastics. They point back to the time of the first seal (Rev.6:1-2) when the rider on the white horse, in his first brief appearance brings false peace to the earth by offering to

Israel a diplomatic solution to the Middle East problem. But he knows what his real intentions are. He will break his promise to Israel. The rider on the white horse of Rev.6:1,2 will become the "abomination of desolation spoken of by Daniel the prophet" (Mt.24:15) three and one half years later.The "peacemaker" will become the "beast." He will capture control of the international market and thus control the economy of the entire world. Thus he will need a capital city. Babylon, with her stragetic position for shipping at the head of the Persian Gulf, and in the middle of the richest oil fields on earth will be chosen and building will begin. Revelation 17:9-11 tells us that the time point is during the second seal. This is perhaps a year or a little more after the beginning of the seven year period. Babylon, the great city is in process of becoming ready to take her place as the queen of the international commercial world. Thus her description. In the 18th chapter we move to the last day of the week and see her total destruction at the second coming of Messiah.

Purple and scarlet as a color combination is garish, vulgar and ostentatious - the gaudy evidence of personal insecurity and bad taste. A sign of the times is the current disregard in clothing fashion for color clash. The gold, costly gems and pearls is an example of Thorstein Veblen's "conspicuous consumption," a mark of a morally decadent, sensate culture. The whore is certainly no example of Aristotle's "golden mean" or the New Testament teaching about temperance . Babylon, the whore, is the exemplification of total depravity in economic, political, philosophical, moral, theological, cultural, psychological and aesthetic senses. She represents the totality of sin in all of its blasphemous expressions. The golden cup from which she drinks is a symbolic evidence of her taste for ethical abnormality with all of its disgusting ramifications.

She will be the source of all of earth's abominations as we learn in

Verse 5 - "And upon her forehead was a name written, Mystery, Babylon the Great, the Mother of Harlots and Abominations of the earth."

καὶ ἐπὶ τὸ μέτωπον αὐτῆς ὄνομα γεγραμμένον, μυστήριον, Βαβυλὼν ἡ μεγάλη, ἡ μήτηρ τῶν πορνῶν καὶ τῶν βδελυγμάτων τῆς γῆς.

"and on her forehead was written a name of mystery: 'Babylon the great, mother of harlots and of earth's abominations.' " . . . RSV

καὶ (continuative conjunction) 14.

ἐπὶ (preposition with the accusative, extent) 47.

τὸ (acc.sing.neut.of the article in agreement with μέτωπον) 9.

μέτωπον (acc.sing.neut.of μέτωπον, extent) 5356.

αὐτῆς (gen.sing.fem.of αὐτός, possession) 16.

ὄνομα (acc.sing.neut.of ὄνομα, direct object of εἶδον, verse 3) 108.

γεγραμμενον (perf.pass.part.acc.sing.neut.of γράφω, adjectival, predicate position, restrictive, in agreement with ὄνομα) 156.

μυστήριον (acc.sing.neut.of μυστήριον, in apposition with ὄνομα) 1038.

Βαβυλὼν (nom.sing.fem.of Βαβυλών, appellation) 49.

ἡ (nom.sing.fem.of the article in agreement with μεγάλη) 9.

μεγάλη (nom.sing.fem.of μέγας, in agreement with Βαβυλῶν) 9.
ἡ (nom.sing.fem.of the article in agreement with μήτηρ) 9.
μήτηρ (nom.sing.fem.of μήτηρ, apposition) 76.
τῶν (gen.pl.fem.of the article in agreement with πορνῶν) 9.
πορνῶν (gen.pl.fem.of πόρνη, relationship) 1374.
καὶ (adjunctive conjunction joining nouns) 14.
τῶν (gen.pl.neut.of the article in agreement with βδελυγμάτων) 9.
βδελυγμάτων (gen.pl.neut.of βδέλυγμα, relationship) 1492.
τῆς (gen.sing.fem.of the article in agreement with γῆς) 9.
γῆς (gen.sing.fem.of γῆ, description) 157.

Translation - "And upon her forehead (I saw) a name that had been written: 'Mystery. Babylon the Great, the Mother of Harlots and of the Abominations of the Earth.' "

Comment: The perfect participles continue as the Apostle adds γεγραμμένον, the adjectival participle, defining ὄνομα. The woman is clothed and bedecked and her name fits her appearance. She is Confusion *a fortiori* (*Cf.* Gen.11:1-9).

In contradistinction to the clarity of the truth of God's revelation, she is confusion personified. Thus we have a clue as to who or what the whore represents. She represents error. Thus she is totally Antichrist (John 8:32,36). Thus she is total bondage. Truth liberates; error enslaves. Trust is light; error is darkness. Truth yields fruit that is eternally constructive (Gal.5:22,23). Error works activities that are ultimately destructive (Gal.5:17-19).

The woman in the city of the seven hills is Catholicism only to the degree that Catholicism is in error. She represents all error, including that found among Protestant Christians, as well as Catholic Christians.

God has a mystery. Satan also has a mystery. *Cf.*#1038 for references on both the "mystery of Godliness" and the "mystery of iniquity." These two programs have been arrayed against each other since Satan's original and unsuccessful attempt at *coup d'etat* in heaven (Ezek.28:11-19; Isa.14:12-15). The divine mystery culminates in Christ, the Incarnate Saviour (1 Tim.3:16). It includes His calling out the elect, a work of grace to be finished at the very close of the "times of the Gentiles" (Lk.21:24; Rev.10:7). The "mystery of iniquity" (2 Thess.2:7) culminates in Antichrist and his whore (Rev.17:5). It involves and embraces all deviation from the revealed Word of God. So, if the whore is Roman Catholicism, as some paranoid protestants teach, she is much more. She is also the amoral existential philosophical basis for situation ethics; she is the democratic assumption that unregenerate man is good, kind and rational; she is the Gnostic error that matter is inherently evil and hence that Jesus is not God — the error that the early Christians fought; she is the doctrine of legalism that teaches that man is saved by his own meritorious contribution to a salvation equation that says that God plus man equals salvation. The whore's panoply of error includes the lunacies of the late 20th century flood of false teaching about the gifts, because of which the charismatic fanatics, vomit forth gibberish which they dare to call a gift of the Holy Spirit, drive out demons which they claim to find in everyone except themselves, lay hands of healing on hypochondriacs who enjoy being unhappy, feel good because they are sick and bask in the sunlight of national television coverage. One deacon suggested that he "lay hands on" an ailing air conditioning unit in the church building, thus to heal it and save a repair bill of ten thousand dollars. Thus the whore of Babylon offers the contents of her golden cup to the unsaved world.

Her abominations include all of the false teaching of the heretics to whatever extent we indulge them. But, though the Christian may, because of human frailty, be guilty of some heresy, he is, by divine regeneration, not a fundamental component of the whore's makeup. In the flesh he is the whore's bastard, for the flesh in its fallen condition is always wrong. It produces nothing profitable (John 6:63b). There comes a time when the true Christian, who has been associating with Babylon will realize his error. When? When the mark of the Beast, the permanent badge of the whore's consort will be presented. Then the Christian will choose. And he will choose properly, for those who receive the mark of the Beast are damned (Rev.19:20). When Babylon loses some of her previously duped followers, as Christians are forced to choose, she will turn in fury upon those who forsake her. This is the point in

Verse 6 - "And I saw the woman drunken with the blood of the saints, and with the blood of the martyrs of Jesus: and when I saw her, I wondered with great admiration."

καὶ εἶδον τὴν γυναῖκα μεθύουσαν ἐκ τοῦ αἵματος τῶν ἀγίων καὶ ἐκ τοῦ αἵματος τῶν μαρτύρων Ἰησοῦ. Καὶ ἐθαύμασα ἰδὼν αὐτὴν θαῦμα μέγα.

"And I saw the woman, drunk with the blood of the saints, and the blood of the martyrs of Jesus. When I saw her I marveled greatly." . . . RSV

καὶ (continuative conjunction) 14.

εἶδον (1st.per.sing.aor.act.ind.of ὁράω, ingressive) 144.

τὴν (acc.sing.fem.of the article in agreement with γυναῖκα) 9.

γυναῖκα (acc.sing.fem.of γυνή, direct object of εἶδον) 103.

μεθύουσαν (pres.act.part.acc.sing.fem.of μεθύω, adjectival, predicate position, restrictive, in agreement with γυναῖκα) 1527.

ἐκ (preposition with the ablative, cause) 19.

τοῦ (abl.sing.neut.of the article in agreement with αἵματος) 9.

αἵματος (abl.sing.neut.of αἷμα, cause) 1203.

τῶν (gen.pl.masc.of the article in agreement with ἀγίων) 9.

ἀγίων (gen.pl.masc.of ἄγιος, possession) 84.

καὶ (adjunctive conjunction joining prepositional phrases) 14.

ἐκ (preposition with the ablative of cause) 19.

τοῦ (abl.sing.neut.of the article in agreement with αἵματος) 9.

αἵματος (abl.sing.neut.of αἷμα, cause) 1203.

τῶν (gen.pl.masc.of the article in agreement with μαρτύρων) 9.

μαρτύρων (gen.pl.masc.of μάρτυς, possession) 1263.

Ἰησοῦ (gen.sing.masc.of Ἰησοῦς, relationship) 3.

καὶ (adjunctive conjunction joining verbs) 14.

ἐθαύμασα (1st.per.sing.aor.act.ind.of θαυμάζω, ingressive) 726.

ἰδὼν (aor.act.part.nom.sing.masc.of ὁράω, adverbial, temporal) 144.

αὐτὴν (acc.sing.fem.of αὐτός, direct object of ἰδὼν) 16.

θαῦμα (acc.sing.neut.of θαῦμα, cognative accusative) 4378.

μέγα (acc.sing.neut.of μέγας, in agreement with θαῦμα) 184.

Translation - "And I saw the woman getting drunk on the blood of the saints and on the blood of the witnesses of Jesus. And when I saw her I was seized with great amazement.

Comment: μεθύουσαν is a present participle, indicating simultaneous time with the verb εἶδον. Since this is during the time of the second seal (verse 8) Babylon, the capital city and capital institution of depravity of the Beast, now mortally wounded and in the abyss, but destined to rise and reign for forty two months in the middle of the week, will already be persecuting the saints, before he reappears.

Temperance and tolerance are divinely given virtues (Gal.5:22,23; 2 Peter 1:5-7). Intolerance and intemperance will be two of the earmarks of Babylon. Democracy, with its purely theoretical assumption of freedom of thought for the individual, with its accompanying protection of civil rights, will have been proved fallacious. The whore of Babylon will have none of it. She will kill all who disagree with her. Already her harlot offspring shows signs of bigotry. Indeed some true Christians are intolerant to the point of bigotry, because they forget Matthew 7:1, and take the matter of judgment upon others unto themselves. Indeed, we will be judges, after the second coming, but only with the delegated authority given to us by the only true Judge (1 Cor.6:2,3; John 5:22). Neither now, in any sense, nor even then, will we be personally permitted to assess blame and measure punishment. But the unsaved have already judged Christ as unworthy of their consideration and it is no small wonder that they should also judge Christ's witnesses worthy of death (Acts 13:46). So why should John have been amazed when he saw the woman? Perhaps it was the degree of her gaudy splendor, not her hatred for Christ and His saints. He also did not know what Babylon represented. Note the inner content cognate accusative.

Verse 7 - "And the angel said unto me, Wherefore didst thou marvel? I will tell thee the mystery of the woman, and of the beast that carrieth her, which hath the seven heads and ten horns."

καὶ εἶπέν μοι ὁ ἄγγελος, Διὰ τί ἐθαύμασας; ἐγὼ ἐρῶ σοι τὸ μυστήριον τῆς γυναικὸς καὶ τοῦ θηρίου τοῦ βαστάζοντος αὐτήν, τοῦ ἔχοντος τὰς ἑπτὰ κεφαλὰς καὶ τὰ δέκα κέρατα.

"But the angel said to me, 'Why marvel? I will tell you the mystery of the woman, and of the beast with seven heads and ten horns that carries her." . . . RSV

καὶ (inferential conjunction) 14.

εἶπέν (3d.per.sing.aor.act.ind.of εἶπον, constative) 155.

μοι (dat.sing.masc.of ἐγώ, indirect object of εἶπεν) 123.

ὁ (nom.sing.masc.of the article in agreement with ἄγγελος) 9.

ἄγγελος (nom.sing.masc.of ἄγγελος, subject of εἶπεν) 96.

Διὰ (preposition with the accusative, cause) 118.

τί (acc.sing.neut.of τίς, interrogative pronoun, in direct question) 281.

ἐθαύμασας (2d.per.sing.aor.act.ind.of θαυμάζω, direct question) 726.

ἐγὼ (nom.sing.masc.of ἐγώ, subject of ἐρῶ, emphatic) 123.

ἐρῶ (1st.per.sing.fut.act.ind.of εἴρω, predictive) 155.

σοι (dat.sing.masc.of σύ, indirect object of ἐρῶ) 104.

τὸ (acc.sing.neut.of the article in agreement with μυστήριον) 9.

μυστήριον (acc.sing.neut.of μυστήριον, direct object of ἐρῶ) 1038.

τῆς (gen.sing.fem.of the article in agreement with γυναικὸς) 9.

γυναικὸς (gen.sing.fem.of γυνή, description) 103.

καὶ (adjunctive conjunction joining nouns) 14.

τοῦ (gen.sing.neut.of the article in agreement with θηρίου) 9.

θηρίου (gen.sing.neut.of θηρίον, description) 1951.

τοῦ (gen.sing.neut.of the article in agreement with βαστάζοντος) 9.

βαστάζοντος (pres.act.part.gen.sing.neut.of βαστάζω, adjectival, emphatic attributive position, ascriptive, in agreement with θηρίου) 306.

αὐτὴν (acc.sing.fem.of αὐτός, direct object of βαστάζοντος) 16.

τοῦ (gen.sing.neut.of the article in agreement with ἔχοντος) 9.

ἔχοντος (pres.act.part.gen.sing.neut.of ἔχω, adjectival, emphatic attributive position, ascriptive, in agreement with θηρίου) 82.

τὰς (acc.pl.fem.of the article in agreement with κεφαλὰς) 9.

κεφαλὰς (acc.pl.fem.of κεφαλή, direct object of ἔχοντας) 521.

καὶ (adjunctive conjunction joining nouns) 14.

τὰ (acc.pl.neut.of the article in agreement with κέρατα) 9.

δέκα (numeral) 1330.

κέρατα (acc.pl.neut.of κέρας, direct object of ἔχοντος) 1851.

Translation - "So the angel said to me, 'Why did you wonder? I will explain to you the mystery of the woman and of the Beast who is carrying her, who has the seven heads and the ten horns. . . ." . . . RSV

Comment: καὶ is inferential. The angel seems amazed that John is amazed and apparently feels that John needs the explanation which he promises to offer. Note διὰ τί in a causal sense. The two participles are adjectival, describing τοῦ θηρίου. He is the carrying and having Beast.

Since the Beast will be given power by Satan to rule the world for 42 months (Rev.13:1-8), Babylon's position in the world will be dependent upon his support. He will have begun rebuilding the ancient city when he appears at the beginning of the week as the rider on the white horse (Rev.6:1,2), unless the city is rebuilt before the tribulation week begins. This is a possibility, due to the strategic position of the area in relation to the oil fields and the Persian Gulf. On the same day that the Beast is thrown into the lake of fire (Rev.19:20), Babylon will be destroyed (Rev.18:1-24; 14:8). The promised explanation follows in verses 8-14.

Verse 8 - "The beast that thou sawest was and is not; and shall ascend out of the bottomless pit, and go into perdition: and they that dwell on the earth shall wonder, whose names are not written in the book of life from the foundation of the world, when they behold the beast that was, and is not, and yet is."

τὸ θηρίον ὃ εἶδες ἦν καὶ οὐκ ἔστιν, καὶ μέλλει ἀναβαίνειν ἐκ τῆς ἀβύσσου, καὶ εἰς ἀπώλειαν ὑπάγει. καὶ θαυμασθήσονται οἱ κατοικοῦντες ἐπὶ τῆς γῆς, ὧν οὐ γέγραπται τὸ ὄνομα ἐπὶ τό βιβλίον τῆς ζωῆς ἀπὸ καταβολῆς κόσμου, βλεπόντων τὸ θηρίον ὅτι ἦν καὶ οὐκ ἔστιν καὶ παρέσται.

"The beast that you saw was, and is not, and is to ascend from the bottomless pit and go to perdition; and the dwellers on earth whose names have not been written in the book of life from the foundation of the world, will marvel to behold the beast, because it was and is not and is to come." . . . RSV

τὸ (nom.sing.neut.of the article in agreement with θηρίον) 9.

θηρίον (nom.sing.neut.of θηρίον, subject of ἦν, ἔστιν, μέλλει and ὑπάγει) 1951.

ὃ (acc.sing.neut.of ὅς, relative pronoun, direct object of εἶδες) 65.

εἶδες (2d.per.sing.aor.act.ind.of ὁράω, culminative) 144.

ἦν (3d.per.sing.imp.ind.of εἰμί, progressive duration) 86.

καὶ (adversative conjunction) 14.

οὐκ (negative conjunction with the indicative) 130.

ἔστιν (3d.per.sing.pres.ind.of εἰμί, aoristic) 86.

καὶ (adversative conjunction) 14.

μέλλει (3d.per.sing.pres.act.ind.of μέλλω, aoristic) 206.

ἀναβαίνειν (pres.act.inf.of ἀναβαίνω, complementary) 323.

ἐκ (preposition with the ablative of separation) 19.

τῆς (abl.sing.fem.of the article in agreement with ἀβύσσου) 9.

ἀβύσσου (abl.sing.fem.of ἄβυσσος, separation) 2231.

καὶ (adjunctive conjunction joining verbs) 14.

εἰς (preposition with the accusative of extent) 140.

ἀπώλειαν (acc.sing.fem.of ἀπώλεια, extent) 666.

ὑπάγει (3d.per.sing.pres.act.ind.of ὑπάγω, futuristic) 364.

καὶ (inferential conjunction) 14.

θαυμασθήσονται (3d.per.pl.fut.pass.ind.of θαυμάζω, predictive) 726.

οἱ (nom.pl.masc.of the article in agreement with κατοικοῦντες) 9.

κατοικοῦντες (pres.act.part.nom.pl.masc.of κατοικέω substantival, subject of θαυμασθήσονται) 242.

ἐπὶ (preposition with the genitive of place description) 47.

τῆς (gen.sing.fem.of the article in agreement with γῆς) 9.

γῆς (gen.sing.fem.of γῆ, place description) 157.

ὧν (gen.pl.masc.of ὅς, relative pronoun, possession) 65.

οὐ (negative conjunction with the indicative) 130.

γέγραπται (3d.per.sing.perf.pass.ind.of γράφω, intensive) 156.

τὸ (nom.sing.neut.of the article in agreement with ὄνομα) 9.

ὄνομα (nom.sing.neut.of ὄνομα, subject of γέγραπται) 108.

ἐπὶ (preposition with the accusative, extent) 47.

τὸ (acc.sing.neut.of the article in agreement with βιβλίον) 9.

βιβλίον (acc.sing.neut.of βίβλιον, extent) 1292.

τῆς (gen.sing.fem.of the article in agreement with ζωῆς) 9.

ζωῆς (gen.sing.fem.of ζωή, description) 668.

ἀπὸ (preposition with the ablative of time separation) 70.

καταβολῆς (abl.sing.fem.of καταβολή, time separation) 1079.

κόσμου (gen.sing.masc.of κόσμος, description) 360.

βλεπόντων (pres.act.part.gen.pl.masc.of βλέπω, adverbial, temporal/causal) 499.

τὸ (acc.sing.neut.of the article in agreement with θηρίον) 9.

θηρίον (acc.sing.neut.of θηρίον, direct object of βλεπόντων) 1951.

ὅτι (conjunction introducing a subordinate causal clause) 211.

ἦν (3d.per.sing.imp.ind.of εἰμί, progressive duration) 86.

καὶ (adversative conjunction) 14.

οὐκ (negative conjunction with the indicative) 130.

ἔστιν (3d.per.sing.pres.ind.of εἰμί, aoristic) 86.

καὶ (adversative conjunction) 14.

παρέσται (3d.per.sing.fut.ind.of πάρειμι, predictive) 1592.

Translation - "The Beast which you saw used to be but is not now present, but he is about to ascend from the abyss and he will go into perdition. Therefore those who are dwelling on the earth, whose names are not now inscribed upon the Book of Life, having been written there since the foundation of the world, are going to be astounded, when (and because) they see the Beast, because he used to be, but is not now present, and yet he shall be here again."

Comment: This long and involved compound/complex sentence is really not difficult. In it John has two relative clauses, a complementary infinitive, five prepositional phrases, a substantival participle and a temporal/causal participle. These clauses and phrases are tied together with six uses of καί, adversative five times and inferential once.

Verse 10 contains the details that explain the material in verse 8. The time point is that of the sixth beast (of eight) and thus is the time of the second seal (Rev.6:3-4). The beast in question who supports Babylon will have already appeared as the White Horse Rider (Rev.6:1-2). He was (ἦν) But (adversative καί) he is not now present (at the point in time of the text), having been killed (Rev.13:3,14). But (adverstive καί) he will soon arise from the abyss (Rev.9:11) and appear as the Beast of Rev.13:1-10. But (adversative καί) after 42 months (Rev.13:5) he will go to destruction (Rev.19:20).

The rest of the verse describes the reaction of the non-elect who will be living upon the earth at the time. They will be astounded to see him who was dead but is now alive again. Satan will have produced his hellish counterpart to the resurrection of our Lord. The difference is that Jesus is described after His resurrection in terms of Rom.6:9, while the Beast's destiny after his "resurrection" is described in Rev.19:20. But the unsaved who do not believe in the resurrection of Jesus will have the proof of the resurrection of the Beast before their very eyes. This is indeed "strong delusion" because of which they will believe his lie (2 Thess.2:9-11). Those who reject the sign of the prophet Jonah (Mt.12:38-41) will be happy to see a sign that they can believe, because they are a "wicked and adulterous generation." (Rev.17:4).

However one group of people still living upon the earth at the time will not worship the Beast. These are the elect whose names have been inscribed in the Book of Life since (ἀπὸ καταβολῆς κόσμου) the beginning of creation (Mt.24:24). Note the perfect tense in γέγραπται. Once written there and hence still written there, even though some of them will not yet have been irresistibly called (Rev.10:7). Cf.#1079 for ἀπό in this same sense with καταβολῆς. The point in this research will provide some fruitful preaching material. Those whom God has chosen cannot be deceived by hell's clever stunts (1 John 4:4).

Our Lord knew that at this point in our study we would need more direction in our thinking. This is why we have the guidance of the rest of the chapter.

Verse 9 - "And here is the mind which hath wisdom. The seven heads are seven mountains on which the woman sitteth."

"ὧδε ὁ νοῦς ὁ ἔχων σοφίαν. αἱ ἑπτὰ κεφαλαὶ ἑπτὰ ὄρη εἰσίν, ὅπου ἡ γυνὴ κάθηται ἐπ' αὐτῶν. καὶ βασιλεῖς ἑπτὰ εἰσιν.

"This calls for a mind with wisdom: the seven heads are seven hillson which the woman is seated;" . . . RSV

ὧδε (local adverb) 766.

ὁ (nom.sing.masc.of the article in agreement with νοῦς) 9.

νοῦς (nom.sing.masc.of νοῦς, nominative absolute) 2928.

ὁ (nom.sing.masc.of the article in agreement with ἔχων) 9.

ἔχων (pres.act.part.nom.sing.masc.of ἔχω, substantival, apposition) 82.

σοφίαν (acc.sing.fem.of σοφία, direct object of ἔχων) 934.

αἱ (nom.pl.fem.of the article in agreement with κεφαλαὶ) 9.

ἑπτὰ (numeral) 1024.

κεφαλαὶ (nom.pl.fem.of κεφαλή, subject of εἰσίν) 521.

ἑπτὰ (numeral) 1024.

ὄρη (nom.pl.neut.of ὄρος, predicate nominative) 357.

εἰσίν (3d.per.pl.pres.ind.of εἰμί, aoristic) 86.

ὅπου (adverb with the indicative in a definite local clause) 592.

ἡ (nom.sing.fem.of the article in agreement with γυνὴ) 9.

γυνὴ (nom.sing.fem.of γυνή, subject of κάθηται) 377.

ἐπ' (preposition with the genitive of place description) 47.

αὐτῶν (gen.pl.neut.of αὐτός, place description) 16.

καὶ (continuative conjunction) 14.

βασιλεῖς (nom.pl.masc.of βασιλεύς, subject of εἰσιν) 31.

ἑπτὰ (numeral) 1024.

εἰσιν (3d.per.pl.pres.ind.of εἰμί, aoristic) 86.

Translation - "Here is the rationale that has validity. The seven heads represent seven mountains upon which the woman is sitting. And there are seven kings."

Comment: The first clause indicates that what follows is a key to interpretation of the mystery of the woman, her political consort and their allies. The seven heads of the Beast represent the seven hills upon which the woman sits. These "hills" are not topographical phenomena, but they are the seven kings as the next clause tells us. This weakens the case of those who contend that the city of Rome is in view, and by implication, that the Catholic Church is meant.

"No other city in the world has ever been celebrated, as the city of Rome has, for its situation on seven hills. Pagan poets and orators, who had no thought of elucidating prophecy, have alike characterised it as 'the seven hilled city.' " (Alexander Hislop, *The Two Babylons*, 2).

"Virgil wrote, *Scilicet et rerum facta est pulcherrima Roma. Septemquenna sibe muro circumdedit arces.* (Virgil, *Georg., lib.* ii. v. 534, 535, as cited in *Ibid.*). — "Rome has both become the most beautiful (city) in the world, and alone has surrounded for herself seven heights with a wall."

Again, *Septem urbs alta jugis toto quae praesidet orbi.* — "The lofty city on seven hills, which governs the whole world." (Propertius, *Lib. iii,* Eleg. 9, p.721, as cited in *Ibid*) *Cf.* Rev.17:18.

Again, *Diis, quibus septem placuere colles.* (Horace, *Carmen Seculare,* v. 7, p.497, as cited in *Ibid.*).

Again, *Septem dominoes montes* — "The seven dominating mountains." (Martial, *Lib.* iv.*Ep.* 64, p.254, as cited in *Ibid.*).

Finally, *de septem montibus virum* - "A man from the seven mountains." (Symmachus, *Lib.* ii, *Epis.* 9, f.n.p.63, as cited in Hislop).

The Hislop study is worth reading. It can be conceded that Rome is known more than any other city on earth as being situated on seven hills. It must also be said that a part of the Catholic system of theology is a perversion of the Christian revelation. But Catholicism is not the only source of error in the history of the Church. Hence, we suggest that though Babylon may represent the false doctrines of the Medieval Church it means much more, to include all that is evil.

The last clause of the Greek text, (included in verse 10 in the King James Version) associates the seven hills which support the woman with seven kings, and then goes on to identify these seven world rulers.

Verse 10 - "And there are seven kings: five are fallen, and one is, and the other is not yet come; and when he cometh, he must continue a short space."

οἱ πέντε ἔπεσαν, ὁ εἷς ἔστιν, ὁ ἄλλος οὔπω ἦλθεν, καὶ ὅταν ἔλθῃ ὀλίγον αὐτὸν δεῖ μεῖναι.

"*. . . they are also seven kings, five of whom have fallen, one is, the other has not yet come, and when he comes he must remain only a little while."* . . . *RSV*

οἱ (nom.pl.masc.of the article in agreement with βασιλεῖς understood) 9.
πέντε (numeral) 1119.

ἔπεσαν (3d.per.pl.aor.act.ind.of πίπτω, culminative) 187.

ὁ (nom.sing.masc.of the article in agreement with εἷς) 9.

εἷς (nom.sing.masc.of εἷς, subject of ἔστιν) 469.

ἔστιν (3d.per.sing.pres.ind.of εἰμί, aoristic) 86.

ὁ (nom.sing.masc.of the article in agreement with ἄλλος) 9.

ἄλλος (nom.sing.masc.of ἄλλος, subject of ἦλθεν) 198.

οὔπω (temporal adverb) 1198.

ἦλθεν (3d.per.sing.aor.ind.of ἔρχομαι, ingressive) 146.

καὶ (adversative conjunction) 14.

ὅταν (conjunction with the subjunctive in an indefinite temporal clause) 436.

ἔλθη (3d.per.sing.aor.subj.of ἔρχομαι, indefinite temporal clause) 146.

ὀλίγον (acc.sing.neut.of ὀλίγος, time extent) 669.

αὐτὸν (acc.sing.masc.of αὐτός, general reference) 16.

δεῖ (impersonal, indicative of δεῖ) 1207.

μεῖναι (aor.act.inf.of μένω, complementary) 864.

Translation - "The (first) five have fallen; the present one now rules; the other one has not yet come, but when he comes he must continue for a short time."

Comment: This is an analysis of the political history of the "times of the Gentiles" (Dan.9:24-27; Lk.21:24). Jerusalem has been and will continue to be overrun by the Gentiles during this time. There are seven kings involved in this period of history. The double imagery of Daniel 2,7,8 demands that Daniel was being given information concerning both Israel in his day and also concerning the years following Messiah's death (Dan.9:24-27) and also concerning Israel's history in the final week of Daniel's prophecy. The time gap between the close of the 69th week and the beginning of the 70th week, so clearly indicated by Dan.9:24-27 exists. Thus the seven kings, who are involved are the seven different world powers who will have dominated Israel and the land of the Abrahamic covenant during the course of the 490 years. They are the kings (hills) upon which the city of Babylon has sat and will sit again during the tribulation. They are ancient Babylon, who carried Israel into captivity, ancient Medio-Persia, under whom Nehemiah returned to rebuild Jerusalem, ancient Greece under Alexander the Great and ancient Rome under the imperial Caesars. These four dominated the Jews and overran the promised land as well as imposing their rule over the then known civilized earth. It was the Roman Emperor, Titus who in A.D.70 sacked the city of Jerusalem and scattered the Jews throughout the world.

The Christian world during the Middle Ages became interested in Palestine and the Middle East, not because they understood the prophecy that designates the area as the home land of national Israel, but because the holy places in Jerusalem were under the control of the pagan Turks. Political and economic considerations, with reference to trade with the Levant and thus with the Orient had as much to do with the zeal of the Crusaders from Europe as the desire to restore the control of the holy city of Jerusalem to Christian hands.

In the sixteenth and seventeenth centuries the Puritans in England, who had been studying their Bibles, came to understand that Messiah could not return to earth to bring the Kingdom Age of peace and prosperity until the Jews had been regathered from their wanderings of the diaspora which began in A.D.70. The Puritans were particularly concerned about the fact that Edward I, in the latter part of the 13th century had banished the Jews from England. Before that they had been tolerated, chiefly because some of them were wealthy and, being Jews, were not under the ban on usury which the Scholastics imposed upon the Christians. Thus they were sources of venture capital, at a time when England was beginning to awake to the possibilities of international trade. Though Walter Scott's *Ivanhoe* is only a novel, it is true to the history of the times. Thus Scott portrays Isaac of York and his beautiful daughter Rebecca as objects of contempt in the eyes of both Saxons and Normans, but tolerated for pecuniary reasons. Three centuries later the Puritans, inspired and guided by their Bible study and led by Cromwell tried to persuade the Stewarts, James I and Charles I, to open the doors of the British realm to the Jews, who would then be helped to migrate to their own land of promise. They failed and came to America, and in the next hundred years the Stewart was beheaded, the Cromwellian interregnum had its brief day, the Stewarts were restored and the Glorious Revolution drove James II from his throne and brought William and Mary to a throne that was bereft of any real governmental power. But England, though now free from the dogma of the divine right of kings, be they Tudors or Stewarts, was beset with the Age of Reason of Locke, Hume and Hobbes. As a result there was little interest in England during the 18th century in what the Bible said about Palestine and the destiny of God's chosen people.

But the philosophical and theological pendulum returned to its 17th century interest in the Bible in the Victorian Age, as Lord Shaftesbury revived the program of the Puritans of two centuries before. The Jew was now the centerpiece of the Mid-East question for the Victorians. Palestine was his home and he should be established there. The hated Turk, who had been the motivation for the Crusades eight hundred years before, was no longer the reason for British interest in Palestine. The holy land was the covenant home of God's chosen people.

This is not to say that the Victorians were not also interested in Palestine for economic reasons, as the Crusaders had been. Victoria recognized Russia as a threat to the balance of power on the continent, and was alarmed as the Russian drive to the south in search of a warm water port for her naval and merchant marine interests. Thus the Crimean War and Disraeli's interest in the Suez Canal. Religious interests have often been more forcefully pursued when it can be shown that what is good for religion is also good for business.

British interest in Palestine revived again in the 20th century with the Balfour Declaration that Palestine should become the home land of the nation Israel and the British mandate over Palestine under the League of Nations, finally brought us to 1948 when Zionist hopes were realized and, for the first time, since the Babylonian Captivity, Israel took her place in the family of sovereign nations, if only in possession of a very small portion of the territory which God had promised to Abraham.*

*Cf. Barbara W. Tuchman, *Bible and Sword: England and Palestine from the Bronze Age to Balfour,* et passim.

But Israel is to be suppressed again, though not driven from her land. It is important to realize that the prophecy given to Daniel was sealed, and Daniel was ordered to "shut up the words, ... even to the time of the end." (Dan.12:4). When the prophet, unwilling to accept the verdict that the book should be sealed, asked, "O my Lord, what shall be the end of these things?" he was told, "Go thy way, Daniel: for the words are closed up and sealed till the time of the end." (Dan.12:9). This book will remain sealed until the "Lion of the Tribe of Judah, the Root of David (prevails) to open the book, and to loose the seven seals thereof" (Rev.5:5). When He does the "time of the end" will be upon us, and once again Gentile powers will overrun Jerusalem, despite Israel's short period of national sovereignty. This will continue for seven years, after which Messiah will return and Israel shall live forever under his aegis in the land that God promised to Abraham in the covenant.

This is why we learn that there are seven kings, not the four of ancient time (Nebuchadnezzar of Babylon, Darius the Mede, Alexander the Greek and Caesar of Rome). The fifth king will be the White Horse Rider of Rev.6:1-2, who will "confirm the covenant with many for one week" (Dan.9:27a) and, in the middle of the week, return as the "abomination of desolation spoken of by Daniel the prophet" (Dan.9:27b; Mt.24:25). He is the last of the first five who will have fallen at the time point of Rev.17:10. Note the culminative aorist tense in ἔπεσαν. Babylon, Medio-Persia, Geece, Rome and the White Horse Rider will have fallen. The angel goes on to tell John that "one is." He will be the Red Horse Rider of the second seal (Rev.6:3-4). The other (not the others) of the seven (note the singular in ὁ ἄλλος, because out of a total of seven we have accounted for six and only one is left) "has not yet come" (οὔπω ἦλθεν) and when he does he will continue only a short time. He will be the Black Horse Rider of the third seal (Rev.6:5-6).

Now since we have eight places to fill and only seven different kings to fill them, it is obvious that one must fill two positions. This is precisely what verse 11 says. The eighth is one of the preceding seven (*viz.* the fifth). Before his death he was number five, the first in the end-time series. After his resurrection he will be the eighth. He will dominate not only the land of promise but also the entire world for the last 42 months (Rev.13:5) of "the times of the Gentiles" (Luke 21:24) and then meet his match and be cast into the lake of fire by Messiah at the second coming (Rev.19:20). This is the thought of

Verse 11 - "And the beast that was, and is not, even he is the eighth, and is of the seven, and goeth into perdition."

καὶ τὸ θηρίον ὃ ἦν καὶ οὐκ ἔστιν, καὶ αὐτὸς ὄγδοός ἐστιν καὶ ἐκ τῶν ἑπτά ἐστιν, καὶ εἰς ἀπώλειαν ὑπάγει.

"As for the beast that was and is not, it is an eighth but it belongs to the seven, and it goes to perdition." ... RSV

καὶ (explanatory conjunction) 14.

τὸ (nom.sing.neut.of the article in agreement with θηρίον) 9.

ὅ (nom.sing.neut.of ὅς, relative pronoun, subject of ἦν and ἔστιν) 65.

ἦν (3d.per.sing.imp.ind.of εἰμί, progressive duration) 86.

καὶ (adversative conjunction) 14.

οὐκ (negative conjunction with the indicative) 130.

ἔστιν (3d.per.sing.pres.ind.of εἰμί, aoristic) 86.

καὶ (adjunctive conjunction) 14.

αὐτὸς (nom.sing.masc.of αὐτός, subject of ἔστιν) 16.

ὄγδοός (nom.sing.neut.of ὄγδοός, predicate nominative) 1841.

ἔστιν (3d.per.sing.pres.ind.of εἰμί, futuristic) 86.

καὶ (concessive conjunction) 14.

ἐκ (preposition with the ablative of source) 19.

τῶν (abl.pl.neut.of the article joined with ἑπτά) 9.

ἑπτά (numeral) 1024.

ἔστιν (3d.per.sing.pres.ind.of εἰμί, aoristic) 86.

καὶ (adversative conjunction) 14.

εἰς (preposition with the accusative of extent) 140.

ἀπώλειαν (acc.sing.fem.of ἀπωλεία, extent) 666.

ὑπάγει (3d.per.sing.pres.act.ind.of ὑπάγω, futuristic) 364.

Translation - "And the Beast which was but is no longer here — he is also eighth although he is one of the seven, but he will go to perdition."

Comment: Goodspeed, with an interesting twist, which is not wrong, has construed the first καὶ as adjunctive and translated "So (in the sense of also) must it be with the animal that was and is no more." Just as the seventh (the Black Horse Rider) has a short stay, so also does the eighth (albeit a little longer than the seventh — 42 months). Thus Goodspeed shows that both seventh and eighth are to have temporary periods of rule. This translation, grammatically possible and contextually correct, points out what Rev.13:5 says. We have the first καὶ as explanatory, as the angel continues his exposition to John. The Beast who was here (Rev.6:1-2), but (adversative καὶ) is now gone to the abyss, he also (adjunctive καὶ) is the eighth. He fills two slots, *viz.*, numer five and number eight, although (concessive καὶ) he is one of the seven, but (adversative καὶ) lest we think that when he is resurrected as the eighth (number five restored to life - Rev.9:1-11; 13:3,14) he will be permanent, we are told that he will be cast into the lake of fire (Rev.19:20) after only 42 months (Rev.13:5).

The writer well remembers a moment in 1937 when he discovered that the word is ἑπτά (seven) and not ἕβδομος (seventh). Careless reading had resulted in the erroneous "he is the eighth and is of the seventh"!! Thus we were trying to explain the Beast as of the seventh, immediately preceding him, rather than "of the seven" *viz.* the fifth. When we read what John wrote, the scheme of the Revelation in relation to Daniel came into clear and consistent focus.

The warning to all of us is that we read slowly, carefully, precisely and above all, with the supernatural guidance of the Author, the Holy Spirit.

Verse 11 says that the Beast of Rev.17:3 is the same Beast as the one of Rev.13:1. He is the Pale Horse Rider of Rev.6:7-8. In his first appearance three and one half years before, he had been the White Horse Rider (Rev.6:1-2) who "confirme(d) the covenant" with Israel (Dan.9:27a) to start God's clock on its last seven year countdown. Then he was the fifth. Now, as the eighth, he breaks his promise to Israel (Dan.9:28b) and is the "Abomination of Desolation" (Mt.24:15; 2 Thess.2:7-12). He supports Babylon politically, economically and philosophically and is doomed with her to swift destruction after 42 months of blasphemous rule.

Thus we have the identification of the seven heads, the seven mountains and the seven kings. The seven mountains are kings, not mountains. Rome, the seat of the Catholic Church has not been under the rule of Babylon, Medio-Persia or Greece. Nor has she been under the rule of a single king, since the end of the Caesar rule. But the land of covenant promise to Israel has. The Babylonians, the Medes and Persians, the Greeks and the Romans have dominated this territory in the past, and the prophecy is that she will be subject to the dictatorship of three more rulers, one of whom will exercise his power twice — once before he is killed and again, for 42 months, after his resurrection. Rome is not in a position to become the commercial and financial center of the world in the future. But a rebuilt Babylon is. She will represent all that is evil, politically, economically, culturally, theologically and ethically. She will demand that all who come to her court to buy and sell will worship the Beast and receive his mark.

The Beast will have some subordinate allies who will appear with him briefly in the last half of the tribulation period. This is the statement of

Verse 12 - "And the ten horns which thou sawest are ten kings, which have received no kingdom as yet; but receive power as kings one hour with the beast."

καὶ τὰ δέκα κέρατα ἃ εἶδες δέκα βασιλεῖς εἰσιν, οἵτινες βασιλείαν οὔπω ἔλαβον, ἀλλὰ ἐξουσίαν ὡς βασιλεῖς μίαν ὥραν λαμβάνουσιν μετὰ τοῦ θηρίου.

"And the ten horns that you saw are ten kings who have not yet received royal power, but they are to receive authority as kings for one hour, together with the beast." . . . RSV

καὶ (continuative conjunction) 14.
τὰ (nom.pl.neut.of the article in agreement with κέρατα) 9.
δέκα (numeral) 1330.
κέρατα (nom.pl.neut.of κέρας, subject of εἰσιν) 1851.
ἃ (acc.pl.neut.of ὅς, relative pronoun, direct object of εἶδες) 65.
εἶδες (2d.per.sing.aor.act.ind.of ὁράω, constative) 144.
δέκα (numeral) 1330.
βασιλεῖς (nom.pl.masc.of βασιλεύς, predicate nominative) 31.
εἰσιν (3d.per.pl.pres.ind.of εἰμί, aoristic) 86.
οἵτινες (nom.pl.masc.of ὅστις, relative pronoun, subject of ἔλαβον) 163.
βασιλείαν (acc.sing.fem.of βασιλεία, direct object of ἔλαβον) 253.
οὔπω (temporal adverb) 1198.

ἔλαβον (3d.per.pl.aor.act.ind.of λαμβάνω, ingressive) 533.
ἀλλά (adversative conjunction) 342.
ἐξουσίαν (acc.sing.fem.of ἐξουσία, direct object of ἔλαβον) 707.
ὡς (comparative particle) 128.
βασιλεῖς (nom.pl.masc.of βασιλεύς, subject of λαμβάνουσιν, understood) 31.
μίαν (acc.sing.fem.of εἷς, in agreement with ὥραν) 469.
ὥραν (acc.sing.fem.of ὥρα, time extent) 735.
λαμβάνουσιν (3d.per.pl.pres.act.ind.of λαμβάνω, futuristic) 533.
μετά (preposition with the genitive, association) 50.
τοῦ (gen.sing.neut.of the article in agreement with θηρίου) 9.
θηρίου (gen.sing.neut.of θηρίον, accompaniment) 1951.

Translation - "And the ten horns which you saw represent ten kings who as yet have received no kingdom, but they will receive authority as kings with the Beast for one hour."

Comment: The Beast will have in his political sphere of influence ten puppet kings who will serve with him temporarily. The duration of time is short, whether μίαν ὥραν is to be taken literally or not, is of small concern to us who try to see the future. Their relations to the Beast, to Christ and to Babylon are described in verses 13-17. Any attempt to identify these ten puppet powers in terms of modern national politics could at best be only conjectual, and at worst a sophomoric attempt to assume the role of a prophet. *Cf.* Dan.7:24-28. We do prophetic study a great disservice when we try to speak when the text has not spoken clearly. Those who will live in that future time will see who the ten kings are and what they role will be. That they will be in complete agreement with the Beast is clear from

Verse 13 - "These have one mind, and shall give their power and strength unto the beast."

οὗτοι μίαν γνώμην ἔχουσιν, καὶ τὴν δύναμιν καὶ ἐξουσίαν αὐτῶν τῷ θηρίῳ διδόασιν.

"These are of one mind and give over their power and authority to the beast;". . . *RSV*

οὗτοι (nom.pl.masc.of οὗτος, subject of ἔχουσιν) 93.
μίαν (acc.sing.fem.of εἷς, in agreement with γνώμην) 469.
γνώμην (acc.sing.fem.of γνώμη, direct object of ἔχουσιν) 3499.
ἔχουσιν (3d.per.pl.pres.act.ind.of ἔχω, futuristic) 82.
καὶ (adjunctive conjunction joining verbs) 14.
τὴν (acc.sing.fem.of the article in agreement with δύναμιν) 9.
δύναμιν (acc.sing.fem.of δύναμις, direct object of διδόασιν) 687.
καὶ (adjunctive conjunction joining nouns) 14.
ἐξουσίαν (acc.sing.fem.of ἐξουσία, direct object of διδόασιν) 707.
αὐτῶν (gen.pl.masc.of αὐτός, possession) 16.

τῷ (dat.sing.neut.of the article in agreement with ϑηρίῳ) 9.
ϑηρίῳ (dat.sing.neut.of ϑηρίον, indirect object of διδόασιν) 1951.
διδόασιν (3d.per.pl.pres.act.ind.(for διδοῦσι) of δίδωμι, futuristic) 362.

Comment: Unity of policy, domestic and foreign, will characterize these ten puppet national powers. They will give all of their power, economic, social, political and military and all of their influence to the Beast. Because they are aligned with him they also will oppose Christ, as he does; and just as the Beast will be destroyed by the Lamb, so indeed will his puppets.

Verse 14 - "These shall make war with the Lamb, and the Lamb shall overcome them: for He is Lord of lords, and King of kings: and they that are with Him are called, and chosen, and faithful."

οὗτοι μετὰ τοῦ ἀρνίου πολεμήσουσιν, καὶ τὸ ἀρνίον νικήσει αὐτούς, ὅτι κύριος κυρίων ἐστὶν καὶ βασιλεὺς βασιλέων, καὶ οἱ μετ' αὐτοῦ κλητοὶ καὶ ἐκλεκτοὶ καὶ πιστοί.

"and they will make war on the Lamb, and the Lamb will conquer them, for he is Lord of lords and King of kings, and those with him are called and chosen and faithful." . . . RSV

οὗτοι (nom.pl.masc.of οὗτος, subject of πολεμήσουσιν) 93.
μετὰ (preposition with the genitive, hostility) 50.
τοῦ (gen.sing.neut.of the article in agreement with ἀρνίου) 9.
ἀρνίου (gen.sing.neut.of ἀρνίον, hostility) 2923.
πολεμήσουσιν (3d.per.pl.fut.act.ind.of πολεμέω, predictive) 5140.
καὶ (adversative conjunction) 14.
τὸ (nom.sing.neut.of the article in agreement with ἀρνίον) 9.
ἀρνίον (nom.sing.neut.of ἀρνίον, subject of νικήσει) 2923.
νικήσει (3d.per.sing.fut.act.ind.of νικάω, predictive) 2454.
αὐτούς (acc.pl.masc.of αὐτός, direct object of νικήσει) 16.
ὅτι (conjunction introducing a subordinate causal clause) 211.
κύριος (nom.sing.masc.of κύριος, predicate nominative) 97.
κυρίων (gen.pl.masc.of κύριος, relationship) 97.
ἐστὶν (3d.per.sing.pres.ind.of εἰμί, aoristic) 86.
καὶ (adjunctive conjunction joining nouns) 14.
βασιλεὺς (nom.sing.masc.of βασιλεύς, predicate nominative) 31.
βασιλέων (gen.pl.masc.of βασιλεύς, relationship) 31.
καὶ (continuative conjunction) 14.
οἱ (nom.pl.masc.of the article, subject of εἰσίν, understood) 9.
μετ' (preposition with the genitive, association) 50.
αὐτοῦ (gen.sing.masc.of αὐτός, association) 16.
κλητοὶ (nom.pl.masc.of κλητός, predicate adjective) 1411.
καὶ (inferential conjunction) 14.
ἐκλεκτοὶ (nom.pl.masc.of ἐκλεκτός, predicate adjective) 1412.
καὶ (adjunctive conjunction joining adjectives) 14.

πιστοί (nom.pl.masc.of πιστός, predicate adjective) 1522.

Translation - "These will wage war against the Lamb, but the Lamb will defeat them, because He is Lord of lords and King of kings, and those with him are called and therefore chosen and faithful."

Comment: *Cf.* Dan.2:47; Deut.10:17; 1 Tim.6:15; Rev.19:16. Only unregenerate men, driven insane by Satan (Eph.2:1-3; 2 Cor.4:4) would dare to "rage" and "imagine a vain thing" (Psalm 2:1-3). Psalm 2:4-6 is parallel to the second clause of our verse. The Lamb is certain to win and those with Him are to share His victory. But they are with Him, not by virtue of their own merit. They are the objects of His electing grace — called, chosen and faithful. Note the inferential conjunction. The reason that we are chosen is because we have been called (Rom.8:29-30).

The angel has identified the woman (verse 5), the Beast (vss.8-11) and the horns (vss.12-14). He now indentifies the waters of verse 1 in

Verse 15 - "And he saith unto me, The waters which thou sawest, where the whore sitteth, are peoples, and multitudes and nations and tongues."

Καὶ λέγει μοι, Τὰ ὕδατα ἃ εἶδες, οὗ ἡ πόρνη κάθηται, λαοὶ καὶ ὄχλοι εἰσὶν καὶ ἔθνη καὶ γλῶσσαι.

"And he said to me, 'The waters that you saw, where the harlot is seated, are peoples and multitudes and nations and tongues." . . . *RSV*

Καὶ (continuative conjunction) 13.
λέγει (3d.per.sing.pres.act.ind.of λέγω, historical) 66.
μοι (dat.sing.masc.of ἐγώ, indirect object of λέγει) 123.
Τὰ (nom.pl.neut.of the article in agreement with ὕδατα) 9.
ὕδατα (nom.pl.neut.of ὕδωρ, subject of εἰσὶν) 301.
ἃ (acc.pl.neut.of ὅς, relative pronoun, direct object of εἶδες) 65.
εἶδες (2d.per.sing.aor.act.ind.of ὁράω, constative) 144.
οὗ (gen.sing.neut.of ὅς, relative pronoun, place description) 65.
ἡ (nom.sing.fem.of the article in agreement with πόρνη) 9.
πόρνη (nom.sing.fem.of πόρνη, subject of κάθηται) 1374.
κάθηται (3d.per.sing.pres.mid.ind.of κάθημαι, aoristic) 377.
λαοὶ (nom.pl.masc.of λαός, predicate nominative) 110.
καὶ (adjunctive conjunction joining nouns) 14.
ὄχλοι (nom.pl.masc.of ὄχλος, predicate nominative) 418.
εἰσὶν (3d.per.pl.pres.ind.of εἰμί, aoristic) 86.
καὶ (adjunctive conjunction joining nouns) 14.
ἔθνη (nom.pl.neut.of ἔθνος, predicate nominative) 376.
καὶ (adjunctive conjunction joining nouns) 14.
γλῶσσαι (nom.pl.fem.of γλῶσσα, predicate nominative) 1846.

Translation - "And he said to me, 'The waters which you saw, upon which the whore is seated, are peoples and multitudes and nations and languages.' "

Comment: Note in verse 1 that the waters in question were many. They represent the multitudinous dupes who will be deceived by Babylon and who will support her. It is a world-wide description — peoples, nations, hordes, multitudes, throngs, crowds of every dialect. Satan's "mystery of iniquity" (2 Thess.2:7) reaches out to condemn, just as the "mystery of godliness" (1 Tim.3:16) reaches out to save (Rev.5:9).

In a kingdom of confusion unity would be too much to expect. Thus the ten kings are going to find their selfish interests diverse from those of the great industrial and commercial city of Babylon. And they will go to war against her.

Verse 16 - "And the ten horns which thou sawest upon the beast, these shall hate the whore, and shall make her desolate and naked, and shall eat her flesh, and burn her with fire."

καὶ τὰ δέκα κέρατα ἃ εἶδες καὶ τὸ θηρίον, οὗτοι μισήσουσιν τὴν πόρνην, καὶ ἠρημωμένην ποιήσουσιν αὐτὴν καὶ γυμνήν, καὶ τὰς σάρκας αὐτῆς φάγονται, καὶ αὐτὴν κατακαύσουσιν ἐν πυρί.

"And the ten horns that you saw, they and the beast will hate the harlot; they will make her desolate and naked, and devour her flesh and burn her up with fire, . . ." . . . RSV

καὶ (continuative conjunction) 14.

τὰ (nom.pl.neut.of the article in agreement with κέρατα) 9.

δέκα (numeral) 1330.

κέρατα (nom.pl.neut.of κέρας, subject of ποιήσουσιν, φάγονται and κατακαύσουσιν) 1851.

ἃ (acc.pl.neut.of ὅς, relative pronoun, direct object of εἶδες) 65.

εἶδες (2d.per.sing.aor.act.ind.of ὁράω, constative) 144.

καὶ (adjunctive conjunction joining nouns) 14.

τὸ (acc.sing.neut.of the article in agreement with θηρίον) 9.

θηρίον (acc.sing.neut.of θηρίον, direct object of εἶδες) 1951.

οὗτοι (nom.pl.masc.of οὗτος, deictic, subject of ποιήσουσιν, φάγονται and κατακαύσουσιν) 93.

μισήσουσιν (3d.per.pl.fut.act.ind.of μισέω, predictive) 542.

τὴν (acc.sing.fem.of the article in agreement with πόρνην) 9.

πόρνην (acc.sing.fem.of πόρνη, direct object of μισήσουσιν) 1374.

καὶ (adjunctive conjunction joining verbs) 14.

ἠρημωμένην (perf.pass.part.acc.sing.fem.of ἐρημόω, predicate adjective) 994.

ποιήσουσιν (3d.per.pl.fut.act.ind.of ποιέω, predictive) 127.

αὐτὴν (acc.sing.fem.of αὐτός, direct object of ποιήσουσιν) 16.

καὶ (adjunctive conjunction joining adjectives) 14.

γυμνήν (acc.sing.fem.of γυμνός, predicate adjective) 1548.

καὶ (adjunctive conjunction joining verbs) 14.

τὰς (acc.pl.fem.of the article in agreement with σάρκας) 9.

σάρκας (acc.pl.fem.of σάρξ, direct object of φάγονται) 1202.

αὐτῆς (gen.sing.fem.of αὐτός, possession) 16.

φάγονται (3d.per.pl.2d.fut.act.ind.of ἐσθίω, predictive) 610.
καὶ (adjunctive conjunction joining verbs) 14.
αὐτὴν (acc.sing.fem.of αὐτός, direct object of κατακαύσουσιν) 16.
κατακαύσουσιν (3d.per.pl.fut.act.ind.of κατακαίω, predictive) 314.
ἐν (preposition with the instrumental, means) 80.
πυρί (instru.sing.neut.of πῦρ, means) 298.

Translation - "And the ten horns and the Beast which you saw — these will hate the whore and they will reduce her to desolation and strip her naked and they will eat her flesh and they will burn her with fire."

Comment: Thus we learn that the destruction of Babylon, so graphically described in Chapter 18, will be the work of the Beast and his ten puppet kings. It is likely that economic competition will have something to do with their displeasure with the great city, since she will be a great entrepot of commercial activity. Some commentators have suggested that the ten puppet kings will come from the European Common Market. There is nothing in the text to suggest this, any more than that they will represent the Arab world. It is significant that northwest Europe is almost totally dependent upon the Persian Gulf area for petroleum, though this situation may change before the time when the prophecy will be fulfilled.

Whatever the reason for their attack upon Babylon, neither the Beast nor his allies will know that in the destruction they are heaping upon Babylon, they will be doing God's will, as we learn in

Verse 17 - "For God hath put in their hearts to fulfil his will, and to agree, and give their kingdom unto the beast, until the words of God shall be fulfilled."

ὁ γὰρ θεὸς ἔδωκεν εἰς τὰς καρδίας αὐτῶν ποιῆσαι τὴν γνώμην αὐτοῦ, καὶ ποιῆσαι μίαν γνώμην καὶ δοῦναι τὴν βασιλείαν αὐτῶν τῷ θηρίῳ, ἄχρι τελεσθήσονται οἱ λόγοι τοῦ θεοῦ.

"for God has put it into their hearts to carry out his purpose by being of one mind and giving over their royal power to the beast, until the words of God shall be fulfilled." . . . RSV

ὁ (nom.sing.masc.of the article in agreement with θεὸς) 9.
γὰρ (causal conjunction) 105.
θεὸς (nom.sing.masc.of θεός, subject of ἔδωκεν) 124.
ἔδωκεν (3d.per.sing.aor.act.ind.of δίδωμι, culminative) 362.
εἰς (preposition with the accusative of extent) 140.
τὰς (acc.pl.fem.of the article in agreement with καρδίας) 9.
καρδίας (acc.pl.fem.of καρδία, extent) 432.
αὐτῶν (gen.pl.masc.of αὐτός, possession) 16.
ποιῆσαι (aor.act.inf.of ποιέω, purpose) 127.
τὴν (acc.sing.fem.of the article in agreement with γνώμην) 9.
γνώμην (acc.sing.fem.of γνώμη, direct object of ποιῆσαι) 3499.
αὐτοῦ (gen.sing.masc.of αὐτός, possession) 16.
καὶ (adjunctive conjunction joining infinitives) 14.

ποιῆσαι (aor.act.inf.of ποιέω, purpose) 127.

μίαν (acc.sing.fem.of εἷς, in agreement with γνώμην) 469.

γνώμην (acc.sing.fem.of γνώμη, direct object of ποιῆσαι) 3499.

καὶ (adjunctive conjunction joining infinitives) 14.

δοῦναι (aor.act.inf.of δίδωμι, purpose) 362.

τὴν (acc.sing.fem.of the article in agreement with βασιλείαν) 9.

βασιλείαν (acc.sing.fem.of βασιλεία, direct object of δοῦναι) 253.

αὐτῶν (gen.pl.masc.of αὐτός, possession) 16.

τῷ (dat.sing.neut.of the article in agreement with θηρίῳ) 9.

θηρίῳ (dat.sing.neut.of θηρίον, indirect object of δοῦναι) 1951.

ἄχρι (conjunction with the indicative in a definite temporal clause) 1517.

τελεσθήσονται (3d.per.pl.fut.pass.ind.of τελέω, in a definite temporal clause) 704.

οἱ (nom.pl.masc.of the article in agreement with λόγοι) 9.

λόγοι (nom.pl.masc.of λόγος, subject of τελεσθήσονται) 510.

τοῦ (gen.sing.masc.of the article in agreement with θεοῦ) 9.

θεοῦ (gen.sing.masc.of θεός, description) 124.

Translation - "Because God put it into their hearts to execute His plan and to come to agreement to give their authority to the Beast until the words of God should be fulfilled."

Comment: Three infinitives of purpose follow ἔδωκεν. God put it into the hearts of these godless little politicians (1) to carry out His battle plan, (2) to agree among themselves to do so, and (3) to yield their political influence to the Beast until Babylon is destroyed. Thus God moves godless men about on the chess board of history and makes the wrath of men to praise Him (Rom.9:17; Psalm 76:10). God was the indirect Agent for the destruction of Babylon, but he used men as direct agents.

Finally we learn in verse 18 that Babylon is a city, not a quasi political-religious organization.

Verse 18 - "And the woman which thou sawest is that great city, which reigneth over the kings of the earth."

καὶ ἡ γυνὴ ἣν εἶδες ἔστιν ἡ πόλις ἡ μεγάλη ἡ ἔχουσα βασιλείαν ἐπὶ τῶν βασιλέων τῆς γῆς.

"And the woman that you saw is the great city which has dominion over the kings of the earth." . . . RSV

Καὶ (continuative conjunction) 14.

ἡ (nom.sing.fem.of the article in agreement with γυνή) 9.

γυνή (nom.sing.fem.of γυνή, subject of ἔστιν) 103.

ἣν (acc.sing.fem.of ὅς, relative pronoun, direct object of εἶδες) 65.

εἶδες (2d.per.sing.aor.act.ind.of ὁράω, constative) 144.

ἔστιν (3d.per.sing.pres.ind.of εἰμί, aoristic) 86.

ἡ (nom.sing.fem.of the article in agreement with πόλις) 9.

πόλις (nom.sing.fem.of πόλις, predicate nominative) 243.
ἡ (nom.sing.fem.of the article in agreement with μεγάλη) 9.
μεγάλη (nom.sing.fem.of μέγας, in agreement with πόλις) 184.
ἡ (nom.sing.fem.of the article in agreement with ἔχουσα) 9.
ἔχουσα (pres.act.part.nom.sing.fem.of ἔχω, adjectival, emphatic attributive position, ascriptive, in agreement with πόλις) 82.
βασιλείαν (acc.sing.fem.of βασιλεία, direct object of ἔχουσα) 253.
ἐπὶ (preposition with the genitive, metaphorical, over) 47.
τῶν (gen.pl.masc.of the article in agreement with βασιλέων) 9.
βασιλέων (gen.pl.masc.of βασιλεύς, metaphorical, over) 31.
τῆς (gen.sing.fem.of the article in agreement with γῆς) 9.
γῆς (gen.sing.fem.of γῆ, description) 157.

Translation - *"And the woman whom you saw is the great city which exercises dominion over the kings of the earth."*

Comment: Finally we learn that the woman does indeed represent a city and that the reference to the seven hills upon which she sits is to the seven world governments, four of which have ruled her in the past and three others which will rule her for the seven years of the tribulation period. Revelation 18 describes her as a sea port city, highly involved in commercial activities, with whom merchantes from all over the world will trade.

The Fall of Babylon

(Revelation 18:1-19:4)

Revelation 18:1 - "And after these things I saw another angel come down from heaven, having great power; and the earth was lightened with his glory."

Μετὰ ταῦτα εἶδον ἄλλον ἄγγελον καταβαίνοντα ἐκ τοῦ οὐρανοῦ ἔχοντα ἐξουσίαν μεγάλην, καὶ ἡ γῆ ἐφωτίσθη ἐκ τῆς δόξης αὐτοῦ.

"After this I saw another angel coming down from heaven, having great authority; and the earth was made bright with his splendor." . . . RSV

Μετὰ (preposition with the accusative of time extent) 50.
ταῦτα (acc.pl.neut.of οὗτος, in a time expression) 93.
εἶδον (1st.per.sing.aor.act.ind.of ὁράω, ingressive) 144.
ἄλλον (acc.sing.masc.of ἄλλος, in agreement with ἄγγελον) 198.
ἄγγελον (acc.sing.masc.of ἄγγελος, direct object of εἶδον) 96.
καταβαίνοντα (pres.act.part.acc.sing.masc.of καταβαίνω, adjectival, predicate position, restrictive, in agreement with ἄγγελον) 324.
ἐκ (preposition with the ablative of separation) 19.
τοῦ (abl.sing.masc.of the article in agreement with οὐρανοῦ) 9.
οὐρανοῦ (abl.sing.masc.of οὐρανός, separation) 254.
ἔχοντα (pres.act.part.acc.sing.masc.of ἔχω, adjectival, predicate position, restrictive, in agreement with ἄγγελον) 82.

ἐξουσίαν (acc.sing.fem.of ἐξουσία, direct object of ἔχοντα) 707.
μεγάλην (acc.sing.fem.of μέγας, in agreement with ἐξουσίαν) 184.
καὶ (continuative conjunction) 14.
ἡ (nom.sing.fem.of the article in agreement with γῆ) 9.
γῆ (nom.sing.fem.of γῆ, subject of ἐφωτίσθη) 157.
ἐφωτίσθη (3d.per.sing.aor.pass.ind.of φωτίζω, constative) 1697.
ἐκ (preposition with the ablative, means) 19.
τῆς (abl.sing.fem.of the article in agreement with δόξης) 9.
δόξης (abl.sing.fem.of δόξα, means) 361.
αὐτοῦ (gen.sing.masc.of αὐτός, possession) 16.

Translation - *"After these things I began to watch another angel coming down from heaven with great authority; and the earth was illuminated by his glory."*

Comment: Here we have another example of the present participle, after εἶδον. (*Cf.* Rev.10:1; 13:1,11; 14:6; 18:1; 20:1, etc.). The time is near the end of the week, as the angel's announcement in verse two indicates. All of the material from Rev.18:1 through Rev.20:6 is descriptive of events at the actual second coming of our Lord.

Verse 2 - *"And he cried mightily with a strong voice, saying, Babylon the great is fallen, is fallen, and is become the habitation of devils, and the hold of every foul spirit, and a cage of every unclean and hateful bird."*

καὶ ἔκραξεν ἐν ἰσχυρᾷ φωνῇ λέγων, Ἔπεσεν, ἔπεσεν Βαβυλὼν ἡ μεγάλη, καὶ ἐγένετο κατοικητήριον δαιμονίων καὶ φυλακὴ παντὸς πνεύματος ἀκαθάρτου καὶ μεμισημένου, καὶ φυλακὴ παντὸς ὀρνέου ἀκαθάρτου καὶ μεμισημένου,

"And he called out with a mighty voice, 'Fallen, fallen is Babylon the great! It has become a dwelling place of demons, a haunt of every foul spirit, a haunt of every foul and hateful bird; . . . " . . . *RSV*

καὶ (continuative conjunction) 14.
ἔκραξεν (3d.per.sing.aor.act.ind.of κράζω, ingressive) 765.
ἐν (preposition with the instrumental, means) 80.
ἰσχυρᾷ (instru.sing.fem.of ἰσχυρός, in agreement with φωνῇ) 303.
φωνῇ (instru.sing.fem.of φωνή, means) 222.
λέγων (pres.act.part.nom.sing.masc.of λέγω, recitative) 66.
Ἔπεσεν (3d.per.sing.aor.act.ind.of πίπτω, culminative) 187.
ἔπεσεν (3d.per.sing.aor.act.ind.of πίπτω, culminative) 187.
Βαβυλὼν (nom.sing.fem.of Βαβυλών, subject of ἔπεσεν) 49.
ἡ (nom.sing.fem.of the article in agreement with μεγάλη) 9.
μεγάλη (nom.sing.fem.of μέγας, in agreement with Βαβυλὼν) 184.
καὶ (adjunctive conjunction joining verbs) 14.
ἐγένετο (3d.per.sing.aor.ind.of γίνομαι, culminative) 113.
κατοικητήριον (nom.sing.neut.of κατοικητήριον, predicate nominative) 4480.
δαιμονίων (gen.pl.neut.of δαιμόνιον, description) 686.

καὶ (adjunctive conjunction joining nouns) 14.

φυλακὴ (nom.sing.fem.of φυλακή, predicate nominative) 494.

παντὸς (gen.sing.neut.of πᾶς, in agreement with πνεύματος) 67.

πνεύματος (gen.sing.neut.of πνεῦμα, description) 83.

ἀκαθάρτου (gen.sing.neut.of ἀκάθαρτος, in agreement with πνεύματος) 843.

καὶ (adjunctive conjunction joining nouns) 14.

φυλακὴ (nom.sing.fem.of φυλακή, predicate nominative) 494.

παντὸς (gen.sing.neut.of πᾶς, in agreement with ὀρνέου) 67.

#5399 ὀρνέου (gen.sing.neut.of ὄρνεον, description).

King James Version

bird - Rev.18:2.
fowl - Rev.19:17,21.

Revised Standard Version

bird - Rev.18:2; 19:17,21.

Meaning: bird. The context in Rev.19:17,21 indicates a scavenger, while in Rev.18:2 it is joined to ἀκαθάρτου καὶ μεμισημένου to indicate revulsion. This idea, however,is not implicit in ὄρνεον itself but in its adjuncts and contextual affiliation.

ἀκαθάρτου (gen.sing.neut.of ἀκάθαρτος, in agreement with ὀρνέου) 843.

καὶ (adjunctive conjunction joining an adjective and an adjectival participle) 14.

μεμισημένου (perf.pass.part.gen.sing.neut.of μισέω, adjectival, predicate position, restrictive, in agreement with ὀρνέου) 542.

Translation - "And he began to shout with a strong voice saying, 'Babylon the Great has fallen, has fallen, and she has become a dwelling place for demons and the haunt of every unclean spirit and a cage for every dirty and despised bird. . ."

Comment: Instead of ὄρνις (#1478) John uses an older word, ὄρνεον. *Cf.* Rev.19:17,21.

The announcement is made from heaven of the fall of Babylon. She is then described in wholly uncomplimentary terms — the dwelling place of demons; the haunt of unclean spirits and the cage of dirty, loathsome birds, who are indicated in Rev.19:17,21 to be scavengers, like the replusive turkey buzzard. *Cf.* Eph.2:22 to appreciate the fact that a local church of regenerated saints is the habitation of God, while Babylon is the habitation of everything opposed to God. Babylon is at the opposite end of the continuum from the local body of born again believers.

The reason for the total corruption and depraved condition of Babylon is given in

Verse 3 - "For all nations have drunk of the wine of the wrath of her fornication, and the kings of the earth have committed fornication with her, and

the merchants of the earth are waxed rich through the abundance of her delicacies."

ὅτι ἐκ τοῦ οἴνου τοῦ θυμοῦ τῆς πορνείας αὐτῆς πεπότικεν πάντα τὰ ἔθνη, καὶ οἱ βασιλεῖς τῆς γῆς μετ' αὐτῆς ἐπόρνευσαν, καὶ οἱ ἔμποροι τῆς γῆς ἐκ τῆς δυνάμεως τοῦ στρήνους αὐτῆς ἐπλούτησαν.

"... for all nations have drunk the wine of her impure passion, and the kings of the earth have committed fornication with her, and the merchants of the earth have grown rich with the wealth of her wantonness.' " ... RSV

ὅτι (conjunction introducing a subordinate causal clause) 211.

ἐκ (preposition with the ablative of source) 19.

τοῦ (abl.sing.masc.of the article in agreement with οἴνου) 9.

οἴνου (abl.sing.masc.of οἶνος, source) 808.

τοῦ (gen.sing.masc.of the article in agreement with θυμοῦ) 9.

θυμοῦ (gen.sing.masc.of θυμός, description) 2034.

τῆς (gen.sing.fem.of the article in agreement with πορνείας) 9.

πορνείας (abl.sing.fem.of πορνεία, cause) 511.

αὐτῆς (gen.sing.fem.of αὐτός, possession) 16.

πεπότικεν (3d.per.sing.perf.act.ind.of ποτίζω, intensive) 900.

πάντα (nom.pl.neut.of πᾶς, in agreement with ἔθνη) 67.

τὰ (nom.pl.neut.of the article in agreement with ἔθνη) 9.

ἔθνη (nom.pl.neut.of ἔθνος, subject of πεπότικεν) 376.

καὶ (continuative conjunction) 14.

οἱ (nom.pl.masc.of the article in agreement with βασιλεῖς) 9.

βασιλεῖς (nom.pl.masc.of βασιλεύς, subject of ἐπόρνευσαν) 31.

τῆς (gen.sing.fem.of the article in agreement with γῆς) 9.

γῆς (gen.sing.fem.of γῆ, description) 157.

μετ' (preposition with the genitive, accompaniment) 50.

αὐτῆς (gen.sing.fem.of αὐτός, accompaniment) 16.

ἐπόρνευσαν (3d.per.pl.aor.act.ind.of πορνεύω, culminative) 4152.

καὶ (continuative conjunction) 14.

οἱ (nom.pl.masc.of the article in agreement with ἔμποροι) 9.

ἔμποροι (nom.pl.masc.of ἔμπορος, subject of ἐπλούτησαν) 1086.

τῆς (gen.sing.fem.of the article in agreement with γῆς) 9.

γῆς (gen.sing.fem.of γῆ, description) 157.

ἐκ (preposition with the ablative of source) 19.

τῆς (abl.sing.fem.of the article in agreement with δυνάμεως) 9.

δυνάμεως (abl.sing.fem.of δύναμις, source) 687.

τοῦ (gen.sing.masc.of the article in agreement with στρήνους) 9.

#5400 στρήνους (gen.sing.masc.of στρῆνος, description).

King James Version

delicacy - Rev.18:3.

Revised Standard Version

wantonness - Rev.18:3.

Meaning: "The earliest instance of this word is in the IV/B.C. comic poet Licostratus (see Kock CAF II, p.230, No.42), if the fragment is genuine. Unfortunately the word stands alone without context. It occurs later in Lycophron 438 (III/B.C.) and the LXX: *cf.* 4 Kings 19:28 τὸ στρῆνός σου ἀνέβη ἐν τοῖς ὠσίν μου - said of the Assyraian King." (Moulton & Milligan, 594). Thayer thinks it is allied with στερεός (#4827). Apparently it refers to an excess of something. In 2 Kings 19:28, of hatred and military activity against Israel. In Rev.18:3, an excessive supply of saleable products, profits from which make merchants who traffic in them rich. Hence, luxury, over indulgence, frenetic participation. The context defines in what manner the excess is exhibited. Babylon's affluence is described in Rev.18:12-13.

αὐτῆς (gen.sing.fem.of αὐτός, possession) 16.

ἐπλούτησαν (3d.per.pl.aor.act.ind.of πλουτέω, culminative) 1834.

Translation - "Because all of the nations have been drinking of the wine of the wrath aroused because of her fornication, and the kings of the earth have committed fornication with her, and the merchants of the earth have got rich off the profits that her affluence yielded."

Comment: Babylon's destruction is due to her world-wide influence for sin, error and debauchery. No nation will escape her corruption. Apostate Israel (not the elect 144,000) will be guilty also. Every king will have yielded to her political, economic, industrial and financial claims. Her productive output will be so great and varied (vss.12,13) that profits from its sale will be prodigious. Note that her ability to corrupt the world's philosophy, theology and morals is linked with her dominate position in the world market — a striking proof of 1 Tim.6:10. Babylon's economic domination of the world, coupled with the present (1984) world dependence upon petroleum for power would seem to suggest that Babylon is not Rome, but some Arab city, perhaps not yet built, nearer to the center of the Middle East oil fields. But we do not press this point.

   The student may wish to reseach #'s 5399 and 615 in connection with false teaching and the ultimate development of error in Babylon.

   Just as the canon of truth is holistic, since the divine Logos is the truth, so the Satanic canon of error confronts the truth at every point of contact. The "mystery of iniquity" always opposes the "mystery of godliness." Every false philosophy and theology, is based either upon denial of Scripture or, what is more prevalent, misinterpretation of it. The canon of error will find its full and final development in the confusion of Babylon. The proliferation of cults in the late 20th century produces new, seductive, intellectual and emotional excesses which will find their resting place and fulfillment in Babylon. Truth can find no place in the system of error.

Verse 4 - "And I heard another voice from heaven, saying, Come out of her, my people, that ye be not partaker of her sins, and that ye receive not of her plagues."

Καὶ ἤκουσα ἄλλην φωνὴν ἐκ τοῦ οὐρανοῦ λέγουσαν, Ἐξέλθατε, ὁ λαός μου, ἐξ αὐτῆς, ἵνα μὴ συγκοινωνήσητε ταῖς ἁμαρτίαις αὐτῆς, καὶ ἐκ τῶν πληγῶν αὐτῆς ἵνα μὴ λάβητε.

"Then I heard another voice from heaven saying, 'Come out of her, my people, lest you take part in her sins, lest you share in her plagues; . . . " . . . RSV

Καὶ (continuative conjunction) 14
ἤκουσα (1st.per.sing.aor.act.ind.of ἀκούω, ingressive) 148.
ἄλλην (acc.sing.fem.of ἄλλος, in agreement with φωνὴν) 198.
φωνὴν (acc.sing.fem.of φωνή, direct object of ἤκουσα) 222.
ἐκ (preposition with the ablative of source) 19.
τοῦ (abl.sing.masc.of the article in agreement with οὐρανοῦ) 9.
οὐρανοῦ (abl.sing.masc.of οὐρανός, source) 254.
λέγουσαν (pres.act.part.acc.sing.fem.of λέγω, recitative) 66.
Ἐξέλθατε (2d.per.pl.aor.mid.impv.of ἐξέρχομαι, command) 161.
ὁ (nom.sing.masc.of the article in agreement with λαός) 9.
λαός (nom.sing.masc.of λαός, (for vocative), address) 110.
μου (gen.sing.masc.of ἐγώ, relationship) 123.
ἐξ (preposition with the ablative of separation) 19.
αὐτῆς (abl.sing.fem.of αὐτός, separation) 16.
ἵνα (conjunction with the subjunctive, negative purpose) 114.
μὴ (negative conjunction with the subjunctive) 87.
συγκοινωνήσητε (2d.per.pl.aor.act.subj.of συγκοινωνέω, negative purpose) 4512.
ταῖς (instrumental pl.fem.of the article in agreement with ἁμαρτίαις) 9.
ἁμαρτίαις (instru.pl.fem.of ἁμαρτία, association, after σύν in composition) 111.
αὐτῆς (gen.sing.fem.of αὐτός, description) 16.
καὶ (adjunctive conjunction joining negative purpose clauses) 14.
ἐκ (preposition with the ablative of source) 19.
τῶν (abl.pl.fem.of the article in agreement with πλαγῶν) 9.
πληγῶν (gen.pl.fem.of πληγή, source) 2421.
αὐτῆς (gen.sing.fem.of αὐτός, description) 16.
ἵνα (conjunction with the subjunctive in a negative purpose clause) 114.
μὴ (negative conjunction with the subjunctive) 87.
λάβητε (2d.per.pl.2d.aor.act.subj.of λαμβάνω, negative purpose) 533.

Translation - "And I began to hear another voice from heaven, saying, 'Come out, come out of her, my people, lest you participate in her sins and suffer from her plagues."

Comment: We have noted before (Rev.17:16) that the destruction of Babylon is the work of the Beast and of his puppet kings and not that of God at the second coming. Thus the time of her destruction could be shortly before the second coming, which serves to explain how it is that some Christians are still in Babylon at the time of her destruction. They are now called out. This summons is not necessarily the rapture, though it could be. We have a similar story in God's call to Lot to leave Sodom (Genesis 19:15-16). *Cf.* Isa.48:20; 52:11; Jer.50:8; 51:6,9,45; 2 Cor.6:17.

Verse 5 - "For her sins have reached unto heaven, and God hath remembered her iniquities."

ὅτι ἐκολλήθησαν αὐτῆς αἱ ἁμαρτίαι ἄχρι τοῦ οὐρανοῦ, καὶ ἐμνημόνευσεν ὁ θεὸς τὰ ἀδικήματα αὐτῆς.

". . . for her sins are heaped high as heaven, and God has remembered her iniquities. . . ." . . . RSV

ὅτι (conjunction introducing a subordinate causal clause) 211.
ἐκολλήθησαν (3d.per.pl.aor.act.ind.of κολλάομαι, culminative) 1288.
αὐτῆς (gen.sing.fem.of αὐτός, possession) 16.
αἱ (nom.pl.fem.of the article in agreement with ἁμαρτίαι) 9.
ἁμαρτίαι (nom.pl.fem.of ἁμαρτία, subject of ἐκολλήθησαν) 111.
ἄχρι (preposition with the genitive of place description) 1517.
τοῦ (gen.sing.masc.of the article in agreement with οὐρανοῦ) 9.
οὐρανοῦ (gen.sing.masc.of οὐρανός, place description) 254.
καὶ (continuative conjunction) 14.
ἐμνημόνευσεν (3d.per.sing.aor.act.ind.of μνημονεύω, culminative) 1199.
ὁ (nom.sing.masc.of the article in agreement with θεὸς) 9.
θεὸς (nom.sing.masc.of θεός, subject of ἐμνημόνευσεν) 124.
τὰ (acc.pl.neut.of the article in agreement with ἀδικήματα) 9.
ἀδικήματα (acc.pl.neut.of ἀδίκημα, direct object of ἐμνημόνευσεν) 3446.
αὐτῆς (gen.sing.fem.of αὐτός, possession) 16.

Translation - "Because her sins have reached into the sky and God has kept her injustices in mind."

Comment: The causal clause indicates that not only the Beast and his puppets will attack the city, but that God also will take a hand in punishing her. *Cf.* Rev.16:19.

Verse 6 - "Reward her even as she rewarded you, and double unto her double according to her works: in the cup, which she hath filled fill to her double."

ἀπόδοτε αὐτῇ ὡς καὶ αὐτὴ ἀπέδωκεν, καὶ διπλώσατε (τὰ) διπλᾶ κατὰ τὰ ἔργα αὐτῆς. ἐν τῷ ποτηρίῳ ᾧ ἐκέρασεν κεράσατε αὐτῇ διπλοῦν.

"Render to her as she herself has rendered, and repay her double for her deeds; mix a double draught for her in the cup she mixed." . . . RSV

ἀπόδοτε (2d.per.pl.2d.aor.act.impv.of ἀποδίδωμι, command) 495.
αὐτῇ (dat.sing.fem.of αὐτός, indirect object of ἀπόδοτε) 16.
ὡς (comparative particle) 128.

καὶ (emphatic conjunction) 14.
αὐτὴ (nom.sing.fem.of αὐτός, subject of ἀπέδωκεν, intensive) 16.
ἀπέδωκεν (3d.per.sing.aor.act.ind.of ἀποδίδωμι, culminative) 495.
καὶ (adjunctive conjunction joining verbs) 14.

#5401 διπλώσατε (2d.pl.aor.act.impv.of διπλόω, command).

King James Version

double - Rev.18:6.

Revised Standard Version

repay double - Rev.18:6.

Meaning: Cf. #1446. Hence, to double. To multiply by two. In Rev.18:6, in a cognate accusative of inner content. To repay twice as much, followed by κατὰ and the accusative.

τὰ (acc.pl.neut.of the article in agreement with διπλᾶ) 9.
διπλᾶ (acc.pl.neut.of διπλοῦς, direct object of διπλώσατε) 1446.
κατὰ (preposition with the accusative, according to) 98.
τὰ (acc.pl.neut.of the article in agreement with ἔργα) 9.
ἔργα (acc.pl.neut.of ἔργον, according to) 460.
αὐτῆς (gen.sing.fem.of αὐτός, possession) 16.
ἐν (preposition with the locative of place) 80.
τῷ (loc.sing.neut.of the article in agreement with ποτηρίῳ) 9.
ποτηρίῳ (loc.sing.neut.of ποτήριον, place) 902.
ᾧ (loc.sing.neut.of ὅς, relative pronoun, place where) 65.
ἐκέρασεν (3d.per.sing.aor.act.ind.of κεράννυμι, constative) 5390.
κεράσατε (2d.per.pl.aor.act.impv.of κεράννυμι, command) 5390.
αὐτῇ (dat.sing.fem.of αὐτός, indirect object of κεράσατε) 16.
διπλοῦν (acc.sing.neut.of διπλοῦς, adverbial accusative) 1446.

Translation - "Give to her as she in fact herself has given and double to her twice, according to her deeds; in the cup in which she mixed a drink, mix for her a double drink."

Comment: Goodspeed translates, "Pay her back in her own coin." While that is not precisely what the text says, the concept is true to the text. Note the cognate accusative - διπλώσατε τὰ διπλᾶ. It is the same thought as that in Gal.6:7 and Mt.7:2. These admonitions of verse 4 must have been directed to Christians in Babylon only for purposes of witnessing for Christ, since they could have no part in the commercial activities of the city (Rev.13:16).

Verse 7 - "How much she hath glorified herself, and lived deliciously, so much torment and sorrow give her: for she saith in her heart, I sit a queen, and am no widow, and shall see no sorrow."

ὅσα ἐδόξασεν αὐτὴν καὶ ἐστρηνίασεν, τοσοῦτον δότε αὐτῇ βασανισμὸν καὶ πένθος. ὅτι ἐν τῇ καρδίᾳ αὐτῆς λέγει ὅτι Κάθημαι βασίλισσα, καὶ χήρα οὐκ εἰμί, καὶ πένθος οὐ μὴ ἴδω.

"As she glorified herself and played the wanton, so give her a like measure of torment and mourning. Since in her heart she says, 'A queen I sit, I am no widow, mourning I shall never see,' " . . . RSV

ὅσα (acc.pl.neut.of ὅσος, relative pronoun, extent) 660.
ἐδόξασεν (3d.per.sing.aor.act.ind.of δοξάζω, constative) 461.
αὐτὴν (acc.sing.fem.of σεαυτοῦ, reflexive personal pronoun) 347.
καὶ (adjunctive conjunction joining verbs) 14.

#5402 ἐστρηνίασεν (3d.per.sing.aor.act.ind.of στρηνιάω, constative).

King James Version

live deliciously - Rev.18:7,9.

Revised Standard Version

play the wanton - Rev.18:7.
be wanton - Rev.18:9.

Meaning: Cf.στρῆνος (#5400). In a bad sense, to be completely intemperate. To live luxuriously. To be wanton - Rev.18:7,9. *Cf.* 1 Tim.5:11 where we have the verb in composition with κατα (#98). Properly the verb means to exert all of one's energies. To intensify effort.

τοσοῦτον (acc.sing.neut.of τοσοῦτος, adverbial) 727.
δότε (2d.per.pl.aor.act.impv.of δίδωμι, command) 362.
αὐτῇ (dat.sing.fem.of αὐτός, indirect object of δότε) 16.
βασανισμὸν (acc.sing.masc.of βασανισμός, direct object of δότε) 5368.
καὶ (adjunctive conjunction, joining nouns) 14.
πένθος (acc.sing.neut.of πένθος, direct object of δότε) 5145.
ὅτι (conjunction introducing a subordinate causal clause) 211.
ἐν (preposition with the locative of sphere) 80.
τῇ (loc.sing.fem.of the article in agreement with καρδίᾳ) 9.
καρδίᾳ (loc.sing.fem.of καρδία, sphere) 432.
αὐτῆς (gen.sing.fem.of αὐτός, possession) 16.
λέγει (3d.per.sing.pres.act.ind.of λέγω, customary) 66.
ὅτι (recitative) 211.
Κάθημαι (1st.per.sing.pres.mid.ind.of κάθημαι, progressive) 377.
βασίλισσα (nom.sing.fem.of βασίλισσα, predicate nominative) 1014.
καὶ (continuative conjunction) 14.
χήρα (nom.sing.fem.of χήρα, predicate nominative) 1910.
οὐκ (negative conjunction with the indicative) 130.
εἰμί (1st.per.sing.pres.ind.of εἰμί, aoristic) 86.
καὶ (continuative conjunction) 14.

πένθος (acc.sing.neut.of πένθος, direct object of ἴδω) 5145.
οὐ (conjunction with the subjunctive, emphatic negation) 130.
μή (conjunction with οὐ and the subjunctive, emphatic negation) 87.
ἴδω (1st.per.sing.2d.aor.subj.of ὁράω, emphatic negative) 144.

Translation - "To the degree that she glorified herself and lived intemperately, to that same degree give to her torment and sorrow. Because she says in her heart, 'I sit here like a queen; and I am not a widow, and I shall never experience sorrow, . . .'"

Comment: Note the relative pronoun ὅσα together with the correlative demonstrative τοσοῦτον - "To the degree that . . . to the same degree."
The ultimate in depravity is human self-sufficiency with its supreme confidence exuding in groundless optimism. Man must believe that his society is viable because he made it. To foretell its doom is to imply that he did not build it permanently. That all unregenerate systems are doomed to failure is obvious to the Bible believer. John 6:63; 9:4b; Gal.6:8; Mt.6:22,23, etc.
This city, like the original Babel (Gen.11) was to reach to heaven and live forever on her own licentious terms. Here there is no humility nor repentance. Jas.4:6; 1 Pet.5:5; Lk.13:3,5. Her doom is a foregone conclusion.

Verse 8 - "Therefore shall her plagues come in one day, death, and mourning, and famine; and she shall be utterly burned with fire: for strong is the Lord who judgeth her."

διὰ τοῦτο ἐν μιᾷ ἡμέρᾳ ἥξουσιν αἱ πληγαὶ αὐτῆς, θάνατος καὶ πένθος καὶ λιμός, καὶ ἐν πυρὶ κατακαυθήσεται, ὅτι ἰσχυρὸς κύριος ὁ θεὸς ὁ κρίνας αὐτήν.

"so shall her plagues come in a single day, pestilence and mourning and famine, and she shall be burned with fire; for mighty is the Lord God who judges her." . . . RSV

διὰ (preposition with the accusative, cause) 118.
τοῦτο (acc.sing.neut.of οὗτος, cause) 93.
ἐν (preposition with the locative, time point) 80.
μιᾷ (loc.sing.fem.of εἷς, in agreement with ἡμέρᾳ) 469.
ἡμέρᾳ (loc.sing.fem.of ἡμέρα, time point) 135.
ἥξουσιν (3d.per.pl.fut.act.ind.of ἥκω, predictive) 730.
αἱ (nom.pl.fem.of the article in agreement with πληγαὶ) 9.
πληγαὶ (nom.pl.fem.of πληγή, subject of ἥξουσιν) 2421.
αὐτῆς (gen.sing.fem.of αὐτός, description) 16.
θάνατος (nom.sing.masc.of θάνατος, apposition) 381.
καὶ (adjunctive conjunction joining nouns) 14.
πένθος (nom.sing.neut.of πένθος, in apposition) 5145.
καὶ (adjunctive conjunction joining nouns) 14.
λιμός (nom.sing.masc.of λιμός, in apposition) 1485.
καὶ (continuative conjunction) 14.
ἐν (preposition with the instrumental, means) 80.

πυρὶ (instru.sing.neut.of πῦρ, means) 298.

κατακαυθήσεται (3d.per.sing.fut.pass.ind.of κατακαίω, predictive) 314.

ὅτι (conjunction introducing a subordinate causal clause) 211.

ἰσχυρὸς (nom.sing.masc.of ἰσχυρός, predicate adjective) 303.

κύριος (nom.sing.masc.of κύριος, apposition) 97.

ὁ (nom.sing.masc.of the article in agreement with ϑεὸς) 9.

ϑεὸς (nom.sing.masc.of ϑεός, subject of ἔστιν understood) 124.

ὁ (nom.sing.masc.of the article in agreement with κρίνας) 9.

κρίνας (aor.act.part.nom.sing.masc.of κρίνω, substantival, in apposition with ϑεὸς) 531.

αὐτήν (acc.sing.fem.of αυτός, direct object of κρίνας) 16.

Translation - *"So in one day her plagues will come — death and mourning and famine. And she will be burned down with fire, because God, the Lord Who has judged her is mighty."*

Comment: διὰ τοῦτο in a causal sense often. The reason for her destruction of verse 8 is her self-exaltation and self-exultation of verse 7. The plagues will come upon her suddenly — in one day, and with devastating effect. ϑάνατος καὶ πένϑος καὶ λιμὸς are all in apposition. The fiery destruction will be complete. Why? The last ὅτι clause points to Almighty God, the Judge. (Mt.28:18; Eph.1:22; Acts 17:31; 2 Thess.1:7).

The reaction of the politicians is described in verses 9 and 10. That this is a scene to be enacted before the actual second coming is clear from what they say and do. When they see the Lord descending from heaven, they will not be thinking of the destruction of Babylon, but crying for the rocks and mountains to fall upon them and hide them from the face of the Judge who sits upon the throne (Rev.6:16,17).

Verse 9 - "And the kings of the earth, who have committed fornication and lived deliciously with her, shall bewail her, and lament for her, when they shall see the smoke of her burning."

Καὶ κλαύσουσιν καὶ κόφονται ἐπ' αὐτὴν οἱ βασιλεῖς τῆς γῆς οἱ μετ' αὐτῆς πορνεύσαντες καὶ στρηνιάσαντες, ὅταν βλέπωσιν τὸν καπνὸν τῆς πυρώσεως αὐτῆς,

"And the kings of the earth, who committed fornication and were wanton with her, will weep and wail over her when they see the smoke of her burning;" . . . RSV

Καὶ (continuative conjunction) 14.

κλαύσουσιν (3d.per.pl.fut.act.ind.of κλαίω, predictive) 225.

καὶ (adjunctive conjunction joining verbs) 14.

κόφονται (3d.per.pl.fut.mid.ind.of κόπτω, predictive) 929.

ἐπ' (preposition with the accusative, cause) 47.

αὐτὴν (acc.sing.fem.of αυτός, cause) 16.

οἱ (nom.pl.masc.of the article in agreement with βασιλεῖς) 9.

βασιλεῖς (nom.pl.masc.of βασιλεύς, subject of κλαύσουσιν and κόψονται) 31.

τῆς (gen.sing.fem.of the article in agreement with γῆς) 9.

γῆς (gen.sing.fem.of γῆ, description) 157.

οἱ (nom.pl.masc.of the article in agreement with πορνεύσαντες and στρηιάσαντες) 9.

μετ᾽ (preposition with the genitive, accompaniment) 50.

αὐτῆς (gen.sing.fem.of αὐτός, accompaniment) 16.

πορνεύσαντες (aor.act.part.nom.pl.masc.of πορνεύω, substantival, in apposition with βασιλεῖς) 4152.

καὶ (adjunctive conjunction joining participles) 14.

στρηνιάσαντες (aor.act.part.nom.pl.masc.of στρηνίαω, substantival, in apposition with βαιλεῖς) 5402.

ὅταν (conjunction introducing the subjunctive in an indefinite temporal clause) 436.

βλέπωσιν (3d.per.pl.pres.act.subj.of βλέπω, indefinite temporal clause) 499.

τὸν (acc.sing.masc.of the article in agreement with καπνὸν) 9.

καπνὸν (acc.sing.masc.of καπνός, direct object of βλέπωσιν) 2986.

τῆς (abl.sing.fem.of the article in agreement with πυρώσεως) 9.

πυρώσεως (abl.sing.fem.of πύρωσις, source) 5210.

αὐτῆς (gen.sing.fem.of αὐτός, description) 16.

Translation - "And the kings of the earth who had committed fornication and lived intemperately with her will weep and beat their breasts because of her, when they see the smoke from her burning."

Comment: The weeping and lamenting is emphasized by position in the sentence. ἐπ᾽ with the accusative to indicate cause. The participles joined with οἱ are in apposition to οἱ βασιλεῖς.

These minor politicians who have been forced to worship the Beast would of course be forced into league with his capital city. The destruction of the city means that the Beast, for all of his boasting, is unable to maintain himself. His judgment also means the judgment of lesser political figures. These kings who weep are not the ten horns, in league with the Beast, since they burned the city (Rev.17:16). Verse 10 continues to describe the reaction of the kings of the earth.

Verse 10 - "Standing afar off for the fear of her torment, saying, Alas, Alas that great city Babylon, that mighty city! For in one hour is thy judgment come."

ἀπὸ μακρόθεν ἑστηκότες διὰ τὸν φόβον τοῦ βασανισμοῦ αὐτῆς, λέγοντες, Οὐαὶ οὐαί, ἡ πόλις ἡ μεγάλη, Βαβυλὼν ἡ πόλις ἡ ἰσχυρά ὅτι μιᾷ ὥρᾳ ἦλθεν ἡ κρίσις σου.

"they will stand far off, in fear of her torment, and say, 'Alas! alas! thou great city, thou mighty city, Babylon! In one hour has thy judgment come.'" ... RSV

ἀπὸ (preposition, place separation, with an adverb) 70.

μακρόθεν (adverbial) 1600.
ἑστηκότες (perf.act.part.nom.pl.masc.of ἵστημι, adverbial, circumstantial) 180.
διὰ (preposition with the accusative, cause) 118.
τὸν (acc.sing.masc.of the article in agreement with φόβον) 9.
φόβον (acc.sing.masc.of φόβος, cause) 1131.
τοῦ (abl.sing.masc.of the article in agreement with βασανισμοῦ) 9.
βασανισμοῦ (abl.sing.masc.of βασανισμός, source) 5368.
αὐτῆς (gen.sing.fem.of αὐτός, possession) 16.
λέγοντες (pres.act.part.nom.pl.masc.of λέγω, recitative) 66.
Οὐαὶ (interjection) 936.
οὐαὶ (interjection) 936.
ἡ (nom.sing.fem.of the article in agreement with πόλις) 9.
πόλις (nom.sing.fem.of πόλις, nominative absolute) 243.
ἡ (nom.sing.fem.of the article in agreement with μεγάλη) 9.
μεγάλη (nom.sing.fem.of μέγας, in agreement with πόλις) 184.
Βαβυλὼν (nom.sing.masc.of Βαβυλών, in apposition) 49.
ἡ (nom.sing.fem.of the article in agreement with πόλις) 9
πόλις (nom.sing.fem.of πόλις, apposition) 243.
ἡ (nom.sing.fem.of the article in agreement with ἰσχυρά) 9.
ἰσχυρά (nom.sing.fem.of ἰσχυρός, in agreement with πόλις) 303.
ὅτι (conjunction introducing a subordinate causal clause) 211.
μιᾷ (loc.sing.fem.of εἷς, in agreement with ὥρᾳ) 469.
ὥρᾳ (loc.sing.fem.of ὥρα, time point) 735.
ἦλθεν (3d.per.sing.aor.ind.of ἔρχομαι, culminative) 146.
ἡ (nom.sing.fem.of the article in agreement with κρίσις) 9.
κρίσις (nom.sing.fem.of κρίσις, subject of ἦλθεν) 478.
σου (gen.sing.fem.of σύ, description) 104.

Translation - "Standing far away because they fear her torture, they say, 'Alas! Alas! The great Babylon, the mighty city! Because in one hour your condemnation has come.'"

Comment: *Cf.* Dan.4:30; Ezek.26:17.*Cf.* Mt.4:17 for another instance of ἀπό with an adverb - ἀπὸ τότε.

Verse 11 - "And the merchants of the earth shall weep and mourn over her; for no man buyeth her merchandise any more."

Καὶ οἱ ἔμποροι τῆς γῆς κλαίουσιν καὶ πενθοῦσιν ἐπ' αὐτήν, ὅτι τὸν γόμον αὐτῶν οὐδεὶς ἀγοράζει οὐκέτι,

"And the merchants of the earth weep and mourn for her, since no one buys her cargo any more, . . . " . . . RSV

Καὶ (continuative conjunction) 14.
οἱ (nom.pl.masc.of the article in agreement with ἔμποροι) 9.
ἔμποροι (nom.pl.masc.of ἔμπορος, subject of κλαίουσιν and πενθοῦσιν) 1086.

τῆς (gen.sing.fem.of the article in agreement with γῆς) 9.

γῆς (gen.sing.fem.of γῆ, description) 157.

κλαίουσιν (3d.per.pl.pres.act.ind.of κλαίω, progressive description) 225.

καὶ (adjunctive conjunction joining verbs) 14.

πενθοῦσιν (3d.per.pl.pres.act.ind.of πενθέω, progressive description) 424.

ἐπ' (preposition with the accusative, cause) 47.

αὐτὴν (acc.sing.fem.of αὐτός, cause) 16.

ὅτι (conjunction introducing a subordinate causal clause) 211.

τὸν (acc.sing.masc.of the article in agreement with γόμον) 9.

γόμον (acc.sing.masc.of γόμος, direct object of ἀγοράζει) 3542.

αὐτῶν (gen.pl.masc.of αὐτός, possession) 16.

οὐδεὶς (nom.sing.masc.of οὐδείς, subject of ἀγοράζει) 446.

ἀγοράζει (3d.per.sing.pres.act.ind.of ἀγοράζω, present progressive, existing results) 1085.

οὐκέτι (temporal adverb) 1289.

Translation - "And the merchants of the earth are weeping and mourning because of her, because no one is buying their cargo."

Comment: That ἔμποροι here means merchants engaged in import/export business is clear from the meaning of γόμον (#3542). Thus it is clear that until her destruction Babylon was the commercial nerve center of the entire world. The products comprising this worldwide market are listed in verses 12 and 13. Merchant mariners are sad because their capital is invested in an inventory that no one will buy, since the Beast and his puppet kings have destroyed Babylon and evidently ordered a boycott on all her goods. Though the merchants, who will have the mark of the Beast had been able to buy in Babylon, now they cannot sell, not because they do not have his mark but because they cannot find a buyer. Thus they are bankrupt. Not that it should make any difference to them. They are all going to hell very soon.

Verse 12 - "The merchandise of gold, and silver, and precious stones, and of pearls, and fine linen, and purple, and silk, and scarlet, and all thyine wood, and all manner vessels of ivory, and all manner vessels of most precious wood, and of brass, and iron and marble.

γόμον χρυσοῦ καὶ ἀργύρου καὶ λίθου τιμίου καὶ μαργαριτῶν καὶ βυσσίνου καὶ πορφύρας καὶ σιρικοῦ καὶ κοκκίνου, καὶ πᾶν ξύλον θύϊνον καὶ πᾶν σκεῦος ἐλεφάντινον καί πᾶν σκεῦος ἐκ ξύλου τιμιωτάτου καὶ χαλκοῦ καὶ σιδήρου καὶ μαρμάρου,

"cargo of gold, silver, jewels and pearls, fine linen, purple, silk and scarlet, all kinds of scented wood, all articles of ivory, all articles of costly wood, bronze, iron and marble, . . . " . . . RSV

γόμον (acc.sing.masc.of γόμος, in apposition) 3542.

χρυσοῦ (gen.sing.masc.of χρυσός, description) 192.

καὶ (adjunctive conjunction joining nouns) 14.

ἀργύρου (gen.sing.masc.of ἄγυρος, description) 860.
καὶ (adjunctive conjunction joining nouns) 14.
λίθου (gen.sing.masc.of λίθος, description) 290.
τιμίου (gen.sing.masc.of τίμιος, in agreement with λίθου) 3070.
καὶ (adjunctive conjunction joining nouns) 14.
μαργαριτῶν (gen.pl.masc.of μαργαρίτης, description) 652.
καὶ (adjunctive conjunction joining nouns) 14.

#5403 βυσσίνου (gen.sing.masc.of βύσσινος, description).

King James Version

fine linen - Rev.18:12,16; 19:8,8,14.

Revised Standard Version

fine linen - Rev.18:12,16; 19:8,8,14.

Meaning: Cf. βύσσος (#2577). Cloth of fine linen - a product of Babylon in Rev.18:12,16. Typical of imputed righteousness of the saints in Rev.19:8,8,14.

καὶ (adjunctive conjunction joining nouns) 14.
πορφύρας (gen.sing.fem.of πορφύρα, description) 2576.
καὶ (adjunctive conjunction joining nouns) 14.

#5404 σιρικοῦ (gen.sing.neut.of σηρικόν, description).

King James Version

silk - Rev.18:12.

Revised Standard Version

silk - Rev.18:12.

Meaning: Cf. Σῆρ, Σῆρες, the people of India (probably modern China), the land of silk. Hence, a garment made of silk - Rev.18:12.

καὶ (adjunctive conjunction joining nouns) 14.
κοκκίνου (gen.sing.masc.of κόκκινος, description) 1638.
καὶ (adjunctive conjunction joining nouns) 14.
πᾶν (acc.sing.neut.of πᾶς, in agreement with ξύλον) 67.
ξύλον (acc.sing.neut.of ξύλον, in agreement with γόμον) 1590.

#5405 θύϊνον (acc.sing.neut.of θύϊνος, in agreement with ξύλον).

King James Version

thyine - Rev.18:12.

Revised Standard Version

scented - Rev.18:12.

Meaning: fr. ϑυία - the citrus, an odiferous North African tree used for incense. Evidently a valuable product - Rev.18:12.

καὶ (adjunctive conjunction joining nouns) 14.
πᾶν (acc.sing.neut.of πᾶς, in agreement with σκεῦος) 67.
σκεῦος (acc.sing.neut.of σκεύος, in agreement with γόμον) 997.

#5406 ἐλεφάντινον (acc.sing.neut.of ἐλεφάντινος, in agreement with σκεῦος).

King James Version

of ivory - Rev.18:12.

Revised Standard Version

ivory - Rev.18:12.

Meaning: Cf. ἐλέφας - "ivory." Of ivory - Rev.18:12.

καὶ (adjunctive conjunction joining nouns) 14.
πᾶν (acc.sing.neut.of πᾶς, in agreement with σκεῦος) 67.
σκεῦος (acc.sing.neut.of σκεῦος, in agreement with γόμον) 997.
ἐκ (preposition with the ablative of source) 19.
ξύλου (abl.sing.neut.of ξύλον, source) 1590.
τιμιωτάτου (abl.sing.neut.of τίμιος, superlative, in agreement with ξύλου) 3070.

καὶ (adjunctive conjunction joining nouns) 14.
χαλκοῦ (gen.sing.masc.of χαλκός, description) 861.
καὶ (adjunctive conjunction joining nouns) 14.

#5407 σιδήρου (gen.sing.masc.of σίδηρος, description).

King James Version

iron - Rev.18:17; 19:15.

Revised Standard Version

iron - Rev.18:12; 19:15.

Meaning: iron - Rev.18:12; 19:15.

καὶ (adjunctive conjunction joining nouns) 14.

#5408 μαρμάρου (gen.sing.masc.of μάρμαρος, description).

King James Version

marble - Rev.18:12.

Revised Standard Version

marble - Rev.18:12.

Meaning: Cf. μαρμαίρω - "to sparkle," "to glisten." Hence, a stone that sparkles - marble - Rev.18:12.

Translation - "a cargo of gold and silver and costly stones and pearls, and fine linen and purple and silk and scarlet and all kinds of scented wood and every vessel of ivory and every vessel of costly wood and brass and iron and marble . . . "

Comment: The list continues in

Verse 13 - "And cinnamon, and odours, and ointments, and franckincense, and wine, and oil, and fine flour, and wheat, and beasts, and sheep, and horses, and chariots, and slaves, and souls of men."

καὶ κιννάμωμον καὶ ἄμωμον καὶ θυμιάματα καὶ μύρον καὶ λίβανον καί οἶνον καὶ ἔλαιον καὶ σεμίδαλιν καί σῖτον καὶ κτήνη καὶ πρόβατα, καὶ ἵππων καὶ ῥεδῶν καὶ σωμάτων, καὶ φυχὰς ἀνθρώπων.

"cinnamon, spice, incense, myrrh, frankincense, wine, oil, fine flour and wheat, cattle and sheep, horses and chariots, and slaves, that is, human souls.". . . RSV

καὶ (adjunctive conjunction joining nouns) 14.

#5409 κιννάμωμον (acc.sing.neut.of κιννάμωμον, in agreement with γόμον).

King James Version

cinnamon - Rev.18:13.

Revised Standard Version

cinnamon - Rev.18:13.

Meaning: cinnamon - Rev.18:13.

καὶ (adjunctive conjunction joining nouns) 14.

#5410 ἄμωμον (acc.sing.neut.of ἄμωμον, in agreement with γόμον).

King James Version

odours - Rev.18:13.

Revised Standard Version

spice - Rev.18:13.

Meaning: a fragrant plant of India, from which ointment was made - Rev.18:13.

καὶ (adjunctive conjunction) 14.

ϑυμιάματα (acc.pl.neut.of ϑυμιάμα, in agreement with γόμον) 193.

καὶ (adjunctive conjunction) 14.

μύρον (acc.sing.neut.of μύρον, in agreement with γόμον) 1562.

καὶ (adjunctive conjunction joining nouns) 14.

λίβανον (acc.sing.masc.of λίβανος, in agreement with γόμον) 808.

καὶ (adjunctive conjunction joining nouns) 14.

οἶνον (acc.sing.masc.of οἶνος, in agreement with γύμον) 808.

καὶ (adjunctive conjunction joining nouns) 14.

ἔλαιον (acc.sing.neut.of ἔλαιον, in agreement with γόμον) 1530.

καὶ (adjunctive conjunction joining nouns) 14.

#5411 σεμίδαλιν (acc.sing.fem.of σεμίδαλις in agreement with γόμον).

King James Version

fine flour - Rev.18:13.

Revised Standard Version

fine flour - Rev.18:13.

Meaning: The finest wheat flour - Rev.18:13.

καὶ (adjunctive conjunction joining nouns) 14.

σῖτον (acc.sing.masc.of σῖτος, in agreement with γόμον) 311.

καὶ (adjunctive conjunction joining nouns) 14.

κτήνη (acc.sing.neut.of κτῆνος, in agreement with γόμον) 2430.

καὶ (adjunctive conjunction joining nouns) 14.

πρόβατα (acc.sing.neut.of πρόβατον, in agreement with γόμον) 671.

καὶ (adjunctive conjunction joining nouns) 14.

ἵππων (gen.pl.masc.of ἵππος, description) 5121.

καὶ (adjunctive conjunction joining nouns) 14.

#5412 ῥεδῶν (gen.pl.fem.of ῥέδα, description).

King James Version

chariot - Rev.18:13.

Revised Standard Version

chariot - Rev.18:13.

Meaning: a chariot - Rev.18:13.

καὶ (adjunctive conjunction joining nouns) 14.

σωμάτων (gen.pl.neut.of σῶμα, description) 507.

καὶ (ascensive conjunction) 14.

φυχὰς (acc.pl.fem.of φυχή, in agreement with ·γόμον) 233.

ἀνϑρώπων (gen.pl.masc.of ἄνϑρωπος, description) 341.

Translation - ". . . and cinnamon and perfume and spice and ointments and frankincense and wine and oil and fine flour and wheat and beasts of burden and sheep and horses and chariots and slaves, even human souls."

Comment: The list covers a wide variety of classes of products — monetary, jewelry, fabrics, wood products, metals, stone products, spices, perfumes, cooking oils, wines, grain, live stock, military equipment and slaves. We may change the names of some of these to include modern counterparts to these first century products.

The point is that Babylon will be a great entrepot for world trade - a position that will gain for her, first the support and later the hatred of the Beast and other lesser political powers and because of which she will be able to corrupt the earth with her heresy and immorality.

Verse 14 - "And the fruits that thy soul lusted after are departed from thee, and all things which were dainty and goodly are departed from thee, and thou shalt find them no more at all."

καὶ ἡ ὀπώρα σου τῆς ἐπιθυμίας τῆς φυχῆς ἀπῆλθεν ἀπὸ σοῦ, καὶ πάντα τὰ λιπαρὰ καὶ τὰ λαμπρὰ ἀπώλετο ἀπὸ σοῦ, καὶ οὐκέτι οὐ μὴ αὐτὰ εὑρήσουσιν.

" 'The fruit for which thy soul longed has gone from thee, and all thy dainties and thy splendor are lost to thee, never to be found again!' " . . . RSV

καὶ (adversative conjunction) 14.
ἡ (nom.sing.fem.of the article in agreement with ὀπώρα) 9.

#5413 ὀπώρα (nom.sing.fem.of ὀπώρα, subject of ἀπῆλθεν).

King James Version

fruits - Rev.18:14.

Revised Standard Version

fruit - Rev.18:14.

Meaning: Some think ὀπώρα is derived from ὄπις (cf.ὀπίσω, #302), ἕπομαι and ὥρα, hence, the time that follows the ὥρα. Others point to ὀπός - "juice" and ὥρα; thus the time of juicy fruits, which fruits become ripe. Hence, harvest. The season after θέρος and before φθινόπωρον. The seven seasons of the year are ἔαρ, θέρος, ὀπώρα, φθινόπωρον, σπορητός, χειμών φυταλία. Thus ὀπώρα - late summer or early autumn. Astronomically ὀπώρα began with the rising of Sirius and ended with the rise of Arcturus. In Rev.18:14 it seems to mean the ripe fruit of trees (Thayer, 450). The etymology, says Moulton and Milligan indicates "the season that follows summer."

σου (gen.sing.masc.of σύ, possession) 104.

τῆς (gen.sing.fem.of the article in agreement with ἐπιθυμίας) 9.
ἐπιθυμίας (gen.sing.fem.of ἐπιθυμία, description) 2186.
τῆς (gen.sing.fem.of the article in agreement with ψυχῆς) 9.
ψυχῆς (gen.sing.fem.of ψυχή, description) 233.
ἀπῆλθεν (3d.per.sing.aor.ind.of ἀπέρχομαι, culminative) 239.
ἀπό (preposition with the ablative of separation) 70.
σοῦ (abl.sing.fem.of σύ, separation) 104.
καὶ (continuative conjunction) 14.
πάντα (nom.pl.neut.of πᾶς, in agreement with λιπαρά) 67.
τὰ (nom.pl.neut.of the article in agreement with λιπαρά) 9.

#5414 λιπαρά (nom.pl.neut.of λιπαρός, subject of ἀπώλετο).

King James Version

dainty - Rev.18:14.

Revised Standard Version

dainties - Rev.18:14.

Meaning: Cf. λίπος — "grease" or "fat." Akin to ἀλείφω (#589). Hence that lotion used for anointing. Hence a dainty cosmetic. Rev.18:14. Used with λαμπρός (#2832) to denote sumptuous living.

καὶ (adjunctive conjunction joining nouns) 14.
τὰ (nom.pl.neut.of the article in agreement with λαμπρά) 9.
λαμπρά (nom.pl.neut.of λαμπρός, subject of ἀπώλετο) 2832.
ἀπώλετο (3d.per.sing.2d.aor.mid.ind.of ἀπόλλυμι, culminative) 208.
ἀπό (preposition with the ablative of separation) 70.
σοῦ 9abl.sing.fem.of σύ, separation) 104.
καὶ (inferential conjunction) 14.
οὐκέτι (temporal adverb) 1289.
οὐ (negative conjunction with μή and the future indicatve, emphatic negation) 130.
μή (negative conjunction with οὐ and the future indicative, emphatic negation) 87.
αὐτὰ (acc.pl.neut.of αὐτός, direct object of εὑρήσουσιν) 16.
εὑρήσουσιν (3d.per.pl.fut.act.ind.of εὑρίσκω, predictive) 79.

Translation - "But the harvest of the passion of your soul has gone from you; and all the dainty things and the splendor have been destroyed, and they will never again find them."

Comment: Here is a godless and therefore a thoroughly materialistic culture, where the expansability of human wants is indefinite and the sum of human satisfcation is infinite. Here is Adam Smith's "economic man" guided by a natural "invisible hand" which finds work distasteful and demands more and more in consumption. The intemperance that ignores diminishing marginal utility is the hallmark of Babylon and the world culture at the end of the age. Thus she will grow and thus after growth to the level of affluence, described in verses 12 and 13 she will be destroyed. And thus she will be frustrated. She was looking forward to a golden harvest of lustful satiation, but at the end it will all come down in wreckage and go up in smoke.

We have already seen the reaction of the kings of earth (vss.9,10). Verse 11 is a partial description of the merchants whose ships have plied between Babylon and other ports. Verses 15-19 resume the description of the reaction of the commercial world to Babylon's destruction.

Verse 15 - "The merchants of these things, which were made rich by her, shall stand afar off for the fear of her torment, weeping and wailing."

οἱ ἔμποροι τούτων οἱ πλουτήσαντες ἀπ᾽ αὐτῆς, ἀπὸ μακρόθεν στήσονται, διὰ τὸν φόβον τοῦ βασανισμοῦ αὐτῆς, κλαίοντες καὶ πενθοῦντες.

"The merchants of these wares, who gained wealth from her, will stand far off, in fear of her torment, weeping and mourning aloud, . . . " . . . RSV

οἱ (nom.pl.masc.of the article in agreement with ἔμποροι) 9.

ἔμποροι (nom.pl.masc.of ἔμπορος, subject of στήσονται) 1086.

τούτων (gen.pl.neut.of οὗτος, description) 93.

οἱ (nom.pl.masc.of the article in agreement with πλουτήσαντες) 9.

πλουτήσαντες (aor.act.part.nom.pl.masc.of πλουτέω, adjectival, emphatic attributive position, ascriptive, in agreement with ἔμποροι) 1834.

ἀπ᾽ (preposition with the ablative, agency) 70.

αὐτῆς (abl.sing.fem.of αὐτός, agency) 16.

ἀπὸ (preposition with the local adverb) 70.

μακρόθεν (local adverb) 1600.

στήσονται (3d.per.pl.fut.mid.ind.of ἵστημι, predictive) 180.

διὰ (preposition with the accusative, cause) 118.

τὸν (acc.sing.masc.of the article in agreement with φόβον) 9.

φόβον (acc.sing.masc.of φόβος, cause) 1131.

τοῦ (gen.sing.masc.of the article in agreement with βασανισμοῦ) 9.

βασανισμοῦ (gen.sing.masc.of βασανισμός, description) 5368.

αὐτῆς (gen.sing.fem.of αὐτός, possession) 16.

κλαίοντες (pres.act.part.nom.pl.masc.of κλαίω, adverbial, circumstantial) 225.

καὶ (adjunctive conjunction joining participles) 14.

πενθοῦντες (pres.act.part.nom.pl.masc.of πενθέω, adverbial, circumstantial) 424.

Translation - "The merchants who dealt in these things who were enriched by her, will stand afar off because of the fear of her torture, weeping and wailing."

Comment: It is the same description as that applied to the kings in verse 10. τούτων is anaphoric, referring to the items of verses 12 and 13. The trade had made the merchants rich. ἀπ᾽ αὐτῆς - an ablative of agent. διὰ τὸν φόβον is cause. Their comment is similar to that of the kings (verse 10).

It is inevitable that rejection of the true God, His incarnate Logos and His written Word, and persecution of His Church, "which is His body" results in rejection of His ethics with its value priorities. The end-time Babylonians and their trading partners and customers will have ignored our Lord's teaching of Mt.6:19-24 with its warning about stumbling in the dark, and also Paul's admonition, assurance and promise of Col.3:1-4. None of the destruction to be visited upon Babylon will fall upon the house of the wise man, which is built upon the Rock, Christ Jesus. The fools who built their houses and cities on the sand will suffer the destruction described in Mt.7:27.

The inventory list which Babylon will have advertized and the sea merchants will have peddled throughout the earth resembles an Amway catalogue. Amway dealers who are getting rich at the expense of the sweat of their sponsorial subjects, while they prate about their lofty Chrisian ethics, had better take notice. Where in the Bible is there support for any necessary correlation between Christian sanctification and the wealth of Babylon? If God has blessed the Christian with great wealth, or any wealth beyond his reasonable needs, he had better read Mt.7:12, obey the command of Mt.19:21 and Lev.19:18, answer James' question of James 2:14-17 and heed his warning in James 5:1-5. The far-right fundamentalists who are neither moral nor a majority, speaking from the depths of their abysmal ignorance of economics and political science find it convenient to ignore the ethical teachings of the Word of God with reference to the Christians attitude toward wealth in this affluent age, with its unjust differential in living standards. Can a Christian who would never think of taking the mark of the Beast nor of worshipping his image, nevertheless emulate Babylon?

Verse 16 - "And saying, Alas, Alas that great city, that was clothed in fine linen, and purple, and scarlet, and decked with gold, and precious stones and pearls!"

λέγοντες, Οὐαὶ οὐαί, ἡ πόλις ἡ μεγάλη, ἡ περιβεβλημένη βύσσινον καὶ πορφυροῦν καὶ κόκκινον, καὶ κεχρυσωμένη (ἐν) χρυσίῳ καὶ λίθῳ τιμίῳ καὶ μαργαρίτῃ,

" 'Alas, alas, for the great city that was clothed in fine linen, in purple and scarlet, bedecked with gold, with jewels, and with pearls! ... " . . . RSV

λέγοντες (pres.act.part.nom.pl.masc.of λέγω, recitative) 66.

Οὐαὶ (interjection) 936.

οὐαί (interjection) 936.

ἡ (nom.sing.fem.of the article in agreement with πόλις) 9.

πόλις (nom.sing.fem.of πόλις, nominative absolute) 243.

ἡ (nom.sing.fem.of the article in agreement with μεγάλη) 9.

μεγάλη (nom.sing.fem.of μέγας, in agreement with πόλις) 184.

ἡ (nom.sing.fem.of the article in agreement with περιβεβλημένη) 9.

περιβεβλημένη (perf.pass.part.nom.sing.fem.of περιβάλλω, adjectival, emphatic attributive position, ascriptive, in agreement with πόλις) 631.

βύσσινον (acc.sing.masc.of βύσσινος, adverbial accusative) 5403.

καὶ (adjunctive conjunction) 14.

πορφυροῦν (acc.sing.fem.of πορφύρεος, adverbial accusative) 2844.

καὶ (adjunctive conjunction joining nouns) 14.

κόκκινον (acc.sing.masc.of κόκκινος, adverbial accusative) 1638.

καὶ (adjunctive conjunction joining participles) 14.

κεχρυσωμένη (perf.pass.part.nom.sing.fem.of χρυσόω, adjectival, emphatic attributive position, ascriptive, in agreement with πόλις) 5398.

(ἐν) (preposition with the instrumental, means) 80.

χρυσίῳ (instru.sing.masc.of χρυσός, means) 192.

καὶ (adjunctive conjunction joining nouns) 14.

λίθῳ (instru.sing.masc.of λίθος, means) 290.

τιμίῳ (instru.sing.masc.of τίμιος, in agreement with λίθῳ) 3070.

καὶ (adjunctive conjunction joining nouns) 14.

μαργαρίτῃ (instru.sing.masc.of μαργαρίτης, means) 652.

Translation - "saying, 'Alas! Alas! The great city clothed in fine linen and purple and scarlet and adorned with gold and a precious stone and a pearl."

Comment: Here we have another case of περιβάλλω, which in its passive form retains the accusative. This is true of verbs that have only one accusative in the active voice. For example cf.περιεβάλετε με (Mt.25:36,43; Mk.14:51; John 19:2) In the passive we have περιβεβλημένη βύσσινον - "having been (and therefore now) clothed with fine lines." Cf. Mk.16:5; Rev.7:9,13; 10:1; 11:3; 12:1; 17:4; 19:13. But note κεχρυσωμένη followed by the instrumental of means ἐν χρυσίῳ καὶ λίθῳ, etc.

We should follow the inspired text faithfully unless there is good reason to do otherwise. Note that λίθῳ τιμίῳ καὶ μαργαρίτῃ are singular in number! Whether the whore had one precious stone and only one pearl or many the point is the same. She was vulgar.

Verse 17 - "For in one hour so great riches is come to nought. And every ship master and all the company in ships, and sailors, and as many as trade by sea, stood afar off."

ὅτι μιᾷ ὥρᾳ ἠρημώθη ὁ τοσοῦτος πλοῦτος. Καὶ πᾶς κυβερνήτης καὶ πᾶς ὁ ἐπὶ τόπων πλέων καὶ ναῦται   καὶ ὅσοι τὴν θάλασσαν ἐργάζονται ἀπὸ μακρόθεν ἔστησαν

"In one hour all this wealth has been laid waste.' And all shipmasters and seafaring men, sailors and all whose trade is on the sea, stood far off..."... RSV

ὅτι (conjunction introducing a subordinate causal clause) 211.

μιᾷ (loc.sing.fem.of εἷς, in agreement with ὥρᾳ) 469.

ὥρᾳ (loc.sing.fem.of ὥρα, time point) 735.

ἠρημώθη (3d.per.sing.aor.pass.ind.of ἐρημόω, culminative) 994.

ὁ (nom.sing.masc.of the article in agreement with πλοῦτος) 9.

τοσοῦτος (nom.sing.masc.of τοσοῦτος, in agreement with πλοῦτος) 727.

πλοῦτος (nom.sing.masc.of πλοῦτος, subject of ἠρημώθη) 1050.

καὶ (continuative conjunction) 14.

πᾶς (nom.sing.masc.of πᾶς, subject of κυβερνήτης) 67.

κυβερνήτης (nom.sing.masc.of κυβερνήτης, subject of ἔστησαν) 3696.

καὶ (adjunctive conjunction joining nouns) 14.

πᾶς (nom.sing.masc.of πᾶς, in agreement with πλέων) 67.

ὁ (nom.sing.masc.of the article in agreement with πλέων) 9.

ἐπὶ (preposition with the accusative of extent) 47.

τόπον (acc.sing.masc.of τόπος, extent) 1019.

πλέων (pres.act.part.nom.sing.masc.of πλέω, substantival, subject of ἔστησαν) 2209.

καὶ (adjunctive conjunction joining nouns) 14.

ναῦται (nom.pl.masc.of ναύτης, subject of ἔστησαν) 3730.

καὶ (adjunctive conjunction joining substantives) 14.

ὅσοι (nom.pl.masc.of ὅσος, subject of ἐργάζονται) 660.

τὴν (acc.sing.fem.of the article in agreement with θάλασσαν) 9.

θάλασσαν (acc.sing.fem.of θάλασσα, direct object of ἐργάζονται) 374.

ἐργάζονται (3d.per.pl.pres.mid.ind.of ἐργάζομαι customary) 691.

ἀπὸ (preposition with the adverb) 70.

μακρόθεν (adverbial of place) 1600.

ἔστησαν (3d.per.pl.2d.aor.act.ind.of ἵστημι, constative) 180.

Translation - "Because in a single hour such great wealth was laid waste; and every pilot and every passenger on board and sailors and whoever trades at sea stood afar off . . . "

Comment: The reading ὁ ἐπὶ τόπον πλέων ("he who sails for (any) port") is strongly supported by A C about 100 minuscules, including 1006 1854 it₆₁ vg, as well as by Sinaiticus 046 0229 *al*, which insert τὸν before τόπον. The unusual expression with τόπον (though one similar to it occurs in Acts 27:2) prompted copyists to substitute one or another interpretations, as (a) ἐπὶ τῶν πλοίων πλέων (P 051 about 100 minuscules *al*), (b) ὁ ἐπὶ πόντον πλέων (469 582 2076* 2254 cop_bo), (c) ὁ ἐπὶ τῶν πλοίων ἐπὶ τόπον πλέων (syr_ph), (d) ὁ ἐπὶ τὸν ποταμὸν πλέων (2053 2062 cf. cop_sa "who sail in the rivers"), (e) "those who sail from a distance" (Ps-Ambrose), and (f) ἐπὶ τῶν πλοίων ὁ ὅμιλος (1 296 2049 2186 Hippolytus), which passed into the Textus Receptus ("the company in ship" AV)." (Metzger, *A Textual Commentary on the Greek New Testament*, 761). Our translation does full justice to ἐπὶ with the accusative of extent, and fits the context. Those involved were close enough to see the smoke (verse 18). Who are involved? Merchants (verse 15), ship pilots and passengers, sailors, and those who trade at sea. *Cf.* Mt.25:16 for ἐργάζομαι, a transitive verb in the same sense, though Robertson's comment "but τὴν θάλασσαν ἐργάζονται . . . is somewhat unusual to say the least" (Robertson, *Grammar*, 474) is well taken. Yet the main thrust of the passage is clear. Everyone close enough to see the sight, was dismayed at the destruction of the city.

Verse 18 - "And cried when they saw the smoke of her burning, saying, What city is like unto this great city!"

καὶ ἔκραζον βλέποντες τὸν καπνὸν τῆς πυρώσεως αὐτῆς λέγοντες, Τίς ὁμοία τῇ πόλει τῇ μεγαλλη;

". . . and cried out as they saw the smoke of her burning, 'What city was like the great city?' " . . . RSV

καὶ (adjunctive conjunction joining verbs) 14.

ἔκραζον (3d.per.pl.imp.act.ind.of κράζω, progressive description) 765.

βλέποντες (pres.act.part.nom.pl.masc.of βλέπω, adverbial, temporal/causal) 499.

τὸν (acc.sing.masc.of the article in agreement with καπνὸν) 9.

καπνὸν (acc.sing.masc.of καπνός, direct object of βλέποντες) 2986.

τῆς (gen.sing.fem.of the article in agreement with πυρώσεως) 9.

πυρώσεως (gen.sing.fem.of πύρωσις, description) 5210.

αὐτῆς (gen. sing.fem.of αὐτός, possession) 16.

λέγοντες (pres.act.part.nom.pl.masc.of λέγω, recitative) 66.

Τίς (nom.sing.masc.of τίς, interrogative pronoun, subject of ἔστιν understood, direct question) 281.

ὁμοία (nom.sing.fem.of ὅμοιος, predicate adjective) 923.

τῇ (dat.sing.fem.of the article in agreement with πόλει) 9.

πόλει (dat.sing.fem.of πόλις,comparison) 243.

τῇ (dat.sing.fem.of the article in agreement with μεγάλῃ) 9.

μεγάλῃ (dat.sing.fem.of μέγας, in agreement with πόλει) 184.

Translation - "And they were crying out as they watched the smoke of her burning, saying, 'What city is like the great city!' "

Comment: ὁμοία followed here by the dative of comparison, though sometimes by the ablative. Cf. #923.

Verse 19 - "And they cast dust on their heads, and cried, weeping and wailing, saying, Alas, Alas that great city, wherein were made rich all that had ships in the sea by reason of her costliness! For in one hour is she made desolate."

καὶ ἔβαλον χοῦν ἐπὶ τὰς κεφαλὰς αὐτῶν καὶ ἔκραζον κλαίοντες καὶ πενθούντες, λέγοντες, Οὐαὶ οὐαί, ἡ πόλις ἡ μεγάλη, ἐν ᾗ ἐπλούτησαν πάντες οἱ ἔχοντες τὰ πλοῖα ἐν τῇ θαλάσσῃ ἐκ τῆς τιμιότητος αὐτῆς, ὅτι μιᾷ ὥρᾳ ἠρημώθη.

"And they threw dust on their heads, as they wept and mourned, crying out, 'Alas, alas, for the great city where all who had ships at sea grew rich by her wealth! In one hour she has been laid waste.' " . . . RSV

καὶ (adjunctive conjunction joining verbs) 14.

ἔβαλον (3d.per.pl.aor.act.ind.of βάλλω, inceptive) 299.

χοῦν (acc.sing.neut.of χόος, direct object of ἔβαλον) 2250.

ἐπὶ (preposition with the accusative of extent) 47.

τὰς (acc.pl.fem.of the article in agreement with κεφαλὰς) 9.

κεφαλὰς (acc.pl.fem.of κεφαλή, extent) 521.
αὐτῶν (gen.pl.masc.of αὐτός, possession) 16.
καὶ (adjunctive conjunction joining verbs) 14.
ἔκραζον (3d.per.pl.imp.act.ind.of κράζω, inceptive) 765.
κλαίοντες (pres.act.part.nom.pl.masc.of κλαίω, adverbial, modal) 225.
καὶ (adjunctive conjunction joining participles) 14.
πενθοῦντες (pres.act.part.nom.pl.masc.of πενθέω, adverbial, modal) 424.
λέγοντες (pres.act.part.nom.pl.masc.of λέγω, recitative) 66.
Οὐαὶ (interjection) 936.
οὐαί (interjection) 936.
ἡ (nom.sing.fem.of the article in agreement with πόλις) 9.
πόλις (nom.sing.fem.of πόλις, nominative absolute) 243.
ἡ (nom.sing.fem.of the article in agreement with μεγάλη) 9.
μεγάλη (nom.sing.fem.of μέγας, in agreement with πόλις) 184.
ἐν (preposition with the locative of place) 80.
ᾗ (loc.sing.fem.of ὅς, relative pronoun, place) 65.
ἐπλούτησαν (3d.per.pl.aor.act.ind.of πλουτέω, ingressive) 1834.
πάντες (nom.pl.masc.of πᾶς, in agreement with ἔχοντες) 67.
οἱ (nom.pl.masc.of the article in agreement with ἔχοντες) 9.
ἔχοντες (pres.act.part.nom.pl.masc.of ἔχω, substantival, subject of ἐπλούτησαν) 82.
τὰ (acc.pl.neut.of the article in agreement with πλοῖα) 9.
πλοῖα (acc.pl.neut.of πλοῖον, direct object of ἔχοντες) 400.
ἐν (preposition with the locative of place) 80.
τῇ (loc.sing.fem.of the article in agreement with θαλάσσῃ) 9.
θαλάσσῃ (loc.sing.fem.of θάλασσα, place) 374.
ἐκ (preposition with the ablative of source) 19.
τῆς (abl.sing.fem.of the article in agreement with τιμιότητος) 9.

#**5415** τιμιότητος (abl.sing.fem.of τιμιότης, source).

King James Version

costliness - Rev.18:19.

Revised Standard Version

wealth - Rev.18:19.

Meaning: Cf. τίμιος (#3070). Abundance of costly things. Wealth - Rev.18:19.

αὐτῆς (gen.sing.fem.of αὐτός, possession) 16.
ὅτι (conjunction introducing a subordinate causal clause) 211.
μιᾷ (loc.sing.fem.of εἷς, in agreement with ὥρᾳ) 469.
ὥρᾳ (loc.sing.fem.of ὥρα, time point) 735.
ἠρημώθη (3d.per.sing.aor.pass.ind.of ἐρημόω, culminative) 994.

Translation - "And they began to pour dust on their heads, and they began to cry

out, weeping and mourning, as they said, 'Alas! Alas, the great city, in which
all those having ships in the sea became rich, because in a single hour she has
been devastated."

Comment: To pour dust on one's head is an example of irrational behavior.
Fallen men who reject Jesus Christ, Who is the Truth are subject to such
aberrations. For them the destruction of Babylon was a tragedy. How different
are the points of view of heaven and hell. They wept because the city in which
they had gained wealth was now destroyed. They did not consider that the
wealth which they had gained was something that they could not keep. But how
would one who pours dust on his own head know this?
     The reaction of the saints is quite different as we learn in

Verse 20 - "Rejoice over her, thou heaven, and ye holy apostles and prophets: for
God hath avenged you on her."

Εὐφραίνου ἐπ' αὐτῇ, οὐρανέ, καὶ οἱ ἅγιοι καὶ οἱ ἀπόστολοι καὶ οἱ προφῆται,
ὅτι ἔκρινεν ὁ θεὸς τὸ κρίμα ὑμῶν ἐξ αὐτῆς.

"Rejoice over her, O heaven, O saints and apostles and prophets, for God has
given judgment for you against her!" . . . RSV

Εὐφραίνου (2d.per.sing.pres.act.impv.of εὐφραίνω, command) 2479.
ἐπ' (preposition with the locative, with a verb of emotion) 47.
αὐτῇ (loc.sing.fem.of αὐτός, with a verb of emotion) 16.
οὐρανέ (voc.sing.masc.of οὐρανός, address) 254.
καὶ (adjunctive conjunction joining nouns) 14.
οἱ (article with the vocative noun) 9.
ἅγιοι (voc.pl.masc.of ἅγιος, address) 84. ·
καὶ (adjunctive conjunction joining nouns) 14.
οἱ (article with the vocative noun) 9.
ἀπόστολοι (voc.pl.masc.of ἀπόστολος, address) 844.
καὶ (adjunctive conjunction joining nouns) 14.
οἱ (article with the vocative noun) 9.
προφῆται (voc.pl.masc.of προφήτης, address) 119.
ὅτι (conjunction introducing a subordinate causal clause) 211.
ἔκρινεν (3d.per.sing.aor.act.ind.of κρίνω, culminative) 531.
ὁ (nom.sing.masc.of the article in agreement with θεὸς) 9.
θεὸς (nom.sing.masc.of θεός, subject of ἔκρινεν) 124.
τὸ (acc.sing.neut.of the article in agreement with κρίμα) 9.
κρίμα (acc.sing.neut.of κρίμα, direct object of ἔκρινεν) 642.
ὑμῶν (gen.pl.masc.of σύ, possession) 104.
ἐξ (preposition with the ablative of source) 19.
αὐτῆς (abl.sing.fem.of αὐτός, source) 16.

Translation - "Rejoice over her, O heaven and the saints and the apostles and the
prophets, because God has settled your account with her."

Comment: Note that the article with ἅγιοι, ἀπόστολοι and προφῆται in apposition with the vocative οὐρανέ makes these vocative. *Cf.* Deut.32:43; Psalm 96:11; Isa.44:23; 49:13; Jer.51:48,49.

Verse 21 - "And a mighty angel took up a stone like a great millstone, and cast it into the sea, saying, Thus with violence shall that great city Babylon be thrown down, and shall be found no more at all."

Καὶ ἦρεν εἷς ἄγγελος ἰσχυρὸς λίθον ὡς μύλινον μέγαν καὶ ἔβαλεν εἰς τὴν θάλασσαν λέγων, Οὕτως ὁρμήματι βληθήσεται Βαβυλὼν ἡ μεγάλη πόλις, καὶ οὐ μὴ εὑρεθῇ ἔτι.

"Then a mighty angel took up a stone like a great millstone and threw it into the sea, saying, 'So shall Babylon the great city be thrown down with violence, and shall be found no more; . . ." . . . RSV

Καὶ (continuative conjunction) 14.
ἦρεν (3d.per.sing.aor.act.ind.of αἴρω, constative) 350.
εἷς (nom.sing.masc.of εἷς, in agreement with ἄγγελος) 469.
ἄγγελος (nom.sing.masc.of ἄγγελος, subject of ἦρεν and ἔβαλεν) 96.
ἰσχυρὸς (nom.sing.masc.of ἰσχυρός, in agreement with ἄγγελος) 303.
λίθον (acc.sing.masc.of λίθος, direct object of ἦρεν and ἔβαλεν) 290.
ὡς (comparative particle) 128.
μύλινον (nom.sing.masc.of μύλινος, subject of ἔστιν) 1250.
μέγαν (acc.sing.masc.of μέγας, in agreement with λίθον) 184.
καὶ (adjunctive conjunction joining verbs) 14.
ἔβαλεν (3d.per.sing.aor.act.ind.of βάλλω, constative) 299.
εἰς (preposition with the accusative of extent) 140.
τὴν (acc.sing.fem.of the article in agreement with θάλασσαν) 9.
θάλασσαν (acc.sing.fem.of θάλασσα, extent) 374.
λέγων (pres.act.part.nom.sing.masc.of λέγω, recitative) 66.
Οὕτως (comparative adverb) 74.

#5416 ὁρμήματι   (instru.sing.neut.of ὅρμημα, means).

King James Version

violence - Rev.18:21.

Revised Standard Version

violence - Rev.18:21.

Meaning: Cf. ὁρμάω (#772); ὁρμή (#3309). A rush; an impulse; sudden decision to take action; sudden impulse; incitement - Rev.18:21.

βληθήσεται (3d.per.sing.fut.pass.ind.of βάλλω, predictive) 299.
Βαβυλὼν (nom.sing.fem.of Βαβυλών, subject of βληθήσεται) 49.
ἡ (nom.sing.fem.of the article in agreement with πόλις) 9.
μεγάλη (nom.sing.fem.of μέγας, in agreement with πόλις) 184.
πόλις (nom.sing.fem.of πόλις, in apposition) 243.

καὶ (adjunctive conjunction joining verbs) 14.
οὐ (negative conjunction with μὴ and the subjunctive, emphatic negation) 130.
μὴ (negative conjunction with οὐ and the subjunctive, emphatic negation) 87.
εὑρεθῇ (3d.per.sing.aor.pass.subj.of εὑρίσκω, emphatic negation) 79.
ἔτι (temporal adverb) 448.

Translation - "And one mighty angel took up a stone that looked like a mill stone and he cast it into the sea, saying, 'Thus with sudden violence Babylon the great city shall be cast down and shall never again be found . . . "

Comment: The point in ὁρήματι is not only the violence of the action but its suddenness. God, as if prompted by sudden impulse, will move against the city, using as His destructive agents the ten kings allied with the Beast. Note μύλινον for μύλον. The negative in the last clause, οὐ μὴ is further intensified by the subjunctive in εὑρέθη and the temporal adverb ἔτι. The city's life, both at work and play will suddenly be terminated.

Verse 22 - "And the voice of harpers, and musicians, and of pipers, and trumpeters, shall be heard no more at all in thee; and no craftsmen, of whatsoever craft be he, shall be found any more in thee: and the sound of a millstone shall be heard no more at all in thee."

καὶ φωνὴ κιθαρίδων καὶ μουσικῶν καὶ αὐλητῶν καὶ σαλπιστῶν οὐ μὴ ἀκουσθῇ ἐν σοὶ ἔτι, καὶ πᾶς τεχνίτης πάσης τέχνης οὐ μὴ εὑρεθῇ ἐν σοὶ ἔτι, καὶ φωνὴ μύλου οὐ μὴ ἀκουσθῇ ἐν σοὶ ἔτι.

"and the sound of harpers and minstrels, of flute players and trumpeters, shall be heard in thee no more; and a craftsman of any craft shall be found in thee no more; and the sound of the millstone shall be heard in thee no more;..."... RSV

καὶ (continuative conjunction) 14.
φωνὴ (nom.sing.fem.of φωνή, subject of ἀκουσθῇ) 222.
κιθαρῳδῶν (gen.pl.masc.of κιθάρῳδος, description) 5389.
καὶ (adjunctive conjunction joining nouns) 14.

#5417 μουσικῶν (gen.pl.masc.of μουσικός, description).

King James Version

musician - Rev.18:22.

Revised Standard Version

minstrels - Rev.18:22.

Meaning: Cf. μοῦσα - "music, eloquence." Hence a musician; a minstrel. One trained in music arts - Rev.18:22.
καὶ (adjunctive conjunction) 14.
αὐλητῶν (gen.pl.masc.of αὐλητής, description) 824.
καὶ (adjunctive conjunction joining nouns) 14.

#5418 σαλπιστῶν (gen.pl.masc.of σαλπιστής, description).

King James Version

trumpeter - Rev.18:22.

Revised Standard Version

trumpeter - Rev.18:22.

Meaning: Cf. σάλπιγξ (#1507), σαλπίζω (#559). Hence, a trumpeter; one who plays a trumpet - Rev.18:22.

οὐ (negative conjunction with μή and the subjunctive, emphatic negation) 130.
μή (negative conjunction with οὐ and the subjunctive, emphatic negation) 87.
ἀκουσθῇ (3d.per.sing.aor.pass subj.of ἀκούω, emphatic negation) 148.
ἐν (preposition with the locative of place) 80.
σοὶ (loc.sing.masc.of σύ, place) 104.
ἔτι (temporal adverb) 448.
καὶ (continuative conjunction) 14.
πᾶς (nom.sing.masc.of πᾶς, in agreement with τεχνίτης) 67.
τεχνίτης (nom.sing.masc.of τεχνίτης, subject of εὑρεθῇ) 3477.
πάσης (gen.sing.fem.of πᾶς, in agreement with τέχνης) 67.
τέχνης (gen.sing.fem.of τέχνη, description) 3421.
οὐ (negative conjunction with μή and the subjunctive, emphatic negation) 130.
μή (negative conjunction with οὐ and the subjunctive, emphatic negation) 87.
εὑρεθῇ (3d.per.sing.aor.pass.subj.of εὑρίσκω, emphatic negation) 79.
ἐν (preposition with the locative of place) 80.
σοὶ (loc.sing.masc.of σύ, place) 104.
ἔτι (temporal adverb) 448.
καὶ (continuative conjunction) 14.
φωνὴ (nom.sing.fem.of φωνή, subject of ἀκουσθῇ) 222.
μύλου (gen.sing.masc.of μύλος, description) 1250.
οὐ (negative conjunction with μή and the subjunctive, emphatic negation) 130.
μή (negative conjunction with οὐ and the subjunctive, emphatic negation) 87.
ἀκουσθῇ (3d.per.sing.aor.pass.subj.of ἀκούω, emphatic negation) 148.
ἐν (preposition with the locative of place) 80.
σοὶ (loc.sing.masc.of σύ, place) 104.
ἔτι (temporal adverb) 448.

Translation - "And the sound of harpers and musicians and flutists and trumpet players will never be heard in thee again; no artisan of whatever craft will ever be found in you again, and the sound of the millstone will never be heard in you again."

Comment: Babylon, the entertainer; Babylon the manufacturer and Babylon the food producer is destroyed. The description of her complete destruction continues in

Verse 23 - "*And the light of a candle shall shine no more at all in thee; and the voice of the bridegroom and of the bride shall be heard no more at all in thee: for thy merchants were the great men of the earth: for by thy sorceries were all nations deceived.*"

καὶ φῶς λύχνου οὐ μὴ φάνῃ ἐν σοὶ ἔτι, καὶ φωνὴ νυμφίου καὶ νύμφης οὐ μὴ ἀκουσθῇ ἐν σοὶ ἔτι, ὅτι οἱ ἔμποροί σου ἦσαν οἱ μεγιστᾶνες τῆς γῆς, ὅτι ἐν τῇ φαρμακείᾳ σου ἐπλανήθησαν πάντα τὰ ἔθνη,

"*. . . and the light of a lamp shall shine in thee no more: and the voice of bridegroom and bride shall be heard in thee no more; for thy merchants were the great men of the earth, and all nations were deceived by thy sorcery.*" . . . RSV

καὶ (continuative conjunction) 14.

φῶς (nom.sing.neut.of φῶς, subject of φάνῃ) 379.

λύχνου (gen.sing.masc.of λύχνος, description) 454.

οὐ (negative conjunction with μή and the subjunctive, emphatic negation) 130.

μὴ (negative conjunction with οὐ and the subjunctive, emphatic negation) 87.

φάνῃ (3d.per.sing.aor.pass.subj.of φαίνω, emphatic negation) 100.

ἐν (preposition with the locative of place) 80.

σοὶ (loc.sing.fem.of σύ, place) 104.

ἔτι (temporal adverb) 448.

καὶ (continuative conjunction) 14.

φωνὴ (nom.sing.fem.of φωνή, subject of ἀκουσθῇ) 222.

νυμφίου (gen.sing.masc.of νυμφίος, description) 798.

καὶ (adjunctive conjunction joining nouns) 14.

νύμφης (gen.sing.fem.of νύμφη, description) 898.

οὐ (negative conjunction with μή and the subjunctive, emphatic negation) 130.

μὴ (negative conjunction with οὐ and the subjunctive, emphatic negation) 87.

ἀκουσθῇ (3d.per.sing.aor.pass.subj.of ἀκούω, emphatic negation) 148.

ἐν (preposition with the locative of place) 80.

σοὶ (loc.sing.fem.of σύ, place) 104.

ἔτι (temporal adverb) 448.

ὅτι (conjunction introducing a subordinate causal clause) 211.

οἱ (nom.pl.masc.of the article in agreement with ἔμποροί) 9.

ἔμποροί (nom.pl.masc.of ἔμπορος, subject of ἦσαν) 1086.

σου (gen.sing.fem.of σύ, possession) 104.

ἦσαν (3d.per.pl.imp.ind.of εἰμί, progressive description) 86.

οἱ (nom.pl.masc.of the article in agreement with μεγιστᾶνες) 9.

μεγιστᾶνες (nom.pl.masc.of μεγιστάν, predicate nominative) 2257.

τῆς (gen.sing.fem.of the article in agreement with γῆς) 9.

γῆς (gen.sing.fem.of γῆ, description) 157.

ὅτι (conjunction introducing a subordinate causal clause) 211.

ἐν (preposition with the instrumental, means) 80.

τῇ (instru.sing.fem.of the article in agreement with φαρμακείᾳ) 9.

φαρμακείᾳ (instru.sing.fem.of φαρμακεία, means) 4451.

σου (gen.sing.fem.of σύ, possession) 104.

ἐπλανήθησαν (3d.per.pl.aor.pass.ind.of πλανάω, culminative) 1257.
πάντα (nom.pl.neut.of πᾶς, in agreement with ἔθνη) 67.
τὰ (nom.pl.neut.of the article in agreement with ἔθνη) 9.
ἔθνη (nom.pl.neut.of ἔθνος, subject of ἐπλανήθησαν) 376.

Translation - *"And candle light will never again shine in you, and the voice of bridegroom and bride will never again be heard in you, because your merchants were the great men of the earth because by your sorcery the nations were led astray."*

Comment: The form φάνη is passive but the context demands that it be active. Passive forms "have a decidedly mixed origin and history. There is nothing special to note about these passive endings in the N.T. save the increase use of them when ever the passive idea does not exist." (Robertson, *Grammar*, 340).

Babylon's motivation and *modus operandi* will be totally Satanic. Thus her machinations, philosophical, religious, moral, economic and political will impress the non-elect. She will deceive the nations by them and thus elevate her statesmen to positions of world leadership. They will have received the mark of the Beast and of course they will ban from their markets all those Christians who have not received the mark. The customers in her market places, both wholesale and retail will be those who will share with her destiny in the lake of fire.

Through commerce, with its materialistic emphasis on things instead of ideas, she will conquer the world and then seduce it to the short-run analysis which materialistic ethics professors have always taught. Christians sing

With eternity's values in view —

but this will not be one of the featured songs on Babylon's television stations. And thus her judgment will be total, decisive and final.

We dare not attempt to lift the curtain that hides the future to peek, when God has not put something in the Word to guide, but it is difficult, with our present insights (1984) to understand how any city could rise to the heights of world domination without controlling the production and flow of petroleum in the world market. And this suggests that Babylon is not Rome, despite what Rev.17:9 says, but a rebuilt city on the ancient site at the head of the Persian Gulf. It is difficult to imagine Rome as we view the city now, as an industrial and commercial center that fits the description in Revelation 18.

Babylon will be wholly evil, and thus she will incorporate into her system the false theology of the Catholic Church to be sure, and she will also make a place for the false theology of the Baptists, the Methodists, the "Moonies" and the church of the homosexuals, who will probably be demonstrating in her streets along with the "holy rollers" who will be "speaking in tongues" and anointing everything in sight in order to drive out the demons. There will be no place for error in the Body and Bride of Christ and no place for truth in Babylon.

Verse 24 - "And in you was found the blood of prophets and of saints, and of all that were slain upon the earth."

καὶ ἐν αὐτῇ αἷμα προφητῶν καὶ ἁγίων εὑρέθη καὶ πάντων τῶν ἐσφαγμένων ἐπὶ τῆς γῆς.

"And in her was found the blood of prophets and of saints, and of all who have been slain on earth." . . . RSV

καὶ (continuative conjunction) 14.
ἐν (preposition with the locative of place) 80.
αὐτῇ (loc.sing.fem.of αὐτός, place) 16.
αἷμα (acc.sing.neut.of αἷμα, direct object of εὑρέθη) 1203.
προφητῶν (gen.pl.masc.of προφήτης, description) 119.
καὶ (adjunctive conjunction joining nouns) 14.
ἁγίων (gen.pl.masc.of ἅγιος, description) 84.
εὑρέθη (3d.per.sing.aor.pass.ind.of εὑρίσκω, constative) 79.
καὶ (adjunctive conjunction joining substantives) 14.
πάντων (gen.pl.masc.of πᾶς, in agreement with ἐσφαγμένων) 67.
τῶν (gen.pl.masc.of the article in agreement with ἐσφαγμένων) 9.
ἐσφαγμένων (perf.pass.part.gen.pl.masc.of σφάζω, substantival, description) 5292.
ἐπὶ (preposition with the genitive of place description) 47.
τῆς (gen.sing.fem.of the article in agreement with γῆς) 9.
γῆς (gen.sing.fem.of γῆ, place description) 157.

Translation - "*And in her was found blood of prophets and saints and all those slain upon the earth.*"

Comment: ἐν αὐτῇ is a sudden change from ἐν σοι in verses 22 and 23, but "it is not strictly reflexive. The same use of αὐτήν rather than σε occurs in Mt.23:37 and parallel Lk.13:34. Also Lk.1:45" (Robertson, *Grammar*, 689).

This verse recalls Rev.17:6.

It is important not to miss the fact that Babylon, the city of the time of the end is also charged with the blood of the prophets, although there have been no prophets upon the earth since the first century of the Christian era (1 Cor.13:8). Prophecy was phased out of the divine program of revelation when the literature of the New Testament was completed in the last decade of the first century. Yet Babylon is charged with the deaths, not only of the prophets of the first century, but also, presumably with the deaths of the prophets of the Old Testament period. This is proper because Satan is the designer of the city and the Antichrist and the False Prophet are her Mayor and Vice Mayor. It is the spirit of error that has murdered the prophets and the saints. Modern Babylon will not murder any prophets, for there are none now, and there have not been any since the first century, although self-appointed "prophets" and "apostles" will be among her most respected citizens (Mt.7:21-23).

Chapter 18 describes the judgment of Christ upon the Babylon whore on earth. It is only fitting that Chapter 19 should describe for us the marriage of the Lamb and His Bride. After that we have, at last, the thrilling description of the second coming of our Lord.

Revelation 19:1 - "And after these things I heard a great voice of much people in
heaven, saying, Alleluia; Salvation, and glory, and honour, and power, unto the
Lord our God."

Μετὰ ταῦτα ἤκουσα ὡς φωνὴν μεγάλην ὄχλου πολλοῦ ἐν τῷ οὐρανῷ
λεγόντων,'Αλληλουϊά, ἡ σωτηρία καὶ ἡ δόξα καὶ ἡ δύναμις τοῦ θεοῦ ἡμῶν,

"After this I heard what seemed to be the mighty voice of a great multitude in
heaven, crying, 'Hallelujah! Salvation and glory and power belong to our God,.
.."... RSV

Μετὰ (preposition with the accusative, time extent) 50.

ταῦτα (acc.pl.neut.of οὗτος, time extent) 93.

ἤκουσα (1st.per.sing.aor.act.ind.of ἀκούω, ingressive) 148.

ὡς (comparative particle) 128.

φωνὴν (acc.sing.fem.of φωνή, direct object of ἤκουσα) 222.

μεγάλην (acc.sing.fem.of μέγας, in agreement with φωνὴν) 184.

ὄχλου (abl.sing.masc.of ὄχλος, comparison) 418.

πολλοῦ (abl.sing.masc.of πολύς, in agreement with ὄχλου) 228.

ἐν (preposition with the locative of place) 80.

τῷ (loc.sing.masc.of the article in agreement with οὐρανῷ) 9.

οὐρανῷ (loc.sing.masc.of οὐρανός, place) 254.

λεγόντων (pres.act.part.gen.pl.masc. of λέγω, recitative) 66.

5419'Αλληλουϊά (exclamation).

King James Version

Alleluia - Rev.19:1,3,4,6.

Revised Standard Version

Hallelujah - Rev.19:1,3,4,6.

Meaning: "Praise ye the Lord." Hallelujah! - Rev.19:1,3,4,6.

ἡ (nom.sing.fem.of the article in agreement with σωτηρία) 9.

σωτηρία (nom.sing.fem.of σωτηρία, nominative absolute) 1852.

καὶ (adjunctive conjunction joining nouns) 14.

ἡ (nom.sing.fem.of the article in agreement with δόξα) 9.

δόξα (nom.sing.fem.of δόξα, nominative absolute) 361.

καὶ (adjunctive conjunction joining nouns) 14.

ἡ (nom.sing.fem.of the article in agreement with δύναμις) 9.

δύναμις (nom.sing.fem.of δύναμις, nominative absolute) 687.

τοῦ (gen.sing.masc.of the article in agreement with θεοῦ) 9.

θεοῦ (gen.sing.masc.of θεός, possession) 124.

ἡμῶν (gen.pl.masc.of ἐγώ, relationship) 123.

Translation - "After these things I heard what sounded like the mighty voice of a great multitude in heaven saying, 'Hallelujah! Salvation and glory and power belong to our God. . . "

Comment: Once again we warn that μετὰ ταῦτα and μετὰ τοῦτο mean "after" in the order in which John saw the scenes and heard the accompanying sound effects, not "after" necessarily in a chronological scheme of interpretation of sequence of prophetic events. God could not show it all to John at once. In a sequence of three scenes, scene three need not be thought to follow scene two and two is not necessarily after one on the countdown of God's clock. The context must decide. In the scene before us we are at the end of the tribulation week. The second coming of Christ is immanent.

The text does not tell us who the people in the great multitude are. They could be the martyred saints or the saints of all ages since the resurrection of Christ. *Cf.* verse 6, where another (or is it the same?) multitude is heard. They begin a doxology which continues through the second verse.

Verse 2 - "For true and righteous are his judgments: for he hath judged the great whore, which did corrupt the earth with her fornication and hath avenged the blood of his servants at her hand."

ὅτι ἀληθιναὶ καὶ δίκαιαι αἱ κρίσεις αὐτοῦ, ὅτι ἔκρινεν τὴν πόρνην τὴν μεγάλην ἥτις ἔφθειρεν τὴν γῆν ἐν τῇ πορνείᾳ αὐτῆς, καὶ ἐξεδίκησεν τὸ αἷμα τῶν δούλων αὐτοῦ ἐκ χειρὸς αὐτῆς.

"for his judgments are true and just; he has judged the great harlot who corrupted the earth with her fornication, and he has avenged on her the blood of his servants.'" . . . *RSV*

ὅτι (conjunction introducing a subordinate causal clause) 211.
ἀληθιναὶ (nom.pl.fem.of ἀληθινός, predicate adjective) 1696.
καὶ (adjunctive conjunction joining adjectives) 14.
δίκαιαι (nom.pl.fem.of δίκαιος, predicate adjective) 85.
αἱ (nom.pl.fem.of the article in agreement with κρίσεις) 9.
κρίσεις (nom.pl.fem.of κρίσις, subject of εἰσιν understood) 478.
αὐτοῦ (gen.sing.masc.of αὐτός, possession) 16.
ὅτι (conjunction introducing a subordinate causal clause) 211.
ἔκρινεν (3d.per.sing.imp.act.ind.of κρίνω, progressive description) 531.
τὴν (acc.sing.fem.of the article in agreement with πόρνην) 9.
πόρνην (acc.sing.fem.of πόρνη, direct object of ἔκρινεν) 1374.
τὴν (acc.sing.fem.of the article in agreement with μεγάλην) 9.
μεγάλην (acc.sing.fem.of μέγας, in agreement with πόρνην) 184.
ἥτις (nom.sing.fem.of ὅστις, relative pronoun, subject of ἔφθειρεν) 163.
ἔφθειρεν (3d.per.sing.imp.act.ind.of φθείρω, progressive duration) 4119.
τὴν (acc.sing.fem.of the article in agreement with γῆν) 9.
γῆν (acc.sing.fem.of γῆ, direct object of ἔφθειρεν) 157.
ἐν (preposition with the instrumental, means) 80.
τῇ (instru.sing.fem.of the article in agreement with πορνείᾳ) 9.

πορνείᾳ (instru.sing.fem.of πορνεία, means) 511.
αὐτῆς (gen.sing.fem.of αὐτός, possession) 16.
καὶ (adjunctive conjunction joining verbs) 14.
ἐξεδίκησεν (3d.per.sing.aor.act.ind.of ἐκδικέω, culminative) 2623.
τὸ (acc.sing.neut.of the article in agreement with αἷμα) 9.
αἷμα (acc.sing.neut.of αἷμα, direct object of ἐξεδίκησεν) 1203.
τῶν (gen.pl.masc.of the article in agreement with δούλων) 9.
δούλων (gen.pl.masc.of δοῦλος, possession) 725.
αὐτοῦ (gen.sing.masc.of αὐτός, relationship) 16.
ἐκ (preposition with the ablative of source) 19.
χειρὸς (abl.sing.fem.of χείρ, source) 308.
αὐτῆς (gen.sing.fem.of αὐτός, possession) 16.

Translation - "... because His judgments are true and just on the basis of which He has judged the great whore, who has been corrupting the earth with her immorality; and He has avenged the blood of His bondservants at her expense."

Comment: The doxology to God is on the basis of the truth and fairness of His judgment. The ὅτι clauses are causal. God's true and righteous judgment is demonstrated by the judgment which God has visited upon Babylon. The relative clause is definite. ἥτις refers to τὴν πόνην. Note the imperfect tense in ἔφθειρεν. For three and one half years Babylon will have been corrupting the world with her monopoly on world trade and her blasphemous idolatry. Note in Rev.18:23 that Babylon's merchants will be the great men of the earth (world leaders) *because* by her sorcery (economic domination as well as philosophical error) she has led all nations astray. Marxian philosophy that teaches that all values are determined by economics will have its little day upon the earth in Babylon's domination of the world. In her quest, by economic determinism, for world domination, she will find God's servants standing athwart her path. These she will kill. But God will get even with her. The law of *lex talonis* is a part of God's moral code. (Mt.5:38).

Verse 3 - "And again they said, Alleluia. And her smoke rose up forever and ever."

καὶ δεύτερον εἴρηκαν, Ἀλληλουϊαί, καὶ ὁ καπνὸς αὐτῆς ἀναβαίνει εἰς τοὺς αἰῶνας τῶν αἰώνων.

"Once more they cried, 'Hallelujah! The smoke from her goes up for ever and ever.' " ... RSV

καὶ (continuative conjunction) 14.
δεύτερον (acc.sing.neut.of δεύτερος, adverbial) 1371.
εἴρηκαν (3d.per.pl.perf.ind (Attic) of ῥέω) 116.
Ἀλληλουϊά (exclamation) 5419.
καὶ (continuative conjunction) 14.
ὁ (nom.sing.masc.of the article in agreement with καπνὸς) 9.
καπνὸς (nom.sing.masc.of καπνός, subject of ἀναβαίνει) 2986.

αὐτῆς (gen.sing.fem.of αὐτός, description) 16.
ἀναβαίνει (3d.per.sing.pres.act.ind.of ἀναβαίνω, static) 323.
εἰς (preposition with the accusative, time extent) 140.
τοὺς (acc.pl.masc.of the article in agreement with αἰῶνας) 9.
αἰῶνας (acc.pl.masc.of αἰών, time extent) 1002.
τῶν (gen.pl.masc.of the article in agreement with αἰώνων) 9.
αἰώνων (gen.pl.masc.of αἰών, partitive genitive) 1002.

Translation - "*And again they said, 'Hallelujah! And her smoke ascends for ever and ever.*"

Comment: That the smoke of Babylon's destruction should forever ascend is only another way of saying that the eternity of hell is as eternal as the eternity of heaven and of the throne of God. *Cf.#* 1002. Both heaven and hell are eternal because God is eternal and His judgments, being true and just are eternal. The passage does not say that the smoke of Babylon's destruction will ascend eternally on the earth. There is to be "a new heaven and a new earth wherein dwelleth righteounsess" (2 Peter 3:13) and in which a remembrance of the former will have passed away. (Rev.21:4).

Verse 4 - "*And the four and twenty elders and the four beasts fell down and worshipped God that sat on the throne, saying, Amen; Alleluia.*"

καὶ ἔπεσαν οἱ πρεσβύτεροι οἱ εἴκοσι τέσσαρες καὶ τὰ τέσσαρα ζῷα, καὶ προσεκύνησαν τῷ θεῷ τῷ καθημένῳ ἐπὶ τῷ θρόνῳ, λέγοντες, Ἀμήν, Ἁλληλουϊά.

"*And the twenty-four elders and the four living creatures fell down and worshipped God who is seated on the throne, saying, 'Amen. Hallelujah!*" . . . RSV

καὶ (continuative conjunction) 14.
ἔπεσαν (3d.per.pl.aor.act.ind.of πίπτω, constative) 187.
οἱ (nom.pl.masc.of the article in agreement with πρεσβύτεροι) 9.
πρεσβύτεροι (nom.pl.masc.of πρεσβύτερος, subject of ἔπεσαν and προσεκύνησαν) 1141.
οἱ (nom.pl.masc.of the article in agreement with εἴκοσι τέσσαρες) 9.
εἴκοσι (numeral) 2283.
τέσσαρες (numeral) 1508.
καὶ (adjunctive conjunction joining nouns) 14.
τὰ (nom.pl.neut.of the article in agreement with ζῷα) 9.
τεσσαρα (nom.pl.neut.of τέσσαρες, in agreement with ζῷα) 1508.
ζῷα (nom.pl.neut.of ζῷον, subject of ἔπεσαν and προσεκύνησαν) 5086.
καὶ (adjunctive conjunction joining verbs) 14.
προσεκύνησαν (3d.per.pl.aor.act.ind.of προσκυνέω, ingressive) 147.
τῷ (dat.sing.masc.of the article in agreement with θεῷ) 9.
θεῷ (dat.sing.masc.of θεός, indirect object of προσεκύνησαν) 124.
τῷ (dat.sing.masc.of the article in agreement with καθημένῳ) 9.

καθημένῳ (pres.mid.part.dat.sing.masc.of κάθημαι, substantival, apposition) 377.

ἐπί (preposition with the locative, place) 47.

τῷ (loc.sing.masc.of the article in agreement with θρόνῳ) 9.

θρόνῳ (loc.sing.masc.of θρόνος, place) 519.

λέγοντες (pres.act.part.nom.pl.masc.of λέγω, recitative) 66.

Ἀμήν (exclamation) 466.

Ἀλληλουϊά (exclamation) 466.

Translation - *"And the twenty-four elders and the four living creatures fell down and began to worship the God Who was sitting on the throne, saying, 'Amen. Hallelujah!' "*

Comment: Not only the saints in heaven offer the doxology of verses 1 and 2, with a repeat (verse 3) but the heavenly order of creatures, elders and living creatures concur (Rev.4:4-10).

God has dealt with the enemy on earth. Now He turns to a happier scene. There is to be a wedding. The Lamb of God, Who has taken away the sins of the world (John 1:29) is about to meet His bride.

The Marriage Supper of the Lamb

(Revelation 19:5-10)

Verse 5 - "And a voice came out of the throne, saying, Praise our God, all ye his servants, and ye that fear him, both small and great."

Καὶ φωνὴ ἀπὸ τοῦ θρόνου ἐξῆλθεν λέγουσα, Αἰνεῖτε τῷ θεῷ ἡμῶν, πάντες οἱ δοῦλοι αὐτοῦ, (καὶ) οἱ φοβούμενοι αὐτόν, οἱ μικροὶ καὶ οἱ μεγάλοι.

"And from the throne came a voice crying, 'Praise our God, all you his servants, you who fear him, small and great.' " . . . RSV

Καὶ (continuative conjunction) 14.

φωνὴ (nom.sing.fem.of φωνή, subject of ἐξῆλθεν) 222.

ἀπὸ (preposition with the ablative of source) 70.

τοῦ (abl.sing.masc.of the article in agreement with θρόνου) 9.

θρόνου (abl.sing.masc.of θρόνος, source) 519.

ἐξῆλθεν (3d.per.sing.aor.ind.of ἐξέρχομαι, constative) 161.

λέγουσα (pres.act.part.nom.sing.fem.of λέγω, recitative) 66.

Αἰνεῖτε (2d.per.pl.pres.act.impv.of αἰνέω, command) 1881.

τῷ (dat.sing.masc.of the article in agreement with θεῷ) 9.

θεῷ (dat.sing.masc.of θεός, indirect object of Αἰνεῖτε) 124.

ἡμῶν (gen.pl.masc.of ἐγώ, relationship) 123.

πάντες (nom.pl.masc.of πᾶς, in agreement with δοῦλοι) 67.

οἱ (nom.pl.masc.of the article in agreement with δοῦλοι) 9.

δοῦλοι (nom.pl.masc.of δοῦλος, address) 725.

αὐτοῦ (gen.sing.masc.of αὐτός, relationship) 16.
(καὶ) (adjunctive conjunction joining substantives) 14.
οἱ (nom.pl.masc.of the article in agreement with φοβούμενοι) 9.
φοβούμενοι (pres.mid.part.nom.pl.masc.of φοβέομαι, substantival, address) 101.
αὐτόν (acc.sing.masc.of αὐτός, direct object of φοβούμενοι) 16.
οἱ (nom.pl.masc.of the article in agreement with μικροὶ) 9.
μικροὶ (nom.pl.masc.of μικρός, address) 901.
καὶ (adjunctive conjunction joining substantives) 14.
οἱ (nom.pl.masc.of the article in agreement with μεγάλοι) 9.
μεγάλοι (nom.pl.masc.of μέγας, address) 184.

Translation - "And a voice came from the throne saying, 'Praise our Lord, all His servants, and those who fear Him, small and great.'"

Comment: The nominative forms for the vocative are often found in the Revelation. The voice of verse 5 gives the order. The voices of verse 6 obey the order.

Verse 6 - "And I heard as it were the voice of a great multitude, and as the voice of many waters, and as the voice of mighty thunderings, saying, Alleluia: for the Lord God omnipotent reigneth."

καὶ ἤκουσα ὡς φωνὴν ὄχλου πολλοῦ καὶ ὡς φωνὴν ὑδάτων πολλῶν καὶ ὡς φωνὴν βροντῶν ἰσχυρῶν λεγόντων, Ἀλληλουϊά, ὅτι ἐβασίλευσεν κύριος ὁ θεὸς (ἡμῶν) ὁ παντοκράτωρ.

"Then I heard what seemed to be the voice of a great multitude, like the sound of many waters and like the sound of mighty thunderpeals, crying, 'Hallelujah! For the Lord our God the Almighty reigns. . ."... RSV

καὶ (continuative conjunction) 14.
ἤκουσα (1st.per.sing.aor.act.ind.of ἀκούω, ingressive) 148.
ὡς (comparative particle) 128.
φωνὴν (acc.sing.fem.of φωνή, direct object of ἤκουσα) 222.
ὄχλου (gen.sing.masc.of ὄχος, description) 418.
πολλοῦ (gen.sing.masc.of πολύς, in agreement with ὄχλου) 228.
καὶ (adjunctive conjunction joining comparative phrases) 128.
ὡς (comparative particle) 128.
φωνὴν (acc.sing.fem.of φωνή, direct object of ἤκουσα) 222.
ὑδάτων (gen.pl.neut.of ὕδωρ, description) 301.
πολλῶν (gen.pl.neut.of πολύς, in agreement with ὑδάτων) 228.
καὶ (adjunctive conjunction joining comparative phrases) 14.
ὡς (comparative particle) 128.
φωνὴν (acc.sing.fem.of φωνή, direct object of ἤκουσα) 222.
βροντῶν (gen.pl.fem.of βροντή, description) 2117.
ἰσχυρῶν (gen.pl.fem.of ἰσχυρός, in agreement with βροντῶν) 303.
λεγόντων (pres.act.part.gen.pl.masc.of λέγω, recitative) 66.

'Αλληλουϊά (exclamation) 5419.

ὅτι (conjunction introducing a subordinate causal clause) 211.

ἐβασίλευσεν (3d.per.sing.aor.act.ind.of βασιλεύω, ingressive) 236.

κύριος (nom.sing.masc.of κύριος, in apposition) 97.

ὁ (nom.sing.masc.of the article in agreement with θεὸς) 9.

θεὸς (nom.sing.masc.of θεός, subject of ἐβασίλευσεν) 124.

ἡμῶν (gen.pl.masc.of ἐγώ, relationship) 123.

ὁ (nom.sing.masc.of the article in agreement with παντοκράτωρ) 9.

παντοκράτωρ (nom.sing.masc.of παντοκράτωρ, apposition) 4325.

Translation - "And I heard what sounded like the roar of a great crowd and like the sound of many waters and like the crash of mighty thunders saying, 'Hallelujah! Because our God, the Lord Almighty has begun to reign.' "

Comment: As Jesus descends from the right hand of God (Psalm 110:1) to take up His place upon David's throne (Lk.1:32; 2 Sam.7:12-13) the roar of heaven's acclaim grows and reverberates. Multiplied millions of saints (the vast majority of Adam's race died in infancy, so they will be there), sounding like a mighty Niagra or like the crash of gigantic thunderings will fill the universe with the joyous sound.

As our Lord descends we will be caught up to meet Him in the air, after which we will return with him immediately to the marriage supper of the Lamb (1 Thess.4:13-18; 1 Cor.15:51-58; Phil.3:20-21; 1 John 3:1-3).

Note the ingressive aorist tense in ἐβασίλευσεν, as we have it also in Rev.11:17. Our Lord's enemies will have been made His footstool (Psalm 110:1). The Holy Spirit will have completed His ministry of calling out from the Gentiles a people for His name (Acts 15:14-18; Rev.10:7) and the mystery, revealed to Paul (Eph.3:1-8) will have been made complete. The "times of the Gentiles" are fulfilled and Jerusalem will no longer be overrun (Lk.21:24) by the Beast and his dupes. Israel's partial blindness will be healed (Rom.11:25). The promise of the angel Gabriel to the Virgin Mary is about to be fulfilled (Lk.1:30-33).

The assumption of power upon the earth, destined to be delayed until His foes are subjected to His authority is also the occasion of His wedding.

Verse 7 - "Let us be glad and rejoice, and give honour to him: for the marriage of the Lamb is come, and his wife hath made herself ready."

χαίρωμεν καὶ ἀγαλλιῶμεν, καὶ δώσωμεν τὴν δόξαν αὐτῷ, ὅτι ἦλθεν ὁ γάμος τοῦ ἀρνίου, καὶ ἡ γυνὴ αὐτοῦ ἡτοίμασεν ἑεαυτήν.

"Let us rejoice and exult and give him the glory, for the marriage of the Lamb has come, and his Bride has made herself ready; . . . " . . . RSV

χαίρωμεν (1st.per.pl.pres.act.subj.of χαίρω, hortatory) 182.

καὶ (adjunctive conjunction joining verbs) 14.

ἀγαλλιῶμεν (1st.per.pl.pres.act.subj.of ἀγαλλιάω, hortatory) 440.

καὶ (adjunctive conjunction joining verbs) 14.

δώσωμεν (1st.per.pl.aor.act.subj.of δίδωμι, hortatory) 362.

τὴν (acc.sing.fem.of the article in agreement with δόξαν) 9.

δόξαν (acc.sing.fem.of δόξα, direct object of δώσωμεν) 361.

αὐτῷ (dat.sing.masc.of αὐτός, indirect object of δώσωμεν) 16.

ὅτι (conjunction introducing a subordinate causal clause) 211.

ἦλθεν (3d.per.sing.aor.ind.of ἔρχομαι, culminative) 146.

ὁ (nom.sing.masc.of the article in agreement with γάμος) 9.

γάμος (nom.sing.masc.of γάμος, subject of ἦλθεν) 1394.

τοῦ (gen.sing.neut.of the article in agreement with ἀρνίου) 9.

ἀρνίου (gen.sing.neut.of ἀρνίον, description) 2923.

καὶ (continuative conjunction) 14.

ἡ (nom.sing.fem.of the article in agreement with γυνὴ) 9.

γυνὴ (nom.sing.fem.of γυνή, subject of ἡτοίμασεν) 103.

αὐτοῦ (gen.sing.masc.of αὐτός, relationship) 16.

ἡτοίμασεν (3d.per.sing.aor.act.ind.of ἑτοιμάζω, culminative) 257.

ἑαυτήν (acc.sing.fem.of ἑαυτός, direct object of ἡτοίμασεν) 288.

Translation - "Let us be glad and jubilate and let us give the glory to Him; because the marriage of the Lamb has come and his wife has prepared herself."

Comment: The hortatory subjunctives set the mood for the occasion. Joy, jubilation, exultation, delight — the mood that properly surrounds a wedding. Note that the first two hortatory subjunctives are in the present tense. The third is aorist. Let us keep on rejoicing and let us give the glory to Him once and for all, because He is the only one who deserves it. The causal clause gives the reason for the celebration. The Bridegroom is coming and His Bride is eager to meet Him in person. The wedding day has arrived.

Note that the preparation is the work of the Bride, a fact which may help us to identify her properly in verse 8. "If δῶμεν (Sinaiticus* 046 051 most minuscules) were original, it is not easy to account for the origin of the other readings. The future tense δώσομεν, though attested by Sinaiticusₐ A 2053 *al*, is intolerable Greek after two hortatory subjunctive verbs and must be judged as a scribal blunder (P and 25 minucsules), which, being the irregular aorist subjunctive and used only rarely (4.9 in Sinaiticus and six minucsules; Mk.6:37 in Sinaiticus and D), seems to have been intentionally or unintentionally altered in the other witnesses to one or another of the other readings." (Metzger, *A Textual Commentary on the Greek New Testament*, 762).

The manner in which the Lamb's wife is dressed gives us a hint as to who is to be included in this fortunate group. Review thoroughly our comments on Mt.25:1-13.

Verse 8 - "And to her was granted that she should be arrayed in fine linen, clean and white: for the fine linen is the righteousness of saints."

καὶ ἐδόθη αὐτῇ ἵνα περιβάληται βύσσινον λαμπρὸν καθαρόν, τὸ γὰρ βύσσινον τὰ δικαιώματα τῶν ἁγίων ἐστίν.

"it was granted her to be clothed with fine linen, bright and pure' — for the fine

linen is the righteous deeds of the saints." . . . RSV

καὶ (continuative conjunction) 14.

ἐδόθη (3d.per.sing.aor.pass.ind.of δίδωμι, constative) 362.

αὐτῇ (dat.sing.fem.of αὐτός, indirect object of ἐδόθη) 16.

ἵνα (conjunction with the subjunctive, consecutive) 114.

περιβάληται (3d.per.sing.2d.aor.mid.subj.of περιβάλλω, result) 631.

βύσσινον (acc.sing.masc.of βύσσινος, adverbial accusative) 5403.

λαμπρὸν (acc.sing.masc.of λαμπρός, in agreement with βύσσινον) 2832.

καθαρόν (acc.sing.masc.of καθαρός, in agreement with βύσσινον) 431.

τὸ (nom.sing.neut.of the article in agreement with βύσσινον) 9.

γὰρ (explanatory conjunction) 105.

βύσσινον (nom.sing.neut.of βύσσινος, subject of ἐστίν) 5403.

τὰ (nom.pl.neut.of the article in agreement with δικαιώματα) 9.

δικαιώματα (nom.pl.neut.of δικαίωμα, predicate nominative) 1781.

τῶν (gen.pl.masc.of the article in agreement with ἁγίων) 9.

ἁγίων (gen.pl.masc.of ἅγιος, possession) 84.

ἐστίν (3d.per.sing.pres.ind.of εἰμί, aoristic) 86.

Translation - *"And she was given the privilege of clothing herself with clean glistening linen: now the linen is the righteous deeds of the saints."*

Comment: The parable of the virgins in Mt.25:1-13 makes it clear that at the second coming all of the regenerate children of God will be watching, waiting and ready to go in to the marriage feast. These people are not necessarily the Bride, but they are guests at the supper. *Cf.* comment on Mt.25:1-13. The foolish virgins are unregenerate professors, not possessors, of Christianity. The wise virgins, though regenerate and hence admitted to the festivities, do not necessarily make up the most favored personnel - that of the Bride of the Lamb. There is no partial or selective rapture, but not all who are raptured are included in the group here called "the Lamb's wife." How then shall we identify her? By the way she is dressed, of course. This is how one identifies the bride at any wedding. The fine linen is composed of the righteous acts (δικαιώματα) of the saints. *Cf.* Eph.2:10; 2 Tim.4:7.

God has saved us for specific service. We can do what He has planned for us only as we yield to the indwelling Holy Spirit (1 Cor.6:19). Paul finished his course (2 Tim.4:7 and he will be a part of the Bride.

The righteous acts of the saints (δικαιώματα #1781) are not to be confused with the righteousness of the saints (δικαιοσύνη #322). The latter is imputed righteousness — God's gift to all who are justified. Every one who has δικαιωσύνη will be at the wedding. Only those who have been sufficiently obedient to the Holy Spirit to have performed the δικαιώματα which "He has before ordained that we should walk in them" (Eph.2:10) will be a part of the Bride

This raises an unanswered and unanswerable question. How may righteous acts are required? Does membership in the Bride require sinless perfection after regeneration? Obviously not as 1 John 1:18 makes clear, because, if so, no one would qualify. Only our Lord, the Bridegroom, unto whom all the judicial powers of the Godhead have been given (John 5:22; Acts 17:31) can grade the performance of the saint. He is the Bridegroom and He has the right and can be expected to choose His Bride according to His standards. Does unconfessed and unforsaken sin in the life of the Christian disqualify him for membership in the Bride? It would seem so, since the Holy Spirit cannot work His works in the life of the rebellious saint. But does a sin, however great, which is later confessed and forsaken disqualify us? Again, No, since 1 John 1:9 applies. Thus Paul admonishes us in terms of Romans 12:1-2.

The opportunity cost of sin in the life of the believer is that while he is sinning he is not performing δικαιώματα which he needs for his wedding garment. The moments of our life and the days and years which they comprise are numbered. A moment lost can never be regained. Thus the time, strength, money and talents spend in disobedience to the divine will are assets which otherwise could have been spent in doing what God wanted us to do.

Since no one knows how obedient the Christian must be in order to qualify as a part of the Bride of Christ, the safe policy is to be totally obedient to the Holy Spirit, or as nearly so as possible. Gal.5:16; Rom.8:14-17; 1 Cor.3:14; 2 Cor.5:10.

Some Christian groups have insisted that correct doctrine qualifies for membership in the Bride. Thus for them, a Presbyterian, however victorious a Christian he might be in all other respects, will be disqualified because he has not been immersed in water! One denomination insists that only those who are members of their group will qualify, even for salvation, much less for the Bride of Christ. Indeed correct theology as a result of diligent Bible study (2 Tim.2:15) is a virtue, but a doctrine, if corectly understood,   will also be adorned (Titus 2:10). After studying the personal lives of some who insist that they only are the Bride of Christ, it is clear that in their case a lack of adornment indicates a lack of understanding of theology. Thus their claim is refuted. Indeed one might, due to intellectual lack of depth, have an incorrect doctrinal position, and yet humbly yield to the Holy Spirit, with the result that his righteous acts (δικαιώματα) are of sufficient number to dress him as Christ's Bride. This statement must not be construed however as a denigration of correct theology. The loss, suffered by the defeated Christian is real enough (1 Cor.3:15) but it is not a loss of his salvation.

One wonders about the relative merits, before the judgment throne of Christ, the Bridegroom of a Landmark Baptist, properly immersed upon proper local church authority, who has insisted upon closed communion with wine (or grapejuice?!) only and who claims unbroken apostolic succession from John the Baptist, but who does not tithe, nor study his Bible, nor pray, nor attend church regularly, nor win souls, but who drinks, smokes and yields compliance to the flesh in other ways, as opposed to the Presbyterian who has lived a victorious life for Christ in all respects except that he was only sprinkled?

Shall not the Judge of all the earth do right? (Gen.18:25).

Verse 9 - "And he saith unto me, Write, Blessed are they which are called unto the marriage supper of the Lamb. And he saith unto me, These are the true sayings of God."

Καὶ λέγει μοι, Γράφον. Μακάριοι οἱ εἰς τὸ δεῖπνον τοῦ γάμου τοῦ ἀρνίου κεκλημένοι. καὶ λέγει μοι, Οὗτοι οἱ λόγοι ἀληθινοὶ τοῦ θεοῦ εἰσιν.

"And the angel said to me, 'Write this: Blessed are those who are invited to the marriage supper of the Lamb.' And he said to me, 'These are the true words of God.' " . . . RSV

Καὶ (continuative conjunction) 14.

λέγει (3d.per.sing.pres.act.ind.of λέγω, historical) 66.

μοι (dat.sing.masc.of ἐγώ, indirect object of λέγει) 123.

Γράφον (2d.per.sing.aor.act.impv.of γράφω, command) 156.

Μακάριοι (nom.pl.masc.of μακάριος, predicate adjective) 422.

οἱ (nom.pl.masc.of the article in agreement with κεκλημένοι) 9.

εἰς (preposition with the accusative of extent) 140.

τὸ (acc.sing.neut.of the article in agreement with δεῖπνον) 9.

δεῖπνον (acc.sing.neut.of δεῖπνον, extent) 1440.

τοῦ (gen.sing.masc.of the article in agreement with γάμου) 9.

γαμοῦ (gen.sing.masc.of γάμος, description) 1394.

τοῦ (gen.sing.neut.of the article in agreement with ἀρνίου) 9.

ἀρνίου (gen.sing.neut.of ἀρνίου, description) 2923.

κεκλημένοι (perf.pass.part.nom.pl.masc.of καλέω, substantival, subject of εἰσίν understood) 107.

καὶ (adjunctive conjunction joining verbs) 14.

λέγει (3d.per.sing.pres.act.ind.ofd λέγω, historical) 66.

μοι (dat.sing.masc.of ἐγώ, indirect object of λέγει) 123.

Οὗτοι (nom.pl.masc.of οὗτος, predicate nominative) 93.

οἱ (nom.pl.masc.of the article in agreement with λόγοι) 9.

λόγοι (nom.pl.masc.of λόγος, subject of εἰσίν) 510.

ἀληθινοὶ (nom.pl.masc.of ἀληθινός, in agreement with λόγοι) 1696.

τοῦ (gen.sing.masc.of the article in agreement with θεοῦ) 9.

θεοῦ (gen.sing.masc.of θεός, description) 124.

εἰσίν (3d.per.pl.pres.ind.of εἰμί, aoristic) 86.

Translation - "And he said to me, 'Write: Blessed are those who have been called to the supper of the marriage of the Lamb.' And he added, 'These are the true sayings of God.' "

Comment: *Cf.* Mt.22:1-14 and let us study with care What follows is suggestive, not dogmatic. Those wedding guests who were called were saved (Rom.8:29,30). They wore the wedding garment which is Christ's imputed righteousness, and hence were allowed to stay. One unregenerate had "crashed the party" and was ejected. But of those who were called (Mt.22:14) only a few were the "choice ones" who are a part of the Bride. It is blessed to be "called" because attendance at the marriage supper is better than what happened to the man who was not dressed properly for the occasion (Mt.22:13).

The statement οὗτοι οἱ λόγοι ἀληθινοὶ τοῦ θεοῦ εἰσίν seems to challenge John and us to study this matter carefully. Mt.22:1-14; 25:1-13 and Rev.19:5-10 comprise a closely coordinated unit of study. We can draw some tentative conclusions: (a) Old Testament Israel was invited to the wedding. Some of them looked forward in God given faith to the incarnation, which they only imperfectly understood, and were saved, and are thus members of the Body of Christ. Others did not; (b) some of the Jews who heard John the Baptist accepted his message; others did not; (c) of those in John's audience who refused his invitation, some murdered the Messiah and persecuted His apostles and other Christian believers; (d) so God turned to the Gentiles and called many, all of whom are saved, and hence have a wedding garment and will be allowed to see the festivities, but (e) of the many who will be present only a few are in the Bride - "the choice ones" (Mt.22:14).

There must be some way in this scenario to explain the fact that those who built upon the foundation, which is Christ Jesus, a superstructure of wood, hay and stubble, and who thus are destined to see their works burned at the judgment seat of Christ, will suffer loss (1 Cor.3:15), although they themselves will be saved. Paul feared that after he had won others to Christ he himself would be disapproved (1 Cor.9:27). The field of Heb.6:7 grew a profitable harvest for the farmer and will receive blessing from God. The field of Heb.6:8 grew only thorns and briers and was ἀδόκιμος ("disapproved" — cf.#3818 and see how this word is used). What is the difference between the man who received few stripes and the man who received many stripes? (Lk.12:47-48). What is the difference between the soil that was thin, the soil that was deep but infested with thorns and the good soil? And, indeed, between the good soil that yielded thirty, sixty and one hundred fold? (Mt.13:1-9; 18-23). We should avoid the Bible student who seems to have all of the answers. The Judge of all the earth has told us plainly that we are not the judge and warned us that those who think they are will be judged. He will decide who is caught up to meet Him in the air and He will decide which of that great number He will have as members of His bride. The older we get and the more we study the less dogmatic we tend to become about some things.

> *I dream't death came the other night*
> *and heaven's gate swung wide;*
> *With kindly grace, an angel came*
> *and ushered me inside.*

> *And there, to my astonishment,*
> *stood folks I'd known on earth;*
> *Some I judged as quite unfit,*
> *or of but little worth.*

> *Indignant words rose to my lips,*
> *but never were set free:*
> *For every face showed stunned surprise,*
> *no one expected ME.*

Verse 10 - "And I fell at his feet to worship him. And he said unto me, See thou do

it not; I am thy fellowservant, and of thy brethren that have the testimony of
Jesus: worship God: for the testimony of Jesus is the spirit of prophecy."

καὶ ἔπεσα ἔμπροσθεν τῶν ποδῶν αὐτοῦ προσκυνῆσαι αὐτῷ. καὶ λέγει μοι,
῞Ορα μή, σύνδουλός σού εἰμι καὶ τῶν ἀδελφῶν σου τῶν ἐχόντων τὴν μαρτυρίαν
᾽Ιησοῦ. τῷ θεῷ προσκύνησον. ἡ γὰρ μαρτυρία ᾽Ιησοῦ ἐστιν τὸ πνεῦμα τῆς
προφητείας.

"Then I fell down at his feet to worship him, but he said to me, 'You must not
do that! I am a fellow servant with you and your brethren who hold the
testimony of Jesus. Worship God.' For the testimony of Jesus is the spirit of
prophecy." . . . RSV

καὶ (continuative conjunction) 14.

ἔπεσα (1st.per.sing.aor.act.ind.of πίπτω, constative) 187.

ἔμπροσθεν (preposition with the genitive of place description) 459.

τῶν (gen.pl.masc.of the article in agreement with ποδῶν) 9.

ποδῶν (gen.pl.masc.of πούς, place description) 353.

αὐτοῦ (gen.sing.masc.of αὐτός, possession) 16.

προσκυνῆσαι (aor.act.inf.of προσκυνέω, purpose) 147.

αὐτῷ (dat.sing.masc.of αὐτός, indirect object of προσκυνῆσαι) 16.

καὶ (adversative conjunction) 14.

λέγει (3d.per.sing.pres.act.ind.of λέγω, historical) 66.

μοι (dat.sing.masc.of ἐγώ, indirect object of λέγει) 123.

῞Ορα (2d.per.sing.pres.act.impv.of ὁράω, prohibition) 144.

μή (negative conjunction with the imperative, prohibition) 87.

σύνδουλός (nom.sing.masc.of σύνδουλος, predicate nominative) 1276.

σού (gen.sing.masc.of σύ, relationship) 104.

εἰμί (1st.per.sing.pres.ind.of εἰμί, aoristic) 86.

καὶ (adjunctive conjunction joining nouns) 14.

τῶν (gen.pl.masc.of the article in agreement with ἀδελφῶν) 9.

ἀδελφῶν (gen.pl.masc.of ἀδελφός, partitive) 15.

σου (gen.sing.masc.of σύ, relationship) 104.

τῶν (gen.pl.masc.of the article in agreement with ἐχόντων) 9.

ἐχόντων (pres.act.part.gen.pl.masc.of ἔχω, substantival, in apposition with
ἀδελφῶν) 82.

τὴν (acc.sing.fem.of the article in agreement with μαρτυρίαν) 9.

μαρτυρίαν (acc.sing.fem.of μαρτυρία, direct object of ἐχόντων) 1695.

᾽Ιησοῦ (gen.sing.masc.of ᾽Ιησοῦς, description) 3.

τῷ (dat.sing.masc.of the article in agreement with θεῷ) 9.

θεῷ (dat.sing.masc.of θεός, indirect object of προσκύνησον) 124.

προσκύνησον (2d.per.sing.aor.act.impv.of προσκυνέω, command) 147.

ἡ (nom.sing.fem.of the article in agreement with μαρτυρία) 9.

μαρτυρία (nom.sing.fem.of μαρτυρία, subject of ἐστιν) 1695.

᾽Ιησοῦ (gen.sing.masc.of ᾽Ιησοῦς, description) 3.

ἐστιν (3d.per.sing.pres.ind.of εἰμί, static) 86.

τὸ (nom.sing.neut.of the article in agreement with πνεῦμα) 9.

πνεῦμα (nom.sing.neut.of πνεῦμα, predicate nominative) 83.
τῆς (gen.sing.fem.of the article in agreement with προφητείας) 9.
προφητείας (gen.sing.fem.of προφητεία, description) 1041.

Translation - "And I fell at his feet to worship him. But he said to me, 'Take care never to do that. I am the fellow servant of you and your brothers who have the witness of Jesus. Worship God. For the testimony of Jesus is the spirit of prophecy.' "

Comment: John, overcome with gratitude and excitement, mistakes his informant for a heavenly creature and falls at his feet to worship. Ὅρα μή is a case of asyndeton. The verb to go with μή is missing. But the thought is clear. His informant associates himself both with John and John's Christian brethren, who have faithfully witnessed for Jesus. The δικαιώματα of verse 8 are identified as testimonies and service for Christ.

Note that the last clause is causal. The reason John was told not to worship his informant is that the essence and the sum and substance of prophecy is the testimony that Jesus Christ is Lord to the glory of God the Father. Thus as Messiah returns to judge Babylon, destroy them that destroy the earth, rapture His saints and take His place on His throne as King David's greater Son, to begin His glorious reign, it is out of place to worship anyone but Him. It is impossible to separate the incarnation of His first coming to earth from the glory of His second coming. Unfortunately there have been prophecy preachers who majored upon the events of His second coming at the expense of the theology of His first coming. And there have been those who have put their emphasis upon His first coming and forgotten or at least minimized the importance of His second coming. Neither emphasis is correct. Isaiah said, 'Unto us a child is born and unto us a son is given (the incarnation) and the government shall be upon His shoulder (His second coming) (Isaiah 9:6). Note also how Isaiah spoke of both comings in Isaiah 61:1-2, and how Jesus dealt with this passage in Luke 4:16-21. *Cf.* our comment *en loc.* In keeping with the last clause of our verse, theologians can never divorce soteriology from eschatology, to emphasize either at the expense of the other.

The remainder of the chapter depicts the second coming of our Lord.

The Rider on the White Horse

(Revelation 19:11-21)

Verse 11 - "And I saw heaven opened, and behold a white horse; and he that sat upon him was called Faithful and True, and in righteousness he doth judge and make war."

Καὶ εἶδον τὸν οὐρανὸν ἠνεῳγμένον, καὶ ἰδοὺ ἵππος λευκός, καὶ ὁ καθήμενος ἐπ᾽ αὐτὸν πιστὸς (καλούμενος) καὶ ἀληθινός, καὶ ἐν δικαιοσύνῃ κρίνει καὶ πολεμεῖ.

"Then I saw heaven opened, and behold, a white horse! He who sat upon it is called Faithful and True, and in righteousness he judges and makes war." . . . RSV

Καὶ (continuative conjunction) 14.

εἶδον (1st.per.sing.aor.act.ind.of ὁράω, ingressive) 144.

τὸν (acc.sing.masc.of the article in agreement with οὐρανὸν) 9.

οὐρανὸν (acc.sing.masc.of οὐρανός, direct object of εἶδον) 254.

ἠνεῳγμένον (perf.pass.part.acc.sing.masc.of ἀνοίγω, adjectival, predicate position, restrictive, in agreement with οὐρανὸν) 188.

καὶ (continuative conjunction) 14.

ἰδοὺ (exclamation) 95.

ἵππος (nom.sing.masc.of ἵππος, nominative absolute) 5121.

λευκός (nom.sing.masc.of λευκός, in agreement with ἵππος) 522.

καὶ (adjunctive conjunction joining substantives) 14.

ὁ (nom.sing.masc.of the article in agreement with καθήμενος) 9.

καθήμενος (pres.mid.part.nom.sing.masc.of κάθημαι, substantival, nominative absolute) 377.

ἐπ' (preposition with the accusative of extent, rest) 47.

αὐτὸν (acc.sing.masc.of αὐτός, rest) 16.

πιστὸς (nom.sing.masc.of πιστός, predicate nominative) 1522.

(καλούμενος) (pres.pass.part.nom.sing.masc.of καλέω, adjectival, predicate position, restrictive, in agreement with καθήμενος) 107.

καὶ (adjunctive conjunction joining adjectives) 14.

ἀληθινός (nom.sing.masc.of ἀληθινός, predicate nominative) 1696.

καὶ (continuative conjunction) 14.

ἐν (preposition with the instrumental, means) 80.

δικαιοσύνῃ (instru.sing.fem.of δικαιοσύνη, means) 322.

κρίνει (3d.per.sing.pres.act.ind.of κρίνω, static) 531.

καὶ (adjunctive conjunction joining verbs) 14.

πολεμεῖ (3d.per.sing.pres.act.ind.of πολεμέω, static) 5140.

Translation - "And I looked up into the opened heaven and Look! A white horse and the One sitting upon him, called Faithful and True! And in righteousness He is about to judge and wage war."

Comment: Satan's man also rode a white horse (Rev.6:1-2). Now the God-Man appears on a white horse. The heaven is opened (Mt.24:30; Rev.6:14; 11:19). *Cf.* also Ezek.1:1; Rev.4:1; Zech.1:8; 6:3,6; Rev.1:5; 3:14; Psalm 96:13; Isa.11:4.

The events described in Rev.19:11-21 occur simultaneously with those shown on the chart in comment on Rev.16:17 (*supra*, page 305). Into this pattern of events they fit with perfect correlation. The rapture of those Christians who survived on earth until the last day is taking place at this time. They are caught up to meet the Lord in the air and they immediately return with Him. *Cf.* #1533 and comment upon the three places where it is used - Mt.25:6; Acts 28:15; 1 Thess.4:17.

Verse 12 - "His eyes were as a flame of fire, and on his head were many crowns:

and he had a name written that no man knew, but he himself."

οἱ δὲ ὀφθαλμοὶ αὐτοῦ (ὡς) φλὸξ πυρός, καὶ ἐπὶ τὴν κεφαλὴν αὐτοῦ διαδήματα πολλά, ἔχων ὄνομα γεγραμμένον ὃ οὐδεὶς οἶδεν εἰ μὴ αὐτός,

"His eyes are like a flame of fire, and on his head are many diadems; and he has a name inscribed which no one knows but himself." . . . RSV

οἱ (nom.pl.masc.of the article in agreement with ὀφθαλμοὶ) 9.

δὲ (continuative conjunction) 11.

ὀφθαλμοὶ (nom.pl.masc.of ὀφθαλμός, subject of εἰσίν understood) 501.

αὐτοῦ (gen.sing.masc.of αὐτός, possession) 16.

(ὡς) (comparative particle) 128.

φλὸξ (nom.sing.fem.of φλόξ, subject of ἔστιν understood) 2586.

πυρός (gen.sing.neut.of πῦρ, description) 298.

καὶ (continuative conjunction) 14.

ἐπὶ (preposition with the accusative, extent, rest) 47.

τὴν (acc.sing.fem.of the article in agreement with κεφαλὴν) 9.

κεφαλὴν (acc.sing.fem.of κεφαλή, extent, rest) 521.

αὐτοῦ (gensing.masc.of αὐτός, possession) 16.

διαδήματα (nom.pl.neut.of διάδημα, subject of ἔστιν understood) 5383.

πολλά (nom.pl.neut.of πολύς, in agreement with διαδήματα) 228.

ἔχων (pres.act.part.nom.sing.masc.of ἔχω, adjectival, predicate position, restrictive) 82.

ὄνομα (acc.sing.neut.of ὄνομα, direct object of ἔχων) 108.

γεγραμμένον (perf.pass.part.acc.sing.neut.of γράφω, adjectival, predicate position, restrictive, in agreement with ὄνομα) 156.

ὃ (acc.sing.neut.of ὅς, relative pronoun, direct object of οἶδεν) 65.

οὐδεὶς (nom.sing.masc.of οὐδείς, subject of οἶδεν) 446.

οἶδεν (3d.per.sing.perf.act.ind.of ὁράω) 144b.

εἰ (conditional particle in an elliptical clause) 337.

μὴ (negative conjunction in an elliptical clause) 87.

αὐτός (nom.sing.masc.of αὐτός, subject of ellided verb in an elliptical clause, intensive) 16.

Translation - "And His eyes looked like a flame of fire, and upon His head were many crowns. He had a name written which no one has ever known except Himself."

Comment: In his excitement John omitted his verbs except for the participle ἔχων which is only loosely connected. It agrees in gender neither with κεφαλὴν (feminine) nor διαδήματα (neuter). Were the names written on His head or upon the crowns upon His head? The crowns which Satan presumed to display as his own (Rev.12:3) and which the Beast wore (Rev.13:1) are properly worn by Messiah (Rev.19:12).

John's vision of Christ is similar to the first sight which he had of Him (Rev.1:14; 2:18; Dan.10:6).

This name which no one has ever known except Christ Himself (intensive αὐτός) was given to Him in exaltation in return for His *kenosis* at Calvary (Phil.2:6-11). It is above every name, the mention of which results in universal submission to Messiah.

Verse 13 - "And he was clothed with a vesture dipped in blood: and his name is called The Word of God."

καὶ περιβεβλημένος ἱμάτιον βεβαμμένον αἵματι, καὶ κέκληται τὸ ὄνομα αὐτοῦ ὁ λόγος τοῦ θεοῦ.

"He is clad in a robe dipped in blood, and the name by which he is called is The Word of God." . . . RSV

καὶ (continuative conjunction) 14.

περιβεβλημένος (perf.pass.part.nom.sing.masc.of περιβάλλω, adjectival, predicate position, restrictive, in agreement with καθήμενος, verse 11) 631.

ἱμάτιον (acc.sing.neut.of ἱμάτιον, adverbial accusative) 534.

βεβαμμένον (perf.pass.part.acc.sing.neut.of βάπτω, adjectival, predicate position, restrictive, in agreement with ἱμάτιον) 2584.

αἵματι (loc.sing.neut.of αἷμα, place) 1203.

καὶ (continuative conjunction) 14.

κέκληται (3d.per.sing.perf.pass.ind.of καλέω, intensive) 107.

τὸ (nom.sing.neut.of the article in agreement with ὄνομα) 9.

ὄνομα (nom.sing.neut.of ὄνομα, subject of κέκληται) 108.

αὐτοῦ (gen.sing.masc.of αὐτός, possession) 16.

ὁ (nom.sing.masc.of the article in agreement with λόγος) 9.

λόγος (nom.sing.masc.of λόγος, predicate nominative) 510.

τοῦ (gen.sing.masc.of the article in agreement with θεοῦ) 9.

θεοῦ (gen.sing.masc.of θεός, description) 124.

Translation - "And He was clothed in a garment dipped in blood, and His name was called The Word of God."

Comment: Once again we find the passive form of περιβάλλω followed by the accusative. We have noted this before. The list includes Mk.14:51; 16:5; Rev.7:9,13; 10:1; 11:3; 12:1; 17:4; 18:16; 19:13. (Robertson, *Grammar*, 485).

Other manuscripts read ἐρραντισμένον or ῥεραντισμένον, ῥεραμμένον, περιρεραμμένον or περιρεραντισμένον, for βεβαμμένον. Metzger says, in part, "Among the many variant readings βεβαμμένον appears to be both the best supported (A 046 051 most minuscules cop^sa arm *al*) and most likely to provoke change. Either the absence of ἐν with the following αἵματι or, more probably, the feeling that the context (and perhaps also the recollection of Isa.63:3) made βάπτω less appropriate to express the sense than ῥαίνω or its collateral ῥαντίζω, prompted copyists to substitute . . . " the other readings (*A Textual Commentary on the Greek New Testament*, 763, 764). Whether Christ's garment was red by virtue of having been dipped (βεβαμμένον) or splattered (ἐρραντισμένον) with blood is immaterial. The thrust of the passage is that our Lord is there on the business of judgment and that bloodshed is involved. As

John introduced Jesus in John 1:1,14 and 1 John 1;1, he now sees Him in His second coming with the same name (Heb.13:8).

Verse 14 - "And the armies which were in heaven followed him upon white horses, clothed in fine linen, white and clean."

καὶ τὰ στρατεύματα (τὰ) ἐν τῷ οὐρανῷ ἠκολούθει αὐτῷ ἐφ' ἵπποις λευκοῖς, ἐνδεδυμένοι βύσσινον λευκὸν καθαρόν.

"And the armies of heaven, arrayed in fine linen, white and pure, followed him on white horses." . . . RSV

καὶ (continuative conjunction) 14.

τὰ (nom.pl.neut.of the article in agreement with στρατεύματα) 9.

στρατεύματα (nom.pl.neut.of στράτευμα, subject of ἠκολούθει) 1404.

τὰ (nom.pl.neut.of the article in agreement with στρατεύματα) 9.

ἐν (preposition with the locative of place) 80.

τῷ (loc.sing.masc.of the article in agreement with οὐρανῷ) 9.

οὐρανῷ (loc.sing.masc.of οὐρανός, place) 254.

ἠκολούθει (3d.per.sing.imp.act.ind.of ἀκολουθέω, progressive description) 394.

αὐτῷ (dat.sing.masc.of αὐτός, with persons) 16.

ἐφ' (preposition with the locative of place) 47.

ἵπποις (loc.pl.masc.of ἵππος, place) 5121.

λευκοῖς (loc.pl.masc.of λευκός, in agreement with ἵπποις) 522.

ἐνδεδυμένοι (perf.pass.part.nom.pl.masc.of ἐνδύω, adjectival, predicate position, restrictive, for ἐνδεδυμένα, in agreement with στρατεύματα) 613.

βύσσινον (acc.sing.neut.of βύσσινος, adverbial accusative) 5403.

λευκὸν (acc.sing.neut.of λευκός, in agreement with βύσσινον) 522.

καθαρόν (acc.sing.neut.of καθαρός, in agreement with βύσσινον) 431.

Translation - "And the armies of heaven, clothed in clean white fine linen were following Him upon white horses."

Comment: It is the armies, not the white horses, who are clothed in clean white linen, although the participle ἐνδεδυμένοι, which is masculine does not agree in gender with στρατεύματα nor in case with ἵπποις. Another one of John's grammatical errors. These heavenly mounted soldiers are not identified, but it is proper to assume that they are angels. They, the angelic troops under the direction of Michael, have had encounters with Lucifer and his demons before on at least two occasions (Isa.14:12-16; Ezek.28:11-19; Rev.12:7-9). There is to be another battle, at the end of the millenium (Rev.20:7-10), though it is not clear that the angels of heaven will be involved in this fight.

Verse 15 - "And out of his mouth goeth a sharp sword, that with it he should smite the nations; and he shall rule them with a rod of iron: and he treadeth the winepress of the fierceness and wrath of Almighty God."

καὶ ἐκ τοῦ στόματος αὐτοῦ ἐκπορεύεται ῥομφαία ὀξεῖα, ἵνα ἐν αὐτῇ πατάξῃ τὰ ἔθνη, καὶ αὐτὸς ποιμανεῖ αὐτοὺς ἐν ῥάβδῳ σιδηρᾷ. καὶ αὐτὸς πατεῖ τὴν ληνὸν τοῦ οἴνου τοῦ θυμοῦ τῆς ὀργῆς τοῦ θεοῦ τοῦ παντοκράτορος.

"From his mouth issues a sharp sword with which to smite the nations, and he will rule them with a rod of iron; he will tread the wine press of the fury of the wrath of God the Almighty." . . . RSV

καὶ (continuative conjunction) 14.
ἐκ (preposition with the ablative of source) 19.
τοῦ (abl.sing.neut.of the article in agreement with στόματος) 9.
στόματος (abl.sing.neut.of στόμα, source) 344.
αὐτοῦ (gen.sing.masc.of αὐτός, possession) 16.
ἐκπορεύεται (3d.per.sing.pres.mid.ind.of ἐκπορεύομαι, aoristic) 270.
ῥομφαία (nom.sing.fem.of ῥομφαία, subject of ἐκπορεύεται) 1904.
ὀξεῖα (nom.sing.fem.of ὀξύς, in agreement with ῥομφαία) 3867.
ἵνα (conjunction with the subjunctive, purpose) 114.
ἐν (preposition with the instrumental, means) 80.
αὐτῇ (instru.sing.fem.of αὐτός, means) 16.
πατάξῃ (3d.per.sing.aor.act.subj.of πατάσσω, purpose) 1579.
τὰ (acc.pl.neut.of the article in agreement with ἔθνη) 9.
ἔθνη (acc.pl.neut.of ἔθνος, direct object of πατάξῃ) 376.
καὶ (continuative conjunction) 14.
αὐτὸς (nom.sing.masc.of αὐτός, subject of ποιμανεῖ, emphatic) 16.
ποιμανεῖ (3d.per.sing.fut.act.ind.of ποιμαίνω, predictive) 164.
αὐτοὺς (acc.pl.masc.of αὐτός, direct object of ποιμανεῖ) 16.
ἐν (preposition with the instrumental, means) 80.
ῥάβδῳ (instru.sing.masc.of ῥάβδος, means) 863.
σιδηρᾷ (instru.sing.masc.of σίδηρος, in agreement with ῥάβδῳ) 5407.
καὶ (adjunctive conjunction joining verbs) 14.
αὐτὸς (nom.sing.masc.of αὐτός, subject of πατεῖ, emphatic) 16.
πατεῖ (3d.per.sing.fut.act.ind.of πατέω, predictive) 2415.
τὴν (acc.sing.fem.of the article in agreement with ληνὸν) 9.
ληνὸν (acc.sing.fem.of ληνός, direct object of πατεῖ) 1378.
τοῦ (gen.sing.masc.of the article in agreement with οἴνου) 9.
οἴνου (gen.sing.masc.of οἶνος, description) 808.
τοῦ (gen.sing.masc.of the article in agreement with θυμοῦ) 9.
θυμοῦ (gen.sing.masc.of θυμός, description) 2034.
τῆς (gen.sing.fem.of the article in agreement with ὀργῆς) 9.
ὀργῆς (gen.sing.fem.of ὀργή, description) 283.
τοῦ (gen.sing.masc.of the article in agreement with θεοῦ) 9.
θεοῦ (gen.sing.masc.of θεός, possession) 124.
τοῦ (gen.sing.masc.of the article in agreement with παντοκράτορος) 9.
παντοκράτορος (gen.sing.masc.of παντοκράτωρ, apposition) 4325.

Translation - *"And out of His mouth there goes a sharp sword with which He will smite the nations, and He will rule them with an iron rod, and He will tread the winepress of the wine of the intensity of the wrath of God the Almighty."*

Comment: The ἵνα clause "usurps the province of the relative clause" (Robertson, *Grammar*, 1001) here. It is used where the relative could have been used. Robertson points to 2 Cor.12:7; John 5:7; 9:36 and Gal.4:5 (*Ibid.*, 960). Literally the translation is "so that (or in order that) by means of it, he might smite . . . κ.τ.λ." The passage recalls many others. *Cf.* Isa.49:2; Rev.1:16; 2:12,16; Psalm 2:9; Rev.12:5; Isa.63:3; Lam.1:15; Joel 3:13; Rev.14:20. *Cf.*#4325 for all the places where the word applies to Christ. Here is His decisive assertion of authority. Plato's Philosopher-King has arrived. (*Republic*, V, 473, D).

Verse 16 - "And he hath on his vesture and on his thigh a name written, King of Kings, and Lord of Lords."

καὶ ἔχει ἐπὶ τὸ ἱμάτιον καὶ ἐπὶ τὸν μηρὸν αὐτοῦ ὄνομα γεγραμμένον, Βασιλεὺς βασιλέων καὶ κύριος κυρίων.

"On his robe and on his thigh he has a name inscribed, King of kings and Lord of lords." . . . RSV

καὶ (continuative conjunction) 14.
ἔχει (3d.per.sing.pres.act.ind.of ἔχω, aoristic) 82.
ἐπὶ (preposition with the accusative, place) 47.
τὸ (acc.sing.neut.of the article in agreement with ἱμάτιον) 9.
ἱμάτιον (acc.sing.neut.of ἱμάτιον, place) 534.
καὶ (adjunctive conjunction joining prepositional phrases) 14.
ἐπὶ (preposition with the accusative, place) 47.
τὸν (acc.sing.masc.of the article in agreement with μηρὸν) 9.

#5420 μηρὸν (acc.sing.masc.of μηρός, place).

King James Version

thigh - Rev.19:16.

Revised Standard Version

thigh - Rev.19:16.

Meaning: the thigh - Rev.19:16.

αὐτοῦ (gen.sing.masc.of αὐτός, possession) 16.
ὄνομα (acc.sing.neut.of ὄνομα, direct object of ἔχει) 108.
γεγραμμένον (perf.pass.part.acc.sing.neut.of γράφω, adjectival, predicate position, restrictive, in agreement with ὄνομα) 156.
Βασιλεὺς (nom.sing.masc.of βασιλεύς, appellation) 31.
βασιλέων (gen.pl.masc.of βασιλεύς, relationship) 31.
καὶ (adjunctive conjunction joining nouns) 14.
κύριος (nom.sing.masc.of κύριος, appellation) 97.
κυρίων (gen.pl.masc.of κύριος, relationship) 97.

*Translation - "And He has upon His robe and upon His thigh a name written —
'King of kings and Lord of lords.' "*

Comment: *Cf.* 1 Tim.6:15; Rev.17:14. The grisly results of the conflict are set
forth in verses 17 and 18.

*Verse 17 - "And I saw an angel standing in the sun, and he cried with a loud voice,
saying to all the fowls that fly in the midst of heaven, Come and gather
yourselves together unto the supper of the great God."*

Καὶ εἶδον ἕνα ἄγγελον ἑστῶτα ἐν τῷ ἡλίῳ, καὶ ἔκραξεν (ἐν) φωνῇ μεγάλῃ
λέγων πᾶσιν τοῖς ὀρνέοις τοῖς πετομένοις ἐν μεσουρανήματι, Δεῦτε
συνάχθητε εἰς τὸ δεῖπνον τὸ μέγα τοῦ θεοῦ,

*"Then I saw an angel standing in the sun, and with a loud voice he called to all
the birds that fly in midheaven, 'Come, gather for the great supper of God,...".*.
. RSV

Καὶ (continuative conjunction) 14.

εἶδον (1st.per.sing.aor.act.ind.of ὁράω, constative) 144.

ἕνα (acc.sing.masc.of εἷς, in agreement with ἄγγελον) 469.

ἄγγελον (acc.sing.masc.of ἄγγελος, direct object of εἶδον) 96.

ἑστῶτα (perf.act.part.acc.sing.masc.of ἵστημι, adjectival, predicate position,
restrictive, in agreement with ἄγγελον) 180.

ἐν (preposition with the locative of place) 80.

τῷ (loc.sing.masc.of the article in agreement with ἡλίῳ) 9.

ἡλίῳ (loc.sing.masc.of ἥλιος, place) 546.

καὶ (continuative conjunction) 14.

ἔκραξεν (3d.per.sing.aor.act.ind.of κράζω, ingressive) 765.

(ἐν) (preposition with the instrumental, means) 80.

φωνῇ (instru.sing.fem.of φωνή, means) 222.

μεγάλῃ (instru.sing.fem.of μέγας, in agreement with φωνῇ) 184.

λέγων (pres.act.part.nom.sing.masc.of λέγω, recitative) 66.

πᾶσιν (dat.pl.neut.of πᾶς, in agreement with ὀρνέοις) 67.

τοῖς (dat.pl.neut.of the article in agreement with ὀρνέοις) 9.

ὀρνέοις (dat.pl.neut.of ὄρνεον, indirect object of ὄρνεον) 5399.

τοῖς (dat.pl.neut.of the article in agreement with πετομένοις) 9.

πετομένοις (pres.mid.part.dat.pl.masc.of πετάομαι, adjectival, emphatic
attributive position, ascriptive, in agreement with ὀρνέοις) 5346.

ἐν (preposition with the locative, place) 80.

μεσουρανήματι (loc.sing.neut.of μεσουράνημα, place) 5367.

Δεῦτε (imperative particle) 391.

συνάχθητε (2d.per.pl.aor.pass.impv.of συνάγω, command) 150.

εἰς (preposition with the accusative of extent) 140.

τὸ (acc.sing.neut.of the article in agreement with δεῖπνον) 9.

δεῖπνον (acc.sing.neut.of δεῖπνον, extent) 1440.

τὸ (acc.sing.neut.of the article in agreement with μέγα) 9.

μέγα (acc.sing.neut.of μέγας, in agreement with δεῖπνον) 184.
τοῦ (gen.sing.masc.of the article in agreement with θεοῦ) 9.
θεοῦ (gen.sing.masc.of θεός, description) 124.

Translation - "And I saw one angel standing in the sun and he began to cry with a loud voice, saying to all the scavangers that fly across the sky, 'Come! Assemble yourselves unto the great supper of God.' "

Comment: This is irony. In Rev.19:7-9 we have the joyous marriage supper of the Lamb and His bride. Now the buzzards are invited to another great supper of a different kind. The menu is described in

Verse 18 - ". . . that ye may eat the flesh of kings and the flesh of captains, and the flesh of mighty men, and the flesh of horses, and of them that sit on them, and the flesh of all men, both small and great."

ἵνα φάγητε σάρκας βασιλέων καὶ σάρκας χιλιάρχων καὶ σάρκας ἰσχυρῶν καὶ σάρκας ἵππων καὶ τῶν καθημένων ἐπ' αὐτῶν καὶ σάρκας πάντων ἐλευθέρων τε καὶ δούλων καὶ μικρῶν καὶ μεγάλων.

". . . to eat the flesh of kings, the flesh of captains, the flesh of mighty men, the flesh of horses and their riders, and the flesh of all men, both free and slave, both small and great.' " . . . RSV

ἵνα (conjunction with the subjunctive, sub-final) 114.
φάγητε (2d.per.pl.aor.act.subj.of ἐσθίω, purpose/result) 610.
σάρκας (acc.pl.fem.of σάρξ, direct object of φάγητε) 1202.
βασιλέων (gen.pl.masc.of βασιλεύς, description) 31.
καὶ (adjunctive conjunction joining nouns) 14.
σάρκας (acc.pl.fem.of σάρξ, direct object of φάγητε) 1202.
χιλιάρχων (gen.pl.masc.of χιλίαρχος, description) 2258.
καὶ (adjunctive conjunction joining nouns) 14.
σάρκας (acc.pl.fem.of σάρξ, direct object of φάγητε) 1202.
ἰσχυρῶν (gen.pl.masc.of ἰσχυρός, description) 303.
καὶ (adjunctive conjunction joining nouns) 14.
σάρκας (acc.pl.fem.of σάρξ, direct object of φάγητε) 1202.
ἵππων (gen.pl.masc.of ἵππος, description) 5121.
καὶ (adjunctive conjunction joining substantives) 14.
τῶν (gen.pl.masc.of the article in agreement with καθημένων) 9.
καθημένων (pres.mid.part.gen.pl.masc.of κάθημαι, substantival, description) 377.
ἐπ' (preposition with the gentive, place description) 47.
αὐτῶν (gen.pl.masc.of αὐτός, place description) 16.
καὶ (adjunctive conjunction joining nouns) 14.
σάρκας (acc.pl.fem.of σάρξ, direct object of φάγητε) 1202.
πάντων (gen.pl.masc.of πᾶς, in agreement with ἐλευθέρων) 67.
ἐλευθέρων (gen.pl.masc.of ἐλεύθερος, description) 1245.
τε (correlative particle) 1408.

καὶ (adjunctive conjunction joining nouns) 14.
δούλων (gen.pl.masc.of δοῦλος, description) 725.
καὶ (adjunctive conjunction joining nouns) 14.
μικρῶν (gen.pl.masc.of μικρός, description) 901.
καὶ (adjunctive conjunction joining adjectives) 14.
μεγάλων (gen.pl.masc.of μέγας, description) 184.

Translation - *"So that you may eat the flesh of kings and captains and strong men and horses and those who ride upon them and of all, both free men and slaves, both small and great."*

Comment: *Cf.* Ezek.39:5-16, though this passage may refer to a clean-up operation following an earlier battle, but it gives us an idea of the intensity of the conflict.

The battle of Armageddon is joined in

Verse 19 - *"And I saw the beast, and the kings of the earth, and their armies, gathered together to make war against him that sat on the horse, and against his army."*

Καὶ εἶδον τὸ θηρίον καὶ τοὺς βασιλεῖς τῆς γῆς καὶ τὰ στρατεύματα αὐτῶν συνηγμένα ποιῆσαι τὸν πόλεμον μετὰ τοῦ καθημένου ἐπὶ τοῦ ἵππου καὶ μετὰ τοῦ στρατεύματος αὐτοῦ.

"And I saw the beast and the kings of the earth with their armies gathered to make war against him who sits upon the horse and against his army." . . . RSV

Καὶ (continuative conjunction) 14.
εἶδον (1st.per.sing.aor.act.ind.of ὁράω, constative) 144.
τὸ (acc.sing.neut.of the article in agreement with θηρίον) 9.
θηρίον (acc.sing.neut.of θηρίον, direct object of εἶδον) 1951.
καὶ (adjunctive conjunction joining nouns) 14.
τοὺς (acc.pl.masc.of the article in agreement with βασιλεῖς) 9.
βασιλεῖς (acc.pl.masc.of βασιλεύς, direct object of εἶδον) 31.
τῆς (gen.sing.fem.of the article in agreement with γῆς) 9.
γῆς (gen.sing.fem.of γῆ, description) 157.
καὶ (adjunctive conjunction joining nouns) 14.
τὰ (acc.pl.neut.of the article in agreement with στρατεύματα) 9.
στρατεύματα (acc.pl.neut.of στράτευμα, direct object of εἶδον) 1404.
αὐτῶν (gen.pl.masc.of αὐτός, possession) 16.
συνηγμένα (perf.pass.part.acc.pl.neut.of συνάγω, adjectival, predicate position, restrictive, in agreement with στρατεύματα) 150.
ποιῆσαι (aor.act.inf.of ποιέω, purpose) 127.
τὸν (acc.sing.masc.of the article in agreement with πόλεμον) 9.
πόλεμον (acc.sing.masc.of πολεμος, direct object of ποιῆσαι) 1483.
μετὰ (preposition with the genitive, opposition) 50.
τοῦ (gen.sing.masc.of the article in agreement with καθημένου) 9.
καθημένου (pres.mid.part.gen.sing.masc.of κάθημαι, opposition) 377.

ἐπί (preposition with the genitive, place description) 47.
τοῦ (gen.sing.masc.of the article in agreement with ἵππου) 9.
ἵππου (gen.sing.masc.of ἵππος, place description) 5121.
καί (adjunctive conjunction joining prepositional phrases) 14.
μετά (preposition with the genitive, opposition) 50.
τοῦ (gen.sing.neut.of the article in agreement with στρατεύματος) 9.
στρατεύματος (gen.sing.neut.of στράτευμα, opposition) 1404.
αὐτοῦ (gen.sing.masc.of αὐτός, possession) 16.

Translation - "And I saw the Beast and the kings of the earth and their armies mobilized to do battle with Him Who sits upon the horse and with His army."

Comment: *Cf.* Zech.14:1-21; Psalm 2:2. This is the moment of showdown. The conflict between Satan and his Creator began in heaven (Isa.14:12-14) and it will end on earth. Satan's representatives will be cast into the lake of fire.

Verse 20 - "And the beast was taken, and with him the false prophet that wrought miracles before him, with which he deceived them that had received the mark of the beast, and them that worshipped his image. These both were cast alive into a lake of fire burning with brimstone."

καὶ ἐπιάσθη τὸ θηρίον καὶ μετ᾽ αὐτοῦ ὁ ψευδοπροφήτης ὁ ποιήσας τὰ σημεῖα ἐνώπιον αὐτοῦ, ἐν οἷς ἐπλάνησεν τοὺς λαβόντας τὸ χάραγμα τοῦ θηρίου καὶ τοὺς προσκυνοῦντας τῇ εἰκόνι αὐτοῦ. ζῶντες ἐβλήθησαν οἱ δύο εἰς τὴν λίμνην τοῦ πυρὸς τῆς καιομένης ἐν θείῳ.

"And the beast was captured, and with it the false prophet who in its presence had worked the signs by which he deceived those who had received the mark of the beast and those who worshipped its image. These two were thrown alive into the lake of fire that burns with brimstone." . . . RSV

καί (continuative conjunction) 14.
ἐπιάσθη (3d.per.sing.aor.pass.ind.of πιάζω,constative) 2371.
τό (nom.sing.neut.of the article in agreement with θηρίον) 9.
θηρίον (nom.sing.neut.of θηρίον, subject of ἐπιάσθη) 1951.
καί (adjunctive conjunction joining nouns) 14.
μετ᾽ (preposition with the genitive, accompaniment) 50.
αὐτοῦ (gen.sing.masc.of αὐτός, accompaniment) 16.
ὁ (nom.sing.masc.of the article in agreement with ψευδοπροφήτης) 9.
ψευδοπροφήτης (nom.sing.masc.of ψευδοπροφήτης, subject of ἐπιάσθη) 670.
ὁ (nom.sing.masc.of the article in agreement with ποιήσας) 9.
ποιήσας (aor.act.part.nom.sing.masc.of ποιέω, substantival, apposition) 127.
τά (acc.pl.neut.of the article in agreement with σημεῖα) 9.
σημεῖα (acc.pl.neut.of σημεῖον, direct object of ποιήσας) 1005.
ἐνώπιον (preposition with the genitive of place description) 1798.
αὐτοῦ (gen.sing.masc.of αὐτός, place description) 16.

ἐν (preposition with the instrumental, means) 80.

οἷς (instru.pl.neut.of ὅς, relative pronoun, means) 65.

ἐπλάνησεν (3d.per.sing.aor.act.ind.of πλανάω, constative) 1257.

τοὺς (acc.pl.masc.of the article in agreement with λαβόντας) 9.

λαβόντας (2d.aor.act.part.acc.pl.masc.of λαμβάνω, substantival, direct object of ἐπλάνησεν) 533.

τὸ (acc.sing.neut.of the article in agreement with χάραγμα) 9.

χάραγμα (acc.sing.neut.of χάραγμα, direct object of λαβόντας) 3420.

τοῦ (gen.sing.neut.of the article in agreement with θηρίου) 9.

θηρίου (gen.sing.neut.of θηρίον, description) 1951.

καὶ (adjunctive conjunction joining participles) 14.

τοὺς (acc.pl.masc.of the article in agreement with προσκυνοῦντας) 9.

προσκυνοῦντας (pres.act.part.acc.pl.masc.of προσκυνέω, substantival, direct object of ἐπλάνσεν) 147.

τῇ (dat.sing.fem.of the article in agreement with εἰκόνι) 9.

εἰκόνι (dat.sing.fem.of εἰκών, indirect object of προσκυνοῦντας) 1421.

αὐτοῦ (gen.sing.masc.of αὐτός, description) 16.

ζῶντες (pres.act.part.nom.pl.masc.of ζάω, adverbial, temporal) 340.

ἐβλήθησαν (3d.per.pl.aor.pass.ind.of βάλλω, constative) 299.

οἱ (nom.pl.masc.of the article in agreement with δύο) 9.

δύο (nom.masc., subject of ἐβλήθησαν) 385.

εἰς (preposition with the accusative, extent) 140.

τὴν (acc.sing.fem.of the article in agreement with λίμνην) 9.

λίμνην (acc.sing.fem.of λίμνη, extent) 2041.

τοῦ (gen.sing.neut.of the article in agreement with πυρὸς) 9.

πυρὸς (gen.sing.neut.of πῦρ, description) 298.

τῆς (gen.sing.fem.of the article in agreement with καιομένης) 9.

καιομένης (pres.mid.part.gen.sing.fem.of καίω, adjectival, emphatic attributive position, ascriptive, in agreement with λίμνην) 453.

ἐν (preposition with the instrumental, means) 80.

θείῳ (instru.sing.neut.of θεῖον, means) 2619.

Translation - "And the Beast was captured and with him the False Prophet, who performed the miracles before him, by which he deceived those who had taken the mark of the Beast and who were worshipping his image. While yet alive, these two were cast into the lake of fire burning with brimstone."

Comment: καιομένης agrees in gender with λίμνην and in case with πυρὸς. We have often observed that the phrase ἡ λίμνη τοῦ πυρός means "a lake characterized as being on fire" in the sense that a field of fire is a field with patches of fire here and there. Thus it is possible to be in a lake of fire or a field of fire without actually being *in* the flame. The phrase ἐν τῇ φλογὶ τούτῃ (Luke 16:24) can be translated "by this flame." *Cf.* comment *en loc.* The doctrine of eternal punishment in a "lake of fire" does not require us to believe that souls and bodies are to be perpetually suspended in a flame and thus subject to physical combustion. Any fire fighter in a forest or blazing field has had the experience of being inside a field of fire and tormented by the heat, though not actually in the blaze.

The Beast (Rev.13:1-10) and his hellish colleague (Rev.13:11-18) will be cast alive into the lake of fire at the second coming. Their dupes, the unregenerates who received the mark of the Beast and worshipped his image will not be sent to hell at this time (Rev.20:5). They will be slain and their bodies will be eaten by the scavengers, while the bones will be left to be buried. Their bodily resurrection comes at the end of the thousand years. Satan however is to have a temporary incarceration in the abyss. Our sovereign Lord will not yet have finished with Lucifer (Rev.20:1-2; 7-10).

Verse 21 - "And the remnant were slain with the sword of him that sat upon the horse, which sword proceeded out of his mouth; and all the fouls were filled with their flesh."

καὶ οἱ λοιποὶ ἀπεκτάνθησαν ἐν τῇ ῥομφαίᾳ τοῦ καθημένου ἐπὶ τοῦ ἵππου τῇ ἐξελθούσῃ ἐκ τοῦ στόματος αὐτοῦ, καὶ πάντα τὰ ὄρνεα ἐχορτάσθησαν ἐκ τῶν σαρκῶν αὐτῶν.

"And the rest were slain by the sword of him who sits upon the horse, the sword that issues from his mouth; and all the birds were gorged with their flesh."

καὶ (continuative conjunction) 14.

οἱ (nom.pl.masc.of the article in agreement with λοιποὶ) 9.

λοιποὶ (nom.pl.masc.of λοιπός, subject of ἀπεκτάνθησαν) 1402.

ἀπεκτάνθησαν (3d.per.pl.aor.pass.ind.of ἀποκτείνω, constative) 889.

ἐν (preposition with the instrumental, means) 80.

τῇ (instrumental sing.fem.of the article in agreement with ῥομφαίᾳ) 9.

ῥομφαίᾳ (instru.sing.fem.of ῥμφαία, means) 1904.

τοῦ (gen.sing.masc.of the article in agreement with καθημένου) 9.

καθημένου (pres.mid.part.gen.sing.masc.of κάθημαι, substantival, possession) 377.

ἐπὶ (preposition with the genitive, place description) 47.

τοῦ (gen.sing.masc.of the article in agreement with ἵππου) 9.

ἵππου (gen.sing.masc.of ἵππος, place description) 5121.

τῇ (instru.sing.fem.of the article in agreement with ἐξελθούσῃ) 9.

ἐξελθούσῃ (aor.mid.part.instr.sing.fem.of ἐξέρχομαι, substantival, in apposition with ῥομφαίᾳ) 161.

ἐκ (preposition with the ablative of source) 19.

τοῦ (abl.sing.neut.of the article in agreement with στόματος) 9.

στόματος (abl.sing.neut.of στόμα, source) 344.

αὐτοῦ (gen.sing.masc.of αὐτός, possession) 16.

καὶ (continuative conjunction) 14.

πάντα (nom.pl.neut.of πᾶς, in agreement with ὄρνεα) 67.

τὰ (nom.pl.neut.of the article in agreement with ὄρνεα) 9.

ὄρνεα (nom.pl.neut.of ὄρνεα, subject of ἐχορτάσθησαν) 5399.

ἐχορτάσθησαν (3d.per.pl.aor.pass.ind.of χορτάζω, culminative) 428.

ἐκ (preposition with the ablative, source) 19.

τῶν (abl.pl.fem.of the article in agreement with σαρκῶν) 9.
σαρκῶν (abl.pl.fem.of σάρξ, source) 1202.
αὐτῶν (gen.pl.masc.of αὐτός, description) 16.

Translation - "And the rest were killed by the sword coming out of the mouth of Him Who sits upon the horse, and all the scavengers were surfeited upon the flesh of the dead."

Comment: *Cf.* Ezekiel 39:17-20. A periodical devoted to Bible prophecy has reported that the vulture population in Palestine has been increasing in recent years, due to the increase in the number of eggs laid.

The Thousand Years

(Revelation 20:1-6)

Revelation 20:1 - "And I saw an angel come down from heaven, having the key of the bottomless pit and a great chain in his hand."

Καὶ εἶδον ἄγγελον καταβαίνοντα ἐκ τοῦ οὐρανοῦ, ἔχοντα τὴν κλεῖν τῆς ἀβύσσου καὶ ἄλυσιν μεγάλην ἐπὶ τὴν χεῖρα αὐτοῦ.

"Then I saw an angel coming down from heaven, holding in his hand the key of the bottomless pit and a great chain." . . . *RSV*

Καὶ (continuative conjunction) 14.
εἶδον (1st.per.sing.aor.act.ind.of ὁράω, ingressive) 144.
ἄγγελον (acc.sing.masc.of ἄγγελος, direct object of εἶδον) 96.
καταβαίνοντα (pres.act.part.acc.sing.masc.of καταβαίνω, adjectival, predicate position, restrictive, in agreement with ἄγγελον) 324.
ἐκ (preposition with the ablative of source) 19.
τοῦ (abl.sing.masc.of the article in agreement with οὐρανοῦ) 9.
οὐρανοῦ (abl.sing.masc.of οὐρανός, source) 254.
ἔχοντα (pres.act.part.acc.sing.masc.of ἔχω, adjectival, predicate position, restrictive, in agreement with ἄγγελον) 82.
τὴν (acc.sing.fem.of the article in agreement with κλεῖν) 9.
κλεῖν (acc.sing.fem.of κλεῖς, Attic, direct object of ἔχοντα) 1206.
τῆς (gen.sing.fem.of the article in agreement with ἀβύσσου) 9.
ἀβύσσου (gen.sing.fem.of ἄβυσσος, description) 2231.
καὶ (adjunctive conjunction joining nouns) 14.
ἄλυσιν (acc.sing.fem.of ἄλυσις, direct object of ἔχοντα) 2216.
μεγάλην (acc.sing.fem.of μέγας, in agreement with ἄλυσιν) 184.
ἐπὶ (preposition with the accusative, place) 47.
τὴν (acc.sing.fem.of the article in agreement with χεῖρα) 9.
χεῖρα (acc.sing.fem.of χείρ, place) 308.
αὐτοῦ (gen.sing.masc.of αὐτός, possession) 16.

Translation - "*And I saw an angel coming down from heaven with the key of the abyss and a great chain in his hand.*"

Comment: Again we have an instance of the present participle (ἔχοντα) with an object (τὴν κλεῖν) after a verb of sensation (εἶδον). Robertson calls it "a sort of indirect discourse with verbs of sensation." Others are Lk.9:49; Rev.10:1; 13:1,11; 14:6; 18:1) (Robertson, *Grammar*, 892).

It is idle to quibble about whether the chain is literal or whether one needs a literal chain to chain an unholy spirit. No one is sure whether Satan has a physical form or not, except God, and He won't tell. The point is that Christ, at His second coming, will not only win the war against the Beast, the False Prophet and the kings and their armies of this world, but that He will also capture, bind and incarcerate the god of this world (2 Cor.4:4).

To win the argument that the chain which binds Satan must be allegorical is not to win the argument that the phrase χίλαι ἔτη is also allegorical. See our comments on this point in Comment upon verse 2.

Verse 2 - "*And he laid hold on the dragon, that old serpent, which is the Devil, and Satan, and bound him a thousand years.*"

καὶ ἐκράτησεν τὸν δράκοντα, ὁ ὄφις ὁ ἀρχαῖος, ὅς ἐστιν Διάβολος καὶ ὁ Σατανᾶς, καὶ ἔδησεν αὐτὸν χίλια ἔτη.

"*And he seized the dragon, that ancient serpent, who is the Devil and Satan, and bound him for a thousand years, . . .*" . . . RSV

καὶ (continuative conjunction) 14.
ἐκράτησεν (3d.per.sing.aor.act.ind.of κρατέω, constative) 828.
τὸν (acc.sing.masc.of the article in agreement with δράκοντα) 9.
δράκοντα (acc.sing.masc.of δράκων, direct object of ἐκράτησεν) 5382.
ὁ (nom.sing.masc.of the article in agreement with ὄφις) 9.
ὄφις (nom.sing.masc.of ὄφις, apposition) 658.
ὁ (nom.sing.masc.of the article in agreement with ἀρχαῖος) 9.
ἀρχαῖος (nom.sing.masc.of ἀρχαῖος, in agreement with ὄφις) 475.
ὅς (nom.sing.masc.of ὅς, relative pronoun, subject of ἐστιν) 65.
ἐστιν (3d.per.sing.pres.ind.of εἰμί, aoristic) 86.
Διάβολος (nom.sing.masc.of διάβολος, predicate nominative) 331.
καὶ (adjunctive conjunction joining nouns) 14.
ὁ (nom.sing.masc.of the article in agreement with Σατανᾶς) 9.
Σατανᾶς (nom.sing.masc.of Σατανᾶς, predicate nominative) 365.
καὶ (adjunctive conjunction joining verbs) 14.
ἔδησεν (3d.per.sing.aor.act.ind.of δέω, constative) 998.
αὐτὸν (acc.sing.masc.of αὐτός, direct object of ἔδησεν) 16.
χίλια (acc.sing.neut.of χίλιος, in agreement with ἔτη) 5278.
ἔτη (acc.pl.neut.of ἔτος, time extent) 821.

Translation - "*And He seized the dragon, the old serpent, who is known as the Devil and Satan, and He bound him for a thousand years.*"

Comment: We have a failure of case concord in ὁ ὄφις in apposition with the accusative τὸν δράκοντα. John spares no effort to identify the dragon who is bound. *Cf.*#'s 5382, 658, 331 and 365 and run all of the references. The god of this world (2 Cor.4:4) is also the evil spirit that works in the unsaved (Eph.2:1-3); he is the thief bent on killing and destroying (John 10:10); he is the accuser of the Christian (Rev.12:10).

For a thousand years the Kingdom of God will be rid of him as he languishes in the abyss. The attempt of the amillenialists to escape this passage by pointing to 2 Peter 3:8, thus to find authority for interpreting Rev.20:2 in a figurative sense, is futile. Thus they attempt to telescope the events of Revelation 20, which are separated by one thousand years into the time scope of one day. This overlooks Peter's point. From God's point of view there is no difference between a thousand years and a day, or indeed an hour, minute or second, since God is eternal and not subject to the time category. If indeed the amillenialists are correct, then no mention of time, when God is involved means anything and the Scriptures are reduced to nonesense, as they try to communicate to us who are creatures subject to the time and space categories. How long was Jesus in the heart of the earth if time expressions are to be interpreted allegorically? (Mt.12:40). But in Revelation 20 God is communicating to John and through him to us, and we, unlike God, do see a difference between a thousand years and a day. For God, the millenium will seem only as a day, or indeed as a fleeting moment, for He has no sense of the passing of time. If the phrase χίλια ἔτη is to mean nothing to us, then the entire passage that serves to separate some events from others by a thousand years is pointless. Either God wants us to understand that 1000 years, *as we count time*, will elapse between Satan's incarceration in the abyss and his release, or Rev.20:2,3,5,7 mean nothing significant to us who are creatures of time and space and thus unable to dismiss 1000 years with the snap of a finger. What shall we say of other passages, the understanding of which depends upon time expressions as we understand them? If a thousand years means only one day, what, pray does 42 months mean?(Rev.13:5). Or 1260 days (Rev.12:6)? Or five months? (Rev.9:10). Or about eight days? (Lk.9:28).

Clear communication depends upon the ability of the speaker or writer to use words, not as he understands them, but as he knows the listener or the reader understands them. If both speaker and listener or writer and reader understand the words in the same way, then there is no problem. But if the communicator uses words which he knows the one to whom his communication is directed will misunderstand, there is no communication. Ordinary time expressions like second, minute, hour, day, week, fortnight, month and year are clearly understood by man. These terms sustain numerical and mathematical relations to each other. It is possible for man to know how many seconds of time there are in 1000 years. But God is not interested in time. But He is interested in communicating His thoughts clearly to us.

The issue between the amillenialists and the premillenialists is whether or not God's covenant promise to Abraham about an earthly kingdom is to be taken literally or whether we are to consider that His promise to Israel is fulfilled in the Body of Christ. When James said in Acts 15:14-18 that the prophecy of Amos

9:11-12 was fulfilled in Paul's ministry to the Gentiles, and thus that God had begun in the latter days to rebuild the Tabernacle of David, premillenialists find nothing in his statement with which to disagree. To be sure, the mystery which was revealed to Paul, as he describes it in Eph.3:1-8, that the Gentiles should be "fellow heirs and of the same body" is the truth that the elect Gentiles are the spiritual seed of Abraham (Gal.3:7). The Holy Spirit, both in the Old Testament and New Testament ages has called out and is still calling out from among both Jews and Gentiles a people for His name. These are the Body of Christ. And thus the Tabernacle of David finds its place in the economy of God in the Kingdom Age and throughout eternity. There will be no Tabernacle, such as Moses built at the foot of Mount Sinai with its animal sacrifices. The Book of Hebrews makes this clear. But James said the Tabernacle of David. He did not say his throne. The Body of Christ, wherein God dwells (1 Cor.6:19) and in which His glory rests, as it rested upon the mercy seat within the inner veil, is the tabernacle of God. But King David's greater Son (Heb.1:5; 2 Sam.7:14) is also to have His throne (Luke 1:30-33). And He is to rule upon the throne of His father David over a kingdom that shall have no end, and His administrative national unit shall be the House of Israel. This was the angel's promise to Mary before her baby was born.

Now the promise becomes the bone of contention between the amillenialists and the premillenialists. Is God obligated to keep that promise which He made to Abraham, Isaac, Jacob and David? Was his covenant promise conditional or unconditional? Does it depend for its fulfillment upon certain conditions laid down for man to keep, or is it unconditional? Upon what, if anything, is it contingent? If it is conditional, then it is null and void for Israel sinned against God, and at last murdered His Son, the only Man in Israel Who had any legal right to sit on David's throne. Thus, if the Abrahamic Covenant is conditional, there is no future history for Israel as a nation, although individual Jews may find Christ as personal Saviour and find their place in the Church which is His Body.

But if the promise of God is without condition, then God is obligated to fulfill it to the letter. This is the position of the premillenialists. We reject the notion that Abraham and all of his descendants disobeyed the law of God and thus forfeited their rights in the covenant. To be sure, some Jews did sin against God, because some of them were of their father "the devil, and the lusts of their father" they did (John 8:44). Is the covenant conditional or not? If so, there is no future for national Israel. If not, there is.

The premillenial position, that God's promise to Abraham is unconditional and thus that the Kingdom prophecy of the thousand years is literal is convincingly presented in an unpublished letter by John L. Benson, the following digest of which is presented with his consent:

Premillenial Calvinism is the only position that is both biblical and logical. Amillenial Calvinists are illogical, though they are soteriologically correct when they insist upon unconditional election. The calling of God is without repentance.

The premillenial Arminians are also illogical, although they are correct when they teach that God's covenant with Abraham is unconditional. They are eschatologically scriptural.

The deciding factor in both the Abrahamic and the salvation covenant is God's sovereign and immutable counsel. There are no "if clauses" in either of God's promises to Abraham or to the believer. Calvinists say that there is nothing contingent in the salvation covenant, and they are quite correct. But some Calvinists say that the Kingdom covenant is contingent upon Israel's obedience and that God was released from His promise to Abraham by Israel's disobedience. These Calvinists are also amillenialists.

Premillenial Arminians disagree on both questions. For them God's promise to Abraham about the Kingdom is unconditional and therefore Israel's national future in the promised land is certain, but nothing is certain about the future salvation of the individual believer, since God's promise to him is contingent upon his faithfulness. All may be lost in the last moment of his life by any indiscretion, however minor. Each school borrows from the other to say that one of God's promises is conditional and the other unconditional, but they disagree on which one is which.

Premillenial Calvinism is consistent with itself and also consistent with the Scriptures, both in its eschatology and in its soteriology. Amillenial Arminianism is also consistent with itself, but inconsistent with Scripture, both in its eschatology and in its soteriology.

Benson correctly says, "When a Calvinist talks about unconditional election, he does not mean that in salvation no conditional factors are involved. In order to be saved a man must believe, repent and obey the gospel. But God's purpose to save him is not contingent upon these factors. God will save His elect according to His own eternal purpose and sovereign grace through working in them the very conditions which He demands.If a man cannot be saved apart from faith, God will generate the necessary faith in him. The condition (faith) is never really in question, for it is a foregone conclusion that God will cause His elect people to believe.

The same thing is true of the Abrahamic Covenant. When premillenialists speak of the unconditionality of the covenant, they do not mean that there are no conditional factors involved. They see it in the same light as unconditional election. The fulfillment of the promise does not depend ultimately upon the faithfulness and obedience of men, but upon the immutable purpose of God. The deciding and determining factor is God's faithfulness to promise. The fulfillment of the covenant does not rest in the hands of men for its realization.

Naturally we are the first to affirm that the promises of the Abrahamic Covenant will not be fulfilled to unbelieving Israel any more than the promises of salvation will be realized by unbelieving people. But it is a foregone conclusion that when God gets ready to restore Israel to the land according to the interpretation of Old and New Testament, unbelief willnot bar the way, for God will cause the nation to believe in order that He can keep faith with the patriarchs. The response of men can never ultimately thwart the divine purpose — either in soteriology or in eschatology. In the so-called covenant of grace God purposes to save His elect people, and because they do not have the ability in themselves to meet the conditions of faith, obedience, repentance and perseverance is no hindrance to the divine purpose; God will enable them to believe by regenerating them. In the Abrahamic Covenant God purposes that the seed of Abraham (his physical descendants) come to a glorious destiny in their own land. All of Israel's long history of rebellion and unbelief will not ultimately thwart God's purpose, for in His own good time He will enable them to believe by regenerating them, by giving them a new spirit of repentance and supplication, by causing them to walk in His statutes.

Man's unbelief is never a deterrent to God's purposes. Amillenialists believe this about soteriology, but not about eschatology. Until this hour God has not given to Israel an heart to perceive and eyes to see, and ears to hear, but the time will come when in faithfulness to His covenant promises, the Lord . . . God will circumcise their heart and the heart of their seed "to love the Lord thy God with all thine heart, and with all thy mind, that thou mayest live." (Deuteronomy 29:4; 30:6).

In the new covenant of Ezekiel 36, note carefully that the promise involves not only regeneration (verse 26) but restoration to the land which God promised to the patriarchs (verse 23). . . . The prophets of Israel evidently did not dream that Israel had forfeited the Abrahamic and Davidic promises through unbelief, for all of the prophets predicted that golden age when the covenant promises would be fulfilled and Israel would be released from worldwide dispersion and return home to the land of promise. I have just taught the whole book of Isaiah and there is scarcely a page that does not contain this hope. Just read A. Barnes, E.J.Young, and other amillenial writers on Isaiah if you want to see what strained exegesis these men use in spiritualizing away the literal fulfillment of the prophecies connected with the second advent. Calvin is no exception. Their basic presupposition is that God has finished with the Jews as a nation and that all of the promises to Israel are now being fulfilled in the Church. (Strange that these men do not transfer the curses upon Israel also to the Church). This basic presupposition causes them to interpret all passages in harmony with their preconceived system of theology."

The above observations by Benson are devastatingly logical. However a system built up deductively suffers from the assumption that the depraved human mind is always logical. Logic is a safe guide to validity if it is good logic. Only the Holy Spirit is capable of total logic. Hence Benson's argument is sound only if the promises of God to Abraham and His promise to His elect are based on sound exegesis. And we believe that they are. If individual election of the members of the Body of Christ is taught in Scripture as an unconditioned act of God's will, and if the Abrahamic covenant as unconditional is also taught, then no logical mind, least of all that of the Holy Spirit, could make the fulfillment of one promise certain and that of the other contingent.

Verse 3 - "And cast him into the bottomless pit, and shut him up, and set a seal upon him, that he should deceive the nations no more, till the thousand years should be fulfilled: and after that he must be loosed for a little season."

καὶ ἔβαλεν αὐτὸν εἰς τὴν ἄβυσσον καὶ ἔκλεισεν καὶ ἐσφράγισεν ἐπάνω
αὐτοῦ ἵνα μὴ πλανήσῃ ἔτι τὰ ἔθνη ἄχρι τελεσθῇ τὰ χίλια ἔτη. μετὰ ταῦτα δεῖ
λυθῆναι αὐτὸν μικρὸν χρόνον.

". . . and threw him into the pit, and shut it and sealed it over him, that he
should deceive the nations no more, till the thousand years were ended. After
that he must be loosed for a little while." . . . RSV

καὶ (continuative conjunction) 14.

ἔβαλεν (3d.per.sing.aor.act.ind.of βάλλω, constative) 299.

αὐτὸν (acc.sing.masc.of αὐτός, direct object of ἔβαλεν) 16.

εἰς (preposition with the accusative of extent) 140.

τὴν (acc.sing.fem.of the article in agreement with ἄβυσσον) 9.

ἄβυσσον (acc.sing.fem.of ἄβυσσος, extent) 2231.

καὶ (adjunctive conjunction joining verbs) 14.

ἔκλεισεν (3d.per.sing.aor.act.ind.of κλείω, constative) 570.

καὶ (adjunctive conjunction joining verbs) 14.

ἐσφράγισεν (3d.per.sing.aor.act.ind.of σφραγίζω, constative) 1686.

ἐπάνω (preposition with the genitive of place description) 181.

αὐτοῦ (gen.sing.masc.of αὐτός, place description) 16.

ἵνα (conjunction with the subjunctive, negative purpose) 114.

μὴ (negative conjunction with the subjunctive, negative purpose) 87.

πλανήσῃ (3d.per.sing.aor.act.subj.of πλανάω, negative purpose) 1257.

ἔτι (temporal adverb) 448.

τὰ (acc.pl.neut.of the article in agreement with ἔθνη) 9.

ἔθνη (acc.pl.neut.of ἔθνος, direct object of πλανήσῃ) 376.

ἄχρι (temporal adverb) 1517.

τελεσθῇ (3d.per.sing.aor.pass.subj.of τελέω, indefinite temporal clause) 704.

τὰ (nom.pl.neut.of the article in agreement with ἔτη) 9.

χίλια (nom.pl.neut.of χίλιος, in agreement with ἔτη) 5278.

ἔτη (nom.pl.neut.of ἔτος, subject of τελεσθῇ) 821.

μετὰ (preposition with the accusative, time extent) 50.

ταῦτα (acc.pl.neut.of οὗτος, time extent) 93.

δεῖ (3d.impersonal, singular, pres.ind.of δεῖ) 1207.

λυθῆναι (aor.pass.inf.of λύω, epexegetical) 471.

αὐτὸν (acc.sing.masc.of αὐτός, general reference) 16.

μικρὸν (acc.sing.masc.of μικρός, in agreement with χρόνον) 901.

χρόνον (acc.sing.masc.of χρόνος, time extent) 168.

*Translation - "And he hurled him into the abyss, and he closed and sealed it over
him, so that he would not again deceive the nations until the thousand years have
run their course. After that it is decreed that he should be set free for a short
time."*

Comment: Is this angel of verses 2 and 3 Michael, the archangel who threw
Satan out of heaven three and one half years before? (Rev.12:7-9). Who threw
him out originally when Jesus saw him fall? (Lk.10:18). The answer is not

essential to the point of the passage, which is that Almighty Christ is greater than mighty Satan (1 John 4:4). The Devil will become a prisoner in the ἀβύσσῳ, the key to which he had three and one half years before (Rev.9:1-2). Having opened the pit then to unleash the Beast upon the world, he will now find himself sealed inside for one thousand years, while the Beast, the former occupant of the pit finds his permanent residence in the lake of fire (Rev.19:20).

One thousand years after the second coming Satan will join the Beast and his hellish colleague, the False Prophet in the lake of fire (Rev.20:10). The abyss is God's cell block on execution row; the lake of fire is His execution chamber, although in it the executed criminal is never pronounced dead.

Satan will make one last attempt to overthrow God, albeit an abortive one (Rev.20:7-9).

The temporal conjunction ἄχρι introduces the subjunctive in the temporal clause, following the negative purpose clause with ἵνα μή and the subjunctive in πλανήσῃ - "in order that he will not again deceive the nations until the thousand years are over." This sentence makes no sense at all if we are to regard the phrase τὰ χίλια ἔτη as a figurative expression. If one thousand years means to us what it means to God — only one day (2 Peter 3:8) then the sentence should read "until the next day" or "until tomorrow." Peter could just as well have said "an hour, minute or second." The eternal God knows nothing of time. Thus Satan will not be imprisoned at all if we are to accept the figurative interpretation of τὰ χίλια ἔτη. Likewise μετὰ ταῦτα has no meaning for the same reason. As it stands in the text ταῦτα is anaphoric, in reference to the 1000 years, but if "one thousand years" means nothing then μετὰ ταῦτα also means nothing. So also ἄχρι in verse 5 is without meaning as is the temporal conjunction ὅταν in verse 7.

How essential good exegesis is if we are to refute wrong ideas.

It is thriling, though delightfully impossible to imagine the progress that the world society will make during those one thousand years, with Christ, Plato's Philosopher-King, upon the throne and Satan, the seductive author of confusion locked out of the play. A hockey team finds it easier to score when the goal keeper is in the penalty box. But though world peace and human progress will be realized, since Christ will rule with a rod of iron (#863), social and economic progress will not bring spiritual regeneration to all, as the environmentalists teach. After the thousand years have passed unbelievers will be found on earth who will follow Satan to their death (Rev.20:7-10). But not all of those born during the kingdom age will be lost. God's elect will be saved as a result of the preaching of the gospel (Rev.14:6). At the Great White Throne judgment at the end of the millenium those saved during the millenium will be found written in the Book of Life.

Verse 4 - "And I saw thrones, and they sat upon them, and judgment was given unto them: and I saw the souls of them that were beheaded for the witness of Jesus, and for the word of God, and which had not worshipped the beast, neither his image, neither had received his mark upon their foreheads or in their hands: and they lived and reigned with Christ a thousand years."

Καὶ εἶδον θρόνους, καὶ ἐκάθισαν ἐπ' αὐτούς, καὶ κρίμα ἐδόθη αὐτοῖς, καὶ τὰς φυχὰς τῶν πεπελεκισμένων διὰ τὴν μαρτυρίαν Ἰησοῦ καὶ διὰ τὸν λόγον τοῦ θεοῦ, καὶ οἵτινες οὐ προσεκύνησαν τὸ θηρίον οὐδὲ τὴν εἰκόνα αὐτοῦ καὶ οὐκ ἔλαβαν τὸ χάραγμα ἐπὶ τὸ μέτωπον καὶ ἐπὶ τὴν χεῖρα αὐτῶν, καὶ ἔζησαν καὶ ἐβασίλευσαν μετὰ τοῦ Χριστοῦ χίλια ἔτη.

"Then I saw thrones, and seated on them were those to whom judgment was committed. Also I saw the souls of those who had been beheaded for their testimony to Jesus and for the word of God, and who had not worshipped the beast or its image and had not received its mark on their foreheads or their hands. They came to life, and reigned with Christ a thousand years." . . . RSV

Καὶ (continuative conjunction) 14.
εἶδον (1st.per.sing.aor.act.ind.of ὁράω, ingressive) 144.
θρόνους (acc.pl.masc.of θρόνος, direct object of εἶδον) 519.
καὶ (continuative conjunction) 14.
ἐκάθισαν (3d.per.pl.aor.act.ind.of καθίζω, constative) 420.
ἐπ' (preposition with the accusative of extent, rest) 47.
αὐτούς (acc.pl.masc.of αὐτός, rest) 16.
καὶ (continuative conjunction) 14.
κρίμα (nom.sing.neut.of κρίμα, subject of ἐδόθη) 642.
ἐδόθη (3d.per.sing.aor.pass.ind.of δίδωμι, ingressive) 363.
αὐτοῖς (dat.pl.masc.of αὐτός, indirect object of ἐδόθη) 16.
καὶ (adjunctive conjunction joining nouns) 14.
τὰς (acc.pl.fem.of the article in agreement with φυχὰς) 9.
φυχὰς (acc.pl.fem.of φυχή, direct object of εἶδον) 233.
τῶν (gen.pl.masc.of the article in agreement with πεπελεκισμένων) 9.

#5421 πεπελεκισμένων (perf.pass.part.gen.pl.fem.of πελεκίζω, substantival, possession).

King James Version

behead - Rev.20:4.

Revised Standard Version

behead - Rev.20:4.

Meaning: Cf. πέλεκυς - "an axe or two-edged hatchet." Hence, to behead; cut off with an axe - Rev.20:4.

διὰ (preposition with the accusative, cause) 118.
τὴν (acc.sing.fem.of the article in agreement with μαρτυρίαν) 9.
μαρτυρίαν (acc.sing.fem.of μαρτυρία, cause) 1695.
Ἰησοῦ (gen.sing.masc.of Ἰησοῦς, description) 3.
καὶ (adjunctive conjunction joining prepositional phrases) 14.
διὰ (preposition with the accusative, cause) 118.
τὸν (acc.sing.masc.of the article in agreement with λόγον) 9.

λόγον (acc.sing.masc.of λόγος, cause) 510.

τοῦ (gen.sing.masc.of the article in agreement with θεοῦ) 9.

θεοῦ (gen.sing.masc.of θεός, description) 124.

οἵτινες (nom.pl.masc.of ὅστις, indefinite relative, subject of προσεκύνησαν and ἔλαβον) 163.

οὐ (negative conjunction with the indicative) 130.

προσεκύνησαν (3d.per.pl.aor.act.ind.of προσκυνέω, constative) 147.

τό (acc.sing.neut.of the article in agreement with θηρίον) 9.

θηρίον (acc.sing.neut.of θηρίον, direct object of προσεκύνησαν) 1951.

οὐδὲ (disjunctive particle) 452.

τὴν (acc.sing.fem.of the article in agreement with εἰκόνα) 9.

εἰκόνα (acc.sing.fem.of εἰκών, direct object of προσκύνησαν) 1421.

αὐτοῦ (gen.sing.neut.of αὐτός, description) 16.

καὶ (adjunctive conjunction joining verbs) 14.

οὐκ (negative conjunction with the indicative) 130.

ἔλαβον (3d.per.pl.aor.act.ind.of λαμβάνω, constative) 533.

τό (acc.sing.neut.of the article in agreement with χάραγμα) 9.

χάραγμα (acc.sing.neut.of χάραγμα, direct object of ἔλαβον) 3420.

ἐπὶ (preposition with the accusative, place) 47.

τό (acc.sing.neut.of the article in agreement with μέτωπον) 9.

μέτωπον (acc.sing.neut.of μέτωπον, place) 5356.

καὶ (adjunctive conjunction joining prepositional phrases) 14.

ἐπὶ (preposition with the accusative, place) 47.

τὴν (acc.sing.fem.of the article in agreement with χεῖρα) 9.

χεῖρα (acc.sing.fem.of χείρ, place) 308.

αὐτῶν (gen.pl.masc.of αὐτός, possession) 16.

καὶ (continuative conjunction) 14.

ἔζησαν (3d.per.pl.aor.act.ind.of ζάω, constative) 340.

καὶ (adjunctive conjunction joining verbs) 14.

ἐβασίλευσαν (3d.per.pl.aor.act.ind.of βασιλεύω, constative) 236.

μετὰ (preposition with the genitive, accompaniment) 50.

τοῦ (gen.sing.masc.of the article in agreement with Χριστοῦ) 9.

Χριστοῦ (gen.sing.masc.of Χριστός, accompaniment) 4.

χίλια (acc.pl.neut.of χίλιος, in agreement with ἔτη) 5278.

ἔτη (acc.pl.neut.of ἔτος, time extent) 821.

Translation - "And I saw thrones, and they sat upon them; and jurisdiction was given to them, and I saw the souls of those who had been beheaded because of the testimony of Jesus and because of the Word of God, and those who had never worshipped the Beast nor His statue, and had not taken His mark upon their forehead nor upon their hand. And they were resurrected and ruled with the Messiah for a thousand years."

Comment: Whose thrones and who sat upon them as judges? We can be sure of two groups. The twelve Apostles (the original twelve whom Jesus chose, minus Judas Iscariot plus Paul) will each occupy one of twelve thrones in courts with jurisdiction given to each over one of the twelve tribes of Israel (Mt.19:27,28;

Lk.22:30). The other group is composed of martyrs who lost their heads because they were true witnesses who refused the worship of the Beast and His statue and His mark. There have been many Christians in the past who were martyred who cannot be included in the group described as having refused to worship the Beast and his statue, only because they died before the Beast came to power. There is nothing in the grammar to exclude them from judges who will reign with Messiah. They will be made to live (ingressive aorist in ἔζησαν) and they will continue to reign (constative aorist in ἐβασίλευσαν) for 1000 years. Note ἐβασίλευσας in Rev.11:17 as an ingressive aorist). *Cf.* 2 Tim.2:12, where Paul holds out the promise to suffering saints of all ages, not only to end-time saints, who meet all of the conditions of Rev.20:4. Christians who lost their heads as martyrs for Christ before the Beast arrives on the scene, fulfill the ethical though not all of the detailed requirements. If they would not worship Caligula and his horse, they would not worship the Antichrist. If we take the definite relative οἵτινες as the object of εἶδον as we did τὰς ψυχάς, then it should be οἵτινας (accusative plural), rather than the nominative plural. Otherwise we have anacoluthon, since we have only οἵτινες as the subject of προσεκύνησαν and ἔλαβον.

Verse 5 - "But the rest of the dead lived not again until the thousand years were finished. This is the first resurrection."

οἱ λοιποὶ τῶν νεκρῶν οὐκ ἔζησαν ἄχρι τελεσθῇ τὰ χίλια ἔτη. αὕτη ἡ ἀνάστασις ἡ πρώτη.

"The rest of the dead did not come to life until the thousand years were ended. This is the first resurrection." . . . RSV

οἱ (nom.pl.masc.of the article in agreement with λοιποὶ) 9.
λοιποὶ (nom.pl.masc.of λοιπός, subject of ἔζησαν) 1402.
τῶν (gen.pl.masc.of the article in agreement with νεκρῶν) 9.
νεκρῶν (gen.pl.masc.of νεκρός, partitive genitive) 749.
οὐκ (negative conjunction with the indicative) 130.
ἔζησαν (3d.per.pl.aor.act.ind.of ζάω, ingressive) 340.
ἄχρι (conjunction with the subjunctive in an indefinite temporal clause) 1517.
τελεσθῇ (3d.per.sing.aor.pass.subj.of τελέω, indefinite temporal clause) 704.
τὰ (nom.pl.neut.of the article in agreement with ἔτη) 9.
χίλια (nom.pl.neut.of χίλιος, in agreement with ἔτη) 5278.
ἔτη (nom.pl.neut.of ἔτος, subject of τελεσθῇ) 821.
αὕτη (nom.sing.fem.of οὗτος, subject of ἔστιν understood) 93.
ἡ (nom.sing.fem.of the article in agreement with ἀνάστασις) 9.
ἀνάστασις (nom.sing.fem.of ἀνάστασις, predicate nomiantive) 1423.
ἡ (nom.sing.fem.of the article in agreement with πρώτη) 9.
πρώτη (nom.sing.fem.of πρώτη, in agreement with ἀνάστασις) 487.

Translation - "The rest of the dead were not brought to life until the thousand years were past. This is the first resurrection."

Comment: When exegetes are in doubt they should say so. Who are the other dead (τῶν νεκρῶν) who are not resurrected until the end of the millenium? There is no doubt that the text divides the resurrections into two events. Some will be raised to reign with Christ for 1000 years (verse 4). Other will not (verse 5). That the thousand years is literal is demanded by this fact. Otherwise there is no distinction between the first resurrection and the one following when the "rest of the dead will rise."

If we say that all regenerated saints will take part in the first resurrection, and support it with 1 Thess.4:13-18; 1 Cor.15:51-58, *et al.*, we are faced with verse 6, which says that all such are blessed, because saved, since the second death (Rev.20:14) has no power over them. This is no problem. But verse 6 goes on to say that all such shall be priests of God and of Christ and that they shall reign with Him for 1000 years.

Do all first resurrection saints reign with Christ? Are all regenerated saints, living and dead at the second coming to be resurrected and raptured? Including backsliders? And if so, the question becomes, "How backslidden?" In view of 1 John 1:8 all saints have been backslidden at some time(s) in their life, and thus the question becomes one of establishing the degree of inconsistency in which the Christian may indulge before losing his privilege of reigning with Christ.

This writer has always thought that the rapture and resurrection would be complete, not partial nor selective. But verse 6 says that they will also reign with Christ! Live and enjoy perhaps, but reign?

The "rest of the dead" must mean the unsaved dead, since 1 Thess.4:13-18 says (a) all who sleep in Jesus will God bring with Him; (b) the living saints will accompany those who at the time had already died. We will not go ahead (before) the dead; (c) the dead in Christ, including all Old Testament saints, will rise first; (d) then we shall be raptured with them and (e) all of us, dead, but resurrected saints in Christ and living but transfigured saints, will be raptured together, and finally (f) all of us, once resurrected, transfigured and raptured shall be forever with the Lord. That this coming is post-tribulational but premillenial is obvious.

It seems to the writer, in the light of 1 Thess.4:13-18 that a selective (partial) rapture is impossible. There is nothing in 1 Cor.15:51-58 to indicate otherwise. Not all Christians are going to die before the second coming, though most will, but all will be transfigured. This will be sudden and will occur at the last (seventh) trump (Rev.11:15-18). There seems to be no room for a selective rapture. Thus if all saints of all ages, living and dead, at the second coming of Messiah are to be raised, and if this is the first resurrection, then the remaining dead at that time must be the unsaved dead. They too are to be raised (John 5:28-29) to a resurrection of condemnation (Rev.20:11-15).

There is no problem in any of this analysis until we read in Rev.20:6 that all of these Christians will reign with Christ. Perhaps John means that while Messiah, the twelve Apostles and martyrs and other victorious saints reign (verse 4) the rest of us will enjoy the reign. Not all who reign, if not all do, will be entrusted with the same degree of authority (Luke 19:16-19). Is this the answer?

Verse 6 - "Blessed and holy is he that hath part in the first resurrection: on such the second death hath no power, but they shall be priests of God and of Christ, and shall reign with him a thousand years."

μακάριος καὶ ἅγιος ὁ ἔχων μέρος ἐν τῇ ἀναστάσει τῇ πρώτῃ. ἐπὶ τούτων ὁ δεύτερος θάνατος οὐκ ἔχει ἐξουσίαν, ἀλλ' ἔσονται ἱερεῖς τοῦ θεοῦ καὶ τοῦ Χριστοῦ, καὶ βασιλεύσουσιν μετ' αὐτοῦ (τὰ) χίλια ἔτη.

"Blessed and holy is he who shares in the first resurrection! Over such the second death has no power, but they shall be priests of God and of Christ, and they shall reign with him a thousand years." . . . RSV

μακάριος (nom.sing.masc.of μακάριος, predicate adjective) 422.

καὶ (adjunctive conjunction joining adjectives) 14.

ἅγιος (nom.sing.masc.of ἅγιος, predicate adjective) 84.

ὁ (nom.sing.masc.of the article in agreement with ἔχων) 9.

ἔχων (pres.act.part.nom.sing.masc.of ἔχω, substantival, subject of ἔστιν understood) 82.

μέρος (acc.sing.neut.of μέρος, direct object of ἔχων) 240.

ἐν (preposition with the locative of sphere) 80.

τῇ (loc.sing.fem.of the article in agreement with ἀναστάσει) 9.

ἀναστάσει (loc.sing.fem.of ἀνάστασις, sphere) 1423.

τῇ (loc.sing.fem.of the article in agreement with πρώτῃ) 9.

πρώτῃ (loc.sing.fem.of πρῶτος, in agreement with ἀναστάσει) 487.

ἐπὶ (preposition with the genitive, metaphorical, over) 47.

τούτων (gen.pl.masc.of οὗτος, metaphorical, over, anaphoric) 93.

ὁ (nom.sing.masc.of the article in agreement with θάνατος) 9.

δεύτερος (nom.sing.masc.of δεύτερος, in agreement with θάνατος) 1371.

θάνατος (nom.sing.masc.of θάνατος, subject of ἔχει) 381.

οὐκ (negative conjunction with the indicative) 130.

ἔχει (3d.per.sing.pres.act.ind.of ἔχω, static) 82.

ἐξουσίαν (acc.sing.fem.of ἐξουσία, direct object of ἔχει) 707.

ἀλλ' (alternative conjunction) 342.

ἔσονται (3d.per.pl.fut.ind.of εἰμί, predictive) 86.

ἱερεῖς (nom.pl.neut.of ἱερεύς, predicate nominative) 714.

τοῦ (gen.sing.masc.of the article in agreement with θεοῦ) 9.

θεοῦ (gen.sing.masc.of θεός, relationship) 124.

καὶ (adjunctive conjunction joining nouns) 14.

τοῦ (gen.sing.masc.of the article in agreement with Χριστοῦ) 9.

Χριστοῦ (gen.sing.masc.of Χριστός, relationship) 4.

καὶ (adjunctive conjunction joining verbs) 14.

βασιλεύσουσιν (3d.per.pl.fut.act.ind.of βασιλεύω, predictive) 236.

μετ' (preposition with the genitive, association) 50.

αὐτοῦ (gen.sing.masc.of αὐτός, association) 16.

(τὰ) (acc.pl.neut.of the article in agreement with ἔτη) 9.

χίλια (acc.pl.neut.of χίλιος, in agreement with ἔτη) 5278.

ἔτη (acc.pl.neut.of ἔτος, time extent) 821.

Translation - "Happy and holy is he who participates in the first resurrection.

Upon these the second death has no power, but they will be priests of God and of Christ, and they will reign with Him throughout the thousand years."

Comment: Since the second death is the lot of the unsaved, the inference here is that all Christians will experience the first resurrection. *Cf.* our comments on verse 5. If the second death were the lot of the Christian who missed the first resurrection, the Arminian conclusion would follow that a child of God can ultimately be lost. But our verse says that we will be kings and priests unto God. *Cf.* Rev.15:10; 1 Pet.2:5,9; Rev.1:6; Exodus 19:6; Isaiah 61:6.

The Defeat of Satan

(Revelation 20:7-10)

Verse 7 - "And when the thousand years are expired, Satan shall be loosed out of his prison."

Καὶ ὅταν τελεσθῇ τὰ χίλια ἔτη, λυθήσεται ὁ Σατανᾶς ἐκ τῆς φυλακῆς αὐτοῦ,

"And when the thousand years are ended, Satan will be loosed from his prison . . ." . . . RSV

Καὶ (continuative conjunction) 14.

ὅταν (conjunction introducing the subjunctive in an indefinite temporal clause) 436.

τελεσθῇ (3d.per.sing.aor.pass.subj.of τελέω, indefinite temporal clause) 704.

τὰ (nom.pl.neut.of the article in agreement with ἔτη) 9.

χίλια (nom.pl.neut.of χίλιος, in agreement with ἔτη) 5278.

ἔτη (nom.pl.neut.of ἔτος, subject of τελεσθῇ) 821.

λυθήσεται (3d.per.sing.fut.pass.ind.of λύω, predictive) 471.

ὁ (nom.sing.masc.of the article in agreement with Σατανᾶς) 9.

Σατανᾶς (nom.sing.masc.of Σατανᾶς, subject of λυθήσεται) 365.

ἐκ (preposition with the ablative of separation) 19.

τῆς (abl.sing.fem.of the article in agreement with φυλακῆς) 9.

φυλακῆς (abl.sing.fem.of φυλακή, separation) 494.

αὐτοῦ (gen.sing.masc.of αὐτός, description) 16.

Translation - "And when the thousand years have run their course, Satan will be released from his prison."

Comment: Again we make the point that temporal conjunctions, such as ὅταν and ἄχρι (verses 3,5) are meaningless when they are joined to the phrase τὰ χίλια ἔτη, if the phrase is not to have the usual meaning of the passing of a period of time normally understood by human beings as one thousand years. If the time period involved is more or less than one thousand years, why did not the Holy Spirit say so? To be sure, in God's view, one thousand years and one day mean the same, because in fact neither of them mean anything to the eternal God. But God did not write this passage to edify, inform or amuse Himself. He write it for our instruction and therefore He wrote it in terms which we can understand and with which we can identify.

Satan is not bound and released at all or he is bound at the beginning of some time span and released at the end of it. Now if the time span is not one thousand years, but something less, it can be expressed as 500 years, 100 years, a year of five minutes. If God did not mean for us to understand a period of one millenium, He could have defined a shorter (or longer) period as easily. If no time period is involved at all, then Satan will be neither bound nor released. However, he is to be bound (whether with a literal chain or not) and wherever confined (in an abyss or not) is immaterial. The point is that he is to be bound (verse 3) and later released (verse 7). In between the two events, Messiah will reign, in fulfillment of the unconditional covenant of God to Abraham.

In this period it will be demonstrated that unregenerate man, even under ideal social, moral, economic, environmental and political conditions cannot think God's thoughts after Him and is still determined in his rebellious heart to strike God from the skies. Thus the Marxian ideal, and those of other environmental determinists (Rousseau, Godwin, Pavlov, Watson, Skinner *al*), that man is bad only superficially and that because of external stimulii, will become demonstrably false, as we see in verses 8 and 9.

Verse 8 - "And shall go out to deceive the nations which are in the four quarters of the earth, Gog and Magog, to gather them together to battle: the number of whom is as the sand of the sea."

καὶ ἐξελεύσεται πλανῆσαι τὰ ἔθνη τὰ ἐν ταῖς τέσσαρσιν γωνίαις τῆς γῆς, τὸν Γὼγ καὶ Μαγώγ, συναγαγεῖν αὐτοὺς εἰς τὸν πόλεμον, ὧν ὁ ἀριθμὸς αὐτῶν ὡς ἡ ἄμμος τῆς θαλάσσης.

". . . and will come out to deceive the nations which are at the four corners of the earth, that is, Gog and Magog, to gather them for battle; their number is like the sand of the sea." . . . RSV

καὶ (adjunctive conjunction joining verbs) 14.
ἐξελεύσεται (3d.per.sing.fut.mid.ind.of ἐξέρχομαι, predictive) 161.
πλανῆσαι (aor.act.inf.of πλανάω, purpose) 1257.
τὰ (acc.pl.neut.of the article in agreement with ἔθνη) 9.
ἔθνη (acc.pl.neut.of ἔθνος, direct object of πλανῆσαι) 376.
τὰ (acc.pl.neut.of the article in agreement with ἔθνη) 9.
ἐν (preposition with the locative of place) 80.
ταῖς (loc.pl.fem.of the article in agreement with γωνίαις) 9.
τέσσαρσιν (loc.pl.fem.of τέσσαρες, in agreement with γωνίαις) 1508.
γωνίαις (loc.pl.fem.of γωνία, place) 567.
τῆς (gen.sing.fem.of the article in agreement with γῆς) 9.
γῆς (gen.sing.fem.of γῆ, description) 157.
τὸν (acc.sing.masc.of the article in agreement with Γὼγ) 9.

#5422 Γὼγ (acc.sing.masc.of Γώγ, apposition).

King James Version

Gog - Rev.20:8.

Revised Standard Version

Gog - Rev.20:8.

Meaning: Cf. Ezekiel 38. In Ezekiel a term used to describe the King of Magog, leader of the northern confederate attempt to destroy Israel. At the end of the millenium, all unregenerates in nations throughout the world will be incited by Satan to attack the Messianic Kingdom in Jerusalem. The terms Gog and Magog (#'s 5422, 5423) are applied to all of these nations in the final Satanic revolt against God. Rev.20:8.

καὶ (adjunctive conjunction joining nouns) 14.

#5423 Μαγώγ (acc.sing.masc.of Μαγώγ, apposition).

King James Version

Magog - Rev.20:8.

Revised Standard Version

Magog - Rev.20:8.

Meaning: Cf. the *Meaning* article, *supra,* #5422.

συναγαγεῖν (aor.act.inf.of συνάγω, purpose) 150.
αὐτοὺς (acc.pl.masc.of αὐτός, direct object of συναγαγεῖν) 16.
εἰς (preposition with the accusative of extent) 140.
τὸν (acc.sing.masc.of the article in agreement with πόλεμον) 9.
πόλεμον (acc.sing.masc.of πόλεμος, extent) 1483.
ὧν (gen.pl.neut.of ὅς, relative pronoun, description) 65.
ὁ (nom.sing.masc.of the article in agreement with ἀριθμὸς) 9.
ἀριθμὸς (nom.sing.masc.of ἀριθμός, subject of ἐστιν understood) 2278.
αὐτῶν (gen.pl.masc.of αὐτός, description, redundant) 16.
ὡς (comparative particle) 128.
ἡ (nom.sing.fem.of the article in agreement with ἄμμος) 9.
ἄμμος (nom.sing.fem.of ἄμμος, subject of ἐστιν understood) 701.
τῆς (gen.sing.fem.of the article in agreement with θαλάσσης) 9.
θαλάσσης (gen.sing.fem.of θάλασσα, description) 374.

Translation - "And he will go out to deceive the nations in the four corners of the earth, Gog and Magog, in order to mobilize them for the battle, the number of whom is as the sand of the sea."

Comment: Two purpose infinitives πλανῆσαι and συναγαγεῖν, follow the main verb. Satan, always the liar and deceiver, released and having learned nothing from a thousand years of imprisonment, will go forth to deceive and mobilize his victims. From the day that God in His infinite and ineffable wisdom chose to create Lucifer, and permit the evil which was to be found in him (Ezekiel 28:15) the finite god of this insignificant world (2 Cor.4:4) has dreamed of destroying the infinite God of the universe. This unholy spirit who is allowed by sovereignty to work in the children of disobedience (Eph.2:1-3) will make his last attempt to dethrone his Creator. The mobilization of the unsaved at the end of the millenium will be the result of his deception and in turn will result in his total defeat, as verse 9 tells us. Satan used this deception a thousand years earlier to mobilize his troops at Armageddon (Rev.16:14).

Though this study is not passionately committed to the extreme dispensational views of some, it is interesting to point out that man, apart from God, has failed in every age of his history, regardless of circumstance. The age of innocence ended when Satan deceived Eve and Adam chose with total knowledge of the consequences to disobey God (1 Tim.2:14). The antediluvians failed at a time when they had only their conscience to guide them (Romans 1:18-31; Mt.24:37-39). Human government led only to a scheme to build a tower to heaven and resulted in universal confusion and loss of communication, as a result of which man has spent his time contriving means to and justification for killing each other with the least possible cost to the survivors in the event that they survive. The dispensation of promise followed as God, Who had determined to save some, announced that He would do so, without regard to man and his schemes. As a result the elect have been, are and will continue to be called out of the world that cares nothing for the promises of God. Meanwhile the vast majority of the human race has died in infancy and thus are to be numbered among those whom God has chosen to save — a fact which makes the picture of human history brighter.

There followed a period from Sinai to Pentecost when man was told in specific terms what was sin and what was not and challenged to obey the law of Moses or face the consequences. Israel, the people to whom God chose to deliver his moral code, transgressed it before Moses could deliver it to them and continued to transgress it, until they murdered the One Who had written it in letters of fire upon the rock.

The dispensation of grace, as it is called by the hyper-dispensationalists, has always been God's way of dealing with those whom He has chosen to save. It was grace that clothed Adam and Eve in the garden of Eden; it was grace that warned Noah to build an ark; it was grace that brought the ancestors of Abraham through the confusion at Babel; it was grace that called Abraham out of Babylon; it was grace that convinced men, that under law they could not be saved, and thus that they should cry to God for mercy; it is grace that has been calling out from among the Gentiles a people for His name, and it will be grace that will save those born during the kingdom age, after Armageddon. Grace has always been God's way, for there is no other way that man can be saved.

But during the kingdom age, man will be denied his last and best excuse for his moral failures. His story is that he is not inherently evil, but only superficially so and that his sins are the result of environmental circumstances over which he had no control. Driven by his own lust and the hatred and contempt for divine law in his evil heart (Mk.7:21-23) he has been cheap enough to blame the devil for his failures. The television comedian, Skip Wilson, is not the first to deny personal responsibility for his sins by saying, "The devil made me do it." Satan deserves no defense for the things that he does, but he is not personally responsible for much of man's sins. He need not tempt the sinner, for the sinner has the flesh, which is motivation enough to commit the most heinous crimes.

If we reject the view of the sociologists that environment directs history and seek the reason for man's failure within his own heart, we can look forward to the kingdom age for the experiment that will prove the case one way or the other. If man is evil because he is poor, why should he rebel against God after a thousand years of affluence. For "the desert shall rejoice, and blossom as a rose" (Isa.35:1). If man fights back because he is attacked, and pleads self-defense, why should he start a fight after a thousand years during which time "they shall not hurt nor destroy in all my holy mountain: for the earth shall be full of the knowledge of the Lord, as the waters cover the sea" (Isa.11:9). If he pleads ignorance, with the theory that if he had known God's will better he would have obeyed it, what excuse shall he give after a reign of peace and righteousness in which "the mountain of the Lord's house shall be established in the top of the mountains, and shall be exalted above the hills; and all nations shall flow unto it. And many people shall go and say, Come ye, and let us go up to the mountain of the Lord, to the house of the God of Jacob; and he will teach us of his ways, and we will walk in his paths: for out of Zion shall go forth the law, and the word of the Lord from Jerusalem" (Isa.2:2-3).

The environment will be perfect for one thousand years. The curse that God placed upon the earth will be lifted. Even the animals, previously wild and forced to kill in order to survive, will teach men how to live together amicably. There will be no air pollution and the chemists will cease trying to poison the human race, with the result that when a man dies at the age of one hundred years, he will be considered as having died as a child.

If it is the environment that makes man evil, the question to ask is this: How did the first environment become bad? Thus we see that at the end of the millenium man will no longer be able to blame the circumstances that surround him, and plead that he is a victim of forces over which he has no control. When he rises to follow Satan to Zion to destroy the Lord and His Anointed, "He that sitteth in the heavens shall laugh" (Psalm 2:4). It will be a short fight, as we learn in

Verse 9 - "And they went up on the breadth of the earth, and compassed the camp of the saints about, and the beloved city: and fire came down from God out of heaven, and devoured them."

καὶ ἀνέβησαν ἐπὶ τὸ πλάτος τῆς γῆς καὶ ἐκύκλευσαν τὴν παρεμβολὴν τῶν ἁγίων καὶ τὴν πόλιν τὴν ἠγαπημένην, καὶ κατέβη πῦρ ἐκ τοῦ οὐρανοῦ καὶ κατέφαγεν αὐτούς.

"And they marched up over the broad earth and surrounded the camp of the

saints and the beloved city; but fire came down from heaven and consumed them, . . . " . . . RSV.

καὶ (continuative conjunction) 14.

ἀνέβησαν (3d.per.pl.aor.act.ind.of ἀναβαίνω, constative) 323.

ἐπὶ (preposition with the accusative of extent) 47.

τὸ (acc.sing.neut.of the article in agreement with πλάτος) 9.

πλάτος (acc.sing.neut.of πλάτος, extent) 4487.

τῆς (gen.sing.fem.of the article in agreement with γῆς) 9.

γῆς (gen.sing.fem.of γῆ, description) 157.

καὶ (adjunctive conjunction joining verbs) 14.

ἐκύκλευσαν (3d.per.pl.aor.act.ind.of κυκλόω, constative) 2509.

τὴν (acc.sing.fem.of the article in agreement with παρεμβολὴν) 9.

παρεμβολὴν (acc.sing.fem.of παρεμβολή, direct object of ἐκύκλευσαν) 3566.

τῶν (gen.pl.masc.of the article in agreement with ἁγίων) 9.

ἁγίων (gen.pl.masc.of ἅγιος, possession) 84.

καὶ (adjunctive conjunction joining nouns) 14.

τὴν (acc.sing.fem.of the article in agreement with πόλιν) 9.

πόλιν (acc.sing.fem.of πόλις, direct object of ἐκύκλευσαν) 243.

τὴν (acc.sing.fem.of the article in agreement with ἠγαπημένην) 9.

ἠγαπημένην (perf.pass.part.acc.sing.fem.of ἀγαπάω, adjectival, emphatic attributive position, ascriptive, in agreement with πόλιν) 540.

καὶ (adversative conjunction) 14.

κατέβη (3d.per.sing.aor.act.ind.of καταβαίνω, ingressive) 324.

πῦρ (nom.sing.neut.of πῦρ, subject of κατέβη and κατέφαγεν) 298.

ἐκ (preposition with the ablative of source) 19.

τοῦ (abl.sing.masc.of the article in agreement with οὐρανοῦ) 9.

οὐρανοῦ (abl.sing.masc.of οὐρανός, source) 254.

καὶ (adjunctive conjunction joining verbs) 14.

κατέφαγεν (3d.per.sing.aor.act.ind.of κατεσθίω, constative) 1028.

αὐτούς (acc.pl.masc.of αὐτός, direct object of κατέφαγεν) 16.

Translation - "And they went up upon the broad plain of the earth and encircled the encampment of the saints and the beloved city; but fire came down out of heaven and consumed them."

Comment: τὸ πλάτος τῆς γῆς - "the broad plain of the earth" is an unusual way to refer to the topography. Is the topographical picture of Isa.40:4 to be interpreted literally and if so does this mean that in the Kingdom Age there will be no mountains and valleys? Or is this a reference to the plain area along the Palestinian coast as one approaches Jerusalem, the city which now is surrounded by mountains? However this may be the point is that this end-time army will come from all parts of the globe as was made clear in verse 8. The encampment of the saints and the beloved city refer to Jerusalem and environs. The hostile armies of the nations, deceived by Satan will surround the city. The war will be brief. *Cf.* comment on 2 Peter 3:10-13. Verse 10 tells us of the fate of the Devil.

Verse 10 - "And the devil that deceived them was cast into the lake of fire and brimstone, where the beast and the false prophet are, and shall be tormented day and night forever and ever."

καὶ ὁ διάβολος ὁ πλανῶν αὐτοὺς ἐβλήθη εἰς τὴν λίμνην τοῦ πυρὸς καὶ θείου, ὅπου καὶ τὸ θηρίον καὶ ὁ ψευδοπροφήτης, καὶ βασανισθήσονται ἡμέρας καὶ νυκτὸς εἰς τοὺς αἰῶνας τῶν αἰώνων.

"and the devil who deceived them was thrown into the lake of fire and brimstone where the beast and the false prophet were, and they will be tormented day and night for ever and ever." . . . RSV

καὶ (continuative conjunction) 14.

ὁ (nom.sing.masc.of the article in agreement with διάβολος) 9.

διάβολος (nom.sing.masc.of διάβολος, subject of ἐβλήθη) 331.

ὁ (nom.sing.masc.of the article in agreement with πλανῶν) 9.

πλανῶν (pres.act.part.nom.sing.masc.of πλανάω, substantival, in apposition) 1257.

αὐτοὺς (acc.pl.masc.of αὐτός, direct object of πλανῶν) 16.

ἐβλήθη (3d.per.sing.aor.pass.ind.of βάλλω, constative) 299.

εἰς (preposition with the accusative of extent) 140.

τὴν (acc.sing.fem.of the article in agreement with λίμνην) 9.

λίμνην (acc.sing.fem.of λίμνη, extent) 2041.

τοῦ (gen.sing.neut.of the article in agreement with πυρὸς) 9.

πυρὸς (gen.sing.neut.of πῦρ, description) 298.

καὶ (adjunctive conjunction joining nouns) 14.

θείου (gen.sing.neut.of θεῖον, description) 2619.

ὅπου (local adverb in a definite local clause) 592.

καὶ (correlative conjunction) 14.

τὸ (nom.sing.neut.of the article in agreement with θηρίον) 9.

θηρίον (nom.sing.neut.of θηρίον, subject of ἔστιν understood) 1951.

καὶ (adjunctive conjunction joining nouns) 14.

ὁ (nom.sing.masc.of the article in agreement with ψευδοπροφήτης) 9.

ψευδοπροφήτης (nom.sing.masc.of ψευδοπροφήτης, subject of ἔστιν understood) 670.

καὶ (continuative conjunction) 14.

βασανισθήσονται (3d.per.pl.fut.pass.ind.of βασανίζω, predictive) 719.

ἡμέρας (gen.sing.fem.of ἡμέρα, time description) 135.

καὶ (adjunctive conjunction joining nouns) 14.

νυκτὸς (gen.sing.fem.of νύξ, time description) 209.

εἰς (preposition with the accusative, time extent) 140.

τοὺς (acc.pl.masc.of the article in agreement with αἰῶνας) 9.

αἰῶνας (acc.pl.masc.of αἰών, time extent) 1002.

τῶν (gen.pl.masc.of the article in agreement with αἰώνων) 9.

αἰώνων (gen.pl.masc.of αἰών, partitive genitive) 1002.

Translation - "And the devil who was deceiving them was hurled into the lake of fire and brimstone, where both the Beast and the False Prophet were, and they will be tormented by day and by night into the ages of the ages."

Comment: Thus we have the final disposition of Satan in the eternal plan of the ages. The "anointed cherub" (Ezek.28:14) finds his eternal destiny in hell. His sin? Pride! (James 4:6; 1 Peter 5:5). Deception, error, heresy, extremism, sanctimony, fanaticism, cant, tartuffery, hypocrisy and unctuous affectation will be forever at an end in the Kingdom of God. The "Truth" (John 8:32,36) will have made free His elect. Satan joins the two beasts of Revelation 13 in the lake of fire into which they were hurled one thousand years before (Rev.19:20).

The description of the Great White Throne judgment occupies the rest of the material dealing with what men call time, after which God's eternity begins for us.

The Judgment at the Great White Throne

(Revelation 20:11-15)

Verse 11 - "And I saw a great white throne, and him that sat on it, from whose face the earth and the heaven fled away; and there was found no place for them."

Καὶ εἶδον θρόνον μέγαν λευκὸν καὶ τὸν καθήμενον ἐπ' αὐτόν, οὗ ἀπὸ τοῦ προσώπου ἔφυγεν ἡ γῆ καὶ ὁ οὐρανός, καὶ τόπος οὐχ εὑρέθη αὐτοῖς.

"Then I saw a great white throne and him who sat upon it; from his presence earth and sky fled away, and no place was found for them." . . . RSV

Καὶ (continuative conjunction) 14.

εἶδον (1st.per.sing.aor.act.ind.of ὁράω, ingressive) 144.

θρόνον (acc.sing.masc.of θρόνος, direct object of εἶδον) 519.

μέγαν (acc.sing.masc.of μέγας, in agreement with θρόνον) 184.

λευκὸν (acc.sing.masc.of λευκός, in agreement with θρόνον) 522.

καὶ (adjunctive conjunction joining substantives) 14.

τὸν (acc.sing.masc.of the article in agreement with καθήμενον) 9.

καθήμενον (pres.mid.part.acc.sing.masc.of κάθημαι, substantival, direct object of εἶδον) 377.

ἐπ' (preposition with the accusative of extent, rest) 47.

αὐτόν (acc.sing.masc.of αὐτός, extent, rest) 16.

οὗ (gen.sing.masc.of ὅς, relative pronoun, possession) 65.

ἀπὸ (preposition with the ablative of separation) 70.

τοῦ (abl.sing.neut.of the article in agreement with προσώπου) 9.

προσώπου (abl.sing.neut.of πρόσωπον, separation) 588.

ἔφυγεν (3d.per.sing.aor.act.ind.of φεύγω, ingressive) 202.

ἡ (nom.sing.fem.of the article in agreement with γῆ) 9.

γῆ (nom.sing.fem.of γῆ, subject of ἔφυγεν) 157.

καὶ (adjunctive conjunction joining nouns) 14.

ὁ (nom.sing.masc.of the article in agreement with οὐρανός) 9.

οὐρανός (nom.sing.masc.of οὐρανός, subject of ἔφυγεν) 254.

καὶ (adversative conjunction) 14.
τόπος (nom.sing.masc.of τόπος, subject of εὑρέθη) 1019.
οὐχ (negative conjunction with the indicative) 130.
εὑρέθη (3d.per.sing.aor.pass.ind.of εὑρίσκω, constative) 79.
αὐτοῖς (dat.pl.masc.of αὐτ ός, personal advantage) 16.

Translation - *"And I saw a great white throne and the One sitting upon it, from the face of Whom the earth and the heaven fled; but a place was not found for them."*

Comment: The point here is the universality of the jurisdiction of the court. Our Lord is the Judge (John 5:22; Acts 17:31) and He is God and therefore His rule is omnipresent. The earth and the heaven, a poetic way of saying "all creation," fled from the face of the Judge but they were unsuccessful in their search for a place where they could escape His jurisdiction. (Psalm 114:3,7). If the lost souls now fleeing from His face had had David's experience in Psalm 139:7-12 they would not have need to flee from Him at the judgment. The jurisdiction of this Judge is universal (Col.1:14-20).

Verse 12 - *"And I saw the dead, small and great, stand before God, and the books were opened; and another book was opened, which is the book of life: and the dead were judged out of those things which were written in the books, according to their works."*

καὶ εἶδον τοὺς νεκρούς, τοὺς μεγάλους καὶ τοὺς μικρούς, ἑστῶτας ἐνώπιον τοῦ θρόνου, καὶ βιβλία ἠνοίχθησαν, καὶ ἄλλο βιβλίον ἠνοίχθη, ὅ ἐστιν τῆς ζωῆς, καὶ ἐκρίθησαν οἱ νεκροὶ ἐκ τῶν γεγραμμένων ἐν τοῖς βιβλίοις κατὰ τὰ ἔργα αὐτῶν.

"And I saw the dead, great and small, standing before the throne, and books were opened. Also another book was opened, which is the book of life. And the dead were judged by what was written in the books, by what they had done." ...
RSV

καὶ (continuative conjunction) 14.
εἶδον (1st.per.sing.aor.act.ind.of ὁράω, ingressive) 144.
τοὺς (acc.pl.masc.of the article in agreement with νεκρούς) 9.
νεκρούς (acc.pl.masc.of νεκρός, direct object of εἶδον) 749.
τοὺς (acc.pl.masc.of the article in agreement with μεγάλους) 9.
μεγάλους (acc.pl.masc.of μέγας, in agreement with νεκρούς) 184.
καὶ (adjunctive conjunction joining adjectives) 14.
τοὺς (acc.pl.masc.of the article in agreement with μικρούς) 9.
μικρούς (acc.pl.masc.of μικρός, in agreement with νεκρούς) 901.
ἑστῶτας (perf.act.part.acc.pl.masc.of ἵστημι, adjectival, predicate position, restrictive, in agreement with νεκροὺς) 180.
ἐνώπιον (preposition with the genitive of place description) 1798.
τοῦ (gen.sing.masc.of the article in agreement with θρόνου) 9.
θρόνου (gen.sing.masc.of θρόνος, place description) 519.

καὶ (continuative conjunction) 14.

βιβλία (nom.pl.neut.of βιβλίον, subject of ἠνοίχθησαν) 1292.

ἠνοίχθησαν (3d.per.pl.aor.pass.ind.of ἀνοίγω, constative) 188.

καὶ (continuative conjunction) 14.

ἄλλο (nom.sing.neut.of ἄλλος, in agreement with βιβλίον) 198.

βιβλίον (nom.sing.neut.of βιβλίον, subject of ἠνοίχθη) 1292.

ἠνοίχθη (3d.per.sing.aor.pass.ind.of ἀνοίγω, constative) 188.

ὅ (nom.sing.neut.of ὅς, relative pronoun, subject of ἐστιν) 65.

ἐστιν (3d.per.sing.pres.ind.of εἰμί, aoristic) 86.

τῆς (gen.sing.fem.of the article in agreement with ζωῆς) 9.

ζωῆς (gen.sing.fem.of ζωή, description) 668.

καὶ (continuative conjunction) 14.

ἐκρίθησαν (3d.per.pl.aor.pass.ind.of κρίνω, constative) 531.

οἱ (nom.pl.masc.of the article in agreement with νεκροὶ) 9.

νεκροὶ (nom.pl.masc.of νεκρός, subject of ἐκρίθησαν) 749.

ἐκ (preposition with the ablative, source) 19.

τῶν (abl.pl.neut.of the article in agreement with γεγραμμένων) 9.

γεγραμμένων (perf.pass.part.abl.pl.neut.of γράφω, source) 156.

ἐν (preposition with the locative of place) 80.

τοῖς (loc.pl.neut.of the article in agreement with βιβλίοις) 9.

βιβλίοις (loc.pl.neut.of βιβλίον, place) 1292.

κατὰ (preposition with the accusative, according to) 98.

τὰ (acc.pl.neut.of the article in agreement with ἔργα) 9.

ἔργα (acc.pl.neut.of ἔργον, according to) 460.

αὐτῶν (gen.pl.masc.of αὐτός, description) 16.

Translation - *"And I saw the dead, the great and the small, standing before the throne; and books were opened, and another book was opened, which is concerned with life; and the dead were judged on the basis of what was written in the books, according to their deeds."*

Comment: Who are the dead? Obviously the unsaved dead of all ages (Rev.20:5) will be there standing before the throne. The saints of all ages, up to the second coming of Messiah, at the beginning of the millenium will have been resurrected/raptured then. Their judgment was effected at Calvary, and the issue of their salvation will not be in doubt, though they will face the judgment for rewards of believers' works (2 Cor.5:10,11; 1 Cor.3:11-15; Rev.11:18). Now, 1000 years later,the unsaved dead who were not disturbed by the second coming, 1000 years before, plus all of the unsaved dead who died during or at the end of the millenium (Rev.20:9) are standing before the throne.

But this accounting leaves one group yet unaccounted for. That is the group of saints, born to unsaved parents who survived Armageddon and saved during the Kingdom Age, as a result of the preaching of the everlasting gospel (Rev.14:6). This accounts for the presence at the great white throne of the Book of Life. The Kingdom saints will have their names written there. All unregenerates whose names are not in the Book of Life will have their deeds recorded in the other books of record and will be judged by them. Since the wages of sin is death (Rom.6:23) and since they did not accept Christ, they will be judged on the basis of strict legality (Rom.3:26). The just Judge Who justifies him to believes in Jesus, in whatever age, will, with the same standard of justice judge others according to their works. *Cf.* Psalm 28:4; 62:12; Proverbs 24:12; Isa.59:18; Jer.17:10; Rom.2:6; 2 Cor.11:15; 2 Tim.4:14; 1 Pet.1:17; Rev.2:23; 18:6; 22:12.

Verse 13 - "And the sea gave up the dead which were in it; and death and hell delivered up the dead which were in them: and they were judged every man according to their works."

καὶ ἔδωκεν ἡ θάλασσα τοὺς νεκροὺς τοὺς ἐν αὐτῇ, καὶ ὁ θάνατος καὶ ὁ ᾅδης ἔδωκαν τοὺς νεκροὺς τοὺς ἐν αὐτοῖς, καὶ ἐκρίθησαν ἕκαστος κατὰ τὰ ἔργα αὐτῶν.

"And the sea gave up the dead in it, Death and Hades gave up the dead in them, and all were judged by what they had done." . . . RSV

καὶ (continuative conjunction) 14.
ἔδωκεν (3d.per.sing.aor.act.ind.of δίδωμι, constative) 362.
ἡ (nom.sing.fem.of the article in agreement with θάλασσα) 9.
θάλασσα (nom.sing.fem.of θάλασσα, subject of ἔδωκεν) 374.
τοὺς (acc.pl.masc.of the article in agreement with νεκροὺς) 9.
νεκροὺς (acc.pl.masc.of νεκρός, direct object of ἔδωκεν) 749.
τοὺς (acc.pl.masc.of the article in agreement with νεκροὺς) 9.
ἐν (preposition with the locative of place) 80.
αὐτῇ (loc.sing.fem.of αὐτός, place) 16.
καὶ (continuative conjunction) 14.
ὁ (nom.sing.masc.of the article in agreement with θάνατος) 9.
θάνατος (nom.sing.masc.of θάνατος, subject of ἔδωκαν) 381.
καὶ (adjunctive conjunction joining nouns) 14.
ὁ (nom.sing.masc.of the article in agreement with ᾅδης) 9.
ᾅδης (nom.sing.masc.of ᾅδης, subject of ἔδωκαν) 947.
ἔδωκαν (3d.per.pl.aor.act.ind.of δίδωμι, constative) 362.
τοὺς (acc.pl.masc.of the article in agreement with νεκροὺς) 9.
νεκροὺς (acc.pl.masc.of νεκρός, direct object of ἔδωκαν) 749.
τοὺς (acc.pl.masc.of the article in agreement with νεκροὺς) 9.
ἐν (preposition with the locative of place) 80.
αὐτοῖς (loc.pl.masc.of αὐτός, place) 16.
καὶ (continuative conjunction) 14.
ἐκρίθησαν (3d.per.pl.aor.pass.ind.of κρίνω, constative) 531.
ἕκαστος (nom.sing.masc.of ἕκαστος,subject of ἐκρίθησαν) 1217.
κατὰ (preposition with the accusative, according to) 98.
τὰ (acc.pl.neut.of the article in agreement with ἔργα) 9.
ἔργα (acc.pl.neut.of ἔργον, according to) 460.
αὐτῶν (gen.pl.masc.of αὐτος, description) 16.

Translation - "And the sea gave up the dead in it; and Death and Hades gave up the dead in them; and each one was judged in keeping with his works."

Comment: Here is the description of the resurrection of the bodies of the unsaved dead. Critics have often objected that one cannot torture an unclothed spirit with heat. Scripture nowhere teaches the eternal punishment of unsaved souls apart from the resurrection of their bodies. *Cf.* John 5:27-29 and comment *en loc.* John 5:29 does not say that the resurrection of saved and unsaved comes at the same time. Jesus was contrasting the spiritual hearing of His voice in John 5:25 with the auditory hearing of His voice in verse 28.

It is clear from Rev.20:4-6 that a thousand years elapses between the first resurrection of saints (John 5:29a) and the second death resurrection of the lost (John 5:29b). The saints are resurrected, transfigured, judge for rewards and rewarded premillenially. The lost are resurrected, judged on the basis of their works without faith and condemned postmillenially.

The unsaved who died at sea will be raised. That human bodies, long since dead and buried have decomposed by chemical entropy and have by biodegradability, returned to the basic elements is, of course true. But this is no problem for a sovereign God.

Death is associated here with *ᾅδης* as an abiding place of the wicked dead. *Cf.* #947 and run the references. Bodies of the lost in earthly graves or in the sea and souls of the lost in *ᾅδης* will be reunited to face judgment. Death and *ᾅδης*, no longer needed as execution cells on death row, for those awaiting execution, will also be hurled into the lake of fire.

Verse 14 - "And death and hell were cast into the lake of fire. This is the second death." . . . RSV

καὶ ὁ θάνατος καὶ ὁ ᾅδης ἐβλήθησαν εἰς τὴν λίμνην τοῦ πυρός. οὗτος ὁ θάνατος ὁ δεύτερος ἐστιν, ἡ λίμνην τοῦ πυρός.

"Then Death and Hades were thrown into the lake of fire. This is the second death, the lake of fire;" . . . RSV

καὶ (continuative conjunction) 14.
ὁ (nom.sing.masc.of the article in agreement with *θάνατος*) 9.
θάνατος (nom.sing.masc.of *θάνατος*, subject of *ἐβλήθησαν*) 381.
καὶ (adjunctive conjunction joining nouns) 14.
ὁ (nom.sing.masc.of the article in agreement with *ᾅδης*) 9.
ᾅδης (nom.sing.masc.of *ᾅδης*, subject of *ἐβλήθησαν*) 947.
ἐβλήθησαν (3d.per.pl.aor.pass.ind.of *βάλλω*, constative) 299.
εἰς (preposition with the accusative of extent) 140.
τὴν (acc.sing.fem.of the article in agreement with *λίμνην*) 9.
λίμνην (acc.sing.fem.of *λίμνη*, extent) 2041.
τοῦ (gen.sing.neut.of the article in agreement with *πυρός*) 9.
πυρός (gen.sing.neut.of *πῦρ*, description) 298.
οὗτος (nom.sing.masc.of *οὗτος*, subject of *ἐστιν*) 93.

ὁ (nom.sing.masc.of the article in agreement with θάνατος) 9.
θάνατος (nom.sing.masc.of θάνατος, predicate nominative) 381.
ὁ (nom.sing.masc.of the article in agreement with δεύτερος) 9.
δεύτερος (nom.sing.masc.of δεύτερος, in agreement with θάνατος) 1371.
ἐστιν (3d.per.sing.pres.ind.of εἰμί, aoristic) 86.
ἡ (nom.sing.fem.of the article in agreement with λίμνην) 9.
λίμνη (nom.sing.fem.of λίμνη, in apposition) 2041.
τοῦ (gen.sing.neut.of the article in agreement with πυρός) 9.
πυρός (gen.sing.neut.of πῦρ, description) 298.

Translation - *"And Death and Hades were hurled into the lake of fire; this, the lake of fire, is the second death."*

Comment: The redeemed need not fear it (Rev.20:6). It is the final destiny of all who reject Christ as Saviour. Its chief victim will be Satan and his two demonic prophets,the Beast and the False Prophet.

Verse 15 - *"And whosoever was not found written in the book of life was cast into the lake of fire."*

καὶ εἴ τις οὐχ εὑρέθη ἐν τῇ βίβλῳ τῆς ζωῆς γεγραμμένος ἐβλήθη εἰς τὴν λίμνην τοῦ πυρός.

"and if any one's name was not found written in the book of life, he was thrown into the lake of fire." . . . RSV

καὶ (continuative conjunction) 14.
εἴ (conditional particle in a first-class condition) 337.
τις (nom.sing.masc.of τις, indefinite pronoun, subject of εὑρέθη) 486.
οὐχ (negative conjunction with the indicative) 130.
εὑρέθη (3d.person, singular, aorist passive indicative in a first-class condition) 79.
ἐν (preposition with the locative of place) 80.
τῇ (loc.sing.fem.of the article in agreement with βίβλῳ) 9.
βίβλῳ (loc.sing.fem.of βίβλος, place) 1.
τῆς (gen.sing.fem.of the article in agreement with ζωῆς) 9.
ζωῆς (gen.sing.fem.of ζωή, description) 668.
γεγραμμένος (perf.pass.part.nom.sing.masc.of γράφω, adverbial, modal) 156.
ἐβλήθη (3d.per.sing.aor.pass.ind.of βάλλω, constative) 299.
εἰς (preposition with the accusative of extent) 140.
τὴν (acc.sing.fem.of the article in agreement with λίμνην) 9.
λίμνην (acc.sing.fem.of λίμνη, extent) 2041.
τοῦ (gen.sing.neut.of the article in agreement with πυρός) 9.
πυρός (gen.sing.neut.of πῦρ, description) 298.

Translation - *"And if anyone was not found having been written in the Book of Life he was cast into the lake of fire."*

Comment: The first class condition "*assumes* the condition to be a reality and the conclusion follows logically and naturally from that assumption. . . . The construction is εἰ (sometimes ἐάν) and any tense of the indicative in the protasis. The apodosis varies greatly. It all depends on what one is after, whether mere statement, prediction, command, prohibition, suggestion, question. Hence the apodosis may be in the indicative (any tense) or the subjunctive or the imperative. There is no necessary correspondence in tense between protasis and apodosis. The variation in the mode of the apodosis has no essential bearing on the force of the condition. This condition, therefore, taken at its face value, assumes the condition to be true. The context or other light must determine the actual situation." (Robertson, *Grammar*, 1007, 1008).

In our verse it is clear from other scriptures that someone will be found whose name is not written in the Book of Life. This is not, therefore, a second-class condition, which expresses an assumption, contrary to fact, although the verbs, both in the protasis and the apodosis are aorist tense.

This judgment is postmillenial and hence there will be found present before the throne the unsaved, who are not found in the Book of Life. But there will also be present those who were saved during the millenium (the children of unsaved parents, whose parents survived Armageddon. The parents cannot be saved, because they received the mark of the Beast during the tribulation. But their children and children's children will have the gospel offer, to which they can respond. Their names will be in the Book of Life. That is why both the books, which record the sins of the unsaved and the Book of Life which records the names of those saved during the millenium are present at the judgment.

The Book of Life was written before the foundation of the world (Rev.17:8)

With the close of chapter 20 we turn away from the story of Generation, Degeneration and Regeneration and turn in Rev.21:1-22:5 to the beautiful picture of the New and Eternal Heaven and Earth.

The play has ended. The curtain is down on the last act. Christ is totally triumphant. His enemy, Satan was doomed by His death at Calvary (Heb.2:14) and His elect will have been saved by the same event. The divine plan of the ages, conceived by Him who does everything after the counsel of His own will (Eph.1:11) has run its predestined course. There remains only to show the scene where the eternal drama of Christian service and worship will be enacted. For it is in the new heavens and the new earth, wherein dwelleth righteousness (2 Peter 3:13), the new creation which the saints have been looking for, that we will spend eternity.

The New Heaven and the New Earth

(Revelation 21:1-8)

Revelation 21:8 - "And I saw a new heaven and a new earth: for the first heaven and the first earth were passed away; and there was no more sea."

Καὶ εἶδον οὐρανὸν καινὸν καὶ γῆν καινήν. ὁ γὰρ πρῶτος οὐρανὸς καὶ ἡ πρώτη γῆ ἀπῆλθαν, καὶ ἡ θάλασσα οὐκ ἔστιν ἔτι.

"Then I saw a new heaven and a new earth; for the first heaven and the first earth had passed away, and the sea was no more." . . . RSV

Καὶ (continuative conjunction) 14.
εἶδον (1st.per.sing.aor.act.ind.of ὁράω, ingressive) 144.
οὐρανὸν (acc.sing.masc.of οὐρανός, direct object of εἶδον) 254.
καινὸν (acc.sing.masc.of καινός, in agreement with οὐρανὸν) 812.
καὶ (adjunctive conjunction joining nouns) 14.
γῆν (acc.sing.fem.of γῆ, direct object of εἶδον) 157.
καινήν (acc.sing.fem.of καινός, in agreement with γῆν) 812.
ὁ (nom.sing.masc.of the article in agreement with οὐρανὸς) 9.
γὰρ (causal conjunction) 105.
πρῶτος (nom.sing.masc.of πρῶτος, in agreement with οὐρανὸς) 487.
οὐρανὸς (nom.sing.masc.of οὐρανός, subject of ἀπῆλθαν) 254.
καὶ (adjunctive conjunction joining nouns) 14.
ἡ (nom.sing.fem.of the article in agreement with γῆ) 9.
πρώτη (nom.sing.fem.of πρῶτος, in agreement with γῆ) 487.
γῆ (nom.sing.fem.of γῆ, subject of ἀπῆλθαν) 157.
ἀπῆλθαν (3d.per.pl.aor.ind.of ἀπέρχομαι, culminative) 239.
καὶ (continuative conjunction) 14.
ἡ (nom.sing.fem.of the article in agreement with θάλασσα) 9.
θάλασσα (nom.sing.fem.of θάλασσα, subject of ἔστιν) 374.
οὐκ (negative conjunction with the indicative) 130.
ἔστιν (3d.per.sing.pres.ind.of εἰμί, static) 86.
ἔτι (temporal adverb) 448.

Translation - "*And I saw a new heaven and a new earth, for the first heaven and the first earth had passed away, and the sea existed no longer.*

Comment: The eternal order of things of course will be a viable society. The present order, both the cursed earth and its atmospheric and stellar heavens will have passed away as described in 2 Peter 3:10-13. Note that both the earth and the heavens are to be disintegrated in that nuclear fire storm. It is idle for us to speculate as to why the new earth will need no oceans. We will understand that when we get there. *Cf.* Isa.65:17: 66:22.

Verse 2 - "And I, John saw the holy city, new Jerusalem, coming down from God out of heaven, prepared as a bride adorned for her husband."

καὶ τὴν πόλιν τὴν ἁγίαν Ἰερουσαλὴμ καινὴν εἶδον καταβαίνουσαν ἐκ τοῦ οὐρανοῦ ἀπὸ τοῦ θεοῦ, ἡτοιμασμένην ὡς νύμφην κεκοσμημένην τῷ ἀνδρὶ αὐτῆς.

"And I saw the holy city, new Jerusalem, coming down out of heaven from God, prepared as a bride adorned for her husband;" . . . RSV

καὶ (continuative conjunction) 14.

τὴν (acc.sing.fem.of the article in agreement with πόλιν) 9.

πόλιν (acc.sing.fem.of πόλις, direct object of εἶδον) 243.

τὴν (acc.sing.fem.of the article in agreement with ἁγίαν) 9.

ἁγίαν (acc.sing.fem.of ἅγιος, in agreement with πόλιν) 84.

Ἰερουσαλὴμ (acc.sing.fem.of Ἱεροσόλυμα, in apposition with πόλιν) 141.

καινὴν (acc.sing.fem.of καινός, in agreement with Ἰερουσαλὴμ) 812.

εἶδον (1st.per.sing.aor.act.ind.of ὁράω, ingressive) 144.

καταβαίνουσαν (pres.act.part.acc.sing.fem.of καταβαίνω, adjectival, predicate position, ascriptive, in agreement with πόλιν) 324.

ἐκ (preposition with the ablative of separation) 19.

τοῦ (abl.sing.masc.of the article in agreement with οὐρανοῦ) 9.

οὐρανοῦ (abl.sing.masc.of οὐρανός, separation) 254.

ἀπὸ (preposition with the ablative of source) 70.

τοῦ (abl.sing.masc.of the article in agreement with θεοῦ) 9.

θεοῦ (abl.sing.masc.of θεός, source) 124.

ἡτοιασμένην (perf.pass.part.acc.sing.fem.of ἑτοιμάζω, adjectival, predicate position, ascriptive, in agreement with πόλιν) 257.

ὡς (comparative particle) 128.

νύμφην (acc. sing.fem.of νύμφη, in agreement with πόλιν) 898.

κεκοσμημένην (perf.pass.part.acc.sing.fem.of κοσμέω, adjectival, predicate position, ascriptive, in agreement with νύμφην) 1023.

τῷ (dat.sing.masc.of the article in agreement with ἀνδρὶ) 9.

ἀνδρὶ (dat.sing.masc.of ἀνήρ, personal advantage) 63.

αὐτῆς (gen.sing.fem.of αὐτός, relationship) 16.

Translation - "And I saw the holy city, New Jerusalem, coming down out of heaven from God, prepared like a bride adorned for her husband."

Comment: *Cf.*#254 to note that οὐρανός is used in three senses: atmospheric, stellar and God's heaven. The latter was not destroyed in the fire of 2 Peter 3:10-13. God's throne will always be secure. The city is prepared. *Cf.* John 14:2. Built by One Who grew up in a carpenter's shop (Mt.13:55; Mk.6:3), the city is beautiful. Heaven, the Holy City, is a prepared place for a prepared people.

It is significant that the New Jerusalem is a holy city, not a holy countryside. A city, where human contacts are closest, more intimate and hence sociologically more dangerous, is not a holy place on earth. But, thanks to redemption, regeneration and transfiguration, we shall live together in a city of holiness. The crime and sin ridden cities of earth testify that only Christ can build a holy city, where saints can live together with God. Population density, far greater in New York city than in Montana means that crime is more prevalent in New York, not because New Yorkers are more wicked than Montana ranchers, but because one must travel further in Montana before coming in contact with another sinner. There are ten thousand sinners in the same city block in New York.

Verse 3 - "And I heard a great voice out of heaven saying, Behold the tabernacle of God is with men, and he will dwell with them, and they shall be his people, and God himself shall be with them, and be their God."

καὶ ἤκουσα φωνῆς μεγάλης ἐκ τοῦ θρόνου λεγούσης, Ἰδοὺ ἡ σκηνὴ τοῦ θεοῦ μετὰ τῶν ἀνθρώπων, καὶ σκηνώσει μετ' αὐτῶν, καὶ αὐτοὶ λαοὶ αὐτοῦ ἔσονται, καὶ αὐτὸς ὁ θεὸς μετ' αὐτῶν ἔσται, (αὐτῶν θεός,)

"and I heard a great voice from the throne saying, 'Behold the dwelling of God is with men. He will dwell with them, and they shall be his people, and God himself will be with them;" . . . RSV

καὶ (continuative conjunction) 14.

ἤκουσα (1st.per.sing.aor.act.ind.of ἀκούω, ingressive) 148.

φωνῆς (gen.sing.fem.of φωνή, objective genitive) 222.

μεγάλης (gen.sing.fem.of μέγας, in agreement with φωνῆς) 184.

ἐκ (preposition with the ablative of source) 19.

τοῦ (abl.sing.masc.of the article in agreement with θρόνου) 9.

θρόνου (abl.sing.masc.of θρόνος, source) 519.

λεγούσης (pres.act.part.gensing.fem.of λέγω, recitative) 66.

Ἰδοὺ (exclamation) 95.

ἡ (nom.sing.fem.of the article in agreement with σκηνὴ) 9.

σκηνὴ (nom.sing.fem.of σκηνή, subject of ἔστιν understood) 1224.

τοῦ (gen.sing.masc.of the article in agreement with θεοῦ) 9.

θεοῦ (gen.sing.masc.of θεός, description) 124.

μετὰ (preposition with the genitive, accompaniment) 50.

τῶν (gen.pl.masc.of the article in agreement with ἀνθρώπων) 9.

ἀνθρώπων (gen.pl.masc.of ἄνθρωπος, accompaniment) 341.

καὶ (continuative conjunction) 14.

σκηνώσει (3d.per.sing.fut.act.ind.of σκηνόω, predictive) 1698.

μετ' (preposition with the genitive, association) 50.

αὐτῶν (gen.pl.masc.of αὐτός, association) 16.

καὶ (continuative conjunction) 14.

αὐτοὶ (nom.pl.masc.of αὐτός, subject of ἔσονται) 16.

λαοὶ (nom.pl.masc.of λαός, predicate nominative) 110.

αὐτοῦ (gen.sing.masc.of αὐτός, relationship) 16.

ἔσονται (3d.per.pl.fut.ind.of εἰμί, predictive) 86.

καὶ (continuative conjunction) 14.

αὐτὸς (nom.sing.masc.of αὐτός, intensive) 16.

ὁ (nom.sing.masc.of the article in agreement with θεὸς) 9.

θεὸς (nom.sing.masc.of θεός, subject of ἔσται) 124.

μετ' (preposition with the genitive, association) 50.

αὐτῶν (gen.pl.masc.of αὐτός, association) 16.

ἔσται (3d.per.sing.fut.ind.of εἰμί, predictive) 86.

αὐτῶν (gen.pl.masc.of αὐτός, realtionship) 16.

θεός (nom.sing.masc.of θεός, apposition) 124.

Translation - "And I heard a loud voice from the throne saying, 'Look! The tabernacle of God is with men, and He will always dwell with them, and they will always be His people, and God Himself will always be with them as their God."

Comment: Here is the final sociological result of which John 17:21 is the spiritual and psychological foundation and preparation. Christ's prayer of John 17:9-26 will be totally answered, in its most complete sense. The verse breathes intimacy between God and His saints. We are going to be neighbors in the same city. This is the ultimate result of the incarnation of the Logos. This is the goal which the trinune Godhead had in mind when it was said, "Let us make man in our image, after our likeness. . . " (Gen.1:26).

Verse 4 - "And God shall wipe away all tears from their eyes; and there shall be no more death, neither sorrow, nor crying, neither shall there be any more pain: for the former things are passed away."

καὶ ἐξαλείφει πᾶν δάκρυον ἐκ τῶν ὀφθαλμῶν αὐτῶν, καὶ ὁ θάνατος οὐκ ἔσται ἔτι, οὔτε πένθος οὔτε κραυγὴ οὔτε πόνος οὐκ ἔσται ἔτι (ὅτι) τὰ πρῶτα ἀπῆλθαν.

"he will wipe away every tear from their eyes, and death shall be no more, neither shall there be mourning nor crying nor pain any more, for the former things have passed away." . . . RSV

καὶ (continuative conjunction) 14.

ἐξαλείφει (3d.per.sing.fut.act.ind.of ἐξαλείφω, predictive) 3017.

πᾶν (acc.sing.neut.of πᾶς, in agreement with δάκρυον) 67.

δάκρυον (acc.sing.neut.of δάκρυ, direct object of ἐξαλείφει) 2166.

ἐκ (preposition with the ablative of separation) 19.

τῶν (abl.pl.masc.of the article in agreement with ὀφθαλμῶν) 9.

ὀφθαλμῶν (abl.pl.masc.of ὀφθαλμός, separation) 501.

αὐτῶν (gen.pl.masc.of αὐτός, possession) 16.

καὶ (continuative conjunction) 14.

ὁ (nom.sing.masc.of the article in agreement with θάνατος) 9.

θάνατος (nom.sing.masc.of θάνατος, subject of ἔσται) 381.

οὐκ (negative conjunction with the indicative) 130.

ἔσται (3d.per.sing.fut.ind.of εἰμί, predictive) 86.

ἔτι (temporal adverb) 448.

οὔτε (negative copulative conjunction) 598.

πένθος (nom.sing.masc.of πένθος, subject of ἔσται) 5145.

οὔτε (negative copulative conjunction) 598.

κραυγὴ (nom.sing.fem.of κραυγή, subject of ἔσται) 1532.

οὔτε (negative copulative conjunction) 598.

πόνος (nom.sing.masc.of πόνος, subject of ἔσται) 4643.

οὐκ (negative conjunction with the indicative) 130.

ἔσται (3d.per.sing.fut.ind.of εἰμί, predictive) 86.

ἔτι (temporal adverb) 448.

ὅτι (conjunction introducing a subordinate causal clause) 211.

τὰ (nom.pl.neut.of the article in agreement with πρῶτα) 9.

πρῶτα (nom.pl.neut.of πρῶτος, subject of ἀπῆλθαν) 487.

ἀπῆλθαν (3d.per.pl.aor.mid.ind.of ἀπέρχομαι, culminative) 239.

Translation - "And He shall wipe away all tears out of their eyes, and death shall never occur again, nor shall sorrow nor crying nor pain ever be again, because the former things have passed away."

Comment: *Cf.* Rev.7:17; Isa.35:10; 65:19. Tears, death, crying, sorrow and pain are the results of sin. Since sin will be a thing of the past, so indeed will be its results.

Verse 5 - "And he that sat upon the throne said, Behold, I make all things new. And he said unto me, Write: for these words are true and faithful."

Καὶ εἶπεν ὁ καθήμενος ἐπὶ τῷ θρόνῳ, Ἰδοὺ καινὰ ποιῶ πάντα. καὶ λέγει, Γράφον, ὅτι οὗτοι οἱ λόγοι πιστοὶ καὶ ἀληθινοί εἰσιν.

"And he who sat upon the throne said, 'Behold, I make all things new.' Also he said, 'Write this, for these words are trustworthy and true.' " . . . RSV

Καὶ (continuative conjunction) 14

εἶπεν (3d.per.sing.aor.act.ind.of εἶπον, ingressive) 155.

ὁ (nom.sing.masc.of the article in agreement with καθήμενος) 9.

καθήμενος (pres.mid.part.nom.sing.masc.of κάθημαι, substantival, subject of εἶπεν) 377.

ἐπὶ (preposition with the locative of place) 47.

τῷ (loc.sing.masc.of the article in agreement with θρόνῳ) 9.

θρόνῳ (loc.sing.masc.of θρόνος, place) 519.

Ἰδοὺ (exclamation) 95.

καινὰ (acc.pl.neut.of καινός, predicate adjective) 812.

ποιῶ (1st.per.sing.pres.act.ind.of ποιέω, static) 127.

πάντα (acc.pl.neut.of πᾶς, direct object of ποιῶ) 67.

καὶ (adjunctive conjunction joining verbs) 14.

λέγει (3d.per.sing.pres.act.ind.of λέγω, aoristic) 66.

Γράφον (2d.per.sing.aor.act.impv.of γράφω, command) 156.

ὅτι (recitative) 211.

οὗτοι (nom.pl.masc.of οὗτος, in agreement with λόγοι) 93.

οἱ (nom.pl.masc.of the article in agreement with λόγοι) 9.

λόγοι (nom.pl.masc.of λόγος, subject of εἰσιν) 510.

πιστοὶ (nom.pl.masc.of πιστός, predicate adjective) 1522.

καὶ (adjunctive conjunction joining adjectives) 14.

ἀληθινοί (nom.pl.masc.of ἀληθινός, predicate adjective) 1696.

εἰσιν (3d.per.pl.pres.ind.of εἰμί, static) 86.

Translation - "And the One sitting upon the throne said, 'Look! I am making everything new.' And he added, 'Write: These words are faithful and true.' "

Comment: The One on the throne is our Lord (John 5:22). Only He can say καινὰ ποιῶ πάντα, since He is the One Who created them originally (John 1:2; Heb.1:2; Col.1:16,17). Just as regeneration is a new experience that admits us to a new life-style (2 Cor.5:17), as a result of which regenerated people are unable to conform to a ruined world, so now Christ regenerates the universe to fit the

the regenerated saints. Until He makes the universe new, as He did His elect when He saved us, there is conflict within the Christian. His new life rejects the response to the environmental stimuli that are evil. The need for what Thorndike called "intervening variables" as an ethical court of review to determine what stimuli should be obeyed and what rejected, will be no more. All stimuli will be holy and all responses moral. Freud's conflict between super ego, ego and id will be a thing of the past. The Christian was given a new personality at regeneration (2 Cor.5:17). He will be given a new body to go with the personality at the rapture (1 John 3:2; Phil.3:20,21; 1 Thess.4:16; 1 Cor.15:44,51). Finally, as time yields to eternity he will be introduced into a new universe, as an environment for his new body and personality.

Before the rapture the Christian is in a struggle with himself (Rom.7:11-25; Gal.5:16), as the old man fights against the new inner man. He also resists a godless world societal environment. At last all struggle will be over as the new creation, free from the curse, will provide him an eternal play ground. This new creation is not an accommodation in the sociological sense. There will be no compromise. There will be no Hegelian synthesis. Evil will be sent to hell in total banishment. Only God, Christ, the Holy Spirit and the Body of Christ will remain in a universe totally obedient to the divine will and hence, from a scientific point of view, capable of infinite development.

But these are things that cannot be predicted — only experienced. He adds for John's benefit, and for ours, the last clause. There is no doubt about it. *Cf.* 1 Kings 22:59; 2 Chron.18:18; Psalm 47:8; Ezek.1:26,27; Rev.4:2,9; 5:1,7,13; 6:16; 7:10,15; 19:4.

Verse 6 - "And he said unto me, It is done. I am Alpha and Omega, the beginning and the end. I will give unto him that is athirst of the fountain of the water of life freely."

καὶ εἶπέν μοι, Γέγοναν, ἐγώ (εἰμι) τὸ Ἄλφα καὶ τὸ Ὦ, ἡ ἀρχὴ καὶ τὸ τέλος. ἐγὼ τῷ διφῶντι δώσω ἐκ τῆς πηγῆς τοῦ ὕδατος τῆς ζωῆς δωρεάν.

"And he said to me, 'It is done! I am the Alpha and the Omega, the beginning and the end. To the thirsty I will give water without price from the fountain of the water of life. . . . " . . . RSV

καὶ (continuative conjunction) 14.

εἶπέν (3d.per.sing.aor.act.ind.of εἶπον, constative) 155.

μοι (dat.sing.masc.of ἐγώ, indirect object of εἶπέν) 123.

Γέγοναν (3d.per.sing.2d.per. ind.of γίνομαι, culminative) 113.

ἐγώ (nom.sing.masc.of ἐγώ, subject of εἰμι) 123.

(εἰμι) (1st.per.sing.pres.ind.of εἰμί, aoristic) 86.

τὸ (nom.sing.neut.of the article in agreement with Ἄλφα) 9.

Ἄλφα (nom.sing.neut.of Ἄλφα, predicate nominative) 5318.

καὶ (adjunctive conjunction joining nouns) 14.

Ὦ (nom.sing.neut.of Ὦ, predicate nominative) 5319.

ἡ (nom.sing.fem.of the article in agreement with ἀρχή) 9.

ἀρχῆ (nom.sing.fem.of ἀρχή, in apposition) 1285.
καὶ (adjunctive conjunction joining nouns) 14.
τὸ (nom.sing.neut.of the article in agreement with τέλος) 9.
τέλος (nom.sing.neut.of τέλος, in apposition) 881.
ἐγὼ (nom.sing.masc.of ἐγώ, subject of δώσω, emphatic) 123.
τῷ (dat.sing.masc.of the article in agreement with διφῶντι) 9.
διφῶντι (pres.act.part.dat.sing.masc.of διφάω, indirect object of δώσω) 427.
δώσω (1st.per.sing.fut.act.ind.of δίδωμι, predictive) 362.
ἐκ (preposition with the ablative of source) 19.
τῆς (abl.sing.fem.of the article in agreement with πηγῆς) 9.
πηγῆς (abl.sing.fem.of πηγή, source) 2001.
τοῦ (gen.sing.neut.of the article in agreement with ὕδατος) 9.
ὕδατος (gen.sing.neut.of ὕδωρ, description) 301.
τῆς (gen.sing.fem.of the article in agreement with ζωῆς) 9.
ζωῆς (gen.sing.fem.of ζωή, description) 668.
δωρεάν (adverbial) 858.

Translation - "And He said to me, 'It is done. I am the Alpha and the Omega, the beginning and the end. I will give to the one who is thirsty from the fountain of the water of life, without cost.' "

Comment: Because Jesus said τετέλεσται (John 19:30) He can now say γέγοναν. Redemption was accomplished on the cross and hence the entire redemptive program of God is finished. It is all over. "I was before anything was here and I will be here after everything is gone." (Col.1:17; John 1:1). Thus the Origin and End of all things is sovereign. *Cf.*#3013.

Note how John is careful to use the definite article to accentuate τὸ Ἄλφα καὶ τὸ Ὦ and ἡ ἀρχὴ καὶ τὸ τέλος. The thirsty one (Mt.5:6; Rev.22:17) will be led to the fountain (Rev.7:17; Psalm 23:2). *Cf.* John 4:10,14,14; 7:38. What Jesus said to the Samaritan woman (John 4:10,14) and on the last day of the Feast (John 7:38) He will again say in Eternity.

Jesus thirsted and was tortured with vinegar (John 19:28-30; Psalm 22:15). the eternal result is that His Bride will never thirst because of the eternal spring of the water of life.

Verse 7 - "He that overcometh shall inherit all things; and I will be his God, and he shall be my son."

ὁ νικῶν κληρονομήσει ταῦτα, καὶ ἔσομαι αὐτῷ θεός, καὶ αὐτὸς ἔσται μοι υἱόν.

"He who conquers shall have this heritage, and I will be his God and he shall be my son." ... RSV

ὁ (nom.sing.masc.of the article in agreement with νικῶν) 9.
νικῶν (pres.act.part.nom.sing.masc.of νικάω, substantival, subject of κληρονομήσει) 2454.
κληρονομήσει (3d.per.sing.fut.act.ind.of κληρονομέω, predictive) 426.
ταῦτα (acc.pl.neut.of οὗτος, direct object of κληρονομήσει) 93.

καὶ (continuative conjunction) 14.
ἔσομαι (1st.per.sing.fut.ind.of εἰμί, predictive) 86.
αὐτῷ (dat.sing.masc.of αὐτός, personal advantage) 16.
θεὸς (nom.sing.masc.of θεός, predicate nominative) 124.
καὶ (continuative conjunction) 14.
αὐτὸς (nom.sing.masc.of αὐτός, subject of ἔσται) 16.
ἔσται (3d.per.sing.fut.ind.of εἰμί, predictive) 86.
μοι (dat.sing.masc.of ἐγώ, personal advantage) 123.
υἱός (nom.sing.masc.of υἱός, predicate nominative) 5.

Translation - *"The overcomer shall inherit these things: and I will be God to him and he will be a son to me."*

Comment: *Cf.* #'s 2454 and 426 for a study on overcoming and overcomers and inheritance. *Cf.* also #'s 4462, 1648 and 1386 to expand your research on inheritance.

The interpersonal relation between God and son emphasizes again the intimacy of verse 3. *Cf.* John 17:21; 15:13-15.

Heaven is described not only by its positive characteristics but also by what is excluded. We have the list of excluded elements in verses 8 and 27 and in Rev.22:15.

Verse 8 - *"But the fearful, and unbelieving, and the abominable, and murderers, and whoremongers, and sorcerers, and idolators, and all liars, shall have their part in the lake which burneth with fire and brimstone: which is the second death."*

τοῖς δὲ δειλοῖς καὶ ἀπίστοις καὶ ἐβδελυγμένοις καὶ φονεῦσιν καὶ πόρνοις καὶ φαρμάκοις καὶ εἰδωλολάτραις καὶ πᾶσιν τοῖς ψευδέσιν τὸ μέρος αὐτῶν ἐν τῇ λίμνῃ τῇ καιομένῃ πυρὶ καὶ θείῳ, ὅ ἐστιν ὁ θάνατος ὁ δεύτερος.

"But as for the cowardly, the faithless, the polluted, as for murderers, fornicators, sorcerers, idolaters, and all liars, their lot shall be in the lake that burns with fire and brimstone, which is the second death." . . . *RSV*

τοῖς (dat.pl.masc.of the article in agreement with δειλοῖς) 9.
δὲ (adversative conjunction) 11.
δειλοῖς (dat.pl.masc.of δειλός, reference) 756.
καὶ (adjunctive conjunction joining nouns) 14.
ἀπίστοις (dat.pl.masc.of ἄπιστος, reference) 1231.
καὶ (adjunctive conjunction joining nouns) 14.
ἐβδελυγμένοις (perf.pass.part.dat.pl.masc.of βδελύσσομαι, substantival, reference) 3849.
καὶ (adjunctive conjunction joining substantives) 14.
φονεῦσιν (dat.pl.masc.of φονεύς, reference) 1405.
καὶ (adjunctive conjunction joining nouns) 14.
πόρνοις (dat.pl.masc.of πόρνος, reference) 4140.
καὶ (adjunctive conjunction joining nouns) 14.

#5424 φαρμάκοις (dat.pl.masc.of φαρμακός, reference).

King James Version

sorcerer - Rev.21:8; 22:15.

Revised Standard Version

sorcerer - Rev.21:8; 22:15.

Meaning: Cf. φαρμακεία (#4457) One who uses magical arts; a sorcerer. - Rev.21:8; 22:15.

καὶ (adjunctive conjunction joining nouns) 14.
εἰδωλολάτραις (dat.pl.masc.of εἰδωλολάτρης, reference) 4142.
καὶ (adjunctive conjunction joining nouns) 14.
πᾶσιν (dat.pl.masc.of πᾶς, in agreement with ψευδέσιν) 67.
τοῖς (dat.pl.masc.of the article in agreement with ψευδέσιν) 9.
ψευδέσιν (dat.pl.masc.of ψευδής, reference) 3096.
τὸ (nom.sing.neut.of the article in agreement with μέρος) 9.
μέρος (nom.sing.neut.of μέρος, subject of ἔσται understood) 240.
αὐτῶν (gen.pl.masc.of αὐτός, possession) 16.
ἐν (preposition with the locative of place) 80.
τῇ (loc.sing.fem.of the article in agreement with λίμνη) 9.
λίμνῃ (loc.sing.fem.of λίμνη, place) 2041.
τῇ (loc.sing.fem.of the article in agreement with καιομένη) 9.
καιομένῃ (pres.mid.part.loc.sing.fem.of καίω, adjectival, emphatic attributive position, ascriptive, in agreement with λίμνη) 453.
πυρὶ (instru.sing.neut.of πῦρ, means) 298.
καὶ (adjunctive conjunction joining nouns) 14.
θείῳ (instru.sing.neut.of θεῖον, means) 2619.
ὅ (nom.sing.neut.of ὅς, relative pronoun, subject of ἐστιν) 65.
ἐστιν (3d.per.sing.pres.ind.of εἰμί, static) 86.
ὁ (nom.sing.masc.of the article in agreement with θάνατος) 9.
θάνατος (nom.sing.masc.of θάνατος, predicate nominative) 381.
ὁ (nom.sing.masc.of the article in agreement with δεύτερος) 9.
δεύτερος (nom.sing.masc.of δεύτερος, in agreement with θάνατος) 1371.

Translation - "But as for the cowards and skeptics and boors and killers and libertines and sorcerers and idolaters and all the liars — their place is in the lake burning with fire and brimstone, which is the second death."

Comment: Cowards are excluded (Psalm 23:4; 27:1; 1 John 4:18) for where perfect love is, there is no fear. Skeptics, with their worship of William James and his "tough minded" induction will not be there to find the empirical evidence that they sought in life. The unregenerate impatience for "proof" that could not afford to have faith and wait until God got ready to present it, will never find it while, ironically enough, the "babes" (Mt.11:25) and little children (Mt.18:3) and "fools" (1 Cor.3:18) who believed what they had not yet seen (John 20:29) will be there with the opportunity for chemical analysis, if they wish (!) of the golden streets.

Of course knowledge is grounded in sensation if one waits until he has seen it all. The skeptic's sin, which will get him damned, is his arrogance, that since he has not seen it, it does not exist! He must believe only what he has seen. No one else is a reliable witness.

The murderers (1 John 2:9; 3:15; 4:20), fornicators and adulterers, witches, idolators and all the liars (note the extra emphasis here - *cf.* 1 John 2:22) will also be excluded. Fruitful research on all of these groups is available by referring to their respective numbers. John omits the verb with τὸ μέρος. The lake of fire is identified as the second death. It holds no fears for the happy and holy participants in the first resurrection (Rev.20:6).

We are now to be treated to a breathtaking description of the heavenly city, the New Jerusalem. This description occupies the remainder of the Revelation proper - Rev.21:9-22:5.

The New Jerusalem

(Revelation 21:9-22:5)

Verse 9 - "And there came unto me one of the seven angels which had the seven vial full of the seven last plagues, and talked with me, saying, Come hither, I will shew thee the bride, the Lamb's wife."

Καὶ ἦλθεν εἷς ἐκ τῶν ἑπτὰ ἀγγέλων τῶν ἐχόντων τὰς ἑπτὰ φιάλας, τῶν γεμόντων τῶν ἑπτὰ πληγῶν τῶν ἐσχάτων, καὶ ἐλάλησεν μετ' ἐμοῦ λέγων, Δεῦρο, δείξω σοι τὴν νύμφην τὴν γυναῖκα τοῦ ἀρνίου.

"Then came one of the seven angels who had the seven bowls full of the seven last plagues, and spoke to me, saying, 'Come, I will show you the Bride, the wife of the Lamb.' " . . . RSV

Καὶ (continuative conjunction) 14.

ἦλθεν (3d.per.sing.aor.ind.of ἔρχομαι, constative) 146.

εἷς (nom.sing.masc.of εἷς, subject of ἦλθεν and ἐλάλησεν) 469.

ἐκ (preposition with the partitive genitive) 19.

τῶν (gen.pl.masc.of the article in agreement with ἀγγέλων) 9.

ἑπτὰ (numeral) 1024.

ἀγγέλων (gen.pl.masc.of ἄγγελος, partitive genitive) 96.

τῶν (gen.pl.masc.of the article in agreement with ἐχόντων) 9.

ἐχόντων (pres.act.part.gen.pl.masc.of ἔχω, adjectival, emphatic attributive postion, restrictive, in agreement with ἀγγέλων) 82.

τὰς (acc.pl.fem.of the article in agreement with φιάλας) 9.

ἑπτὰ (numeral) 1024.

φιάλας (acc.pl.fem.of φιάλη, direct object of ἐχόντων) 5348.

τῶν (gen.pl.fem.of the article in agreement with γεμόντων) 9.

γεμόντων (pres.act.participle, gen.pl.fem.of γέμω) 1457.

τῶν (abl.pl.fem.of the article in agreement with πληγῶν) 9.
ἑπτὰ (numeral) 1024.
πληγῶν (abl.pl.fem.of πληγή, source) 2421.
τῶν (abl.pl.fem.of the article in agreement with ἐσχάτων) 9.
ἐσχάτων (abl.pl.fem.of ἔσχατος, in agreement with πληγῶν) 496.
καὶ (adjunctive conjunction joining verbs) 14.
ἐλάλησεν (3d.per.sing.aor.act.ind.of λαλέω, ingressive) 815.
μετ' (preposition with the genitive, association) 50.
ἐμοῦ (gen.sing.masc.of ἐμοῦ, association) 1267.
λέγων (pres.act.part.nom.sing.masc.of λέγω, recitative) 66.
Δεῦρο (adverbial interjection, imperative) 1304.
δείξω (1st.per.sing.fut.act.ind.of δείκνυμι, predictive) 359.
σοι (dat.sing.masc.of σύ, indirect object of δείξω) 104.
τὴν (acc.sing.fem.of the article in agreement with νύμφην) 9.
νύμφην (acc.sing.fem.of νύμφη, direct object of δείξω) 898.
τὴν (acc.sing.fem.of the article in agreement with γυναῖκα) 9.
γυναῖκα (acc.sing.fem.of γυνή, in apposition with νύμφην) 103.
τοῦ (gen.sing.neut.of the article in agreement with ἀρνίου) 9.
ἀρνίου (gen.sing.neut.of ἀρνίον, relationship) 2923.

Translation - "And one of the seven angels who had the seven bowls which were full of seven last plagues approached and began to talk to me, saying, 'Come. I will show you the bride, the wife of the Lamb.'"

Comment: It is interesting that an angel who had been involved in visiting the punishment of God uponthe unsaved would be just as ready to conduct a tour of the Holy City. In verse 2, the city was described as prepared like a bride. Now the city is identified as the Bride. It has been traditional to refer to some superior group of the family of God as "the Bride of Christ." Yet νύμφη (#898) is never used in this sense, except perhaps in Rev.22:17. The group normally referred to as νύμφη (#898) is called ἡ γυνή (#103) in Rev.19:7. Yet in Rev.21:9 γυναῖκα (#103) is associated in apposition with τὴν νύμφην (#898). It is clear that in Rev.19:7 we have a group of saints. Thus apparently the terms "bride" (νύμφη) and "wife" (γυνή) are applied both to the saints and to the city.

Verse 10 - "And he carried me away in the spirit to a great and high mountain and shewed me that great city, the holy Jerusalem, descending out of heaven from God."

καὶ ἀπήνεγκέν με ἐν πνεύματι ἐπὶ ὄρος μέγα καὶ ὑψηλόν, καὶ ἔδειξέν μοι τὴν πόλιν τὴν ἁγίαν Ἰερουσαλὴμ καταβαίνουσαν ἐκ τοῦ οὐρανοῦ ἀπὸ τοῦ θεοῦ.

"And in the Spirit he carried me away to a great, high mountain, and showed me the holy city Jerusalem coming down out of heaven from God, ..."... RSV

καὶ (adjunctive conjunction joining verbs) 14.
ἀπήνεγκέν (3d.per.sing.aor.act.ind.of ἀποφέρω, constative) 2583.
με (acc.sing.masc.of ἐγώ, direct object of ἀπήνεγκέν) 123.

ἐν (preposition with the instrumental, means) 80.
πνεύματι (instru.sing.neut.of πνεῦμα, means) 83.
ἐπὶ (preposition with the accusative, extent, place) 47.
ὄρος (acc.sing.neut.of ὄρος, place) 357.
μέγα (acc.sing.neut.of μέγας, in agreement with ὄρος) 184.
καὶ (adjunctive conjunction joining adjectives) 14.
ὑψηλόν (acc.sing.neut.of ὑψηλός, in agreement with ὄρος) 358.
καὶ (adjunctive conjunction joining verbs) 14.
ἔδειξέν (3d.per.sing.aor.act.ind.of δείκνυμι, ingressive) 359.
μοι (dat.sing.masc.of ἐγώ, indirect object of ἔδειξεν) 123.
τὴν (acc.sing.fem.of the article in agreement with πόλιν) 9.
πόλιν (acc.sing.fem.of πόλις, direct object of ἔδειξεν) 243.
τὴν (acc.sing.fem.of the article in agreement with ἁγίαν) 9.
ἁγίαν (acc.sing.fem.of ἅγιος, in agreement with Ἰερουσαλήμ) 84.
Ἰερουσαλήμ (acc.sing.fem.of Ἰεροσολύμων, apposition) 141.
καταβαίνουσαν (pres.act.part.acc.sing.fem.of καταβαίνω, adjectival,
predicate position, ascriptive, in agreement with πόλιν) 324.
ἐκ (preposition with the ablative of separation) 19.
τοῦ (abl.sing.masc.of the article in agreement with οὐρανοῦ) 9.
οὐρανοῦ (abl.sing.masc.of οὐρανός, separation) 254.
ἀπὸ (preposition with the ablative of source) 70.
τοῦ (abl.sing.masc.of the article in agreement with θεοῦ) 9.
θεοῦ (abl.sing.masc.of θεός, source) 124.

Translation - *"And he carried me away in the Spirit unto a mountain, great and high, and he began to show to me the city, the holy Jerusalem, coming down out of heaven from God."*

Comment: There is little need to comment beyond what the text says. God is the source of this city. It was built in heaven and now is ready for occupancy upon earth. That the New Jerusalem is in earthly city, heavenly in its origin and character, but earthly in its situation is clear. *Cf.* John 14:1-3. We are reminded of Ezek.40:2.

Verse 11 - "Having the glory of God: and her light was like unto a stone most precious, even like a jasper stone, clear as crystal;"

ἔχουσαν τὴν δόξαν τοῦ θεοῦ. ὁ φωστὴρ αὐτῆς ὅμοιος λίθῳ τιμιωτάτῳ, ὡς λίθῳ ἰάσπιδι κρυσταλλίζοντι,

"having the glory of God, its radiance like a most rare jewel, like a jasper, clear as crystal." . . . RSV

ἔχουσαν (pres.act.part.acc.sing.fem.of ἔχω, adjectival, predicate position, ascriptive, in agreement with πόλιν) 82.
τὴν (acc.sing.fem.of the article in agreement with δόξαν) 9.
δόξαν (acc.sing.fem.of δόξα, direct object of ἔχουσαν) 361.
τοῦ (gen.sing.masc.of the article in agreement with θεοῦ) 9.

θεοῦ (gen.sing.masc.of θεός, description) 124.
ὁ (nom.sing.masc.of the article in agreement with φωστήρ) 9.
φωστήρ (nom.sing.masc.of φωστήρ, subject of ἔστιν understood) 4557.
αὐτῆς (gen.sing.fem.of αὐτός, possession) 16.
ὅμοιος (nom.sing.masc.of ὅμοιος, predicate adjective) 923.
λίθῳ (dat.sing.masc.of λίθος, comparison) 290.
τιμιωτάτῳ (dat.sing.masc.superlative of τίμιος, in agreement with λίθῳ) 3070.
ὡς (comparative particle) 128.
ἰάσπιδι (dat.sing.fem.of ἴασπις, comparison) 5339.

#5425 κρυσταλλίζοντι (pres.act.part.dat.sing.masc.of κρυσταλλίζω, adjectival, predicate position, restrictive, in agreement with ἰάσπιδι).

King James Version

clear as crystal - Rev.21:11.

Revised Standard Version

clear as crystal - Rev.21:11.

Meaning: Cf. κρύσταλλας (#5345). Hence, to shine with the clarity and brightness of crystal. To be transparent. Found only here in Greek literature - Rev.21:11.

Translation - "having the glory of God. Her light was like a most precious stone. It looked like a clear as crystal jasper."

Comment: τιμιωτάτῳ is an elative superlative, *i.e.* of the highest possible degree of comparison. The first clause belongs to the preceding sentence. The Holy City, coming down from heaven had the glory of God. The first thing that impressed John was the radiance of her light. He struggled for words — like the most costly of precious stones. Perhaps like a jasper (some think the word means a diamond). Clear as crystal.

So much for the general appearance of the city. The detailed description follows in the remainder of the chapter.

Verse 12 - "And had a wall great and high and had twelve gates, and at the gates twelve angels, and names written thereon, which are the names of the twelve tribes of the children of Israel."

ἔχουσα τεῖχος μέγα καὶ ὑψηλόν, ἔχουσα πυλῶνας δώδεκα, καὶ ἐπὶ τοῖς πυλῶσιν ἀγγέλους δώδεκα, καὶ ὀνόματα ἐπιγεγραμμένα ἅ ἐστιν τῶν δώδεκα φυλῶν υἱῶν Ἰσραήλ.

"It had a great, high wall, with twelve gates, and at the gates twelve angels, and on the gates the names of the twelve tribes of the sons of Israel were inscribed;" .. . RSV

ἔχουσα (pres.act.part.nom.sing.fem.of ἔχω, joined with πόλιν) 82.

τεῖχος (acc.sing.neut.of τεῖχος, direct object of ἔχουσα) 3196.
μέγα (acc.sing.neut.of μέγας, in agreement with τεῖχος) 184.
καὶ (adjunctive conjunction joining adjectives) 14.
ὑφηλόν (acc.sing.neut.of ὑφαλός, in agreement with τεῖχος) 358.
ἔχουσα (pres.act.part.nom.sing.fem.of ἔχω, joined with πόλιν) 82.
πυλῶνας (acc.pl.masc.of πυλών, direct object of ἔχουσα) 1610.
δώδεκα (numeral) 820.
καὶ (adjunctive conjunction joining nouns) 14.
ἐπὶ (preposition with the locative, place) 47.
τοῖς (loc.pl.masc.of the article in agreement with πυλῶσιν) 9.
πυλῶσιν (loc.pl.masc.of πυλών, place) 1610.
ἀγγέλους (acc.pl.masc.of ἄγγελος, direct object of ἔχουσα) 96.
δώδεκα (numeral) 820.
καὶ (adjunctive conjunction joining nouns) 14.
ὀνόματα (acc.pl.neut.of ὄνομα, direct object of ἔχουσα) 108.
ἐπιγεγραμμένα (perf.pass.part.acc.pl.neut.of ἐπιγράφω, adjectival, predicate position, restrictive, in agreement with ὀνόματα) 2853.
ἅ (nom.pl.neut.of ὅς, relative pronoun, subject of ἐστιν) 65.
ἐστιν (3d.per.sing.pres.ind.of εἰμί, aoristic) 86.
τῶν (gen.pl.fem.of the article in agreement with φυλῶν) 9.
δώδεκα (numeral) 820.
φυλῶν (gen.pl.fem.of φυλή, description) 1313.
υἱῶν (gen.pl.masc.of υἱός, description) 5.
Ἰσραήλ (gen.sing.indeclin. of Ἰσραήλ, relationship) 165.

Translation - ". . . having a great and high wall with twelve gates, and at the gates twelve angels, and on the gates inscribed names, which names are those of the twelve sons of Israel."

Comment: Robertson says that ἔχουσα in verse 12 is both proper gender and case (Robertson, *Grammar*, 414). I agree that the feminine gender is correct, but the participle is joined to πόλιν (verse 10) as is ἔχουσαν (verse 11), which is correct — accusative singular feminine. It would seem that in verse 12 we should have ἔχουσαν as in verse 11.

The city had the glory of God, and the wall and the twelve gates. Of course, the names are written, not upon the angels, but upon the gates. A high wall, twelve gates, twelve angel guards or sentries and on each gate the twelve names listed in Rev.7:1-8.

Since these gates are to be eternally open (verse 25), just why they should be there and what the function of the angels is, is not revealed. Certainly they do not act as guards since there will be no enemies.

Verse 13 - "On the east three gates; on the north three gates; on the south three gates; and on the west three gates."

ἀπὸ ἀνατολῆς πυλῶνες τρεῖς, καὶ ἀπὸ βορρᾶ πυλῶνας τρεῖς, καὶ ἀπὸ νότου πυλῶνας τρεῖς, καὶ ἀπὸ δυσμῶν πυλῶνες τρεῖς.

"on the east three gates, on the north three gates, on the south three gates, and on the west three gates." . . . RSV

ἀπό (preposition with the ablative, source) 70.
ἀνατολῆς (abl.sing.fem.of ἀνατολή, source) 138.
πυλῶνες (nom.pl.masc.of πυλών, nominative absolute) 1610.
τρεῖς (numeral) 1010.
καὶ (adjunctive conjunction joining prepositional phrases) 14.
ἀπό (preposition with the ablative, source) 70.
βορρᾶ (abl.sing.masc.of βορρᾶς, source) 2513.
πυλῶνες (nom.pl.masc.of πυλών, nominative absolute) 1610.
τρεῖς (numeral) 1010.
καὶ (adjunctive conjunction joining prepositional phrases) 14.
ἀπό (preposition with the ablative, source) 70.
νότου (abl.sing.masc.of νότος, source) 1015.
πυλῶνες (nom.pl.masc.of πυλών, nominative absolute) 1610.
τρεῖς (numeral) 1010.
καὶ (adjunctive conjunction joining prepositional phrases) 14.
ἀπό (preposition with the ablative, source) 70.
δυσμῶν (abl.pl.fem.of δυσμή, source) 729.
πυλῶνες (nom.pl.masc.of πυλών, nominative absolute) 1610.
τρεῖς (numeral) 1010.

Translation - *"From the east three gates; and from the north three gates; and from the south three gates; and from the west three gates."*

Comment: ἀπό with the ablative suggests the idea of the appearance of the city wall as one approaches from the east, north, south or west. Just why δυσμῶν should be plural, while the others are singular we do not know.

Verse 14 - *"And the wall of the city had twelve foundations, and on them the names of the twelve apostles of the Lamb."*

καὶ τὸ τεῖχος τῆς πόλεως ἔχων θεμελίους δώδεκα, καὶ ἐπ᾽ αὐτῶν δώδεκα ὀνόματα τῶν δώδεκα ἀποστόλων τοῦ ἀρνίου.

"And the wall of the city had twelve foundations, and on them the twelve names of the twelve apostles of the Lamb." . . . RSV

καὶ (continuative conjunction) 14.
τὸ (nom.sing.neut.of the article in agreement with τεῖχος) 9.
τεῖχος (nom.sing.neut.of τεῖχος, joined with ἔχων) 3196.
τῆς (gen.sing.fem.of the article in agreement with πόλεως) 9.
πόλεως (gen.sing.fem.of πόλις, description) 243.
ἔχων (pres.act.part.nom.sing.masc.of ἔχω) 82.
θεμελίους (acc.pl.masc.of θεμέλιος, direct object of ἔχων) 2143.
δώδεκα (numeral) 820.
καὶ (continuative conjunction) 14.

ἐπ' (preposition with the genitive of place description) 47.
αὐτῶν (gen.pl.masc.of αὐτός, place description) 16.
δώδεκα (numeral) 820.
ὀνόματα (acc.pl.neut.of ὄνομα, direct object of ἔχων) 108.
τῶν (gen.pl.masc.of the article in agreement with ἀποστόλων) 9.
δώδεκα (numeral) 820.
ἀποστόλων (gen.pl.masc.of ἀπόστολος, description) 844.
τοῦ (gen.sing.neut.of the article in agreement with ἀρνίου) 9.
ἀρνίου (gen.sing.neut.of ἀρνίον, relationship) 2923.

Translation - "And the wall of the city has twelve foundations, and upon them twelve names of the twelve Apostles of the Lamb."

Comment: ἔχων, the present participle with τὸ τεῖχος is for ἔχει. In Acts 16:26 the accusative plural of θεμέλιος is τὰ θεμέλια, as though neuter, though in Heb.11:10 and Rev.21:19 we have the masculine as in verse 14.

Abraham had the eye of faith on this city (Heb.11:10) and was content therefore to dwell in tents. The twelve Apostles, previously mentioned as judges over Israel (Mt.19:28; Lk.22:3) will have their names on the foundations of the city. *Cf.* Eph.2:19,20. The household of God is built upon the Apostles and we will live forever in a beautiful city also built upon foundations that bear their names. Thus we see the connection between the covenants which God made with Abraham, by reason of which Israel is assured a national future and the covenant of grace by which His elect, even those from among the Gentiles are also assured everlasting life. This is the essence of the Judeo-Christian revelation.

Verse 15 - "And he that talked with me had a golden reed to measure the city, and the gates thereof, and the wall thereof."

Καὶ ὁ λαλῶν μετ' ἐμοῦ εἶχεν μέτρον κάλαμον χρυσοῦν, ἵνα μετρήσῃ τὴν πόλιν καὶ τοὺς πυλῶνας αὐτῆς καὶ τὸ τεῖχος αὐτῆς.

"And he who talked to me had a measuring rod of gold to measure the city and its gates and walls." . . . RSV

Καὶ (continuative conjunction) 14.
ὁ (nom.sing.masc.of the article in agreement with λαλῶν) 9.
λαλῶν (pres.act.part.nom.sing.masc.of λαλέω, substantival, subject of εἶχεν) 815.
μετ' (preposition with the genitive of association) 50.
ἐμοῦ (gen.sing.masc.of ἐμοῦ, association) 1267.
εἶχεν (3d.per.sing.imp.act.ind.of ἔχω, progressive description) 82.
μέτρον (acc.sing.neut.of μέτρον, direct object of εἶχεν) 643.
κάλαμον (acc.sing.masc.of κάλαμος, in apposition) 910.
χρυσοῦν (acc.sing.masc.of χρύσεος, in agreement with κάλαμον) 4828.
ἵνα (conjunction with the subjunctive, purpose) 114.
μετρήσῃ (3d.per.sing.aor.act.subj.of μετρέω, purpose) 644.

τὴν (acc.sing.fem.of the article in agreement with πόλιν) 9.
πόλιν (acc.sing.fem.of πόλις, direct object of μετρήσῃ) 243.
καὶ (adjunctive conjunction joining nouns) 14.
τοὺς (acc.pl.masc.of the article in agreement with πυλῶνας) 9.
πυλῶνας (acc.pl.masc.of πυλών, direct object of μετρήσῃ) 1610.
αὐτῆς (gen.sing.fem.of αὐτός, description) 16.
καὶ (adjunctive conjunction joining nouns) 14.
τὸ (acc.sing.neut.of the article in agreement with τεῖχος) 9.
τεῖχος (acc.sing.neut.of τεῖχος, direct object of μετρήσῃ) 3196.
αὐτῆς (gen.sing.fem.of αὐτός, description) 16.

Translation - *"And the one speaking with me was holding a golden measuring
stick, in order to measure the city and her gates and her wall."*

Comment: *Cf.* Ezekiel 40:3,5.

Verse 16 - *"And the city lieth foursquare, and the length is as large as the breadth;
and he measured the city with the reed, twelve thousand furlongs. The length
and the breadth and the height of it are equal."*

καὶ ἡ πόλις τετράγωνος κεῖται, καὶ τό μῆκος αὐτῆς ὅσον τό πλάτος. καὶ
ἐμέτρησεν τὴν πόλιν τῷ καλάμῳ ἐπὶ σταδίων δώδεκα χιλιάδων, τὸ μῆκος καὶ
τὸ πλάτος καὶ τὸ ἤφος αὐτῆς ἴσα ἐστίν.

*"The city lies foursquare, its length the same as its breadth; and he measured
the city with his rod, twelve thousand stadia; its length and breadth and height
are equal."* . . . RSV

καὶ (continuative conjunction) 14.
ἡ (nom.sing.fem.of the article in agreement with πόλις) 9.
πόλις (nom.sing.fem.of πόλις, subject of κεῖται) 243.

#5426 τετράγωνος (nom.sing.fem.of τετράγωνος, in agreement with πόλις).

King James Version

foursquare - Rev.21:16.

Revised Standard Version

foursquare - Rev.21:16.

Meaning: A combination of τέτρα and γωνία (#567). Four cornered. Four
quarters; four equal angles. Hence, square - Rev.21:16.

κεῖται (3d.per.sing.pres.ind.of κεῖμαι, progressive duration) 295.
καὶ (inferential conjunction) 14.
τὸ (nom.sing.neut.of the article in agreement with μῆκος) 9.
μῆκος (nom.sing.neut.of μῆκος, subject of ἐστιν understood) 4488.
αὐτῆς (gen.sing.fem.of αὐτός, description) 16.
ὅσον (nom.sing.neut.of ὅσος, predicate adjective) 660.

τό (nom.sing.neut.of the article in agreement with πλάτος) 9.

πλάτος (nom.sing.neut.of πλάτος, subject of ἔστιν understood) 4487.

καὶ (continuative conjunction) 14.

ἐμέτρησεν (3d.per.sing.aor.act.ind.of μετρέω, ingressive) 644.

τὴν (acc.sing.fem.of the article in agreement with πόλιν) 9.

πόλιν (acc.sing.fem.of πόλις, direct object of ἐμέτρησεν) 243.

τῷ (instru.sing.masc.of the article in agreement with καλάμῳ) 9.

καλάμῳ (instru.sing.masc.of κάλαμος, means) 910.

ἐπὶ (preposition with the genitive, description of measure) 47.

σταδίων (gen.pl.masc.of στάδιος, description of measure) 1127.

δώδεκα (numeral) 820.

χιλιάδων (gen.pl.fem.of χίλιος, description of measure) 2536.

τό(nom.sing.neut.of the article in agreement with μῆκος) 9.

μῆκος (nom.sing.neut.of μῆκος, subject of ἐστίν) 4488.

καὶ (adjunctive conjunction joining nouns) 14.

τὸ (nom.sing.neut.of the article in agreement with πλάτος) 9.

πλάτος (nom.sing.neut.of πλάτος, subject of ἐστίν) 4487.

καὶ (adjuntive conjunction joining nouns) 14.

τὸ (nom.sing.neut.of the article in agreement with ὕψος) 9.

ὕψος (nom.sing.neut.of ὕψος, subject of ἐστίν) 1858.

αὐτῆς (gen.sing.fem.of αὐτός, possession) 16.

ἴσα (nom.pl.neut.of ἴσος, predicate adjective) 1323.

ἐστίν (3d.per.sing.pres.ind.of εἰμί, aoristic) 86.

Translation - "And the city is laid out foursquare: thus the length is as great as the width. And he measured the city with a reed at twelve thousand furlongs; the length and the width and the height of it are equal."

Comment: Note ἴσα the neuter plural predicate adjective with the singular ἐστίν, which is good Greek. The city is thus a cube, a little more than 1377 miles in length, width and height. The length and width are not hard for us to grasp. There are many areas, 1000 miles or more in length that are heavily populated. Boston-Miami, Chicago-New York and San Diego-San Francisco are examples. Another megapolis is developing linking Corpus Christi, Austin, Dallas, Fort Worth, Oklahoma City, Kansas City, Omaha, St. Louis and Chicago. These urban developments give us some idea of the picture. But the height of the New Jerusalem staggers the imagination.

Verse 17 - "And he measured the wall thereof, an hundred and forty and four cubits, according to the measure of a man, that is, of the angel."

καὶ ἐμέτρησεν τὸ τεῖχος αὐτῆς ἑκατὸν τεσσαράκοντα τεσσάρων πηχῶν, μέτρον ἀνθρώπου, ὅ ἐστιν ἀγγέλου.

"He also measured its wall, a hundred and forty-four cubits by a man's measure, that is, an angel's." . . . RSV

καὶ (continuative conjunction) 14.

ἐμέτρησεν (3d.per.sing.aor.act.ind.of μετρέω ingressive) 644.
τὸ (acc.sing.neut.of the article in agreement with τεῖχος) 9.
τεῖχος (acc.sing.neut.of τεῖχος, direct object of ἐμέτρησεν) 3196.
αὐτῆς (gen.sing.fem.of αὐτός, possession) 16.
ἑκατὸν (numeral) 1035.
τεσσαράκοντα (numeral) 333.
τεσσάρων (gen.pl.masc.of τέσσαρες, in agreement with πηχῶν) 1508.
πηχῶν (gen.pl.masc.of πῆχος, measurement) 623.
μέτρον (acc.sing.neut.of μέτρον, extent) 643.
ἀνθρώπου (gen.sing.masc.of ἄνθρωπος, description) 341.
ὅ (nom.sing.masc.of ὅς, relative pronoun, subject of ἐστιν) 65.
ἐστιν (3d.per.sing.pres.ind.of εἰμί, aoristic) 86.
ἀγγέλου (gen.sing.masc.of ἄγγελος, description) 96.

Translation - "And he measured her wall at one hundred, forty-four cubits, as men measure, which is how the angel measured."

Comment: The cubit is equal to eighteen inches. Thus the wall was two hundred, sixteen feet high. This is not relatively high, since the city within the walls is 1377 miles high.

Ancient China built her wall and East Germany has her iron curtain. Boundary impedimenta, either physical or legal, or both are designed by men for protection from invasion or, in the case of the iron curtain between East and West Europe to prevent emigration to the West. The wall of the New Jerusalem cannot be thought of in these terms. There will be no need for protection since there will be no enemies, and the gates will never close.

The description of verse 18 tends to leave us breathless with anticipation. Let every Christian reflect upon the fact that we are going to see this city and live in it. And let us give thanks and pledge total obedience to the will of Him Who has built this beautiful city.

Verse 18 - "And the building of the wall of it was of jasper: and the city was pure gold, like unto clear glass."

καὶ ἡ ενδώμησις τοῦ χείχους αὐτῆς ἴασπις, καὶ ἡ πόλις χρυσίον καθαρὸν ὅμοιον ὑάλω καθαρῷ.

"The wall was built of jasper, while the city was pure gold, clear as glass." . . . RSV

καὶ (continuative conjunction) 14.
ἡ (nom.sing.fem.of the article in agreement with ἐνδώμησις) 9.

#5427 ἐνδώμησις (nom.sing.fem.of ἐνδώμησις, subject of ἐστιν understood).

     King James Version

building - Rev.21:18.

Revised Standard Version

built - Rev.21:28.

Meaning: Cf. ἐνδομέω - "to build in" - Hence, construction; the manner in which something is built - Rev.21:18.

τοῦ (gen.sing.neut.of the article in agreement with τείχους) 9.
τείχους (gen.sing.neut.of τεῖχος, description) 3196.
αὐτῆς (gen.sing.fem.of αὐτός, description) 16.
ἴασπις (nom.sing.fem.of ἴασπις, predicate nominative) 5339.
καὶ (continuative conjunction) 14.
ἡ (nom.sing.fem.of the article in agreement with πόλις) 9.
πόλις (nom.sing.fem.of πόλις, subject of ἐστιν understood) 243.
χρυσίον (nom.sing.neut.of χρυσίον, predicate nominative) 3006.
καθαρὸν (nom.sing.neut.of καθαρός, in agreement with χρυσίον) 431.
ὅμοιον (nom.sing.neut.of ὅμοιος, in agreement with χρυσίον) 923.

#**5428** ὑάλῳ (dat.sing.masc.of ὕαλος, comparison).

King James Version

glass - Rev.21:18,21.

Revised Standard Version

glass - Rev.21:18,21.

Meaning: Any stone as transparent as glass - Rev.21:18,21. Perhaps related to ὑέτος (#3327). As clear as a raindrop.

καθαρῷ (dat.sing.masc.of καθαρός, in agreement with ὑάλῳ) 431.

Translation - "And the building material of her wall was jasper; and the city was of pure gold ike clear glass."

Comment: *Cf.* #5339. Whether jasper is the diamond or something else, the jasper walls, surrounding a pure gold city is beyond human imagination. Thus God is building a city out of that which men fight over on earth.

Next we come to a description of the foundation of the walls, of which there are twelve.

Verse 19 - "And the foundations of the wall of the city were garnished with all manner of precious stones. The first foundation was jasper; the second, sapphire; the third, a chalcedony; the fourth, an emerald."

οἱ θεμέλιοι τοῦ τείχους τῆς πόλεως παντὶ λίθῳ τιμίῳ κεκοσμημένοι. ὁ θεμέλιος ὁ πρῶτος ἴασπις, ὁ δεύτερος σάπφιρος, ὁ τρίτος χαλκηδών, ὁ τέταρτος σμάραγδος,

"The foundations of the wall of the city were adorned with every jewel; the first

was jasper, the second sapphire, the third agate, the fourth emerald, . . . " . . .
RSV

οἱ (nom.pl.masc.of the article in agreement with θεμέλιοι) 9.
θεμέλιοι (nom.pl.masc.of θεμέλιος, subject of verb understood) 2143.
τοῦ (gen.sing.neut.of the article in agreement with τείχους) 9.
τείχους (gen.sing.neut.of τεῖχος, description) 3196.
τῆς (gen.sing.fem.of the article in agreement with πόλεως) 9.
πόλεως (gen.sing.fem.of πόλις, description) 243.
παντὶ (instru.sing.masc.of πᾶς, in agreement with λίθῳ) 67.
λίθῳ (instru.sing.masc.of λίθος, means) 290.
τιμίῳ (instru.sing.masc.of τίμιος, in agreement with λίθῳ) 3070.
κεκοσμημένοι (perf.pass.part.nom.pl.masc.of κοσμέω, pluperfect periphrastic, with ἦν supplied) 1023.
ὁ (nom.sing.masc.of the article in agreement with θεμέλιος) 9.
θεμέλιος (nom.sing.masc.of θεμέλιος, nominative absolute) 2143.
ὁ (nom.sing.masc.of the article in agreement with πρῶτος) 9.
πρῶτος (nom.sing.masc.of πρῶτος, in agreement with θεμέλιος) 487.
ἴασπις (nom.sing.fem.of ἴασπις, predicate nomintive) 5339.
ὁ (nom.sing.masc.of the article in agreement with δεύτερος) 9.
δεύτερος (nom.sing.masc.of δεύτερος, nominative absolute) 1371.

#5429 σάπφιρος (nom.sing.masc.of σάπφιρος).

King James Version

sapphire - Rev.21:19.

Revised Standard Version

sapphire - Rev.21:19.

Meaning: A precious tone in various shades of blue; in hardness, next to the diamond - Rev.21:19.

ὁ (nom.sing.masc.of the article in agreement with τρίτος) 9.
τρίτος (nom.sing.masc.of τρίτος, nominative absolute) 1209.

#5430 χαλκηδών (nom.sing.masc.of χαλκηδών).

King James Version

chalcedony - Rev.21:19.

Revised Standard Version

agate - Rev.21:19.

Meaning: Chalcedony - a gem described by Pliny, h.n.37,5 (18), 72. A translucent variety of quartz in various colors - often milky and clouded - Rev.21:19.

ὁ (nom.sing.masc.of the article in agreement with τέταρτος) 9.
τέταρτος (nom.sing.masc.of τέταρτος, nominative absolute) 1129.

#5431 σμάραγδος (nom.sing.masc.of σμάραγδος).

King James Version

emerald - Rev.21:19.

Revised Standard Version

emerald - Rev.21:19.

Meaning: A transparent precious stone noted for its light green color - Rev.21:19. *Cf.*#5343.

Translation - "The foundations of the wall of the city had been decorated with every precious stone. The first foundation jasper; the second sapphire; the third chalcedony; the fourth emerald."

Comment: Comment at this point would be almost obscene! We shall have eternity to gaze at these beautiful foundation stones under the wall. Note that θεμέλιοι is plural and τείχους is singular. There is one wall with twelve foundations. The order of the foundations is not revealed. Are they placed side by side under the wall, or is there a vertical order? If so, is the order from top to bottom or bottom to top? Note that both the wall and the first foundation are of jasper (verses 18,19).

Verse 20 - "The fifth sardonyx; the sixth sardius; the seventh chrysolyte; the eighth, beryl; the ninth, a topaz;   the tenth, a chrysoprasus; the eleventh, a jacinth; tne twelfth, an amethyst."

ὁ πέμπτος σαρδόνυξ, ὁ ἕκτος σάρδιον, ὁ ἕβδομος χρυσόλιθος, ὁ ὄγδοος βήρυλλος, ὁ ἔνατος τοπάζιον, ὁ δέκατος χρυσόπρασος, ὁ ἑνδέκατος ὑάκινθος, ὁ δωδέκατος ἀμέθυστος.

"the fifth onyx, the sixth carnelian, the seventh chrysolite, the eighth beryl, the ninth topaz, the tenth chrysoprase, the eleventh jacinth, the twelfth amethyst.". . . RSV

ὁ (nom.sing.masc.of the article in agreement with πέμπτος) 9.
πέμπτος (nom.sing.masc.of πέμπτος, nominative absolute) 5353.

#5432 σαρδόνυξ (nom.sing.masc.of σαρδόνυξ)

King James Version

sardonyx - Rev.21:20.

Revised Standard Version

onyx - Rev.21:20.

Meaning: A gem mixing carnelion red (sard) with the white of the onyx - Rev.21:20.

ὁ (nom.sing.masc.of the article in agreement with ἕκτος) 9.
ἕκτος (nom.sing.masc.of ἕκτος, nominative absolute) 1317.

#5433 σάρδιον (nom.sing.neut.of σάρδιος)

King James Version

sardius - Rev.21:20.

Revised Standard Version

carnelian - Rev.21:20.

Meaning: sard, sardius - a precious stone of which these are two kinds. Theophr. *de lapid*, 16, 5 paragraph 30 ed. Schneid says, τοῦ γὰρ σαρδίου τὸ μὲν διαφανὲς ἐρύθρότερον δὲ καλεῖται θῆλυ, τὸ δε διαφανὲς μὲν μελάντερον δὲ καὶ ἄρσεν. The former of which is called carnelian, because flesh colored. - Rev.21:20.

ὁ (nom.sing.masc.of the article in agreement with ἕβδομος) 9.
ἕβδομος (nom.sing.masc.of ἕβδομος, nominative absolute) 2020.

#5434 χρυσόλιθος (nom.sing.masc.of χρυσόλιθος).

King James Version

chrysolite - Rev.21:20

Revised Standard Version

chrysolite - Rev.21:20.

Meaning: A combination of χρυσός (#192) and λίθος (#290). A precious stone of gold color. Some think it is our topaz, but *cf.* τοπάζιον (#5436), *infra*. Rev.21:20.

ὁ (nom.sing.masc.of the article in agreement with ὄγδοος) 9.
ὄγδοος (nom.sing.masc.of ὄγδοος, nominative absolute) 1841.

#5435 βήρυλλος (nom.sing.masc.of βήρυλλος).

King James Version

beryl - Rev.21:20.

Revised Standard Version

beryl - Rev.21:20.

Meaning: a precious stone of pale green color. "A mineral $Be_3Al_2Si_6O_{18}$ consisting of a silicate of beryllium and aluminum of great hardness and occurring in green, bluish green, yellow, pink, or white hexagonal prisms." (*Websters New Seventh Collegiate Dictionary*).

ὁ (nom.sing.masc.of the article in agreement with ἔνατος) 9.
ἔνατος (nom.sing.masc.of ἔνατος, nominative absolute) 1318.

#**5436** τοπάζιον (nom.sing.neut.of τοπάζξιον).

King James Version

topaz - Rev.21:20.

Revised Standard Version

topaz - Rev.21:20.

Meaning: "a mineral $Al_2SiO_4(F,OH)$ consisting of a silicate of aluminum and usa.occurring in white orthorhombic translucent or transparent crystals or in white translucent masses." (*Ibid.*) A greenish yellow precious stone - Rev.21:20.

ὁ (nom.sing.masc.of the article in agreement with δέκατος) 9.
δέκατος (nom.sing.masc.of δέκατος, nominative absolute) 1961.

#**5437** χρυσόπρασος (nom.sing.masc.of χρυσόπρασος).

King James Version

chryoprasas - Rev.21:20.

Revised Standard Version

chryoprase - Rev.21:20.

Meaning: A combination of χρυσός (#192) and πράσον - "a leek." A precious stone colored in translucent golden-green. Leek colored - Rev.21:20. "An apple-green chalcedony valued as a gem." (*Ibid.*)

ὁ (nom.sing.masc.of the article in agreement with ἐνδέκατος) 9.
ἐνδέκατος (nom.sing.masc.of ἐνδέκατος, nominative absolute) 1320.

#**5438** ὑάκινθος (nom.sing.masc.of ὑάκινθος).

King James Version

jacinth - Rev.21:20.

Revised Standard Version

jacinth - Rev.21:20.

Meaning: Cf.#5376. A precious stone of dark blue, verging toward black - Rev.21:20.

ὁ (nom.sing.masc.of the article in agreement with δωδέκατος) 9.

#5439 δωδέκατος (nom.sing.masc.of δωδέκατος, nominative absolute).

King James Version

twelfth - Rev.21:20.

Revised Standard Version

twelfth - Rev.21:20.

Meaning: A combination of δύo (#385) and δέκα (#1330). Twelfth - Rev.21:20.

#5440 ἀμέθυστος (nom.sing.fem.of ἀμέθυστος).

King James Version

amethyst - Rev.21:20.

Revised Standard Version

amethyst - Rev.21:20.

Meaning: "A clear purple or bluish violet variety of crystallized quartz much used as a jeweler's stone." (*Ibid.*) - Rev.21:20.

Translation - "the fifth, a red onyx, the sixth, a carnelian, the seventh, a chrysolite, the eighth, a beryl, the ninth, a topaz, the tenth, a chryoprase, the eleventh, a jacinth, the twelfth, an amethyst."

Comment: Thus the foundations under the wall of the city presented a combination of colors — purple, blue, green (#5339), blue (#5429), variegated (#5430), light green (#5431), red and white (#5432), flesh colored (#5433), gold color (#5434), pale green (#5435), greenish yellow (#5436), golden green (#5437), dark blue and black (#5438) and violet and purple (#5440). One cannot imagine the beauty of the foundation.

We do not know how thick the foundations were, nor how thick the wall above them. The wall was 216 feet high and 1377 miles long and wide. The city arose within the wall to a height of 1377 miles. That these measurements are to be thought of in human terms, not figuratively, is clear from verse 17.

There were three pearl gates on each side of the city, each of which led to a street of pure gold. When the light of the Lamb (Rev.21:23) shines on that wall, foundations and its gates, the effect will be eternally startling. The gates are described in

Verse 21 - "And the twelve gates were twelve pearls; every several gate was one pearl: and the street of the city was pure gold, as it were transparent glass."

καὶ οἱ δώδεκα πυλῶνες δώδεκα μαργαρῖται, ἀνὰ εἷς ἕκαστος τῶν πυλώνων ἦν ἐξ ἑνὸς μαργαρίτου. καὶ ἡ πλατεῖα τῆς πόλεως χρυσίον καθαρὸν ὡς ὕαλος διαυγής.

"And the twelve gates were twelve pearls, each of the gates made of a single pearl, and the street of the city was pure gold, transparent as glass." . . . RSV

καί (continuative conjunction) 14.

οἱ (nom.pl.masc.of the article in agreement with πυλῶνες) 9.

δώδεκα (numeral) 820.

πυλῶνες (nom.pl.masc.of πυλών, suspended subject) 1610.

δώδεκα (numeral) 820.

μαργαρῖται (nom.pl.masc.of μαργαρίτης, predicate nominative) 652.

ἀνά (adverbial) 1059.

εἷς (nom.sing.masc.of εἷς, parenthetic nominative with ἀνά) 469.

ἕκαστος (nom.sing.masc.of ἕκαστος, subject of ἦν) 1217.

τῶν (gen.pl.masc.of the article in agreement with πυλώνων) 9.

πυλώνων (gen.pl.masc.of πυλών, partitive genitive) 1610.

ἦν (3d.per.sing.imp.ind.of εἰμί, progressive description) 86.

ἐξ (preposition with the ablative of source) 19.

ἑνός (abl.sing.masc.of εἷς, in agreement with μαργαρίτου) 469.

μαργαρίτου (abl.sing.masc.of μαργαρίτης, source) 652.

καί (continuative conjunction) 14.

ἡ (nom.sing.fem.of the article in agreement with πλατεῖα) 9.

πλατεῖα (nom.sing.fem.of πλατεῖα, suspended subject) 568.

τῆς (gen.sing.fem.of the article in agreement with πόλεως) 9.

πόλεως (gen.sing.fem.of πόλις, description) 243.

χρυσίον (nom.sing.neut.of χρυσίον, predicate nominative) 3006.

καθαρόν (nom.sing.neut.of καθαρός, in agreement with χρυσίον) 431.

ὡς (comparative particle) 128.

ὕαλος (nom.sing.masc.of ὕαλός, subject of ἔστιν understood) 5428.

#**5441** διαυγής (nom.sing.masc.of διαυγής, in agreement with ὕαλος).

King James Version

transparent - Rev.21:21.

Revised Standard Version

transparent - Rev.21:21.

Meaning: A combination of διά (#118) and αὐγή (#3516). Hence that which allows the light to shine through. Transparent - Rev.21:21.

Translation - "And the twelve gates are twelve pearls; each one of the gates was made out of one pearl. And the street of the city was pure gold, as transparent as glass."

Comment: Note ἀνά εἷς in an adverbial distributive sense. *Cf.* καθ' εἷς - Mk.14:19; John 8:9; Rom.12:5. εἷς here is a parenthetic nominative with an adverb (the only place where ἀνά (#1059) is used as an adverb, not as a preposition). *Cf.* also ἐν καθ' ἔν in Rev.4:8.

The beauty of the sight is so great that John forgot to put in his verbs in the first and last clauses. That ἡ πλατεῖα, means "the main street" is probable since it is singular. In a city so large there are many streets. We learned in verse 18 that the entire city is made of gold. The magnificance of this scene is so great and super-earthly that any human attempt to describe it before the time, except in terms of the Revelation, becomes presumption. Yet God wishes us to have some conception of the city or He would not have described it for us. Since the wall is 216 feet high, above the twelve foundations, is each gate that high? Or are the gates archways such as are seen in many ancient cities? Is there a ramp sloping upward to the height of the twelve foundations? The saints some day will know by empirical investigation!

Metallurgists agree that pure, unalloyed gold is transparent. The city has many beautiful features. In verses 22 and 23 we learns of those things which it does not have.

Verse 22 - "And I saw no temple therein: for the Lord God Almighty and the Lamb are the temple of it."

Καὶ ναὸν οὐκ εἶδον ἐν αὐτῇ, ὁ γὰρ κύριος ὁ θεὸς ὁ παντοκράτωρ ναὸς αὐτῆς ἐστιν, καὶ τὸ ἀρνίον.

"And I saw no temple in the city, for its temple is the Lord God the Almighty and the Lamb." . . . RSV

Καὶ (adversative conjunction) 14.
ναὸν (acc.sing.masc.of ναός, direct object of εἶδον) 1447.
οὐκ (negative conjunction with the indicative) 130.
εἶδον (1st.per.sing.aor.act.ind.of ὁράω, constative) 144.
ἐν (preposition with the locative of place) 80.
αὐτῇ (loc.sing.fem.of αὐτός, place) 16.
ὁ (nom.sing.masc.of the article in agreement with κύριος) 9.
γὰρ (causal conjunction) 105.
κύριος (nom.sing.masc.of κύριος, subject of ἐστιν) 97.
ὁ (nom.sing.masc.of the article in agreement with θεὸς) 9.
θεὸς (nom.sing.masc.of θεός, in apposition) 124.
ὁ (nom.sing.masc.of the article in agreement with παντοκράτωρ) 9.
παντοκράτωρ (nom.sing.masc.of παντοκράτωρ, apposition) 4325.
ναὸς (nom.sing.masc.of ναός, predicate nominative) 1447.
αὐτῆς (gen.sing.fem.of αὐτός, possession) 16.
ἐστιν (3d.per.sing.pres.ind.of εἰμί, aoristic) 86.
καὶ (ascensive conjunction) 14.
τὸ (nom.sing.neut.of the article in agreement with ἀρνίον) 9.
ἀρνίον (nom.sing.neut.of ἀρνίον, subject of ἐστιν) 2923.

Translation - "But I saw no temple in her, because the Lord, the Almighty God, even the Lamb is her temple."

Comment: The temple on earth was provided that the saints might worship in symbol Him Whom we are not yet able to see. It represents Him in all of His sovereign characteristics. We find Him in the written Word and we worship Him in an earthly building. Thus our worship now is shadow of which He is the substance - the anti-type of which He is the type. When we see Him face to face we will no longer need a temple. Plato's Allegory of the Cave makes the point. If the saints in heaven worshipped in a temple they would be like Plato's prisoners in the cave who "recognize as reality nothing but the shadows . . . " instead of the reality. Plato's discussion of the need of the former occupants in the cave to become accustomed to the light outside the cave suggests that the saints in glory, worshipping the Lamb, not in a temple, will have an instantaneous adjustment to heaven's glory at the rapture (1 John 3:1-3; Phil.3:20,21). Enlightened by the Holy Spirit at regeneration to see the difference between shadows on the wall and reality, we will at last see Him with physical vision. Who will need a temple? Note that the Lamb is referred to as the Almighty Lord God. The Lamb, with His glorified body in which He suffered will be visible to you and we will learn from Him throughout eternity.

Verse 23 - "And the city had no need of the sun, neither of the moon to shine in it: for the glory of God did lighten it, and the Lamb is the light thereof."

καὶ ἡ πόλις οὐ χρείαν ἔχει τοῦ ἡλίου οὐδὲ τῆς σελήνης, ἵνα φαίνωσιν αὐτῇ, ἡ γὰρ δόξα τοῦ θεοῦ ἐφώτισεν αὐτήν, καὶ ὁ λύχνος αὐτῆς τὸ ἀρνίον.

"And the city has no need of sun or moon to shine upon it, for the glory of God is its light, and its lamp is the Lamb." . . . RSV

καὶ (continuative conjunction) 14.

ἡ (nom.sing.fem.of the article in agreement with πόλις) 9.

πόλις (nom.sing.fem.of πόλις, subject of ἔχει) 243.

οὐ (negative conjunction with the indicative) 130.

χρείαν (acc.sing.fem.of χρεία, direct object of ἔχει) 317.

ἔχει (3d.per.sing.pres.act.ind.of ἔχω, aoristic) 82.

τοῦ (gen.sing.masc.of the article in agreement with ἡλίου) 9.

ἡλίου (gen.sing.masc.of ἥλιος, description) 546.

οὐδὲ (disjunctive compound particle) 452.

τῆς (gen.sing.fem.of the article in agreement with σελήνης) 9.

σελήνης (gen.sing.fem.of σελήνη, description) 1505.

ἵνα (conjunction with the subjunctive, epexegetical) 114.

φαίνωσιν (3d.per.pl.pres.act.subj.of φαίνω) 100.

αὐτῇ (dat.sing.fem.of αὐτός, personal advantage) 16.

ἡ (nom.sing.fem.of the article in agreement with δόξα) 9.

γὰρ (causal conjunction) 105.

δόξα (nom.sing.fem.of δόξα, subject of ἐφώτισεν) 361.

τοῦ (gen.sing.masc.of the article in agreement with θεοῦ) 9.

θεοῦ (gen.sing.masc.of θεός, description) 124.

ἐφώτισεν (3d.per.sing.aor.act.ind.of φωτίζω, culminative) 1697.

αὐτήν (acc.sing.fem.of αὐτός, direct object of ἐφώτισεν) 16.
καί (continuative conjunction) 14.
ὁ (nom.sing.masc.of the article in agreement with λύχνος) 9.
λύχνος (nom.sing.masc.of λύχνος, predicate nominative) 454.
αὐτῆς (gen.sing.fem.of αὐτός, possession) 16.
τό (nom.sing.neut.of the article in agreement with ἀρνίον) 9.
ἀρνίον (nom.sing.neut.of ἀρνίον, subject of ἐστιν understood) 2923.

Translation - "And the city has no need of the sun nor of the moon, that they should shine on her, because the glory of God has illuminated her and the Lamb is her lamp."

Comment: It is not said that there is neither sun nor moon in the eternal order. The New Jerusalem has no need for them. The statement applies only to the city, not to the universe outside the city. Nor does it say that the sun and moon will not shine - only that their light will go unnoticed in the city because of her superior lighting system. She has been once illuminated, for all time (aorist tense in ἐφώτισεν) and the Lamb is the medium of illumination. He is not only "the Light of the world" (John 8:12), but He is also the Light of the New Jerusalem. God's glory illuminates as it shines through the Agent, Who is the Lamb. *Cf.* Rev.22:5). Outside the city, upon the earth and in other parts of the universe (solar systems, suns, moons, galaxies) the light will shine.

The ἵνα clause seems epexegetical or appositive, as it explains χρείαν. Though ἀρχηγός (#3013) is joined only with ζωη, πίστις and σωτηρία, is He not also ὁ ἀρχηγὸς τοῦ φωτός?

Verse 24 - "And the nations of them which are saved shall walk in the light of it: and the kings of the earth do bring their glory and honour into it."

καὶ περιπατήσουσιν τὰ ἔθνη διὰ τοῦ φωτὸς αὐτῆς. καὶ οἱ βασιλεῖς τῆς γῆς φέρουσιν τὴν δόξαν αὐτῶν εἰς αὐτήν.

"By its light shall the nations walk; and the kings of the earth shall bring their glory into it, . . . " . . . RSV

καί (continuative conjunction) 14.
περιπατήσουσιν (3d.per.pl.fut.act.ind.of περιπατέω, predictive) 384.
τά (nom.pl.neut.of the article in agreement with ἔθνη) 9.
ἔθνη (nom.pl.neut.of ἔθνος, subject of περιπατήσουσιν) 376.
διά (preposition with the ablative, means, with abstract ideas) 118.
τοῦ (abl.sing.neut.of the article in agreement with φωτός) 9.
φωτός (abl.sing.neut.of φῶς, means) 379.
αὐτῆς (gen.sing.fem.of αὐτός, possession) 16.
καί (continuative conjunction) 14.
οἱ (nom.pl.masc.of the article in agreement with βασιλεῖς) 9.
βασιλεῖς (nom.pl.masc.of βασιλεύς, subject of φέρουσιν) 31.
τῆς (gen.sing.fem.of the article in agreement with γῆς) 9.
γῆς (gen.sing.fem.of γῆ, description) 157.

φέρουσιν (3d.per.pl.pres.act.ind.of φέρω, customary) 683.
τὴν (acc.sing.fem.of the article in agreement with δόξαν) 9.
δόξαν (acc.sing.fem.of δόξα, direct object of φέρουσιν) 361.
αὐτῶν (gen.pl.masc.of αὐτός, direct object of φέρουσιν) 16.
εἰς (preposition with the accusative of extent) 140.
αὐτήν (acc.sing.fem.of αὐτός, extent) 16.

Translation - "And the nations will walk about by means of her light; and the kings of the earth bring their glory into her."

Comment: *Cf.* Isa.60:3,5; Micah 4:1-7. Some elements in the Micah prophecy apply to the Kingdom more than to the eternal state, but verse 2 especially fits Rev.21:24. Here we have evidence that outside the foursquare city, the earth (and possibly other planets) will be inhabited and will be governed by kings. An anarchist system will be possible since there will be no sin but life will not be unorganized. The King of kings will receive eternal homage from the kings of earth. Access will never be denied.

Verse 25 - "And the gates of it shall not be shut at all by day: for there shall be no night there."

καὶ οἱ πυλῶνες αὐτῆς οὐ μὲ κλεισθῶσιν ἡμέρας, νὺξ γὰρ οὐκ ἔσται ἐκεῖ.

"and the gates shall never be shut by day — and there shall be no night there." .
. . RSV

καὶ (continuative conjunction) 14.
οἱ (nom.pl.masc.of the article in agreement with πυλῶνες) 9.
πυλῶνες (nom.pl.masc.of πυλών, subject of κλεισθῶσιν) 1610.
οὐ (negative conjunction with μὴ and the subjunctive, emphatic negation) 130.
μὴ (negative conjunction with οὐ and the subjunctive, emphatic negation) 87.
κλεισθῶσιν (3d.per.pl.aor.pass.subj.of κλείω, emphatic negation) 570.
ἡμέρας (gen.sing.fem.of ἡμέρα, time description) 135.
νὺξ (nom.sing.fem.of νύξ, subject of ἔσται) 209.
οὐκ (negative conjunction with the indicative) 130.
ἔσται (3d.per.sing.fut.ind.of εἰμί, predictive) 86.
ἐκεῖ (local adverb) 204.

Translation - "And her gates will never be closed during the day: there will be no night there."

Comment: What a beautifully emphatic way to say that the gates will never be closed. Night and day, in the sense of periods of light and darkness, will still be known elsewhere in heaven, but not in the New Jerusalem. *Cf.* Isa.60:11.

Verse 26 - "And they shall bring the glory and honor of the nations into it."

καὶ οἴσουσιν τὴν δόξαν καὶ τὴν τιμὴν τῶν ἐθνῶν εἰς αὐτήν.

"they shall bring into it the glory and honor of the nations. "... RSV

καὶ (continuative conjunction) 14.
οἴσουσιν (3d.per.pl.fut.act.ind.of φέρω, predictive) 683.
τὴν (acc.sing.fem.of the article in agreement with δόξαν) 9.
δόξαν (acc.sing.fem.of δόξα, direct object of οἴσουσιν) 361.
καὶ (adjunctive conjunction joining nouns) 14.
τὴν (acc.sing.fem.of the article in agreement with τιμὴν) 9.
τιμὴν (acc.sing.fem.of τιμή, direct object of οἴσουσιν) 1619.
τῶν (gen.pl.neut.of the article in agreement with ἐθνῶν) 9.
ἐθνῶν (gen.pl.neut.of ἔθνος, description) 376.
εἰς (preposition with the accustative of extent) 140.
αὐτήν (acc.sing.fem.of αὐτός, extent) 16.

Translation - "And they will bring the glory and the wealth of the nations into her."

Comment: All the kings (verse 24) and all of the nations (verse 26) will do for the New Jerusalem what all of the unregenerate kings did for Babylon (Rev.17-18). τιμή means wealth as well as honor. Splendor and wealth will be theirs in abundance because holiness is always profitable, because it is always constructive.

Verse 27 - "And there shall in no wise enter into it any thing that defileth, neither whatsoever worketh abomination, or maketh a lie; but they which are written in the Lamb's book of life."

καὶ οὐ μὴ εἰσέλθῃ εἰς αὐτὴν πᾶν κοινὸν καὶ ποιῶν βδέλυγμα καὶ φεῦδος, εἰ μὴ οἱ γεγραμμένοι ἐν τῷ βιβλίῳ τῆς ζωῆς τοῦ ἀρνίου.

"But nothing unclean shall enter it, nor any one who practices abomination or falsehood, but only those who are written in the Lamb's book of life."... RSV

καὶ (adversative conjunction) 14.
οὐ (negative conjunction with μὴ and the subjunctive, emphatic negation) 130.
μὴ (negative conjunction with οὐ and the subjunctive, emphatic negation) 87.
εἰσέλθῃ (3d.per.sing.aor.subj.of εἰσέρχομαι, emphatic negation) 161.
εἰς (preposition with the accusative of extent) 140.
αὐτὴν (acc.sing.fem.of αὐτός, extent) 16.
πᾶν (nom.sing.masc.of πᾶς, in agreement with κοινὸν) 67.
κοινὸν (nom.sing.masc.of κοινός, subject of εἰσέλθῃ) 2295.
καὶ (adjunctive conjunction joining substantives) 14.
ποιῶν (pres.act.part.nom.sing.masc.of ποιέω, substantival, subject of εἰσέλθῃ) 127.
βδέλυγμα (acc.sing.neut.of βδέλυγμα, direct object of ποιῶν) 1492.
καὶ (adjunctive conjunction joining nouns) 14.
φεῦδος (acc.sing.neut.of φεῦδος, direct object of ποιῶν) 2388.

εἰ (conditional particle in an elliptical condition) 337.

μὴ (negative conjunction in an elliptical condition) 87.

οἱ (nom.pl.masc.of the article in agreement with γεγραμμένοι) 9.

γεγραμμένοι (perf.pass.part.nom.pl.masc.of γράφω, substantival, subject of verb understood) 156.

ἐν (preposition with the locative of place) 80.

τῷ (loc.sing.neut.of the article in agreement with βιβλίῳ) 9.

βιβλίῳ (loc.sing.neut.of βιβλίον, place) 1292.

τῆς (gen.sing.fem.of the article in agreement with ζωῆς) 9.

ζωῆς (gen.sing.fem.of ζωή, description) 668.

τοῦ (gen.sing.neut.of the article in agreement with ἀρνίου) 9.

ἀρνίου (gen.sing.neut.of αρνίον, possession) 2923.

Translation - "But there shall never enter into her anything mediocre or that generates abomination or promotes falsehood, but only those written in the Lamb's book of life."

Comment: *Cf.* #2295 for the basic idea. The New Jerusalem will be a sophisticated society. Those saints who, though saved, unfortunately did not develop their spiritual potential (Mt.22:14; 13:5,6), who are members of the family of God (John 1:12), and wedding guests (Mt.25:2a) if not the Bride (Rev.19:7-8), but have not attained Paul's goal (Phil.3:10-14) will be permitted inside the city because their names are written in the Lamb's book of life. They did not promote the lie, but rather the truth (1 John 2:22). Nevertheless, due to their failure to fulfill God's total blueprint for their lives (Eph.2:10), they will be to some degree κοινός - mediocre. Indeed, relative to the perfection which is demonstrated by Jesus Christ, no saint totally escapes mediocrity.But since nothing mediocre from the "lie promoting" and "abomination working" outside world of unregenerate philosophy will be allowed to enter, the mediocrity of the saints, by sociological accommodations with the perfection of Christ, given an eternity to work, will disappear until we all achieve the goal of Eph.4:13. There will be growth in the New Jerusalem. The most infantile Christian, who, though saved, wasted his life (Mt.13:7), or because of a lack of intellectual endowment (Mt.13:5) was unable to grow as he should, will grow up in Christ. A society with a sociology of holiness and nothing militating against it, is certain to be a society where an entropy of righteousness will ultimately be achieved. Rev.21:8,27; 22:15 list those excluded, which is only a negative way of describing those who will be admitted.

The thrilling description of the New Jerusalem continues in Chapter 22, for the last five verses of the Revelation proper, after which we have the sixteen verse epilogue.

Revelation 22:1 - "And he shewed me a pure river of water of life, clear as crystal, proceeding out of the throne of God and of the Lamb."

Καὶ ἔδειξέν μοι ποταμὸν ὕδατος ζωῆς λαμπρὸν ὡς κρύσταλλον, ἐκπορευόμενον ἐκ τοῦ θρόνου τοῦ θεοῦ καὶ τοῦ ἀρνίου.

"Then he showed me the river of the water of life, bright as crystal, flowing from the throne of God and of the Lamb . . . " . . . RSV

Καὶ (continuative conjunction) 14.
ἔδειξέν (3d.per.sing.aor.act.ind.of δείκνυμι, ingressive) 359.
μοι (dat.sing.masc.of ἐγώ, indirect object of ἔδειξέν) 123.
ποταμὸν (acc.sing.masc.of ποταμός, direct object of ἔδειξέν) 274.
ὕδατος (gen.sing.neut.of ὕδωρ, description) 301.
ζωῆς (gen.sing.fem.of ζωή, description) 668.
λαμπρὸν (acc.sing.masc.of λαμπρός, predicate adjective) 2832.
ὡς (comparative particle) 128.
κρύσταλλον (acc.sing.masc.of κρύσταλλος, in a comparative phrase) 5345.
ἐκπορευόμενον (pres.mid.part.acc.sing.masc.of ἐκπορεύομαι, adjectival, predicate position, ascriptive, in agreement with ποταμὸν) 270.
ἐκ (preposition with the ablative of source) 19.
τοῦ (abl.sing.masc.of the article in agreement with θρόνου) 9.
θρόνου (abl.sing.masc.of θρόνος, source) 519.
τοῦ (gen.sing.masc.of the article in agreement with θεοῦ) 9.
θεοῦ (gen.sing.masc.of θεός, possession) 124.
καὶ (adjunctive conjunction joining nouns) 14.
τοῦ (gen.sing.neut.of the article in agreement with ἀρνίου) 9.
ἀρνίου (gen.sing.neut.of ἀρνίον, possession) 2923.

Translation - "And he showed me a river of living water, clear as crystal, flowing from the throne of God and of the Lamb . . . "

Comment: *Cf.* Ezekiel 47:1-5; Joel 3:18; John 7:38,39; Zech.14:8. The beauty of the Holy City has been described chiefly in terms of precious metals and gems. Now the rustic and majestic scene of a great river with all of the fruits adds to the beauty. This river is clear; there is no pollution. It is life giving and refreshing.

Verse 2 - "In the midst of the street of it, and on either side of the river, was there the tree of life, which bare twelve manner of fruits, and yielded her fruit every month: and the leaves of the tree were for the healing of the nations."

ἐν μέσῳ τῆς πλατείας αὐτῆς καὶ τοῦ ποταμοῦ ἐντεῦθεν καὶ ἐκεῖθεν ξύλον ζωῆς ποιοῦν καρποὺς δώδεκα, κατὰ μῆνα ἕκαστον ἀποδιδοῦν τὸν καρπὸν αὐτοῦ, καὶ τὰ φύλλα τοῦ ξύλου εἰς θεραπείαν τῶν ἐθνῶν.

". . . through the middle of the street of the city; also, on either side of the river, the tree of life with its twelve kinds of fruit, yielding its fruit each month: and the leaves of the tree were for the healing of the nations." . . . RSV

ἐν (preposition with the locative of place) 80.
μέσῳ (loc.sing.masc.of μέσος, place) 873.
τῆς (gen.sing.fem.of the article in agreement with πλατείας) 9.
πλατείας (gen.sing.fem.of πλατεῖα, description) 568.
αὐτῆς (gen.sing.fem.of αὐτός, possession) 16.

καὶ (adjunctive conjunction joining nouns) 14.

τοῦ (gen.sing.masc.of the article in agreement with ποταμοῦ) 9.

ποταμοῦ (gen.sing.masc.of ποταμός, description) 274.

ἐντεῦθεν (local adverb) 1236.

καὶ (adjunctive conjunction joining adverbs) 14.

ἐξεῖθεν (local adverb) 396.

ξύλον (acc.sing.neut.of ξύλον, direct object of ἔδειξέν) 1590.

ζωῆς (gen.sing.fem.of ζωή, description) 668.

ποιοῦν (pres.act.part.acc.sing.neut.of ποιέω, adjectival, predicate position, restrictive, in agreement with ξύλον) 127.

καρποὺς (acc.pl.masc.of καρπός, direct object of ποιοῦν) 284.

δώδεκα (numeral) 820.

κατὰ (preposition with the accusative, distributive) 98.

μῆνα (acc.sing.fem.of μήν, distributive) 1809.

ἕκαστον (acc.sing.fem.of ἕκαστος, in agreement with ξύλον) 1217.

ἀποδιδοῦν (pres.act.part.acc.sing.neut. of ἀποδίδωμι, adjectival, predicate position, restrictive, in agreement with ἕκαστον) 495.

τὸν (acc.sing.masc.of the article in agreement with καρπὸν) 9.

καρπὸν (acc.sing.masc.of καρπός, direct object of ἀποδιδοῦν) 284.

αὐτοῦ (gen.sing.masc.of αὐτός, possession) 16.

καὶ (continuative conjunction) 14.

τὰ (nom.pl.neut.of the article in agreement with φύλλα) 9.

φύλλα (nom.pl.neut.of φύλλον, subject of ἐστι understood) 1367.

τοῦ (gen.sing.neut.of the article in agreement with θύλου) 9.

ξύλου (gen.sing.neut.of ξύλον, description) 1590.

εἰς (preposition with the accusative, purpose) 140.

θεραπείαν (acc.sing.fem.of θεραπεία, purpose) 2270.

τῶν (gen.pl.neut.of the article in agreement with ἐθνῶν) 9.

ἐθνῶν (gen.pl.neut.of ἔθνος, description) 376.

Translation - "*In the middle of the street. And from that point on, on both sides of the river, the tree of life, yielding twelve fruits, one fruit each month: and the leaves of the tree are for the healing of the nations.*"

Comment: The prepositional phrase ἐν μέσῳ τῆς πλατείας αὐτῆς belongs with the sentence in verse 1. The river flowed from the throne down the middle of the street. From that point (ἐκεῖθεν) and on both sides of the river (ἐντεῦθεν) grew a tree of life. ξύλον is singular with reference to the species, not to the number of trees. There was more than one tree, but the species was known as the "tree of life." We need not think that the tree produced twelve different kinds of fruit, only that it produced a crop each month. The leaves are for the purpose (εἰς θεραπείαν) of the nations. This is a difficult passage, since the nations in eternity will not be ill or sinful. Perhaps John means that the leaves of the eternal tree of life would heal sick nations now.

Verse 3 - "*And there shall be no more curse: but the throne of God and of the Lamb shall be in it; and his servants shall serve him.*"

καὶ πᾶν κατάθεμα οὐκ ἔσται ἔτι. καὶ ὁ θρόνος τοῦ θεοῦ καὶ τοῦ ἀρνίου ἐν αὐτῇ ἔσται, καὶ οἱ δοῦλοι αὐτοῦ λατρεύσουσιν αὐτῷ.

"There shall no more be anything accursed, but the throne of God and of the Lamb shall be in it, and his servants shall worship him;" . . . RSV

καὶ (continuative conjunction) 14.

πᾶν (nom.sing.neut.of πᾶς, in agreement with κατάθεμα) 67.

#5442 κατάθεμα (nom.sing.neut.for κατανάθεμα, subject of ἔσται).

King James Version

curse - Rev.22:3.

Revised Standard Version

accursed - Rev.22:3.

Meaning: an accursed thing; worthy of execration. - Rev.22:3.

οὐκ (negative conjunction with the indicative) 130.
ἔσται (3d.per.sing.fut.ind.of εἰμί, predictive) 86.
ἔτι (temporl adverb) 448.
καὶ (continuative conjunction) 14.
ὁ (nom.sing.masc.of the article in agreement with θρόνος) 9.
θρόνος (nom.sing.masc.of θρόνος, subject of ἔσται) 519.
τοῦ (gen.sing.masc.of the article in agreement with θεοῦ) 9.
θεοῦ (gen.sing.masc.of θεός, possession) 124.
καὶ (adjunctive conjunction joining nouns) 14.
τοῦ (gen.sing.neut.of the article in agreement with ἀρνίου) 9.
ἀρνίου (gen.sing.neut.of ἀρνίον, possession) 2923.
ἐν (preposition with the locative of place) 80.
αὐτῇ (loc.sing.fem.of αὐτός, place) 16.
ἔσται (3d.per.sing.fut.ind.of εἰμί, predictive) 86.
καὶ (continuative conjunction) 14.
οἱ (nom.pl.masc.of the article in agreement with δοῦλοι) 9.
δοῦλοι (nom.pl.masc.of δοῦλος, subject of λατρεύσουσιν) 725.
αὐτοῦ (gen.sing.masc.of αὐτός, relationship) 16.
λατρεύσουσιν (3d.per.pl.fut.act.ind.of λατρεύω, predictive) 366.
αὐτῷ (dat.sing.masc.of αὐτός, personal advantage) 16.

Translation - "And there shall never be a curse there. But the throne of God and of the Lamb will be in her, and His servants will serve Him."

Comment: Positive and negative descriptions. No more curse or accursed thing ever in the city, but God's throne and of the Lamb and His servants will always serve Him.

Verse 4 - "And they shall see His face: and His name shall be in their foreheads."

καὶ ὄφονται τὸ πρόσωπον αὐτοῦ, καὶ τὸ ὄνομα αὐτοῦ ἐπὶ τῶν μετώπων αὐτῶν.

"they shall see his face, and his name shall be on their foreheads." . . . RSV

καὶ (continuative conjunction) 14.
ὄφονται (3d.per.pl.fut.ind.of ὁράω, predictive) 144.
τὸ (acc.sing.neut.of the article in agreement with πρόσωπον) 9.
πρόσωπον (acc.sing.neut.of πρόσωπον, direct object of ὄφονται) 588.
αὐτοῦ (gen.sing.masc.of αὐτός, possession) 16.
καὶ (continuative conjunction) 14.
τὸ (nom.sing.neut.of the article in agreement with ὄνομα) 9.
ὄνομα (nom.sing.neut.of ὄνομα, subject of ἔσται understood) 108.
αὐτοῦ (gen.sing.masc.of αὐτός, possession) 16.
ἐπὶ (preposition with the genitive of place description) 47.
τῶν (gen.pl.neut.of the article in agreement with μετώπων) 9.
μετώπων (gen.pl.neut.of μέτωπον, place description) 5356.
αὐτῶν (gen.pl.masc.of αὐτός, possession) 16.

Translation - "And they will always see His face, and His name will be upon their foreheads."

Comment: This is not too anthropomorphic. Our Lord is there at the Father's right hand in the resurrection body in which He suffered. We shall see Him just as the early Christians saw Him on the day that He arose from the grave. *Cf.* #5356. Both Christ and Antichrist seal their servants in the forehead.

Verse 5 - "And there shall be no night there: and they need no candle, neither light of the sun; for the Lord God giveth them light: and they shall reign forever and ever."

καὶ νὺξ οὐκ ἔσται ἔτι, καὶ οὐκ ἔχουσιν χρείαν φωτὸς λύχνου καὶ φῶς ἡλίου, ὅτι κύριος ὁ θεὸς φωτίσει ἐπ' αὐτούς, καὶ βασιλεύσουσιν εἰς τοὺς αἰῶνας τῶν αἰώνων.

"And night shall be no more; they need no light of lamp or sun, for the Lord God will be their light, and they shall reign for ever and ever." . . . RSV

καὶ (continuative conjunction) 14.
νὺξ (nom.sing.fem.of νύξ, subject of ἔσται) 209.
οὐκ (negative conjunction with the indicative) 130.
ἔσται (3d.per.sing.fut.ind.of εἰμί, predictive) 86.
ἔτι (temporal adverb) 448.
καὶ (continuative conjunction) 14.
οὐκ (negative conjunction with the indicative) 130.
ἔχουσιν (3d.per.pl.pres.act.ind.of ἔχω, aoristic) 82.
χρείαν (acc.sing.fem.of χρεία, direct object of ἔχουσιν) 317.

φωτὸς (gen.sing.neut.of φῶς, description) 379.
λύχνου (abl.sing.masc.of λύχνος, source) 454.
καὶ (adjunctive conjunction joining nouns) 14.
φῶς (acc.sing.neut.of φῶς, in apposition with χρείαν) 379.
ἡλίου (abl.sing.masc.of ἥλιος, source) 546.
ὅτι (conjunction introducing a subordinate causal clause) 211.
κύριος (nom.sing.masc.of κύριος, in apposition) 97.
ὁ (nom.sing.masc.of the article in agreement with θεὸς) 9.
θεὸς (nom.sing.masc.of θεός, subject of φωτίσει) 124.
φωτίσει (3d.per.sing.fut.act.ind.of φωτίζω, predictive) 1697.
ἐπ' (preposition with the accusative, extent) 47.
αὐτούς (acc.pl.masc.of αὐτός, extent) 16.
καὶ (continuative conjunction) 14.
βασιλεύσουσιν (3d.per.pl.fut.act.ind.of βασιλεύω, predictive) 236.
εἰς (preposition with the accusative of time extent) 140.
τοὺς (acc.pl.masc.of the article in agreement with αἰῶνας) 9.
αἰῶνας (acc.pl.masc.of αἰών, time extent) 1002.
τῶν (gen.pl.masc.of the article in agreement with αἰώνων) 9.
αἰώνων (gen.pl.masc.of αἰών, partitive genitive) 1002.

Translation - *"But there will never again be night; and they have no need for lamp light or light from the sun, because God the Lord will cast light upon them and they will reign into the ages of the ages."*

Comment: There is an air of finality as this verse closes. It is a happy denouement. What began with God, the Creator ends with His creatures reigning with Him into the eternal ages to come. Sin came and brought darkness (Gen.1:2) but here we have God shining His light upon them. Then there was chaos (Gen.1:2); now we have κόσμος. Then God drove them from the garden; now they behold His face in His city and His seal is upon their foreheads. Generation was followed by degeneration, but incarnation and redemption intervened and regeneration was the eternal result.

The last sixteen verses are epilogue. John's preview of the judgment of God during the last week of the "times of the Gentiles" (Lk.21:24) is over. The curtain on the thrilling drama is now down. John is back at Patmos in the first century.

Epilogue

(Revelation 22:6-21)

Verse 6 - "And he saith unto me, These sayings are faithful and true: and the Lord God of the holy prophets sent his angel to shew unto his servants the things which must shortly be done."

Καὶ εἶπέν μοι, Οὗτοι οἱ λόγοι πιστοὶ καὶ ἀληθινοί, καὶ ὁ κύριος, ὁ θεὸς τῶν πνευμάτων τῶν προφητῶν, ἀπέστειλεν τὸν ἄγγελον αὐτοῦ δεῖξαι τοῖς δούλοις αὐτοῦ ἃ δεῖ γενέσθαι ἐν τάχει.

"And he said to me, 'These words are trustworthy and true. And the Lord, the God of the spirits of the prophets, has sent his angel to show his servants what must soon take place. . . . " . . . RSV

Καὶ (continuative conjunction) 14.
εἶπέν (3d.per.sing.aor.act.ind.of εἶπον, constative) 155.
μοι (dat.sing.masc.of ἐγώ, indirect object of εἶπεν) 123.
Οὗτοι (nom.pl.masc.of οὗτος, in agreement with λόγοι) 93.
οἱ (nom.pl.masc.of the article in agreement with λόγοι) 9.
λόγοι (nom.pl.masc.of λόγος, subject of ἐστιν understood) 510.
πιστοὶ (nom.pl.masc.of πιστός, predicate adjective) 1522.
καὶ (adjunctive conjunction joining adjectives) 14.
ἀληθινοί (nom.pl.masc.of ἀληθινός, predicate adjective) 1696.
καὶ (continuative conjunction) 14.
ὁ (nom.sing.masc.of the article in agreement with κύριος) 9.
κύριος (nom.sing.masc.of κύριος, subject of ἀπέστειλεν) 97.
ὁ (nom.sing.masc.of the article in agreement with θεὸς) 9.
θεὸς (nom.sing.masc.of θεός, apposition) 124.
τῶν (gen.pl.neut.of the article in agreement with πνευμάτων) 9.
πνευμάτων (gen.pl.neut.of πνεῦμα, description) 83.
τῶν (gen.pl.masc.of the article in agreement with προφητῶν) 9.
προφητῶν (gen.pl.masc.of προφήτης, description) 119.
ἀπέστειλεν (3d.per.sing.aor.act.ind.of ἀποστέλλω, constative) 215.
τὸν (acc.sing.masc.of the article in agreement with ἄγγελον) 9.
ἄγγελον (acc.sing.masc.of ἄγγλος, direct object of ἀπέστειλεν) 96.
αὐτοῦ (gen.sing.masc.of αὐτός, relationship) 16.
δεῖξαι (aor.act.inf.of δείκνυμι, purpose) 359.
τοῖς (dat.pl.masc.of the article in agreement with δούλοις) 9.
δούλοις (dat.pl.masc.of δοῦλος, indirect object of δεῖξαι) 725.
αὐτοῦ (gen.sing.masc.of αὐτός relationship) 16.
ἃ (acc.pl.neut.of ὅς, relative pronoun, general reference) 65.
δεῖ (present indicative impersonal) 1207.
γενέσθαι (aor.inf.of γίνομαι, complementary) 113.
ἐν (preposition with the locative of time point) 80.
τάχει (loc.sing.neut.of τάχος, time point) 2626.

Translation - "And he said to me, 'These messages are trustworthy and true; and the Lord God of the spirits of the prophets sent His messenger to show to His servants those things which must happen soon."

Comment: *Cf.* Rev.1:1. It is clear that in point of time we are back at the beginning of the Revelation. *Cf.* comment *en loc.* John is adding a few words of epilogue. The angel adds another word.

Verse 7 - "Behold, I come quickly: blessed is he that keepeth the sayings of the prophecy of this book."

καὶ ἰδοὺ ἔρχομαι ταχύ. μακάριος ὁ τηρῶν τοὺς λόγους τῆς προφητείας τοῦ βιβλίου τούτου.

"And behold, I am coming soon.' Blessed is he who keeps the words of the prophecy of this book." . . . RSV

καὶ (continuative conjunction) 14.
ἰδοὺ (exclamation) 95.
ἔρχομαι (1st.per.sing.pres.mid.ind.of ἔρχομαι, futuristic) 146.
ταχύ (acc.sing.neut.of ταχύς, temporal adverb) 491.
μακάριος (nom.sing.masc.of μακάριος, predicate adjective) 422.
ὁ (nom.sing.masc.of the article in agreement with τηρῶν) 9.
τηρῶν (pres.act.part.nom.sing.masc.of τηρέω, substantival, subject of ἐστιν, understood) 1297.
τοὺς (acc.pl.masc.of the article in agreement with λόγους) 9.
λόγους (acc.pl.masc.of λόγος, direct object of τηρῶν) 510.
τῆς (gen.sing.fem.of the article in agreement with προφητείας) 9.
προφητείας (gen.sing.fem.of προφητεία, description) 1041.
τοῦ (gen.sing.neut.of the article in agreement with βιβλίου) 9.
βιβλίου (gen.sing.neut.of βιβλίον, description) 1292.
τούτου (gen.sing.neut.of οὗτος, in agreement with βιβλίου) 93.

Translation - "And Look! I am coming soon! Happy is the one who is keeping the words of the prophecy of this book."

Comment: This repeats the thought of Rev.1:3 in the prologue. The importance of the Revelation is indicated by these two special promises of blessing for those who study it - at the beginning (Rev.1:3) and again at the close of the book (Rev.22:7).

Verse 8 - "And I John saw these things and heard them. And when I had heard and seen, I fell down to worship before the feet of the angel which shewed me these things."

Κἀγὼ Ἰωάννης ὁ ἀκούων καὶ βλέπων ταῦτα. καὶ ὅτε ἤκουσα καὶ ἔβλεφα, ἔπεσα προσκυνῆσαι ἔμπροσθεν τῶν ποδῶν τοῦ ἀγγέλου τοῦ δεικνύοντός μοι ταῦτα.

"I John am he who heard and saw these things. And when I heard and saw them, I fell down to worship at the feet of the angel who showed them to me;..."
. . . RSV

Κἀγὼ (continuative conjunction and first personal pronoun, crasis) 178.
Ἰωάννης (nom.sing.masc.of Ἰωάννης, subject of εἰμί understood) 399.
ὁ (nom.sing.masc.of the article in agreement with ἀκούων and βλέπων) 9.
ἀκούων (pres.act.part.nom.sing.masc.of ἀκούω, substantival, predicate nominative) 148.
καὶ (adjunctive conjunction joining participles) 14.

βλέπων (pres.act.part.nom.sing.masc.of βλέπω, substantival, predicate nominative) 499.

ταῦτα (acc.pl.neut.of οὗτος, deictic, direct object of ἀκούων and βλέπων) 93.

καὶ (continuative conjunction) 14.

ὅτε (conjunction in a definite temporal clause) 703.

ἤκουσα (1st.per.sing.aor.act.ind.of ἀκούω, constative) 148.

καὶ (adjunctive conjunction joining verbs) 14.

ἔβλεφα (1st.per.sing.aor.act.ind.of βλέπω, constative) 499.

ἔπεσα (1st.per.sing.aor.act.ind.of πίπτω, constative) 187.

προσκυνῆσαι (aor.act.inf.of προσκυνέω, purpose) 147.

ἔμπροσθεν (preposition with the genitive of place description) 459.

τῶν (gen.pl.masc.of the article in agreement with ποδῶν) 9.

ποδῶν (gen.pl.masc.of πούς, place description) 353.

τοῦ (gen.sing.masc.of the article in agreement with ἀγγέλου) 9.

ἀγγέλου (gen.sing.masc.of ἄγγελος, possession) 96.

τοῦ (gen.sing.masc.of the article in agreement with δεικνύοντός) 9.

δεικνύοντός (pres.act.part.gen.sing.masc.of δείκνυμι, adjectival, emphatic attributive position, ascriptive, in agreement with ἀγγέλου) 359.

μοι (dat.sing.masc.of ἐγώ, indirect object of δεικνύοντός) 123.

ταῦτα (acc.pl.neut.of ουτος, direct object of δεικνύοντός) 93.

Translation - "And I, John, am the one who heard and saw these things. And when I heard and saw, I fell down to worship at the feet of the messenger who showed these things to me."

Comment: John made this mistake once before (Rev.19:10) and received the same rebuke, which follows in verse 9. Now we learn that the messenger of Rev.1:1 was not an angel but a man.

Verse 9 - "Then saith he unto me, See thou do it not; for I am thy fellow servant, and of thy brethren, the prophets, and of them which keep the sayings of this book: worship God."

καὶ λέγει μοι, ῎Ορα μή. σύνδουλός σού εἰμι καὶ τῶν ἀδελφῶν σου τῶν προφητῶν καὶ τῶν τηρούντων τοὺς λόγους τού βιβλίου τούτου. τῷ θεῷ προσκύνησον.

"but he said to me, 'You must not do that! I am a fellow servant with you and your brethren the prophets, and with those who keep the words of this book. Worship God." . . . RSV

καὶ (adversative conjunction) 14.

λέγει (3d.per.sing.pres.act.ind.of λέγω, historical) 66.

μοι (dat.sing.masc.of ἐγώ, indirect object of λέγει) 123.

῎Ορα (2d.per.sing.pres.act.impv.of ὁράω, prohibition) 144.

μή (negative conjunction with the imperative, prohibition) 87.

σύνδουλός (nom.sing.masc.of σύνδουλος, predicate nominative) 1276.

σού (gen.sing.masc.of σύ, relationship) 104.

εἰμι (1st.pers.sing.pres.ind.of εἰμί, aoristic) 86.

καὶ (adjunctive conjunction joining nouns) 14.

τῶν (gen.pl.masc.of the article in agreement with ἀδελφῶν) 9.

ἀδελφῶν (gen.pl.masc.of ἀδελφός, partitive genitive) 15.

σου (gen.sing.masc.of σύ, relationship) 104.

τῶν (gen.pl.masc.of the article in agreement with προφητῶν) 9.

προφητῶν (gen.pl.masc.of προφήτης, apposition) 119.

καὶ (adjunctive conjunction joining substantives) 14.

τῶν (gen.pl.masc.of the article in agreement with τηρούντων) 9.

τηρούντων (pres.act.part.gen.pl.masc.of τηρέω, substantival, partitive genitive) 1297.

τοὺς (acc.pl.masc.of the article in agreement with λόγους) 9.

λόγους (acc.pl.masc.of λόγος, direct object of τηρούντων) 510.

τοῦ (gen.sing.neut.of the article in agreement with βιβλίου) 9.

βιβλίου (gen.sing.neut.of βιβλίον, description) 1292.

τούτου (gen.sing.neut.of οὗτος, in agreement with βιβλίου) 93.

τῷ (dat.sing.masc.of the article in agreement with θεῷ) 9.

θεῷ (dat.sing.masc.of θεός, personal advantage) 124.

προσκύνησον (2d.per.sing.aor.act.impv.of προσκυνέω, command) 147.

Translation - "But he said to me, 'Never do that! I am your fellow servant and one of your brothers of the prophets, and one of those who is keeping the messages of this book. Worship God."

Comment: ποιήσῃς can be supplied with ὅρα μή, though the man's prohibition is perfectly clear. *Cf.* Rev.19:10. He introduces himself as one of the fellow servants - indeed one of the prophets and as one who is observing the messages of the Revelation, just as he admonishes John and all of its readers to do (Rev.1:3). It is similar to Rev.19:10.

Let us respect the divine reticencies. The text does not identify the messenger beyond saying that he is a Christian, a brother of John and a prophet. But there is a hint that he is Daniel or perhaps Ezekiel. It was Daniel to whom the message of the "times of the Gentiles" was given (Dan.9:24-27; Lk.21:24). It would seem appropriate that he should reveal the events and scenes of its final week, and the events to follow the second coming of our Lord. There is a further hint in verse 10. But until further evidence is available no one should dogmatize about the messenger's identity.

Verse 10 - "And he saith unto me, Seal not the sayings of the prophecy of this book. For the time is at hand."

καὶ λέγει μοι, Μὴ σφραγίσῃς τοὺς λόγους τῆς προφητείας τοῦ βιβλίου τούτου, ὁ καιρὸς γὰρ ἐγγὺς ἐστιν.

"And he said to me, 'Do not seal up the words of the prophecy of this book, for the time is near." . . . RSV

καὶ (continuative conjunction) 14.

λέγει (3d.per.sing.pres.act.ind.of λέγω, historical) 66.
μοι (dat.sing.masc.of ἐγώ, indirect object of λέγει) 123.
Μὴ (negative conjunction with the subjunctive, prohibition) 87.
σφραγίσῃς (2d.per.sing.aor.act.subj.of σφραγίζω, prohibition) 1686.
τοὺς (acc.pl.masc.of the article in agreement with λόγους) 9.
λόγους (acc.pl.masc.of λόγος, direct object of σφραγίσῃς) 510.
τῆς (gen.sing.fem.of the article in agreement with προφητείας) 9.
προφητείας (gen.sing.fem.of προφητεία, description) 1041.
τοῦ (gen.sing.neut.of the article in agreement with βιβλίου) 9.
βιβλίου (gen.sing.neut.of βιβλίον, description) 1292.
τούτου (gen.sing.neut.of οὗτος, in agreement with βιβλίου) 93.
ὁ (nom.sing.masc.of the article in agreement with καιρὸς) 9.
καιρὸς (nom.sing.masc.of καιρός, subject of ἐστιν) 767.
γὰρ (causal conjunction) 105.
ἐγγύς (nom.sing.masc.of ἐγγύς, predicate adjective) 1512.
ἐστιν (3d.per.sing.pres.ind.of εἰμί, aoristic) 86.

Translation - "And he added, 'Do not seal the messages of the prophecy of this book, because the time is at hand.' "

Comment: *Cf.* Dan.12:9 and Rev.5:1-14. Daniel's book, containing the information about "the times of the Gentiles" (Lk.21:24) was sealed until the time of the end. Then it was unsealed (Rev.5). Now John is ordered to leave the Revelation, which unseals Daniel's book and describes "the time of the end" unsealed, since the time is near. ἐγγύς to an eternal God means "immanent" since time to him means nothing. In the first centiry A.D. the next scheduled event was the "time of the end." Since this καιρὸς has not yet begun as we write (4 July 1984) it is still immanent. 1900 years have elapsed since John was told that the time was immanent, but this is only a moment to God, and hence immanent. There are no necessary intervening events in God's prophetic program. Is the fellow servant whom John tried to worship the prophet Daniel?

Verse 11 - "He that is unjust, let him be unjust still: and he which is filthy, let him be filthy still; and he that is righteous, let him be righteous still; and he that is holy, let him be holy still."

ὁ ἀδικῶν ἀδικησάτω ἔτι, καὶ ὁ ῥυπαρὸς ῥυπανθήτω ἔτι, καὶ ὁ δίκαιος δικαιοσύνην ποιησάτω ἔτι, καὶ ὁ ἅγιος ἁγιασθήτω ἔτι.

"Let the evildoer still do evil, and the filthy still be filthy, and the righteous still do right, and the holy still be holy." . . . RSV

ὁ (nom.sing.masc.of the article in agreement with ἀδικῶν) 9.
ἀδικῶν (pres.act.part.nom.sing.masc.of ἀδικέω, substantival, subject of ἀδικησάτω) 1327.
ἀδικησάτω (3d.per.sing.aor.act.impv.of ἀδικέω, command) 1327.
ἔτι (temporal adverb) 448.
καὶ (continuative conjunction) 14.
ὁ (nom.sing.masc.of the article in agreement with ῥυπαρὸς) 9.

ῥυπαρὸς (nom.sing.masc.of ῥυπαρός, subject of ῥυπανθήτω) 5115.

#5443 ῥυπανθήτω (3d.per.sing.aor.pass.impv.of ῥυπαίνω, command).

King James Version

be filthy - Rev.22:11.

Revised Standard Version

be filthy - Rev.22:11.

Meaning: Cf. #'s 5115, 5201. Hence, to be filthy; to defile - Rev.22:11.

ἔτι (temporal adverb) 448.
καὶ (continuative conjunction) 14.
ὁ (nom.sing.masc.of δίκαιος, subject of ποιησάτω) 85.
δικαιοσύνην (acc.sing.fem.of δικαιοσύνη, direct object of ποιησάτω) 322.
ποιησάτω (3d.per.sing.aor.act.impv.of ποιέω, command) 127.
ἔτι (temporal adverb) 448.
καὶ (continuative conjunction) 14.
ὁ (nom.sing.masc.of the article in agreement with ἅγιος) 9.
ἅγιος (nom.sing.masc.of ἅγιος, subject of ἁγιασθήτω) 84.
ἁγιασθήτω (3d.per.sing.aor.pass.impv.of ἁγιάζω, command) 576.
ἔτι (temporal adverb) 448.

Translation - "Let the law breaker always be a law breaker, and let the filthy be forever filthy and let the righteous always produce righteousness, and let the holy always be holy."

Comment: The point is that in eternity all conditions which prevail at the end of time will prevail eternally. ἔτι in each clause means "forever" or "from this point onward." The transgressor will always be a transgressor; so also with the filthy and disreputable, the righteous and the holy ones. Goodspeed's concept — "... worse and worse . . . baser and baser . . . more and more upright. . . more and more holy" that ἔτι denotes an intensification is probably true but not supported by ἔτι as such.Certainly in eternity the saved will grow into greater and greater status in holiness (completion) and righteousness (Eph.4:13) and there is nothing in the lake of fire to make the filthy and the lawless less so. Just as the sociology of heaven will lead to higher and nobler accommodation to the standard of Christ, the sociology of hell will lead to deeper and deeper levels of degeneration. But this verse does not say so.

Verse 12 - "And behold I come quickly: and my reward is with me, to give every man according as his work shall be."

Ἰδοὺ ἔρχομαι ταχύ, καὶ ὁ μισθός μου μετ' ἐμοῦ, ἀποδοῦναι ἑκάστῳ ὡς τὸ ἔργον αὐτοῦ.

"Behold, I am coming soon, bringing my recompense, to repay every one for

what he has done." . . . RSV

Ἰδοὺ (exclamation) 95.
ἔρχομαι (1st.per.sing.pres.ind.of ἔρχομαι, futuristic) 146.
ταχύ (temporal adverb) 491.
καὶ (continuative conjunction) 14.
ὁ (nom.sing.masc.of the article in agreement with μισθός) 9.
μισθός (nom.sing.masc.of μισθός, subject of ἔστιν understood) 441.
μου (gen.sing.masc.of ἐγώ, possession) 123.
μετ' (preposition with the genitive, accompaniment) 50.
ἐμοῦ (gen.sing.masc.of ἐμός, accompaniment) 1267.
ἀποδοῦναι (2d.aor.act.inf.of ἀποδίδωμι, purpose) 495.
ἑκάστῳ (dat.sing.masc.of ἕκαστος, indirect object of ἀποδοῦναι) 1217.
ὡς (comparative particle) 128.
τὸ (nom.sing.neut.of the article in agreement with ἔργον) 9.
ἔργον (3d.per.sing.pres.ind.of ἐστίν) 460.
ἐστίν (3d.per.sing.pres.ind.of εἰμί, aoristic) 86.
αὐτοῦ (gen.sing.masc.of αὐτός, possession) 16.

Translation - "Look! I will come quickly and my reward is with me, to recompense to each one in keeping with his performance."

Comment: This can apply both to saint and sinner. For the saints it is in keeping with Mt.16:27; 2 Cor.5:10; 1 Cor.3:11-15; Rev.11:18. For the unsaved it is a statement that the wages of sin is death and that he that sows to the flesh shall of the flesh reap corruption (Gel.6:8a). However the saints, who sow to the Spirit shall of the Spirit reap everlasting life (Gal.6:8b). There is nothing in the context to indicate that ἑκάστῳ is to be applied only to one category or the other, but normally it means both.

There are two statements of immanency in the Prologue (Rev.1:1,3). There are five such statements in the Epilogue (Rev.22:6, 7, 10, 12, 20).There is another in Rev.3:11, which is appropriate since the Philadelphian church is the church on earth just before the rapture at the end of the tribulation period.

Verse 13 - "I am Alpha and Omega, the beginning and the end, the first and the last."

ἐγώ τὸ Ἄλφα καὶ τὸ Ὦ, ὁ πρῶτος καὶ ὁ ἔσχατος, ἡ ἀρχὴ καὶ τὸ τέλος.

"I am the Alpha and the Omega, the first and the last, the beginning and the end." . . . RSV

ἐγὼ (nom.sing.masc.of ἐγώ, subject of εἰμί supplied) 123.
τὸ (nom.sing.neut.of the article in agreement with Ἄλφα) 9.
Ἄλφα (nom.sing.neut.of Ἄλφα, predicate nominative) 5318.
καὶ (adjunctive conjunction joining substantives) 14.
τὸ (nom.sing.neut.of the article in agreement with Ὦ) 9.
Ὦ (nom.sing.neut.of Ὦ, predicate nominative) 5319.

ὁ (nom.sing.masc.of the article in agreement with πρῶτος) 9.
πρῶτος (nom.sing.masc.of πρῶτος, apposition) 487.
καὶ (adjunctive conjunction joining substantives) 14.
ὁ (nom.sing.masc.of the article in agreement with ἔσχατος) 9.
ἔσχατος (nom.sing.masc.of ἔσχατος, apposition) 496.
ἡ (nom.sing.fem.of the article in agreement with ἀρχή) 9.
ἀρχή (nom.sing.fem.of ἀρχή, apposition) 1285.
καὶ (adjunctive conjunction joining substantives) 14.
τὸ (nom.sing.neut.of the article in agreement with τέλος) 9.
τέλος (nom.sing.neut.of τέλος, apposition) 881.

Translation - "I am the Alpha and the Omega; the first and the last, the beginning and the end."

Comment: *Cf.*#'s 5318, 5319, 487, 496, 1285 and 881 for other similar designations of Christ. He is First and Last in a chronological sense and Beginning and End in a cause and result sense. He is thus Alpha and Omega. As Ἀρχή, He is the creative First Cause and as such Deists have known Him. But He is also a redemptive Ἀρχη, Who brings the salvation result. Only the Christian knows Him in this sense. Theists have no objection when the philosopher calls God "first cause" if the philosopher means Jesus Christ as First Cause, both of creation and redemption. To call God "first cause" only in a creative sense is to damn Him with faint praise, or indeed to insult Him, since He Who creates without providing redemption, at least for the elect, is worthy of no praise.

Verse 14 - "Blessed are they that do his commandments, that they may have right to the tree of life, and may enter in through the gates of the city."

Μακάριοι οἱ πλύνοντες τὰς στολὰς αὐτῶν, ἵνα ἔσται ἡ ἐξουσία αὐτῶν ἐπὶ τὸ ξύλον τῆς ζωῆς καὶ τοῖς πυλῶσιν εἰσέλθωσιν εἰς τὴν πόλιν.

"Blessed are those who wash their robes, that they may have the right to the tree of life and that they may enter the city by the gates." . . . RSV

Μακάριοι (nom.pl.masc.of μακάριος, predicate adjective) 422.
οἱ (nom.pl.masc.of the article in agreement with πλύνοντες) 9.
πλύνοντες (pres.act.part.nom.pl.masc.of πλύνω, substantival, subject of εἰσίν understood) 2043.
τὰς (acc.pl.fem.of the article in agreement with στολὰς) 9.
στολὰς (acc.pl.fem.of στολή, direct object of πλύνοντες) 2552.
αὐτῶν (gen.pl.masc.of αὐτός, possession) 16.
ἵνα (conjunction with the future indicative, consecutive) 114.
ἔσται (3d.per.sing.fut.ind.of εἰμί, consecutive) 86.
ἡ (nom.sing.fem.of the article in agreement with ἐξουσία) 9.
ἐξουσία (nom.sing.fem.of ἐξουσία, subject of ἔσται) 707.
αὐτῶν (gen.pl.masc.of αὐτός, possession) 16.
ἐπὶ (preposition with the accusative, ground) 47.
τὸ (acc.sing.neut.of the article in agreement with ξύλον) 9.

ξύλον (acc.sing.neut.of ξύλον, ground) 1590.
τῆς (gen.sing.fem.of the article in agreement with ζωῆς) 9.
ζωῆς (gen.sing.fem.of ζωή, description) 668.
καὶ (adjunctive conjunction joining result clauses) 14.
τοῖς (instrumental pl.masc.of the article in agreement with πυλῶσιν) 9.
πυλῶσιν (instru.pl.masc.of πυλών, means) 1610.
εἰσέλθωσιν (3d.per.pl.2d.aor.mid.subj.of εἰσέρχομαι, consecutive) 234.
εἰς (preposition with the accusative of extent) 140.
τὴν (acc.sing.fem.of the article in agreement with πόλιν) 9.
πόλιν (acc.sing.fem.of πόλις, extent) 243.

Translation - "Happy are those who wash their robes so that theirs will be the right to the tree of life and so that they may enter by the gates into the city."

Comment: Jesus began His ministry with a series of Beatitudes (Mt.5:1-12). Now He closes with another. "Instead of πλύνοντες τὰς στολὰς αὐτῶν, supported by Sinaiticus A about 15 minuscules (including 1006 2020 2053) it₆₁ vg cop_sa *al*, the Textus Receptus, following 046 most minuscules it_gig syr_ph,b cop_bo *al*, reads the somewhat similar sounding words ποιοῦντες τὰς ἐντολὰς αὐτοῦ. The latter reading appears to be a scribal emendation, for elsewhere the author uses the expression τηρεῖν τὰς ἐντολάς (12.17; 14.12). "Moreover the prepossessions of the scribes would have favoured ποιοῦντες τὰς ἐντολάς rather than πλύνοντες τὰς στολάς" (H.B.Swete, *in loc.*). (Metzger, *A Textual Commentary on the Greek New Testament*, 767, 768).

Both readings express the idea of the victorious Christian life. The implication in the result clause with ἵνα is that entrance into the Holy City will be restricted only to the Christian who has obeyed the admonition and met the condition. How does one wash his robe? (1 John 1:9). The cleansing of all unrighteousness (washing our robes) is the result of confession of sin and forsaking it. The reward is two-fold. He will have access to the tree of life and he will be permitted to walk through the pearl gates into the city. Note both the subjunctive and the future indicative afte ἵνα in the result clause. Robertson lists the following, a partial list, where ἵνα, either in final or consecutive clauses has the future indicative: John 7:3; Acts 21:24; Lk.14:10; 1 Cor.9:18; Lk.20:10; 1 Cor.9:15; 1 Pet.3:1; Rev.6:4; 8:3; 3:9; 22:14 and adds "in some of these examples the subj.and ind.future occur side by side." (Robertson, *Grammar*, 984). *Cf.*#114.

The New Testament, totally Calvinistic with respect to salvation by grace and not by works is nevertheless opposed to antinomian thought. It warns again and again that certain special rewards and privileges are reserved only for obedient Christians. The Christian with unwashed robes will be saved and in the eternal Kingdom of God, but the implication of this verse is that he will be forever denied entrance into the city.

Verse 15 - "For without are dogs, and sorcerers, and whoremongers, and murderers, and idolaters, and whosoever loveth and maketh a lie."

ἔξω οἱ κύνες καὶ οἱ φάρμακοι καὶ οἱ πόρνοι καὶ οἱ φονεῖς καὶ οἱ εἰδωλολάτραι καὶ πᾶς φιλῶν καὶ ποιῶν φεῦδος.

"Outside are the dogs and sorcerers and fornicators and murderers and idolaters, and every one who lives and practices falsehood." . . . *RSV*

ἔξω (adverbial form of ἐξ, local) 449.
οἱ (nom.pl.masc.of the article in agreement with κύνες) 9.
κύνες (nom.pl.masc.of κύων, subject of ellided verb) 651.
καὶ (adjunctive conjunction joining nouns) 14.
οἱ (nom.pl.masc.of the article in agreement with φάρμακοι) 9.
φάρμακοι (nom.pl.masc.of φάρμακος, subject of ellided verb) 5424.
καὶ (adjunctive conjunction joining nouns) 14.
οἱ (nom.pl.masc.of the article in agreement with πόρνοι) 9.
πόρνοι (nom.pl.masc.of πόρνος, subject of ellided verb) 4140.
καὶ (adjunctive conjunction joining nouns) 14.
οἱ (nom.pl.masc.of the article in agreement with φονεῖς) 9.
φονεῖς (nom.pl.masc.of φονεύς, subject of ellided verb) 1405.
καὶ (adjunctive conjunction joining nouns) 14.
οἱ (nom.pl.masc.of the article in agreement with εἰδωλολάτραι) 9.
εἰδωλολάτραι (nom.pl.masc.of εἰδωλολάτρης, subject of ellided verb) 4142.
καὶ (adjunctive conjunction joining substantives) 14.
πᾶς (nom.sing.masc.of πᾶς, in agreement with φιλῶν and ποιῶν) 67.
φιλῶν (pres.act.part.nom.sing.masc.of φιλέω, substantival, subject of ellided verb) 566.
καὶ (adjunctive conjunction joining participles) 14.
ποιῶν (pres.act.part.nom.sing.masc.of ποιέω, substantival, subject of ellided verb) 127.
ψεῦδος (acc.sing.neut.of ψεῦδος, direct object of φιλῶν and ποιῶν) 2388.

Translation - "Outside are the dogs and the sorcerers and the fornicators and the muderers and the idolators and every one who loves and practices a lie."

Comment: Once again the New Jerusalem is described negatively in terms of the types not to be admitted. *Cf.* Rev.21:8. Those who love and practise lying are described in 1 John 2:22. The "dogs" are the legalists (Phil.3:2), not your little friend to whom you serve Alpo. The passage does not say that all of these evil people are immediately outside the Holy City. They are in the lake of fire, which is outside (ἔξω).

Verse 16 - "I Jesus have sent mine angel to testify unto you these things in the churches. I am the root and the offspring of David, and the bright and morning star."

Ἐγὼ Ἰησοῦς ἔπεμφα τὸν ἄγγελόν μου μαρτυρῆσαι ὑμῖν ταῦτα ἐπὶ ταῖς ἐκκλησίαις. ἐγώ εἰμι ἡ ῥίζα καὶ τὸ γένος Δαυίδ, ὁ ἀστὴρ ὁ λαμπρὸς ὁ πρωϊνός.

"I Jesus have sent my angel to you with this testimony for the churches. I am the root and the offspring of David, the bright and morning star." . . . *RSV*

Ἐγώ (nom.sing.masc.of ἐγώ, subject of ἔπεμφα) 123.

Ἰησοῦς (nom.sing.masc.of Ἰησοῦς, apposition) 3.
ἔπεμψα (1st.per.sing.aor.act.ind.of πέμπω, culminative) 169.
τὸν (acc.sing.masc.of the article in agreement with ἄγγελον) 9.
ἄγγελόν (acc.sing.masc.of ἄγγελος, direct object of ἔπεμψα) 96.
μου (gen.sing.masc.of ἐγώ, relationship) 123.
μαρτυρῆσαι (aor.act.inf.of μαρτυρέω, purpose) 1471.
ὑμῖν (dat.pl.masc.of σύ, indirect object of μαρτυρῆσαι) 104.
ταῦτα (acc.pl.neut.of οὗτος, direct object of μαρτυρῆσαι) 93.
ἐπὶ (preposition with the dative, indirect object of μαρτυρῆσαι) 47.
ταῖς (dat.pl.fem.of the article in agreement with ἐκκλησίαις) 9.
ἐκκλησίαις (dat.pl.fem.of ἐκκλεσία, indirect object of μαρτυρῆσαι) 1204.
ἐγώ (nom.sing.masc.of ἐγώ, subject of εἰμι) 123.
εἰμι (1st.per.sing.pres.ind.of εἰμί, static) 86.
ἡ (nom.sing.fem.of the article in agreement with ῥίζα) 9.
ῥίζα (nom.sing.fem.of ῥίζα, apposition) 293.
καὶ (adjunctive conjunction joining nouns) 14.
τὸ (nom.sing.neut.of the article in agreement with γένος) 9.
γένος (nom.sing.neut.of γένος, apposition) 1090.
Δαυίδ, (gen.sing.masc.of Δαυίδ, relationship) 6.
ὁ (nom.sing.masc.of the article in agreement with ἀστήρ) 9.
ἀστὴρ (nom.sing.masc.of ἀστήρ, apposition) 145.
ὁ (nom.sing.masc.of the article in agreement with λαμπρὸς) 9.
λαμπρὸς (nom.sing.masc.of λαμπρός, in agreement with ἀστήρ) 2832.
ὁ (nom.sing.masc.of the article in agreement with πρωϊνός) 9.
πρωϊνός (nom.sing.masc.of πρωϊνος, in agreement with ἀστήρ) 5333.

Translation - "I, Jesus, sent my messenger to relate to you these things for the chaurches. I, I am the Root and Descendant of David, the Bright and Morning Star."

Comment: It is fitting that at the close of a book that reveals Jesus as the Almighty Creator, Redeemer and Judge, taking vengeance upon the ungodly (2 Thess.1:7) that He should remind us again that He is the incarnate Son of Man as well. He points to His lineage in the house of David and thus reminds us of His mission in fulfilling the Davidic covenant (2 Sam.7). *Cf.* Isa.11:1,10; Rom.1:3; Rev.5:5. He is the star that Balaam saw in vision (Numbers 24:17; Rev.2:28). His coming will herald the dawning of a new day. His last words are in terms of a gospel invitation (Mt.11:28).

Verse 17 - "And the Spirit and the Bride say, Come. And let him that heareth say, come. And let him that is athirst come. And whosoever will, let him take the water of life freely."

Καὶ τὸ πνεῦμα καὶ ἡ νύμφη λέγουσιν, Ἔρχου. καὶ ὁ ἀκούων εἰπάτω, Ἔρχου. καὶ ὁ διψῶν ἐρχέσθω, ὁ θέλων λαβέτω ὕδωρ ζωῆς δωρεάν.

"The Spirit and the Bride say, 'Come.' And let him who hears say, 'Come.' And let him who is thirsty come, let him who desires take the water of life without price." . . . RSV

καὶ (explanatory conjunction) 14.
τὸ (nom.sing.neut.of the article in agreement with πνεῦμα) 9.
πνεῦμα (nom.sing.neut.of πνεῦμα, subject of λέγουσιν) 83.
καὶ (adjunctive conjunction joining nouns) 14.
ἡ (nom.sing.fem.of the article in agreement with νύμφη) 9.
νύμφη (nom.sing.fem.of νύμφη, subject of λέγουσιν) 898.
λέγουσιν (3d.per.pl.pres.act.ind.of λέγω, present progressive) 66.
Ἔρχου (2d.per.sing.pres.mid.impv.of ἔρχομαι, entreaty) 146.
καὶ (continuative conjunction) 14.
ὁ (nom.sing.masc.of the article in agreement with ἀκούων) 9.
ἀκούων (pres.act.part.nom.sing.masc.of ἀκούω, substantival, subject of εἰπάτω) 148.
εἰπάτω (3d.per.sing.aor.act.impv.of εἶπον, command) 155.
Ἔρχου (2d.per.sing.pres.mid.impv.of ἔρχομαι, entreaty) 146.
καὶ (continuative conjunction) 14.
ὁ (nom.sing.masc.of the article in agreement with διψῶν) 9.
διψῶν (pres.act.part.nom.sing.masc.of διψάω, subject of ἐρχέσθω) 427.
ἐρχέσθω (3d.per.sing.pres.mid.impv.of ἔρχομαι, entreaty) 146.
ὁ (nom.sing.masc.of the article in agreement with θέλων) 9.
θέλων (pres.act.part.nom.sing.masc.of θέλω, subject of λαβέτω) 88.
λαβέτω (3d.per.sing.aor.act.impv.of λαμβάνω, entreaty) 533.
ὕδωρ (acc.sing.neut.of ὕδωρ, direct object of λαβέτω) 301.
ζωῆς (gen.sing.fem.of αωή, description) 668.
δωρεάν (adverbial) 858.

Translation - "Now the Spirit and the Bride are saying, 'Come.' And let the one who is hearing say, 'Come.' And let the thirsty one come. Let him who wishes, take living water without cost."

Comment: A further evidence that the Bride of Christ is a body of select saints (Rev.19:8, on which *cf.* comment) is found here in that what the Holy Spirit says, he says through the Bride. The gospel invitation comes from the Holy Spirit (John 16:7-11), through the lips of those saints who are responsive to His promptings. Hence, when the Holy Spirit says, "Come" she says, "Come." Unfortunately, many of the elect saints have never witnessed for Christ nor invited the lost to come to Him. Therefore, since the gospel invitation is "Come" every Chrsitian who has studied the Revelation should be saying, "Come." Thus the first imperative.

The hearer should start inviting the lost to Christ. When we do, some will get thirsty. Indeed all who will to do so are entreated to drink of the living water freely. The Bride (Rev.21:9) has a river of living water. The King of the city will give the water freely (Rev.21:6; John 4:10, 13-14; 7:37-39).

Not all can come (John 6:44) but he who can and thus wishes to do so (Rev.22:17) and does (Mt.11:27-28) will be saved. And God's method of drawing him involves the Holy Spirit and the Bride, the Father and the Son. The Greek New Testament, a document that teaches the Reformed Theology closes on the note of a gospel invitation. Since we do not know whom the Father will draw to Christ, our task is to invite all. Some will come and others will not. There is no excuse for a hyper-Calvinistic disregard for the Great Commission (Mt.28:18-20). *Cf.* Acts 20:31.

Verse 18 - "For I testify unto every man that heareth the words of the prophecy of this book. If any man shall add unto these things God shall add unto him the plagues that are written in this book."

Μαρτυρῶ ἐγὼ παντὶ τῷ ἀκούοντι τοὺς λόγους τῆς προφητείας τοῦ βιβλίου τούτου, ἐάν τις ἐπιθῇ ἐπ’ αὐτά, ἐπιθήσει ἐπ’ αὐτὸν ὁ θεὸς τὰς πληγὰς τὰς γεγραμμένας ἐν τῷ βιβλίῳ τούτῳ.

"I warn every one who hears the words of the prophecy of this book: if any one adds to them, God will add to him the plagues described in this book, . . ." . . . RSV

Μαρτυρῶ (1st.per.sing.pres.act.ind.of μαρτυρέω, aoristic) 1471.
ἐγὼ (nom.sing.masc.of ἐγώ, subject of μαρτυρῶ) 123.
παντί (dat.sing.masc.of πᾶς, in agreement with ἀκούοντι) 67.
τῷ (dat.sing.masc.of the article in agreement with ἀκούοντι) 9.
ἀκούοντι (pres.act.part.dat.sing.masc.of ἀκούω, indirect object of μαρτυρῶ) 148.
τοὺς (acc.pl.masc.of the article in agreement with λόγους) 9.
λόγους (acc.pl.masc.of λόγος, direct object of ἀκούοντι) 510.
τῆς (gen.sing.fem.of the article in agreement with προφητείας) 9.
προφητείας (gen.sing.fem.of προφητεία, description) 1041.
τοῦ (gen.sing.neut.of the article in agreement with βιβλίου) 9.
βιβλίου (gen.sing.neut.of βιβλίον, description) 1292.
τούτου (gen.sing.neut.of οὗτος, in agreement with βιβλίου) 93.
ἐάν (conditional particle with the subjunctive in a third-class condition) 363.
τις (nom.sing.masc.of τις, indefinite pronoun, subject of ἐπιθῇ) 486.
ἐπιθῇ (3d.per.sing.aor.act.subj.of ἐπιτίθημι, third-class condition) 818.
ἐπ’ (preposition with the accusative, extent) 47.
αὐτά (acc.pl.neut.of αὐτός, extent) 16.
ἐπιθήσει (3d.per.sing.fut.act.ind.of ἐπιτίθημι, predictive) 818.
ἐπ’ (preposition with the accusative of extent) 47.
αὐτὸν (acc.sing.masc.of αὐτός, extent) 16.
ὁ (nom.sing.masc.of the article in agreement with θεὸς) 9.
θεὸς (nom.sing.masc.of θεός, subject of ἐπιθήσει) 124.
τὰς (acc.pl.fem.of the article in agreement with πληγὰς) 9.
πληγὰς (acc.pl.fem.of πληγή, direct object of ἐπιήσει) 2421.
τὰς (acc.pl.fem.of the article in agreement with γεγραμμένας) 9.
γεγραμμένας (perf.pass.part.acc.pl.fem.of γράφω, adjectival, emphatic attributive position, ascriptive, in agreement with πληγὰς) 156.
ἐν (preposition with the locative of place) 80.

τῷ (loc.sing.neut.of the article in agreement with βιβλίῳ) 9.
βιβλίῳ (loc.sing.neut.of βιβλίον, place) 1292.
τούτῳ (loc.sing.neut.of οὗτος, in agreement with βιβλίῳ) 93.

Translation - "I serve notice to every one who hears the words of the prophecy of this book that if any one adds to them, God will add to him the plagues that stand written in this book."

Comment: This solemn warning, coupled with its counterpart in verse 19 accentuates the importance of the Revelation as does the special promises of blessing available to those who give it special study (Rev.1:3; 22:7). Eisegesis (ἐάν τις ἐπιθῇ ἐπ' αὐτά) is just as dangerous as denial. The superficial prophecy buff who imagines fulfillment of prophecy before the time is in danger here.

Verse 19 - "And it any man shall take away from the words of the book of this prophecy, God shall take away his part out of the book of life, and out of the holy city, and from the things which are written in this book."

καὶ ἐάν τις ἀφέλῃ ἀπὸ τῶν λόγων τοῦ βιβλίου τῆς προφητείας ταύτης, ἀφελεῖ ὁ θεὸς τὸ μέρος αὐτοῦ ἀπὸ τοῦ ξύλου τῆς ζωῆς καὶ ἐκ τῆς πόλεως τῆς ἁγίας, τῶν γεγραμμένων ἐν τῷ βιβλίῳ τούτῳ.

"and if any one takes away from the words of the book of this prophecy, God will take away his share in the tree of life and in the holy city, which are described in this book." . . . RSV

καὶ (continuative conjunction) 14.
ἐάν (condition particle with the subjunctive in a third-class condition) 363.
τις (nom.sing.masc.of τις, indefinite pronoun, subject of ἀφέλῃ) 486.
ἀφέλῃ (3d.per.sing.2d.aor.act.subj.of ἀφαιρέω, third-class condition) 1594.
ἀπὸ (preposition with the ablative of separation) 70.
τῶν (abl.pl.masc.of the article in agreement with λόγων) 9.
λόγων (abl.pl.masc.of λόγος, separation) 510.
τοῦ (gen.sing.neut.of the article in agreement with βιβλίου) 9.
βιβλίου (gen.sing.neut.of βιβλίον, separation) 1292.
τῆς (gen.sing.fem.of the article in agreement with προφητείας) 9.
προφητείας (gen.sing.fem.of προφητεία, description) 1041.
ταύτης (gen.sing.fem.of οὗτος, in agreement with προφητείας) 93.
ἀφελεῖ (3d.per.sing.fut.act.ind.of ἀφαιρέω, predictive) 1594.
ὁ (nom.sing.masc.of the article in agreement with θεὸς) 9.
θεὸς (nom.sing.masc.of θεός, subject of ἀφελεῖ) 124.
τὸ (acc.sing.neut.of the article in agreement with μέρος) 9.
μέρος (acc.sing.neut.of μέρος, direct object of ἀφελεῖ) 240.
αὐτοῦ (gen.sing.masc.of αὐτός, possession) 16.
ἀπὸ (preposition with the ablative of separation) 70.
τοῦ (gen.sing.neut.of the article in agreement with ξύλου) 9.
ξύλου (gen.sing.neut.of ξύλον, separation) 1590.

τῆς (gen.sing.fem.of the article in agreement with ζωῆς) 9.
ζωῆς (gen.sing.fem.of ζωή, description) 668.
καὶ (adjunctive conjunction joining prepositional phrases) 14.
ἐκ (preposition with the ablative of separation) 19.
τῆς (abl.sing.fem.of the article in agreement with πόλεως) 9.
πόλεως (abl.sing.fem.of πόλις, separation) 243.
τῆς (gen.sing.fem.of the article in agreement with ἀγίας) 9.
ἀγίας (abl.sing.fem.of ἄγιος, in agreement with πόλεως) 84.
τῶν (gen.pl.neut.of the article in agreement with γεγραμμένων) 9.
γεγραμμένων (perf.pass.part.abl.pl.neut.of γράφω, adjectival, emphatic attributive position, ascriptive, in agreement with μέρος, ξύλου and πόλεως) 156.
ἐν (preposition with the locative of place) 80.
τῷ (loc.sing.neut.of the article in agreement with βιβλίῳ) 9.
βιβλίῳ (loc.sing.neut.of βιβλίον, place) 1292.
τούτῳ (loc.sing.neut.of οὗτος, in agreement with βιβλίῳ) 93.

Translation - "And if any one takes away from the words of the book of this prophecy, God will take away his portion from the tree of life, and out of the Holy City, which are written in this book."

Comment: The higher critic with his documentary hypothesis and polychrome Bible had better beware!

Verse 20 - "He which testifieth these things saith, Surely I come quickly. Amen. Even so, come, Lord Jesus."

Λέγει ὁ μαρτυρῶν ταῦτα, Ναί, ἔρχομαι ταχύ. Ἀμήν, ἔρχου, κύριε Ἰησοῦ.

"He who testifies to these things says, 'Surely I am coming soon.' Amen. Come, Lord Jesus!" . . . RSV

λέγει (3d.per.sing.pres.act.ind.of λέγω, aoristic) 66.
ὁ (nom.sing.masc.of the article in agreement with μαρτυρῶν) 9.
μαρτυρῶν (pres.act.part.nom.sing.masc.of μαρτυρέω, substantival, subject of λέγει) 1471.
ταῦτα (acc.pl.neut.of οὗτος, direct object of μαρτυρῶν) 93.
Ναί (affirmative particle) 524.
ἔρχομαι (1st.per.sing.pres.mid.ind.of ἔρχομαι, predictive) 146.
ταχύ (temporal adverb) 491.
Ἀμήν (exclamation) 466.
ἔρχου (2d.per.sing.pres.mid.impv.of ἔρχομαι, entreaty) 146.
κύριε (voc.sing.masc.of κύριος, address) 97.
Ἰησοῦ (voc.sing.masc.of Ἰησοῦς, address) 3.

Translation - "The one who witnesses to these things is saying, 'Indeed I am coming quickly.' Be it so. Come, Lord, Jesus."

Comment: Our Lord's promise to come in what to a timeless God is "quickly," since back on Patmos in the first century, He looked forward to "the time of the end" is heartily echoed by the aged apostle John, who can scarcely wait for the glorious day. Nor can we, 1900 years later.

Verse 21 - "The grace of our Lord Jesus Christ be with you all. Amen."

Ἡ χάρις τοῦ κυρίου Ἰησοῦ μετὰ πάντων.

"The grace of the Lord Jesus be with all the saints. Amen." . . . RSV

Ἡ (nom.sing.fem.of the article in agreement with χάρις) 9.
χάρις (nom.sing.fem.of χάρις, subject of ἔστω understood) 1700.
τοῦ (gen.sing.masc.of the article in agreement with κυρίου) 9.
κυρίου (gen.sing.masc.of κύριος, description) 97.
Ἰησοῦ (gen.sing.masc.of Ἰησοῦς, appellation) 3.
μετὰ (preposition with the genitive of accompaniment) 50.
πάντων (gen.pl. masc.of πᾶς, accompaniment and fellowship) 67.

Translation - "The grace of the Lord Jesus be with all."

Comment: There are various readings in the MSS for the close, none of which improve upon the one in the opinion of the United Bible Societies' Committee.

Gracious Father, lovely Lord Jesus and ever patient Holy Spirit, what began in my mind as a research project in your Word more than fifty years ago, has at this moment (12:55 P.M., 4 July 1984) come to a close. I dedicate it all to you and ask that whatever further blessing it may provide may be used to glorify only you. In the name and for the eternal glory of Father, Son and Holy Spirit, the Almighty Triune God.

Randy Yeager

Index to Volume 18

Vocabulary Index to The Renaissance New Testament

#	Volume	Page
1	1	1
2	1	1
3	1	1
4	1	1
5	1	2
6	1	2
7	1	3
8	1	5
9	1	5
10	1	6
11	1	7
12	1	7
13	1	7
14	1	8
15	1	9
16	1	10
17	1	11
18	1	12
19	1	12
20	1	12
21	1	12
22	1	13
23	1	13
24	1	13
25	1	13
26	1	14
27	1	14
28	1	14
29	1	15
30	1	15
31	1	16
32	1	16
33	1	16
34	1	18
35	1	18
36	1	19
37	1	19
38	1	19
39	1	20
40	1	21
41	1	21
42	1	22
43	1	22
44	1	22
45	1	23
46	1	23
47	1	24
48	1	24

49	1	24	73	1	43
50	1	25	74	1	44
51	1	26	75	1	45
52	1	26	76	1	46
53	1	26	77	1	46
54	1	26	78	1	46
55	1	27	79	1	47
56	1	27	80	1	48
57	1	27	81	1	48
58	1	27	82	1	48
59	1	28	83	1	49
60	1	28	84	1	50
61	1	28	85	1	53
62	1	29	86	1	54
63	1	29	87	1	54
64	1	30	88	1	54
65	1	30	89	1	55
66	1	30	90	1	55
67	1	34	91	1	56
68	1	36	92	1	56
69	1	41	93	1	57
70	1	41	94	1	58
71	1	41	95	1	58
72	1	42	96	1	59

97	1	59	121	1	83
98	1	60	122	1	84
99	1	61	123	1	84
100	1	61	124	1	84
101	1	61	125	1	88
102	1	62	126	1	89
103	1	62	127	1	89
104	1	63	128	1	91
105	1	63	129	1	93
106	1	65	130	1	93
107	1	65	131	1	94
108	1	66	132	1	95
109	1	66	133	1	97
110	1	67	134	1	97
111	1	67	135	1	97
112	1	71	136	1	100
113	1	72	137	1	100
114	1	75	138	1	100
115	1	76	139	1	100
116	1	77	140	1	101
117	1	78	141	1	101
118	1	78	142	1	102
119	1	81	143	1	103
120	1	83	144	1	103

145	1	106	169	1	129
146	1	106	170	1	130
147	1	109	171	1	130
148	1	111	172	1	130
149	1	113	173	1	130
150	1	114	174	1	130
151	1	115	175	1	132
152	1	116	176	1	132
153	1	116	177	1	132
154	1	116	178	1	133
155	1	120	179	1	135
156	1	122	180	1	135
157	1	123	181	1	136
158	1	124	182	1	138
159	1	124	183	1	138
160	1	124	184	1	138
161	1	124	185	1	139
162	1	125	186	1	140
163	1	126	187	1	141
164	1	126	188	1	142
165	1	126	189	1	142
166	1	128	190	1	142
167	1	128	191	1	143
168	1	128	192	1	143

193	1	144	217	1	160
194	1	144	218	1	161
195	1	145	219	1	161
196	1	145	220	1	161
197	1	146	221	1	162
198	1	146	222	1	164
199	1	147	223	1	164
200	1	148	224	1	164
201	1	148	225	1	165
202	1	150	226	1	165
203	1	150	227	1	165
204	1	150	228	1	165
205	1	151	229	1	167
206	1	151	230	1	168
207	1	152	231	1	169
208	1	153	232	1	171
209	1	155	233	1	171
210	1	156	234	1	174
211	1	158	235	1	175
212	1	158	236	1	175
213	1	159	237	1	175
214	1	159	238	1	176
215	1	159	239	1	178
216	1	160	240	1	179

241	1	180	265	1	198
242	1	181	266	1	198
243	1	181	267	1	198
244	1	182	268	1	199
245	1	182	269	1	199
246	1	184	270	1	200
247	1	184	271	1	200
248	1	185	272	1	201
249	1	185	273	1	201
250	1	185	274	1	203
251	1	186	275	1	204
252	1	187	276	1	207
253	1	188	277	1	208
254	1	189	278	1	208
255	1	194	279	1	208
256	1	194	280	1	209
257	1	194	281	1	209
258	1	195	282	1	211
259	1	196	283	1	211
260	1	197	284	1	213
261	1	197	285	1	213
262	1	197	286	1	214
263	1	197	287	1	216
264	1	198	288	1	217

289	1	219	313	1	236
290	1	220	314	1	236
291	1	222	315	1	236
292	1	222	316	1	239
293	1	222	317	1	239
294	1	222	318	1	243
295	1	223	319	1	244
296	1	223	320	1	245
297	1	224	321	1	245
298	1	225	322	1	246
299	1	225	323	1	249
300	1	227	324	1	250
301	1	228	325	1	251
302	1	229	326	1	252
303	1	230	327	1	255
304	1	230	328	1	255
305	1	231	329	1	258
306	1	231	330	1	259
307	1	234	331	1	259
308	1	234	332	1	261
309	1	235	333	1	261
310	1	235	334	1	261
311	1	235	335	1	261
312	1	236	336	1	263

337	1	263	361	1	284
338	1	264	362	1	286
339	1	266	363	1	288
340	1	267	364	1	291
341	1	268	365	1	291
342	1	270	366	1	292
343	1	271	367	1	293
344	1	272	368	1	295
345	1	274	369	1	296
346	1	274	370	1	297
347	1	275	371	1	297
348	1	275	372	1	298
349	1	276	373	1	298
350	1	276	374	1	300
351	1	277	375	1	300
352	1	278	376	1	301
353	1	278	377	1	302
354	1	280	378	1	303
355	1	280	379	1	303
356	1	281	380	1	304
357	1	282	381	1	304
358	1	282	382	1	305
359	1	283	383	1	306
360	1	283	384	1	307

385	1	308	409	1	321
386	1	308	410	1	321
387	1	309	411	1	322
388	1	309	412	1	322
389	1	310	413	1	322
390	1	310	414	1	323
391	1	310	415	1	323
392	1	312	416	1	324
393	1	312	417	1	324
394	1	313	418	1	325
395	1	313	419	1	326
396	1	314	420	1	327
397	1	314	421	1	327
398	1	314	422	1	330
399	1	314	423	1	330
400	1	315	424	1	332
401	1	315	425	1	333
402	1	317	426	1	333
403	1	318	427	1	334
404	1	318	428	1	334
405	1	319	429	1	336
406	1	319	430	1	336
407	1	320	431	1	337
408	1	320	432	1	337

433	1	339
434	1	340
435	1	341
436	1	343
437	2	343
438	1	344
439	1	344
440	1	346
441	1	346
442	1	347
443	1	349
444	1	349
445	1	350
446	1	350
447	1	351
448	1	352
449	1	353
450	1	353
451	1	355
452	1	356
453	1	357
454	1	357
455	1	358
456	1	359

457	1	359
458	1	359
459	1	360
460	1	361
461	1	362
462	1	364
463	1	364
464	1	365
465	1	366
466	1	368
467	1	369
468	1	369
469	1	369
470	1	370
471	1	372
472	1	372
473	1	374
474	1	375
475	1	377
476	1	378
477	1	378
478	1	378
479	1	380
480	1	380

481	1	380	505	1	402
482	1	381	506	1	403
483*	1	381	507	1	403
484	1	383	508	1	406
485	1	383	509	1	408
486	1	384	510	1	408
487	1	388	511	1	411
488	1	389	512	1	411
489	1	390	513	1	411
490	1	390	514	1	413
491	1	391	515	1	413
492	1	391	516	1	414
493	1	392	517	1	414
494	1	392	518	1	415
495	1	394	519	1	415
496**	1	395	520	1	417
497	1	395	521	1	418
498	1	396	522	1	418
499	1	397	523	1	419
500	1	398	524	1	419
501	1	400	525	1	420
502	1	401	526	1	422
503	1	401	527	1	422
504	1	401	528	1	423

* #**483** γέεvvαv (acc.sing.fem.of γέεvvα, extent).

** Inadvertently numbered 395 in the first edition of Volume 1.

529	1	423	553	1	444
530	1	423	554	1	444
531	1	425	555	1	446
532	1	426	556	1	446
533	1	426	557	1	447
534	1	428	558	1	448
535	1	429	559	1	448
536	1	430	560	1	448
537	1	430	561	1	449
538	1	431	562	1	449
539	1	431	563	1	450
540	1	432	564	1	451
541	1	434	565	1	452
542	1	434	566	1	453
543	1	435	567	1	454
544	1	436	568	1	454
545	1	436	569	1	456
546	1	438	570	1	456
547	1	439	571	1	456
548	1	440	572	1	458
549	1	440	573	1	458
550	1	441	574	1	458
551	1	442	575	1	459
552	1	443	576	1	461

577	1	462		601	1	484
578	1	464		602	1	484
579	1	464		603	1	485
580	1	465		604	1	486
581	1	465		605	1	486
582	1	467		606	1	487
583	1	467		607	1	487
584	1	467		608	1	488
585	1	469		609	1	489
586	1	471		610	1	489
587	1	472		611	1	490
588	1	472		612	1	490
589	1	474		613	1	491
590	1	474		614	1	493
591	1	476		615	1	493
592	1	476		616	1	493
593	1	477		617	1	494
594	1	477		618	1	494
595	1	478		619	1	495
596	1	478		620	1	495
597	1	478		621	1	497
598	1	479		622	1	497
599	1	482		623	1	497
600	1	482		624	1	499

625	1	499	649	1	516
626	1	499	650	1	518
627	1	499	651	1	519
628	1	500	652	1	519
629	1	501	653	1	519
630	1	501	654	1	520
631	1	502	655	1	522
632	1	503	656	1	524
633	1	503	657	1	525
634	1	504	658	1	525
635	1	504	659	1	526
636	1	504	660	1	528
637	1	506	661	1	531
638	1	506	662	1	531
639	1	507	663	1	531
640	1	509	664	1	532
641	1	509	665	1	532
642	1	511	666	1	532
643	1	512	667	1	535
644	1	512	668	1	535
645	1	514	669	1	536
646	1	514	670	1	537
647	1	514	671	1	538
648	1	515	672	1	538

673	1	538	697	1	557
674	1	539	698	1	558
675	1	540	699	1	558
676	1	540	700	1	558
677	1	541	701	1	561
678	1	541	702	1	563
679	1	541	703	1	566
680	1	541	704	1	567
681	1	541	705	1	567
682	1	543	706	1	568
683	1	544	707	1	569
684*	1	546	708	2	1
685	1	548	709	2	2
686	1	549	710	2	3
687	1	549	711	2	3
688	1	551	712	2	4
689	1	552	713	2	5
690	1	552	714	2	6
691	1	552	715	2	6
692	1	553	716	2	6
693	1	554	717	2	8
694	1	554	718	2	9
695	1	555	719	2	9
696	1	557	720	2	10

*Number inadvertently omitted in first edition of Volume 1.
ἄραγε (inferential conjunction).

497

721	2	11	745	2	31
722	2	12	746	2	32
723	2	13	747	2	34
724	2	13	748	2	34
725	2	14	749	2	35
726	2	16	750	2	37
727	2	17	751	2	38
728	2	17	752	2	38
729	2	19	753	2	39
730	2	19	754	2	40
731	2	19	755	2	40
732	2	21	756	2	43
733	2	21	757	2	43
734	2	21	758	2	44
735	2	23	759	2	45
736	2	24	760	2	46
737	2	24	761	2	48
738	2	25	762	2	48
739	2	26	763	2	49
740	2	28	764	2	49
741	2	29	765	2	50
742	2	30	766	2	51
743	2	31	767	2	51
744	2	31	768	2	53

69	2	53	793	2	79
70	2	54	794	2	80
71	2	55	795	2	80
72	2	56	796	2	81
'73	2	57	797	2	84
'74	2	57	798	2	84
'75	2	60	799	2	84
'76	2	60	800	2	86
'77	2	61	801	2	86
'78	2	61	802	2	86
779	2	63	803	2	86
780	2	63	804	2	87
781	2	65	805	2	87
782	2	66	806	2	88
783	2	67	807	2	88
784	2	68	808	2	89
785	2	71	809	2	89
786	2	73	810	2	89
787	2	73	811	2	90
788	2	73	812	2	91
789	2	74	813	2	91
790	2	75	814	2	91
791	2	76	815	2	93
792	2	76	816	2	94

817	2	94	841	2	120
818	2	95	842	2	121
819	2	98	843	2	121
820	2	98	844	2	124
821	2	98	845	2	125
822	2	99	846	2	126
823	2	99	847	2	126
824	2	102	848	2	126
825	2	102	849	2	126
826	2	103	850	2	126
827	2	103	851	2	127
828	2	104	852	2	127
829	2	105	853	2	127
830	2	106	854	2	127
831	2	109	855	2	128
832	2	100	856	2	129
833	2	111	857	2	131
834	2	114	858	2	132
835	2	116	859	2	133
836	2	116	860	2	133
837	2	117	861	2	134
838	2	117	862	2	134
839	2	119	863	2	135
840	2	119	864	2	136

865	2	139	889	2	166
866	2	140	890	2	168
867	2	142	891	2	169
868	2	143	892	2	169
869	2	143	893	2	169
870	2	146	894	2	171
871	2	146	895	2	174
872	2	146	896	2	177
873	2	147	897	2	180
874	2	148	898	2	181
875	2	150	899	2	183
876	2	150	900	2	188
877	2	155	901	2	188
878	2	155	902	2	189
879	2	155	903	2	189
880	2	156	904	2	191
881	2	157	905	2	192
882	2	161	906	2	194
883	2	161	907	2	196
884	2	162	908	2	196
885	2	162	909	2	197
886	2	163	910	2	199
887	2	165	911	2	199
888	2	165	912	2	200

913	2	201	937	2	221
914	2	203	938	2	221
915	2	204	939	2	221
916	2	205	940	2	222
917	2	205	941	2	222
918	2	206	942	2	222
919	2	207	943	2	223
920	2	207	944	2	224
921	2	210	945	2	225
922	2	212	946	2	225
923	2	212	947	2	226
924	2	213	948	2	227
925	2	213	949	2	229
926	2	214	950	2	230
927	2	214	951	2	230
928	2	214	952	2	232
929	2	215	953	2	239
930	2	216	954	2	242
931	2	216	955	2	242
932	2	217	956	2	245
933	2	217	957	2	246
934	2	218	958	2	246
935	2	220	959	2	251
936	2	220	960	2	251

961	2	251	985	2	279
962	2	253	986	2	280
963	2	253	987	2	280
964	2	254	988	2	280
965	2	254	989	2	280
966	2	255	990	2	281
967	2	256	991	2	285
968	2	257	992	2	287
969	2	259	993	2	289
970	2	260	994	2	290
971	2	262	995	2	293
972	2	265	996	2	294
973	2	265	997	2	296
974	2	266	998	2	296
975	2	268	999	2	297
976	2	268	1000	2	298
977	2	270	1001	2	299
978	2	271	1002	2	301
979	2	272	1003	2	306
980	2	273	1004	2	308
981	2	275	1005	2	310
982	2	276	1006	2	312
983	2	278	1007	2	313
984	2	278	1008	2	314

1009	2	314	1033	2	340
1010	2	315	1034*	2	341
1011	2	316	1035	2	342
1012	2	316	1036	2	342
1013	2	317	1037	2	343
1014	2	319	1038	2	345
1015	2	319	1039	2	348
1016	2	319	1040	2	349
1017	2	321	1041	2	349
1018	2	322	1042	2	351
1019	2	322	1043	2	351
1020	2	324	1044	2	351
1021	2	325	1045	2	360
1022	2	325	1046	2	360
1023	2	325	1047	2	361
1024	2	327	1048	2	362
1025	2	332	1049	2	363
1026	2	335	1050	2	363
1027	2	336	1051	2	364
1028	2	337	1052	2	364
1029	2	338	1053	2	366
1030	2	339	1054	2	366
1031	2	339	1055	2	368
1032	2	340	1056	2	369

*Cf.note and #1279.

1057	2	370	1081	2	392
1058	2	370	1082	2	395
1059	2	370	1083	2	396
1060	2	372	1084	2	397
1061	2	373	1085	2	399
1062	2	375	1086	2	401
1063	2	376	1087	2	402
1064	2	377	1088	2	402
1065	2	377	1089	2	403
1066	2	377	1090	2	403
1067	2	379	1091	2	405
1068	2	379	1092	2	405
1069	2	380	1093	2	407
1070	2	380	1094	2	409
1071	2	381	1095	2	411
1072	2	383	1096	2	411
1073	2	383	1097	2	413
1074	2	383	1098	2	413
1075	2	383	1099	2	413
1076	2	384	1100	2	414
1077	2	385	1101	2	414
1078	2	386	1102	2	415
1079	2	387	1103	2	417
1080	2	389	1104	2	418

1105	2	419	1129	2	449
1106	2	420	1130	2	451
1107	2	421	1131	2	451
1108	2	421	1132	2	456
1109*	2	423	1133	2	457
1110	2	424	1134	2	457
1111	2	425	1135	2	458
1112	2	426	1136	2	459
1113	2	426	1137	2	460
1114	2	428	1138	2	462
1115	2	429	1139	2	464
1116	2	431	1140	2	465
1117	2	432	1141	2	465
1118	2	433	1142	2	469
1119	2	436	1143	2	469
1120	2	439	1144	2	471
1121	2	439	1145	2	472
1122	2	441	1146	2	474
1123	2	442	1147	2	474
1124	2	442	1148	2	475
1125	2	443	1149	2	475
1126	2	445	1150	2	476
1127	2	448	1151	2	476
1128	2	448	1152	2	477

* # inadvertently omitted in first edition of Volume 1. γενεσίοις (loc.pl.neut.of γενέσια, time point).

1153	2	479	1177	2	500
1154	2	480	1178	2	503
1155	2	481	1179	2	505
1156	2	481	1180	2	506
1157	2	482	1181	2	506
1158	2	483	1182	2	507
1159	2	483	1183	2	509
1160	2	484	1184	2	509
1161	2	484	1185	2	510
1162	2	485	1186	2	512
1163	2	485	1187	2	512
1164	2	486	1188	2	513
1165	2	487	1189	2	514
1166	2	488	1190	2	516
1167	2	488	1191	2	516
1168	2	488	1192	2	516
1169	2	488	1193	2	517
1170	2	489	1194	2	517
1171	2	491	1195	2	517
1172	2	493	1196	2	522
1173	2	496	1197	2	524
1174	2	497	1198	2	525
1175	2	498	1199	2	525
1176	2	498	1200	2	531

1201	2	535	1225	2	577
1202	2	535	1226	2	577
1203	2	536	1227	2	581
1204	2	541	1228	2	582
1205	2	543	1229	2	588
1206	2	546	1230	2	589
1207	2	550	1231	2	590
1208	2	551	1232	2	591
1209	2	552	1233	2	591
1210	2	554	1234	2	591
1211	2	554	1235	2	594
1212	2	555	1236	2	595
1213	2	558	1237	2	595
1214	2	561	1238	2	597
1215	2	561	1239	2	597
1216	2	562	1240	2	598
1217	2	564	1241	2	600
1218	2	564	1242	2	601
1219	2	567	1243	2	602
1220	2	569	1244	2	602
1221	2	571	1245	2	604
1222	2	571	1246	2	605
1223	2	573	1247	2	605
1224	2	575	1248	2	611

1249	2	613	1273*	2	641
1250	2	614	1274	2	643
1251	2	614	1275	2	644
1252	2	614	1276	2	645
1253	2	614	1277	2	646
1254	2	615	1278	2	646
1255	2	617	1279	2	647
1256	2	619	1280	2	651
1257	2	622	1281	2	651
1258	2	622	1282	2	651
1259	2	622	1283	3	3
1260	2	626	1284	3	4
1261	2	626	1285	3	5
1262	2	627	1286	3	6
1263	2	629	1287	3	6
1264	2	630	1288	3	7
1265	2	633	1289	3	8
1266	2	634	1290	3	9
1267	2	635	1291	3	9
1268	2	637	1292	3	11
1269	2	638	1293	3	12
1270	2	639	1294	3	16
1271	2	640	1295	3	17
1272	2	640	1296	3	20

* Number inadvertently omitted. ταλάντων (gen.pl.neut.of τάλαντον, objective genitive).

1297	3	23	1321	3	56
1298	3	25	1322	3	59
1299	3	26	1323	3	60
1300	3	29	1324	3	60
1301	3	29	1325	3	61
1302	3	30	1326	3	62
1303	3	32	1327	3	62
1304	3	33	1328	3	68
1305	3	35	1329	3	70
1306	2	36	1330	3	74
1307	3	37	1331	3	75
1308	3	38	1332	3	76
1309	3	38	1333	3	77
1310	3	40	1334	3	78
1311	3	40	1335	3	80
1312	3	43	1336	3	82
1313	3	44	1337	3	84
1314	3	46	1338	3	85
1315	3	49	1339	3	87
1316	3	49	1340	3	88
1317	3	52	1341	3	88
1318	3	53	1342	3	89
1319	3	53	1343	3	89
1320	3	54	1344	3	90

1345	3	92	1369	3	113
1346	3	92	1370	3	115
1347	3	93	1371	3	126
1348	3	94	1372	3	129
1349	3	95	1373	3	131
1350	3	96	1374	3	131
1351	3	96	1375	3	135
1352	3	98	1376	3	135
1353	3	99	1377	3	136
1354	3	100	1378	3	136
1355	3	102	1379	3	136
1356	3	103	1380	3	136
1357	3	103	1381	3	137
1358	3	104	1382	3	137
1359	3	104	1383	3	139
1360	3	106	1384	3	139
1361	3	108	1385	3	141
1362	3	108	1386	3	143
1363	3	109	1387	3	143
1364	3	110	1388	3	146
1365	3	110	1389	3	148
1366	3	111	1390	3	148
1367	3	112	1391	3	149
1368	3	112	1392	3	152

1393	3	152	1417	3	180
1394	3	156	1418	3	182
1395	3	159	1419	3	183
1396	3	159	1420	3	185
1397	3	159	1421	3	186
1398	3	159	1422	3	186
1399	3	160	1423	3	190
1400	3	161	1424	3	191
1401	3	162	1425	3	194
1402	3	163	1426	3	198
1403	3	164	1427	3	203
1404	3	165	1428	3	205
1405	3	165	1429	3	213
1406	3	165	1430	3	216
1407	3	167	1431	3	220
1408	3	168	1432	3	220
1409	3	170	1433	3	221
1410	3	174	1434	3	221
1411*	3	176	1435	3	221
1412	3	176	1436	3	223
1413	3	178	1437	3	223
1414	3	179	1438	3	223
1415	3	179	1439	3	224
1416	3	180	1440	3	225

* 1411 κλητοί.

1441	3	225	1465	3	250
1442	3	226	1466	3	251
1443	3	226	1467	3	251
1444	3	229	1468	3	252
1445	3	233	1469	3	252
1446	3	233	1470	3	254
1447	3	235	1471	3	256
1448	3	242	1472	3	261
1449	3	242	1473	3	262
1450	3	243	1474	3	262
1451	3	243	1475	3	262
1452	3	245	1476	3	265
1453	3	245	1477	3	266
1454	3	245	1478	3	266
1455	3	246	1479	3	266
1456	3	246	1480	3	266
1457	3	247	1481	3	269
1458	3	247	1482	3	272
1459	3	247	1483	3	276
1460	3	248	1484	3	277
1461	3	248	1485	3	278
1462	3	250	1486	3	279
1463	3	250	1487	3	282
1464	3	250	1488	3	285

1489	3	285	1513	3	318
1490	3	285	1514	3	325
1491	3	288	1515	3	327
1492	3	291	1516	3	327
1493	3	291	1517	3	327
1494	3	291	1518	3	328
1495	3	297	1519	3	332
1496	3	298	1520	3	333
1497	3	298	1521	3	336
1498	3	301	1522	3	338
1499	3	304	1523	3	339
1500	3	304	1524	3	339
1501	3	306	1525	3	342
1502	3	308	1526	3	344
1503	3	309	1527	3	344
1504	3	310	1528	3	346
1505	3	311	1529	3	348
1506	3	311	1530	3	349
1507	3	315	1531	3	351
1508	3	315	1532	3	352
1509	3	315	1533	3	352
1510	3	317	1534	3	355
1511	3	317	1535	3	365
1512	3	318	1536	3	369

1537	3	373	1561	3	415
1538	3	373	1562	3	415
1539	3	376	1563	3	416
1540	3	378	1564	3	416
1541	3	378	1565	3	419
1542	3	378	1566	3	419
1543	3	379	1567	3	420
1544	3	383	1568	3	422
1545	3	386	1569	3	423
1546	3	389	1570	3	427
1547	3	391	1571	3	428
1548	3	392	1572	3	430
1549	3	393	1573	3	435
1550	3	398	1574	3	435
1551	3	402	1575	3	442
1552	3	405	1576	3	443
1553	3	408	1577	3	445
1554	3	410	1578	3	447
1555	3	410	1579	3	449
1556	3	411	1580	3	449
1557	3	411	1581	3	452
1558	3	412	1582	3	452
1559	3	413	1583	3	454
1560	3	415	1584	3	455

1585	3	456	1609	3	502
1586	3	457	1610	3	504
1587	3	459	1611	3	507
1588	3	463	1612	3	507
1589	3	466	1613	3	508
1590	3	470	1614	3	511
1591	3	473	1615	3	512
1592	3	473	1616	3	513
1593	3	475	1617	3	517
1594	3	475	1618	3	518
1595	3	476	1619	3	518
1596	3	478	1620	3	520
1597	3	479	1621	3	521
1598	3	482	1622	3	521
1599	3	482	1623	3	529
1600	3	487	1624	3	529
1601	3	488	1625	3	530
1602	3	491	1626	3	531
1603	3	493	1627	3	533
1604	3	494	1628	3	534
1605	3	497	1629	3	536
1606	3	499	1630	3	540
1607	3	500	1631	3	541
1608	3	501	1632	3	542

1633	3	544	1657	3	572
1634	3	546	1658	3	573
1635	3	546	1659	3	573
1636	3	547	1660	3	573
1637	3	547	1661	3	576
1638	3	547	1662	3	576
1639	3	548	1663	3	577
1640	3	548	1664	3	578
1641	3	553	1665	3	580
1642	3	553	1666	3	580
1643	3	554	1667	3	583
1644	3	554	1668	3	584
1645	3	555	1669	3	585
1646	3	555	1670	3	585
1647	3	556	1671	3	585
1648	3	556	1672	3	586
1649	3	559	1673	3	586
1650	3	556	1674	3	586
1651	3	568	1675	3	588
1652	3	569	1676	3	589
1653	3	569	1677	3	590
1654	3	569	1678	3	590
1655	3	571	1679	3	592
1656	3	571	1680	3	592

1681	3	593	1705	4	47
1682	3	594	1706	4	48
1683	3	596	1707	4	48
1684	3	596	1708	4	48
1685	3	598	1709	4	50
1686	3	599	1710	4	51
1687	3	601	1711	4	51
1688	3	601	1712	4	52
1689	3	603	1713	4	52
1690	3	604	1714	4	52
1691	3	604	1715	4	53
1692	3	618	1716	4	55
1693	3	620	1717	4	56
1694	4	16	1718	4	56
1695	4	21	1719	4	56
1696	4	24	1720	4	56
1697	4	24	1721	4	56
1698	4	35	1722	4	56
1699	4	35	1723	4	56
1700	4	36	1724	4	56
1701	4	44	1725	4	57
1702	4	45	1726	4	57
1703	4	45	1727	4	57
1704	4	47	1728	4	57

1729	4	57	1753	4	58
1730	4	57	1754	4	58
1731	4	57	1755	4	58
1732	4	57	1756	4	60
1733	4	57	1757	4	60
1734	4	57	1758	4	60
1735	4	57	1759	4	60
1736	4	57	1760	4	60
1737	4	57	1761	4	60
1738	4	57	1762	4	60
1739	4	57	1763	4	60
1740	4	57	1764	4	60
1741	4	57	1765	4	60
1742	4	57	1766	4	60
1743	4	57	1767	4	60
1744	4	57	1768	4	60
1745	4	57	1769	4	60
1746	4	57	1770	4	60
1747	4	58	1771	4	60
1748	4	58	1772	4	60
1749	4	58	1773	4	60
1750	4	58	1774	4	60
1751	4	58	1775	4	61
1752	4	58	1776	4	62

1777	4	62			
1778	4	62	1801	4	79
1779	4	62	1802	4	82
1780	4	64	1803	4	83
1781	4	64	1804	4	87
1782	4	65	1805	4	88
1783	4	65	1806	4	88
1784	4	66	1807	4	89
1785	4	67	1808	4	90
1786	4	67	1809	4	91
1787	4	67	1810	4	91
1788	4	68	1811	4	92
1789	4	68	1812	4	95
1790	4	69	1813	4	96
1791	4	69	1814	4	104
1792	4	70	1815	4	106
1793	4	70	1816	4	106
1794	4	72	1817	4	107
1795	4	73	1818	4	110
1796	4	73	1819	4	110
1797	4	74	1820	4	112
1798	4	75	1821	4	112
1799	4	76	1822	4	113
1800	4	79	1823	4	117
			1824	4	119

520

1825	4	121	1849	4	155
1826	4	122	1850	4	156
1827	4	122	1851	4	157
1828	4	125	1852	4	157
1829	4	125	1853	4	161
1830	4	126	1854	4	162
1831	4	130	1855	4	164
1832	4	130	1856	4	165
1833	4	135	1857	4	167
1834	4	135	1858	4	168
1835	4	136	1859	4	168
1836	4	136	1860	4	169
1837	4	139	1861	4	170
1838	4	141	1862	4	171
1839	4	143	1863	4	172
1840	4	144	1864	4	172
1841	4	145	1865	4	172
1842	4	145	1866	4	173
1843	4	148	1867	4	174
1844	4	148	1868	4	174
1845	4	150	1869	4	174
1846	4	151	1870	4	176
1847	4	152	1871	4	178
1848	4	152	1872	4	179

1873	4	180	1897	4	209
1874	4	180	1898	4	210
1875	4	180	1899	4	211
1876*	4	181	1900	4	212
1877	4	183	1901	4	213
1878	4	184	1902	4	215
1879	4	187	1903	4	218
1880	4	188	1904	4	219
1881	4	188	1905	4	220
1882	4	191	1906	4	221
1883	4	192	1907	4	221
1884	4	193	1908	4	221
1885	4	196	1909	4	221
1886	4	198	1910	4	222
1887	4	200	1911	4	223
1888	4	201	1912	4	223
1889	4	202	1913	4	224
1890	4	203	1914	4	232
1891	4	203	1915	4	234
1892	4	203	1916	4	234
1893	4	204	1917	4	234
1894	4	204	1918	4	239
1895	4	205	1919	4	239
1896	4	205	1920	4	241

* # inadvertently omitted. ἀγραυλοῦντες.

1921	4	244	1945	4	275
1922	4	245	1946	4	275
1923	4	246	1947	4	275
1924	4	251	1948	4	284
1925	4	254	1949	4	288
1926	4	254	1950	4	289
1927	4	255	1951	4	291
1928	4	256	1952	4	293
1929	4	256	1953	4	297
1930	4	256	1954	4	305
1931	4	256	1955	4	308
1932	4	257	1956	4	312
1933	4	257	1957	4	315
1934	4	257	1958	4	316
1935	4	257	1959	4	318
1936	4	258	1960	4	321
1937	4	261	1961	4	332
1938	4	261	1962	4	333
1939	4	262	1963	4	335
1940	4	262	1964	4	335
1941	4	262	1965	4	335
1942	4	270	1966	4	338
1943	4	273	1967	4	341
1944	4	274	1968	4	348

1969	4	353	1993	4	428
1970	4	354	1994	4	430
1971	4	354	1995	4	438
1972	4	356	1996	4	445
1973	4	356	1997	4	451
1974	4	357	1998	4	453
1975	4	358	1999	4	454
1976	4	360	2000	4	454
1977	4	360	2001	4	455
1978	4	365	2002	4	455
1979	4	365	2003	4	458
1980	4	366	2004	4	460
1981	4	366	2005	4	462
1982	4	367	2006	4	462
1983	4	367	2007	4	463
1984	4	369	2008	4	464
1985	4	370	2009	4	467
1986	4	383	2010	4	468
1987	4	391	2011	4	477
1988	4	406	2012	4	482
1989	4	407	2013	4	484
1990	4	421	2014	4	492
1991	4	427	2015	4	493
1992	4	428	2016	4	506

2017	4	508	2041	4	547
2018	4	515	2042	4	548
2019	4	515	2043	4	548
2020	4	515	2044	4	550
2021	4	522	2045	4	551
2022	4	522	2046	4	551
2023	4	522	2047	4	552
2024	4	523	2048	4	554
2025	4	524	2049	4	555
2026	4	524	2050	4	555
2027	4	525	2051	4	556
2028	4	526	2052	4	557
2029	4	529	2053	4	558
2030	4	535	2054	4	558
2031	4	536	2055	4	560
2032	4	536	2056	4	561
2033	4	537	2057	4	565
2034	4	537	2058	4	567
2035	4	539	2059	4	569
2036	4	539	2060	4	569
2037	4	540	2061	4	570
2038	4	542	2062	4	571
2039	4	546	2063*	4	573
2040	4	546	2064	4	576

* # 2063a, p.573; #2063b, p.574.

2065	4	578	2089	4	647
2066	4	579	2090	4	650
2067	4	588	2091	5	2
2068	4	589	2092	5	2
2069	4	591	2093	5	2
2070	4	591	2094	5	2
2071	4	593	2095	5	2
2072	4	601	2096	5	3
2073	4	602	2097	5	12
2074	4	606	2098	5	22
2075	4	610	2099	5	45
2076	4	610	2100	5	53
2077	4	610	2101	5	54
2078	4	619	2102	5	57
2079	4	620	2103	5	62
2080	4	622	2104	5	67
2081	4	622	2105	5	68
2082	4	622	2106	5	69
2083	4	628	2107	5	70
2084	4	629	2108	5	70
2085	4	632	2109	5	70
2086	4	632	2110	5	77
2087	4	640	2111	5	80
2088	4	642	2112	5	81

2113	5	82	2137	5	118
2114	5	83	2138	5	126
2115	5	87	2139	5	126
2116	5	89	2140	5	127
2117	5	89	2141	5	130
2118	5	92	2142	5	130
2119	5	93	2143	5	130
2120	5	95	2144	5	131
2121	5	95	2145	5	131
2122	5	96	2146	5	133
2123	5	96	2147	5	133
2124	5	97	2148	5	135
2125	5	97	2149	5	136
2126	5	98	2150	5	138
2127	5	100	2151	5	141
2128	5	102	2152	5	146
2129	5	108	2153	5	147
2130	5	110	2154	5	147
2131	5	113	2155	5	148
2132	5	115	2156	5	150
2133	5	115	2157	5	153
2134	5	116	2158	5	159
2135	5	118	2159	5	164
2136	5	118	2160	5	164

2161	5	164	2185	5	230
2162	5	165	2186	5	232
2163	5	170	2187	5	234
2164	5	170	2188	5	236
2165	5	177	2189	5	240
2166	5	179	2190	5	242
2167	5	180	2191	5	243
2168	5	183	2192	5	244
2169	5	184	2193	5	251
2170	5	184	2194	5	251
2171	5	184	2195	5	252
2172	5	185	2196	5	254
2173	5	186	2197	5	254
2174	5	186	2198	5	255
2175	5	189	2199*	5	255
2176	5	190	2200	5	256
2177	5	191	2201	5	262
2178	5	196	2202	5	262
2179	5	198	2203	5	262
2180	5	198	2204	5	263
2181	5	198	2205	5	270
2182	5	206	2206	5	271
2183	5	210	2207	5	271
2184	5	212	2208	5	272

* #2199 συμφυεῖσαι

2209	5	276	2233	5	315
2210	5	277	2234	5	316
2211	5	277	2235	5	316
2212	5	277	2236	5	318
2213	5	278	2237	5	318
2214	5	281	2238	5	319
2215	5	282	2239	5	326
2216	5	283	2240	5	331
2217	5	284	2241	5	332
2218	5	284	2242	5	335
2219	5	284	2243	5	335
2220	5	285	2244	5	337
2221	5	287	2245	5	339
2222	5	291	2246	5	344
2223	5	293	2247	5	345
2224	5	294	2248	5	362
2225	5	295	2249	5	363
2226	5	300	2250	5	365
2227	5	300	2251	5	367
2228	5	303	2252	5	371
2209	5	304	2253	5	377
2230	5	304	2254	5	378
2231	5	306	2255	5	379
2232	5	315	2256	5	380

2257	5	380	2281	5	430
2258	5	381	2282	5	440
2259	5	383	2283	5	443
2260	5	385	2284	5	446
2261	5	387	2285	5	447
2262	5	390	2286	5	448
2263	5	395	2287	5	451
2264	5	397	2288	5	463
2265	5	402	2289	5	483
2266	5	403	2290	5	485
2267	5	404	2291	5	494
2268	5	405	2292	5	498
2269	5	406	2293	5	506
2270	5	409	2294	5	519
2271	5	411	2295	5	520
2272	5	413	2296	5	522
2273	5	419	2297	5	523
2274	5	422	2298	5	524
2275	5	423	2299	5	524
2276	5	423	2300	5	524
2277	5	423	2301	5	534
2278	5	425	2302	5	544
2279	5	426	2303	5	545
2280	5	428	2304	5	546

2305	5	546	2329	5	631
2306	5	549	2330	5	635
2307	5	549	2331	6	6
2308	5	555	2332	6	9
2309	5	556	2333	6	9
2310	5	558	2334	6	12
2311	5	558	2335	6	12
2312	5	560	2336	6	15
2313	5	561	2337	6	15
2314	5	569	2338	6	16
2315	5	572	2339	6	22
2316	5	585	2340	6	26
2317	5	587	2341	6	28
2318	5	603	2342	6	28
2319	5	608	2343	6	30
2320	5	619	2344	6	32
2321	5	620	2345	6	35
2322	5	620	2346	6	36
2323	5	622	2347	6	36
2324	5	624	2348	6	38
2325	5	626	2349	6	42
2327	5	629	2350	6	44
2328	5	630	2351	6	56
			2352	6	57

531

2353	6	61	2377	6	154
2354	6	63	2378	6	155
2355	6	63	2379	6	157
2356	6	63	2380	6	158
2357	6	65	2381	6	158
2358	6	77	2382	6	160
2359	6	77	2383	6	177
2360	6	81	2384	6	189
2361	6	85	2385	6	195
2362	6	87	2386	6	204
2363	6	87	2387	6	218
2364	6	91	2388	6	218
2365	6	95	2389	6	219
2366	6	98	2390	6	229
2367	6	102	2391	6	243
2368	6	106	2392	6	249
2369	6	108	2393	6	249
2370	6	109	2394	6	249
2371	6	117	2395	6	250
2372	6	123	2396	6	252
2373	6	123	2397	6	252
2374	6	143	2398	6	254
2375	6	150	2399	6	256
2376	6	153	2400	6	266

2401	6	267
2402	6	271
2403	6	275
2404	6	288
2405	6	292
2406	6	297
2407	6	301
2408	6	316
2409	6	318
2410	6	318
2411	6	320
2412	6	321
2413	6	323
2414	6	329
2415	6	338
2416	6	338
2417	6	340
2418	6	342
2419	6	351
2420	6	356
2421	6	356
2422	6	356
2423	6	358
2424	6	359

2425	6	361
2426	6	362
2427	6	362
2428	6	362
2429	6	363
2430	6	363
2431	6	363
2432	6	363
2433	6	365
2434	6	365
2435	6	365
2436	6	369
2437	6	369
2438	6	369
2439	6	370
2440	6	370
2441	6	371
2442	6	372
2443*	6	372
2444	6	373
2445	6	374
2446	6	379
2447	6	379
2448	6	381

* Inadvertent error in numbering. #2442 - διακόνιαν; #2443 - συναντιλάβηται, pp.371, 372.

2449	6	383	2473	6	440
2450	6	383	2474	6	441
2451	6	386	2475	6	445
2452	6	392	2476	6	450
2453	6	399	2477	6	454
2454	6	400	2478	6	456
2455	6	401	2479	6	458
2456	6	401	2480	6	463
2457	6	406	2481	6	469
2458	6	407	2482	6	472
2459	6	408	2483	6	474
2560	6	417	2484	6	474
2461	6	421	2485	6	474
2462	6	423	2486	6	476
2463	6	424	2487	6	477
2464	6	426	2488	6	483
2465	6	428	2489	6	484
2466	6	430	2490	6	493
2467	6	430	2491	6	495
2468	6	432	2492	6	499
2469	6	434	2493	6	500
2470	6	438	2494	6	503
2471	6	439	2495	6	503
2472	6	439	2496	6	504

2498	6	505	2521	6	569
2499	6	512	2522	6	570
2500	6	513	2523	6	572
2501	6	515	2524	6	573
2502	6	517	2525	6	573
2503	6	517	2526	6	576
2504	6	519	2527	6	576
2505	6	523	2528	6	577
2506	6	524	2529	6	577
2507	6	526	2530	6	582
2508	6	528	2531	6	585
2509	6	529	2532	6	593
2510	6	548	2533	6	593
2511	6	550	2534	6	593
2512	6	551	2535	6	595
2513	6	557	2536	6	597
2514	6	559	2537	6	601
2515	6	559	2538	6	608
2516	6	561	2539	6	609
2517	6	562	2540	6	615
2518	6	566	2541	6	616
2519	6	567	2542	6	617
2520	6	568	2543	6	619
			2544	6	620

2545	6	620	2569	7	11
2546	6	622	2570	7	13
2547	6	622	2571	7	15
2548	6	624	2572	7	17
2549	6	625	2573	7	20
2550	6	626	2574	7	20
2551	6	631	2575	7	26
2552	6	632	2576	7	26
2553	6	632	2577	7	26
2554	6	633	2578	7	27
2555	6	633	2579	7	27
2556	6	634	2580	7	28
2557	6	636	2581	7	29
2558	6	636	2582	7	29
2559	7	1	2583	7	30
2560	7	3	2584	7	34
2561	7	4	2585	7	34
2562	7	5	2586	7	35
2563	7	5	2587	7	37
2564	7	6	2588	7	38
2565	7	8	2589	7	40
2566	7	9	2590	7	45
2567	7	10	2591	7	46
2568	7	10	2592	7	47

2593	7	50	2617	7	125
2594	7	52	2618	7	130
2595	7	53	2619	7	132
2596	7	56	2620	7	136
2597	7	65	2621	7	136
2598	7	66	2622	7	141
2599	7	68	2623	7	142
2600	7	68	2624	7	145
2601	7	70	2625	7	146
2602	7	71	2626	7	148
2603	7	87	2627	7	149
2604	7	91	2628	7	150
2605	7	91	2629	7	152
2606	7	94	2630	7	153
2607	7	96	2631	7	155
2608	7	96	2632	7	155
2609	7	96	2633	7	161
2610	7	101	2633A	7	162
2611	7	105	2634	7	170
2612	7	111	2635	7	176
2613	7	113	2636	7	177
2614	7	113	2637	7	179
2615	7	117	2638	7	181
2616	7	119	2639	7	188
			2640	7	192

537

2641	7	194	2665	7	261
2642	7	200	2666	7	263
2643	7	207	2667	7	271
2644	7	216	2668	7	274
2645	7	216	2669	7	280
2646	7	216	2670	7	281
2647	7	220	2671	7	282
2648	7	220	2672	7	287
2649	7	221	2673	7	287
2650	7	229	2674	7	289
2651	7	230	2675	7	296
2652	7	232	2676	7	296
2653	7	232	2677	7	296
2654	7	238	2678	7	297
2655	7	241	2679	7	298
2656	7	243	2680	7	311
2657	7	244	2681	7	313
2658	7	244	2682	7	327
2659	7	247	2683	7	330
2660	7	249	2684	7	342
2661	7	249	2685	7	344
2662	7	252	2686	7	349
2663	7	253	2687	7	350
2664	7	259	2688	7	355

2689	7	360	2713	7	471
2690	7	361	2714	7	483
2691	7	361	2715	7	484
2692	7	364	2716	7	486
2693	7	364	2717	7	489
2694	7	366	2718	7	493
2695	7	369	2719	7	493
2696	7	377	2720	7	494
2697	7	381	2721	7	495
2698	7	381	2722	7	497
2699	7	381	2723	7	498
2700	7	383	2724	7	502
2701	7	392	2725	7	503
2702	7	393	2726	7	506
2703	7	398	2727	7	507
2704	7	401	2728	7	508
2705	7	408	2729	7	508
2706	7	409	2730	7	508
2707	7	410	2731	7	509
2708	7	432	2732	7	511
2709	7	440	2733	7	513
2710	7	443	2734	7	516
2711	7	444	2735	7	516
2712	7	460	2736	7	516

2737	7	516	2761	7	566
2738	7	517	2762	7	572
2739	7	518	2763	7	575
2740	7	519	2764	7	583
2741	7	521	2765	7	588
2742	7	526	2766	7	590
2743	7	526	2767	7	591
2744	7	526	2768	8	4
2745	7	528	2769	8	5
2746	7	531	2770	8	6
2747	7	531	2771	8	6
2748	7	531	2772	8	15
2749	7	533	2773	8	19
2750	7	534	2774	8	36
2751	7	536	2775	8	51
2752	7	540	2776	8	52
2753	7	540	2777*	8	52
2754	7	542	2778	8	52
2755	7	544	2779	8	56
2756	7	546	2780	8	61
2757	7	548	2781	8	87
2758	7	561	2782	8	94
2759	7	561	2783	8	116
2760	7	561	2784	8	119

* inadvertently omitted

540

2785	8	129	2809	8	286
2786	8	129	2810	8	286
2787	8	163	2811	8	291
2788	8	167	2812	8	293
2789	8	237	2813	8	293
2790	8	238	2814	8	295
2791	8	241	2815	8	296
2792	8	245	2816	8	298
2793	8	247	2817	8	302
2794	8	248	2818	8	305
2795	8	248	2819	8	306
2796	8	248	2820	8	313
2797	8	248	2821	8	313
2798	8	251	2822	8	319
2799	8	251	2823	8	330
2800	8	253	2824	8	331
2801	8	253	2825	8	331
2802	8	255	2826	8	332
2803	8	266	2827	8	334
2804	8	266	2828	8	343
2805	8	272	2829	8	348
2806	8	273	2830	8	351
2807	8	275	2831	8	352
2808	8	280	2832	8	353

2833	8	354	2857	8	431
2834	8	354	2858	8	434
2835	8	356	2859	8	435
2836	8	356	2860	8	436
2837	8	368	2861	8	438
2838	8	370	2862	8	438
2839	8	371	2863	8	443
2840	8	374	2864	8	453
2841	8	376	2865	8	457
2842	8	377	2866	8	462
2943	8	378	2867	8	463
2844	8	381	2868	8	464
2845	8	384	2869	8	466
2846	8	394	2870	8	467
2847	8	394	2871	8	469
2848	8	402	2872	8	470
2849	8	403	2873	8	470
2850	8	404	2874	8	472
2851	8	409	2875	8	473
2852	8	411	2876	8	473
2853	8	415	2877	8	476
2854	8	417	2878	8	478
2855	8	429	2879	8	480
2856	8	429	2880	8	486

2881	8	488	2905	8	567
2882	8	488	2906	8	570
2883	8	489	2907	8	573
2884	8	490	2908	8	574
2885	8	491	2909	8	574
2886	8	493	2910	8	576
2887	8	496	2911	9	1
2888	8	496	2912	9	3
2889	8	504	2913	9	8
2890	8	510	2914	9	11
2891	8	522	2915	9	11
2892	8	532	2916	9	17
2893	8	533	2917	9	25
2894	8	543	2918	9	25
2895	8	549	2919	9	37
2896	8	550	2920	9	40
2897	8	552	2921	9	43
2898	8	553	2922	9	45
2899	8	556	2923	9	54
2900	8	557	2924	9	59
2901	8	557	2925	9	59
2902	8	562	2926	9	68
2903	8	563	2927	9	72
2904	8	567	2928	9	75

2929	9	79	2953	9	126
2930	9	81	2954	9	127
2931	9	82	2955	9	129
2932	9	82	2956	9	130
2933	9	83	2957	9	132
2934	9	93	2958	9	133
2935	9	93	2959	9	133
2936	9	95	2960	9	135
2937	9	95	2961	9	138
2938	9	98	2962	9	142
2939	9	106	2963	9	142
2940	9	110	2964	9	142
2941	9	110	2965	9	143
2942	9	112	2966	9	143
2943	9	117	2967	9	143
2944	9	118	2968	9	143
2945	9	118	2969	9	144
2946	9	119	2970	9	144
2947	9	119	2971	9	144
2948	9	120	2972	9	144
2949	9	125	2973	9	145
2950	9	125	2974	9	145
2951	9	125	2975	9	145
2952	9	125	2976	9	146

2977	9	147	3001	9	199
2978	9	147	3002	9	204
2979	9	147	3003	9	206
2980	9	149	3004	9	206
2981	9	151	3005	9	211
2982	9	152	3006	9	213
2983	9	153	3007	9	214
2984	9	153	3008	9	214
2985	9	157	3009	9	215
2986	9	157	3010	9	216
2987	9	158	3011	9	219
2988	9	158	3012	9	220
2989	9	162	3013	9	224
2990	9	164	3014	9	227
2991	9	164	3015	9	228
2992	9	164	3016	9	229
2993	9	167	3017	9	231
2994	9	173	3018	9	232
2995	9	174	3019	9	232
2996	9	175	3020	9	234
2997	9	176	3021	9	238
2998	9	176	3022	9	239
2999	9	188	3023	9	239
3000	9	197	3024	9	241

3025	9	244	3049	9	290
3026	9	246	3050	9	290
3027	9	248	3051	9	291
3028	9	248	3052*	9	291
3029	9	249	3053	9	297
3030	9	251	3054	9	297
3031	9	257	3055	9	306
3032	9	257	3056	9	307
3033	9	261	3057	9	307
3034	9	262	3058	9	308
3035	9	263	3059	9	310
3036	9	263	3060	9	313
3037	9	266	3061	9	315
3038	9	266	3062	9	316
3039	9	271	3063	9	319
3040	9	271	3064	9	322
3041	9	272	3065	9	323
3042	9	275	3066	9	325
3043	9	276	3067	9	326
3044	9	285	3068	9	329
3045	9	285	3069	9	331
3046	9	288	3070	9	331
3047	9	288	3071	9	333
3048	9	288	3072	9	333

* *Cf.* #3052A, page 296

3073	9	333	3097	9	357
3074	9	334	3098	9	360
3075	9	334	3099	9	361
3076	9	337	3100	9	362
3077	9	341	3101	9	363
3078	9	341	3102	9	364
3079	9	341	3103	9	365
3080	9	342	3104	9	365
3081	9	346	3105	9	368
3082	9	346	3106	9	370
3083	9	346	3107	9	371
3084	9	346	3108	9	372
3085	9	347	3109	9	372
3086	9	347	3110	9	373
3087	9	347	3111	9	374
3088	9	347	3112	9	375
3089*	9		3113	9	376
3090	9	351	3114	9	376
3091	9	351	3115	9	376
3092	9	352	3116	9	382
3093	9	353	3117	9	383
3094	9	354	3118	9	384
3095	9	355	3119	9	384
3096	9	356	3120	9	385

* #3089 inadvertently omitted

547

3121	9	387	3145	9	419
3122	9	388	3146	9	429
3123	9	388	3147	9	431
3124	9	390	3148	9	431
3125	9	390	3149	9	431
3126	9	391	3150	9	432
3127	9	392	3151	9	433
3128	9	393	3152	9	434
3129	9	394	3153	9	435
3130	9	395	3154	9	439
3131	9	397	3155	9	439
3132	9	397	3156	9	442
3133	9	399	3157	9	442
3134	9	401	3158	9	443
3135	9	404	3159	9	444
3136	9	407	3160	9	444
3137	9	409	3161	9	450
3138	9	410	3162	9	450
3139	9	411	3163	9	452
3140	9	412	3164	9	459
3141	9	413	3165	9	463
3142	9	413	3166	9	464
3143	9	416	3167	9	464
3144	9	416	3168	9	468

3169	9	469	3193	9	512
3170	9	470	3194	9	513
3171	9	470	3195*	9	518
3172	9	470	3196	9	519
3173	9	471	3197	9	522
3174	9	476	3198	9	525
3175	9	476	3199	9	527
3176	9	477	3200	9	529
3177	9	477	3201	9	532
3178	9	486	3202	9	533
3179	9	488	3203	9	533
3180	9	489	3204	9	533
3181	9	489	3205	9	533
3182	9	491	3206	9	535
3183	9	495	3207	9	541
3184	9	495	3208	9	541
3185	9	496	3209	9	542
3186	9	498	3210	9	542
3187	9	500	3211	9	542
3188	9	500	3212	9	543
3189	9	503	3213	9	547
3190	9	508	3214	9	548
3191	9	508	3215	9	551
3192	9	511	3216	9	552

* #3195

3217	9	552	3241	10	50
3218	9	553	3242	10	50
3219	9	554	3243	10	54
3220	9	555	3244	10	59
3221	9	556	3245	10	60
3222	9	559	3246	10	63
3223	9	560	3247	10	63
3224	9	565	3248	10	67
3225	9	567	3249	10	70
3226	9	569	3250	10	70
3227	9	570	3251	10	70
3228	9	571	3252	10	70
3229	9	572	3253	10	72
3230	10	1	3254	10	72
3231	10	8	3255	10	75
3232	10	8	3256	10	77
3233	10	11	3257	10	79
3234	10	12	3258	10	80
3235	10	12	3259	10	80
3236	10	24	3260	10	80
3237	10	38	3261	10	80
3238	10	39	3262	10	81
3239	10	39	3263	10	81
3240	10	48	3264	10	82

3265	10	83	3289	10	108
3266	10	85	3290	10	109
3267	10	90	3291	10	112
3268	10	90	3292	10	114
3269	10	90	3293	10	115
3270	10	91	3294	10	118
3271	10	91	3295	10	118
3272	10	92	3296	10	123
3273	10	94	3297	10	125
3274	10	94	3298	10	125
3275	10	94	3299	10	136
3276	10	95	3300	10	140
3277	10	97	3301	10	144
3278	10	97	3302	10	145
3279	10	97	3303	10	146
3280	10	98	3304	10	148
3281	10	98	3305	10	149
3282	10	98	3306	10	156
3283	10	99	3307	10	156
3284	10	100	3308	10	158
3285	10	102	3309	10	165
3286	10	105	3310	10	167
3287	10	105	3311	10	167
3288	10	107	3312	10	167

3313	10	167	3337	10	212
3314	10	170	3338	10	212
3315	10	171	3339	10	219
3316	10	172	3340	10	221
3317	10	172	3341	10	221
3318	10	174	3342	10	222
3319	10	175	3343	10	222
3320	10	176	3344	10	225
3321	10	176	3345	10	225
3322	10	178	3346	10	228
3323	10	179	3347	10	232
3324	10	179	3348	10	233
3325	10	179	3349	10	233
3326	10	179	3350	10	241
3327	10	179	3351	10	241
3328	10	179	3352	10	242
3329	10	181	3353	10	245
3330	10	186	3354	10	245
3331	10	186	3355	10	251
3332	10	188	3356	10	253
3333	10	190	3357	10	253
3334	10	196	3358	10	255
3335	10	197	3359	10	255
3336	10	197	3360	10	256

3361	10	259	3385	10	291
3362	10	259	3386	10	291
3363	10	259	3387	10	294
3364	10	260	3388	10	297
3365	10	260	3389	10	297
3366	10	262	3390	10	297
3367	10	262	3391	10	299
3368	10	262	3392	10	299
3369	10	265	3393	10	303
3370	10	265	3394	10	303
3371	10	270	3395	10	304
3372	10	271	3396	10	308
3373	10	272	3397	10	308
3374	10	272	3398	10	309
3375	10	273	3399	10	310
3376	10	274	3400	10	310
3377	10	275	3401	10	311
3378	10	276	3402	10	312
3379	10	277	3403	10	313
3380	10	279	3404	10	313
3381	10	285	3405	10	313
3382	10	286	3406	10	314
3383	10	287	3407	10	315
3384	10	291	3408	10	317

3409	10	318	3433	10	344
3410	10	319	3434	10	345
3411	10	319	3435	10	346
3412	10	319	3436	10	347
3413	10	320	3437	10	350
3414	10	320	3438	10	351
3415	10	324	3439	10	352
3416	10	324	3440	10	352
3417	10	326	3441	10	352
3418	10	326	3442	10	357
3419	10	332	3443	10	357
3420	10	334	3444	10	357
3421	10	334	3445	10	358
3422	10	334	3446	10	360
3423	10	335	3447	10	360
3424	10	340	3448	10	362
3425	10	341	3449	10	363
3426	10	341	3450	10	365
3427	10	342	3451	10	365
3428	10	343	3452	10	366
3429	10	344	3453	10	367
3430	10	344	3454	10	372
3431	10	344	3455	10	372
3432	10	344	3456	10	374

3457	10	375	3481	10	413
3458	10	377	3482	10	414
3459	10	378	3483	10	414
3460	10	380	3484	10	414
3461	10	389	3485	10	414
3462	10	389	3486	10	415
3463	10	389	3487	10	416
3464	10	393	3488	10	418
3465	10	393	3489	10	421
3466	10	394	3490	10	421
3467	10	395	3491	10	423
3468	10	396	3492	10	423
3469	10	398	3493	10	423
3470	10	402	3494	10	424
3471	10	402	3495	10	425
3472	10	405	3496	10	426
3473	10	407	3497	10	427
3474	10	407	3498	10	430
3475	10	407	3499	10	431
3476	10	407	3500	10	432
3477	10	408	3501	10	432
3478	10	409	3502	10	433
3479	10	411	3503	10	433
3480	10	411	3504	10	433

3505	10	433	3529	10	451
3506	10	433	3530	10	457
3507	10	433	3531	10	460
3508	10	434	3532	10	461
3509	10	434	3533	10	461
3510	10	437	3534	10	463
3511	10	438	3535	10	463
3512	10	439	3536	10	470
3513	10	439	3537	10	471
3514	10	439	3538	10	471
3515	10	440	3539	10	471
3516	10	442	3540	10	473
3517	10	442	3541	10	473
3518	10	443	3542	10	473
3519	10	444	3543	10	475
3520	10	444	3544	10	477
3521	10	445	3545	10	478
3522	10	445	3546	10	478
3523	10	445	3547	10	478
3524	10	445	3548	10	479
3525	10	446	3549	10	483
3526	10	446	3550	10	484
3527	10	447	3551	10	484
3528	10	450	3552	10	486

3553	10	486	3577	10	520
3554	10	487	3578	10	522
3555	10	491	3579	10	527
3556	10	495	3580	10	529
3557	10	495	3581	10	533
3558	10	498	3582	10	536
3559	10	498	3583	10	537
3560	10	498	3584	10	537
3561	10	503	3585	10	538
3562	10	503	3586	10	539
3563	10	504	3587	10	539
3564	10	505	3588	10	542
3565	10	508	3589	10	542
3566	10	508	3590	10	545
3567	10	509	3591	10	546
3568	10	511	3592	10	546
3569	10	512	3593	10	547
3570	10	513	3594	10	548
3571	10	514	3595	10	553
3572	10	514	3596	10	558
3573	10	515	3597	10	559
3574	10	516	3598	10	560
3575	10	517	3599	10	562
3576	10	517	3600	10	567

557

3601	10	568	3625	11	17
3602	10	568	3626	11	17
3603	10	569	3627	11	24
3604	10	570	3628	11	25
3605	10	573	3629	11	27
3606	10	574	3630	11	28
3607	10	575	3631	11	31
3608	10	577	3632	11	31
3609	10	578	3633	11	31
3610	10	579	3634	11	31
3611	11	1	3635	11	37
3612	11	2	3636	11	39
3613	11	3	3637	11	42
3614	11	3	3638	11	46
3615	11	4	3639	11	48
3616	11	4	3640	11	49
3617	11	5	3641	11	51
3618	11	6	3642	11	52
3619	11	6	3643	11	53
3620	11	7	3644	11	56
3621	11	9	3645	11	56
3622	11	9	3646	11	58
3623	11	11	3647	11	59
3624	11	13	3648	11	60

* #3645A, page 56; #3645B (3646) page 58.

3649	11	60	3673	11	109
3650	11	63	3674	11	110
3651	11	64	3675	11	111
3652	11	67	3676	11	112
3653	11	68	3677	11	112
3654	11	70	3678	11	113
3655	11	70	3679	11	114
3656	11	71	3680	11	114
3657	11	73	3681	11	115
3658	11	74	3682	11	115
3659	11	77	3683	11	116
3660	11	78	3684	11	116
3661	11	79	3685	11	116
3662*	11	81	3686	11	116
3663	11	82	3687	11	116
3664	11	93	3688	11	117
3665	11	94	3689	11	117
3666	11	96	3690	11	118
3667	11	97	3691	11	118
3668	11	97	3692	11	119
3669	11	98	3693	11	119
3670	11	103	3694	11	120
3671	11	104	3695	11	120
3672	11	109	3696	11	121

* #3662A, page 80; #3662B, page 82

3697	11	121	3721	11	131
3698	11	122	3722	11	131
3699	11	122	3723	11	131
3700	11	123	3724	11	132
3701	11	123	3725	11	133
3702	11	123	3726	11	135
3703	11	123	3727	11	135
3704	11	124	3728	11	139
3705	11	124	3729	11	139
3706	11	124	3730	11	140
3707*	11		3731	11	140
3708	11	126	3732	11	140
3709	11	126	3733	11	141
3710	11	127	3734	11	142
3711	11	127	3735	11	145
3712	11	127	3736	11	145
3713	11	127	3737	11	145
3714	11	128	3738	11	149
3715	11	128	3739	11	150
3716	11	128	3740	11	153
3717	11	129	3741	11	153
3718	11	129	3742	11	153
3719	11	130	3743	11	154
3720	11	131	3744	11	154

* number omitted

3745	11	154	3769	11	173
3746	11	155	3770	11	173
3747	11	155	3771	11	174
3748	11	156	3772	11	174
3749	11	156	3773	11	175
3750	11	157	3774	11	175
3751	11	151	3775	11	176
3752	11	157	3776	11	177
3753	11	158	3777	11	177
3754	11	160	3778	11	177
3755	11	161	3779	11	187
3756	11	161	3780	11	189
3757	11	161	3781	11	194
3758	11	162	3782	11	196
3759	11	163	3783	11	201
3760	11	163	3784	11	206
3761	11	164	3785	11	209
3762	11	166	3786	11	216
3763	11	167	3787	11	216
3764	11	168	3788	11	217
3765	11	168	3789	11	218
3766	11	168	3790	11	219
3767	11	169	3791	11	219
3768	11	173	3792	11	220

3793	11	224	3817	11	267
3794	11	236	3818	11	267
3795	11	239	3819	11	269
3796	11	239	3820	11	270
3797	11	239	3821	11	270
3798	11	240	3822	11	271
3799	11	240	3823	11	271
3800	11	247	3824	11	271
3801	11	247	3825	11	272
3802	11	252	3826	11	272
3803	11	252	3827	11	273
3804	11	252	3828	11	273
3805	11	256	3829	11	273
3806	11	256	3830	11	285
3807	11	259	3831	11	286
3808	11	260	3832	11	286
3809	11	260	3833	11	288
3810	11	261	3834	11	288
3811	11	261	3835	11	288
3812	11	263	3836	11	291
3813	11	263	3837	11	294
3814	11	263	3838	11	295
3815	11	264	3839	11	297
3816	11	264	3840	11	298

3841	11	299	3865	11	341
3842	11	302	3866	11	343
3843	11	302	3867	11	343
3844	11	303	3868	11	344
3845	11	303	3869	11	345
3846	11	306	3870	11	348
3847	11	307	3871	11	348
3848	11	310	3872	11	356
3849	11	312	3873	11	361
3850	11	313	3874	11	361
3851	11	313	3875	11	362
3852	11	316	3876	11	362
3853	11	321	3877	11	365
3854	11	323	3878	11	366
3855	11	329	3879	11	369
3856	11	332	3880	11	372
3857	11	334	3881	11	373
3858	11	335	3882	11	376
3859	11	335	3883	11	378
3860	11	338	3884	11	378
3861	11	339	3885	11	379
3862	11	340	3886	11	383
3863	11	340	3887	11	386
3864	11	340	3888	11	390

3889	11	393	3913	11	460
3890	11	402	3914	11	463
3891	11	402	3915	11	464
3892	11	402	3916	11	469
3893	11	403	3917	11	473
3894	11	403	3918	11	480
3895	11	412	3919	11	484
3896	11	416	3920	11	486
3897	11	418	3921	11	489
3898	11	423	3922	11	493
3899	11	426	3923	11	495
3900	11	428	3924	11	497
3901	11	431	3925	11	500
3902	11	436	3926	11	501
3903	11	437	3927	11	503
3904	11	439	3928	11	506
3905	11	441	3929	11	508
3906	11	443	3930	11	509
3907	11	443	3931	11	520
3908	11	444	3932	11	527
3909	11	451	3933	11	532
3910	11	452	3934	11	532
3911	11	453	3935	11	535
3912	11	458	3936	11	535

3937	11	536	3961	12	18
3938	11	538	3962	12	19
3939	11	538	3963	12	22
3940	11	540	3964	12	24
3941	11	540	3965	12	25
3942	11	542	3966	12	25
3943	11	544	3967	12	26
3944	11	548	3968	12	27
3945	11	348	3969	12	30
3946	11	550	3970	12	32
3947	11	554	3971	12	34
3948	11	554	3972	12	35
3949	11	554	3973	12	37
3950	11	560	3974	12	42
3951	11	569	3975	12	64
3952	11	569	3976	12	65
3953	11	571	3977	12	65
3954	11	572	3978	12	66
3955	11	572	3979	12	68
3956	12	2	3980	12	72
3957	12	3	3981	12	73
3958	12	5	3982	12	74
3959	12	14	3983	12	74
3960	12	15	3984	12	74

3985	12	75	4009	12	121
3986	12	77	4010	12	121
3987	12	79	4011	12	122
3988	12	80	4012	12	125
3989	12	82	4013	12	125
3990	12	82	4014	12	129
3991	12	83	4015	12	134
3992	12	86	4016	12	134
3993	12	89	4017	12	135
3994	12	94	4018	12	138
3995	12	94	4019	12	139
3996	12	95	4020	12	139
3997	12	95	4021	12	140
3998	12	96	4022	12	141
3999	12	97	4023	12	143
4000	12	102	4024	12	144
4001	12	104	4025	12	144
4002	12	111	4026	12	146
4003	12	112	4027	12	147
4004	12	113	4028	12	149
4005	12	116	4029	12	151
4006	12	117	4030	12	154
4007	12	118	4031	12	155
4008	12	119	4032	12	155

4033	12	157	4057	12	239
4034	12	169	4058	12	242
4035	12	170	4059	12	243
4036	12	173	4060	12	245
4037	12	176	4061	12	246
4038	12	181	4062	12	248
4039	12	181	4063	12	250
4040	12	184	4064	12	251
4041	12	189	4065	12	252
4042	12	205	4066	12	253
4043	12	208	4067	12	254
4044	12	211	4068	12	256
4045	12	213	4069	12	256
4046	12	214	4070	12	257
4047	12	220	4071	12	257
4048	12	227	4072	12	258
4049	12	228	4073	12	259
4050	12	228	4074	12	260
4051	12	230	4075	12	260
4052	12	230	4076	12	261
4053	12	233	4077	12	261
4054	12	235	4078	12	262
4055	12	237	4079	12	262
4056	12	238	4080	12	263

4081	12	263	4105	12	305
4082	12	264	4106	12	309
4083	12	265	4107	12	319
4084	12	265	4108	12	325
4085	12	265	4109	12	329
4086	12	266	4110	12	329
4087	12	266	4111	12	343
4088	12	267	4112	12	345
4089	12	267	4113	12	346
4090	12	267	4114	12	351
4091	12	269	4115	12	359
4092	12	271	4116	12	360
4093	12	272	4117	12	360
4094	12	273	4118	12	365
4095	12	276	4119	12	372
4096	12	277	4120	12	376
4097	12	278	4121	12	387
4098	12	281	4122	12	388
4099	12	281	4123	12	391
4100	12	289	4124	12	392
4101	12	293	4125	12	393
4102	12	297	4126	12	395
4103	12	298	4127	12	396
4104	12	302	4128	12	397

4129	12	398	4153	12	457
4130	12	398	4154	12	458
4131	12	400	4155	12	460
4132	12	401	4156	12	461
4133	12	407	4157	12	461
4134	12	410	4158	12	462
4135	12	413	4159	12	473
4136	12	415	4160	12	477
4137	12	417	4161	12	482
4138	12	417	4162	12	487
4139	12	419	4163	12	487
4140	12	419	4164	12	492
4141	12	421	4165	12	492
4142	12	421	4166	12	493
4143	12	423	4167	12	493
4144	12	423	4168	12	494
4145	12	427	4169	12	495
4146	12	430	4170	12	496
4147	12	431	4171	12	508
4148	12	431	4172	12	511
4149	12	433	4173	12	515
4150	12	433	4174	12	524
4151	12	438	4175	12	525
4152	12	448	4176	12	526

4177	12	529	4201	13	6
4178	12	529	4202	13	8
4179	12	531	4203	13	9
4180	12	531	4204	13	17
4181	12	532	4205	13	19
4182	12	536	4206	13	19
4183	12	537	4207	13	20
4184	12	544	4208	13	22
4185	12	544	4209	13	25
4186	12	547	4210	13	31
4187	12	547	4211	13	34
4188	12	549	4212	13	47
4189	12	553	4213	13	49
4190	12	556	4214	13	50
4191	12	557	4215	13	54
4192	12	559	4216	13	55
4193	12	561	4217	13	63
4194	12	562	4218	13	69
4195	12	562	4219	13	69
4196	12	565	4220	13	70
4197	12	565	4221	13	75
4198	12	567	4222	13	75
4199	12	576	4223	13	79
4200	12	580	4224	13	79

4225	13	84	4249	13	194
4226	13	84	4250	13	201
4227	13	101	4251	13	213
4228	13	101	4252	13	218
4229	13	109	4253	13	218
4230	13	114	4254	13	221
4231	13	114	4255	13	226
4232	13	115	4256	13	228
4233	13	115	4257	13	228
4234	13	117	4258	13	233
4235	13	128	4259	13	234
4236	13	128	4260	13	236
4237	13	129	4261	13	240
4238	13	139	4262	13	244
4239	13	163	4263	13	244
4240	13	164	4264	13	248
4241	13	174	4265	13	258
4242	13	179	4266	13	259
4243	13	190	4267	13	261
4244	13	191	4268	13	262
4245	13	191	4269	13	266
4246	13	193	4270	13	269
4247	13	193	4271	13	274
4248	13	194	42/2	13	282

4273	13	282	4297	13	324
4274	13	283	4298	13	325
4275	13	284	4299	13	328
4276	13	287	4300	13	329
4277	13	288	4301	13	330
4278	13	290	4302	13	338
4279	13	291	4303	13	339
4280	13	292	4304	13	342
4281	13	296	4305	13	343
4282	13	297	4306	13	343
4283	13	298	4307	13	347
4284	13	300	4308	13	347
4285	13	300	4309	13	348
4286	13	302	4310	13	367
4287	13	304	4311	13	370
4288	13	306	4312	13	372
4289	13	308	4313	13	372
4290	13	309	4314	13	374
4291	13	313	4315	13	375
4292	13	315	4316	13	377
4293	13	316	4317	13	377
4294	13	318	4318	13	382
4295	13	321	4319	13	382
4296	13	322	4320	13	384

4321	13	384	4345	13	442
4322	13	386	4346	13	442
4323	13	387	4347	13	444
4324	13	389	4348	13	445
4325	13	391	4349	13	446
4326	13	392	4350	13	447
4327	13	397	4351	13	447
4328	13	399	4352	13	448
4329	13	405	4353	13	450
4330	13	405	4354	13	451
4331	13	412	4355	13	452
4332	13	414	4356	13	455
4333	13	417	4357	13	456
4334	13	419	4358	13	457
4335	13	421	4359	13	459
4336	13	422	4360	13	464
4337	13	424	4361	13	464
4338	13	426	4362	13	464
4339	13	428	4363	13	470
4340	13	429	4364	13	474
4341	13	430	4365	13	476
4342	13	433	4366	13	477
4343	13	434	4367	13	477
4344	13	440	4368	13	479

4369	13	481	4393	13	518
4370	13	484	4394	13	519
4371	13	485	4395	13	523
4372	13	489	4396	13	528
4373	13	492	4397	13	528
4374	13	493	4398	13	531
4375	13	493	4399	13	531
4376	13	497	4400	13	537
4377	13	497	4401	13	539
4378	13	498	4402	13	540
4379	13	504	4403	13	541
4380	13	507	4404	13	543
4381	13	508	4405	13	545
4382	13	509	4406	13	545
4383	13	509	4407	13	545
4384	13	510	4408	13	547
4385	13	510	4409	13	549
4386	13	510	4410	13	556
4387	13	512	4411	13	557
4388	13	512	4412	13	578
4389	13	513	4413	13	579
4390	13	517	4414	13	580
4391	13	517	4415	13	580
4392	13	518	4416	13	583

4417	13	584	4441	14	71
4418	13	586	4442	14	83
4419	14	5	4443	14	85
4420	14	5	4444	14	88
4421	14	7	4445	14	88
4422	14	12	4446	14	93
4423	14	14	4447	14	94
4424	14	16	4448	14	95
4425	14	19	4449	14	111
4426	14	20	4450	14	120
4427	14	21	4451	14	125
4428	14	21	4452	14	140
4429	14	21	4453	14	141
4430	14	32	4454	14	144
4431	14	33	4455	14	147
4432	14	35	4456	14	152
4433	14	39	4457	14	155
4434	14	41	4458	14	156
4435	14	42	4459	14	162
4436	14	46	4460	14	173
4437	14	50	4461	14	173
4438	14	52	4462	14	186
4439	14	56	4463	14	187
4440	14	70	4464	14	190

4465	14	198	4489	14	266
4466	14	198	4490	14	269
4467	14	202	4491	14	276
4468	14	202	4492	14	276
4469	14	214	4493	14	278
4470	14	215	4494	14	283
4471	14	216	4495	14	287
4472	14	225	4496	14	288
4473	14	226	4497	14	288
4474	14	228	4498	14	291
4475	14	231	4499	14	291
4476	14	236	4500	14	292
4477	14	237	4501	14	296
4478	14	241	4502	14	297
4479	14	242	4503	14	303
4480	14	242	4504	14	306
4481	14	248	4505	14	306
4482	14	248	4506	14	315
4483	14	251	4507	14	318
4484	14	254	4508	14	318
4485	14	261	4509	14	319
4486	14	262	4510	14	319
4487	14	263	4511	14	322
4488	14	263	4512	14	326

4513	14	327	4537	14	375
4514	14	329	4538	14	377
4515	14	330	4539	14	378
4516	14	333	4540	14	393
4517	14	335	4541	14	396
4518	14	335	4542	14	397
4519	14	336	4543	14	400
4520	14	343	4544	14	405
4521	14	345	4545	14	411
4522	14	345	4546	14	412
4523	14	347	4547	14	417
4524	14	348	4548	14	419
4525	14	349	4549	14	422
4526	14	354	4550	14	424
4527	14	356	4551	14	426
4528	14	359	4552	14	426
4529	14	360	4553	14	429
4530	14	361	4554	14	437
4531	14	367	4555	14	438
4532	14	367	4556	14	442
4533	14	371	4557	14	445
4534	14	372	4558	14	448
4535	14	373	4559	14	450
4536	14	374	4560	14	451

4561	14	451	4585	14	500
4562	14	454	4586	14	500
4563	14	455	4587	14	501
4564	14	456	4588	14	501
4565	14	458	4589	14	503
4566	14	459	4590	14	504
4567	14	461	4591	14	504
4568	14	463	4592	14	505
4569	14	466	4593	14	506
4570	14	467	4594	14	509
4571	14	471	4595	14	510
4572	14	474	4596	14	510
4573	14	476	4597	15	2
4574	14	479	4598	15	5
4575	14	481	4599	15	7
4576	14	483	4600	15	12
4577	14	486	4601	15	13
4578	14	489	4602	15	19
4579	14	492	4603	15	25
4580	14	493	4604	15	27
4581	14	493	4605	15	31
4582	14	494	4606	15	33
4583	14	495	4607	15	40
4584	14	496	4608	15	41

4609	15	43	4633	15	101
4610	15	47	4634	15	102
4611	15	48	4635	15	104
4612	15	50	4636	15	1-4
4613	15	55	4637	15	108
4614	15	55	4638	15	110
4615	15	57	4639	15	113
4616	15	57	4640	15	122
4617A	15	61	4641	15	123
4617B	15	64	4642	15	124
4618	15	65	4643	15	126
4619	15	65	4644	15	127
4620	15	67	4645	15	128
4621	15	69	4646	15	128
4622	15	73	4647	15	129
4623	15	73	4648	15	131
4624	15	78	4649	15	146
4625	15	79	4650	15	154
4626	15	81	4651	15	157
4627	15	83	4652	15	161
4628	15	84	4653	15	164
4629	15	84	4654	15	164
4630	15	94	4655	15	165
4631	15	97	4656	15	168
4632	15	100			

4657	15	169	4681	15	297
4658	15	173	4682	15	299
4659	15	175	4683	15	299
4660	15	178	4684	15	306
4661	15	183	4685	15	308
4662	15	199	4686	15	309
4663	15	202	4687	15	317
4664	15	203	4688	15	318
4665	15	210	4689	15	319
4666	15	212	4690	15	319
4667	15	212	4691	15	319
4668	15	224	4692	15	323
4669	15	235	4693	15	323
4670	15	235	4694	15	324
4671	15	246	4695	15	325
4672	15	246	4696	15	327
4673	15	249	4697	15	329
4674	15	253	4698	15	330
4675	15	255	4699	15	330
4676	15	256	4700	15	330
4677	15	261	4701	15	331
4678	15	262	4702	15	331
4679	15	266	4703	15	332
4680	15	281	4704	15	332

4705	15	336	4729	15	375
4706	15	337	4730	15	376
4707	15	338	4731	15	376
4708	15	340	4732	15	377
4709	15	346	4733	15	377
4710	15	346	4734	15	377
4711	15	348	4735	15	378
4712	15	348	4736	15	380
4713	15	349	4737	15	381
4714	15	349	4738	15	383
4715	15	349	4739	15	383
4716	15	351	4740	15	387
4717	15	356	4741	15	389
4718	15	356	4742	15	390
4719	15	359	4743	15	393
4720	15	360	4744	15	396
4721	15	360	4745	15	398
4722	15	360	4746	15	398
4723	15	361	4747	15	400
4724	15	364	4748	15	401
4725	15	370	4749	15	402
4726	15	374	4750	15	404
4727	15	374	4751	15	405
4728	15	375	4752	15	405

4753	15	406	4777	15	451
4754	15	407	4778	15	451
4755	15	412	4779	15	451
4756	15	416	4780	15	453
4757	15	418	4781	15	453
4758	15	418	4782	15	456
4759	15	419	4783	15	456
4760	15	420	4784	15	457
4761	15	421	4785	15	458
4762	15	424	4786	15	458
4763	15	426	4787	15	460
4764	15	426	4788	15	464
4765	15	426	4789	15	467
4766	15	428	4790	15	468
4767	15	429	4791	15	468
4768	15	431	4792	15	469
4769	15	431	4793	15	470
4770	15	431	4794	15	470
4771	15	438	4795	15	471
4772	15	438	4796	15	471
4773	15	440	4797	15	472
4774	15	441	4798	15	473
4775	15	442	4799	15	473
4776	15	444	4800	15	473

4801	15	481	4825	15	523
4802	15	481	4826	15	523
4803	15	482	4827	15	526
4804	15	482	4828	15	529
4805	15	483	4829	15	529
4806	15	484	4830	15	530
4807	15	485	4831	15	532
4808	15	487	4832	15	533
4809	15	497	4833	15	534
4810	15	497	4834	15	535
4811	15	498	4835	15	537
4812	15	498	4836	15	540
4813	15	500	4837	15	541
4814	15	505	4838	15	541
4815	15	505	4839	15	541
4816	15	505	4840	15	541
4817	15	506	4841	15	542
4818	15	507	4842	15	542
4819	15	511	4843	15	543
4820	15	517	4844	15	544
4821	15	517	4845	15	544
4822	15	518	4846	15	545
4823	15	519	4847	15	546
4824	15	520	4848	15	547

583

4849	15	547	4873	15	587
4850	15	547	4874	15	587
4851	15	549	4875	15	588
4852	15	551	4876	16	3
4853	15	553	4877	16	6
4854	15	554	4878	16	8
4855	15	556	4879	16	8
4856	15	557	4880	16	13
4857	15	558	4881	16	13
4858	15	559	4882	16	13
4859	15	559	4883	16	14
4860	15	561	4884	16	15
4861	15	564	4885	16	16
4862	15	568	4886	16	21
4863	15	568	4887	16	23
4864	15	572	4888	16	23
4865	15	576	4889	16	23
4866	15	577	4890	16	24
4867	15	579	4891	16	24
4868	15	579	4892	16	25
4869	15	580	4893	16	25
4870	15	580	4894	16	26
4871	15	581	4895	16	28
4872	15	584	4896	16	29

4897	16	33	4921	16	85
4898	16	33	4922	16	94
4899	16	36	4923	16	99
4900	16	38	4924	16	101
4901	16	41	4925	16	103
4902	16	45	4926	16	104
4903	16	47	4927	16	107
4904	16	47	4928	16	108
4905	16	49	4929	16	108
4906	16	49	4930	16	121
4907	16	50	4931	16	123
4908	16	51	4932	16	133
4909	16	51	4933	16	137
4910	16	55	4934	16	139
4911	16	56	4935	16	140
4912	16	64	4936	16	145
4913	16	68	4937	16	147
4914	16	73	4938	16	148
4915	16	73	4939	16	163
4916	16	74	4940	16	167
4917	16	79	4941	16	167
4918	16	50	4942	16	168
4919	16	84	4943	16	168
4920	16	84	4944	16	169

4945	16	169	4969	16	218
4946	16	169	4970	16	219
4947	16	171	4971	16	219
4948	16	171	4972	16	223
4949	16	174	4973	16	225
4950	16	175	4974	16	226
4951	16	178	4975	16	228
4952	16	183	4976	16	228
4953	16	184	4977	16	229
4954	16	185	4978	16	229
4955	16	189	4979	16	230
4956	16	190	4980	16	231
4957	16	191	4981	16	232
4958	16	194	4982	16	233
4959	16	195	4983	16	234
4960	16	195	4984	16	236
4961	16	204	4985	16	238
4962	16	204	4986	16	239
4963	16	204	4987	16	239
4964	16	205	4988	16	241
4965	16	206	4989	16	247
4966	16	207	4990	16	248
4967	16	208	4991	16	249
4968	16	215	4992	16	251

4993	16	253	5017	16	350
4994	16	255	5018	16	354
4995	16	257	5019	16	354
4996	16	260	5020	16	357
4997	16	266	5021	16	357
4998	16	284	5022	16	364
4999	16	287	5023	16	370
5000	16	288	5024	16	374
5001	16	289	5025	16	376
5002	16	290	5026	16	378
5003	16	292	5027	16	379
5004	16	296	5028	16	385
5005	16	298	5029	16	389
5006	16	301	5030	16	390
5007	16	301	5031	16	392
5008	16	307	5032	16	401
5009	16	309	5033	16	401
5010	16	312	5034	16	403
5011	16	315	5035	16	405
5012	16	327	5036	16	406
5013	16	340	5037	16	407
5014	16	344	5038	16	407
5015	16	348	5039	16	408
5016	16	349	5040	16	411

5041	16	411	5065	16	433
5042	16	413	5066	16	434
5043	16	413	5067	16	437
5044	16	413	5068	16	439
5045	16	414	5069	16	441
5046	16	414	5070	16	442
5047	16	415	5071	16	444
5048	16	417	5072	16	446
5049	16	418	5073	16	448
5050	16	419	5074	16	449
5051	16	419	5075	16	451
5052	16	420	5076	16	451
5053	16	420	5077	16	452
5054	16	420	5078	16	454
5055	16	422	5079	16	455
5056	16	424	5080	16	458
5057	16	426	5081	16	463
5058	16	426	5082	16	463
5059	16	426	5083	16	464
5060	16	428	5084	16	466
5061	16	430	5085	16	470
5062	16	431	5086	16	474
5063	16	432	5087	16	478
5064	16	433	5088	16	480

5089	16	481	5113	16	522
5090	16	482	5114	16	526
5091	16	493	5115	16	527
5092	16	495	5116	16	534
5093	16	497	5117	16	539
5094	16	497	5118	16	541
5095	16	497	5119	16	542
5096	16	499	5120	16	548
5097	16	500	5121	16	559
5098	16	502	5122	16	559
5099	16	503	5123	16	560
5100	16	504	5124	16	562
5101	16	506	5125	16	562
5102	16	508	5126	16	564
5103	16	508	5127	16	565
5104	16	509	5128	16	565
5105	16	511	5129	16	566
5106	16	512	5130	16	567
5107	16	512	5131	16	568
5108	16	516	5132	16	569
5109	16	516	5133	16	574
5110	16	520	5134	16	574
5111	16	520	5135	16	574
5112	16	522	5136	16	575

5137	16	579	5161	17	37
5138	16	582	5162	17	39
5139	16	582	5163	17	39
5140	17	3	5164	17	56
5141	17	5	5165	17	58
5142	17	7	5166	17	63
5143	17	11	5167	17	65
5144	17	12	5168	17	66
5145	17	12	5169	17	70
5146	17	12	5170	17	70
5147	17	14	5171	17	75
5148	17	16	5172	17	77
5149	17	18	5173	17	82
5150	17	22	5174	17	87
5151	17	24	5175	17	88
5152	17	25	5176	17	92
5153	17	25	5177	17	97
5154	17	26	5178	17	102
5155	17	28	5179	17	102
5156	17	28	5180	17	107
5157	17	28	5181	17	108
5158	17	30	5182	17	111
5159	17	33	5183	17	112
5160	17	34	5184	17	113

5185	17	113	5209	17	162
5186	17	115	5210	17	166
5187	17	117	5211	17	170
5188	17	117	5212	17	173
5189	17	121	5213	17	174
5190	17	122	5214	17	175
1591	17	122	5215	17	176
5192	17	126	5216	17	176
5193	17	127	5217	17	177
5194	17	128	5218	17	178
5195	17	128	5219	17	178
5196	17	130	5220	17	180
5197	17	130	5221	17	181
5198	17	131	5222	17	183
5199	17	131	5223	17	185
5200	17	149	5224	17	187
5201	17	149	5225	17	188
5202	17	149	5226	17	190
5203	17	153	5227	17	195
5204	17	155	5228	17	195
5205	17	155	5229	17	197
5206	17	156	5230	17	208
5207	17	157	5231	17	208
5208	17	158	5232	17	213

5233	17	215	5257	17	247
5234	17	215	5258	17	247
5235	17	216	5259	17	248
5236	17	217	5260	17	249
5237	17	218	5261	17	249
5238	17	219	5262	17	250
5239	17	222	5263*		
5240	17	222	5264	17	251
5241	17	222	5265	17	252
5242	17	224	5266	17	252
5243	17	227	5267	17	253
5244	17	227	5268	17	254
5245	17	232	5269	17	255
5246	17	233	5270	17	257
5247	17	233	5271	17	260
5248	17	235	5272	17	260
5249	17	235	5273	17	260
5250	17	238	5274	17	260
5251	17	239	5275	17	264
5252	17	240	5276	17	264
5253	17	240	5277	17	270
5254	17	243	5278	17	274
5255	17	243	5279	17	276
5256	17	246	5280	17	279

* omitted

592

5281	17	279	5305	17	461
5282	17	283	5306	17	462
5283	17	287	5307	17	464
5284	17	290	5308	17	467
5285	17	290	5309	17	469
5286	17	290	5310	17	469
5287	17	293	5311	17	471
5288	17	301	5312	17	471
5289	17	312	5313	17	474
5290	17	332	5314	17	475
5291	17	335	5315	17	475
5292	17	361	5316	17	479
5293	17	401	5317	17	487
5294	17	423	5318	17	509
5295	17	435	5319	17	509
5296	17	439	5320	17	511
5297	17	443	5321	17	525
5298	17	444	5322	17	525
5299	17	444	5323	17	516
5300	17	445	5324	17	516
5301	17	454	5325	17	519
5302	17	456	5326	17	521
5303	17	460	5327	17	536
5304	17	460	5328	17	547

5329	17	549	5353	18	72
5330	17	556	5354	18	77
5331	17	560	5355	18	78
5332	17	566	5356	18	88
5333	17	567	5357	18	92
5334	17	590	5358	18	92
5335	17	591	5359	18	94
5336	17	591	5360	18	94
5337	17	594	5361	18	108
5338	17	595	5362	18	110
5339	18	7	5363	18	112
5340	18	7	5364	18	117
5341	18	7	5365	18	123
5342	18	8	5366	18	124
5343	18	8	5367	18	126
5344	18	12	5368	18	133
5345	18	12	5369	18	137
5346	18	14	5370	18	139
5347	18	20	5371	18	139
5348	18	34	5372	18	142
5349	18	56	5373	18	144
5350	18	62	5374	18	144
5351	18	66	5375	18	145
5352	18	67	5376	18	146

5377	18	146	5401	18	343
5378	18	150	5402	18	344
5379	18	152	5403	18	350
5380	18	154	5404	18	350
5381	18	156	5405	18	350
5382	18	198	5406	18	351
5383	18	199	5407	18	351
5384	18	217	5408	18	351
5385	18	219	5409	18	353
5386	18	225	5410	18	353
5387	18	225	5411	18	353
5388	18	248	5412	18	353
5389	18	252	5413	18	354
5390	18	261	5414	18	355
5391	18	262	5415	18	361
5392	18	271	5416	18	363
5393	18	272	5417	18	365
5394	18	295	5418	18	365
5395	18	299	5419	18	369
5396	18	303	5420	18	388
5397	18	309	5421	18	403
5398	18	314	5422	18	410
5399	18	338	5423	18	410
5400	18	339	5424	18	430

5425	18	434
5426	18	438
5427	18	440
5428	18	441
5429	18	442
5430	18	442
5431	18	443
5432	18	443
5433	18	444
5434	18	444
5435	18	444
5436	18	445
5437	18	445
5438	18	445
5439	18	446
5440	18	446
5441	18	447
5442	18	456
5443	18	464

DATE DUE